In the name of Allah,
the Beneficent, the Merciful.

SAHIH AL–BUKHARI

[Without Repetition]
All Volumes in One Book

Main Author

Imam Muhammad Al–Bukhari (rh)

Compiled By

Muhammad Mohee Uddin Ibn Ahmad

1ST EDITION

PUBLICATION DATE: JUNE 2020

ISBN: 9798640953879

For information about special discounts available for bulk purchases, sales promotions, fund-raising and educational needs, contact

mohee1990@outlook.com

COVER DESIGN BY

Alifa Yeasmin Brishty

alifayeasmin29@gmail.com

SPECIAL THANKS

Aysha Begum

Aftahar Jahan Miagh

Asad Rahman Rakib

Saif Uddin Babor

Nazrul Islam

INTRODUCTION

All praise belongs to Allah Tala, Lord of the worlds. May the peace and blessings be on our beloved Prophet (ﷺ), on his family, on all of his Companions and Muslim ummah.

The Sahih Bukhari collection of Hadith is considered to be the most authentic collection of the teachings and sayings of the Prophet (ﷺ).

These Prophetic traditions, or hadith, were collected by the Uzbek Muslim scholar Muhammad al-Bukhari (RH), after being transmitted orally for generations.

Al-Bukhari (RH) travelled widely throughout the Abbasid Empire from the age of 16, collecting those traditions he thought trustworthy.

At the time when Bukhari (RH) saw [the earlier] works and conveyed them, he found them, in their presentation, combining between what would be considered sahih (correct) and hasan (good) and that many of them included da'īf (weak) hadith.

This aroused his interest in compiling hadith whose authenticity was beyond doubt. What further strengthened his resolve was something his teacher, hadith scholar Ishaq ibn Ibrahim al-Hanthalee – better known as Ishaq Ibn Rahwayh had said.

Muhammad ibn Ismaa'eel al-Bukhari (RH) said, "We were with Ishaq Ibn Rahwayh who said, 'If only you would compile a book of only authentic narrations of the Prophet.' This suggestion remained in my heart so I began compiling the Sahih."

Bukhari (RH) also said, "I saw the Prophet in a dream and it was as if I was standing in front of him. In my hand was a fan with which I was protecting him. I asked some dream interpreters, who said to me, 'You will protect him from lies.' This is what compelled me to produce the Sahih."

MUHAMMAD AL-BUKHARI

Muhammad ibn Ismail al-Bukhari al-Jufi was born after the Jumu'ah prayer on Friday, 21 July 810 (13 Shawwal 194 AH) in the city of Bukhara in Transoxiana (in present-day Uzbekistan).

During his infancy, Imam al-Bukhari (RH) had weak eyesight that manifested into full-blown blindness. Desperate for her son, his mother made excessive, sincere, and constant dua for her son. This period extended for a lengthy two to three years. One night, Imam al-Bukhari's mother received the glad tidings of Ibrahim (AS) in a dream, who said that Allah (SWT) had granted Imam al-Bukhari vision because of her dua. The eyesight was not even restored at a lesser degree, but at full strength. It is reported that Imam al-Bukhari (RH) would write books without a candle but only from the light of the moon.

He memorized the Holy Qur'an at the age of 9. Then began to learn Hadith from scholars of his region. At the age of 16 he travelled to Makkah and stayed there for 16 years collecting Hadiths. He visited Egypt and Syria twice, Basra four times, spent many years in Hijaz and went to Kufa and Baghdad many times. It is said that he learned about 600,000 Hadith from more than 1,000 scholars.

Imam Bukhari (RH) had an extremely strong memory from an early and his memory was considered to be inhuman. His brother Rashid bin Ismail stated that in his childhood:

"Imam Bukhari used to go with us to the scholars of Basra to listen to Hadiths. All of us used to write Hadiths down except Imam Bukhari. After some days, we condemned Imam Bukhari saying that, you had wasted so many days work by not writing down Hadiths. Imam Bukhari asked us to bring our notes to him. So, we all brought our notes, upon which Imam Bukhari began to read Hadiths one by one from the top of his head until he narrated to us more than fifteen thousand Hadiths.

Hearing these Hadiths, it seemed that Imam Bukhari was re-teaching us all of the Hadiths we had noted."

He did not depend on pen and paper as much as he relied on his sharp memory which was a result of Allah Tala's gift of intelligence and superb memory to him.

There is one remarkable incident took place in Baghdad when Imam Bukhari (RH) visited the place. The people having heard of his many accomplishments, and the attributes which were issued to him, decided to test him so as to make him prove himself to them. In order to do that they chose one hundred different Hadiths and changing the testimonials and the text of the Hadiths. The Hadiths were recited by ten people to Imam Bukhari (RH). When the Hadiths were recited, Imam Bukhari (RH) replied to all in one manner, "Not to my knowledge." However, after the completion of all the Hadiths, he repeated each text and testimonial which had been changed followed by the correct text and testimonial.

Imam al-Bukhari (RH) was someone who upheld his credibility and dignity, knowing that he was trusted by the people to narrate hadith. On one occasion, he was traveling by boat while carrying 1,000 gold coins. There was another traveler who devised a plan to steal the coins. In the middle of the night, the traveler woke up screaming that he had lost his gold coins and described the bag that he had "lost" identical to that of Imam al-Bukhari (RH). The other travelers on the boat searched for the bag but none could find it, and when they could not locate the bag, they became upset with the traveler for waking them up. The traveler came to Imam al-Bukhari (RH) and asked him where the bag of coins was. Imam al-Bukhari (RH) said that he had thrown the bag, his life savings, overboard. When further questioned on his actions, Imam al-Bukhari (RH) said, "...don't you know that I have spent my life collecting the hadith of the Prophet (ﷺ), and the world knows me as trustworthy? And that they trust me and take my hadith? Do you want me to sell all of that for a thousand dinars?"

In 250 AH, Imam al-Bukhari (RH) came to area of Nishapur in Khorasan. This is where he would attract thousands of students, including one of the most famous scholars of Hadith, Imam Muslim ibn al-Hajjaj (writer of Sahih Muslim). Scholars in Nishapur were upset that their students were flocking to Imam al-Bukhari (RH), therefore, rumours were spread that Imam al-Bukhari (RH) had come to Nishapur in order to spread false information about the religion. The rumours caused Imam al-Bukhari (RH) to leave Nishapur and return to his home city of Bukhara. In Bukhara, he was pressured by the governor to have Imam al-Bukhari (RH) give private lessons to his children due to their higher social class. Demanding that his lessons be public to people of all walks of life coupled with the envy of other scholars, Imam al-Bukhari (RH) was forced out of his home city. He then went to settle in Khartang, a village on the outskirts of Samarqand. Keep in mind, Imam al-Bukhari (RH) was rejected by his own home community in Bukhara. When he found he had no place to go, he prayed to Almighty Allah saying,

"O Allah, the Earth despite its grandeur is becoming narrow for me and is troubling me greatly. So, take me back to You."

His prayers were answered and at the age of 62 he died at Khartang, a place between Samarqand and Bukhara. It was on the night of Eid Al-Fitr, the first night of Shawwal 256 A.H. He is buried in Muhammad Al-Bukhari mausoleum at Khartang near Samarkand, in Uzbekistan

Abd Al-Wahid ibn Adam Awaysi states:

"I saw the Holy Prophet (peace be upon him) in dream standing with a group of Sahaba and asked, 'For whom are you waiting?' He replied, 'For Bukhari.' After a few days I heard the news of Imam Bukhari's death. He had died at the very moment that I saw the Prophet (ﷺ) in my dream."

TABLE OF CONTENT

1.Revelation 1

2. Belief 3

3. Knowledge 9

4. Ablutions (Wudu') 14

5. Bathing 22

6. Menstrual Periods 24

7. Ablutions with dust (Tayammum) 26

8. Mosque 29

9. Times of the Prayers 43

10. Call to Prayers (Adhaan) 50

11. Benefits of Prayer 54

12. Rules of Prayer 56

13. Friday Prayer 73

14. Eids 77

15. Witr Prayer 80

16. Invoking Allah for Rain 82

17. Eclipses 86

18. Prostration During Recital of Qur'an 91

19. Shortening the Prayers 92

20. Prayer at Night (Tahajjud) 93

21. Virtues of Prayer at Masjid Makkah and Madinah 98

22. Actions while Praying 99

23. Funerals 102

24. Charity 112

25. Zakat 122

26. Hajj (Pilgrimage) 126

27. Umrah 147

28. While on Pilgrimage . 149

29. Virtues of Madinah .. 153

30. Fasting 156

31. Taraweeh 167

32. Virtues of the Night of Qadr 168

33. I'tikaf 169

34. Sales and Trade 170

35. Agricultural Lease ... 178

36. Transference of a Debt 180

37. Agriculture 184

38. Quarrels 187

39. Lost Things 188

40. Oppressions 189

41. Partnership 191

42. Mortgaging 192

43. Gifts 193

44. Witnesses 196

45. Peacemaking 199

46. Conditions 202

47. Wills and Testaments 204

48. Jihaad 209

49. War Booty 225

50. Jizyah and Mawaada'ah 245

51. Beginning of Creation 248

52. Prophets 257

53. Story of Ahl al-Kitab 275

54. Merits of the Prophet (ﷺ) 280

55. Miracles of Prophet (ﷺ) 286

56. Companions 292

57. Merits of Ansaar 311

58. Pre-Migration Period 315

59. Prophet's Migration 325

60. Military Expeditions 335

61. Death of the Prophet (ﷺ) 400

62. Tafseer 407

63. Compilation of The Quran 428

64. VIRTUES OF THE QUR'AN 433

65. MARRIAGE 440

66. MARRIED LIFE............. 452

67. DIVORCE 460

68. SUPPORTING THE FAMILY 467

69. FOOD, MEALS 468

70. AQIQA 473

71. HUNTING, SLAUGHTERING 475

72. AL-ADHA SACRIFICE 479

73. DRINKS 480

74. SICKNESS 485

75. MEDICINE....................488

76. DRESS 497

77. RIGHTS OF RELATIVES ..506

78. GOOD MANNERS 511

79. NAMING THE CHILD...... 517

80. ASKING PERMISSION 520

81. INVOCATIONS (DUA) 523

82. HOPE AND DESIRE 537

83. QIYAMAH (DAY OF JUDGEMENT) 544

84. JANNAH AND JAHANNAM 556

85. DIVINE WILL (DESTINY) 563

86. OATHS AND VOWS........ 565

87. PUNISHMENTS 570

88. COERCION 582

89. INTERPRETATION OF DREAMS 583

90. FITNA 590

91. LEADERSHIP 622

92. WISHES 634

93. ACCEPTING INFORMATION GIVEN BY A TRUTHFUL PERSON 635

94. HOLDING FAST TO THE QUR'AN AND SUNNAH 635

95. ONENESS, UNIQUENESS OF ALLAH 640

Sahih Bukhari contains 7,563 hadith reports, but of these some 2,450 may be considered as distinct, while the others may be called their repetitions in one form or another. Repetitions of the same report very often occur in different books and chapters. The types of repetitions are:

- Hadith that have the same content and same chain of narration.

- Hadith that have the same content with different chains of narration.

- Hadith that have more than one content through the same chain of narration.

This book contains 2,398 hadith. All effort has been taken to omit repetitions, although some has been kept for a clear narrative.

1. Revelation

1. Narrated 'Umar bin Al-Khattab (RA): I heard Allah's Messenger (ﷺ) saying, "The reward of deeds depends upon the intentions and every person will get the reward according to what he has intended. So whoever emigrated for worldly benefits or for a woman to marry, his emigration was for what he emigrated for." (1) ☐ (Please cross/check the box after you finish reading ☒)

2. Narrated 'Aisha (RA): (the mother of the faithful believers) Al-Harith bin Hisham asked Allah's Messenger (ﷺ) "O Allah's Messenger (ﷺ)! How is the Divine Inspiration revealed to you?" Allah's Messenger (ﷺ) replied, "Sometimes it is (revealed) like the ringing of a bell, this form of Inspiration is the hardest of all and then this state passes off after I have grasped what is inspired. Sometimes the Angel comes in the form of a man and talks to me and I grasp whatever he says." 'Aisha added: Verily I saw the Prophet (ﷺ) being inspired divinely on a very cold day and noticed the sweat dropping from his forehead (as the Inspiration was over). (2) ☐

3. Narrated 'Aisha (RA): The commencement of the Divine Inspiration to Allah's Messenger (ﷺ) was in the form of good dreams which came true like bright daylight, and then the love of seclusion was bestowed upon him. He used to go in seclusion in the cave of Hira where he used to worship (Allah alone) continuously for many days before his desire to see his family. He used to take with him the journey food for the stay and then come back to (his wife) Khadija to take his food likewise again till suddenly the Truth descended upon him while he was in the cave of Hira. The angel came to him and asked him to read. The Prophet (ﷺ) replied, "I do not know how to read." The Prophet (ﷺ) added, "The angel caught me (forcefully) and pressed me so hard that I could not bear it any more. He then released me and again asked me to

read and I replied, 'I do not know how to read.' Thereupon he caught me again and pressed me a second time till I could not bear it any more. He then released me and again asked me to read but again I replied, 'I do not know how to read (or what shall I read)?' Thereupon he caught me for the third time and pressed me, and then released me and said, 'Read in the name of your Lord, who has created (all that exists), created man from a clot. Read! And your Lord is the Most Generous." (96.1- 3) Then Allah's Messenger (ﷺ) returned with the Inspiration and with his heart beating severely. Then he went to Khadija bint Khuwailid and said, "Cover me! Cover me!" They covered him till his fear was over and after that he told her everything that had happened and said, "I fear that something may happen to me." Khadija replied, "Never! By Allah, Allah will never disgrace you. You keep good relations with your kith and kin, help the poor and the destitute, serve your guests generously and assist the deserving calamity-afflicted ones." Khadija then accompanied him to her cousin Waraqa bin Naufal bin Asad bin 'Abdul 'Uzza, who, during the pre-Islamic Period became a Christian and used to write the writing with Hebrew letters. He would write from the Gospel in Hebrew as much as Allah wished him to write. He was an old man and had lost his eyesight. Khadija said to Waraqa, "Listen to the story of your nephew, O my cousin!" Waraqa asked, "O my nephew! What have you seen?" Allah's Messenger (ﷺ) described whatever he had seen. Waraqa said, "This is the same one who keeps the secrets (angel Gabriel) whom Allah had sent to Moses. I wish I were young and could live up to the time when your people would turn you out." Allah's Messenger (ﷺ) asked, "Will they drive me out?" Waraqa replied in the affirmative and said, "Anyone (man) who came with something similar to what you have brought was treated with hostility; and if I should remain alive till the day when you will be turned out then I would support you strongly." But after a few days Waraqa died and the Divine Inspiration was also paused for a while. (3) ☐ ("Salla Alahu alayhi wa-ala alihi wa-salam" [often shortened to SAW or ﷺ] translates to 'May God honor him and grant him peace.' And "Peace be upon him" (PBUH) on the other hand is the lesser "Alayhi as-salam" [AS]. "Radeyallahu Anhu/Anha" [RA] means "May Allah be pleased with him/her.")

2. BELIEF

4. NARRATED IBN 'UMAR (RA): Allah's Messenger (ﷺ) said: Islam is based on (the following) five (principles):

1. To testify that none has the right to be worshipped but Allah and Muhammad is Allah's Messenger (ﷺ).

2. To offer the (compulsory congregational) prayers dutifully and perfectly.

3. To pay Zakat (i.e. obligatory charity).

4. To perform Hajj. (i.e. Pilgrimage to Mecca)

5. To observe fast during the month of Ramadan. (8) ☐

5. Narrated Abu Huraira (RA): The Prophet (ﷺ) said, "Faith (Belief) consists of more than sixty branches (i.e. parts). And Haya ("Haya" is self respect, modesty, honor, bashfulness, scruple, decency, shyness, humility etc.) is a part of faith." (9) ☐

6. Narrated 'Abdullah bin 'Amr (RA): The Prophet (ﷺ) said, "A Muslim is the one who avoids harming Muslims with his tongue and hands. And a Muhajir (emigrant) is the one who gives up (abandons) all what Allah has forbidden." (10) ☐

7. Narrated 'Abdullah bin 'Amr (RA): A man asked the Prophet (ﷺ), "What sort of deeds of Islam are good?" The Prophet (ﷺ) replied, 'To feed (the poor) and greet those whom you know and those whom you do not know. (12) ☐

8. Narrated Anas (RA): The Prophet (ﷺ) said, "None of you will have faith till he wishes for his (Muslim) brother what he likes for himself." (13) ☐

9. Narrated Abu Huraira (RA): "Allah's Messenger (ﷺ) said, "By Him in Whose Hands my life is, none of you will have faith till he loves me more than his father and his children." (14) ☐

10. Narrated Anas (RA): The Prophet (ﷺ) said, "Whoever possesses the following three qualities will have the sweetness (delight) of faith:

1) The one to whom Allah and His Apostle becomes dearer than anything else.

2) Who loves a person and he loves him only for Allah's sake.

3) Who hates to revert to Atheism (disbelief) as he hates to be thrown into the fire." (16) □

11. Narrated 'Ubada bin As-Samit (RA): who took part in the battle of Badr and was a Naqib (a person heading a group of six persons), on the night of Al-'Aqaba pledge: Allah's Apostle said while a group of his companions were around him, "Swear allegiance to me for:

1. Not to join anything in worship along with Allah.

2. Not to steal.

3. Not to commit illegal sexual intercourse.

4. Not to kill your children.

5. Not to accuse an innocent person (to spread such an accusation among people).

6. Not to be disobedient (when ordered) to do good deed."

The Prophet (ﷺ) added: "Whoever among you fulfills his pledge will be rewarded by Allah. And whoever indulges in any one of them (except the ascription of partners to Allah) and gets the punishment in this world, that punishment will be an expiation for that sin. And if one indulges in any of them, and Allah conceals his sin, it is up to Him to forgive or punish him (in the Hereafter)." 'Ubada bin As-Samit added: "So we swore allegiance for these." (18) □

12. Narrated 'Aisha (RA): Whenever Allah's Messenger (ﷺ) ordered the Muslims to

do something, he used to order them deeds which were easy for them to do, (according to their strength and endurance). They said, "O Allah's Messenger (ﷺ)! We are not like you. Allah has forgiven your past and future sins." So Allah's Apostle became angry and it was apparent on his face. He said, "I am the most Allah fearing, and know Allah better than all of you do." (20) □

13. Narrated Abu Said Al-Khudri (RA): The Prophet (ﷺ) said, "When the people of Paradise will enter Paradise and the people of Hell will go to Hell, Allah will order those who have had faith equal to the weight of a grain of mustard seed to be taken out from Hell. So they will be taken out but they will be blackened (charred). Then they will be put in the river of Haya' (rain) or Hayat (life) (the Narrator is in doubt as to which is the right term), and they will revive like a grain that grows near the bank of a flood channel. Don't you see that it comes out yellow and twisted" (22) □

14. Narrated 'Abdullah (bin 'Umar): Once Allah's Messenger (ﷺ) passed by an Ansari (man) who was admonishing his brother regarding Haya'. On that Allah's Messenger (ﷺ) said, "Leave him as Haya' is a part of faith." (24) □

15. Narrated Ibn 'Umar (RA): Allah's Messenger (ﷺ) said: "I have been ordered (by Allah) to fight against the people until they testify that none has the right to be worshipped but Allah and that Muhammad is Allah's Messenger (ﷺ), and offer the prayers perfectly and give the obligatory charity, so if they perform that, then they save their lives and property from me except for Islamic laws and then their reckoning (accounts) will be done by Allah." (25) □

16. Narrated 'Abdullah bin 'Amr (RA): The Prophet (ﷺ) said, "Whoever has the following four (characteristics) will be a pure hypocrite and whoever has one of the following four characteristics will have one characteristic of hypocrisy unless and until he gives it up.

1. Whenever he is entrusted, he betrays.

2. Whenever he speaks, he tells a lie.

3. Whenever he makes a covenant, he proves treacherous.

4. Whenever he quarrels, he behaves in a very imprudent, evil and insulting manner." (34) □

17. Narrated Abu Huraira (RA): The Prophet (ﷺ) said, "Religion is very easy and whoever overburdens himself in his religion will not be able to continue in that way. So you should not be extremists, but try to be near to perfection and receive the good tidings that you will be rewarded; and gain strength by worshipping in the mornings, the afternoons, and during the last hours of the nights." (39) □

18. Narrated Abu Sa'id Al Khudri (RA): Allah's Messenger (ﷺ) said, "If a person embraces Islam sincerely, then Allah shall forgive all his past sins, and after that starts the settlement of accounts, the reward of his good deeds will be ten times to seven hundred times for each good deed and one evil deed will be recorded as it is unless Allah forgives it." (41) □

19. Narrated Anas (RA): The Prophet (ﷺ) said, "Whoever said "None has the right to be worshipped but Allah and has in his heart good (faith) equal to the weight of a barley grain will be taken out of Hell. And whoever said: "None has the right to be worshipped but Allah and has in his heart good (faith) equal to the weight of a wheat grain will be taken out of Hell. And whoever said, "None has the right to be worshipped but Allah and has in his heart good (faith) equal to the weight of an atom will be taken out of Hell." (44) □

20. Narrated 'Abdullah (RA): The Prophet (ﷺ) said, "Abusing a Muslim is Fusuq (an evil doing) and killing him is Kufr (disbelief)." (48) □

21. Narrated Abu Huraira (RA): One day while the Prophet (ﷺ) was sitting in the company of some people, (The angel) Gabriel came and asked, "What is faith?" Allah's Messenger (ﷺ) replied, 'Faith is to believe in Allah, His angels, (the) meeting with Him, His Apostles, and to believe in Resurrection." Then he further asked, "What is Islam?" Allah's Messenger (ﷺ) replied, "To worship Allah Alone and none

clse, to offer prayers perfectly to pay the compulsory charity (Zakat) and to observe fasts during the month of Ramadan." Then he further asked, "What is Ihsan (perfection)?" Allah's Messenger (ﷺ) replied, "To worship Allah as if you see Him, and if you cannot achieve this state of devotion then you must consider that He is looking at you." Then he further asked, "When will the Hour be established?" Allah's Messenger (ﷺ) replied, "The answerer has no better knowledge than the questioner. But I will inform you about its portents.

1. When a slave (lady) gives birth to her master.

2. When the shepherds of black camels start boasting and competing with others in the construction of higher buildings. And the Hour is one of five things which nobody knows except Allah.

The Prophet (ﷺ) then recited: "Verily, with Allah (Alone) is the knowledge of the Hour--." (31. 34) Then that man (Gabriel) left and the Prophet (ﷺ) asked his companions to call him back, but they could not see him. Then the Prophet (ﷺ) said, "That was Gabriel who came to teach the people their religion." Abu 'Abdullah said: He (the Prophet) considered all that as a part of faith. (50) □

22. Narrated An-Nu'man bin Bashir (RA): I heard Allah's Messenger (ﷺ) saying, 'Both legal and illegal things are evident but in between them there are doubtful (suspicious) things and most of the people have no knowledge about them. So whoever saves himself from these suspicious things saves his religion and his honor. And whoever indulges in these suspicious things is like a shepherd who grazes (his animals) near the Hima (private pasture) of someone else and at any moment he is liable to get in it. (O people!) Beware! Every king has a Hima and the Hima of Allah on the earth is His illegal (forbidden) things. Beware! There is a piece of flesh in the body if it becomes good (reformed) the whole body becomes good but if it gets spoilt the whole body gets spoilt and that is the heart. (52) □

23. Narrated Abu Jamra (RA): I used to sit with Ibn 'Abbas and he made me sit on his sitting place. He requested me to stay with him in order that he might give me a

share from his property. So I stayed with him for two months. Once he told (me) that when the delegation of the tribe of 'Abdul Qais came to the Prophet, the Prophet (ﷺ) asked them, "Who are the people (i.e. you)? (Or) who are the delegate?" They replied, "We are from the tribe of Rabi'a." Then the Prophet (ﷺ) said to them, "Welcome! O people (or O delegation of 'Abdul Qais)! Neither will you have disgrace nor will you regret." They said, "O Allah's Messenger (ﷺ)! We cannot come to you except in the sacred month and there is the infidel tribe of Mudar intervening between you and us. So please order us to do something good (religious deeds) so that we may inform our people whom we have left behind (at home), and that we may enter Paradise (by acting on them)." Then they asked about drinks (what is legal and what is illegal). The Prophet (ﷺ) ordered them to do four things and forbade them from four things. He ordered them to believe in Allah Alone and asked them, "Do you know what is meant by believing in Allah Alone?" They replied, "Allah and His Apostle know better." Thereupon the Prophet (ﷺ) said, "It means:

1. To testify that none has the right to be worshipped but Allah and Muhammad is Allah's Messenger (ﷺ).

2. To offer prayers perfectly

3. To pay the Zakat (obligatory charity)

4. To observe fast during the month of Ramadan.

5. And to pay Al-Khumus (one fifth of the booty to be given in Allah's Cause).

Then he forbade them four things, namely, Hantam, Dubba,' Naqir Ann Muzaffat or Muqaiyar; (These were the names of pots in which Alcoholic drinks were prepared) (The Prophet (ﷺ) mentioned the container of wine and he meant the wine itself). The Prophet (ﷺ) further said (to them): "Memorize them (these instructions) and convey them to the people whom you have left behind." (53) □

24. Narrated Jarir bin Abdullah (RA): I gave the pledge of allegiance to Allah's Messenger (ﷺ) for the following:

1. offer prayers perfectly

2. pay the Zakat (obligatory charity)

3. And be sincere and true to every Muslim. (57) □

3. KNOWLEDGE

25. NARRATED ABU HURAIRA (RA): While the Prophet (ﷺ) was saying something in a gathering, a Bedouin came and asked him, "When would the Hour (Doomsday) take place?" Allah's Messenger (ﷺ) continued his talk, so some people said that Allah's Messenger (ﷺ) had heard the question, but did not like what that Bedouin had asked. Some of them said that Allah's Messenger (ﷺ) had not heard it. When the Prophet (ﷺ) finished his speech, he said, "Where is the questioner, who inquired about the Hour?" The Bedouin said, "I am here, O Allah's Apostle." Then the Prophet (ﷺ) said, "When honesty is lost, then wait for the Hour." The Bedouin said, "How will that be lost?" The Prophet (ﷺ) said, "When the power or authority comes in the hands of unfit persons, then wait for the Hour (Doomsday.)" (59) □

26. Narrated Ibn Umar (RA): Allah's Messenger (ﷺ) said, "Amongst the trees, there is a tree, the leaves of which do not fall and is like a Muslim. Tell me the name of that tree?" Everybody started thinking about the trees of the desert areas. And I thought of the date-palm tree but felt shy to answer the others then asked, "What is that tree, O Allah's Messenger (ﷺ)?" He replied, "It is the date-palm tree." (61) □

27. Narrated Anas bin Malik (RA): While we were sitting with the Prophet (ﷺ) in the mosque, a man came riding on a camel. He made his camel kneel down in the mosque, tied its foreleg and then said: "Who amongst you is Muhammad?" At that time the Prophet (ﷺ) was sitting amongst us (his companions) leaning on his arm. We replied, "This white man reclining on his arm." The man then addressed him, "O Son of `Abdul Muttalib." The Prophet (ﷺ) said, "I am here to answer your questions."

The man said to the Prophet, "I want to ask you something and will be hard in questioning. So do not get angry." The Prophet (ﷺ) said, "Ask whatever you want." The man said, "I ask you by your Lord, and the Lord of those who were before you, has Allah sent you as an Apostle to all the mankind?" The Prophet (ﷺ) replied, "By Allah, yes." The man further said, "I ask you by Allah. Has Allah ordered you to offer five prayers in a day and night (24 hours)? He replied, "By Allah, Yes." The man further said, "I ask you by Allah! Has Allah ordered you to observe fasts during this month of the year (i.e. Ramadan)?" He replied, "By Allah, Yes." The man further said, "I ask you by Allah. Has Allah ordered you to take Zakat (obligatory charity) from our rich people and distribute it amongst our poor people?" The Prophet (ﷺ) replied, "By Allah, yes." Thereupon that man said, "I have believed in all that with which you have been sent, and I have been sent by my people as a messenger, and I am Dimam bin Tha`laba from the brothers of Bani Sa`d bin Bakr." (63) □

28. Narrated Ibn Mas`ud: The Prophet (ﷺ) used to take care of us in preaching by selecting a suitable time, so that we might not get bored. (He abstained from pestering us with sermons and knowledge all the time). (68) □

29. Narrated Anas bin Malik: The Prophet (ﷺ) said, "Facilitate things to people (concerning religious matters), and do not make it hard for them and give them good tidings and do not make them run away (from Islam). (69) □

30. Narrated Abu Wail: `Abdullah used to give a religious talk to the people on every Thursday. Once a man said, "O Aba `Abdur-Rahman! (By Allah) I wish if you could preach us daily." He replied, "The only thing which prevents me from doing so, is that I hate to bore you, and no doubt I take care of you in preaching by selecting a suitable time just as the Prophet (ﷺ) used to do with us, for fear of making us bored." (70) □

31. Narrated Muawiya: I heard Allah's Messenger (ﷺ) saying, "If Allah wants to do good to a person, He makes him comprehend the religion. I am just a distributor, but the grant is from Allah. (And remember) that this nation (true Muslims) will keep on

following Allah's teachings strictly and they will not be harmed by any one going on a different path till Allah's order (Day of Judgment) is established." (71) □

32. Narrated `Abdullah bin Mas`ud: The Prophet (ﷺ) said, "Do not wish to be like anyone except in two cases. (The first is) A person, whom Allah has given wealth and he spends it righteously; (the second is) the one whom Allah has given wisdom (the Holy Qur'an) and he acts according to it and teaches it to others." (73) □

33. Narrated Abu Musa: The Prophet (ﷺ) said, "The example of guidance and knowledge with which Allah has sent me is like abundant rain falling on the earth, some of which was fertile soil that absorbed rain water and brought forth vegetation and grass in abundance. (And) another portion of it was hard and held the rain water and Allah benefited the people with it and they utilized it for drinking, making their animals drink from it and for irrigation of the land for cultivation. (And) a portion of it was barren which could neither hold the water nor bring forth vegetation (then that land gave no benefits). The first is the example of the person who comprehends Allah's religion and gets benefit (from the knowledge) which Allah has revealed through me (the Prophets and learns and then teaches others. The last example is that of a person who does not care for it and does not take Allah's guidance revealed through me (He is like that barren land.)" (79) □

34. Narrated `Abdullah and Abu Musa: The Prophet (ﷺ) said, "Near the establishment of the Hour there will be days during which Religious ignorance will spread, knowledge will be taken away (vanish) and there will be much Al-Harj, and Al- Harj means killing." (7062) □

35. Narrated Abu Musa: The Prophet (ﷺ) was asked about things which he did not like, but when the questioners insisted, the Prophet got angry. He then said to the people, "Ask me anything you like." A man asked, "Who is my father?" The Prophet (ﷺ) replied, "Your father is Hudhafa." Then another man got up and said, "Who is my father, O Allah's Messenger (ﷺ)?" He replied, "Your father is Salim, Maula (the freed slave) of Shaiba." So when `Umar saw that (the anger) on the face of the Prophet

(☫) he said, "O Allah's Messenger (☫)! We repent to Allah (Our offending you). (92) □

36. Narrated Anas bin Malik: One day Allah's Messenger (☫) came out (before the people) and `Abdullah bin Hudhafa stood up and asked (him) "Who is my father?" The Prophet (☫) replied, "Your father is Hudhafa." The Prophet (☫) told them repeatedly (in anger) to ask him anything they liked. `Umar knelt down before the Prophet (☫) and said thrice, "We accept Allah as (our) Lord and Islam as (our) religion and Muhammad as (our) Prophet." After that the Prophet (☫) became silent. (93) □

37. Narrated Anas: Whenever the Prophet (☫) asked permission to enter, he knocked the door thrice with greeting and whenever he spoke a sentence (said a thing) he used to repeat it thrice. (94) □

38. Narrated Abu Burda's father: Allah's Messenger (☫) said "Three persons will have a double reward:

1. A Person from the people of the scriptures who believed in his prophet (Jesus or Moses) and then believed in the Prophet (☫) Muhammad (i .e. has embraced Islam).

2. A slave who discharges his duties to Allah and his master.

3. A master of a woman-slave who teaches her good manners and educates her in the best possible way (the religion) and manumits her and then marries her." (97) □

39. 'Narrated `Abdullah bin `Amr bin Al-`As: I heard Allah's Messenger (☫) saying, "Allah does not take away the knowledge, by taking it away from (the hearts of) the people, but takes it away by the death of the religious learned men till when none of the (religious learned men) remains, people will take as their leaders ignorant persons who when consulted will give their verdict without knowledge. So they will go astray and will lead the people astray." (100) □

40. Narrated Abu Sa`id Al-Khudri: Some women requested the Prophet (ﷺ) to fix a day for them as the men were taking all his time. On that he promised them one day for religious lessons and commandments. Once during such a lesson the Prophet said, "A woman whose three children die will be shielded by them from the Hell fire." On that a woman asked, "If only two die?" He replied, "Even two (will shield her from the Hell-fire). (101) ☐

41. Narrated `Abdullah bin Az-Zubair: I said to my father, 'I do not hear from you any narration (Hadith) of Allah s Apostle as I hear (his narration) from so and so?" Az-Zubair replied. I was always with him (the Prophet) and I heard him saying "Whoever tells a lie against me (intentionally) then (surely) let him occupy, his seat in Hellfire. (107) ☐

42. Narrated Abu Huraira: People say that I have narrated many Hadiths. Had it not been for two verses in the Qur'an, I would not have narrated a single Hadith, and the verses are: "Verily those who conceal the clear sign and the guidance which We have sent down . . . (up to) Most Merciful." (2:159-160). And no doubt our Muhajir (emigrant) brothers used to be busy in the market with their business (bargains) and our Ansari brothers used to be busy with their property (agriculture). But I (Abu Huraira) used to stick to Allah's Messenger (ﷺ) contented with what will fill my stomach and I used to attend that which they used not to attend and I used to memorize that which they used not to memorize. (118) ☐

43. Narrated Abu Huraira: I said to Allah's Messenger (ﷺ) "I hear many narrations (Hadiths) from you but I forget them." Allah's Apostle said, "Spread your Rida' (garment)." I did accordingly and then he moved his hands as if filling them with something (and emptied them in my Rida') and then said, "Take and wrap this sheet over your body." I did it and after that I never forgot any thing. (119) ☐

44. Narrated Jarir: The Prophet (ﷺ) said to me during Hajjat-al-Wida`: Let the people keep quiet and listen. Then he said (addressing the people), "Do not (become infidels) revert to disbelief after me by striking the necks (cutting the throats) of one

another (killing each other). (121) ☐

45. Narrated Anas bin Malik: "Once Mu`adh was along with Allah's Messenger (ﷺ) as a companion rider. Allah's Messenger (ﷺ) said, "O Mu`adh bin Jabal." Mu`adh replied, "Labbaik and Sa`daik. O Allah's Messenger (ﷺ)!" Again the Prophet (ﷺ) said, "O Mu`adh!" Mu`adh said thrice, "Labbaik and Sa`daik, O Allah's Messenger (ﷺ)!" Allah's Messenger (ﷺ) said, "There is none who testifies sincerely that none has the right to be worshipped but Allah and Muhammad is his Apostle, except that Allah, will save him from the Hell-fire." Mu`adh said, "O Allah's Messenger (ﷺ)! Should I not inform the people about it so that they may have glad tidings?" He replied, "When the people hear about it, they will solely depend on it." Then Mu`adh narrated the above-mentioned Hadith just before his death, being afraid of committing sin (by not telling the knowledge). (128) ☐

46. Narrated Ibn `Umar: The Prophet (ﷺ) said, "We are an illiterate nation; we neither write, nor know accounts. The month is like this and this, i.e. sometimes of 29 days and sometimes of thirty days." (1913) ☐

4. ABLUTIONS (WUDU')

47. NARRATED ABU HURAIRA (RA): Allah's Messenger (ﷺ) said, "The prayer of a person who does Hadath (passes urine, stool or wind) is not accepted till he performs the ablution." A person from Hadaramout asked Abu Huraira, "What is 'Hadath'?" Abu Huraira replied, " 'Hadath' means the passing of wind." (135) ☐

48. Narrated Nu`am Al-Mujmir: Once I went up the roof of the mosque, along with Abu Huraira. He perform ablution and said, "I heard the Prophet (ﷺ) saying, "On the Day of Resurrection, my followers will be called "Al-Ghurr-ul- Muhajjalun" from the trace of ablution and whoever can increase the area of his radiance should do so (i.e. by performing ablution regularly)."' (136) ☐

49. Narrated `Abbad bin Tamim: My uncle asked Allah's Messenger (ﷺ) about a person who imagined to have passed wind during the prayer. Allah' Apostle replied: "He should not leave his prayers unless he hears sound or smells something." (137) ☐

50. Narrated Kuraib: Ibn `Abbas said, "The Prophet (ﷺ) slept till he snored and then prayed (or probably lay till his breath sounds were heard and then got up and prayed)." Ibn `Abbas added: "I stayed overnight in the house of my aunt, Maimuna, the Prophet (ﷺ) slept for a part of the night, and late in the night, he got up and performed ablution from a hanging water skin, a light (perfect) ablution and stood up for the prayer. I, too, performed a similar ablution, then I went and stood on his left. He drew me to his right and prayed as much as Allah wished, and again lay and slept till his breath sounds were heard. Later on the Mu'adh-dhin (call maker for the prayer) came to him and informed him that it was time for Prayer. The Prophet (ﷺ) went with him for the prayer without performing a new ablution." (Sufyan said to `Amr that some people said, "The eyes of Allah's Messenger (ﷺ) sleep but his heart does not sleep." `Amr replied, "I heard `Ubaid bin `Umar saying that the dreams of Prophets were Divine Inspiration, and then he recited the verse: 'I (Abraham) see in a dream, (O my son) that I offer you in sacrifice (to Allah)." (37.102) (138) ☐

51. Narrated Usama bin Zaid: Allah's Messenger (ﷺ) proceeded from `Arafat till when he reached the mountain pass, he dismounted, urinated and then performed ablution but not a perfect one. I said to him, ("Is it the time for) the prayer, O Allah's Messenger (ﷺ)?" He said, "The (place of) prayer is ahead of you." He rode till when he reached Al-Muzdalifa, he dismounted and performed ablution and a perfect one, the (call for) Iqama was pronounced and he led the Maghrib prayer. Then everybody made his camel kneel down at its place. Then the Iqama was pronounced for the `Isha' prayer which the Prophet (ﷺ) led and no prayer was offered in between the two prayers (`Isha' and Maghrib). (139) ☐

52. Narrated `Ata' bin Yasar: Ibn `Abbas performed ablution and washed his face (in the following way): He ladled out a handful of water, rinsed his mouth and washed

his nose with it by putting in water and then blowing it out. He then, took another handful (of water) and did like this (gesturing) joining both hands, and washed his face, took another handful of water and washed his right forearm. He again took another handful of water and washed his left forearm, and passed wet hands over his head and took another handful of water and poured it over his right foot (up to his ankles) and washed it thoroughly and similarly took another handful of water and washed thoroughly his left foot (up to the ankles) and said, "I saw Allah's Messenger (ﷺ) performing ablution in this way." (140) ☐

53. Narrated Anas: Whenever the Prophet (ﷺ) went to answer the call of nature, he used to say, "اللَّهُمَّ إِنِّي أَعُوذُ بِكَ مِنَ الْخُبْثِ وَالْخَبَائِثِ" Allah-umma inni a`udhu bika minal khubuthi wal khaba'ith" (i.e. O Allah, I seek Refuge with You from all offensive and wicked things (evil deeds and evil spirits). (142) ☐

54. Narrated Ibn `Abbas: Once the Prophet (ﷺ) entered a lavatory and I placed water for his ablution. He asked, "Who placed it?" He was informed accordingly and so he said, "O Allah! Make him a learned scholar in religion (Islam). (143) ☐

55. Narrated Abu Aiyub Ansari: Allah's Messenger (ﷺ) said, "If anyone of you goes to an open space for answering the call of nature he should neither face nor turn his back towards the Qibla; he should either face the east or the west. (144)☐

56. Narrated `Abdullah bin `Umar: People say, "Whenever you sit for answering the call of nature, you should not face the Qibla or Baitul-Maqdis (Jerusalem)." I told them. "Once I went up the roof of our house and I saw Allah's Apostle answering the call of nature while sitting on two bricks facing Baitul-Maqdis (Jerusalem) (but there was a screen covering him. (145) ☐

57. Narrated Anas bin Malik: Whenever Allah's Messenger (ﷺ) went to answer the call of nature, I along with another boy used to carry a tumbler full of water (for cleaning the private parts) and a short spear (or stick). (152) ☐

58. Narrated Abu Qatada: Allah's Messenger (ﷺ) said, "Whenever anyone of you

drinks water, he should not breathe in the drinking utensil, and whenever anyone of you goes to a lavatory, he should neither touch his penis nor clean his private parts with his right hand." (153) ☐

59. Narrated Abu Huraira: I followed the Prophet (ﷺ) while he was going out to answer the call of nature. He used not to look this way or that. So, when I approached near him he said to me, "Fetch for me some stones for ' cleaning the privates parts (or said something similar), and do not bring a bone or a piece of dung." So I brought the stones in the corner of my garment and placed them by his side and I then went away from him. When he finished (from answering the call of nature) he used, them. (155) ☐

60. Narrated `Abdullah: The Prophet (ﷺ) went out to answer the call of nature and asked me to bring three stones. I found two stones and searched for the third but could not find it. So took a dried piece of dung and brought it to him. He took the two stones and threw away the dung and said, "This is a filthy thing." (156) ☐

61. Narrated `Abdullah bin Zaid: The Prophet (ﷺ) performed ablution by washing the body parts twice. (158) ☐

62. Narrated Humran: (the slave of 'Uthman) I saw 'Uthman bin 'Affan asking for a tumbler of water (and when it was brought) he poured water over his hands and washed them thrice and then put his right hand in the water container and rinsed his mouth, washed his nose by putting water in it and then blowing it out. Then he washed his face and forearms up to the elbows thrice, passed his wet hands over his head and washed his feet up to the ankles thrice. Then he said, "Allah's Messenger (ﷺ) said 'If anyone performs ablution like that of mine and offers a two-rak'at prayer during which he does not think of anything else (not related to the present prayer) then his past sins will be forgiven.'" (159) ☐

63. After performing the ablution 'Uthman said, "I am going to tell you a Hadith which I would not have told you, had I not been compelled by a certain Holy Verse (the sub narrator 'Urwa said: This verse is: "Verily, those who conceal the clear signs

and the guidance which we have sent down...)" (2:159). I heard the Prophet (ﷺ) saying, 'If a man performs ablution perfectly and then offers the compulsory congregational prayer, Allah will forgive his sins committed between that (prayer) and the (next) prayer till he offers it. (160) ☐

64. Narrated Abu Huraira: Allah's Messenger (ﷺ) said, "If anyone of you performs ablution he should put water in his nose and then blow it out and whoever cleans his private parts with stones should do so with odd numbers. And whoever wakes up from his sleep should wash his hands before putting them in the water for ablution, because nobody knows where his hands were during sleep." (162) ☐

65. Narrated `Abdullah bin `Amr: The Prophet (ﷺ) remained behind us on a journey. He joined us while we were performing ablution for the `Asr prayer which was overdue and we were just passing wet hands over our feet (not washing them thoroughly) so he addressed us in a loud voice saying twice, "Save your heels from the fire." (163) ☐

66. Narrated Anas: When Allah's Messenger (ﷺ) got his head shaved, Abu- Talha was the first to take some of his hair. (171) ☐

67. Narrated Abu Huraira: Allah's Messenger (ﷺ) said, "If a dog drinks from the utensil of anyone of you it is essential to wash it seven times." (172) ☐

68. Narrated Hamza bin 'Abdullah: My father said. "During the lifetime of Allah's Apostle, the dogs used to urinate, and pass through the mosques (come and go), nevertheless they never used to sprinkle water on it (urine of the dog.)" (174) ☐

69. Narrated Abu Huraira: Allah's Messenger (ﷺ) said, "A person is considered in prayer as long as he is waiting for the prayer in the mosque as long as he does not do Hadath." A non-Arab man asked, "O Abu Huraira! What is Hadath?" I replied, "It is the passing of wind (from the anus) (that is one of the types of Hadath). (176) ☐

70. Narrated `Ali: I used to get emotional urethral discharges frequently and felt shy to ask Allah's Messenger (ﷺ) about it. So I requested Al-Miqdad bin Al-Aswad to

ask (the Prophet (ﷺ)) about it. Al-Miqdad asked him and he replied, "One has to perform ablution (after it)." (178) ☐

71. Narrated Zaid bin Khalid: I asked `Uthman bin `Affan about a person who engaged in intercourse but did no discharge. `Uthman replied, "He should perform ablution like the one for an ordinary prayer but he must wash his penis." `Uthman added, "I heard it from Allah's Messenger (ﷺ)." I asked `Ali Az-Zubair, Talha and Ubai bin Ka`b about it and they, too, gave the same reply. (This order was canceled later on and taking a bath became necessary for such cases). (179) ☐

72. Narrated Al-Mughira bin Shu`ba: I was in the company of Allah's Messenger (ﷺ) on one of the journeys and he went out to answer the call of nature (and after he finished) I poured water and he performed ablution; he washed his face, forearms and passed his wet hand over his head and over the two Khuff (socks made from thick fabric or leather). (182) ☐

7ಅ. Narrated `Abdullah bin `Abbas: That he stayed overnight in the house of Maimuna the wife of the Prophet, his aunt. He added: I lay on the bed (cushion transversally) while Allah's Messenger (ﷺ) and his wife lay in the lengthwise direction of the cushion. Allah's Messenger (ﷺ) slept till the middle of the night, either a bit before or a bit after it and then woke up, rubbing the traces of sleep off his face with his hands. He then, recited the last ten verses of Sura Al-`Imran, got up and went to a hanging water-skin. He then performed the ablution from it and it was a perfect ablution, and then stood up to offer the prayer. I, too, got up and did as the Prophet had done. Then I went and stood by his side. He placed his right hand on my head and caught my right ear and twisted it. He prayed two rak`at then two rak`at and two rak`at and then two rak`at and then two rak`at (separately six times), and finally one rak`a (the witr). Then he lay down again in the bed till the Mu'adh-dhin came to him where upon the Prophet (ﷺ) got up, offered a two light rak`at prayer and went out and led the Fajr prayer. (183) ☐

74. Narrated Yahya Al-Mazini: A person asked `Abdullah bin Zaid who was the

grandfather of `Amr bin Yahya, "Can you show me how Allah's Messenger (ﷺ) used to perform ablution?" `Abdullah bin Zaid replied in the affirmative and asked for water. He poured it on his hands and washed them twice, then he rinsed his mouth thrice and washed his nose with water thrice by putting water in it and blowing it out. He washed his face thrice and after that he washed his forearms up to the elbows twice and then passed his wet hands over his head from its front to its back and vice versa (beginning from the front and taking them to the back of his head up to the nape of the neck and then brought them to the front again from where he had started) and washed his feet (up to the ankles). (185) □

75. Narrated 'Abdullah bin 'Umar: "During the lifetime of Allah's Messenger (ﷺ) men and women used to perform ablution together." (193) □

76. Narrated Anas: The Prophet (ﷺ) used to take a bath with one Sa` up to five Mudds (1 Sa` = 4 Mudds, 1 Mudd = 600 Grams) of water and used to perform ablution with one Mudd of water. (201) □

77. Narrated Ja`far bin `Amr: My father said, "I saw the Prophet (ﷺ) passing wet hands over his turban and Khuffs (socks). (205) □

78. Narrated `Urwa bin Al-Mughira: My father said, "Once I was in the company of the Prophet (ﷺ) on a journey and I dashed to take off his Khuffs (socks made from thick fabric or leather). He ordered me to leave them as he had put them after performing ablution. So he passed wet hands over them. (206) □

79. Narrated Ja`far bin `Amr bin Umaiya: My father said, "I saw Allah's Messenger (ﷺ) taking a piece of (cooked) mutton from the shoulder region and then he was called for prayer. He put his knife down and prayed without repeating ablution." (208) □

80. Narrated Suwaid bin Al-Nu`man: In the year of the conquest of Khaibar I went with Allah's Messenger (ﷺ) till we reached Sahba, a place near Khaibar, where Allah's Messenger (ﷺ) offered the `Asr prayer and asked for food. Nothing but saweeq was brought. He ordered it to be moistened with water. He and all of us ate it and the

Prophet (ﷺ) got up for the evening prayer (Maghrib prayer), rinsed his mouth with water and we did the same, and he then prayed without repeating the ablution. (209) ☐

81. Narrated Ibn `Abbas: Allah's Messenger (ﷺ) drank milk, rinsed his mouth and said, "It has fat." (211) ☐

82. Narrated `Aisha: Allah's Messenger (ﷺ) said, "If anyone of you feels drowsy while praying he should go to bed (sleep) till his slumber is over because in praying while drowsy one does not know whether one is asking for forgiveness or for a bad thing for oneself." (212) ☐

83. Narrated `Amr bin `Amir: Anas said, "The Prophet (ﷺ) used to perform ablution for every prayer." I asked Anas, "what did you used to do?' Anas replied, "We used to pray with the same ablution until we break it with Hadath." (214) ☐

84. Narrated Abu Huraira: A Bedouin stood up and started making water in the mosque. The people caught him but the Prophet (ﷺ) ordered them to leave him and to pour a bucket or a tumbler of water over the place where he had passed the urine. The Prophet (ﷺ) then said, "You have been sent to make things easy and not to make them difficult." (220) ☐

85. Narrated Um Qais bint Mihsin: I brought my young son, who had not started eating (ordinary food) to Allah's Messenger (ﷺ) who took him and made him sit in his lap. The child urinated on the garment of the Prophet, so he asked for water and poured it over the soiled (area) and did not wash it. (223) ☐

86. Narrated Hudhaifa: Once the Prophet (ﷺ) went to the dumps of some people and passed urine while standing. He then asked for water and so I brought it to him and he performed ablution. (224) ☐

87. Narrated `Aisha: I used to wash the traces of Janaba (semen) from the clothes of the Prophet (ﷺ) and he used to go for prayers while traces of water were still on it (water spots were still visible). (229) ☐

88. Prophet (ﷺ) had said: "You should not pass urine in stagnant water which is not flowing then (you may need to) wash in it." (239) ☐

89. Narrated Abu Burda: My father said, "I came to the Prophet (ﷺ) and saw him carrying a Siwak (miswak) in his hand and cleansing his teeth, saying, 'U' U'," as if he was retching while the Siwak was in his mouth." (244) ☐

90. Narrated Hudhaifa: Whenever the Prophet (ﷺ) got up at night, he used to clean his mouth with Siwak. (245) ☐

91. Narrated Ibn 'Umar: The Prophet (ﷺ) said, "I dreamt that I was cleaning my teeth with a Siwak and two persons came to me. One of them was older than the other and I gave the Siwak to the younger. I was told that I should give it to the older and so I did." (246) ☐

92. Narrated Sa`id bin Al-Harith: That he asked Jabir bin `Abdullah about performing ablution after taking a cooked meal. He replied, "It is not essential," and added, "We never used to get such kind of food during the lifetime of the Prophet except rarely; and if at all we got such a dish, we did not have any handkerchiefs to wipe our hands with except the palms of our hands, our forearms and our feet. We would perform the prayer thereafter without performing new ablution." (5457) ☐

5. BATHING

93. NARRATED `AISHA (RA): The Prophet (ﷺ) and I used to take a bath from a single pot called 'Faraq'. (250) ☐

94. Narrated Abu Salama: `Aisha's brother and I went to `Aisha and he asked her about the bath of the Prophet. She brought a pot containing about a Sa` of water and took a bath and poured it over her head and at that time there was a screen between her and us. (251) ☐

95. Narrated `Aisha: Whenever the Prophet (ﷺ) took the bath of Janaba (sexual relation or wet dream) he asked for the Hilab or some other scent. He used to take it in his hand, rub it first over the right side of his head and then over the left and then rub the middle of his head with both hands. (258) □

96. Narrated Hisham bin `Urwa: (on the authority of his father) `Aisha said, "Whenever Allah's Messenger (ﷺ) took the bath of Janaba, he cleaned his hands and performed ablution like that for prayer and then took a bath and rubbed his hair, till he felt that the whole skin of the head had become wet, then he would pour water thrice and wash the rest of the body." `Aisha further said, "I and Allah's Messenger (ﷺ) used to take a bath from a single water container, from which we took water simultaneously." (272) □

97. Narrated Maimuna: Water was placed for the ablution of Allah's Messenger (ﷺ) after Janaba. He poured water with his right hand over his left twice or thrice and then washed his private parts and rubbed his hand on the earth or on a wall twice or thrice and then rinsed his mouth, washed his nose by putting water in it and then blowing it out and then washed his face and forearms and poured water over his head and washed his body. Then he shifted from that place and washed his feet. I brought a piece of cloth, but he did not take it and removed the traces of water from his body with his hand." (274) □

98. Narrated Abu Huraira: Allah's Messenger (ﷺ) came across me and I was Junub. He took my hand and I went along with him till he sat down I slipped away, went home and took a bath. When I came back, he was still sitting there. He then said to me,"O Abu Huraira! Where have you been?'I told him about it. The Prophet (ﷺ) said, "Subhan Allah! O Abu Huraira! A believer never becomes impure."(285) □

99. Narrated Abu Salama: I asked `Aisha "Did the Prophet (ﷺ) use to sleep while he was Junub?" She replied, "Yes, but he used to perform ablution (before going to bed). (286) □

100. Narrated Abu Huraira: The Prophet (ﷺ) said, "When a man sits in between the

four parts of a woman and did the sexual intercourse with her, bath becomes compulsory." (291) ☐

6. MENSTRUAL PERIODS

101. NARRATED `AISHA (RA): While in menses, I used to comb the hair of Allah's Messenger (p.b.u.h). (295) ☐

102. Narrated `Aisha: The Prophet (ﷺ) used to lean on my lap and recite Qur'an while I was in menses. (297) ☐

103. Narrated `Abdur-Rahman bin Al-Aswad: (on the authority of his father) `Aisha said: "Whenever Allah's Messenger (ﷺ) wanted to fondle anyone of us during her periods (menses), he used to order her to put on an Izar and start fondling her." `Aisha added, "None of you could control his sexual desires as the Prophet (ﷺ) could." (302) ☐

104. Narrated Abu Sa`id Al-Khudri: Once Allah's Messenger (ﷺ) went out to the Musalla (to offer the prayer) of Eid-al-Adha or Al-Fitr prayer. Then he passed by the women and said, "O women! Give alms, as I have seen that the majority of the dwellers of Hell-fire were you (women)." They asked, "Why is it so, O Allah's Messenger (ﷺ)?" He replied, "You curse frequently and are ungrateful to your husbands. I have not seen anyone more deficient in intelligence and religion than you. A cautious sensible man could be led astray by some of you." The women asked, "O Allah's Messenger (ﷺ)! What is deficient in our intelligence and religion?" He said, "Is not the evidence of two women equal to the witness of one man?" They replied in the affirmative. He said, "This is the deficiency in her intelligence. Isn't it true that a woman can neither pray nor fast during her menses?" The women replied in the affirmative. He said, "This is the deficiency in her religion." (304) ☐

105. Narrated `Aisha: Fatima bint Abi Hubaish said to Allah's Messenger (ﷺ), "O Allah's Messenger (ﷺ)! I do not become clean (from bleeding). Shall I give up my

prayers?" Allah's Messenger (ﷺ) replied: "No, because it is from a blood vessel and not the menses. So when the real menses begins give up your prayers and when it (the period) has finished wash the blood off your body (take a bath) and offer your prayers." (306) □

106. Narrated Asma' bint Abi Bakr: A woman asked Allah's Messenger (ﷺ), "O Allah's Messenger (ﷺ)! What should we do, if the blood of menses falls on our clothes?" Allah's Messenger (ﷺ) replied, "If the blood of menses falls on the garment of anyone of you, she must take hold of the blood spot, rub it, and wash it with water and then pray in (with it). (307) □

107. Narrated `Aisha: "One of the wives of Allah's Messenger (ﷺ) joined him in I`tikaf and she noticed blood and yellowish discharge (from her private parts) and put a dish under her when she prayed." (310) □

108. Narrated `Aisha: None of us had more than a single garment and we used to have our menses while wearing it. Whenever it got soiled with blood of menses we used to apply saliva to the blood spot and rub off the blood with our nails. (312) □

109. Narrated `Aisha: An Ansari woman asked the Prophet (ﷺ) how to take a bath after finishing from the menses. He replied, "Take a piece of cloth perfumed with musk and clean the private parts with it thrice." The Prophet (ﷺ) felt shy and turned his face. So I pulled her to me and told her what the Prophet (ﷺ) meant. (315) □

110. Narrated Mu`adha: A woman asked `Aisha, "Should I offer the prayers that which I did not offer because of menses" `Aisha said, "Are you from the Huraura' (a town in Iraq?) We were with the Prophet (ﷺ) and used to get our periods but he never ordered us to offer them (the Prayers missed during menses)." `Aisha perhaps said, "We did not offer them." (321) □

111. Narrated Zainab bint Abi Salama: Um-Salama said, "I got my menses while I was lying with the Prophet (ﷺ) under a woolen sheet. So I slipped away, took the clothes for menses and put them on. Allah's Messenger (ﷺ) said, 'Have you got your

menses?' I replied, 'Yes.' Then he called me and took me with him under the woolen sheet." Um Salama further said, "The Prophet (ﷺ) used to kiss me while he was fasting. The Prophet (ﷺ) and I used to take the bath of Janaba from a single pot." (322) □

112. Narrated Um `Atiya: We never considered yellowish discharge as a thing of importance (as menses). (326) □

113. Narrated `Aisha: Um Habiba got bleeding in between the periods for seven years. She asked Allah's Messenger (ﷺ) about it. He ordered her to take a bath (after the termination of actual periods) and added that it was (from) a blood vessel. So she used to take a bath for every prayer. (327) □

114. Narrated `Aisha: The Prophet (ﷺ) said to me, "Give up the prayer when your menses begin and when it has finished, wash the blood off your body (take a bath) and start praying." (331) □

115. Narrated Maimuna: during my menses, I never prayed, but used to sit on the mat beside the mosque of Allah's Messenger (ﷺ). He used to offer the prayer on his sheet and in prostration some of his clothes used to touch me." (333) □

7. ABLUTIONS WITH DUST (TAYAMMUM)

116. NARRATED `AISHA (RA): We set out with Allah's Messenger (ﷺ) on one of his journeys till we reached Al- Baida' or Dhatul-Jaish, a necklace of mine was broken (and lost). Allah's Messenger (ﷺ) stayed there to search for it, and so did the people along with him. There was no water at that place, so the people went to Abu- Bakr As-Siddiq and said, "Don't you see what `Aisha has done? She has made Allah's Apostle and the people stay where there is no water and they have no water with them." Abu Bakr came while Allah's Messenger (ﷺ) was sleeping with his head on my thigh, He said, to me: "You have detained Allah's Messenger (ﷺ) and the people

where there is no water and they have no water with them. So he admonished me and said what Allah wished him to say and hit me on my flank with his hand. Nothing prevented me from moving (because of pain) but the position of Allah's Messenger (ﷺ) on my thigh. Allah's Messenger (ﷺ) got up when dawn broke and there was no water. So Allah revealed the Divine Verses of Tayammum. So they all performed Tayammum. Usaid bin Hudair said, "O the family of Abu Bakr! This is not the first blessing of yours." Then the camel on which I was riding was caused to move from its place and the necklace was found beneath it. (334) □

117. Narrated Abu Juhaim Al-Ansari: The Prophet (ﷺ) came from the direction of Bir Jamal. A man met him and greeted him. But he did not return back the greeting till he went to a (mud) wall and wiped his face and hands with its dust (performed Tayammum) and then returned back the greeting. (337) □

118. Narrated `Abdur Rahman bin Abza: A man came to `Umar bin Al-Khattab and said, "I became Junub but no water was available." `Ammar bin Yasir said to `Umar, "Do you remember that you and I (became Junub) were together on a journey and you didn't pray but I rolled myself on the ground and prayed? I informed the Prophet (ﷺ) about it and he said, 'It would have been sufficient for you to do like this.' The Prophet then stroked lightly the earth with his hands and then blew off the dust and passed his hands over his face and hands." (338) □

119. Narrated `Imran: Once we were traveling with the Prophet (ﷺ) and we carried on traveling till the last part of the night and then we (halted at a place) and slept. There is nothing sweeter than sleep for a traveler in the last part of the night. So it was only the heat of the sun that made us to wake up and the first to wake up was so and so, then so and so and then so and so (the narrator `Auf said that Abu Raja' had told him their names but he had forgotten them) and the fourth person to wake up was `Umar bin Al- Khattab. And whenever the Prophet (ﷺ) used to sleep, nobody would wake up him till he himself used to get up as we did not know what was happening (being revealed) to him in his sleep. So, `Umar got up and saw the condition of the people, and he was a strict man, so he said, "Allahu Akbar" and raised

his voice with Takbir, and kept on saying loudly till the Prophet (ﷺ) got up because of it. When he got up, the people informed him about what had happened to them. He said, "There is no harm (or it will not be harmful). Depart!" So they departed from that place, and after covering some distance the Prophet (ﷺ) stopped and asked for some water to perform the ablution. So he performed the ablution and the call for the prayer was pronounced and he led the people in prayer. After he finished from the prayer, he saw a man sitting aloof who had not prayed with the people. He asked, "O so and so! What has prevented you from praying with us?" He replied, "I am Junub and there is no water." The Prophet (ﷺ) said, "Perform Tayammum with (clean) earth and that is sufficient for you." Then the Prophet (ﷺ) proceeded on and the people complained to him of thirst. Thereupon he got down and called a person (the narrator `Auf added that Abu Raja' had named him but he had forgotten) and `Ali, and ordered them to go and bring water. So they went in search of water and met a woman who was sitting on her camel between two bags of water. They asked, "Where can we find water?" She replied, "I was there (at the place of water) this hour yesterday and my people are behind me." They requested her to accompany them. She asked, "Where?" They said, "To Allah's Messenger (ﷺ)." She said, "Do you mean the man who is called the Sabi, (with a new religion)?" They replied, "Yes, the same person. So come along." They brought her to the Prophet (ﷺ) and narrated the whole story. He said, "Help her to dismount." The Prophet (ﷺ) asked for a pot, then he opened the mouths of the bags and poured some water into the pot. Then he closed the big openings of the bags and opened the small ones and the people were called upon to drink and water their animals. So they all watered their animals and they (too) all quenched their thirst and also gave water to others and last of all the Prophet (ﷺ) gave a pot full of water to the person who was Junub and told him to pour it over his body. The woman was standing and watching all that which they were doing with her water. By Allah, when her water bags were returned the looked like as if they were more full than they had been before (Miracle of Allah's Messenger (ﷺ)) Then the Prophet (ﷺ) ordered us to collect something for her; so dates, flour and Sawiq were collected which amounted to a good meal that was put in a piece of cloth. She was helped to ride on her camel and that cloth full of foodstuff was also placed in front of her and then the Prophet (ﷺ) said to her, "We have not taken your water but Allah has given water to us." She returned home late. Her relatives asked her: "O so and so what has delayed you?" She said, "A strange thing! Two men met me and took me to the man who is called the Sabi' and he did such and such a thing. By Allah, he is either the greatest magician between this and this (gesturing with her index and middle fingers raising them towards the sky indicating the heaven and the earth) or he is Allah's true Apostle." Afterwards the Muslims used to attack the pagans around her abode but never touched her village. One day she said to her people, "I think that these people leave you purposely. Have you got any inclination to Islam?" They obeyed her and all of them embraced Islam. Abu `Abdullah said: The word Saba'a means "The one who has deserted his old religion and embraced a new religion." Abul 'Ailya said, "The S`Abis are a sect of people of the Scripture who recite the Book of Psalms." (344) □

8. MOSQUE

120. NARRATED ABU DHAR (RA): Allah's Messenger (ﷺ) said, "While I was at Mecca the roof of my house was opened and Gabriel descended, opened my chest, and washed it with Zamzam water. Then he brought a golden tray full of wisdom and faith and having poured its contents into my chest, he closed it. Then he took my hand and ascended with me to the nearest heaven, when I reached the nearest heaven, Gabriel said to the gatekeeper of the heaven, 'Open (the gate).' The gatekeeper asked, 'Who is it?' Gabriel answered: 'Gabriel.' He asked, 'Is there anyone with you?' Gabriel replied, 'Yes, Muhammad I is with me.' He asked, 'Has he been called?' Gabriel said, 'Yes.' So the gate was opened and we went over the nearest heaven and there we saw a man sitting with some people on his right and some on his left. When he looked towards his right, he laughed and when he looked toward his left he wept. Then he said, 'Welcome! O pious Prophet and pious son.' I asked Gabriel, 'Who is he?' He replied, 'He is Adam and the people on his right and left are the souls of his offspring.

Those on his right are the people of Paradise and those on his left are the people of Hell and when he looks towards his right he laughs and when he looks towards his left he weeps.' Then he ascended with me till he reached the second heaven and he (Gabriel) said to its gatekeeper, 'Open (the gate).' The gatekeeper said to him the same as the gatekeeper of the first heaven had said and he opened the gate. Anas said: "Abu Dhar added that the Prophet (ﷺ) met Adam, Idris, Moses, Jesus and Abraham, he (Abu Dhar) did not mention on which heaven they were but he mentioned that he (the Prophet (ﷺ)) met Adam on the nearest heaven and Abraham on the sixth heaven. Anas said, "When Gabriel along with the Prophet (ﷺ) passed by Idris, the latter said, 'Welcome! O pious Prophet and pious brother.' The Prophet (ﷺ) asked, 'Who is he?' Gabriel replied, 'He is Idris." The Prophet (ﷺ) added, "I passed by Moses and he said, 'Welcome! O pious Prophet and pious brother.' I asked Gabriel, 'Who is he?' Gabriel replied, 'He is Moses.' Then I passed by Jesus and he said, 'Welcome! O pious brother and pious Prophet.' I asked, 'Who is he?' Gabriel replied, 'He is Jesus. Then I passed by Abraham and he said, 'Welcome! O pious Prophet and pious son.' I asked Gabriel, 'Who is he?' Gabriel replied, 'He is Abraham. The Prophet (ﷺ) added, 'Then Gabriel ascended with me to a place where I heard the creaking of the pens." Ibn Hazm and Anas bin Malik said: The Prophet (ﷺ) said, "Then Allah enjoined fifty prayers on my followers when I returned with this order of Allah, I passed by Moses who asked me, 'What has Allah enjoined on your followers?' I replied, 'He has enjoined fifty prayers on them.' Moses said, 'Go back to your Lord (and appeal for reduction) for your followers will not be able to bear it.' (So I went back to Allah and requested for reduction) and He reduced it to half. When I passed by Moses again and informed him about it, he said, 'Go back to your Lord as your followers will not be able to bear it.' So I returned to Allah and requested for further reduction and half of it was reduced. I again passed by Moses and he said to me: 'Return to your Lord, for your followers will not be able to bear it. So I returned to Allah and He said, 'these are five prayers and they are all (equal to) fifty (in reward) for My Word does not change.' I returned to Moses and he told me to go back once again. I replied, 'Now I feel shy of asking my Lord again.' Then Gabriel took me till we " reached Sidrat-il-Muntaha (Lote tree of; the utmost boundary) which was shrouded in colors, indescribable. Then I was admitted into Paradise where I found small (tents or) walls (made) of pearls and its earth was of musk." (349) ☐

121. Narrated `Aisha: the mother of believers: Allah enjoined the prayer when He enjoined it, it was two rak`at only (in every prayer) both when in residence or on journey. Then the prayers offered on journey remained the same, but (the rak`at of) the prayers for non-travelers were increased. (350) ☐

122. Narrated `Umar bin Abi Salama: I saw the Prophet (ﷺ) offering prayers in a single garment in the house of Um-Salama and he had crossed its ends around his shoulders. (355) ☐

123. Narrated Abu Murra: (the freed slave of Um Hani) Um Hani, the daughter of Abi Talib said, "I went to Allah's Messenger (ﷺ) in the year of the conquest of Mecca and found him taking a bath and his daughter Fatima was screening him. I greeted him. He asked, 'Who is she?' I replied, 'I am Um Hani bint Abi Talib.' He said, 'Welcome! O Um Hani.' When he finished his bath he stood up and prayed eight rak`at while wearing a single garment wrapped round his body and when he finished I said, 'O Allah's Messenger (ﷺ) ! My brother has told me that he will kill a person whom I gave shelter and that person is so and so the son of Hubaira.' The Prophet (ﷺ) said, 'We shelter the person whom you have sheltered.'" Um Hani added, "And that was before noon (Duha). (357) ☐

124. Narrated Abu Huraira: The Prophet (ﷺ) said, "None of you should offer prayer in a single garment that does not cover the shoulders." (359) ☐

125. Narrated Sa`id bin Al-Harith: I asked Jabir bin `Abdullah about praying in a single garment. He said, "I traveled with the Prophet (ﷺ) during some of his journeys, and I came to him at night for some purpose and I found him praying. At that time, I was wearing a single garment with which I covered my shoulders and prayed by his side. When he finished the prayer, he asked, 'O Jabir! What has brought you here?' I told him what I wanted. When I finished, he asked, 'O Jabir! What is this garment

which I have seen and with which you covered your shoulders?' I replied, 'It is a (tight) garment.' He said, 'If the garment is large enough, wrap it round the body (covering the shoulders) and if it is tight (too short) then use it as an Izar (tie it around your waist only.)'" (361) ☐

126. Narrated Sahl: The men used to pray with the Prophet (ﷺ) with their Izars tied around their necks as boys used to do; therefore the Prophet (ﷺ) told the women not to raise their heads till the men sat down straight. (362) ☐

127. Narrated Abu Huraira: A man stood up and asked the Prophet (ﷺ) about praying in a single garment. The Prophet (ﷺ) said, "Has every one of you two garments?" A man put a similar question to `Umar on which he replied, "When Allah makes you wealthier then you should clothe yourself properly during prayers. Otherwise one can pray with an Izar and a Rida' (a sheet covering the upper part of the body.) Izar and a shirt, Izar and a Qaba', trousers and a Rida, trousers and a shirt or trousers and a Qaba', Tubban and a Qaba' or Tubban and a shirt." (The narrator added, "I think that he also said a Tubban and a Rida. ") (365) ☐

128. Narrated `Aisha: the Prophet (ﷺ) prayed in a Khamisa (a square garment) having marks. During the prayer, he looked at its marks. So when he finished the prayer he said, "Take this Khamisa of mine to Abu Jahm and get me his Inbijaniya (a woolen garment without marks) as it (the Khamisa) has diverted my attention from the prayer."

Narrated `Aisha: The Prophet (ﷺ) said, 'I was looking at its (Khamisa's) marks during the prayers and I was afraid that it may put me in trial (by taking away my attention). (373) ☐

129. Narrated Anas: `Aisha had a Qiram (a thin marked woolen curtain) with which she had screened one side of her home. The Prophet (ﷺ) said, "Take away this Qiram of yours, as its pictures are still displayed in front of me during my prayer (i.e. they divert my attention from the prayer). (374) ☐

130. Narrated `Uqba bin 'Amir: The Prophet (ﷺ) was given a silken Farruj as a present. He wore it while praying. When he had finished his prayer, he took it off violently as if with a strong aversion to it and said, "It is not the dress of Allah-fearing pious people." (375) ☐

131. Narrated Abu Juhaifa: I saw Allah's Messenger (ﷺ) in a red leather tent and I saw Bilal taking the remaining water with which the Prophet had performed ablution. I saw the people taking the utilized water impatiently and whoever got some of it rubbed it on his body and those who could not get any took the moisture from the others' hands. Then I saw Bilal carrying a short spear (or stick) which he planted in the ground. The Prophet came out tucking up his red cloak, and led the people in prayer and offered two rak`at (facing the Ka`ba) taking a short spear (or stick) as a Sutra for his prayer. I saw the people and animals passing in front of him beyond the stick. (376) ☐

132. Narrated Abu Hazim: Sahl bin Sa`d was asked about the (Prophet's) pulpit as to what thing it was made of? Sahl replied: "None remains alive amongst the people, who knows about it better than I. It was made of tamarisk (wood) of the forest. So and so, the slave of so and so prepared it for Allah's Messenger (ﷺ). When it was constructed and place (in the Mosque), Allah's Messenger (ﷺ) stood on it facing the Qibla and said 'Allahu Akbar', and the people stood behind him (and led the people in prayer). He recited and bowed and the people bowed behind him. Then he raised his head and stepped back, got down and prostrated on the ground and then he again ascended the pulpit, recited, bowed, raised his head and stepped back, got down and prostrate on the ground. So, this is what I know about the pulpit." Ahmad bin Hanbal said, "As the Prophet (ﷺ) was at a higher level than the people, there is no harm according to the above-mentioned Hadith if the Imam is at a higher level than his followers during the prayers." (377) ☐

133. Narrated 'Is-haq: Anas bin Malik said, "My grandmother Mulaika invited Allah's Messenger (ﷺ) for a meal which she herself had prepared. He ate from it and said, 'Get up! I will lead you in the prayer.'" Anas added, "I took my Hasir, washed it

with water as it had become dark because of long use and Allah's Messenger (ﷺ) stood on it. The orphan (Damira or Ruh) and I aligned behind him and the old lady (Mulaika) stood behind us. Allah's Messenger (ﷺ) led us in the prayer and offered two rak`at and then left." (380) □

134. Narrated Anas bin Malik: We used to pray with the Prophet (ﷺ) and some of us used to place the ends of their clothes at the place of prostration because of scorching heat. (385) □

135. Narrated Abu Maslama: Sa`id bin Yazid Al-Azdi: I asked Anas bin Malik whether the Prophet (ﷺ) had ever, prayed with his shoes on. He replied "Yes." (386) □

136. Narrated 'Abdullah bin Malik: Ibn Buhaina, "When the Prophet (ﷺ) prayed, he used to separate his arms from his body so widely that the whiteness of his armpits was visible." (390) □

137. Narrated Bara' bin `Azib: Allah's Messenger (ﷺ) prayed facing Baitul-Maqdis for sixteen or seventeen months but he loved to face the Ka`ba (at Mecca) so Allah revealed: "Verily, We have seen the turning of your face to the heaven!" (2:144) So the Prophet (ﷺ) faced the Ka`ba and the fools amongst the people namely "the Jews" said, "What has turned them from their Qibla (Baitul-Maqdis) which they formerly observed"" (Allah revealed): "Say: 'To Allah belongs the East and the West. He guides whom he will to a straight path'." (2:142) A man prayed with the Prophet (facing the Ka`ba) and went out. He saw some of the Ansar praying the `Asr prayer with their faces towards Baitul-Maqdis, he said, "I bear witness that I prayed with Allah's Messenger (ﷺ) facing the Ka`ba." So all the people turned their faces towards the Ka`ba. (399) □

138. Narrated Jabir: Allah's Messenger (ﷺ) used to pray (non-obligatory prayer) while riding on his mount (Rahila) wherever it turned, and whenever he wanted to pray the compulsory prayer he dismounted and prayed facing the Qibla. (400) □

139. Narrated `Abdullah: The Prophet (峻) prayed (and the sub-narrator Ibrahim said, "I do not know whether he prayed more or less than usual"), and when he had finished the prayers he was asked, "O Allah's Messenger (峻)! Has there been any change in the prayers?" He said, "what is it?' The people said, "You have prayed so much and so much." So the Prophet (峻) bent his legs, faced the Qibla and performed two prostration's (of Sahu) and finished his prayers with Taslim (by turning his face to right and left saying: 'As-Salamu `Alaikum- Warahmat-ullah'). When he turned his face to us he said, "If there had been anything changed in the prayer, surely I would have informed you but I am a human being like you and liable to forget like you. So if I forget remind me and if anyone of you is doubtful about his prayer, he should follow what he thinks to be correct and complete his prayer accordingly and finish it and do two prostrations (of Sahu). (401) □

140. Narrated `Umar (bin Al-Khattab): My Lord agreed with me in three things: 1) I said, "O Allah's Messenger (峻), I wish we took the station of Abraham as our praying place (for some of our prayers). So came the Divine Inspiration: "And take you (people) the station of Abraham as a place of prayer (for some of your prayers e.g. two rak`at of Tawaf of Ka`ba)". (2.125) 2) And as regards the (verse of) the veiling of the women, I said, 'O Allah's Messenger (峻)! I wish you ordered your wives to cover themselves from the men because good and bad ones talk to them.' So the verse of the veiling of the women was revealed. 3) Once the wives of the Prophet (峻) made a united front against the Prophet (峻) and I said to them, 'It may be if he (the Prophet) divorced you, (all) that his Lord (Allah) will give him instead of you wives better than you.' So this verse (the same as I had said) was revealed." (66.5). (402)

Narrated `Amr bin Dinar: I asked Ibn `Umar, "Can a person who has performed the Tawaf around the Ka`ba for `Umra but has not performed the (Sa`i) Tawaf of Safa and Marwa, have a sexual relation with his wife?" Ibn `Umar replied "When the Prophet (峻) reached Mecca he performed the Tawaf around the Ka`ba (circumambulated it seven times) and offered a two-rak`at prayer (at the place) behind the station (of Abraham) and then performed the Tawaf (Sa`i) of Safa and Marwa, and verily in Allah's Messenger (ﷺ) you have a good example." Then we put the same question to Jabir bin `Abdullah and he too replied, "He should not go near his wife (for sexual relation) till he has finished the Tawaf of Safa and Marwa." (420b) □

141. Narrated `Abdullah: "Once the Prophet (ﷺ) offered five rak`at in Zuhr prayer. He was asked, "Is there an increase in the prayer?" The Prophet (ﷺ) said, "And what is it?" They said, "you have prayed five rak`at.' So he bent his legs and performed two prostrations (of Sahu). (404) □

142. Narrated Anas bin Malik: The Prophet (ﷺ) saw some sputum in the direction of the Qibla (on the wall of the mosque) and he disliked that and the sign of disgust was apparent from his face. So he got up and scraped it off with his hand and said, "Whenever anyone of you stands for the prayer, he is speaking in private to his Lord or his Lord is between him and his Qibla. So, none of you should spit in the direction of the Qibla but one can spit to the left or under his foot." The Prophet (ﷺ) then took the corner of his sheet and spat in it and folded it and said, "Or you can do this." (405) □

143. Narrated Anas bin Malik: The Prophet (ﷺ) said, "Spitting in the mosque is a sin and its expiation is to bury it." (415) □

144. Narrated Abu Huraira: Allah's Messenger (ﷺ) said, "Do you consider or see that my face is towards the Qibla? By Allah, neither your submissiveness nor your bowing is hidden from me, surely I see you from my back." (418) □

145. Narrated `Itban bin Malik: who was one of the companions of Allah's Messenger (ﷺ) and one of the Ansar's who took part in the battle of Badr: I came to Allah's Messenger (ﷺ) and said, "O Allah's Messenger (ﷺ) I have weak eyesight and I lead my people in prayers. When it rains the water flows in the valley between me and my people so I cannot go to their mosque to lead them in prayer. O Allah's Messenger (ﷺ)! I wish you would come to my house and pray in it so that I could take that place as a Musalla. Allah's Messenger (ﷺ) said. "Allah willing, I will do so." Next day after the sun rose high, Allah's Messenger (ﷺ) and Abu Bakr came and Allah's Messenger

(ﷺ) asked for permission to enter. I gave him permission and he did not sit on entering the house but said to me, "Where do you like me to pray?" I pointed to a place in my house. So Allah's Messenger (ﷺ) stood there and said, 'Allahu Akbar', and we all got up and aligned behind him and offered a two-rak`at prayer and ended it with Taslim. We requested him to stay for a meal called "Khazira" which we had prepared for him. Many members of our family gathered in the house and one of them said, "Where is Malik bin Al-Dukhaishin or Ibn Al-Dukhshun?" One of them replied, "He is a hypocrite and does not love Allah and His Apostle." Hearing that, Allah's Messenger (ﷺ) said, "Do not say so. Haven't you seen that he said, 'None has the right to be worshipped but Allah' for Allah's sake only?" He said, "Allah and His Apostle know better. We have seen him helping and advising hypocrites." Allah's Messenger (ﷺ) said, "Allah has forbidden the (Hell) fire for those who say, 'None has the right to be worshipped but Allah' for Allah's sake only." (425) □

146. Narrated `Aisha: Um Habiba and Um Salama mentioned about a church they had seen in Ethiopia in which there were pictures. They told the Prophet (ﷺ) about it, on which he said, "If any religious man dies amongst those people they would build a place of worship at his grave and make these pictures in it. They will be the worst creature in the sight of Allah on the Day of Resurrection." (427) □

147. Narrated Anas: When the Prophet (ﷺ) arrived Medina he dismounted at `Awali-i-Medina amongst a tribe called Banu `Amr bin `Auf. He stayed there for fourteen nights. Then he sent for Bani An-Najjar and they came armed with their swords. As if I am looking (just now) as the Prophet (ﷺ) was sitting over his Rahila (Mount) with Abu Bakr riding behind him and all Banu An-Najjar around him till he dismounted at the courtyard of Abu Aiyub's house. The Prophet (ﷺ) loved to pray wherever the time for the prayer was due even at sheep-folds. Later on he ordered that a mosque should be built and sent for some people of Banu-An-Najjar and said, "O Banu An-Najjar! Suggest to me the price of this (walled) piece of land of yours." They replied, "No! By Allah! We do not demand its price except from Allah." Anas added: There were graves of pagans in it and some of it was unleveled and there were some date-

palm trees in it. The Prophet (ﷺ) ordered that the graves of the pagans be dug out and the unleveled land be level led and the date-palm trees be cut down. (So all that was done). They aligned these cut date-palm trees towards the Qibla of the mosque (as a wall) and they also built two stone side-walls (of the mosque). His companions brought the stones while reciting some poetic verses. The Prophet (ﷺ) was with them and he kept on saying, "There is no goodness except that of the Hereafter, O Allah! So please forgive the Ansars and the emigrants." (428) □

148. Anas said, "The Prophet (ﷺ) prayed in the sheep fold." Later on I heard him saying, "He prayed in the sheep folds before the construction of the, mosque." (429) □

149. Narrated Ibn `Umar: The Prophet (ﷺ) had said, "Offer some of your prayers (Nawafil) at home, and do not take your houses as graves." (432) □

150. Narrated Jabir bin `Abdullah: Allah's Messenger (ﷺ) said, "I have been given five things which were not given to any amongst the Prophets before me. These are: 1) Allah made me victorious by awe (by His frightening my enemies) for a distance of one month's journey. 2) The earth has been made for me (and for my followers) a place for praying and a thing to perform Tayammum. Therefore my followers can pray wherever the time of a prayer is due. 3) The booty has been made Halal (lawful) for me (and was not made so for anyone else). 4) Every Prophet used to be sent to his nation exclusively but I have been sent to all mankind. 5) I have been given the right of intercession (on the Day of Resurrection.) (438) □

151. Narrated Nafi`:`Abdullah bin `Umar said: I used to sleep in the mosque of the Prophet (ﷺ) while I was young and unmarried. (440) □

152. Narrated Abu Huraira: I saw seventy of As-Suffa men and none of them had a Rida' (a garment covering the upper part of the body). They had either Izars (only) or sheets which they tied round their necks. Some of these sheets reached the middle of their legs and some reached their heels and they used to gather them with their hands lest their private parts should become naked. (442) □

153. Narrated Jabir bin `Abdullah: I went to the Prophet (ﷺ) in the mosque (the sub-narrator Mas`ar thought that Jabir had said, "In the forenoon.") He ordered me to pray two rak`at. He owed me some money and he repaid it to me and gave more than what was due to me. (443) ☐

154. Narrated Abu Qatada Al-Aslami: Allah's Messenger (ﷺ) said, "If anyone of you enters a mosque, he should pray two rak`at before sitting." (444) ☐

155. Narrated `Abdullah bin `Umar: In the lifetime of Allah's Messenger (ﷺ) the mosque was built of adobes, its roof of the leaves of date-palms and its pillars of the stems of date-palms. Abu Bakr did not alter it. `Umar expanded it on the same pattern as it was in the lifetime of Allah's Messenger (ﷺ) by using adobes, leaves of date-palms and changing the pillars into wooden ones. `Uthman changed it by expanding it to a great extent and built its walls with engraved stones and lime and made its pillars of engraved stones and its roof of teak wood. (446) ☐

156. Narrated Abu Burda bin `Abdullah: (on the authority of his father) The Prophet (ﷺ) said, "Whoever passes through our mosques or markets with arrows should hold them by their heads lest he should injure a Muslim." (452) ☐

157. Narrated Nafi`: Ibn `Umar said, "The Prophet (ﷺ) arrived at Mecca and sent for `Uthman bin Talha. He opened the gate of the Ka`ba and the Prophet, Bilal, Usama bin Zaid and `Uthman bin Talha entered the Ka`ba and then they closed its door (from inside). They stayed there for an hour, and then came out." Ibn `Umar added, "I quickly went to Bilal and asked him (whether the Prophet (ﷺ) had prayed). Bilal replied, 'He prayed in it.' I asked, 'Where?' He replied, 'Between the two pillars.' "Ibn `Umar added, "I forgot to ask how many rak`at he (the Prophet) had prayed in the Ka`ba." (468) ☐

158. Narrated Abu Huraira: Allah's Messenger (ﷺ) sent some horse men to Najd and they brought a man called Thumama bin Uthal from Bani Hanifa. (He was pagan) They fastened him to one of the pillars of the mosque. (469) ☐

159. Narrated Al-Sa'ib bin Yazid: I was standing in the mosque and somebody threw a gravel at me. I looked and found that he was `Umar bin Al-Khattab. He said to me, "Fetch those two men to me." When I did, he said to them, "Who are you? (Or) where do you come from?" They replied, "We are from Ta'if." `Umar said, "Were you from this city (Medina) I would have punished you for raising your voices in the mosque of Allah's Messenger (p.b.u.h)" (470) □

160. Narrated Ka`b bin Malik: During the lifetime of Allah's Messenger (صلى الله عليه وسلم) I asked Ibn Abi Hadrad in the mosque to pay the debts which he owed to me and our voices grew so loud that Allah's Messenger (صلى الله عليه وسلم) heard them while he was in his house. So he came to us after raising the curtain of his room. The Prophet (صلى الله عليه وسلم) said, "O Ka`b bin Malik!" I replied, "Labaik, O Allah's Messenger (صلى الله عليه وسلم)." He gestured with his hand to me to reduce the debt to one half. I said, "O Allah's Messenger (صلى الله عليه وسلم) have done it." Allah's Messenger (صلى الله عليه وسلم) said (to Ibn Hadrad), "Get up and pay it." (471) □

161. Narrated Abu Waqid al-Laithi: While Allah's Messenger (صلى الله عليه وسلم) was sitting in the mosque (with some people) three men came, two of them came in front of Allah's Messenger (صلى الله عليه وسلم) and the third one went away, and then one of them found a place in the circle and sat there while the second man sat behind the gathering, and the third one went away. When Allah's Messenger (صلى الله عليه وسلم) finished his preaching, he said, "Shall I tell you about these three persons? One of them betook himself to Allah and so Allah accepted him and accommodated him; the second felt shy before Allah so Allah did the same for him and sheltered him in His Mercy (and did not punish him), while the third turned his face from Allah, and went away, so Allah turned His face from him likewise. (474) □

162. Narrated `Abbad bin Tamim: that his uncle said, "I saw Allah's Messenger (صلى الله عليه وسلم) lying flat (on his back) in the mosque with one leg on the other." Narrated Sa`id bin Al-Musaiyab that `Umar and `Uthman used to do the same. (475) □

163. Narrated Abu Huraira: The Prophet (صلى الله عليه وسلم) said, "The prayer offered in congregation is twenty five times more superior (in reward) to the prayer offered alone

in one's house or in a business center, because if one performs ablution and does it perfectly, and then proceeds to the mosque with the sole intention of praying, then for each step which he takes towards the mosque, Allah upgrades him a degree in reward and (forgives) crosses out one sin till he enters the mosque. When he enters the mosque he is considered in prayer as long as he is waiting for the prayer and the angels keep on asking for Allah's forgiveness for him and they keep on saying: 'O Allah! Be Merciful to him, O Allah! Forgive him, as long as he keeps on sitting at his praying place and does not pass wind. (477) ☐

164. Narrated Ibn `Abbas: Once I came riding a she-ass when I had just attained the age of puberty. Allah's Messenger (ﷺ) was offering the prayer at Mina with no wall in front of him and I passed in front of some of the row. There I dismounted and let my she-ass loose to graze and entered the row and nobody objected to me about it. (493) ☐

165. Narrated Salama: The distance between the wall of the mosque and the pulpit was hardly enough for a sheep to pass through. (497) ☐

166. Narrated `Abdullah: The Prophet (ﷺ) used to get a Harba planted in front of him (as a Sutra) and pray behind it. (498) ☐

167. Narrated Nafi`: `Abdullah bin `Umar said, "Allah's Messenger (ﷺ) entered the Ka`ba along with Usama bin Zaid, Bilal and `Uthman bin Talha Al-Hajabi and closed the door and stayed there for some time. I asked Bilal when he came out, 'What did the Prophet (ﷺ) do?' He replied, 'He offered prayer with one pillar to his left and one to his right and three behind.' In those days the Ka`ba was supported by six pillars." Malik said: "There were two pillars on his (the Prophet's) right side." (505) ☐

168. Narrated Nafi': Whenever 'Abdullah entered the Ka'bah, he used to go ahead leaving the door of the Ka'bah behind him. He would proceed on till the remaining distance between him and the opposite wall about three cubits. Then he would off prayer there where the Prophet (ﷺ) had offered Salah, as Bilal informed me. Ibn 'Umar said, "It does not matter for any of us to offer prayers at any place inside the

Ka'bah." (506) □

169. Narrated Nafi`: "The Prophet (ﷺ) used to make his she-camel sit across and he would pray facing it (as a Sutra)." I asked, "What would the Prophet (ﷺ) do if the she-camel was provoked and moved?" He said, "He would take its camel-saddle and put it in front of him and pray facing its back part (as a Sutra). And Ibn `Umar used to do the same." (This indicates that one should not pray except behind a Sutra). (507) □

170. Narrated Abu Sa`id: The Prophet (ﷺ) said, (what is ascribed to him in the following Hadith): Narrated Abu Salih As-Samman: I saw Abu Sa`id Al-Khudri praying on a Friday, behind something which acted as a Sutra. A young man from Bani Abi Mu'ait , wanted to pass in front of him, but Abu Sa`id repulsed him with a push on his chest. Finding no alternative he again tried to pass but Abu Sa`id pushed him with a greater force. The young man abused Abu Sa`id and went to Marwan and lodged a complaint against Abu Sa`id and Abu Sa`id followed the young man to Marwan who asked him, "O Abu Sa`id! What has happened between you and the son of your brother?" Abu Sa`id said to him, "I heard the Prophet (ﷺ) saying, 'If anybody amongst you is praying behind something as a Sutra and somebody tries to pass in front of him, then he should repulse him and if he refuses, he should use force against him for he is a Shaitan.'" (509) □

171. Narrated Busr bin Sa`id: that Zaid bin Khalid sent him to Abi Juhaim to ask him what he had heard from Allah's Messenger (ﷺ) about a person passing in front of another person who was praying. Abu Juhaim replied, "Allah's Messenger (ﷺ) said, 'If the person who passes in front of another person in prayer knew the magnitude of his sin he would prefer to wait for 40 (days, months or years) rather than to pass in front of him." Abu An-Nadr said, "I do not remember exactly whether he said 40 days, months or years." (510) □

172. Narrated `Aisha: The things which annul the prayers were mentioned before me. They said, "Prayer is annulled by a dog, a donkey and a woman (if they pass in front

of the praying people)." I said, "You have made us (i.e. women) dogs. I saw the Prophet (ﷺ) praying while I used to lie in my bed between him and the Qibla. Whenever I was in need of something, I would slip away for I disliked to face him." (511) ☐

173. Narrated `Aisha: The Prophet (ﷺ) used to pray while I was sleeping across in his bed in front of him. Whenever he wanted to pray witr, he would wake me up and I would pray witr. (512) ☐

174. Narrated `Aisha: the wife of the Prophet, "I used to sleep in front of Allah's Messenger (ﷺ) with my legs opposite his Qibla (facing him); and whenever he prostrated, he pushed my feet and I withdrew them and whenever he stood, I stretched them." `Aisha added, "In those days there were no lamps in the houses." (513) ☐

175. Narrated Abu Qatada: Allah's Messenger (ﷺ) was praying and he was carrying Umama the daughters of Zainab, the daughter of Allah's Messenger (ﷺ) and she was the daughter of 'As bin Rabi`a bin `Abd Shams. When he prostrated, he put her down and when he stood, he carried her (on his neck). (516) ☐

9. Times of the Prayers

176. Narrated Ibn Shihab (ra): Once Umar bin Abdul Aziz delayed the prayer and Urwa bin Az-Zubair went to him and said, "Once in 'Iraq, Al-Mughira bin Shu`ba delayed his prayers and Abi Mas`ud Al-Ansari went to him and said, 'O Mughira! What is this? Don't you know that once Gabriel came and offered the prayer (Fajr prayer) and Allah's Messenger (ﷺ) prayed too, then he prayed again (Zuhr prayer) and so did Allah's Apostle and again he prayed (Asr prayers and Allah's Messenger (ﷺ) did the same; again he prayed (Maghrib-prayer) and so did Allah's Messenger (ﷺ) and again prayed (Isha prayer) and so did Allah's Apostle and (Gabriel) said, 'I was ordered to do so (to demonstrate the prayers prescribed to you)?'"

Umar (bin Abdul Aziz) said to Urwa, "Be sure of what you Say. Did Gabriel lead Allah's Messenger (ﷺ) at the stated times of the prayers?" Urwa replied, "Bashir bin Abi Masud narrated like this on the authority of his father." Urwa added, "Aisha told me that Allah's Messenger (ﷺ) used to pray Asr prayer when the sunshine was still inside her residence (during the early time of `Asr). (521) □

177. Narrated Ibn Mas`ud: A man kissed a woman (unlawfully) and then went to the Prophet (ﷺ) and informed him. Allah revealed: And offer prayers perfectly at the two ends of the day and in some hours of the night (i.e. the five compulsory prayers). Verily! Good deeds remove (annul) the evil deeds (small sins) (11.114). The man asked Allah's Messenger (ﷺ), "Is it for me?" He said, "It is for all my followers." (526) □

178. Narrated `Abdullah: I asked the Prophet (ﷺ) "Which deed is the dearest to Allah?" He replied, "To offer the prayers at their early stated fixed times." I asked, "What is the next (in goodness)?" He replied, "To be good and dutiful to your parents" I again asked, "What is the next (in goodness)?" He replied, 'To participate in Jihad in Allah's cause." `Abdullah added, "I asked only that much and if I had asked more, the Prophet (ﷺ) would have told me more." (527) □

179. Narrated Abu Huraira: I heard Allah's Messenger (ﷺ) saying, "If there was a river at the door of anyone of you and he took a bath in it five times a day would you notice any dirt on him?" They said, "Not a trace of dirt would be left." The Prophet (ﷺ) added, "That is the example of the five prayers with which Allah blots out (annuls) evil deeds." (528) □

180. Narrated Anas: The Prophet (ﷺ) said, "Do the prostration properly and do not put your forearms flat with elbows touching the ground like a dog. And if you want to spit, do not spit in front, nor to the right for the person in prayer is speaking in private to his Lord." (532) □

181. Narrated Abu Dhar: The Mu'adh-dhin (call-maker) of the Prophet (ﷺ) pronounced the Adhan (call) for the Zuhr prayer but the Prophet said, "Let it be

cooler, let it be cooler." Or said, 'Wait, wait, because the severity of heat is from the raging of the Hell-fire. In severe hot weather, pray when it becomes (a bit) cooler and the shadows of hillocks appear." (535) □

182. Narrated Abu Al-Minhal: Abu Barza said, "The Prophet (ﷺ) used to offer the Fajr (prayer) when one could recognize the person sitting by him (after the prayer) and he used to recite between 60 to 100 Ayat (verses) of the Qur'an. He used to offer the Zuhr prayer as soon as the sun declined (at noon) and the `Asr at a time when a man might go and return from the farthest place in Medina and find the sun still hot. (The sub-narrator forgot what was said about the Maghrib). He did not mind delaying the `Isha prayer to one third of the night or the middle of the night." (541) □

183. Narrated Ibn `Abbas: "The Prophet (ﷺ) prayed eight rak`at for the Zuhr and `Asr, and seven for the Maghrib and `Isha prayers in Medina." Aiyub said, "Perhaps those were rainy nights." Anas said, "May be." (543) □

184. Narrated Anas bin Malik: We used to pray the `Asr prayer and after that if someone happened to go to the tribe of Bani `Amr bin `Auf, he would find them still praying the `Asr (prayer). (548) □

185. Narrated Abu Bakr bin `Uthman bin Sahl bin Hunaif: that he heard Abu Umama saying: We prayed the Zuhr prayer with `Umar bin `Abdul `Aziz and then went to Anas bin Malik and found him offering the `Asr prayer. I asked him, "O uncle! Which prayer have you offered?" He said 'The `Asr and this is (the time of) the prayer of Allah s Apostle which we used to pray with him." (549) □

186. Narrated Anas bin Malik: Allah's Messenger (ﷺ) used to offer the `Asr prayer at a time when the sun was still hot and high and if a person went to Al-`Awali (a place) of Medina, he would reach there when the sun was still high. Some of Al-`Awali of Medina were about four miles or so from the town. (550) □

187. Narrated Ibn `Umar: Allah's Messenger (ﷺ) said, "Whoever misses the `Asr

prayer (intentionally) then it is as if he lost his family and property." (552) □

188. Narrated Abu Al-Mahh: We were with Buraida in a battle on a cloudy day and he said, "Offer the `Asr prayer early as the Prophet said, "Whoever leaves the `Asr prayer, all his (good) deeds will be annulled." (553) □

189. Narrated Qais: Jarir said, "We were with the Prophet (ﷺ) and he looked at the moon--full-moon--and said, 'Certainly you will see your Lord as you see this moon and you will have no trouble in seeing Him. So if you can avoid missing (through sleep or business, etc.) a prayer before the sunrise (Fajr) and a prayer before sunset (`Asr), you must do so.' He then recited Allah's Statement: And celebrate the praises of your Lord before the rising of the sun and before (its) setting." (50.39) Isma`il said, "Offer those prayers and do not miss them." (554) □

190. Narrated Abu Huraira: Allah's Messenger (ﷺ) said, "Angels come to you in succession by night and day and all of them get together at the time of the Fajr and `Asr prayers. Those who have passed the night with you (or stayed with you) ascend (to the Heaven) and Allah asks them, though He knows everything about you, well, "In what state did you leave my slaves?" The angels reply: "When we left them they were praying and when we reached them, they were praying." (555) □

191. Narrated Abu Huraira: Allah's Messenger (ﷺ) said, "If anyone of you can get one rak`a of the `Asr prayer before sunset, he should complete his prayer. If any of you can get one rak`a of the Fajr prayer before sunrise, he should complete his prayer." (556) □

192. Narrated Rafi bin Khadij: We used to offer the Maghrib prayer with the Prophet (ﷺ) and after finishing the prayer one of us may go away and could still see as Par as the spots where one's arrow might reach when shot by a bow.(559)□

193. Narrated Talha bin 'Ubaidullah: A man came to Allah's Messenger (ﷺ) asking him about Islam, Allah's Messenger (ﷺ) said, "You have to offer five compulsory prayers in a day and a night (24 hours)." The man asked, "Is there any more

compulsory prayers for me?" Allah's Messenger (ﷺ) said, "No, unless you like to offer Nawafil (i.e. optional prayers)." Allah's Messenger (ﷺ) then added, "You have to observe fasts during the month of Ramadan." The man said, "Am I to fast any other days?' Allah's Messenger (ﷺ) said, "No, unless you wish to observe the optional fast voluntarily." Then Allah's Messenger (ﷺ) told him about the compulsory Zakat. The man asked, "Do I have to give anything besides?" Allah's Messenger (ﷺ) said, "No, unless you wish to give in charity voluntarily." So, the man departed saying, "By Allah I will neither do more nor less than that." Allah's Messenger (ﷺ) said, "If he has said the truth he will be successful." (2678) ☐

194. Narrated Jabir bin `Abdullah: The Prophet (ﷺ) used to pray the Zuhr at midday, and the `Asr at a time when the sun was still bright, the Maghrib after sunset (at its stated time) and the `Isha at a variable time. Whenever he saw the people assembled (for `Isha' prayer) he would pray earlier and if the people delayed, he would delay the prayer. And they or the Prophet (ﷺ) used to offer the Fajr Prayers when it still dark. (560) ☐

195. Narrated Salama: We used to pray the Maghrib prayer with the Prophet (ﷺ) when the sun disappeared from the horizon. (561) ☐

196. Narrated Abu Musa: My companions, who came with me in the boat and I landed at a place called Baqi Buthan. The Prophet (ﷺ) was in Medina at that time. One of us used to go to the Prophet (ﷺ) by turns every night at the time of the `Isha prayer. Once I along with my companions went to the Prophet (ﷺ) and he was busy in some of his affairs, so the `Isha' prayer was delayed to the middle of the night. He then came out and led the people (in prayer). After finishing from the prayer, he addressed the people present there saying, "Be patient! Don't go away. Have the glad tiding. It is from the blessing of Allah upon you that none amongst mankind has prayed at this time save you." Or said, "None except you has prayed at this time." Abu Musa added, 'So we returned happily after what we heard from Allah's Messenger (peace be upon him)." (567) ☐

197. Narrated Abu Barza: Allah's Messenger (ﷺ) disliked to sleep before the `Isha' prayer and to talk after it. (568) ☐

198. Narrated Ibn Juraij from Nafi`: `Abdullah bin `Umar said, "Once Allah's Messenger (ﷺ) was busy (at the time of the `Isha'), so the prayer was delayed so much so that we slept and woke up and slept and woke up again. The Prophet (ﷺ) came out and said, 'None amongst the dwellers of the earth but you have been waiting for the prayer." Ibn `Umar did not find any harm in praying it earlier or in delaying it unless he was afraid that sleep might overwhelm him and he might miss the prayer, and sometimes he used to sleep before the `Isha' prayer. Ibn Juraij said, "I said to `Ata', 'I heard Ibn `Abbas saying: Once Allah's Messenger (ﷺ) delayed the `Isha' prayer to such an extent that the people slept and got up and slept again and got up again. Then `Umar bin Al-Khattab stood up and reminded the Prophet (ﷺ) of the prayer.' `Ata' said, 'Ibn `Abbas said: The Prophet came out as if I was looking at him at this time, and water was trickling from his head and he was putting his hand on his head and then said, 'Hadn't I thought it hard for my followers, I would have ordered them to pray (`Isha' prayer) at this time.' I asked `Ata' for further information, how the Prophet had kept his hand on his head as he was told by Ibn `Abbas. `Ata' separated his fingers slightly and put their tips on the side of the head, brought the fingers downwards approximating them till the thumb touched the lobe of the ear at the side of the temple and the beard on the face. He neither slowed nor hurried in this action but he acted like that. The Prophet (ﷺ) said: "Hadn't I thought it hard for my followers I would have ordered them to pray at this time." (571) ☐

199. Narrated Anas: The Prophet (ﷺ) delayed the `Isha' prayer till midnight and then he offered the prayer and said, "The people prayed and slept but you have been in prayer as long as you have been waiting for it (the prayer)." Anas added: As if I am looking now at the glitter of the ring of the Prophet (ﷺ) on that night. (572) ☐

200. Narrated Abu Bakr bin Musa: My father said, "Allah's Messenger (ﷺ) said, 'whoever prays the two cool prayers (`Asr and Fajr) will go to Paradise.'" (574) ☐

201. Narrated Abu Huraira: Allah's Messenger (ﷺ) said, "Whoever could get one rak`a of a prayer, (in its proper time) he has got the prayer." (580) □

202. Narrated `Umar: "The Prophet (ﷺ) forbade praying after the Fajr prayer till the sun rises and after the `Asr prayer till the sun sets." (581) □

203. Narrated Hisham's father: Ibn `Umar said, "Allah's Messenger (ﷺ) said, 'do not pray at the time of sunrise and at the time of sunset.'" Ibn `Umar said, "Allah's Messenger (ﷺ) said, 'If the edge of the sun appears (above the horizon) delay the prayer till it becomes high, and if the edge of the sun disappears, delay the prayer till it sets (disappears completely).'" (583) □

204. Narrated Muawiya: You offer a prayer which I did not see being offered by Allah's Messenger (ﷺ) when we were in his company and he certainly had forbidden it (i.e. two rak`at after the `Asr prayer). (587) □

205. Narrated Ibn `Umar: I pray as I saw my companions praying. I do not forbid praying at any time during the day or night except at sunset and sunrise. (589) □

206. Narrated `Aisha: By Allah, Who took away the Prophet. The Prophet (ﷺ) never missed them (two rak`at) after the `Asr prayer till he met Allah and he did not meet Allah till it became heavy for him to pray while standing so he used to offer most of the prayers while sitting. (She meant the two rak`at after `Asr) He used to pray them in the house and never prayed them in the mosque lest it might be hard for his followers and he loved what was easy for them. (590) □

207. Narrated `Aisha: Allah's Messenger (ﷺ) never missed two rak`at before the Fajr prayer and after the `Asr prayer openly and secretly. (592) □

208. Narrated `Abdullah bin Abi Qatada: My father said, "One night we were traveling with the Prophet (ﷺ) and some people said, 'We wish that Allah's Messenger (ﷺ) would take a rest along with us during the last hours of the night.' He said, 'I am afraid that you will sleep and miss the (Fajr) prayer.' Bilal said, 'I will make you get up.' So all slept and Bilal rested his back against his Rahila and he too was

overwhelmed (by sleep) and slept. The Prophet (ﷺ) got up when the edge of the sun had risen and said, 'O Bilal! What about your statement?' He replied, 'I have never slept such a sleep.' The Prophet (ﷺ) said, 'Allah captured your souls when He wished, and released them when He wished. O Bilal! Get up and pronounce the Adhan for the prayer.' The Prophet (ﷺ) performed ablution and when the sun came up and became bright, he stood up and prayed." (595) ☐

209. Narrated Jabir bin `Abdullah: On the day of Al-Khandaq (the battle of trench.) `Umar bin Al-Khattab came cursing the disbelievers of Quraish after the sun had set and said, "O Allah's Messenger (ﷺ) I could not offer the `Asr prayer till the sun had set." The Prophet (ﷺ) said, "By Allah! I, too, have not prayed." So we turned towards Buthan, and the Prophet (ﷺ) performed ablution and we too performed ablution and offered the `Asr prayer after the sun had set, and then he offered the Maghrib prayer. (596) ☐

210. Narrated Anas: The Prophet (ﷺ) said, "If anyone forgets a prayer he should pray that prayer when he remembers it. There is no expiation except to pray the same." Then he recited: "Establish prayer for My (i.e. Allah's) remembrance." (20.14). (597) ☐

10. CALL TO PRAYERS (ADHAAN)

211. NARRATED IBN `UMAR (RA): When the Muslims arrived at Medina, they used to assemble for the prayer, and used to guess the time for it. During those days, the practice of Adhan for the prayers had not been introduced yet. Once they discussed this problem regarding the call for prayer. Some people suggested the use of a bell like the Christians, others proposed a trumpet like the horn used by the Jews, but `Umar was the first to suggest that a man should call (the people) for the prayer; so Allah's Messenger (ﷺ) ordered Bilal to get up and pronounce the Adhan for prayers. (604) ☐

212. Narrated Anas bin Malik: When the number of Muslims increased they discussed the question as to how to know the time for the prayer by some familiar means. Some suggested that a fire be lit (at the time of the prayer) and others put forward the proposal to ring the bell. Bilal was ordered to pronounce the wording of Adhan twice and of the Iqama once only. (606) ☐

213. Narrated Abu Huraira: Allah's Messenger (ﷺ) said, "When the Adhan is pronounced Satan takes to his heels and passes wind with noise during his flight in order not to hear the Adhan. When the Adhan is completed he comes back and again takes to his heels when the Iqama is pronounced and after its completion he returns again till he whispers into the heart of the person (to divert his attention from his prayer) and makes him remember things which he does not recall to his mind before the prayer and that causes him to forget how much he has prayed." (608) ☐

214. Narrated `Abdur-Rahman: Abu Sa`id Al-Khudri told my father, "I see you liking sheep and the wilderness. So whenever you are with your sheep or in the wilderness and you want to pronounce Adhan for the prayer raise your voice in doing so, for whoever hears the Adhan, whether a human being, a jinn or any other creature, will be a witness for you on the Day of Resurrection." Abu Sa`id added, "I heard it (this narration) from Allah's Messenger (p.b.u.h)." (609) ☐

215. Narrated Abu Sa`id Al-Khudri: Allah's Messenger (ﷺ) said, "Whenever you hear the Adhan, say what the Mu'adh-dhin is saying. (611) ☐

216. Narrated Abu Sa`id Al-Khudri: I heard Allah's Messenger (ﷺ) saying, "There is no prayer after the morning prayer till the sun rises, and there is no prayer after the `Asr prayer till the sun sets." (586) ☐

217. Narrated Yahya as above (586) and added: "Some of my companions told me that Hisham had said, "When the Mu'adh-dhin said, "Haiyi `alassala (come for the prayer)." Muawiya said,(لَا حَوْلَ وَلَا قُوَّةَ إِلَّا بالله) "La hawla wala quwata illa billah (There is neither might nor any power except with Allah)" and added, "We heard your Prophet saying the same." (613) ☐

218. Narrated Jabir bin `Abdullah: Allah's Messenger (ﷺ) said, "Whoever after listening to the Adhan says,

اللَّهُمَّ رَبَّ هَذِهِ الدَّعْوَةِ التَّامَّةِ وَالصَّلَاةِ الْقَائِمَةِ آتِ مُحَمَّدًا الْوَسِيلَةَ وَالْفَضِيلَةَ وَابْعَثْهُ مَقَامًا مَحْمُودًا الَّذِي وَعَدْتَهُ

'Allahumma Rabba hadhihi-dda` watit-tammah, was-Salahil qa'imah, ati Muhammadan al-wasilata wal-fadilah, wa b`ath-hu maqaman mahmudan-il-ladhi wa`adtahu' [O Allah! Lord of this perfect call (perfect by not ascribing partners to You) and of the regular prayer which is going to be established, give Muhammad the right of intercession and illustriousness, and resurrect him to the best and the highest place in Paradise that You promised him (of)], then my intercession for him will be allowed on the Day of Resurrection". (614) □

219. Narrated `Aisha: Allah's Messenger (ﷺ) offered the `Isha' prayer (and then got up at the Tahajjud time) and offered eight rak`at and then offered two rak`at while sitting. He then offered two rak`at in between the Adhan and Iqama (of the Fajr prayer) and he never missed them. (1159) □

220. Narrated `Abdullah bin Mughaffal Al-Muzani: Allah's Messenger (ﷺ) said thrice, "There is a prayer between the two Adhans (Adhan and Iqama)," and added, "For the one who wants to pray." (624) □

221. Narrated Anas bin Malik: "When the Mu'adh-dhin pronounced the Adhan, some of the companions of the Prophet (ﷺ) would proceed to the pillars of the mosque (for the prayer) till the Prophet (ﷺ) arrived and in this way they used to pray two rak`at before the Maghrib prayer. There used to be a little time between the Adhan and the Iqama." Shu`ba said, "There used to be a very short interval between the two (Adhan and Iqama). (625) □

222. Narrated Malik bin Huwairith: Two men came to the Prophet (ﷺ) with the intention of a journey. The Prophet (ﷺ) said, "When (both of) you set out, pronounce Adhan and then Iqama and the oldest of you should lead the prayer." (630) □

223. Narrated Malik: We came to the Prophet (ﷺ) and stayed with him for twenty

days and nights. We were all young and of about the same age. The Prophet (ﷺ) was very kind and merciful. When he realized our longing for our families, he asked about our homes and the people there and we told him. Then he asked us to go back to our families and stay with them and teach them (the religion) and to order them to do good things. He also mentioned some other things which I have (remembered or) forgotten. The Prophet (ﷺ) then added, "Pray as you have seen me praying and when it is the time for the prayer one of you should pronounce the Adhan and the oldest of you should lead the prayer. (631) □

224. Narrated Nafi`: Once in a cold night, Ibn `Umar pronounced the Adhan for the prayer at Dajnan (the name of a mountain) and then said, "Pray at your homes", and informed us that Allah's Messenger (ﷺ) used to tell the Mu'adh-dhin to pronounce Adhan and say, "Pray at your homes" at the end of the Adhan on a rainy or a very cold night during the journey." (632) □

225. Narrated `Aun bin Abi Juhaifa: My father said, "I saw Bilal turning his face from side to side while pronouncing the Adhan for the prayer." (634) □

226. Narrated `Abdullah bin Abi Qatada: My father said, "While we were praying with the Prophet (ﷺ) he heard the noise of some people. After the prayer he said, 'What is the matter?' They replied 'We were hurrying for the prayer.' He said, 'Do not make haste for the prayer, and whenever you come for the prayer, you should come with calmness, and pray whatever you get (with the people) and complete the rest which you have missed." (635) □

227. Narrated `Abdullah bin Abi Qatada: My father said, "Allah's Messenger (ﷺ) said, 'If the Iqama is pronounced, then do not stand for the prayer till you see me (in front of you) and do it calmly.'" (638) □

228. Narrated Abu Huraira: Allah's Messenger (ﷺ) went out (of the mosque) when the Iqama had been pronounced and the rows straightened. The Prophet (ﷺ) stood at his Musalla (praying place) and we waited for the Prophet (ﷺ) to begin the prayer with Takbir. He left and asked us to remain in our places. We kept on standing till

the Prophet returned and the water was trickling from his head for he had taken a bath (of Janaba). (639) ☐

229. Narrated Anas: Once the Iqama was pronounced and the Prophet (ﷺ) was talking to a man (in a low voice) in a corner of the mosque and he did not lead the prayer till (some of) the people had slept (dozed in a sitting posture). (642) ☐

300. Narrated Abu Huraira: Allah's Messenger (ﷺ) said, "By Him in Whose Hand my soul is I was about to order for collecting firewood (fuel) and then order Someone to pronounce the Adhan for the prayer and then order someone to lead the prayer then I would go from behind and burn the houses of men who did not present themselves for the (compulsory congregational) prayer. By Him, in Whose Hands my soul is, if anyone of them had known that he would get a bone covered with good meat or two (small) pieces of meat present in between two ribs, he would have turned up for the `Isha' prayer.' (644) ☐

11. BENEFITS OF PRAYER

301. NARRATED `ABDULLAH BIN `UMAR (RA): Allah's Messenger (ﷺ) said, "The prayer in congregation is twenty seven times superior to the prayer offered by person alone." (645) ☐

302. Narrated Abu Huraira: Allah's Messenger (ﷺ) said, "The reward of the prayer offered by a person in congregation is twenty five times greater than that of the prayer offered in one's house or in the market (alone). And this is because if he performs ablution and does it perfectly and then proceeds to the mosque with the sole intention of praying, then for every step he takes towards the mosque, he is upgraded one degree in reward and his one sin is taken off (crossed out) from his accounts. When he offers his prayer, the angels keep on asking Allah's Blessings and Allah's forgiveness for him as long as he is (staying) at his Musalla. They say, 'O Allah! Bestow Your blessings upon him, be Merciful and kind to him.' And one is regarded in prayer as long as one

is waiting for the prayer." (647) □

303. Narrated Abu Musa: The Prophet (ﷺ) said, "The people who get tremendous reward for the prayer are those who are farthest away (from the mosque) and then those who are next farthest and so on. Similarly one who waits to pray with the Imam has greater reward than one who prays and goes to bed." (651) □

304. Narrated Abu Huraira: Allah's Messenger (ﷺ) said, "While a man was going on a way, he saw a thorny branch and removed it from the way and Allah became pleased by his action and forgave him for that." Then the Prophet (ﷺ) said, "Five are martyrs: One who dies of plague, one who dies of an Abdominal disease, one who dies of drowning, one who is buried alive (and) dies and one who is killed in Allah's cause." (The Prophet (ﷺ) further said, "If the people knew the reward for pronouncing the Adhan and for standing in the first row (in the congregational prayer) and found no other way to get it except by drawing lots they would do so, and if they knew the reward of offering the Zuhr prayer early (in its stated time), they would race for it and if they knew the reward for `Isha' and Fajr prayers in congregation, they would attend them even if they were to crawl. (653) □

305. Narrated Humaid: Anas said, "The Prophet (ﷺ) said, 'O Bani Salima! Don't you think that for every step of yours (that you take towards the mosque) there is a reward (while coming for prayer)?" Mujahid said: "Regarding Allah's Statement: "We record that which they have sent before (them), and their traces" (36.12). 'Their traces' means 'their steps.' " And Anas said that the people of Bani Salima wanted to shift to a place near the Prophet (ﷺ) but Allah's Messenger (ﷺ) disliked the idea of leaving their houses uninhabited and said, "Don't you think that you will get the reward for your footprints." Mujahid said, "Their foot prints mean their foot steps and their going on foot." (656) □

306. Narrated Abu Huraira: The Prophet (ﷺ) said, "No prayer is heavier upon the hypocrites than the Fajr and the `Isha' prayers and if they knew what is in them (in reward), they would have attended them, even if (it was) crawling. Certainly, I felt

the urge to order the Mu'adh-dhin (call-maker) so that he would pronounce Iqama, then order a man to lead the people (in prayer), then take a flame of fire so that I burn (the houses) upon those who had not left for the prayer yet." (657) □

307. Narrated Abu Huraira: The Prophet (ﷺ) said, "Allah will give shade, to seven, on the Day when there will be no shade but His. (These seven persons are) a just ruler, a youth who has been brought up in the worship of Allah (i.e. worships Allah sincerely from childhood), a man whose heart is attached to the mosques (i.e. to pray the compulsory prayers in the mosque in congregation), two persons who love each other only for Allah's sake and they meet and part in Allah's cause only, a man who refuses the call of a charming woman of noble birth for illicit intercourse with her and says: I am afraid of Allah, a man who gives charitable gifts so secretly that his left hand does not know what his right hand has given (i.e. nobody knows how much he has given in charity), and a person who remembers Allah in seclusion and his eyes are then flooded with tears." (660) □

308. Narrated Abu Huraira: The Prophet (ﷺ) said, "Allah will prepare for him who goes to the mosque (every) morning and in the afternoon (for the congregational prayer) an honorable place in Paradise with good hospitality for (what he has done) every morning and afternoon goings. (662) □

12. RULES OF PRAYER

309. NARRATED MALIK IBN BUHAINA (RA): Allah's Messenger (ﷺ) passed by a man praying two rak`at after the Iqama (had been pronounced). When Allah's Messenger (ﷺ) completed the prayer, the people gathered around him (the Prophet) or that man and Allah's Messenger (ﷺ) said to him (protesting), Are there four rak`at in Fajr prayer? Are there four rak`at in Fajr prayer?" (663) □

310. Narrated Anas bin Seereen: I heard Anas saying, "A man from Ansar said to the Prophet, 'I cannot pray with you (in congregation).' He was a very fat man and he

prepared a meal for the Prophet (ﷺ) and invited him to his house. He spread out a mat for the Prophet, and washed one of its sides with water, and the Prophet (ﷺ) prayed two rak`at on it." A man from the family of Al-Jaruid asked, "Did the Prophet (ﷺ) used to pray the Duha (forenoon) prayer?" Anas said, "I did not see him praying the Duha prayer except on that day." (670) □

311. Narrated `Aisha: The Prophet (ﷺ) said, "If supper is served, and Iqama is pronounced one should start with the supper." (671) □

312. Narrated Nafi`: Ibn `Umar said, "Allah's Messenger (ﷺ) said, 'If the supper is served for anyone of you and the Iqama is pronounced, start with the supper and don't be in haste (and carry on eating) till you finish it." If food was served for Ibn `Umar and Iqama was pronounced, he never came to the prayer till he finished it (i.e. food) in spite of the fact that he heard the recitation (of the Qur'an) by the Imam (in the prayer). (673) □

313. Narrated Al-Aswad: That he asked `Aisha "What did the Prophet (ﷺ) use to do in his house?" She replied, "He used to keep himself busy serving his family and when it was the time for prayer he would go for it." (676) □

314. Narrated Sahl bin Sa`d As-Sa`idi: Allah's Messenger (ﷺ) went to establish peace among Bani `Amr bin `Auf. In the meantime the time of prayer was due and the Mu'adh-dhin went to Abu Bakr and said, "Will you lead the prayer, so that I may pronounce the Iqama?" Abu Bakr replied in the affirmative and led the prayer. Allah's Messenger (ﷺ) came while the people were still praying and he entered the rows of the praying people till he stood in the (first row). The people clapped their hands. Abu Bakr never glanced sideways in his prayer but when the people continued clapping, Abu Bakr looked and saw Allah's Messenger (ﷺ). Allah's Messenger (ﷺ) beckoned him to stay at his place. Abu Bakr raised his hands and thanked Allah for that order of Allah's Messenger (ﷺ) and then he retreated till he reached the first row. Allah's Messenger (ﷺ) went forward and led the prayer. When Allah's Messenger (ﷺ) finished the prayer, he said, "O Abu Bakr! What prevented you from staying when I

ordered you to do so?" Abu Bakr replied, "How can Ibn Abi Quhafa (Abu Bakr) dare to lead the prayer in the presence of Allah's Messenger (ﷺ)?" Then Allah's Messenger (ﷺ) said, "Why did you clap so much? If something happens to anyone during his prayer he should say Subhan Allah. If he says so he will be attended to, for clapping is for women." (684) ☐

315. Narrated Anas bin Malik: Once Allah's Messenger (ﷺ) rode a horse and fell down and the right side (of his body) was injured. He offered one of the prayers while sitting and we also prayed behind him sitting. When he completed the prayer, he said, "The Imam is to be followed. Pray standing if he prays standing and bow when he bows; rise when he rises; and if he says, 'Sami`a l-lahu-liman hamidah, say then, 'Rabbana wa laka lhamd' and pray standing if he prays standing and pray sitting (all of you) if he prays sitting." Humaid said: The saying of the Prophet (ﷺ) "Pray sitting, if he (Imam) prays sitting" was said in his former illness (during his early life) but the Prophet (ﷺ) prayed sitting afterwards (in the last illness) and the people were praying standing behind him and the Prophet (ﷺ) did not order them to sit. We should follow the latest actions of the Prophet. (689) ☐

316. Narrated Al-Bara: (and he was not a liar) When Allah's Messenger (ﷺ) said, "Sami`a l-lahu liman hamidah" none of us bent his back (for prostration) till the Prophet (ﷺ) prostrated and then we would prostrate after him. (690) ☐

317. Narrated Abu Huraira: The Prophet (ﷺ) said, "Isn't he who raises his head before the Imam afraid that Allah may transform his head into that of a donkey or his figure (face) into that of a donkey?" (691) ☐

318. Narrated Ibn `Umar: When the earliest emigrants came to Al-`Usba a place in Quba', before the arrival of the Prophet (s), Salim (the slave of Abu Hudhaifa), who knew the Qur'an more than the others used to lead them in prayer. (692) ☐

319. Narrated Abu Huraira: Allah's Messenger (ﷺ) said, "If the Imam leads the prayer correctly then he and you will receive the rewards but if he makes a mistake then you will receive the reward for the prayer and the sin will be his." (694) ☐

320. Narrated 'Ubaid-Ullah bin Adi bin Khiyar: I went to 'Uthman bin Affan while he was besieged, and said to him, "You are the chief of all Muslims in general and you see what has befallen you. We are led in the Salah (prayer) by a leader of Al-Fitan (trials and afflictions etc.) and we are afraid of being sinful in following him." 'Uthman said. "As-Salah (the prayers) is the best of all deeds so when the people do good deeds do the same with them and when they do bad deeds, avoid those bad deeds." Az-Zuhri said, "In our opinion one should not offer Salah behind an effeminate person unless there is no alternative." (695) □

321. Narrated Mu`adh bin Jabal: I used to pray the `Isha prayer with the Prophet (ﷺ) and then go to lead my people in the prayer. (700) □

322. Narrated Abu Mas`ud: A man came and said, "O Allah's Messenger (ﷺ)! By Allah, I keep away from the Morning Prayer only because so and so prolongs the prayer when he leads us in it." The narrator said, "I never saw Allah's Apostle more furious in giving advice than he was at that time. He then said, "Some of you make people dislike good deeds (the prayer). So whoever among you leads the people in prayer should shorten it because among them are the weak, the old and the needy." (702) □

323. Narrated Abu Huraira: Allah's Messenger (ﷺ) said, "If anyone of you leads the people in the prayer, he should shorten it for amongst them are the weak, the sick and the old; and if anyone among you prays alone then he may prolong (the prayer) as much as he wishes." (703) □

324. Narrated Jabir bin `Abdullah Al-Ansari: Once a man was driving two Nadihas (camels used for agricultural purposes) and night had fallen. He found Mu`adh praying so he made his camel kneel and joined Mu`adh in the prayer. The latter recited Surah 'Al-Baqara" or Surah "An-Nisa", (so) the man left the prayer and went away. When he came to know that Mu`adh had criticized him, he went to the Prophet, and complained against Mu`adh. The Prophet said thrice, "O Mu`adh ! Are you putting the people to trial?" It would have been better if you had recited "Sabbih

Isma Rabbika-l-A`la (87)", Wash-shamsi wa duhaha (91)", or "Wal-laili idha yaghsha (92)", for the old, the weak and the needy pray behind you." Jabir said that Mu`adh recited Sura Al-Baqara in the `Isha' prayer. (705) □

325. Narrated Anas: The Prophet (ﷺ) used to pray a short prayer (in congregation) but used to offer it in a perfect manner. (706) □

326. Narrated `Abdullah bin 'Abi Qatada: My father said, "The Prophet (ﷺ) said, 'When I stand for prayer, I intend to prolong it but on hearing the cries of a child, I cut it short, as I dislike to trouble the child's mother.'" (707) □

327. Narrated An-Nu`man bin 'Bashir: The Prophet (ﷺ) said, "Straighten your rows or Allah will alter your faces." (717) □

328. Narrated Anas bin Malik: The Prophet (ﷺ) said, "Straighten your rows as the straightening of rows is essential for a perfect and correct prayer." (723) □

329. Narrated Anas bin Malik: The Prophet (ﷺ) said, "Straighten your rows for I see you from behind my back." Anas added, "Every one of us used to put his shoulder with the shoulder of his companion and his foot with the foot of his companion." (725) □

330. Narrated Ibn `Abbas: One night I stood to the left of the Prophet (ﷺ) in the prayer but he caught hold of me by the hand or by the shoulder (arm) till he made me stand on his right and beckoned with his hand (for me) to go from behind (him). (728) □

331. Narrated Aisha: Allah's Messenger (ﷺ) used to pray in his room at night. As the wall of the room was low, the people saw him and some of them stood up to follow him in the prayer. In the morning they spread the news. The following night the Prophet (ﷺ) stood for the prayer and the people followed him. This went on for two or three nights. Thereupon Allah's Messenger (ﷺ) did not stand for the prayer the following night, and did not come out. In the morning, the people asked him about it. He replied, that he way afraid that the night prayer might become compulsory.

(729) ☐

332. Narrated `Aisha: The Prophet (ﷺ) had a mat which he used to spread during the day and use as a curtain at night. So a number of people gathered at night facing it and prayed behind him. (730) ☐

333. Narrated Zaid bin Thabit: Allah's Messenger (ﷺ) made a small room in the month of Ramadan (Sa`id said, "I think that Zaid bin Thabit said that it was made of a mat") and he prayed there for a few nights, and so some of his companions prayed behind him. When he came to know about it, he kept on sitting. In the morning, he went out to them and said, "I have seen and understood what you did. You should pray in your houses, for the best prayer of a person is that which he prays in his house except the compulsory prayers." (731) ☐

334. Narrated `Abdullah bin `Umar: I saw Allah's Messenger (ﷺ) opening the prayer with the Takbir and raising his hands to the level of his shoulders at the time of saying the Takbir, and on saying the Takbir for bowing he did the same; and when he said, "Sami`a l-lahu liman hamidah ", he did the same and then said, "Rabbana wa laka lhamd." But he did not do the same on prostrating and on lifting the head from it." (738) ☐

335. Narrated Sahl bin Sa`d: The people were ordered to place the right hand on the left forearm in the prayer. Abu Hazim said, "I knew that the order was from the Prophet (peace be upon him). (740) ☐

336. Narrated Anas bin Malik: The Prophet, Abu Bakr and `Umar used to start the prayer with "Al hamdu li l-lahi Rabbi l-`alamin (All praise is but to Allah, Lord of the Worlds). (743) ☐

337. Narrated Abu Huraira: Allah's Messenger (ﷺ) used to keep silent between the Takbir and the recitation of Qur'an and that interval of silence used to be a short one. I said to the Prophet (ﷺ) "May my parents be sacrificed for you! What do you say in the pause between Takbir and recitation?" The Prophet (ﷺ) said, "I say,

اللَّهُمَّ بَاعِدْ بَيْنِي وَبَيْنَ خَطَايَاىَ كَمَا بَاعَدْتَ بَيْنَ الْمَشْرِقِ وَالْمَغْرِبِ، اللَّهُمَّ نَقِّنِي مِنَ الْخَطَايَا كَمَا يُنَقَّى الثَّوْبُ الْأَبْيَضُ مِنَ الدَّنَسِ، اللَّهُمَّ اغْسِلْ خَطَايَاىَ بِالْمَاءِ وَالثَّلْجِ وَالْبَرَدِ

"Allahumma, baaEid baini wa baina khatayaya kama baa`adta baina l-mashriqi wa l-maghrib. Allahumma, naqqini min khatayaya kama yunaqqa th-thawbu l-abyadu mina d-danas. Allahumma, ighsil khatayaya bi l-maa'i wa th-thalji wa l-barad." (O Allah! Set me apart from my sins as the East and West are set apart from each other and clean me from sins as a white garment is cleaned of dirt (after thorough washing). O Allah! Wash off my sins with water, snow and hail.)" (744) □

338. Narrated Abu Ma`mar: We asked Khabbab whether Allah's Messenger (ﷺ) used to recite (the Qur'an) in the Zuhr and the `Asr prayers. He replied in the affirmative. We said, "How did you come to know about it?" He said, "By the movement of his beard." (746) □

339. Narrated Anas bin Malik: The Prophet (ﷺ) said, "What is wrong with those people who look towards the sky during the prayer?" His talk grew stern while delivering this speech and he said, "They should stop (looking towards the sky during the prayer); otherwise their eyesight would be taken away." (750) □

340. Narrated `Aisha: I asked Allah's Messenger (ﷺ) about looking hither and thither in prayer. He replied, "It is a way of stealing by which Satan takes away (a portion) from the prayer of a person." (751) □

341. Narrated Jabir bin Samura: The People of Kufa complained against Sa`d to `Umar and the latter dismissed him and appointed `Ammar as their chief. They lodged many complaints against Sa`d and even they alleged that he did not pray properly. `Umar sent for him and said, "O Aba 'Is-haq! These people claim that you do not pray properly." Abu 'Is-haq said, "By Allah, I used to pray with them a prayer similar to that of Allah's Apostle and I never reduced anything of it. I used to prolong the first two rak`at of `Isha prayer and shorten the last two rak`at." `Umar said, "O Aba 'Is-haq, this was what I thought about you." And then he sent one or more persons with him to Kufa so as to ask the people about him. So they went there and

did not leave any mosque without asking about him. All the people praised him till they came to the mosque of the tribe of Bani `Abs; one of the men called Usama bin Qatada with a surname of Aba Sa`da stood up and said, "As you have put us under an oath; I am bound to tell you that Sa`d never went himself with the army and never distributed (the war booty) equally and never did justice in legal verdicts." (On hearing it) Sa`d said, "I pray to Allah for three things: O Allah! If this slave of yours is a liar and got up for showing off, give him a long life, increase his poverty and put him to trials." (And so it happened). Later on when that person was asked how he was, he used to reply that he was an old man in trial as the result of Sa`d's curse. `Abdul Malik, the sub narrator, said that he had seen him afterwards and his eyebrows were overhanging his eyes owing to old age and he used to tease and assault the small girls in the way. (755) □

342. Narrated 'Ubada bin As-Samit: Allah's Messenger (ﷺ) said, "Whoever does not recite Al-Fatiha in his prayer, his prayer is invalid." (756) □

343. Narrated `Abdullah bin Abi Qatada: My father said, "The Prophet (ﷺ) in Zuhr prayers used to recite Al-Fatiha along with two other Suras in the first two rak`at: a long one in the first rak`a and a shorter (Sura) in the second, and at times the verses were audible. In the Asr prayer the Prophet used to recite Al-Fatiha and two more Suras in the first two rak`at and used to prolong the first rak`a. And he used to prolong the first rak`a of the Fajr prayer and shorten the second. (759) □

344. Narrated `Abdullah bin Abi Qatada: My father said, "The Prophet (ﷺ) used to recite Al-Fatiha along with another Sura in the first two rak`at of the Zuhr and the `Asr prayers and at times a verse or so was audible to us." (762) □

345. Narrated Ibn `Abbas: (My mother) Umu-l-Fadl heard me reciting "Wal MurSalahi `Urfan" (77) and said, "O my son! By Allah, your recitation made me remember that it was the last Sura I heard from Allah's Messenger (ﷺ). He recited it in the Maghrib prayer." (763) □

346. Narrated Marwan bin Al-Hakam: Zaid bin Thabit said to me, "Why do you

recite very short Suras in the Maghrib prayer while I heard the Prophet (ﷺ) reciting the longer of the two long Suras?" (764) □

347. Narrated Jubair bin Mut`im: My father said, "I heard Allah's Messenger (ﷺ) reciting "at-Tur" (52) in the Maghrib prayer." (765) □

348. Narrated Abu Huraira: The Qur'an is recited in every prayer and in those prayers in which Allah's Messenger (ﷺ) recited aloud for us, we recite aloud in the same prayers for you; and the prayers in which the Prophet (ﷺ) recited quietly, we recite quietly. If you recite "Al-Fatiha" only it is sufficient but if you recite something else in addition, it is better. (772) □

349. Narrated Ibn `Abbas: The Prophet (ﷺ) recited aloud in the prayers in which he was ordered to do so and quietly in the prayers in which he was ordered to do so. "And your Lord is not forgetful." "Verily there was a good example for you in the ways of the Prophet." (774) □

350. Narrated Abu Wa'il: A man came to Ibn Mas`ud and said, "I recited the Mufassal (Suras) at night in one rak`a." Ibn Mas`ud said, "This recitation is (too quick) like the recitation of poetry. I know the identical Suras which the Prophet (ﷺ) used to recite in pairs." Ibn Mas`ud then mentioned 20 Mufassal Suras including two Suras from the family of (i.e. those verses which begin with) Ha, Meem (Which the Prophet (ﷺ) used to recite) in each rak`a.) (775) □

351. Narrated Abu Huraira: The Prophet (ﷺ) said, "Say Amin" when the Imam says it and if the Amin of any one of you coincides with that of the angels then all his past sins will be forgiven." Ibn Shihab said, "Allah's Messenger (ﷺ) used to Say "Amin." (780) □

352. Narrated Abu Bakra: I reached the Prophet (ﷺ) in the mosque while he was bowing in prayer and I too bowed before joining the row. Mentioned it to the Prophet (ﷺ) and he said to me, "May Allah increase your love for the good. But do not repeat it again (bowing in that way). (783) □

353. Narrated Abu Huraira: Whenever Allah's Messenger (ﷺ) stood for the prayer, he said Takbir on starting the prayer and then on bowing. On rising from bowing he said, "Sami`a llahu liman hamidah," and then while standing straight he used to say, "Rabbana laka-l hamd" (Al- Laith said, "(The Prophet (ﷺ) said), 'Wa laka l-hamd'." He used to say Takbir on prostrating and on raising his head from prostration; again he would Say Takbir on prostrating and raising his head. He would then do the same in the whole of the prayer till it was completed. On rising from the second rak`a (after at-Tahiyyat), he used to say Takbir. (789) □

354. Narrated Mus`ab bin Sa`d: I offered prayer beside my father and approximated both my hands and placed them in between the knees. My father told me not to do so and said, "We used to do the same but we were forbidden (by the Prophet) to do it and were ordered to place the hands on the knees." (790) □

355. Narrated Al-Bara: The bowing, the prostration the sitting in between the two prostrations and the standing after the bowing of the Prophet (ﷺ) but not qiyam (standing in the prayer) and qu`ud (sitting in the prayer) used to be approximately equal (in duration). (792) □

356. Narrated Abu Huraira: Once the Prophet (ﷺ) entered the mosque, a man came in, offered the prayer and greeted the Prophet. The Prophet returned his greeting and said to him, "Go back and pray again for you have not prayed." The man offered the prayer again, came back and greeted the Prophet. He said to him thrice, "Go back and pray again for you have not prayed." The man said, "By Him Who has sent you with the truth! I do not know a better way of praying. Kindly teach me how to pray." He said, "When you stand for the prayer, say Takbir and then recite from the Qur'an what you know and then bow with calmness till you feel at ease, then rise from bowing till you stand straight. Afterwards prostrate calmly till you feel at ease and then raise (your head) and sit with Calmness till you feel at ease and then prostrate with calmness till you feel at ease in prostration and do the same in the whole of your prayer." (793) □

357. Narrated `Aisha: The Prophet (s) used to say in his bowing and prostrations,

" سُبْحَانَكَ اللَّهُمَّ رَبَّنَا وَبِحَمْدِكَ، اللَّهُمَّ اغْفِرْ لِي " .

"Subhanaka l-lahumma Rabbana wa bihamdika; Allahumma ghfir li." (Exalted [from unbecoming attributes] Are you O Allah our Lord, and by Your praise [do I exalt you]. O Allah! Forgive me). (794) □

358. Narrated Rifa`a bin Rafi` Az-Zuraqi: One day we were praying behind the Prophet. When he raised his head from bowing, he said,

سَمِعَ اللَّهُ لِمَنْ حَمِدَهُ

"Sami`a l-lahu liman hamidah." (Allaah Tala listens to the one who praises Him)

A man behind him said,

رَبَّنَا وَلَكَ الحَمْدُ حَمْداً كَثِيراً طَيِّباً مُبارَكاً فيه

"Rabbana wa laka l-hamdu, hamdan kathiran taiyiban mubarakan fihi" (O our Lord! All the praises are for You, many good and blessed praises.)

When the Prophet completed the prayer, he asked, "Who has said these words?" The man replied, "I." The Prophet said, "I saw over thirty angels competing to write it first." Prophet rose (from bowing) and stood straight till all the vertebrae of his spinal column came to a natural position. (799) □

359. Narrated Thabit: Anas used to demonstrate to us the prayer of the Prophet (ﷺ) and while demonstrating, he used to raise his head from bowing and stand so long that we would say that he had forgotten (the prostration). (800) □

360. Abu Huraira said, "When Allah's Messenger (s) raised his head from (bowing) he used to say,

"سَمِعَ اللَّهُ لِمَنْ حَمِدَهُ رَبَّ نَا وَلَكَ الحَمْدُ

"Sami`a l-lahu liman hamidah, Rabbana wa laka l-hamd." (Allaah listens to the one who praises Him. [O Allaah!] Our Lord, and to You be all Praise)

He Would invoke Allah for some people by naming them: "O Allah! Save Al-Walid bin Al-Walid and Salama bin Hisham and `Aiyash bin Abi Rabi`a and the weak and the helpless people among the faithful believers O Allah! Be hard on the tribe of Mudar and let them suffer from famine years like that of the time of Joseph." In those days the Eastern section of the tribe of Mudar was against the Prophet (s). (804) □

361. Narrated Ibn `Abbas: The Prophet (ﷺ) said, "I have been ordered to prostrate on seven bones i.e. on the forehead along with the tip of the nose and the Prophet (ﷺ) pointed towards his nose, both hands, both knees and the toes of both feet and not to gather the clothes or the hair." (812) □

362. Narrated Anas bin Malik: The Prophet (ﷺ) said, "Be straight in the prostrations and none of you should put his forearms on the ground (in the prostration) like a dog." (822) □

363. Narrated Malik bin Huwairith Al-Laithi: I saw the Prophet (ﷺ) praying and in the odd rak`at, he used to sit for a moment before getting up. (823) □

364. Narrated Aiyub: Abu Qilaba said, "Malik bin Huwairith came to us and led us in the prayer in this mosque of ours and said, 'I lead you in prayer but I do not want to offer the prayer but just to show you how Allah's Apostle performed his prayers." I asked Abu Qilaba, "How was the prayer of Malik bin Huwairith?" He replied, "Like the prayer of this Sheikh of ours-- i.e. `Amr bin Salima." That Sheikh used to pronounce the Takbir perfectly and when he raised his head from the second prostration he would sit for a while and then support himself on the ground and get up. (824) □

365. Narrated `Abdullah bin `Abdullah: I saw `Abdullah bin `Umar crossing his legs while sitting in the prayer and I, a mere youngster in those days, did the same. Ibn `Umar forbade me to do so, and said, "The proper way is to keep the right foot propped up and bend the left in the prayer." I said questioningly, "But you are doing

so (crossing the legs)." He said, "My feet cannot bear my weight." (827) □

366. Narrated Muhammad bin `Amr bin `Ata': I was sitting with some of the companions of Allah's Messenger (ﷺ) and we were discussing about the way of praying of the Prophet. Abu Humaid As-Sa`idi said, "I remember the prayer of Allah's Messenger (ﷺ) better than any one of you. I saw him raising both his hands up to the level of the shoulders on saying the Takbir; and on bowing he placed his hands on both knees and bent his back straight, then he stood up straight from bowing till all the vertebrate took their normal positions. In prostrations, he placed both his hands on the ground with the forearms away from the ground and away from his body, and his toes were facing the Qibla. On sitting In the second rak`a he sat on his left foot and propped up the right one; and in the last rak`a he pushed his left foot forward and kept the other foot propped up and sat over the buttocks." (828) □

367. Narrated `Abdullah bin Buhaina: (he was from the tribe of Uzd Shanu'a and was the ally of the tribe of `Abdul-Manaf and was one of the companions of the Prophet): Once the Prophet (ﷺ) led us in the Zuhr prayer and stood up after the second rak`a and did not sit down. The people stood up with him. When the prayer was about to end and the people were waiting for him to say the Taslim, he said Takbir while sitting and prostrated twice before saying the Taslim and then he said the Taslim." (829) □

368. Narrated Ibn Mas`ud: Allah's Messenger (s) taught me the Tashah-hud as he taught me a Sura from the Quran, while my hand was between his hands. (Tashah-hud was),

التَّحِيَّاتُ لِلَّهِ وَالصَّلَوَاتُ وَالطَّيِّبَاتُ ﴿﴾السَّلَامُ عَلَيْكَ أَيُّهَا النَّبِيُّ وَرَحْمَةُ اللَّهِ وَبَرَكَاتُهُ ﴿﴾ السَّلَامُ عَلَيْنَا وَعَلَى عِبَادِ اللَّهِ الصَّالِحِينَ ﴿﴾ أَشْهَدُ أَنْ لَا إِلَهَ إِلَّا اللَّهُ ﴿﴾ وَأَشْهَدُ أَنَّ مُحَمَّدًا عَبْدُهُ وَرَسُولُهُ

"Attahiyyaatu Lillahi Was Salawatu Wattayyibatu Assalamu Alaika Ayyuhannabi 'yu 'Warahmatullahi Wabarka'tuhu Assalamu Alaina Wa'ala'Ibadillahis Saa'liheen, Ash'had'u'un La ilahaillallahu Wa Ash'hadu Anna Muhammadun Abd'uhu Wa Rasooluh" (All the best compliments and the prayers and the good things are for

Allah. Peace and Allah's Mercy and Blessings be on you, O Prophet! Peace be on us and on the pious slaves of Allah, I testify that none has the right to be worshipped but Allah, and I also testify that Muhammad is Allah's slave and His Apostle. (We used to recite this in the prayer) during the lifetime of the Prophet (s), but when he had died, we used to say, "Peace be on the Prophet.) (6265) ☐

369. Narrated `Aisha: (the wife of the Prophet) Allah's Messenger (s) used to invoke Allah in the prayer saying,

اللَّهُمَّ إِنِّي أَعُوذُ بِكَ مِنْ عَذَابِ الْقَبْرِ وَأَعُوذُ بِكَ مِنْ فِتْنَةِ الْمَسِيحِ الدَّجَّالِ، وَأَعُوذُ بِكَ مِنْ فِتْنَةِ الْمَحْيَا وَفِتْنَةِ الْمَمَاتِ، اللَّهُمَّ إِنِّي أَعُوذُ بِكَ مِنَ الْمَأْثَمِ وَالْمَغْرَمِ

"Allahumma inni a`udhu bika min `adhabi l-qabr, wa a`udhu bika min fitnati l-masihi d-dajjal, wa a`udhu bika min fitnati l-mahya wa fitnati l-mamat. Allahumma inni a`udhu bika mina l-ma'thami wa l-maghram." (O Allah, I seek refuge with You from the punishment of the grave, from the afflictions of the imposter- Messiah, and from the afflictions of life and death. O Allah, I seek refuge with You from sins and from debt.) Somebody said to him, "Why do you so frequently seek refuge with Allah from being in debt?" The Prophet (s) replied, "A person in debt tells lies whenever he speaks, and breaks promises whenever he makes (them)." `Aisha also narrated: I heard Allah's Messenger (s) in his prayer seeking refuge with Allah from the afflictions of Ad-Dajjal. (832) ☐

370. Narrated Abu Bakr As-Siddiq: I asked Allah's Messenger (ﷺ) to teach me an invocation so that I may invoke Allah with it in my prayer. He told me to say,

اللهم إني ظلمت نفسي ظلمًا كثيرًا، ولا يغفر الذنوب إلا أنت، فاغفر لي مغفرة من عندك، وارحمني، إنك أنت الغفور الرحيم

"Allahumma inni zalumtu nafsi zulman kathiran, Wala yaghfiru dh-dhunuba illa anta, fa ghfir li maghfiratan min `indika, wa r-hamni, innaka anta l-ghafuru r-rahim (O Allah! I have considerably wronged myself. There is none to forgive the sins but You. So grant me pardon and have mercy on me. You are the Most Forgiving, the Most Compassionate.) (834) ☐

371. Narrated `Abdullah: When we prayed with the Prophet (s) we used to say, "Peace be on Allah from His slaves and peace be on so and so." The Prophet (s) said, "Don't say As-Salam be on Allah, for He Himself is As-Salam, but say, "At-tahiyatu li l-lahi wa s-salawatu wa t-taiyibat. As-salamu `alaika aiyuha n-Nabiyu wa rahmatu l-lahi wa barakatuh. As-salamu `alaina wa `ala `ibadi l-lahi s-salihin." (If you say this then it will reach all the slaves in heaven or between heaven and earth). Ash-hadu al la-ilaha illa l-lah, wa ash-hadu anna Muhammadan `Abduhu wa Rasuluh.' (Salutations to God and prayers and good deeds. Peace be upon you, O Prophet, and the mercy of God and his blessings. Peace be on us and on the righteous servants of God. I bear witness that there is no god but Allah, and I bear witness that Muhammad is His messenger.) Then select the invocation you like best and recite it." (835). □

372. Narrated Abu Sa`id Al-Khudri: I saw Allah's Messenger (ﷺ) prostrating in mud and water and saw the mark of mud on his forehead. (836) □

373. Narrated `Itban bin Malik: We prayed with the Prophet (ﷺ) and used to finish our prayer with the Taslim along with him. (838) □

374. Narrated Abu Ma`bad: (the freed slave of Ibn `Abbas) Ibn `Abbas told me, "In the lifetime of the Prophet (ﷺ) it was the custom to celebrate Allah's praises aloud after the compulsory congregational prayers." Ibn `Abbas further said, "When I heard the Dhikr, I would learn that the compulsory congregational prayer had ended." (841) □

375. Narrated Abu Huraira: Some poor people came to the Prophet (s) and said, "The wealthy people will get higher grades and will have permanent enjoyment and they pray like us and fast as we do. They have more money by which they perform the Hajj, and `Umra; fight and struggle in Allah's Cause and give in charity." The Prophet said, "Shall I not tell you a thing upon which if you acted you would catch up with those who have surpassed you? Nobody would overtake you and you would be better than the people amongst whom you live except those who would do the same. Say,

سُبْحَانَ اللّٰه "Subhana l-lah", (Glory to God.)

ٱلْحَمْدُ لِلَّٰه "Al hamdu li l-lah" (Praise be to God)

الله أكبر "Allahu Akbar" (God is [the] greatest)

Thirty three times each after every (compulsory) prayer." We differed and some of us said that we should say, "Subhan-al-lah" thirty three times and "Al hamdu li l-lah" thirty three times and "Allahu Akbar" thirty four times. I went to the Prophet (s) who said, "Say, "Subhan-al-lah" and "Al hamdu li l-lah" and "Allahu Akbar" all together, thirty three times." (843) □

376. Narrated Warrad: (the clerk of Al-Mughira bin Shu`ba) Once Al-Mughira dictated to me in a letter addressed to Muawiya that the Prophet (s) used to say after every compulsory prayer,

لَا إِلَٰهَ إِلَّا اللّٰهُ وَحْدَهُ لَا شَرِيكَ لَهُ، لَهُ الْمُلْكُ وَلَهُ الْحَمْدُ وَهُوَ عَلَى كُلِّ شَيْءٍ قَدِيرٌ، اللَّهُمَّ لَا مَانِعَ لِمَا أَعْطَيْتَ، وَلَا مُعْطِيَ لِمَا مَنَعْتَ، وَلَا يَنْفَعُ ذَا الْجَدِّ مِنْكَ الْجَدُّ

"La ilaha illa l-lahu wahdahu la sharika lahu, lahu l-mulku wa lahu l-hamdu, wa huwa `ala kulli shay'in qadir. Allahumma la mani`a lima a`taita, wa la mu`tiya lima mana`ta, wa la yanfa`u dhal-jaddi minka l-jadd." (There is no Deity but Allah, Alone, no Partner to Him. His is the Kingdom and all praise, and Omnipotent is He. O Allah! Nobody can hold back what you gave, nobody can give what You held back, and no struggler's effort can benefit against You.) And Al-Hasan said, "Al-jadd' means prosperity." (844) □

377. Narrated Samura bin Jundub: The Prophet (ﷺ) used to face us on completion of the prayer. (845) □

378. Narrated Um Salama: "The Prophet (ﷺ) after finishing the prayer with Taslim used to stay at his place for a while." Ibn Shihab said, "I think (and Allah knows better), that he used to wait for the departure of the women who had prayed." Ibn Shihab wrote that he had heard it from Hind bint Al-Harith Al-Firasiya from Um Salama, the wife of the Prophet (Hind was from the companions of Um Salama) who said, "When the Prophet (ﷺ) finished the prayer with Taslim, the women would

depart and enter their houses before Allah's Apostle departed." (849) ☐

379. Narrated `Abdullah: You should not give away a part of your prayer to Satan by thinking that it is necessary to depart (after finishing the prayer) from one's right side only; I have seen the Prophet (ﷺ) often leave from the left side. (852) ☐

380. Narrated Jabir bin `Abdullah: The Prophet (ﷺ) said, "Whoever eats garlic or onion should keep away from our mosque or should remain in his house." (Jabir bin `Abdullah, in another narration said, "Once a big pot containing cooked vegetables was brought. On finding unpleasant smell coming from it, the Prophet (ﷺ) asked, 'What is in it?' He was told all the names of the vegetables that were in it. The Prophet (ﷺ) ordered that it should be brought near to some of his companions who were with him. When the Prophet (ﷺ) saw it he disliked to eat it and said, 'Eat. (I don't eat) for I converse with those whom you don't converse with (i.e. the angels). (855) ☐

381. Narrated Ibn `Abbas: Once I came riding a she-ass and I, then, had just attained the age of puberty. Allah's Messenger (ﷺ) was leading the people in prayer at Mina facing no wall. I passed in front of the row and let loose the she-ass for grazing and joined the row and no one objected to my deed. (861) ☐

382. Narrated Ibn `Umar: The Prophet (ﷺ) said, "If your women ask permission to go to the mosque at night, allow them." (865) ☐

383. Narrated Um Salama: In the lifetime of Allah's Messenger (ﷺ) the women used to get up when they finished their compulsory prayers with Taslim. The Prophet (ﷺ) and the men would stay on at their places as long as Allah will. When the Prophet (ﷺ) got up, the men would then get up. (866) ☐

384. Narrated `Aisha: When Allah's Messenger (ﷺ) finished the Fajr prayer, the women would leave covered in their sheets and were not recognized owing to the darkness. (867) ☐

385. Narrated by Majzaa from a man called Uhban bin Aus who was one of those who had witnessed (the Pledge of allegiance beneath) the Tree, and who had some

trouble in his knee so that while doing prostrations, he used to put a pillow underneath his knee. (4174) ☐

13. FRIDAY PRAYER

386. NARRATED ABU HURAIRA (RA): I heard Allah's Messenger (ﷺ) saying, "We are the last (to come) but (will be) the foremost on the Day of Resurrection though the former nations were given the Holy Scriptures before us. And this was their day (Friday) the celebration of which was made compulsory for them but they differed about it. So Allah gave us the guidance for it (Friday) and all the other people are behind us in this respect: the Jews' (holy day is) tomorrow (i.e. Saturday) and the Christians' (is) the day after tomorrow (i.e. Sunday)." (876) ☐

387. Narrated Abu Sa`id: I testify that Allah's Messenger (ﷺ) said, "The taking of a bath on Friday is compulsory for every male Muslim who has attained the age of puberty and (also) the cleaning of his teeth with Siwak, and the using of perfume if it is available." `Amr said, "I confirm that the taking of a bath is compulsory, but as for the Siwak and the using of perfume, Allah knows better whether it is obligatory or not, but according to the Hadith it is as above." (880) ☐

388. Narrated Abu Huraira: Allah's Messenger (ﷺ) said, "Any person who takes a bath on Friday like the bath of Janaba and then goes for the prayer (in the first hour i.e. early), it is as if he had sacrificed a camel (in Allah's cause); and whoever goes in the second hour it is as if he had sacrificed a cow; and whoever goes in the third hour, then it is as if he had sacrificed a horned ram; and if one goes in the fourth hour, then it is as if he had sacrificed a hen; and whoever goes in the fifth hour then it is as if he had offered an egg. When the Imam comes out (i.e. starts Khutba), the angels present themselves to listen to the Khutba." (881) ☐

389. Narrated Salman-Al-Farsi: The Prophet (p.b.u.h) said, "Whoever takes a bath on Friday, purifies himself as much as he can, then uses his (hair) oil or perfumes

himself with the scent of his house, then proceeds (for the Jumua prayer) and does not separate two persons sitting together (in the mosqu, then prays as much as (Allah has) written for him and then remains silent while the Imam is delivering the Khutba, his sins in-between the present and the last Friday would be forgiven." (883) ☐

390. Narrated Abu Huraira: Allah's Messenger (‌ﷺ) said, "If I had not found it hard for my followers or the people, I would have ordered them to clean their teeth with Siwak for every prayer." (887) ☐

391. Narrated Abu Huraira: The Prophet (‌ﷺ) used to recite the following in the Fajr prayer of Friday, "Alif, Lam, Mim, Tanzil" (Surahas- Sajda #32) and "Hal-ata-ala-l-Insani" (i.e. Surah-Ad-Dahr #76). (891) ☐

392. Narrated Ibn `Abbas: The first Jumua prayer which was offered after a Jumua prayer offered at the mosque of Allah's Apostle took place in the mosque of the tribe of `Abdul Qais at Jawathi in Bahrain. (892) ☐

393. Narrated Abu Huraira through different narrators that the Prophet (‌ﷺ) said, "It is Allah's right on every Muslim that he should take a bath (at least) once in seven days." (898) ☐

394. Narrated Ibn `Umar: One of the wives of Umar bin Khattab used to offer the Fajr and the `Isha' prayer in congregation in the Mosque. She was asked why she had come out for the prayer as she knew that `Umar disliked it, and he has great ghaira (self-respect). She replied, "What prevents him from stopping me from this act?" The other replied, "The statement of Allah's Messenger (‌ﷺ): 'Do not stop Allah's women-slaves from going to Allah's Mosques' prevents him." (900) ☐

395. Narrated Muhammad bin Seereen: On a rainy day Ibn `Abbas said to his Mu'adh-dhin, "After saying, 'Ash-hadu anna Muhammadan Rasulullah' (I testify that Muhammad is Allah's Messenger (‌ﷺ)), do not say 'Haiya 'Alas-Salah' (come for the prayer) but say 'Pray in your houses'." (The man did so). But the people disliked it. Ibn `Abbas said, "It was done by one who was much better than I (i.e. the Prophet

(p.b.u.h)). No doubt, the Jumua prayer is compulsory but I dislike to put you to task by bringing you out walking in mud and slush." (901) □

396. Narrated Yahya bin Sa`id: I asked `Amra about taking a bath on Fridays. She replied," Aisha said, 'The people used to work (for their livelihood) and whenever they went for the Jumua prayer, they used to go to the mosque in the same shape as they had been in work. So they were asked to take a bath on Friday.'" (903) □

397. Narrated Anas bin Malik: We used to offer the Jumua prayer early and then have an afternoon nap. (905) □

398. Narrated Anas bin Malik: The Prophet (ﷺ) used to offer the prayer earlier if it was very cold; and if it was very hot he used to delay the prayer, i.e. the Jumua prayer. (906) □

399. Narrated Ibn Juraij: I heard Nafi' saying, "Ibn `Umar, said, 'The Prophet (ﷺ) forbade that a man should make another man to get up to sit in his place' ". I said to Nafi`, 'Is it for Jumua prayer only?' He replied, "For Jumua prayer and any other (prayer)." (911) □

400. Narrated As-Saib bin Yazid: In the lifetime of the Prophet, Abu Bakr and `Umar, the Adhan for the Jumua prayer used to be pronounced when the Imam sat on the pulpit. But during the Caliphate of `Uthman when the Muslims increased in number, a third Adhan at Az-Zaura' was added. Abu `Abdullah said, "Az-Zaura' is a place in the market of Medina." (912) □

401. Narrated Jabir bin `Abdullah: The Prophet (ﷺ) used to stand by a stem of a date-palm tree (while delivering a sermon). When the pulpit was placed for him we heard that stem crying like a pregnant she-camel till the Prophet (ﷺ) got down from the pulpit and placed his hand over it. (918) □

402. Narrated Ibn `Umar: The Prophet (p.b.u.h) used to deliver the Khutba while standing and then he would sit, then stand again as you do now-a-days. (920) □

403. Narrated Abu Hummaid As-Sa`idi: One night Allah's Messenger (ﷺ) stood up after the prayer and recited "Tashah-hud" and then praised Allah as He deserved and said, "Amma ba'du." (925) ☐

404. Narrated Jabir bin `Abdullah: A person entered the mosque while the Prophet (ﷺ) was delivering the Khutba on a Friday. The Prophet (ﷺ) said to him, "Have you prayed?" The man replied in the negative. The Prophet (ﷺ) said, "Get up and pray two rak`at." (930) ☐

405. Narrated Abu Huraira: Allah's Messenger (ﷺ) said, "When the Imam is delivering the Khutba, and you ask your companion to keep quiet and listen, then no doubt you have done an evil act." (934) ☐

406. Narrated Abu Huraira: Allah's Messenger (ﷺ) talked about Friday and said, "There is an hour (opportune time) on Friday and if a Muslim gets it while praying and asks something from Allah, then Allah will definitely meet his demand." And he (the Prophet) pointed out the shortness of that time with his hands. (935) ☐

407. Narrated Jabir bin `Abdullah: While we were praying (Jumua Khutba & prayer) with the Prophet (p.b.u.h), some camels loaded with food, arrived (from Sham). The people diverted their attention towards the camels (and left the mosque), and only twelve persons remained with the Prophet (s). So this verse was revealed: "But when they see Some bargain or some amusement, They disperse headlong to it, And leave you standing." (62.11) (936) ☐

408. Narrated `Abdullah bin `Umar: Allah's Messenger (ﷺ) used to pray two rak`at before the Zuhr prayer and two rak`at after it. He also used to pray two rak`at after the Maghrib prayer in his house, and two rak`at after the `Isha' prayer. He never prayed after Jumua prayer till he departed (from the Mosque), and then he would pray two rak`at at home. (937) ☐

409. Narrated Sahl: We never had an afternoon nap nor meals except after offering the Jumua prayer. (939) ☐

14. EIDS

410. NARRATED AISHA (RA): Allah's Messenger (ﷺ) came to my house while two girls were singing beside me the songs of Buath (a story about the war between the two tribes of the Ansar, the Khazraj and the Aus, before Islam). The Prophet (p.b.u.h) lay down and turned his face to the other side. Then Abu Bakr came and spoke to me harshly saying, "Musical instruments of Satan near the Prophet (p.b.u.h)?" Allah's Messenger (ﷺ) turned his face towards him and said, "Leave them." When Abu Bakr became inattentive, I signaled to those girls to go out and they left. It was the day of Eid, and the Black people were playing with shields and spears; so either I requested the Prophet (p.b.u.h) or he asked me whether I would like to see the display. I replied in the affirmative. Then the Prophet (p.b.u.h) made me stand behind him and my cheek was touching his cheek and he was saying, "Carry on! O Bani Arfida," till I got tired. The Prophet (p.b.u.h) asked me, "Are you satisfied (Is that sufficient for you)?" I replied in the affirmative and he told me to leave. (949) ☐

411. Narrated Aisha: Abu Bakr came to my house while two small Ansari girls were singing beside me the stories of the Ansar concerning the Day of Buath. And they were not singers. Abu Bakr said protestingly, "Musical instruments of Satan in the house of Allah's Messenger (ﷺ)!" It happened on the Eid day and Allah's Messenger (ﷺ) said, "O Abu Bakr! There is an Eid for every nation and this is our Eid." (952) ☐

412. Narrated Anas bin Malik: Allah's Messenger (ﷺ) never proceeded (for the prayer) on the Day of Eid-ul-Fitr unless he had eaten some dates. Anas also narrated: The Prophet (ﷺ) used to eat odd number of dates. (953) ☐

413. Narrated Abu Sa`id Al-Khudri: The Prophet (ﷺ) used to proceed to the Musalla on the days of Id-ul-Fitr and Id-ul-Adha; the first thing to begin with was the prayer and after that he would stand in front of the people and the people would keep sitting in their rows. Then he would preach to them, advise them and give them orders, (i.e.

Khutba). And after that if he wished to send an army for an expedition, he would do so; or if he wanted to give and order, he would do so, and then depart. The people followed this tradition till I went out with Marwan, the Governor of Medina, for the prayer of Id-ul-Adha or Id-ul-Fitr. When we reached the Musalla, there was a pulpit made by Kathir bin As-Salt. Marwan wanted to get up on that pulpit before the prayer. I got hold of his clothes but he pulled them and ascended the pulpit and delivered the Khutba before the prayer. I said to him, "By Allah, you have changed (the Prophet's tradition)." He replied, "O Abu Sa`id! Gone is that which you know." I said, "By Allah! What I know is better than what I do not know." Marwan said, "People do not sit to listen to our Khutba after the prayer, so I delivered the Khutba before the prayer." (956) □

414. Narrated Ibn Juraij: `Ata' said, "Jabir bin `Abdullah said, 'The Prophet (ﷺ) went out on the Day of Eid-ul-Fitr and offered the prayer before delivering the Khutba, Ata told me that during the early days of Ibn Az-Zubair, Ibn `Abbas had sent a message to him telling him that the Adhan for the Eid Prayer was never pronounced (in the life time of Allah's Messenger (ﷺ)) and the Khutba used to be delivered after the prayer. Ata told me that Ibn `Abbas and Jabir bin `Abdullah, had said, "There was no Adhan for the prayer of Eid-ul-Fitr and Eid-ul-Aqha." `Ata' said, "I heard Jabir bin `Abdullah saying, 'The Prophet (ﷺ) stood up and started with the prayer, and after it he delivered the Khutba. When the Prophet (ﷺ) of Allah (p.b.u.h) finished (the Khutba), he went to the women and preached to them, while he was leaning on Bilal's hand. Bilal was spreading his garment and the ladies were putting alms in it.'" I said to Ata, "Do you think it incumbent upon an Imam to go to the women and preach to them after finishing the prayer and Khutba?" `Ata' said, "No doubt it is incumbent on Imams to do so, and why should they not do so?" (961) □

415. Narrated Sa`id bin Jubair: I was with Ibn `Umar when a spear head pierced the sole of his foot and his foot stuck to the paddle of the saddle and I got down and pulled his foot out, and that happened in Mina. Al-Hajjaj got the news and came to inquire about his health and said, "Alas! If we could only know the man who wounded

you!" Ibn `Umar said, "You are the one who wounded me." Al-Hajjaj said, "How is that?" Ibn `Umar said, "You have allowed the arms to be carried on a day on which nobody used to carry them and you allowed arms to be carried in the Haram even though it was not allowed before." (966) ☐

416. Narrated Ibn `Abbas: The Prophet (ﷺ) said, "No good deeds done on other days are superior to those done on these (first ten days of Dhul Hijja)." Then some companions of the Prophet (ﷺ) said, "Not even Jihad?" He replied, "Not even Jihad, except that of a man who does it by putting himself and his property in danger (for Allah's sake) and does not return with any of those things." (969) ☐

417. Narrated Um `Atiya: We used to be ordered to come out on the Day of Eid and even bring out the virgin girls from their houses and menstruating women so that they might stand behind the men and say Takbir along with them and invoke Allah along with them and hope for the blessings of that day and for purification from sins. (971) ☐

418. Narrated Ibn `Umar: The Prophet (ﷺ) used to proceed to the Musalla and an 'Anaza used to be carried before him and planted in the Musalla in front of him and he would pray facing it (as a Sutra). (973) ☐

419. Al-Hasan bin Muslim told me that Ibn `Abbas had said, "I joined the Prophet, Abu Bakr, `Umar and `Uthman in the Eid ul Fitr prayers. They used to offer the prayer before the Khutba and then they used to deliver the Khutba afterwards. Once the Prophet (ﷺ) I came out (for the Eid prayer) as if I were just observing him waving to the people to sit down. He, then accompanied by Bilal, came crossing the rows till he reached the women. He recited the following verse: 'O Prophet! When the believing women come to you to take the oath of fealty to you . . . (to the end of the verse) (60.12).' After finishing the recitation he said, "O ladies! Are you fulfilling your covenant?" None except one woman said, "Yes." Hasan did not know who that woman was. The Prophet (ﷺ) said, "Then give alms." Bilal spread his garment and said, "Keep on giving alms. Let my father and mother sacrifice their lives for you

(ladies)." So the ladies kept on putting their Fatkhs (big rings) and other kinds of rings in Bilal's garment." `Abdur-Razaq said, " 'Fatkhs' is a big ring which used to be worn in the (Pre-Islamic) period of ignorance. (979) ☐

420. Narrated Um-`Atiya: We were ordered to go out (for Eid) and also to take along with us the menstruating women, mature girls and virgins staying in seclusion. (Ibn `Aun said, "Or mature virgins staying in seclusion)." The menstruating women could present themselves at the religious gathering and invocation of Muslims but should keep away from their Musalla. (981) ☐

421. Narrated Jabir bin `Abdullah: On the Day of Eid the Prophet (ﷺ) used to return (after offering the Eid prayer) through a way different from that by which he went. (986) ☐

15. WITR PRAYER

422. NARRATED IBN `UMAR (RA): Once a person asked Allah's Messenger (ﷺ) about the night prayer. Allah's Apostle (ﷺ) replied, "The night prayer is offered as two Rak`at followed by two Rak`at and so on and if anyone is afraid of the approaching dawn (Fajr prayer) he should pray one Rak`ah and this will be a Witr for all the Rak`at which he has prayed before." (990) ☐

423. Narrated `Abdullah bin `Umar: The Prophet (ﷺ) said, "Night prayer is offered as two rak`at followed by two rak`at and so on, and if you want to finish it, pray only one rak`a which will be witr for all the previous rak`at." Al-Qasim said, "Since we attained the age of puberty we have seen some people offering a three-rak`at prayer as witr and all that is permissible. I hope there will be no harm in it." (993) ☐

424. Narrated `A'isha: Allah's Messenger (ﷺ) used to pray eleven rak`at at night and that was his night prayer and each of his prostrations lasted for a period enough for one of you to recite fifty verses before Allah's Messenger (ﷺ) raised his head. He also

used to pray two rak`at (Sunnah) before the (compulsory) Fajr prayer and then lie down on his right side till the Mu'adh-dhin came to him for the prayer. (994) □

425. Narrated Anas bin Seereen: I asked Ibn `Umar, "What is your opinion about the two rak`at before the Fajr (compulsory) prayer, as to prolonging the recitation in them?" He said, "The Prophet (ﷺ) used to pray at night two rak`at followed by two and so on, and end the prayer by one rak`ah witr. He used to offer two rak`at before the Fajr prayer immediately after the Adhan." (Hammad, the sub-narrator said, "That meant (that he prayed) quickly.)" (995) □

426. Narrated `Aisha: Allah's Messenger (ﷺ) offered witr prayer at different nights at various hours extending (from the `Isha' prayer) up to the last hour of the night. (996) □

427. Narrated `A'isha: The Prophet (ﷺ) used to offer his night prayer while I was sleeping across in his bed. Whenever he intended to offer the witr prayer, he used to wake me up and I would offer the witr prayer too. (997) □

428. Narrated Sa`id bin Yasar: I was going to Mecca in the company of `Abdullah bin `Umar and when I apprehended the approaching dawn, I dismounted and offered the witr prayer and then joined him. `Abdullah bin `Umar said, "Where have you been?" I replied, "I apprehended the approaching dawn so I dismounted and prayed the witr prayer." `Abdullah said, "Isn't it sufficient for you to follow the good example of Allah's Messenger (ﷺ)?" I replied, "Yes, by Allah." He said, "Allah's Messenger (ﷺ) used to pray witr on the back of the camel (while on a journey)." (999) □

429. Narrated Ibn `Umar: The Prophet (ﷺ) used to offer (Nawafil) prayers on his Rahila (mount) facing its direction by signals, but not the compulsory prayer. He also used to pray witr on his (mount) Rahila. (1000) □

430. Narrated `Asim: I asked Anas bin Malik about the Qunut. Anas replied, "Definitely it was (recited)". I asked, "Before bowing or after it?" Anas replied, "Before bowing." I added, "So and so has told me that you had informed him that it had been

after bowing." Anas said, "He told an untruth (i.e. "was mistaken," according to the Hijazi dialect). Allah's Messenger (ﷺ) recited Qunut after bowing for a period of one month." Anas added, "The Prophet (ﷺ) sent about seventy men (who knew the Qur'an by heart) towards the pagans (of Najd) who were less than they in number and there was a peace treaty between them and Allah's Messenger (ﷺ) (but the Pagans broke the treaty and killed the seventy men). So Allah's Messenger (ﷺ) recited Qunut for a period of one month asking Allah to punish them." (1002) ☐

431. Narrated Anas: The Qunut used to be recited in the Maghrib and the Fajr prayers. (1004) ☐

432. Narrated Abu Jamra: I asked Aidh bin Amr, who was one of the companions of the Prophet (ﷺ) (who gave the allegiance to the Prophet (ﷺ) the Tree: "Can the witr prayer be repeated (in one night)?" He said, "If you have offered it in the first part of the night, you should not repeat it in the last part 'of the night. (4176) ☐

16. Invoking Allah for Rain

433. Narrated Masruq (ra): We were with `Abdullah and he said, "When the Prophet (ﷺ) saw the refusal of the people to accept Islam he said, "O Allah! Send (famine) years on them for (seven years) like the seven years (of famine during the time) of (Prophet) Joseph." So famine overtook them for one year and destroyed every kind of life to such an extent that the people started eating hides, carcasses and rotten dead animals. Whenever one of them looked towards the sky, he would (imagine himself to) see smoke because of hunger. So Abu Sufyan went to the Prophet (ﷺ) and said, "O Muhammad! You order people to obey Allah and to keep good relations with kith and kin. No doubt the people of your tribe are dying, so please pray to Allah for them." So Allah revealed: "Then watch you For the day that The sky will bring forth a kind Of smoke Plainly visible ... Verily! You will return (to disbelief) On the day when We shall seize You with a mighty grasp. (44.10-16) Ibn Mas`ud added, "Al-

Batsha (i.e. grasp) happened in the battle of Badr and no doubt smoke, Al-Batsha, Al-Lizam, and the verse of Surah Ar-Rum have all passed . (1007) ☐

434. Narrated `Abdullah bin Dinar: My father said, "I heard Ibn `Umar reciting the poetic verses of Abu Talib: "And a white (person) (i.e. the Prophet) who is requested to pray for rain and who takes care of the orphans and is the guardian of widows." Salim's father (Ibn `Umar) said, "The following poetic verse occurred to my mind while I was looking at the face of the Prophet (p.b.u.h) while he was praying for rain. He did not get down till the rain water flowed profusely from every roof-gutter: "And a white (person) who is requested to pray for rain and who takes care of the orphans and is the guardian of widows . . ." And these were the words of Abu Talib." (1008) ☐

435. Narrated Anas: Whenever drought threatened them, `Umar bin Al-Khattab, used to ask Al-Abbas bin `Abdul Muttalib to invoke Allah for rain. He used to say, "O Allah! We used to ask our Prophet to invoke You for rain, and You would bless us with rain, and now we ask his uncle to invoke You for rain. O Allah! Bless us with rain." And so it would rain. (1010) ☐

436. Narrated Sharik bin `Abdullah bin Abi Namir: I heard Anas bin Malik saying, "On a Friday a person entered the main Mosque through the gate facing the pulpit while Allah's Messenger (ﷺ) was delivering the Khutba. The man stood in front of Allah's Apostle and said, 'O Allah's Messenger (ﷺ)! The livestock are dying and the roads are cut off; so please pray to Allah for rain.'" Anas added, "Allah's Messenger (ﷺ) raised both his hands and said,

اللَّهُمَّ اسْقِنَا، اللَّهُمَّ اسْقِنَا، اللَّهُمَّ اسْقِنَا

"Allahumma asqina, allahumma asqina, allahumma asqina." (O Allah! Bless us with rain! O Allah! Bless us with rain! O Allah! Bless us with rain!) Anas added, "By Allah, we could not see any trace of cloud in the sky and there was no building or a house between us and (the mountains of) Sila." Anas added, "A heavy cloud like a shield appeared from behind it (i.e. Sila' Mountain). When it came in the middle of the sky, it spread and then rained." Anas further said, "By Allah! We could not see the sun for a week. Next Friday a person entered through the same gate and at that time Allah's Messenger (ﷺ) was delivering the Friday's Khutba. The man stood in front of him and said, 'O Allah's Messenger (ﷺ)! The livestock are dying and the roads are cut off, please pray to Allah to withhold rain.'" Anas added, "Allah's Messenger (ﷺ) raised both his hands and said,

لَّهُمَّ حَوَالَيْنَا وَلا عَلَيْنَا ، اللَّهُمَّ عَلَى الآكَامِ وَالظِّرَابِ ، وَبُطُوْنِ الأَوْدِيَةِ ، وَمَنابِتِ الشَّجَر

"Allahumma hawalayna wa la 'alayna. Allahumma alal akaami (wal ajaami) wal dhiraabi wa butunil 'awdiyaati wa mana bi tish shajar." (O Allah! Round about us and not on us. O Allah! On the plateaus, on the mountains, on the hills, in the valleys and on the places where trees grow.) So the rain stopped and we came out walking in the sun." Sharik asked Anas whether it was the same person who had asked for the rain (the last Friday). Anas replied that he did not know. (1013) □

437. Narrated Anas bin Malik: In the lifetime of Allah's Messenger (ﷺ) the people were afflicted with a (famine) year. While the Prophet was delivering the Khutba (sermon) on the pulpit on a Friday, a Bedouin stood up and said, "O Allah's Messenger (ﷺ)! The livestock are dying and the families (offspring) are hungry: please pray to Allah to bless us with rain." Allah's Messenger (ﷺ) raised both his hands towards the sky and at that time there was not a trace of cloud in they sky. Then the clouds started gathering like mountains. Before he got down from the pulpit I saw rainwater trickling down his beard. It rained that day, the next day, the third day, the fourth day and till the next Friday, when the same Bedouin or some other person stood up (during the Friday Khutba) and said, "O Allah's Messenger (ﷺ)! The houses have collapsed and the livestock are drowned. Please invoke Allah for us." So Allah's Messenger (ﷺ) raised both his hands and said, "O Allah! Around us and not on us." Whichever side the Prophet (ﷺ) directed his hand, the clouds dispersed from there till a hole (in the clouds) was formed over Medina. The valley of Qanat remained flowing (with water) for one month and none, came from outside who didn't talk about the abundant rain. (1033) □

438. Narrated `Abbad bin Tamim: that his uncle (who was one of the companions of the Prophet) had told him, "The Prophet (ﷺ) went out with the people to invoke Allah for rain for them. He stood up and invoked Allah for rain, then faced the Qibla and turned his cloak (inside out) and it rained." (1023) ☐

439. Narrated `Abbad bin Tamim from his uncle: "I saw the Prophet (ﷺ) on the day when he went out to offer the Istisqa' prayer. He turned his back towards the people and faced the Qibla and asked Allah for rain. Then he turned his cloak inside out and led us in a two rak`at prayer and recited the Qur'an aloud in them." (1025) ☐

440. Narrated Anas bin Malik: The Prophet (ﷺ) never raised his hands for any invocation except for that of Istisqa' and he used to raise them so much that the whiteness of his armpits became visible. (Note: It may be that Anas did not see the Prophet (ﷺ) raising his hands, but it is narrated that the Prophet (ﷺ) used to raise his hands for invocations other than Istisqa. (1031) ☐

441. Narrated Aisha: Whenever Allah's Messenger (ﷺ) saw the rain, he used to say, اللَّهُمَّ صَيِّبًا نَافِعًا " Allaahumma Sayyibann Naafi'aa" (O Allah! Let it be a strong fruitful rain.) (1032) ☐

442. Narrated Anas: Whenever a strong wind blew, anxiety appeared on the face of the Prophet (fearing that wind might be a sign of Allah's wrath). (1034) ☐

443. Narrated Ibn Abbas: The Prophet (ﷺ) said, "I was granted victory with As-Saba and the nation of Ad was destroyed by Ad-Dabur (westerly wind). (1035) ☐

444. Narrated Abu Huraira: The Prophet (ﷺ) said, "The Hour (Last Day) will not be established until (religious) knowledge will be taken away (by the death of religious learned men), earthquakes will be very frequent, time will pass quickly, afflictions will appear, murders will increase and money will overflow amongst you." (1036). ☐

445. Narrated Aisha: Whenever Allah's Messenger (ﷺ) saw clouds or winds, signs of deep concern would appear on his face. I said, "O Allah's Messenger (ﷺ)! When people see clouds they usually feel happy, hoping that it would rain, while I see that

when you see clouds, one could notice signs of dissatisfaction on your face." He said, "O `Aisha! What is the guarantee for me that there will be no punishment in it, since some people were punished with a wind? Verily, some people saw (received) the punishment, but (while seeing the cloud) they said, 'This cloud will give us rain.' (4829) ☐

446. Narrated Ata: `Aisha said, "If the Prophet (ﷺ) saw a cloud in the sky, he would walk to and fro in agitation, go out and come in, and the color of his face would change, and if it rained, he would feel relaxed." So `Aisha knew that state of his. So the Prophet (ﷺ) said, I don't know (am afraid), it may be similar to what happened to some people referred to in the Holy Qur'an in the following Verse: -- "Then when they saw it as a dense cloud coming towards their valleys, they said, 'This is a cloud bringing us rain!' Nay, but, it is that (torment) which you were asking to be hastened a wind wherein is severe torment." (46.24) (3206) ☐

447. Narrated Zaid bin Khalid Al-Juhani: Allah's Messenger (ﷺ) led the Morning Prayer in Al-Hudaibiya and it had rained the previous night. When the Prophet (p.b.u.h) had finished the prayer he faced the people and said, "Do you know what your Lord has said?" They replied, "Allah and His Apostle know better." (The Prophet (ﷺ) said), "Allah says, 'In this morning some of My worshipers remained as true believers and some became non-believers; he who said that it had rained with the blessing and mercy of Allah is the one who believes in Me and does not believe in star, but he who said it had rained because of such and such (star) is a disbeliever in Me and is a believer in star.'" (1038) ☐

17. ECLIPSES

448. NARRATED ABU BAKRA (RA): We were with Allah's Messenger (ﷺ) when the sun eclipsed. Allah's Messenger (ﷺ) stood up dragging his cloak till he entered the Mosque. He led us in a two-rak`at prayer till the sun (eclipse) had cleared. Then the

Prophet (peace be upon him) said, "The sun and the moon do not eclipse because of someone's death. So whenever you see these eclipses pray and invoke (Allah) till the eclipse is over." (1040) □

449. Narrated Al-Mughira bin Shu`ba: "The sun eclipsed in the lifetime of Allah's Messenger (ﷺ) on the day when (his son) Ibrahim died. So the people said that the sun had eclipsed because of the death of Ibrahim. Allah's Messenger (ﷺ) said, "The sun and the moon do not eclipse because of the death or life (i.e. birth) of someone. When you see the eclipse pray and invoke Allah." (1043) □

450. 'Narrated `Aisha: In the lifetime of Allah's Messenger (ﷺ) the sun eclipsed, so he led the people in prayer, and stood up and performed a long Qiyam, then bowed for a long while. He stood up again and performed a long Qiyam but this time the period of standing was shorter than the first. He bowed again for a long time but shorter than the first one, then he prostrated and prolonged the prostration. He did the same in the second rak`a as he did in the first and then finished the prayer; by then the sun (eclipse) had cleared. He delivered the Khutba (sermon) and after praising and glorifying Allah he said, "The sun and the moon are two signs against the signs of Allah; they do not eclipse on the death or life of anyone. So when you see the eclipse, remember Allah and say Takbir, pray and give Sadaqa." The Prophet then said, "O followers of Muhammad! By Allah! There is none who has more ghaira (selfrespect) than Allah as He has forbidden that His slaves, male or female commit adultery (illegal sexual intercourse). O followers of Muhammad! By Allah! If you knew that which I know you would laugh little and weep much. (1044) □

451. Narrated `Aisha: (the wife of the Prophet (p.b.u.h) In the lifetime of the Prophet (ﷺ) the sun eclipsed and he went to the Mosque and the people aligned behind him. He said the Takbir (starting the prayer) and prolonged the recitation (from the Qur'an) and then said Takbir and performed a prolonged bowing; then he (lifted his head and) said, "Sami allahu liman hamidah" (Allah heard him who sent his praises to Him). He then did not prostrate but stood up and recited a prolonged recitation which was shorter than the first recitation. He again said Takbir and then bowed a

prolonged bowing but shorter than the first one and then said, "Sami`a l-lahu Lyman hamidah Rabbana walak-lhamd, (Allah heard him who sent his praises to Him. O our Sustainer! All the praises are for You)" and then prostrated and did the same in the second rak`a; thus he completed four bowing and four prostrations. The sun (eclipse) had cleared before he finished the prayer. (After the prayer) he stood up, glorified and praised Allah as He deserved and then said, "The sun and the moon are two of the signs of Allah. They do not eclipse because of the death or the life (i.e. birth) of someone. When you see them make haste for the prayer." Narrated Az-Zuhri: I said to 'Urwa, "When the sun eclipsed at Medina your brother (`Abdullah bin Az-Zubair) offered only a two-rak`at prayer like that of the morning (Fajr) prayer." 'Urwa replied, "Yes, for he missed the Prophet's tradition (concerning this matter)." (1046) □

452. Narrated `Abdullah bin `Amr: When the sun eclipsed in the lifetime of Allah's Messenger (ﷺ) and an announcement was made that the prayer was to be held in congregation. The Prophet (ﷺ) performed two bowing in one rak`a. Then he stood up and performed two bowing in one rak`a. Then he sat down and finished the prayer; and by then the (eclipse) had cleared `Aisha said, "I had never performed such a long prostration." (1051) □

453. Narrated `Abdullah bin `Abbas: The sun eclipsed in the lifetime of the Prophet (p.b.u.h). Allah's Messenger (ﷺ) offered the eclipse prayer and stood for a long period equal to the period in which one could recite Surah-al-Baqara. Then he bowed for a long time and then stood up for a long period which was shorter than that of the first standing, then bowed again for a long time but for a shorter period than the first; then he prostrated twice and then stood up for a long period which was shorter than that of the first standing; then he bowed for a long time which was shorter than the previous one, and then he raised his head and stood up for a long period which was shorter than the first standing, then he bowed for a long time which was shorter than the first bowing, and then prostrated (twice) and finished the prayer. By then, the sun (eclipse) had cleared. The Prophet (ﷺ) then said, "The sun and the moon are two of

the signs of Allah. They eclipse neither because of the death of somebody nor because of his life (i.e. birth). So when you see them, remember Allah." The people say, "O Allah's Messenger (ﷺ)! We saw you taking something from your place and then we saw you retreating." The Prophet (ﷺ) replied, "I saw Paradise and stretched my hands towards a bunch (of its fruits) and had I taken it, you would have eaten from it as long as the world remains. I also saw the Hell-fire and I had never seen such a horrible sight. I saw that most of the inhabitants were women." The people asked, "O Allah's Messenger (ﷺ)! Why is it so?" The Prophet (ﷺ) replied, "Because of their ungratefulness." It was asked whether they are ungrateful to Allah. The Prophet said, "They are ungrateful to their companions of life (husbands) and ungrateful to good deeds. If you are benevolent to one of them throughout the life and if she sees anything (undesirable) in you, she will say, 'I have never had any good from you.'" (1052) □

454. Narrated Fatima bint Al-Mundhir: Asma' bint Al Bakr said, "I came to `Aisha the wife of the Prophet (p.b.u.h) during the solar eclipse. The people were standing and offering the prayer and she was also praying too. I asked her, 'What has happened to the people?' She pointed out with her hand towards the sky and said, 'Subhan-Allah'. I said, 'Is there a sign?' She pointed out in the affirmative." Asma' further said, "I too then stood up for the prayer till I fainted and then poured water on my head. When Allah's Messenger (ﷺ) had finished his prayer, he thanked and praised Allah and said, 'I have seen at this place of mine what I have never seen even Paradise and Hell. No doubt, it has been inspired to me that you will be put to trial in the graves like or nearly like the trial of (Masih) Ad-Dajjal. (I do not know which one of the two Asma' said.) (The angels) will come to everyone of you and will ask what do you know about this man? (i.e. Muhammad). The believer or a firm believer (I do not know which word Asma' said) will reply, 'He is Muhammad, Allah's Messenger (ﷺ) who came to us with clear evidences and guidance, so we accepted his teachings, believed and followed him.' The angels will then say to him, 'Sleep peacefully as we knew surely that you were a firm believer.' The hypocrite or doubtful person (I do not know which word Asma' said) will say, 'I do not know. I heard the people saying something

so I said it (the same).'" (1053) □

455. Narrated Abu Musa: The sun eclipsed and the Prophet (ﷺ) got up, being afraid that it might be the Hour (i.e. Day of Judgment). He went to the Mosque and offered the prayer with the longest Qiyam, bowing and prostration that I had ever seen him doing. Then he said, "These signs which Allah sends do not occur because of the life or death of somebody, but Allah makes His worshipers afraid by them. So when you see anything thereof, proceed to remember Allah, invoke Him and ask for His forgiveness." (1059) □

456. Narrated `Aisha: The Prophet (p.b.u.h) recited (the Qur'an) aloud during the eclipse prayer and when he had finished the eclipse prayer he said the Takbir and bowed. When he stood straight from bowing he would say "Sami 'allahu liman hamidah Rabbana wa laka l-hamd." And he would again start reciting. In the eclipse prayer there are four bowing and four prostrations in two rak`at. Al-Auza'i and others said that they had heard Az-Zuhri from 'Urwa from `Aisha saying, "In the lifetime of Allah's Messenger (ﷺ) the sun eclipsed, and he made a person to announce: 'Prayer in congregation.' He led the prayer and performed four bowing and four prostrations in two rak`at." Narrated Al-Walid that `Abdur-Rahman bin Namir had informed him that he had heard the same. Ibn Shihab heard the same. Az-Zuhri said, "I asked ('Urwa), 'What did your brother `Abdullah bin Az-Zubair do? He prayed two rak`at (of the eclipse prayer) like the Morning Prayer, when he offered the (eclipse) prayer in Medina.' 'Urwa replied that he had missed (i.e. did not pray according to) the Prophet's tradition." Sulaiman bin Kathir and Sufyan bin Husain narrated from Az-Zuhri that the prayer for the eclipse used to be offered with loud recitation. (1065) □

18. Prostration during Recital of Qur'an

457. Narrated `Abdullah bin Mas`ud (ra): The Prophet (ﷺ) recited Surah Najm (103) at Mecca and prostrated while reciting it and those who were with him did the same except an old man who took a handful of small stones or earth and lifted it to his forehead and said, "This is sufficient for me." Later on, I saw him killed as a non-believer. (1067) ☐

458. Narrated Ibn `Abbas: The prostration of Sa`d is not a compulsory one but I saw the Prophet (ﷺ) prostrating while reciting it. (1069) ☐

459. Narrated Ibn `Abbas: The Prophet (ﷺ) I prostrated while reciting An-Najm and with him prostrated the Muslims, the pagans, the jinns, and all human beings. (1071) ☐

460. Narrated `Ata' bin Yasar: I asked Zaid bin Thabit about prostration on which he said that he had recited An-Najm before the Prophet, yet he (the Prophet) had not performed a prostration. (1072) ☐

461. Narrated Abu Salma: I saw Abu Huraira reciting Idha-Sama' un-Shaqqat and he prostrated during its recitation. I asked Abu Huraira, "Didn't I see you prostrating?" Abu Huraira said, "Had I not seen the Prophet (ﷺ) prostrating, I would not have prostrated." (1074) ☐

462. Narrated Rabi`a: `Umar bin Al-Khattab recited Surah-an-Nahl on a Friday on the pulpit and when he reached the verse of Sajda he got down from the pulpit and prostrated and the people also prostrated. The next Friday `Umar bin Al-Khattab recited the same Sura and when he reached the verse of Sajda he said, "O people! When we recite the verses of Sajda (during the sermon) whoever prostrates does the right thing, yet it is no sin for the one who does not prostrate." And `Umar did not prostrate (that day). Added Ibn `Umar "Allah has not made the prostration of

recitation compulsory but if we wish we can do it." (1077) □

19. SHORTENING THE PRAYERS

463. NARRATED IBN `ABBAS (RA): The Prophet (ﷺ) once stayed for nineteen days and prayed shortened prayers. So when we travelled (and stayed) for nineteen days, we used to shorten the prayer but if we traveled (and stayed) for a longer period we used to offer the full prayer. (1080) □

464. Narrated Yahya bin 'Is-haq: I heard Anas saying, "We traveled with the Prophet (ﷺ) from Medina to Mecca and offered two rak`at (for every prayer) till we returned to Medina." I said, "Did you stay for a while in Mecca?" He replied, "We stayed in Mecca for ten days." (1081) □

465. Narrated `Abdullah bin `Umar: I offered the prayer with the Prophet, Abu Bakr and `Umar at Mina and it was of two rak`at. `Uthman in the early days of his caliphate did the same, but later on he started praying the full prayer. (1082) □

466. Narrated `Abdur Rahman bin Yazid: We offered a four rak`at prayer at Mina behind Ibn `Affan. `Abdullah bin Mas`ud was informed about it. He said sadly, "Truly to Allah we belong and truly to Him we shall return." And added, "I prayed two rak`at with Allah's Messenger (ﷺ) at Mina and similarly with Abu Bakr and with `Umar (during their caliphates)." He further said, "May I be lucky enough to have two of the four rak`at accepted (by Allah)." (1084) □

467. Narrated Ibn `Umar: The Prophet (ﷺ) said, "A woman should not travel for more than three days except with a Dhi-Mahram (i.e. a male with whom she cannot marry at all, e.g. her brother, father, grandfather, etc.) or her own husband.)" (1086) □

468. Narrated Abu Huraira: The Prophet (p.b.u.h) said, "It is not permissible for a woman who believes in Allah and the Last Day to travel for one day and night except

with a Mahram." (1088) □

469. Narrated Ibn `Umar: The Prophet (ﷺ) said, "If the people knew what I know about traveling alone, then nobody would travel alone at night." (2998) □

470. Narrated `Abdullah bin `Umar: "I saw Allah's Messenger (ﷺ) delaying the Maghrib prayer till he offered it along with the `Isha' prayer whenever he was in a hurry during the journey." Salim narrated, "Ibn `Umar used to do the same whenever he was in a hurry during the journey." And Salim added, "Ibn `Umar used to pray the Maghrib and `Isha' prayers together in Al-Muzdalifa." Salim said, "Ibn `Umar delayed the Maghrib prayer because at that time he heard the news of the death of his wife Safiya bint Abi `Ubaid. I said to him, 'The prayer (is due).' He said, 'Go on.' Again I said, 'The prayer (is due).' He said, 'Go on,' till we covered two or three miles. Then he got down, prayed and said, 'I saw the Prophet (ﷺ) praying in this way, whenever he was in a hurry during the journey.' `Abdullah (bin `Umar) added, "Whenever the Prophet was in a hurry, he used to delay the Maghrib prayer and then offer three rak`at (of the Maghrib) and perform Taslim, and after waiting for a short while, Iqama used to be pronounced for the `Isha' prayer when he would offer two rak`at and perform Taslim. He would never offer any optional prayer till the middle of the night (when he used to pray the Tahajjud)." (1092) □

20. PRAYER AT NIGHT (TAHAJJUD)

471. NARRATED IBN `ABBAS (RA): When the Prophet (ﷺ) got up at night to offer the Tahajjud prayer, he used to say:

اللَّهُمَّ لَكَ الْحَمْدُ أَنْتَ قَيِّمُ السَّمَوَاتِ وَالأَرْضِ وَمَنْ فِيهِنَّ وَلَكَ الْحَمْدُ، لَكَ مُلْكُ السَّمَوَاتِ وَالأَرْضِ وَمَنْ فِيهِنَّ، وَلَكَ الْحَمْدُ أَنْتَ نُورُ السَّمَوَاتِ وَالأَرْضِ، وَلَكَ الْحَمْدُ أَنْتَ الْحَقُّ، وَوَعْدُكَ الْحَقُّ، وَلِقَاؤُكَ حَقٌّ، وَقَوْلُكَ حَقٌّ، وَالْجَنَّةُ حَقٌّ، وَالنَّارُ حَقٌّ، وَالنَّبِيُّونَ حَقٌّ، وَمُحَمَّدٌ صلى الله عليه وسلم حَقٌّ، وَالسَّاعَةُ حَقٌّ، اللَّهُمَّ لَكَ أَسْلَمْتُ، وَبِكَ آمَنْتُ وَعَلَيْكَ تَوَكَّلْتُ، وَإِلَيْكَ أَنَبْتُ، وَبِكَ خَاصَمْتُ، وَإِلَيْكَ حَاكَمْتُ، فَاغْفِرْ لِي مَا قَدَّمْتُ وَمَا أَخَّرْتُ، وَمَا أَسْرَرْتُ وَمَا أَعْلَنْتُ، أَنْتَ الْمُقَدِّمُ وَأَنْتَ الْمُؤَخِّرُ، لاَ إِلَهَ إِلاَّ أَنْتَ

"Allahumma lakal-hamd. Anta qaiyyimus-samawati wal-ard wa man fihinna.

Walakal-hamd, Laka mulkus-samawati wal-ard wa man fihinna. Walakal-hamd, anta nurus-samawati wal-ard. Wa lakal-hamd, anta-l-haq wa wa'duka-lhaq, wa liqa'uka Haq, wa qauluka Haq, wal-jannatu Han wan-naru Haq wannabiyuna Haq. Wa Muhammadun, sallal-lahu'alaihi wasallam, Haq, was-sa'atu Haq. Allahumma aslamtu Laka wabika amantu, wa 'Alaika tawakkaltu, wa ilaika anabtu wa bika khasamtu, wa ilaika hakamtu faghfir li ma qaddamtu wama akh-khartu wama as-rartu wama'a lantu, anta-l-muqaddim wa anta-l-mu akh-khir, la ilaha illa anta (or la ilaha ghairuka)." (O Allah! All the praises are for you, You are the Holder of the Heavens and the Earth, And whatever is in them. All the praises are for You; You have the possession of the Heavens and the Earth And whatever is in them. All the praises are for You; You are the Light of the Heavens and the Earth And all the praises are for You; You are the King of the Heavens and the Earth; And all the praises are for You; You are the Truth and Your Promise is the truth, And to meet You is true, Your Word is the truth And Paradise is true And Hell is true And all the Prophets (as) are true; And Muhammad is true, And the Day of Resurrection is true. O Allah! I surrender (my will) to You; I believe in You and depend on You. And repent to You, and with Your help I argue (with my opponents, the non-believers) And I take You as a judge (to judge between us). Please forgive me my previous and future sins; and whatever I concealed or revealed and You are the One who make (some people) forward And (some) backward. There is none to be worshipped but you.) Sufyan said that `Abdul Karim Abu Umaiya added to the above, وَلاَ حَوْلَ وَلاَ قُوَّةَ إِلاَّ بِاللَّ "Wala haula Wala quwata illa billah" (There is neither might nor power except with Allah). (1120) □

472. Narrated `Aisha: Allah's Messenger (ﷺ) used to offer eleven rak`at and that was his prayer. He used to prolong the prostration to such an extent that one could recite fifty verses (of the Qur'an) before he would lift his head. He used to pray two rak`at (Sunnah) before the Fajr prayer and then used to lie down on his right side till the call-maker came and informed him about the prayer. (1123) □

473. Narrated `Ali bin Abi Talib: One night Allah's Messenger (ﷺ) came to me and

Fatima, the daughter of the Prophet (ﷺ) and asked, "Won't you pray (at night)?" I said, "O Allah's Messenger (ﷺ)! Our souls are in the hands of Allah and if He wants us to get up He will make us get up." When I said that, he left us without saying anything and I heard that he was hitting his thigh and saying, "But man is more quarrelsome than anything." (18.54) (1127) ☐

474. Narrated Al-Mughira: The Prophet (ﷺ) used to stand (in the prayer) or pray till both his feets and legs swelled. He was asked why (he offered such an unbearable prayer) and he said, "Should I not be a thankful slave." (1130) ☐

475. Narrated `Abdullah bin `Amr bin Al-`As: Allah's Messenger (ﷺ) told me, "The most beloved prayer to Allah is that of David and the most beloved fasts to Allah are those of David. He used to sleep for half of the night and then pray for one third of the night and again sleep for its sixth part and used to fast on alternate days." (1131) ☐

476. Narrated Masruq: I asked `Aisha which deed was most loved by the Prophet. She said, "A deed done continuously." I further asked, "When did he used to get up (in the night for the prayer)." She said, "He used to get up on hearing the crowing of a cock." (1132) ☐

477. Narrated Abu-Wail: `Abdullah said, "One night I offered the Tahajjud prayer with the Prophet (ﷺ) and he kept on standing till an ill-thought came to me." We said, "What was the ill-thought?" He said, "It was to sit down and leave the Prophet (standing)." (1135) ☐

478. Narrated `Abdullah bin `Umar: A man said, "O Allah's Messenger (ﷺ)! How is the prayer of the night?" He said, "Two rak`at followed by two rak`at and so on, and when you apprehend the approaching dawn, offer one rak`a as witr." (1137) ☐

479. Narrated Masruq: I asked Aisha about the night prayer of Allah's Messenger (ﷺ) and she said, "It was seven, nine or eleven rak`at besides the two rak`at of the Fajr prayer (i.e. Sunnah)." (1139) ☐

480. Narrated `Aisha: The Prophet (peace be upon him) used to offer thirteen rak`at of the night prayer and that included the witr and two rak`at (Sunnah) of the Fajr prayer. (1140) ☐

481. Narrated `Abdullah: A person was mentioned before the Prophet (p.b.u.h) and he was told that he had kept on sleeping till morning and had not got up for the prayer. The Prophet (ﷺ) said, "Satan urinated in his ears." (1144) ☐

482. Narrated Abu Huraira: The Prophet (ﷺ) said, "If anyone of you rouses from sleep and performs the ablution, he should wash his nose by putting water in it and then blowing it out thrice, because Satan has stayed in the upper part of his nose all the night." (3295) ☐

483. Narrated Al-Aswad: I asked `Aisha "How is the night prayer of the Prophet?" She replied, "He used to sleep early at night, and get up in its last part to pray, and then return to his bed. When the Mu'adh-dhin pronounced the Adhan, he would get up. If he was in need of a bath he would take it; otherwise he would perform ablution and then go out (for the prayer)." (1146) ☐

484. Narrated `Aisha: I did not see the Prophet (ﷺ) reciting (the Qur'an) in the night prayer while sitting except when he became old; when he used to recite while sitting, and when thirty or forty verses remained from the Sura, he would get up and recite them and then bow. (1148) ☐

485. Narrated Abu Huraira: At the time of the Fajr prayer the Prophet (ﷺ) asked Bilal, "Tell me of the best deed you did after embracing Islam, for I heard your footsteps in front of me in Paradise." Bilal replied, "I did not do anything worth mentioning except that whenever I performed ablution during the day or night, I prayed after that ablution as much as was written for me." (1149) ☐

486. Narrated Anas bin Malik: Once the Prophet (s) entered the Mosque and saw a rope hanging in between its two pillars. He said, "What is this rope?" The people said, "This rope is for Zainab who, when she feels tired, holds it (to keep standing for the

prayer.)" The Prophet (ﷺ) said, "Don't use it. Remove the rope. You should pray as long as you feel active, and when you get tired, sit down." (1150) □

487. Narrated 'Aisha: A woman from the tribe of Bani Asad was sitting with me and Allah's Apostle (p.b.u.h) came to my house and said, "Who is this?" I said, "(She is) so and so. She does not sleep at night because she is engaged in prayer." The Prophet (ﷺ) said disapprovingly: Do (good) deeds which is within your capacity as Allah never gets tired of giving rewards till you get tired of doing good deeds." (1151) □

488. Narrated `Abdullah bin `Amr bin Al-`As: Allah's Messenger (ﷺ) said to me, "O `Abdullah! Do not be like so and so who used to pray at night and then stopped the night prayer." (1152) □

489. Narrated 'Abdullah bin 'Amr: Once Allah's Messenger (ﷺ) said to me, "I have been informed that you offer Salah (prayer) all the night and observe Saum (fast) during the day." I said, "(Yes) I do so." He said, "If you do so, your eye sight will become weak and you will become weak. No doubt, your body has right on you, and your family has right on you, so observe Saum (for some days) and do not observe it (for some days), offer Salah (for sometime) and then sleep." (1153) □

490. Narrated 'Ubada bin As-Samit: The Prophet (ﷺ) "Whoever gets up at night and says:

لاَ إِلَهَ إِلاَّ اللَّهُ وَحْدَهُ لاَ شَرِيكَ لَهُ، لَهُ الْمُلْكُ، وَلَهُ الْحَمْدُ، وَهُوَ عَلَى كُلِّ شَيْءٍ قَدِيرٌ. الْحَمْدُ لِلَّهِ، وَسُبْحَانَ اللَّهِ، وَلاَ إِلَهَ إِلاَّ اللَّهُ، وَاللهُ أَكْبَرُ، وَلاَ حَوْلَ وَلاَ قُوَّةَ إِلاَّ بِاللَّ

"La ilaha il-lallah Wahdahu la Sharika lahu Lahu-lmulk, waLahu-l-hamd wahuwa 'ala kullishai'in Qadir. Al hamdu lil-lahi wa subhanal-lahi wa la-ilaha il-lal-lah wa-l-lahu akbar wa la hawla Wala Quwata il-la-bil-lah." (None has the right to be worshipped but Allah. He is the Only One and has no partners. For Him is the Kingdom and all the praises are due for Him. He is Omnipotent. All the praises are for Allah. All the glories are for Allah. And none has the right to be worshipped but Allah, And Allah is Great And there is neither Might nor Power Except with Allah). And then says: اللَّهُمَّ اغْفِرْ لِي "Allahumma, Ighfir li." (O Allah! Forgive me). Or invokes

(Allah), he will be responded to and if he performs ablution (and prays), his prayer will be accepted." (1154) ☐

491. Narrated `Aisha: The Prophet (peace be upon him) used to make the two rak`at before the Fajr prayer so light that I would wonder whether he recited Al-Fatiha (or not). (1165) ☐

492. Narrated `Abdur Rahman bin Abi Laila: Only Um Hani narrated to me that she had seen the Prophet (ﷺ) offering the Duha prayer. She said, "On the day of the conquest of Mecca, the Prophet (ﷺ) entered my house, took a bath and offered eight rak`at (of Duha prayers. I had never seen the Prophet (ﷺ) offering such a light prayer but he performed bowing and prostrations perfectly. (1176) ☐

493. Narrated Aisha: The Prophet (ﷺ) never missed four rak`at before the Zuhr prayer and two rak`at before the Fajr prayer. (1182) ☐

494. Narrated `Abdullah Al-Muzni: The Prophet (ﷺ) said, "Pray before the Maghrib (compulsory) prayer." He (said it thrice) and in the third time, he said, "Whoever wants to offer it can do so." He said so because he did not like the people to take it as a tradition. (1183) ☐

21. MOSQUES OF MAKKAH AND MADINAH

495. NRRATED ABU HURAIRA (RA): The Prophet (ﷺ) said, "Do not set out on a journey except for three Mosques (al-Haram, an Nabawi and Al-Aqsa,) (1189) ☐

496. Narrated Abu Huraira: Allah's Messenger (ﷺ) said, "One prayer in my Mosque is better than one thousand prayers in any other mosque excepting Al-Masjid-AI-Haram." (1190) ☐

497. Narrated Nafi`: Ibn `Umar never offered the Duha prayer except on two occasions: (1) whenever he reached Mecca; and he always used to reach Mecca in the

forenoon. He would perform Tawaf round the Ka`ba and then offer two rak`at at the rear of Maqam Ibrahim. (2) Whenever he visited Quba, for he used to visit it every Saturday. When he entered the Mosque, he disliked to leave it without offering a prayer. Ibn `Umar narrated that Allah's Messenger (ﷺ) used to visit the Mosque of Quba (sometime) walking and (sometime) riding. And he (i.e. Ibn `Umar) used to say, "I do only what my companions used to do and I don't forbid anybody to pray at any time during the day or night except that one should not intend to pray at sunrise or sunset." (1191) ☐

498. Narrated Ibn `Umar: The Prophet (ﷺ) used to go to the Mosque of Quba (sometimes) walking and sometimes riding. Added Nafi` (in another narration), "He then would offer two rak`at (in the Mosque of Quba)." (1194) ☐

499. Narrated Abu Huraira: The Prophet (ﷺ) said, "Between my house and my pulpit there is a garden of the gardens of Paradise, and my pulpit is on my fountain tank (i.e. Al-Kauthar)." (1196) ☐

500. Narrated Yazid bin Al Ubaid: I used to accompany Salama bin Al-Akwa and he used to pray behind the pillar which was near the place where the Quran were kept. I said, "O Abu Muslim! I see you always seeking to pray behind this pillar." He replied, "I saw Allah's Messenger (ﷺ) always seeking to pray near that pillar." (502) ☐

22. ACTIONS WHILE PRAYING

501. NARRATED ZAID BIN ARQAM (RA): In the lifetime of the Prophet (ﷺ) we used to speak while praying, and one of us would tell his needs to his companions, till the verse, 'Guard strictly your prayers (2.238) was revealed. After that we were ordered to remain silent while praying. (1200) ☐

502. Narrated Abu Huraira: The Prophet (ﷺ) said, "The saying 'Sub Han Allah' is for men and clapping is for women." (If something happens in the prayer, the men

can invite the attention of the Imam by saying "Sub Han Allah". And women, by clapping their hands). (1203) □

503. Narrated Mu'aiqib: The Prophet (ﷺ) talked about a man leveling the earth on prostrating, and said, "If you have to do so, then do it once." (1207) □

504. Narrated Al-Azraq bin Qais: We were at Al-Ahwaz fighting the Al-Haruriya (tribe). While I was at the bank of a river a man was praying and the reins of his animal were in his hands and the animal was struggling and he was following the animal. (Shu`ba, a sub-narrator, said that man was Abu Barza Al-Aslami). A man from the Khawarij said, "O Allah! Be harsh to this sheik." And when the sheik (Abu Barza) finished his prayer, he said, "I heard your remark. No doubt, I participated with Allah's Messenger (ﷺ) in six or seven or eight holy battles and saw his leniency, and no doubt, I would rather retain my animal than let it return to its stable, as it would cause me much trouble." (1211) □

505. Narrated Jabir bin `Abdullah: Allah's Messenger (ﷺ) sent me for some job and when I had finished it I returned and came to the Prophet (ﷺ) and greeted him but he did not return my greeting. So I felt so sorry that only Allah knows it and I said to myself, 'Perhaps Allah's Messenger (ﷺ) is angry because I did not come quickly, then again I greeted him but he did not reply. I felt even sorrier than I did the first time. Again I greeted him and he returned the greeting and said, "The thing which prevented me from returning the greeting was that I was praying." And at that time he was on his Rahila and his face was not towards the Qibla. (1217) □

506. Narrated Abu Huraira: It was forbidden to keep the hands on the hips during the prayer. (This is narrated by Abu Huraira from the Prophet [s].) (1219) □

507. Narrated `Uqba: I offered the `Asr prayer behind the Prophet (ﷺ) at Medina. When he had finished the prayer with Taslim, he got up hurriedly and went out by crossing the rows of the people to one of the dwellings of his wives. The people got scared at his speed. The Prophet (ﷺ) came back and found the people surprised at his haste and said to them, "I remembered a piece of gold Lying in my house and I did

not like it to divert my attention from Allah's worship, so I have ordered it to be distributed (in charity). (851) ☐

508. Narrated Abu Huraira: Allah's Messenger (ﷺ) said, "When anyone of you stands for the prayers, Satan comes and puts him in doubts till he forgets how many rak`at he has prayed. So if this happens to anyone of you, he should perform two prostrations of Sahu while sitting. (1232) ☐

509. Narrated Kuraib: I was sent to Aisha by Ibn `Abbas, Al-Miswar bin Makhrama and `Abdur-Rahman bin Azhar. They told me to greet her on their behalf and to ask her about the offering of the two rak`at after the `Asr prayer and say to her, "We were informed that you offer those two rak`at and we were told that the Prophet had forbidden offering them." Ibn `Abbas said, "I along with `Umar bin Al-Khattab used to beat the people whenever they offered them." I went to Aisha and told her that message. `Aisha said, "Go and ask Um Salama about them." So I returned and informed them about her statement. They then told me to go to Um Salama with the same question with which they sent me to `Aisha. Um Salama replied, "I heard the Prophet (ﷺ) forbidding them. Later I saw him offering them immediately after he prayed the `Asr prayer. He then entered my house at a time when some of the Ansari women from the tribe of Bani Haram were sitting with me, so I sent my slave girl to him having said to her, 'Stand beside him and tell him that Um Salama says to you, "O Allah's Messenger (ﷺ)! I have heard you forbidding the offering of these (two rak`at after the `Asr prayer) but I have seen you offering them." If he waves his hand then wait for him.' The slave girl did that. The Prophet (ﷺ) beckoned her with his hand and she waited for him. When he had finished the prayer he said, "O daughter of Bani Umaiya! You have asked me about the two rak`at after the `Asr prayer. The people of the tribe of `Abdul-Qais came to me and made me busy and I could not offer the two rak`at after the Zuhr prayer. These (two rak`at that I have just prayed) are for those (missed) ones. (1233) ☐

510. Narrated Alqama: I asked `Aisha "Did Allah s Apostle, use to choose some special days (for fasting)?" She replied, "No, but he used to be regular (constant) (in

his service of worshipping). Who amongst you can endure what Allah's Messenger (ﷺ) used to endure?" (1987) ☐

23. FUNERALS

511. NARRATED ABU DHAR (RA): Allah's Messenger (ﷺ) said, "Someone came to me from my Lord and gave me the news (or good tidings) that if any of my followers dies worshipping none (in any way) along with Allah, he will enter Paradise." I asked, "Even if he committed illegal sexual intercourse and theft?" He replied, "Even if he committed illegal sexual intercourse and theft." (1237) ☐

512. Narrated Abdullah: Allah's Messenger (ﷺ) said, "Anyone who dies worshipping others along with Allah will definitely enter the Fire." I said, "Anyone who dies worshipping none along with Allah will definitely enter Paradise."(1238) ☐

513. Narrated Kharija bin Zaid bin Thabit: Um Al-`Ala', an Ansari woman who gave the pledge of allegiance to the Prophet (ﷺ) said to me, "The emigrants were distributed amongst us by drawing lots and we got in our share `Uthman bin Maz'un. We made him stay with us in our house. Then he suffered from a disease which proved fatal when he died and was given a bath and was shrouded in his clothes, Allah's Messenger (ﷺ) came I said, 'May Allah be merciful to you, O Abu As-Sa'ib! I testify that Allah has honored you'. The Prophet (ﷺ) said, 'How do you know that Allah has honored him?' I replied, 'O Allah's Messenger (ﷺ)! Let my father be sacrificed for you! On whom else shall Allah bestow His honor?' The Prophet (ﷺ) said, 'No doubt, death came to him. By Allah, I too wish him good, but by Allah, I do not know what Allah will do with me though I am Allah's Messenger.' By Allah, I never attested the piety of anyone after that." (1243) ☐

514. Narrated Abu Huraira: Allah's Messenger (ﷺ) informed (the people) about the death of An-Najashi on the very day he died. He went towards the Musalla (praying place) and the people stood behind him in rows. He said four Takbirs (i.e. offered the

Funeral prayer). (1245) ☐

515. Narrated Ibn `Abbas: A person died and Allah's Messenger (ﷺ) used to visit him. He died at night and (the people) buried him at night. In the morning they informed the Prophet. He said, "What prevented you from informing me?" They replied, "It was night and it was a dark night and so we disliked to trouble you." The Prophet (ﷺ) went to his grave and offered the (funeral) prayer. (1247) ☐

516. Narrated Abu Huraira: The Prophet (ﷺ) said, "No Muslim whose three children died will go to the Fire except for Allah's oath (i.e. everyone has to pass over the bridge above the lake of fire)." (1251) ☐

517. Narrated Um 'Atiyya: Allah's Messenger (ﷺ) came to us and we were giving a bath to his (dead) daughter and said, "Wash her three, five or more times with water and Sidr and sprinkle camphor on her at the end; and when you finish, notify me." So when we finished, we informed him and he gave us his waist-sheet and told us to shroud her in it. Aiyub said that Hafsa narrated to him a narration similar to that of Muhammad in which it was said that the bath was to be given for an odd number of times, and the numbers 3, 5 or 7 were mentioned. It was also said that they were to start with the right side and with the parts which were washed in ablution, and that Um 'Atiyya also mentioned, "We combed her hair and divided them in three braids." (1254) ☐

518. Narrated Hafsa bint Seereen: Um 'Atiyya said that they had entwined the hair of the daughter of Allah's Messenger (ﷺ) in three braids. They first undid her hair, washed and then entwined it in three braids." (1260) ☐

519. Narrated `Aisha: Allah's Messenger (ﷺ) was shrouded in three Yemenite white Suhuliya (pieces of cloth) of cotton, and in them there was neither a shirt nor a turban." (1264) ☐

520. Narrated Jabir bin `Abdullah: When it was the day of Badr, prisoners of war were brought including Al-Abbas who was undressed. The Prophet (ﷺ) looked for a

shirt for him. It was found that the shirt of `Abdullah bin Ubai would do, so the Prophet (ﷺ) let him wear it. That was the reason why the Prophet (ﷺ) took off and gave his own shirt to `Abdullah. (The narrator adds, "He had done the Prophet (ﷺ) some favor for which the Prophet liked to reward him.") (3008) □

521. Narrated Ibn `Abbas: When `Abdullah bin 'Ubai died, his son `Abdullah bin `Abdullah came to Allah's Messenger (ﷺ) and asked him to give him his shirt in order to shroud his father in it. He gave it to him and then `Abdullah asked the Prophet (ﷺ) to offer the funeral prayer for him (his father). Allah's Messenger (ﷺ) got up to offer the funeral prayer for him, but `Umar got up too and got hold of the garment of Allah's Messenger (ﷺ) and said, "O Allah's Messenger (ﷺ) Will you offer the funeral prayer for him though your Lord has forbidden you to offer the prayer for him" Allah's Messenger (ﷺ) said, "But Allah has given me the choice by saying: '(Whether you) ask forgiveness for them, or do not ask forgiveness for them; even if you ask forgiveness for them seventy times..' (9.80) so I will ask more than seventy times." `Umar said, "But he (`Abdullah bin 'Ubai) is a hypocrite!" However, Allah's Messenger (ﷺ) did offer the funeral prayer for him whereupon Allah revealed: 'And never (O Muhammad) pray for anyone of them that dies, nor stand at his grave.' (9.84) (4670) □

522. Narrated Khabbab: We emigrated with the Prophet (p.b.u.h) in Allah's cause, and so our reward was then surely incumbent on Allah. Some of us died and they did not take anything from their rewards in this world, and amongst them was Mustab bin `Umar; and the others were those who got their rewards. Mustab bin `Umar was martyred on the day of the Battle of Uhud and we could get nothing except his Burd to shroud him in. And when we covered his head his feet became bare and vice versa. So the Prophet (ﷺ) ordered us to cover his head only and to put idhkhir (a kind of shrub) over his feet. (1276) □

523. Narrated Um 'Atiyya: We (female) were forbidden to accompany funeral processions but not strictly. (1278) □

524. Narrated Zainab bint Abi Salama: When the news of the death of Abu Sufyan reached from Sham, Um Habiba on the third day, asked for a yellow perfume and scented her cheeks and forearms and said, "No doubt, I would not have been in need of this, had I not heard the Prophet (ﷺ) saying: "It is not legal for a woman who believes in Allah and the Last Day to mourn for more than three days for any dead person except her husband, for whom she should mourn for four months and ten days." (1280) □

525. Narrated Anas bin Malik: The Prophet (ﷺ) passed by a woman who was weeping beside a grave. He told her to fear Allah and be patient. She said to him, "Go away, for you have not been afflicted with a calamity like mine." And she did not recognize him. Then she was informed that he was the Prophet (ﷺ). So she went to the house of the Prophet (ﷺ) and there she did not find any guard. Then she said to him, "I did not recognize you." He said, "Verily, the patience is at the first stroke of a calamity." (1283) □

526. Narrated Usama bin Zaid: The daughter of the Prophet (p.b.u.h) sent (a messenger) to the Prophet (ﷺ) requesting him to come as her child was dying (or was gasping), but the Prophet (ﷺ) returned the messenger and told him to convey his greeting to her and say: "Whatever Allah takes is for Him and whatever He gives, is for Him, and everything with Him has a limited fixed term (in this world) and so she should be patient and hope for Allah's reward." She again sent for him, swearing that he should come. The Prophet (ﷺ) got up, and so did Sa`d bin 'Ubada, Mu`adh bin Jabal, Ubai bin Ka`b, Zaid bin Thabit and some other men. The child was brought to Allah's Messenger (ﷺ) while his breath was disturbed in his chest (the sub-narrator thinks that Usama added) as if it was a leather water-skin. On that the eyes of the Prophet (p.b.u.h) started shedding tears. Sa`d said, "O Allah's Messenger (ﷺ)! What is this?" He replied, "It is mercy which Allah has lodged in the hearts of His slaves, and Allah is merciful only to those of His slaves who are merciful (to others). (1284) □

527. Narrated Anas bin Malik: We were (in the funeral procession) of one of the

daughters of the Prophet (ﷺ) and he was sitting by the side of the grave. I saw his eyes shedding tears. He said, "Is there anyone among you who did not have sexual relations with his wife last night?" Abu Talha replied in the affirmative. And so the Prophet told him to get down in the grave. And so he got down in her grave. (1285) ☐

528. Narrated `Aisha: Once Allah's Messenger (ﷺ) passed by (the grave of) a Jewess whose relatives were weeping over her. He said, "They are weeping over her and she is being tortured in her grave." (1289) ☐

529. Narrated Ibn 'Umar from his father: The Prophet (ﷺ) said, "The deceased is tortured in his grave for the wailing done over him."

Narrated Shu'ba: The deceased is tortured for the wailing of the living ones over him. (1292) ☐

530. Narrated `Abdullah: the Prophet (ﷺ) said, "He who slaps his cheeks, tears his clothes and follows the ways and traditions of the Days of Ignorance is not one of us." (1294) ☐

531. Narrated Anas: The Prophet (ﷺ) said, "The real patience is at the first stroke of a calamity." (1302) ☐

532. Narrated Anas bin Malik: We went with Allah's Messenger (ﷺ) to the blacksmith Abu Saif, and he was the husband of the wet-nurse of Ibrahim (the son of the Prophet). Allah's Messenger (ﷺ) took Ibrahim and kissed him and smelled him and later we entered Abu Saif's house and at that time Ibrahim was in his last breaths, and the eyes of Allah's Messenger (ﷺ) started shedding tears. `Abdur Rahman bin `Auf said, "O Allah's Apostle, even you are weeping!" He said, "O Ibn `Auf, this is mercy." Then he wept more and said, "The eyes are shedding tears and the heart is grieved, and we will not say except what pleases our Lord, O Ibrahim! Indeed we are grieved by your separation." (1303) ☐

533. Narrated `Abdullah bin `Umar: Sa`d bin 'Ubada became sick and the Prophet (ﷺ) along with `Abdur Rahman bin `Auf, Sa`d bin Abi Waqqas and `Abdullah bin

Mas`ud visited him to inquire about his health. When he came to him, he found him surrounded by his household and he asked, "Has he died?" They said, "No, O Allah's Apostle." The Prophet (ﷺ) wept and when the people saw the weeping of Allah's Messenger (ﷺ) they all wept. He said, "Will you listen? Allah does not punish for shedding tears, nor for the grief of the heart but he punishes or bestows His Mercy because of this." He pointed to his tongue and added, "The deceased is punished for the wailing of his relatives over him." `Umar used to beat with a stick and throw stones and put dust over the faces (of those who used to wail over the dead). (1304) □

534. Narrated Um 'Atiyya: At the time of giving the pledge of allegiance to the Prophet (ﷺ) one of the conditions was that we would not wail, but it was not fulfilled except by five women and they are Um Sulaim, Um Al-`Ala', the daughter of Abi Sabra (the wife of Mu`adh), and two other women; or the daughter of Abi Sabra and the wife of Mu`adh and another woman. (1306) □

535. Narrated Abu Sa`id Al-Khudri: The Prophet (ﷺ) said, "When you see a funeral procession, you should stand up, and whoever accompanies it should not sit till the coffin is put down." (1310) □

536. Narrated `Abdur Rahman bin Abi Laila: Sahl bin Hunaif and Qais bin Sa`d were sitting in the city of Al-Qadisiya. A funeral procession passed in front of them and they stood up. They were told that funeral procession was of one of the inhabitants of the land i.e. of a non-believer, under the protection of Muslims. They said, "A funeral procession passed in front of the Prophet (ﷺ) and he stood up. When he was told that it was the coffin of a Jew, he said, "Is it not a living being (soul)?" (1312) □

537. Narrated Abu Sa`id Al-Khudri: Allah's Messenger (ﷺ) said, When the funeral is ready and the men carry it on their shoulders, if the deceased was righteous it will say, 'Present me (hurriedly),' and if he was not righteous, it will say, 'Woe to it (me)! Where are they taking it (me)?' Its voice is heard by everything except man and if he heard it he would fall unconscious." (1314) □

538. Narrated Abu Huraira: The Prophet (ﷺ) said, "Hurry up with the dead body for if it was righteous, you are forwarding it to welfare; and if it was otherwise, then you are putting off an evil thing down your necks." (1315) □

539. Narrated Ash-Shaibani: Ash Shu`bi said, "I was informed by a man who had seen the Prophet (ﷺ) going to a grave that was separate from the other graves and he aligned the people in rows and said four Takbir." I said, "O Abu `Amr! Who narrated (that) to you"? He said, "Ibn `Abbas. " (1319) □

540. Narrated Jabir bin `Abdullah: The Prophet (ﷺ) said, "Today a pious man from Ethiopia (i.e. A Najashi) has expired, come on to offer the funeral prayer." (Jabir said): We lined up in rows and after that the Prophet (ﷺ) led the prayer and we were in rows. Jabir added, I was in the second row." (1320) □

541. Narrated Abu Huraira: that Allah's Messenger (ﷺ) said, "Whoever attends the funeral procession till he offers the funeral prayer for it, will get a reward equal to one Qirat, and whoever accompanies it till burial, will get a reward equal to two Qirats." It was asked, "What are two Qirats?" He replied, "Like two huge mountains." (1325) □

542. Narrated Abu Huraira: Allah's Messenger (ﷺ) informed about the news of the death of An-Najash (King of Ethiopia) on the day he expired. He said, "Ask Allah's forgiveness for your brother." Narrated Abu Huraira: The Prophet (ﷺ) made them align in rows at the Musalla and said four Takbir. (1327) □

543. Narrated Samura bin Jundab: I offered the funeral prayer behind the Prophet (ﷺ) for a woman who had died during childbirth and he stood up by the middle of the coffin. (1331) □

544. Narrated Talha bin `Abdullah bin `Auf: I offered the funeral prayer behind Ibn `Abbas and he recited Al-Fatiha and said, "You should know that it (i.e. recitation of Al-Fatiha) is the tradition of the Prophet (ﷺ) Muhammad. (1335) □

545. Narrated Jabir: A man was buried along with my father and I did not like it till

I took him (i.e. my father) out and buried him in a separate grave. (1352) ☐

546. Narrated Anas: A young Jewish boy used to serve the Prophet (ﷺ) and he became sick. So the Prophet (ﷺ) went to visit him. He sat near his head and asked him to embrace Islam. The boy looked at his father, who was sitting there; the latter told him to obey Abul-Qasim and the boy embraced Islam. The Prophet (ﷺ) came out saying: "Praises be to Allah Who saved the boy from the Hell-fire." (1356) ☐

547. Narrated Ibn Shihab: The funeral prayer should be offered for every child even if he were the son of a prostitute as he was born with a true faith of Islam (i.e. to worship none but Allah Alone). If his parents are Muslims, particularly the father, even if his mother were a non-Muslim, and if he after the delivery cries (even once) before his death (i.e. born alive) then the funeral prayer must be offered. And if the child does not cry after his delivery (i.e. born dead) then his funeral prayer should not be offered, and he will be considered as a miscarriage. Abu Huraira, narrated that the Prophet (ﷺ) said, "Every child is born with a true faith (i.e. to worship none but Allah Alone) but his parents convert him to Judaism or to Christianity or to Magainism, as an animal delivers a perfect baby animal. Do you find it mutilated?" Then Abu Huraira recited the holy verses: 'The pure Allah's Islamic nature (true faith i.e. to worship none but Allah Alone), with which He has created human beings.'" (30.30). (1358) ☐

548. Narrated Ibn `Abbas: The Prophet (ﷺ) once passed by two graves, and those two persons (in the graves) were being tortured. He said, "They are being tortured not for a great thing (to avoid). One of them never saved himself from being soiled with his urine, while the other was going about with calumnies (to make enmity between friends). He then took a green leaf of a date-palm tree split it into two pieces and fixed one on each grave. The people said, "O Allah's Messenger (ﷺ)! Why have you done so?" He replied, "I hope that their punishment may be lessened till they (the leaf) become dry." (1361) ☐ (Calumnies - the making of false and defamatory statements about someone in order to damage their reputation)

549. Narrated Anas bin Malik: A funeral procession passed and the people praised the deceased. The Prophet (ﷺ) said, "It has been affirmed to him." Then another funeral procession passed and the people spoke badly of the deceased. The Prophet (ﷺ) said, "It has been affirmed to him". `Umar bin Al-Khattab asked (Allah's Messenger (ﷺ), "What has been affirmed?" He replied, "You praised this, so Paradise has been affirmed to him; and you spoke badly of this, so Hell has been affirmed to him. You people are Allah's witnesses on earth." (1367) □

550. Narrated Abu Al-Aswad: I came to Medina when an epidemic had broken out. While I was sitting with `Umar bin Al-Khattab a funeral procession passed by and the people praised the deceased. `Umar said, "It has been affirmed to him." And another funeral procession passed by and the people praised the deceased. `Umar said, "It has been affirmed to him." A third (funeral procession) passed by and the people spoke badly of the deceased. He said, "It has been affirmed to him." I (Abu Al-Aswad) asked, "O chief of the believers! What has been affirmed?" He replied, "I said the same as the Prophet (ﷺ) had said, that is: if four persons testify the piety of a Muslim, Allah will grant him Paradise." We asked, "If three persons testify his piety?" He (the Prophet) replied, "Even three." Then we asked, "If two?" He replied, "Even two." We did not ask him regarding one witness. (1368) □

551. Narrated Al-Bara' bin 'Azib : The Prophet (p.b.u.h) said, "When a faithful believer is made to sit in his grave, then (the angels) come to him and he testifies that none has the right to be worshipped but Allah and Muhammad is Allah's Apostle. And that corresponds to Allah's statement: Allah will keep firm those who believe with the word that stands firm . . . (14.27).

Narrated Shu'ba: Same as above and added, "Allah will keep firm those who believe . . . (14.27) was revealed concerning the punishment of the grave." (1369) □

552. Narrated Asma' bint Abi Bakr: Allah's Messenger (ﷺ) once stood up delivering a sermon and mentioned the trial which people will face in the grave. When he mentioned that, the Muslims started shouting loudly. (1373) □

553. Narrated Anas bin Malik: Allah's Messenger (ﷺ) said, "When (Allah's) slave is put in his grave and his companions return and he even hears their footsteps, two angels come to him and make him sit and ask, 'What did you use to say about this man (Muhammad)?' The faithful Believer will say, 'I testify that he is Allah's slave and His Apostle.' Then they will say to him, 'Look at your place in the Hell Fire; Allah has given you a place in Paradise instead of it.' So he will see both his places." (Qatada said, "We were informed that his grave would be made spacious." Then Qatada went back to the narration of Anas who said ;) Whereas a hypocrite or a non-believer will be asked, "What did you use to say about this man?" He will reply, "I do not know; but I used to say what the people used to say." So they will say to him, "Neither did you know nor did you take the guidance (by reciting the Qur'an)." Then he will be hit with iron hammers once, that he will send such a cry as everything near to him will hear, except Jinns and human beings. (1374). □

554. Narrated Abi Aiyub: Once the Prophet (ﷺ) went out after sunset and heard a dreadful voice, and said, "The Jews are being punished in their graves."(1375) □

555. Narrated Abu Huraira: Allah's Messenger (ﷺ) used to invoke (Allah):

" اللَّهُمَّ إِنِّي أَعُوذُ بِكَ مِنْ عَذَابِ الْقَبْرِ، وَمِنْ عَذَابِ النَّارِ، وَمِنْ فِتْنَةِ الْمَحْيَا وَالْمَمَاتِ، وَمِنْ فِتْنَةِ الْمَسِيحِ الدَّجَّالِ "

Allahumma ini a`udhu bika min 'adhabi-l-Qabr, wa min 'adhabi-nnar, wa min fitnati-l-mahya wa-lmamat, wa min fitnati-l-masih ad-dajjal. (O Allah! I seek refuge with you from the punishment in the grave and from the punishment in the Hell fire and from the afflictions of life and death, and the afflictions of Al-Masih Ad-Dajjal." (1377) □

556. Narrated `Abdullah bin `Umar: Allah's Messenger (ﷺ) said, "When anyone of you dies, he is shown his place both in the morning and in the evening. If he is one of the people of Paradise; he is shown his place in it, and if he is from the people of the Hell-Fire; he is shown his place there-in. Then it is said to him, 'This is your place till Allah resurrect you on the Day of Resurrection." (1379) □

557. Narrated Anas bin Malik: Allah's Messenger (ﷺ) said, "Any Muslim whose three children died before the age of puberty will be granted Paradise by Allah because of His mercy to them." (1381) ☐

558. Narrated Ibn `Abbas: Allah's Messenger (ﷺ) was asked about the children of (Mushrikeen) pagans. The Prophet (ﷺ) replied, "Since Allah created them, He knows what sort of deeds they would have done." (1383) ☐

559. Narrated Al-Bara': When Ibrahim (the son of Prophet) expired, Allah's Messenger (ﷺ) said, "There is a wet-nurse for him in Paradise." (1382) ☐

560. 'Narrated Aisha: A man said to the Prophet (p.b.u.h), "My mother died suddenly and I thought that if she had lived she would have given alms (charity). So, if I give alms now on her behalf, will she get the reward?" The Prophet (ﷺ) replied in the affirmative. (1388) ☐

561. Narrated `Aisha: The Prophet (p.b.u.h) said, "Don't abuse the dead, because they have reached the result of what they forwarded." (1393) ☐

24. CHARITY

562. NARRATED AL-AHNAF BIN QAIS (RA): While I was sitting with some people from Quraish, a man with very rough hair, clothes, and appearance came and stood in front of us, greeted us and said, "Inform those who hoard wealth, that a stone will be heated in the Hell-fire and will be put on the nipples of their breasts till it comes out from the bones of their shoulders and then put on the bones of their shoulders till it comes through the nipples of their breasts the stone will be moving and hitting." After saying that, the person retreated and sat by the side of the pillar, I followed him and sat beside him, and I did not know who he was. I said to him, "I think the people disliked what you had said." He said, "These people do not understand anything, although my friend told me." I asked, "Who is your friend?" He said, "The Prophet

(☿) said (to me), 'O Abu Dhar! Do you see the mountain of Uhud?' And on that I (Abu Dhar) started looking towards the sun to judge how much remained of the day as I thought that Allah's Messenger (☿) wanted to send me to do something for him and I said, 'Yes!' He said, 'I do not love to have gold equal to the mountain of Uhud unless I spend it all (in Allah's cause) except three Dinars (pounds). These people do not understand and collect worldly wealth. No, by Allah, neither I ask them for worldly benefits nor am I in need of their religious advice till I meet Allah, The Honorable, The Majestic." (1407) □

563. Narrated Abu Huraira: Allah's Messenger (☿) said, "If one give in charity what equals one date-fruit from the honestly earned money and Allah accepts only the honestly earned money --Allah takes it in His right (hand) and then enlarges its reward for that person (who has given it), as anyone of you brings up his baby horse, so much s that it becomes as big as a mountain. (1410) □

564. Narrated `Adi bin Hatim: While I was sitting with Allah's Messenger (☿) two person came to him; one of them complained about his poverty and the other complained about the prevalence of robberies. Allah's Messenger (☿) said, "As regards stealing and robberies, there will shortly come a time when a caravan will go to Mecca (from Medina) without any guard. And regarding poverty, The Hour (Day of Judgment) will not be established till one of you wanders about with his object of charity and will not find anybody to accept it And (no doubt) each one of you will stand in front of Allah and there will be neither a curtain nor an interpreter between him and Allah, and Allah will ask him, 'Did not I give you wealth?' He will reply in the affirmative. Allah will further ask, 'Didn't send a messenger to you?' And again that person will reply in the affirmative. Then he will look to his right and he will see nothing but Hell-fire, and then he will look to his left and will see nothing but Hell-fire. And so, any (each one) of you should save himself from the fire even by giving half of a date-fruit (in charity). And if you do not find a hall datefruit, then (you can do it through saying) a good pleasant word (to your brethren). (1413). □

565. Narrated Abu Mas`ud: When the verses of charity were revealed, we used to

work as porters. A man came and distributed objects of charity in abundance. And they (the people) said, "He is showing off." And another man came and gave a Sa (a small measure of food grains); they said, "Allah is not in need of this small amount of charity." And then the Divine Inspiration came: "Those who criticize the contributors among the believers concerning [their] charities and [criticize] the ones who find nothing [to spend] except their effort, so they ridicule them - Allah will ridicule them, and they will have a painful punishment." (9.79). (1415) □

566. Narrated Abu Huraira: Allah's Messenger (ﷺ) said, "A man said that he would give something in charity. He went out with his object of charity and unknowingly gave it to a thief. Next morning the people said that he had given his object of charity to a thief. (On hearing that) he said, "O Allah! All the praises are for you. I will give alms (charity) again." And so he again went out with his alms and (unknowingly) gave it to an adulteress. Next morning the people said that he had given his alms to an adulteress last night. The man said, "O Allah! All the praises are for you. (I gave my alms) to an adulteress. I will give alms again." So he went out with his alms again and (unknowingly) gave it to a rich person. (The people) next morning said that he had given his alms to a wealthy person. He said, "O Allah! All the praises are for you. (I had given alms) to a thief, to an adulteress and to a wealthy man." Then someone came and said to him, "The alms which you gave to the thief, might make him abstain from stealing, and that given to the adulteress might make her abstain from illegal sexual intercourse (adultery), and that given to the wealthy man might make him take a lesson from it and spend his wealth which Allah has given him, in Allah's cause." (1421) □

567. Narrated Ma'n bin Yazid: My grandfather, my father and I gave the pledge of allegiance to Allah's Messenger (ﷺ). The Prophet (ﷺ) got me engaged and then got me married. One day I went to the Prophet (ﷺ) with a complaint. My father Yazid had taken some gold coins for charity and kept them with a man in the mosque (to give them to the poor) But I went and took them and brought them to him (my father). My father said, "By Allah! I did not intend to give them to you." I took (the

case) to Allah's Messenger (ﷺ). On that Allah's Messenger (ﷺ) said, "O Yazid! You will be rewarded for what you intended. O Man! Whatever you have taken is yours." (1422) □

568. Narrated `Aisha: Allah's Messenger (ﷺ) said, "When a woman gives in charity some of the foodstuff (which she has in her house) without spoiling it, she will receive the reward for what she has spent, and her husband will receive the reward because of his earning, and the storekeeper will also have a reward similar to it. The reward of one will not decrease the reward of the others." (1425) □

569. Narrated Abu Huraira: The Prophet (ﷺ) said, "The best charity is that which is practiced by a wealthy person. And start giving first to your dependents." (1426) □

570. Narrated Hakim bin Hizam: The Prophet (ﷺ) said, "The upper hand is better than the lower hand (i.e. he who gives in charity is better than him who takes it). One should start giving first to his dependents. And the best object of charity is that which is given by a wealthy person (from the money which is left after his expenses). And whoever abstains from asking others for some financial help, Allah will give him and save him from asking others, Allah will make him self-sufficient." (1427) □

571. Narrated Abu Burda bin Abu Musa: that his father said, "Whenever a beggar came to Allah's Messenger (ﷺ) or he was asked for something, he used to say (to his companions), "Help and recommend him and you will receive the reward for it; and Allah will bring about what He will through His Prophet's tongue." (1432) □

572. Narrated Asma: The Prophet (ﷺ) said to me, "Do not withhold your money, (for if you did so) Allah would withhold His blessings from you." □

Narrated `Abda: The Prophet (ﷺ) said, "Do not withhold your money by counting it (i.e. hoarding it), (for if you did so), Allah would also withhold His blessings from you." (1433) □

573. Narrated Asma: Once I said, "O Allah's Messenger (ﷺ)! I have no property except what has been given to me by Az-Zubair (i.e. her husband). May I give in

charity?" The Prophet (ﷺ) said, "Give in charity and do not withhold it; otherwise Allah will withhold it back from you." (2590) ☐

574. Narrated Abu Musa: The Prophet (ﷺ) said, "An honest Muslim storekeeper who carries out the orders of his master and pays fully what he has been ordered to give with a good heart and pays to that person to whom he was ordered to pay, is regarded as one of the two charitable persons." (1438) ☐

575. Narrated Abu Huraira: The Prophet (ﷺ) said, "Every day two angels come down from Heaven and one of them says, 'O Allah! Compensate every person who spends in Your Cause,' and the other (angel) says, 'O Allah! Destroy every miser.'" (1442) ☐

576. Narrated Abu Huraira: The Prophet (ﷺ) said, "The example of a miser and an almsgiver is like the example of two persons wearing iron cloaks." Allah's Messenger (ﷺ) also said, "The example of an almsgiver and a miser is like the example of two persons who have two iron cloaks on them from their breasts to their collar bones, and when the almsgiver wants to give in charity, the cloak becomes capacious till it covers his whole body to such an extent that it hides his fingertips and covers his footprints (obliterates his tracks). (1) And when the miser wants to spend, it (the iron cloak) sticks and every ring gets stuck to its place and he tries to widen it, but it did not become wide. (1443) ☐

577. Narrated Abu Burda: from his father from his grandfather that the Prophet (ﷺ) said, "Every Muslim has to give in charity." The people asked, "O Allah's Prophet! If someone has nothing to give, what will he do?" He said, "He should work with his hands and benefit himself and also give in charity (from what he earns)." The people further asked, "If he cannot find even that?" He replied, "He should help the needy who appeal for help." Then the people asked, "If he cannot do that?" He replied, "Then he should perform good deeds and keep away from evil deeds and this will be regarded as charitable deeds." (1445) ☐

578. Narrated 'Is-haq bin `Abdullah bin Al Talha: I heard Anas bin Malik saying, "Abu Talha had more property of date-palm trees gardens than any other amongst

the Ansar in Medina and the most beloved of them to him was Bairuha garden, and it was in front of the Mosque of the Prophet (ﷺ). Allah's Messenger (ﷺ) used to go there and used to drink its nice water." Anas added, "When these verses were revealed: 'By no means shall you Attain righteousness unless You spend (in charity) of that Which you love.' (3.92) Abu Talha said to Allah's Messenger (ﷺ) 'O Allah's Messenger (ﷺ)! Allah, the Blessed, the Superior says: 'By no means shall you attain righteousness, unless you spend (in charity) of that which you love.' And no doubt, Bairuha' garden is the most beloved of all my property to me. So I want to give it in charity in Allah's Cause. I expect its reward from Allah. O Allah's Messenger (ﷺ)! Spend it where Allah makes you think it feasible.' On that Allah's Apostle said, 'Bravo! It is useful property. I have heard what you have said (O Abu Talha), and I think it would be proper if you gave it to your Kith and kin.' Abu Talha said, I will do so, O Allah's Apostle.' Then Abu Talha distributed that garden amongst his relatives and his cousins." (1461) □

579. Narrated Abu Dhar: I reached him (the Prophet (ﷺ)) while in the shade of the Ka`ba; he was saying, "They are the losers, by the Lord of the Ka`ba! They are the losers, by the Lord of the Ka`ba!" I said (to myself), "What is wrong with me? Is anything improper detected in me? What is wrong with me? Then I sat beside him and he kept on saying his statement. I could not remain quiet, and Allah knows in what sorrowful state I was at that time. So I said, ' Who are they (the losers)? Let My father and mother be sacrificed for you, O Allah's Messenger (ﷺ)!" He said, "They are the wealthy people, except the one who does like this and like this and like this (i.e., spends of his wealth in Allah's Cause). (6638) □

580. Narrated Abu Sa`id Al-Khudri: Once the Prophet (ﷺ) sat on a pulpit and we sat around him. Then he said, "The things I am afraid of most for your sake (concerning what will befall you after me) is the pleasures and splendors of the world and its beauties which will be disclosed to you." Somebody said, "O Allah's Messenger (ﷺ)! Can the good bring forth evil?" The Prophet (ﷺ) remained silent for a while. It was said to that person, "What is wrong with you? You are talking to the Prophet (p.b.u.h)

while he is not talking to you." Then we noticed that he was being inspired divinely. Then the Prophet (ﷺ) wiped off his sweat and said, "Where is the questioner?" It seemed as if the Prophet (ﷺ) liked his question. Then he said, "Good never brings forth evil. Indeed it is like what grows on the banks of a water-stream which either kill or make the animals sick, except if an animal eats its fill the Khadira (a kind of vegetable) and then faces the sun, and then defecates and urinates and grazes again. No doubt this wealth is sweet and green. Blessed is the wealth of a Muslim from which he gives to the poor, the orphans and to needy travelers. (Or the Prophet said something similar to it) No doubt, whoever takes it illegally will be like the one who eats but is never satisfied, and his wealth will be a witness against him on the Day of Resurrection." (1465) □

581. Narrated `Amr bin Al-Harith: Zainab, the wife of `Abdullah said, "I was in the Mosque and saw the Prophet (p.b.u.h) saying, 'O women! Give alms even from your ornaments.' "Zainab used to provide for `Abdullah and those orphans who were under her protection. So she said to `Abdullah, "Will you ask Allah's Messenger (ﷺ) whether it will be sufficient for me to spend part of the Zakat on you and the orphans who are under my protection?" He replied "Will you yourself ask Allah's Messenger (ﷺ)?" (Zainab added): So I went to the Prophet and I saw there an Ansari woman who was standing at the door (of the Prophet (ﷺ)) with a similar problem as mine. Bilal passed by us and we asked him, 'Ask the Prophet (ﷺ) whether it is permissible for me to spend (the Zakat) on my husband and the orphans under my protection.' And we requested Bilal not to inform the Prophet (ﷺ) about us. So Bilal went inside and asked the Prophet (ﷺ) regarding our problem. The Prophet (p.b.u.h) asked, "Who are those two?" Bilal replied that she was Zainab. The Prophet (ﷺ) said, "Which Zainab?" Bilal said, "The wife of `Abdullah (bin Mas`ud)." The Prophet said, "Yes, (it is sufficient for her) and she will receive a double rewards (for that): One for helping relatives, and the other for giving Zakat." (1466) □

582. Narrated Zainab: (the daughter of Um Salama) My mother said, "O Allah's Messenger (ﷺ)! Shall I receive a reward if I spend for the sustenance of Abu Salama's

offspring, and in fact they are also my sons?" The Prophet (ﷺ) replied, "Spend on them and you will get a reward for what you spend on them." (1467)□

583. Narrated Abu Sa`id Al-Khudri: Some Ansari persons asked for (something) from Allah's Messenger (ﷺ) and he gave them. They again asked him for (something) and he again gave them. And then they asked him and he gave them again till all that was with him finished. And then he said "If I had anything. I would not keep it away from you. (Remember) Whoever abstains from asking others, Allah will make him contented, and whoever tries to make himself self-sufficient, Allah will make him self-sufficient. And whoever remains patient, Allah will make him patient. Nobody can be given a blessing better and greater than patience." (1469) □

584. Narrated Abu Huraira: Allah's Messenger (ﷺ) said, "By Him in Whose Hand my life is, it is better for anyone of you to take a rope and cut the wood (from the forest) and carry it over his back and sell it rather than to ask a person for something and that person may give him or not." (1470) □

585. Narrated `Urwa bin Az-Zubair and Sa`id bin Al-Musaiyab: Hakim bin Hizam said, "(Once) I asked Allah's Messenger (ﷺ) (for something) and he gave it to me. Again I asked and he gave (it to me). Again I asked and he gave (it to me). And then he said, "O Hakim! This property is like a sweet fresh fruit; whoever takes it without greediness, he is blessed in it, and whoever takes it with greediness, he is not blessed in it, and he is like a person who eats but is never satisfied; and the upper (giving) hand is better than the lower (receiving) hand." Hakim added, "I said to Allah's Messenger (ﷺ), 'By Him (Allah) Who sent you with the Truth, I shall never accept anything from anybody after you, till I leave this world.' "Then Abu Bakr (during his caliphate) called Hakim to give him his share from the war booty (like the other companions of the Prophet (ﷺ)), he refused to accept anything. Then `Umar (during his caliphate) called him to give him his share but he refused. On that `Umar said, "O Muslims! I would like you to witness that I offered Hakim his share from this booty and he refused to take it." So Hakim never took anything from anybody after the Prophet (ﷺ) till he died. (1472) □

586. Narrated `Umar: Allah's Messenger (ﷺ) used to give me something but I would say to him, "would you give it to a poorer and needier one than I?" The Prophet (p.b.u.h) said to me, "Take it. If you are given something from this property, without asking for it or having greed for it take it; and if not given, do not run for it." (1473) □

587. Narrated `Abdullah bin `Umar: The Prophet (ﷺ) said, "A man keeps on asking others for something till he comes on the Day of Resurrection without any piece of flesh on his face." (1474) □

588. Narrated Ash-Shu`bi: The clerk of Al-Mughira bin Shu`ba narrated, "Muawiya wrote to Al-Mughira bin Shu`ba: Write to me something which you have heard from the Prophet (p.b.u.h)." So Al-Mughira wrote: I heard the Prophet saying, "Allah has hated for you three things: -1. Vain talks, (useless talk) that you talk too much or about others. -2. Wasting of wealth (by extravagance) -3. And asking too many questions (in disputed religious matters) or asking others for something (except in great need). (1477) □

589. Narrated Sa`d (bin Abi Waqqas): Allah's Messenger (ﷺ) distributed something (from the resources of Zakat) amongst a group of people while I was sitting amongst them, but he left a man whom I considered the best of the lot. So, I went up to Allah's Messenger (ﷺ) and asked him secretly, "Why have you left that person? By Allah! I consider him a believer." The Prophet (ﷺ) said, "Or merely a Muslim (Who surrender to Allah)." I remained quiet for a while but could not help repeating my question because of what I knew about him. I said, "O Allah's Apostle! Why have you left that person? By Allah! I consider him a believer." The Prophet (ﷺ) said, "Or merely a Muslim." I remained quiet for a while but could not help repeating my question because of what I knew about him. I said, "O Allah's Messenger (ﷺ)! Why have you left that person? By Allah! I consider him a believer." The Prophet (ﷺ) said, "Or merely a Muslim." Then Allah's Messenger (ﷺ) said, "I give to a person while another is dearer to me, for fear that he may be thrown in the Hell-fire on his face (by reneging from Islam)." (1478) □

590. Narrated Abu Huraira: Allah's Messenger (ﷺ) said, "The poor person is not the one who goes round the people and ask them for a mouthful or two (of meals) or a date or two but the poor is that who has not enough (money) to satisfy his needs and whose condition is not known to others, that others may give him something in charity, and who does not beg of people." (1479) □

591. Narrated Abu Humaid Al-Sa`idi: The Prophet (ﷺ) appointed a man from the tribe of Al-Azd, called Ibn 'Utbiyya for collecting the Zakat. When he returned he said, "This (i.e. the Zakat) is for you and this has been given to me as a present." The Prophet (ﷺ) said, "Why hadn't he stayed in his father's or mother's house to see whether he would be given presents or not? By Him in Whose Hands my life is, whoever takes something from the resources of the Zakat (unlawfully) will be carrying it on his neck on the Day of Resurrection; if it be a camel, it will be grunting; if a cow, it will be mooing; and if a sheep, it will be bleating." The Prophet then raised his hands till we saw the whiteness of his armpits, and he said thrice, "O Allah! Haven't I conveyed Your Message (to them)?" (2597) □

592. Narrated `Umar: Once I gave a horse in Allah's Cause (in charity) but that person did not take care of it. I intended to buy it, as I thought he would sell it at a low price. So, I asked the Prophet (p.b.u.h) about it. He said, "Neither buy, nor take back your alms which you have given, even if the seller were willing to sell it for one Dirham, for he who takes back his alms is like the one who swallows his own vomit." (1490) □

593. Narrated 'Abdullah bin Abu Aufa: Whenever a person came to the Prophet (ﷺ) with his alms, the Prophet (ﷺ) would say, "O Allah! Send your Blessings upon so and so." My father went to the Prophet (ﷺ) with his alms and the Prophet (ﷺ) said, "O Allah! Send your blessings upon the offspring of Abu Aufa." (1497) □

594. Narrated `Aisha: Some of the wives of the Prophet (ﷺ) asked him, "Who amongst us will be the first to follow you (i.e. die after you)?" He said, "Whoever has the longest hand." So they started measuring their hands with a stick and Sauda's

hand turned out to be the longest. (When Zainab bint Jahsh died first of all in the caliphate of `Umar), we came to know that the long hand was a symbol of practicing charity, so she was the first to follow the Prophet (ﷺ) and she used to love to practice charity. (Sauda died later in the caliphate of Muawiya). (1420) ☐

595. Narrated Ibn `Abbas: The mother of Sa`d bin 'Ubada died in his absence. He said, "O Allah's Messenger (ﷺ)! My mother died in my absence; will it be of any benefit for her if I give Sadaqa on her behalf?" The Prophet (ﷺ) said, "Yes," Sa`d said, "I make you a witness that I gave my garden called Al Makhraf in charity on her behalf." (2756) ☐

596. Narrated Ka`b bin Malik: I said, "O Allah's Messenger (ﷺ)! For the acceptance of my repentance I wish to give all my property in charity for Allah's sake through His Apostle." He said, "It is better for you to keep some of the property for yourself." I said, "Then I will keep my share in Khaibar." (2757) ☐

25. ZAKAT

597. NARRATED ABU AIYUB AL-ANSARI (RA): A man said, "O Allah's Messenger (ﷺ)! Inform me of a deed which will make me enter Paradise." The people said, "What is the matter with him? What is the matter with him?" Allah's Messenger (ﷺ) said, "He has something to ask (what he needs greatly)." The Prophet (ﷺ) said (to him), (In order to enter Paradise) you should worship Allah and join none in worship with Him: You should offer prayers perfectly, give obligatory charity (Zakat), and keep good relations with your Kith and kin." He then said, "Leave it!" (The sub-narrator said, "It seems that the Prophet (ﷺ) was riding his she camel.") (5983) ☐

599. Narrated Abu Huraira: When Allah's Messenger (ﷺ) died and Abu Bakr became the caliph some Arabs renegade (reverted to disbelief) (Abu Bakr decided to declare war against them), `Umar, said to Abu Bakr, "How can you fight with these people although Allah's Messenger (ﷺ) said, 'I have been ordered (by Allah) to fight the

people till they say: "None has the right to be worshipped but Allah, and whoever said it then he will save his life and property from me except on trespassing the law (rights and conditions for which he will be punished justly), and his accounts will be with Allah.' "Abu Bakr said, "By Allah! I will fight those who differentiate between the prayer and the Zakat as Zakat is the compulsory right to be taken from the property (according to Allah's orders) By Allah! If they refuse to pay me even a she-kid which they used to pay at the time of Allah's Messenger (ﷺ). I would fight with them for withholding it" Then `Umar said, "By Allah, it was nothing, but Allah opened Abu Bakr's chest towards the decision (to fight) and I came to know that his decision was right." (1399) ☐

600. Narrated Abu Huraira: Allah's Messenger (ﷺ) said, "Whoever is made wealthy by Allah and does not pay the Zakat of his wealth, then on the Day of Resurrection his wealth will be made like a bald-headed poisonous male snake with two black spots over the eyes. The snake will encircle his neck and bite his cheeks and say, 'I am your wealth, I am your treasure.' "Then the Prophet (ﷺ) recited the holy verses: **"And let not those who [greedily] withhold what Allah has given them of His bounty ever think that it is better for them. Rather, it is worse for them. Their necks will be encircled by what they withheld on the Day of Resurrection. And to Allah belongs the heritage of the heavens and the earth. And Allah, with what you do, is [fully] Acquainted."** (3.180). (1403) ☐

601. Narrated Khalid bin Aslam: We went out with 'Abdullah bin 'Umar and a bedouin said (to 'Abdullah), "Tell me about Allah's saying: "And those who hoard up gold and silver (Al-Kanz - money, gold, silver etc., the Zakat of which has not been paid) and spend it not in the Way of Allah (9:34)." Ibn 'Umar said, "Whoever hoarded them and did not pay the Zakat thereof, then woe to him. But these holy Verses were revealed before the Verses of Zakat. So when the Verses of Zakat were revealed, Allah made Zakat a purifier of the property." (1404) ☐

602. Narrated Abu Sa`id: Allah's Messenger (ﷺ) said, "No Zakat is due on property mounting to less than five Uqiyas (of silver), and no Zakat is due on less than five

camels, and there is no Zakat on less than five Wasqs." (A Wasqs equals 60 Sa's) & (1 Sa=3 K gms App.) (1405) □

603. Narrated Anas: When Abu Bakr; sent me to (collect the Zakat from) Bahrain, he wrote to me the following: (In the name of Allah, the Beneficent, the Merciful). These are the orders for compulsory charity (Zakat) which Allah's Messenger (ﷺ) had made obligatory for every Muslim, and which Allah had ordered His Apostle to observe: Whoever amongst the Muslims is asked to pay Zakat accordingly, he should pay it (to the Zakat collector) and whoever is asked more than that (what is specified in this script) he should not pay it; for twenty-four camels or less, sheep are to be paid as Zakat; for every five camels one sheep is to be paid, and if there are between twenty-five to thirty-five camels, one Bint Makhad is to be paid; and if they are between thirty-six to forty-five (camels), one Bint Labun is to be paid; and if they are between forty-six to sixty (camels), one Hiqqa is to be paid; and if the number is between sixty-one to seventy-five (camels), one Jadha is to be paid; and if the number is between seventy-six to ninety (camels), two Bint Labuns are to be paid; and if they are from ninety-one to one-hundredand twenty (camels), two Hiqqas are to be paid; and if they are over one-hundred and-twenty (camels), for every forty (over one-hundred-and-twenty) one Bint Labun is to be paid, and for every fifty camels (over one-hundred-and-twenty) one Hiqqa is to be paid; and who ever has got only four camels, has to pay nothing as Zakat, but if the owner of these four camels wants to give something, he can. If the number of camels increases to five, the owner has to pay one sheep as Zakat. As regards the Zakat for the (flock) of sheep; if they are between forty and one-hundred-and-twenty sheep, one sheep is to be paid; and if they are between one-hundred-and-twenty to two hundred (sheep), two sheep are to be paid; and if they are between two-hundred to three-hundred (sheep), three sheep are to be paid; and for over three-hundred sheep, for every extra hundred sheep, one sheep is to be paid as Zakat. And if somebody has got less than forty sheep, no Zakat is required, but if he wants to give, he can. For silver the Zakat is one-fortieth of the lot (i.e. 2.5%), and if its value is less than two-hundred Dirhams, Zakat is not required, but if the owner wants to pay he can.' (1454) □

604. Narrated Salim bin `Abdullah from his father: The Prophet (ﷺ) said, "On a land irrigated by rain water or by natural water channels or if the land is wet due to a near by water channel Ushr (i.e. one-tenth) is compulsory (as Zakat); and on the land irrigated by the well, half of an Ushr (i.e. one-twentieth) is compulsory (as Zakat on the yield of the land)." (1483) □

605. Narrated Anas: Abu Bakr wrote to me what Allah had ordered His Apostle (about Zakat) which goes: Neither an old nor a defected animal, nor a male-goat may be taken as Zakat except if the Zakat collector wishes (to take it). (1455) □

606. Narrated Abu Ma`bad: (the slave of Ibn `Abbas) Allah's Messenger (ﷺ) said to Mu`adh when he sent him to Yemen, "You will go to the people of the Scripture. So, when you reach there, invite them to testify that none has the right to be worshipped but Allah, and that Muhammad is His Apostle. And if they obey you in that, tell them that Allah has enjoined on them five prayers in each day and night. And if they obey you in that tell them that Allah has made it obligatory on them to pay the Zakat which will be taken from the rich among them and given to the poor among them. If they obey you in that, then avoid taking the best of their possessions, and be afraid of the curse of an oppressed person because there is no screen between his invocation and Allah." (1496) □

607. Narrated Abu Huraira: Allah's Messenger (ﷺ) said, "There is no Zakat either on a horse or a slave belonging to a Muslim." (1463) □

608. Narrated Anas bin Malik: I took `Abdullah bin Abu Talha to Allah's Messenger (ﷺ) to perform Tahnik for him. (Tahnik was a custom among the Muslims that whenever a child was born they used to take it to the Prophet (ﷺ) who would chew a piece of date and put a part of its juice in the child's mouth). I saw the Prophet (ﷺ) and he had an instrument for branding in his hands and was branding the camels of Zakat. (1502) □

609. Narrated Abu Dhar: Once I went to him (the Prophet (ﷺ)) and he said, "By Allah in Whose Hands my life is (or probably said, 'By Allah, except Whom none

has the right to be worshipped) whoever had camels or cows or sheep and did not pay their Zakat, those animals will be brought on the Day of Resurrection far bigger and fatter than before and they will tread him under their hooves, and will butt him with their horns, and (those animals will come in circle): When the last does its turn, the first will start again, and this punishment will go on till Allah has finished the judgments amongst the people." (1460) □

610. Narrated Abu Huraira: Allah's Messenger (ﷺ) ordered (a person) to collect Zakat, and that person returned and told him that Ibn Jamil, Khalid bin Al-Walid, and `Abbas bin `Abdul Muttalib had refused to give Zakat." The Prophet said, "What made Ibn Jamil refuse to give Zakat though he was a poor man, and was made wealthy by Allah and His Apostle? But you are unfair in asking Zakat from Khalid as he is keeping his armor for Allah's Cause (for Jihad). As for `Abbas bin `Abdul Muttalib, he is the uncle of Allah's Apostle (p.b.u.h) and Zakat is compulsory on him and he should pay it double." (1468) □

611. Narrated Ibn `Umar: Allah's Messenger (ﷺ) enjoined the payment of one Sa' of dates or one Sa' of barley as Zakat-ul-Fitr on every Muslim slave or free, male or female, young or old, and he ordered that it be paid before the people went out to offer the Eid prayer. (One Sa' = 3 Kilograms approx.) (1503) □

26. HAJJ (PILGRIMAGE)

612. NARRATED `ABDULLAH BIN `ABBAS (RA): Al-Fadl (his brother) was riding behind Allah's Messenger (ﷺ) and a woman from the tribe of Khath'am came and Al-Fadl started looking at her and she started looking at him. The Prophet (ﷺ) turned Al-Fadl's face to the other side. The woman said, "O Allah's Messenger (ﷺ)! The obligation of Hajj enjoined by Allah on His devotees has become due on my father and he is old and weak, and he cannot sit firm on the Mount; may I perform Hajj on his behalf?" The Prophet (ﷺ) replied, "Yes, you may." That happened during the

Hajj-al-Wida (of the Prophet (p.b.u.h)). (1513) ☐

613. Narrated Abu Huraira: The Prophet (ﷺ) was asked, "Which is the best deed?" He said, "To believe in Allah and His Apostle." He was then asked, "Which is the next (in goodness)?" He said, "To participate in Jihad in Allah's Cause." He was then asked, "Which is the next?" He said, "To perform Hajj-Mabrur." (1519) ☐

614. Narrated `Aisha: I said, "O Allah's Messenger (ﷺ)! We consider Jihad as the best deed." The Prophet (ﷺ) said, "The best Jihad (for women) is Hajj Mabrur (the one accepted by Allah)." (1520) ☐

615. Narrated Abu Huraira: The Prophet (ﷺ) said, "Whoever performs Hajj for Allah's pleasure and does not have sexual relations with his wife, and does not do evil or sins then he will return as if he were born anew." (1521) ☐

616. Narrated Ibn `Abbas: The people of Yemen used to come for Hajj and used not to bring enough provisions with them and used to say that they depend on Allah. On their arrival in Medina they used to beg the people, and so Allah revealed, "And take a provision (with you) for the journey, but the best provision is the fear of Allah." (2.197). (1523) ☐

617. Narrated Ibn `Abbas: Allah's Messenger (ﷺ) made Dhul-Huiaifa as the Miqat for the people of Medina; Al-Juhfa for the people of Sham; Qarn-al-Manazil for the people of Najd; and Yalamlam for the people of Yemen; and these Mawaqit are for the people at those very places, and besides them for those who come thorough those places with the intention of performing Hajj and `Umra; and whoever is living within these boundaries can assume lhram from the place he starts, and the people of Mecca can assume Ihram from Mecca. (1524) ☐

618. Narrated Ibn `Umar: When these two towns (Basra and Kufa) were captured, the people went to `Umar and said, "O the Chief of the faithful believers! The Prophet (ﷺ) fixed Qarn as the Miqat for the people of Najd, it is beyond our way and it is difficult for us to pass through it." He said, "Take as your Miqat a place situated

opposite to Qarn on your usual way. So, he fixed Dhatu-Irq (as their Miqat)." (1531)
□

619. Narrated Ibn `Umar: Allah's Messenger (ﷺ) used to go (for Hajj) via Ash-Shajara way and return via Muarras way; and no doubt, whenever Allah's Messenger (ﷺ) went to Mecca, he used to offer the prayer in the Mosque of Ash-Shajara; and on his return, he used to offer the prayer at Dhul-Hulaifa in the middle of the valley, and pass the night there till morning. (1533) □

620. Narrated `Umar: In the valley of Al-`Aqiq I heard Allah's Messenger (ﷺ) saying, "To night a messenger came to me from my Lord and asked me to pray in this blessed valley and to assume Ihram for Hajj and `Umra together. " (1534) □

621. Narrated Safwan bin Ya'la: Ya'la said to 'Umar, "Show me the Prophet (ﷺ) when he is being inspired Divinely." While the Prophet (ﷺ) was at Ji'rana (in the company of some of his Companions) a person came and asked, "O Allah's Messenger! What is your verdict regarding that person who assumes Ihram for 'Umra and is scented with perfume?" The Prophet (ﷺ) kept quiet for a while and he was Divinely inspired (then). 'Umar beckoned Ya'la. So he came, and the Allah's Messenger (ﷺ) was shaded with sheet. Ya'la put his head in and saw that the face of Allah's Messenger was red and he was snoring. When the state of the Prophet (ﷺ) was over, he (ﷺ) asked, "Where is the person who asked about 'Umra?" Then that person was brought and the Prophet (ﷺ) said, "Wash the perfume off your body thrice and take off the cloak and do the same in 'Umra as you do in Hajj." (1536) □

622. Narrated Sa`id bin Jubair: Ibn `Umar used to oil his hair. I told that to Ibrahim who said, "What do you think about this statement: Narrated Aswad from `Aisha: As if I were now observing the glitter of the scent in the parting of the hair of the Prophet (ﷺ) while he was Muhrim?" (1538) □

623. Narrated `Aisha: (the wife of the Prophet (p.b.u.h) I used to scent Allah's Messenger (ﷺ) when he wanted to assume Ihram and also on finishing Ihram before the Tawaf round the Ka`ba (Tawaf-al-ifada). (1539) □

624. Narrated Salim from his father: I heard that Allah's Messenger (ﷺ) assumed Ihram with his hair matted together. (1540) ☐

625. Narrated `Abdullah bin `Umar: A man asked, "O Allah's Messenger (ﷺ)! What kind of clothes should a Muhrim wear?" Allah's Messenger (ﷺ) replied, "He should not wear a shirt, a turban, trousers, a headcloak or leather socks except if he can find no slippers, he then may wear leather socks after cutting off what might cover the ankles. And he should not wear clothes which are scented with saffron or Wars (kinds of Perfumes)." (1542) ☐

626. Narrated `Abdullah bin `Abbas: The Prophet (ﷺ) with his companions started from Medina after combing and oiling his hair and putting on two sheets of lhram (upper body cover and waist cover). He did not forbid anyone to wear any kind of sheets except the ones colored with saffron because they may leave the scent on the skin. And so in the early morning, the Prophet (ﷺ) mounted his Mount while in Dhul-Hulaifa and set out till they reached Baida', where he and his companions recited Talbiya, and then they did the ceremony of Taqlid (which means to put the colored garlands around the necks of the Budn (camels for sacrifice). And all that happened on the 25th of Dhul-Qa'da. And when he reached Mecca on the 4th of Dhul-Hijja he performed the Tawaf round the Ka`ba and performed the Tawaf between Safa and Marwa. And as he had a Badana and had garlanded it, he did not finish his Ihram. He proceeded towards the highest places of Mecca near Al-Hujun and he was assuming the Ihram for Hajj and did not go near the Ka`ba after he performed Tawaf (round it) till he returned from `Arafat. Then he ordered his companions to perform the Tawaf round the Ka`ba and then the Tawaf of Safa and Marwa, and to cut short the hair of their heads and to finish their Ihram. And that was only for those people who had not garlanded Budn. Those who had their wives with them were permitted to contact them (have sexual intercourse), and similarly perfume and (ordinary) clothes were permissible for them. (1545) ☐

627. Narrated `Abdullah bin `Umar: The Talbiya of Allah's Messenger (ﷺ) was:

لَبَّيْكَ ٱللَّهُمَّ لَبَّيْكَ، لَبَّيْكَ لَا شَرِيكَ لَكَ لَبَّيْكَ، إِنَّ ٱلْحَمْدَ وَٱلنِّعْمَةَ لَكَ وَٱلْمُلْكَ لَا شَرِيكَ لَكَ

'Labbaika Allahumma labbaik, Labbaika la sharika Laka labbaik, Inna-l-hamda wan-ni'mata Laka walmulk, La sharika Laka' (I respond to Your call O Allah, I respond to Your call, and I am obedient to Your orders, You have no partner, I respond to Your call All the praises and blessings are for You, All the sovereignty is for You, And You have no partners with you. (1549) □

628. Narrated Anas bin Malik: Allah's Messenger (ﷺ) offered four rak`at of Zuhr prayer at Medina and we were in his company, and two rak`at of the `Asr prayer at Dhul-Hulaifa and then passed the night there till it was dawn; then he rode, and when he reached Al-Baida', he praised and glorified Allah and said Takbir (i.e. Al hamdu-li l-lah, Subhanallah and Allahu-Akbar). Then he and the people along with him recited Talbiya with the intention of performing Hajj and Umra. When we reached (Mecca) he ordered us to finish the Ihram (after performing the Umra) (only those who had no Hadi (animal for sacrifice) with them were asked to do so) till the day of Tarwiya that is 8th Dhul-Hijja when they assumed Ihram for Hajj. The Prophet sacrificed many camels (slaughtering them) with his own hands while standing. While Allah's Apostle was in Medina he sacrificed two horned rams black and white in color in the Name of Allah." (1551) □

629. Narrated Aisha: (the wife of the Prophet (p.b.u.h) We set out with the Prophet (ﷺ) in his last Hajj and we assumed Ihram for Umra. The Prophet (ﷺ) then said, "Whoever has the Hadi with him should assume Ihram for Hajj along with `Umra and should not finish the Ihram till he finishes both." I was menstruating when I reached Mecca, and so I neither did Tawaf round the Ka`ba nor Tawaf between Safa and Marwa. I complained about that to the Prophet (ﷺ) on which he replied, "Undo and comb your head hair, and assume Ihram for Hajj (only) and leave the Umra." So, I did so. When we had performed the Hajj, the Prophet sent me with my brother `Abdur-Rahman bin Abu Bakr to Tan`im. So I performed the `Umra. The Prophet (ﷺ) said to me, "This `Umra is instead of your missed one." Those who had assumed Ihram for `Umra (Hajj-atTamattu) performed Tawaf round the Ka`ba and between

Safa and Marwa and then finished their Ihram. After returning from Mina, they performed another Tawaf (between Safa and Marwa). Those who had assumed Ihram for Hajj and `Umra together (Hajj-al-Qiran) performed only one Tawaf (between Safa and Marwa). (1556) □

630. Narrated Ibn `Abbas: The people (of the Pre-Islamic Period) used to think that to perform `Umra during the months of Hajj was one of the major sins on earth. And also used to consider the month of Safar as a forbidden (i.e. sacred) month and they used to say, "When the wounds of the camel's back heal up (after they return from Hajj) and the signs of those wounds vanish and the month of Safar passes away then (at that time) `Umra is permissible for the one who wishes to perform it." In the morning of the 4th of Dhul- Hijja, the Prophet (ﷺ) and his companions reached Mecca, assuming Ihram for Hajj and he ordered his companions to make their intentions of the Ihram for `Umra only (instead of Hajj) so they considered his order as something great and were puzzled, and said, "O Allah's Messenger (ﷺ)! What kind (of finishing) of Ihram is allowed?" The Prophet (ﷺ) replied, "Finish the Ihram completely like a non-Muhrim (you are allowed everything)." (1564) □

631. Narrated Ibn `Umar: Hafsa the wife of the Prophet (ﷺ) said, "O Allah's Messenger (ﷺ)! Why have the people finished their Ihram after performing `Umra but you have not finished your Ihram after performing `Umra?" He replied, "I have matted my hair and garlanded (decorate) my Hadi (sacrifice). So I will not finish my Ihram till I have slaughtered (my Hadi)." (1566) □

632. Narrated Shu`ba: Abu Jamra Nasr bin `Imran Ad-Duba'i said, "I intended to perform Hajj-at-Tamattu` (Umrah and Hajj) and the people advised me not to do so. I asked Ibn `Abbas regarding it and he ordered me to perform Hajj-at- Tammatu'. Later I saw in a dream someone saying to me, 'Hajj-Mabrur (Hajj performed in accordance with the Prophet's tradition without committing sins and accepted by Allah) and an accepted `Umra.' So I told that dream to Ibn `Abbas. He said, 'This is the tradition of Abul-Qasim.' Then he said to me, 'Stay with me and I shall give you a portion of my property.'" I (Shu`ba) asked, "Why (did he invite you)?" He said,

"Because of the dream which I had seen." (1567) ☐

633. Narrated Nafi`: On reaching the sanctuary of Mecca, Ibn `Umar used to stop, reciting Talbiya and then he would pass the night at Dhi-Tuwa and then offer the Fajr prayer and take a bath. He used to say that the Prophet (ﷺ) used to do the same. (1573) ☐

634. Narrated `Aisha: When the Prophet (ﷺ) came to Mecca he entered from its higher side and left from its lower side. (1577) ☐

635. Narrated `Aisha: I asked the Prophet (ﷺ) whether the round wall (near Ka`ba) was part of the Ka`ba. The Prophet (ﷺ) replied in the affirmative. I further said, "What is wrong with them, why have they not included it in the building of the Ka`ba?" He said, "Don't you see that your people (Quraish) ran short of money (so they could not include it inside the building of Ka`ba)?" I asked, "What about its gate? Why is it so high?" He replied, "Your people did this so as to admit into it whomever they liked and prevent whomever they liked. Were your people not close to the Pre-Islamic Period of ignorance (i.e. they have recently embraced Islam) and were I not afraid that they would dislike it, surely I would have included the (area of the) wall inside the building of the Ka`ba and I would have lowered its gate to the level of the ground." (1584) ☐

636. That was what urged Ibn-Az-Zubair to demolish the Ka`ba. Jazz said, "I saw Ibn-Az-Zubair when he demolished and rebuilt the Ka`ba and included in it a portion of Al-Hijr (the unroofed portion of Ka`ba which is at present in the form of a compound towards the northwest of the Ka`ba). I saw the original foundations of Abraham which were of stones resembling the humps of camels." So Jarir asked Yazid, "Where was the place of those stones?" Jazz said, "I will just now show it to you." So Jarir accompanied Yazid and entered Al-Hijr, and Jazz pointed to a place and said, "Here it is." Jarir said, "It appeared to me about six cubits from Al-Hijr or so." (1586) ☐

637. Narrated Isma'li bin Abu Khalid: `Abdullah bin Abu `Aufa said, "Allah's

Messenger (ﷺ) performed the `Umra. He performed Tawaf of the Ka`ba and offered two rak`at behind the Maqam Ibrahim and was accompanied by those who were screening him from the people." Somebody asked `Abdullah, "Did Allah's Messenger (ﷺ) enter the Ka`ba?" `Abdullah replied in the negative. (1600) □

638. Narrated Ibn `Abbas: When Allah's Messenger (ﷺ) and his companions came to Mecca, the pagans circulated the news that a group of people were coming to them and they had been weakened by the Fever of Yathrib (Medina). So the Prophet ordered his companions to do Ramal (rapid ritual walk for men) in the first three rounds of Tawaf of the Ka`ba and to walk between the two corners (The Black Stone and Yemenite corner). The Prophet (ﷺ) did not order them to do Ramal in all the rounds of Tawaf out of pity for them. (1602) □

639. Narrated Zaid bin Aslam from his father who said: "`Umar bin Al-Khattab addressed the Corner (Black Stone) saying, 'By Allah! I know that you are a stone and can neither benefit nor harm. Had I not seen the Prophet (ﷺ) touching (and kissing) you, I would never have touched (and kissed) you.' Then he kissed it and said, 'There is no reason for us to do Ramal (in Tawaf) except that we wanted to show off before the pagans, and now Allah has destroyed them.' `Umar added, '(Nevertheless), the Prophet (ﷺ) did that and we do not want to leave it. (1605) □

640. Narrated Nafi`: Ibn `Umar said, "I have never missed the touching of these two stones of Ka`ba (the Black Stone and the Yemenite Corner) both in the presence and the absence of crowds, since I saw the Prophet (ﷺ) touching them." I asked Nafi`: "Did Ibn `Umar use to walk between the two Corners?" Nafi` replied, "He used to walk in order that it might be easy for him to touch it (the Corner Stone)." (1606) □

641. Narrated Ibn `Abbas: The Prophet (ﷺ) performed Tawaf of the Ka`ba riding a camel, and every time he came in front of the Corner (having the Black Stone), he pointed towards it with something he had with him and said Takbir. (1613) □

642. Narrated Abdullah bin Umar: When Allah's Messenger (ﷺ) performed Tawaf of the Kaba for Hajj or Umra, he used to do Ramal during the first three rounds, and

in the last four rounds he used to walk; then after the Tawaf he used to offer two rak`at and then performed Tawaf between Safa and Marwa. (1616) □

643. Narrated Ibn `Abbas: While the Prophet (ﷺ) was performing Tawaf of the Ka`ba, he passed by a person who had tied his hands to another person with a rope or string or something like that. The Prophet (ﷺ) cut it with his own hands and said, "Lead him by the hand." (1620) □

644. Narrated Abu Huraira: In the year prior to the last Hajj of the Prophet (ﷺ) when Allah's Messenger (ﷺ) made Abu Bakr the leader of the pilgrims, the latter (Abu Bakr) sent me in the company of a group of people to make a public announcement: 'No pagan is allowed to perform Hajj after this year, and no naked person is allowed to perform Tawaf of the Ka`ba.' (1622) □

645. Narrated `Amr: We asked Ibn `Umar: "May a man have sexual relations with his wife during the Umra before performing Tawaf between Safa and Marwa?" He said, "Allah's Messenger (ﷺ) arrived (in Mecca) and circumambulated the Ka`ba seven times, then offered two rak`at behind Maqam Ibrahim then performed Tawaf between Safa and Marwa." Ibn `Umar added, "Verily! In Allah's Apostle you have a good example." And I asked Jabir bin `Abdullah (the same question), and he replied, "You should not go near your wives (have sexual relations) till you have finished Tawaf between Safa and Marwa." (1624) □

646. Narrated Um Salama: I informed Allah's Messenger (ﷺ) (about my illness). (Through other sub-narrators, Um Salama narrated that when Allah's Messenger (ﷺ) was at Mecca and had just decided to leave (Mecca) while she had not yet done Tawaf of the Ka`ba (and after listening to her). The Prophet (ﷺ) said, "When the Morning Prayer is established, perform the Tawaf on your camel while the people are in prayer." So she did the same and did not offer the two rak`at of Tawaf until she came out of the Mosque. (1626) □

647. Narrated Abida bin Humaid:`Abdul, `Aziz bin Rufa`i said, "I saw `Abdullah bin Az-Zubair performing Tawaf of the Ka`ba after the morning prayer then offering the

two rak`at prayer." (1630) ☐

648. Narrated Um Salama: I informed Allah's Messenger (ﷺ) that I was sick. He said, "Perform Tawaf (of the Ka`ba) while riding behind the people." So, I performed the Tawaf while Allah's Messenger (ﷺ) was offering the prayer beside the Ka`ba and was reciting Surah-at-Tur. (1633) ☐

649. Narrated Ibn `Umar: Al `Abbas asked the permission of Allah's Messenger (ﷺ) to let him stay in Mecca during the nights of Mina in order to provide the pilgrims with water to drink, so the Prophet (ﷺ) permitted him. (1634) ☐

650. Narrated Ibn `Abbas: Allah's Messenger (ﷺ) came to the drinking place and asked for water. Al-Abbas said, "O Fadl! Go to your mother and bring water from her for Allah's Messenger (ﷺ)." Allah's Messenger (ﷺ) said, "Give me water to drink." Al-Abbas said, "O Allah's Messenger (ﷺ)! The people put their hands in it." Allah's Messenger (ﷺ) again said, 'Give me water to drink. So, he drank from that water and then went to the Zamzam (well) and there the people were offering water to the others and working at it (drawing water from the well). The Prophet (ﷺ) then said to them, "Carry on! You are doing a good deed." Then he said, "Were I not afraid that other people would compete with you (in drawing water from Zamzam), I would certainly take the rope and put it over this (i.e. his shoulder) (to draw water)." On saying that the Prophet (ﷺ) pointed to his shoulder. (1635) ☐

651. Narrated Ibn `Abbas: I gave Zamzam water to Allah's Messenger (ﷺ) and he drank it while standing. 'Asia (a sub-narrator) said that `Ikrima took the oath that on that day the Prophet (ﷺ) had not been standing but riding a camel. (1637) ☐

652. Narrated `Urwa: I asked `Aisha: "How do you interpret the statement of Allah, "Verily! (The mountains) As-Safa and Al-Marwa are among the symbols of Allah, and whoever performs the Hajj to the Ka`ba or performs `Umra, it is not harmful for him to perform Tawaf between them (Safa and Marwa.)" (2.158). By Allah! (it is evident from this revelation) there is no harm if one does not perform Tawaf between Safa and Marwa." Aisha said, "O, my nephew! Your interpretation is not true. Had

this interpretation of yours been correct, the statement of Allah should have been, 'It is not harmful for him if he does not perform Tawaf between them.' But in fact, this divine inspiration was revealed concerning the Ansar who used to assume Ihram for worshiping an idol called "Manat" which they used to worship at a place called Al-Mushallal before they embraced Islam, and whoever assumed Ihram (for the idol), would consider it not right to perform Tawaf between Safa and Marwa. When they embraced Islam, they asked Allah's Messenger (ﷺ) regarding it, saying, "O Allah's Apostle! We used to refrain from Tawaf between Safa and Marwa." So Allah revealed: 'Verily; (the mountains) As-Safa and Al-Marwa are among the symbols of Allah.'" Aisha added, "Surely, Allah's Apostle set the tradition of Tawaf between Safa and Marwa, so nobody is allowed to omit the Tawaf between them." Later on I (`Urwa) told Abu Bakr bin `Abdur-Rahman (of `Aisha's narration) and he said, 'I have not heard of such information, but I heard learned men saying that all the people, except those whom `Aisha mentioned and who used to assume Ihram for the sake of Manat, used to perform Tawaf between Safa and Marwa. When Allah referred to the Tawaf of the Ka`ba and did not mention Safa and Marwa in the Qur'an, the people asked, 'O Allah's Messenger (ﷺ)! We used to perform Tawaf between Safa and Marwa and Allah has revealed (the verses concerning) Tawaf of the Ka`ba and has not mentioned Safa and Marwa. Is there any harm if we perform Tawaf between Safa and Marwa?' So Allah revealed: "Verily As-Safa and Al- Marwa are among the symbols of Allah." Abu Bakr said, "It seems that this verse was revealed concerning the two groups, those who used to refrain from Tawaf between Safa and Marwa in the Pre- Islamic Period of ignorance and those who used to perform the Tawaf then, and after embracing Islam they refrained from the Tawaf between them as Allah had enjoined Tawaf of the Ka`ba and did not mention Tawaf (of Safa and Marwa) till later after mentioning the Tawaf of the Ka`ba.' (1643) □

653. Narrated Nafi`: Ibn `Umar said, "When Allah's Messenger (ﷺ) performed the first Tawaf he did Ramal in the first three rounds and then walked in the remaining four rounds (of Tawaf of the Ka`ba), where as in performing Tawaf between Safa and Marwa he used to run in the midst of the rainwater passage," I asked Nafi`, "Did

`Abdullah (bin `Umar) use to walk steadily on reaching the Yemenite Corner?" He replied, "No, unless people were crowded at the Corner; otherwise he would not leave it without touching it." (1644) □

654. Narrated Jabir bin `Abdullah: The Prophet (ﷺ) and his companions assumed Ihram for Hajj and none except the Prophet (p.b.u.h) and Talha had the Hadi (sacrifice) with them. `Ali arrived from Yemen and had a Hadi with him. `Ali said, "I have assumed Ihram for what the Prophet (ﷺ) has done." The Prophet (ﷺ) ordered his companions to perform the `Umra with the Ihram which they had assumed, and after finishing Tawaf (of Ka`ba, Safa and Marwa) to cut short their hair, and to finish their Ihram except those who had Hadi with them. They (the people) said, "How can we proceed to Mina (for Hajj) after having sexual relations with our wives?" When that news reached the Prophet (ﷺ) he said, "If I had formerly known what I came to know lately, I would not have brought the Hadi with me. Had there been no Hadi with me, I would have finished the state of Ihram." `Aisha got her menses, so she performed all the ceremonies of Hajj except Tawaf of the Ka`ba, and when she got clean (from her menses), she performed Tawaf of the Ka`ba. She said, "O Allah's Messenger (ﷺ)! (All of you) are returning with the Hajj and `Umra, but I am returning after performing Hajj only." So the Prophet (ﷺ) ordered `Abdur-Rahman bin Abu Bakr to accompany her to Tan`im and thus she performed the `Umra after the Hajj. (1651) □

655. Narrated Hafsa: (On Eid) We used to forbid our virgins to go out (for Eid prayer). A lady came and stayed at the Palace of Bani Khalaf. She mentioned that her sister was married to one of the companions of Allah's Messenger (ﷺ) who participated in twelve Ghazawats along with Allah's Messenger (ﷺ) and her sister was with him in six of them. She said, "We used to dress the wounded and look after the patients." She (her sister) asked Allah's Messenger (ﷺ), "Is there any harm for a woman to stay at home if she doesn't have a veil?" He said, "She should cover herself with the veil of her companion and she should take part in the good deeds and in the religious gatherings of the believers." When Um 'Atiyya came, I asked her. "Did you

hear anything about that?" Um 'Atiyya said, "Bi Abi" and she never mentioned the name of Allah's Messenger (ﷺ) without saying "Bi Abi" (i.e. 'let my father be sacrificed for you'). We asked her, "Have you heard Allah's Messenger (ﷺ) saying so and so (about women)?" She replied in the affirmative and said, "Let my father be sacrificed for him. He told us that unmarried mature virgins who stay often screened or unmarried young virgins and mature girls who stay often screened should come out and take part in the good deeds and in the religious gatherings of the believers. But the menstruating women should keep away from the Musalla (praying place)." I asked her, "The menstruating women?" She replied, "Don't they present themselves at `Arafat and at such and such places?" (1652) □

656. Narrated Muhammad bin Abu Bakr Al-Thaqafi: I asked Anas bin Malik while we were proceeding from Mina to `Arafat, "What do you use to do on this day when you were with Allah's Messenger (ﷺ)?" Anas said, "Some of us used to recite Talbiya and nobody objected to that, and others used to recite Takbir and nobody objected to that." (1659) □

657. Narrated Um Al-Fadl bint Al Harith: On the day of `Arafat, some people who were with me, differed about the fasting of the Prophet (ﷺ) some said that he was fasting while others said that he was not fasting. So I sent a bowl full of milk to him while he was riding his camel, and he drank that milk. (1661) □

658. Narrated Muhammad bin Jubair bin Mut`im: My father said, "(Before Islam) I was looking for my camel." The same narration is told by a different sub-narrator. Jubair bin Mut`im said, "My camel was lost and I went out in search of it on the day of `Arafat, and I saw the Prophet (ﷺ) standing in `Arafat. I said to myself: By Allah he is from the Hums (literally: strictly religious, Quraish were called so, as they used to say, 'We are the people of Allah we shall not go out of the sanctuary). What has brought him here?" (1664) □

659. Narrated `Urwa: During the Pre-Islamic period of Ignorance, the people used to perform Tawaf of the Ka`ba naked except the Hums; and the Hums were Quraish

and their offspring. The Hums used to give clothes to the men who would perform the Tawaf wearing them; and women (of the Hums) used to give clothes to the women who would perform the Tawaf wearing them. Those to whom the Hums did not give clothes would perform Tawaf round the Ka`ba naked. Most of the people used to go away (disperse) directly from `Arafat but they (Hums) used to depart after staying at Al-Muzdalifa. `Urwa added, "My father narrated that `Aisha had said, 'the following verses were revealed about the Hums: Then depart from the place where all the people depart--(2.199) `Urwa added, "They (the Hums) used to stay at Al-Muzdalifa and used to depart from there (to Mina) and so they were sent to `Arafat (by Allah's order)." (1665) □

660. Narrated Nafi`:`Abdullah bin `Umar used to offer the Maghrib and `Isha' prayers together at Jam' (Al-Muzdalifa). But he used to pass by that mountain pass where Allah's Messenger (ﷺ) went, and he would enter it and answer the call of nature and perform ablution, and would not offer any prayer till he had prayed at Jam.' (1668) □

661. Narrated Ibn `Abbas: I proceeded along with the Prophet (ﷺ) on the day of `Arafat (9th Dhul-Hijja). The Prophet (ﷺ) heard a great hue and cry and the beating of camels behind him. So he beckoned to the people with his lash, "O people! Be quiet. Hastening is not a sign of righteousness." (1671) □

662. Narrated Ibn `Umar: The Prophet (ﷺ) offered the Maghrib and `Isha' prayers together at Jam' (i.e. Al-Muzdalifa) with a separate Iqama for each of them and did not offer any optional prayer in between them or after each of them. (1673) □

663. Narrated `Abdur-Rahman bin Yazid: `Abdullah; - performed the Hajj and we reached Al-Muzdalifa at or about the time of the `Isha' prayer. He ordered a man to pronounce the Adhan and Iqama and then he offered the Maghrib prayer and offered two rak`at after it. Then he asked for his supper and took it, and then, I think, he ordered a man to pronounce the Adhan and Iqama (for the `Isha' prayer). (`Amr, a sub-narrator said: The intervening statement 'I think', was said by the sub-narrator

Zuhair) (i.e. not by `Abdur-Rahman). Then `Abdullah offered two rak`at of `Isha' prayer. When the day dawned, `Abdullah said, "The Prophet never offered any prayer at this hour except this prayer at this time and at this place and on this day." `Abdullah added, "These two prayers are shifted from their actual times -- the Maghrib prayer (is offered) when the people reached Al-Muzdalifa and the Fajr (morning) prayer at the early dawn." `Abdullah added, "I saw the Prophet (ﷺ) doing that." (1675) □

664. Narrated Salim: `Abdullah bin `Umar used to send the weak among his family early to Mina. So they used to depart from Al-Mash'ar Al-Haram (that is Al-Muzdalifa) at night (when the moon had set) and invoke Allah as much as they could, and then they would return (to Mina) before the Imam had started from Al-Muzdalifa to Mina. So some of them would reach Mina at the time of the Fajr prayer and some of them would come later. When they reached Mina they would throw pebbles on the Jamra (Jamrat-Al-`Aqaba) Ibn `Umar used to say, "Allah's Messenger (ﷺ) gave the permission to them (weak people) to do so." (1676) □

665. Narrated `Abdullah: (the slave of Asma') During the night of Jam', Asma' got down at Al-Muzdalifa and stood up for the prayer and offered the prayer for some time and then asked, "O my son! Has the moon set?" I replied in the negative and she again prayed for another period and then asked, "Has the moon set?" I replied, "Yes." So she said that we should set out (for Mina), and we departed and went on till she threw pebbles at the Jamra (Jamrat-Al-`Aqaba) and then she returned to her dwelling place and offered the morning prayer. I asked her, "O you! I think we have come (to Mina) early in the night." She replied, "O my son! Allah's Messenger (ﷺ) gave permission to the women to do so." (1679) □

666. Narrated `Aisha: We got down at Al-Muzdalifa and Sauda asked the permission of the Prophet (ﷺ) to leave (early) before the rush of the people. She was a slow woman and he gave her permission, so she departed (from Al-Muzdalifa) before the rush of the people. We kept on staying at Al-Muzdalifa till dawn, and set out with the Prophet (ﷺ) but (I suffered so much that) I wished I had taken the permission of Allah's Messenger (ﷺ) as Sauda had done, and that would have been dearer to me

than any other happiness. (1681) ☐

667. Narrated `Abdullah: I never saw the Prophet (ﷺ) offering any prayer not at its stated time except two; he prayed the Maghrib and the `Isha' together and he offered the morning prayer before its usual time. (1682) ☐

668. Narrated `Amr bin Maimun: I saw `Umar, offering the Fajr prayer at Jam'; then he got up and said, "The pagans did not use to depart (from Jam') till the sun had risen, and they used to say, 'Let the sun shine on Thabir (a mountain).' But the Prophet (ﷺ) contradicted them and departed from Jam' before sunrise." (1684)

669. Narrated 'Ubaidullah bin `Abdullah: Ibn `Abbas said, "Usama bin Zaid rode behind the Prophet (ﷺ) from `Arafat to Al-Muzdalifa; and then from Al-Muzdalifa to Mina, Al-Fadl rode behind him." He added, "Both of them (Usama and Al-Fadl) said, 'The Prophet (ﷺ) was constantly reciting Talbiya till he did Rami of the Jamarat-Al-`Aqaba." (1686) ☐

670. Narrated Abu Jamra: I asked Ibn `Abbas about Hajj-at-Tamattu`. He ordered me to perform it. I asked him about the Hadi (sacrifice). He said, "You have to slaughter a camel, a cow or a sheep, or you may share the Hadi with the others." It seemed that some people disliked it (Hajj-at-Tamattu`). I slept and dreamt as if a person was announcing: "Hajj Mabrur and accepted Mut'ah (Hajj-at-Tamattu`)" I went to Ibn `Abbas and narrated it to him. He said, "Allah is Greater. (That was) the tradition of Abu Al-Qasim (i.e. Prophet). Narrated Shu`ba that the call in the dream was. "An accepted `Umra and Hajj-Mabrur. " (1688) ☐

671. Narrated Abu Huraira': Allah's Messenger (ﷺ) saw a man driving his Badana (sacrificial camel). He said, "Ride on it." The man said, "It is a Badana." The Prophet (ﷺ) said, "Ride on it." He (the man) said, "It is a Badana." The Prophet said, "Ride on it." And on the second or the third time he (the Prophet (ﷺ) added, "Woe to you." (1689) ☐

672. Narrated `Abdullah bin Abu Bakr bin `Amr bin Hazm: That `Amra bint

`Abdur-Rahman had told him, "Zaid bin Abu Sufyan wrote to `Aisha that `Abdullah bin `Abbas had stated, 'Whoever sends his Hadi (to the Ka`ba), all the things which are illegal for a (pilgrim) become illegal for that person till he slaughters it (i.e. till the 10th of Dhul-Hijja).'" `Amra added, `Aisha said, 'it is not like what Ibn `Abbas had said: I twisted the garlands of the Hadis of Allah's Messenger (ﷺ) with my own hands. Then Allah's Messenger (ﷺ) put them round their necks with his own hands, sending them with my father; yet nothing permitted by Allah was considered illegal for Allah's Apostle till he slaughtered the Hadis.'" (1700) ☐

673. Narrated `Aisha: Once the Prophet (ﷺ) sent sheep as Hadi. (1701) ☐

674. Narrated Nafi`: Ibn `Umar used to send his Hadi from Jam' (to Mina) in the last third of the night with the pilgrims amongst whom there were free men and slaves, till it was taken into the Manhar (slaughtering place) of the Prophet (p.b.u.h). (1711) ☐

675. Narrated Sahl bin Bakkar: The narration of Anas abridged, saying, "The Prophet (ﷺ) slaughtered seven Budn (camels) while standing, with his own hands. On the day of Eid-ul-Adha he slaughtered (sacrificed) two horned rams, black and white in color. (1712) ☐

676. Narrated Ziyad bin Jubair: I saw Ibn `Umar passing by a man who had made his Badana sit to slaughter it. Ibn `Umar said, "Slaughter it while it is standing with one leg tied up as is the tradition of Muhammad (s)." (1713) ☐

677. Narrated Anas: The Prophet (ﷺ) offered four rak`at of Zuhr prayer at Medina; and two rak`at of `Asr prayer at Dhil- Hulaifa and spent the night there and when (the day) dawned, he mounted his Mount and started saying, "None has the right to be worshipped but Allah, and Glorified be Allah." When he reached Al- Baida' he recited Talbiya for both Hajj and `Umra. And when he arrived at Mecca, he ordered them to finish their Ihram. The Prophet (ﷺ) slaughtered seven Budn (camel) with his own hands while the camels were standing He also sacrificed two horned rams (black and white in color) at Medina. (1714) ☐

678. Narrated `Ali: The Prophet (ﷺ) sent me to supervise the (slaughtering of) Budn (Hadi camels) and ordered me to distribute their meat, and then he ordered me to distribute their covering sheets and skins. 'Ali added, "The Prophet (ﷺ) ordered me to supervise the slaughtering (of the Budn) and not to give anything (of their bodies) to the butcher as wages for slaughtering." (1716) □

679. Narrated Ibn Juraij: `Ata' said, "I heard Jabir bin `Abdullah saying, 'We never ate the meat of the Budn for more than three days of Mina. Later, the Prophet (ﷺ) gave us permission by saying: 'Eat and take (meat) with you. So we ate (some) and took (some) with us.'" I asked `Ata', "Did Jabir say (that they went on eating the meat) till they reached Medina?" `Ata' replied, "No." (1719) □

680. Narrated Ibn `Abbas: A man said to the Prophet (ﷺ) "I performed the Tawaf-al-Ifada before the Rami (throwing pebbles at the Jamra)." The Prophet (ﷺ) replied, "There is no harm." The man said, "I had my head shaved before slaughtering." The Prophet (ﷺ) replied, "There is no harm." He said, "I have slaughtered the Hadi before the Rami." The Prophet (ﷺ) replied, "There is no harm." (1722) □

681. Narrated Ibn `Abbas: The Prophet (ﷺ) was asked by a man who said, "I have done the Rami in the evening." The Prophet (ﷺ) replied, "There is no harm in it." Another man asked, "I had my head shaved before the slaughtering." The Prophet (ﷺ) replied, "There is no harm in it." (1723) □

682. Narrated Abu Musa: I came upon Allah's Messenger (ﷺ) when he was at Al-Batha. He asked me, "Have you intended to perform the Hajj?" I replied in the affirmative. He asked, "For what have you assumed Ihram?" I replied," I have assumed Ihram with the same intention as that of the Prophet (ﷺ)." The Prophet (ﷺ) said, "You have done well! Go and perform Tawaf round the Ka`ba and between Safa and Marwa." Then I went to one of the women of Bani Qais and she took out lice from my head. Later, I assumed the Ihram for Hajj. So, I used to give this verdict to the people till the caliphate of `Umar. When I told him about it, he said, "If we take (follow) the Holy Book, then it orders us to complete Hajj and `Umra (Hajj-at-

Tamattu`) and if we follow the tradition of Allah's Messenger (ﷺ) then Allah's Messenger (ﷺ) did not finish his Ihram till the Hadi had reached its destination (had been slaughtered). (i.e. Hajj-al-Qiran). (1724) □

683. Narrated Abu Huraira: Allah's Messenger (ﷺ) said, "O Allah! Forgive those who get their heads shaved." The people asked. "Also those who get their hair cut short?" The Prophet (ﷺ) said, "O Allah! Forgive those who have their heads shaved." The people said, "Also those who get their hair cut short?" The Prophet (invoke Allah for those who have their heads shaved and) at the third time said, "also (forgive) those who get their hair cut short." (1728) □

684. Narrated Muawiya: I cut short the hair of Allah's Messenger (ﷺ) with a long blade. (1730) □

685. Narrated Ibn `Abbas: When the Prophet (ﷺ) came to Mecca, he ordered his Companions to perform Tawaf round the Ka`ba and between Safa and Marwa, to finish their Ihram and get their hair shaved off or cut short. (1731) □

686. Narrated `Aisha: We performed Hajj with the Prophet (ﷺ) and performed Tawaf-al-ifada on the Day of Nahr (slaughtering). Safiya got her menses and the Prophets desired from her what a husband desires from his wife. I said to him, "O Allah's Messenger (ﷺ)! She is having her menses." He said, "Is she going to detain us?" We informed him that she had performed Tawaf-al-Ifada on the Day of Nahr. He said, "(Then you can) depart." (1733) □

687. Narrated `Abdullah bin `Amr bin Al-`As: I witnessed the Prophet (ﷺ) when he was delivering the sermon on the Day of Nahr. A man stood up and said, "I thought that such and such was to be done before such and such. I got my hair shaved before slaughtering." (Another said), "I slaughtered the Hadi before doing the Rami." So, the people asked about many similar things. The Prophet (ﷺ) said, "Do it (now) and there is no harm in all these cases." Whenever the Prophet (ﷺ) was asked about anything on that day, he replied, "Do it (now) and there is no harm in it." (1737) □

688. Narrated Ibn `Abbas: I heard the Prophet (ﷺ) delivering a sermon at `Arafat. (1740) ☐

689. Narrated Abu Bakra: The Prophet (ﷺ) delivered to us a sermon on the Day of Nahr. He said, "Do you know what the day today is?" We said, "Allah and His Apostle know better." He remained silent till we thought that he might give that day another name. He said, "Isn't it the Day of Nahr?" We said, "It is." He further asked, "Which month is this?" We said, "Allah and His Apostle know better." He remained silent till we thought that he might give it another name. He then said, "Isn't it the month of Dhul-Hijja?" We replied: "Yes! It is." He further asked, "What town is this?" We replied, "Allah and His Apostle know it better." He remained silent till we thought that he might give it another name. He then said, "Isn't it the forbidden (Sacred) town (of Mecca)?" We said, "Yes. It is." He said, "No doubt, your blood and your properties are sacred to one another like the sanctity of this day of yours, in this month of yours, in this town of yours, till the day you meet your Lord. No doubt! Haven't I conveyed Allah's message to you? They said, "Yes." He said, "O Allah! Be witness. So it is incumbent upon those who are present to convey it (this information) to those who are absent because the informed one might comprehend it (what I have said) better than the present audience, who will convey it to him. Beware! Do not renegade (as) disbelievers after me by striking the necks (cutting the throats) of one another." (1741) ☐

690. Narrated Wabra: I asked Ibn `Umar, "When should I do the Rami of the Jimar?" He replied, "When your leader does that." I asked him again the same question. He replied, "We used to wait till the sun declined and then we would do the Rami (i.e. on the 11th and 12th of Dhul-Hijja)." (1746) ☐

691. Narrated Az-Zuhri: Whenever Allah's Messenger (ﷺ) stoned the Jamra near Mina Mosque, he would do Ramy of it with seven small pebbles and say Takbir on throwing each pebble. Then he would go ahead and stand facing the Qiblah with his hands raised, and invoke (Allah) and he sued to stand for a long period. Then he would come to the second Jamra (Al-Wusta) and stone it will seven small stones,

reciting Takbir on throwing each stone. Then he would stand facing the Qiblah with raised hands to invoke (Allah). Then he would come to the Jamra near the 'Aqaba (Jamrat-ul-'Aqaba) and do Ramy of it with seven small pebbles, reciting Takbir on throwing each stone. He then would leave and not stay by it. (1753) ☐

692. Narrated Ibn `Abbas: The people were ordered to perform the Tawaf of the Ka`ba (Tawaf-al-Wada`) as the lastly thing, before leaving (Mecca), except the menstruating women who were excused. (1755) ☐

693. Narrated `Abdul-Aziz bin Rufai: I asked Anas bin Malik, "Tell me something you have observed about the Prophet (ﷺ) concerning where he offered the Zuhr prayer on the Day of Tarwiya (8th Dhul-Hijja)." Anas replied, "He offered it at Mina." I said, "Where did he offer the `Asr prayer on the Day of Nafr (day of departure from Mina)?" He replied, "At Al-Abtah," and added, "You should do as your leaders do." (1763) ☐

694. Narrated Anas bin Malik: The Prophet (ﷺ) offered the Zuhr, `Asr, Maghrib and `Isha' prayers and slept for a while at a place called Al-Mahassab and then he rode towards the Ka`ba and performed Tawaf (al-Wada`). (1764) ☐

695. Narrated Nafi`: Ibn `Umar used to spend the night at Dhi-Tuwa in between the two Thaniyas and then he would enter Mecca through the Thaniya which is at the higher region of Mecca, and whenever he came to Mecca for Hajj or `Umra, he never made his she camel kneel down except near the gate of the Masjid (Sacred Mosque) and then he would enter (it) and go to the Black (stone) Corner and start from there circumambulating the Ka`ba seven times: hastening in the first three rounds (Ramal) and walking in the last four. On finishing, he would offer two rak`at prayer and set out to perform Tawaf between Safa and Marwa before returning to his dwelling place. On returning (to Medina) from Hajj or `Umra, he used to make his camel kneel down at Al-Batha which is at Dhul-Hulaifa, the place where the Prophet used to make his camel kneel down. (1767) ☐

696. Narrated Ibn ' `Abbas: Dhul-Majaz and `Ukaz were the markets of the people

during the Pre-Islamic period of ignorance. When the people embraced Islam, they disliked to do bargaining there till the following Holy Verses were revealed: -- There is no harm for you if you seek of the bounty of your Lord (during Hajj by trading, etc.) (2.198) (1770) □

27. UMRAH

697. NARRATED ABU HURAIRA (RA): Allah's Messenger (ﷺ) said, "`Umra is an expiation for the sins committed (between it and the previous one). And the reward of Hajj Mabrur (the one accepted by Allah) is nothing except Paradise." (1773) □

698. Narrated Ibn Juraij: Ikrima bin Khalid asked Ibn Umar about performing Umra before Hajj. Ibn Umar replied, "There is no harm in it." Ikrima said, "Ibn Umar also said, 'The Prophet (ﷺ) had performed Umra before performing Hajj." (1774) □

699. Narrated Mujahid: Urwa bin Az-Zubair and I entered the Mosque (of the Prophet) and saw `Abdullah bin `Umar sitting near the dwelling place of Aisha and some people were offering the Duha prayer. We asked him about their prayer and he replied that it was a heresy. He (Urwa) then asked him how many times the Prophet (ﷺ) had performed `Umra. He replied, 'Four times; one of them was in the month of Rajab." We disliked to contradict him. Then we heard `Aisha, the Mother of faithful believers cleaning her teeth with Siwak in the dwelling place. 'Urwa said, "O Mother! O Mother of the believers! Don't you hear what Abu `Abdur Rahman is saying?" She said, "What does he say?" 'Urwa said, "He says that Allah's Messenger (ﷺ) performed four `Umra and one of them was in the month of Rajab." `Aisha said, "May Allah be merciful to Abu `Abdur Rahman! The Prophet (ﷺ) did not perform any `Umra except that he was with him, and he never performed any `Umra in Rajab." (1775) □

700. Narrated Qatada: I asked Anas how many times the Prophet (ﷺ) had performed `Umra. He replied, "Four times. 1. `Umra of Hudaibiya in Dhi-l-Qa'da when the pagans hindered him; 2. `Umra in the following year in Dhi-l- Qa'da after the peace

treaty with them (the pagans); 3. `Umra from Al-Ja'rana where he distributed the war booty." I think he meant the booty (of the battle) of Hunain. I asked, "How many times did he perform Hajj?" He replied, "Once." (1778) ☐

701. Narrated Hammam: The Prophet (ﷺ) performed four `Umra (three) in Dhi-l-Qa'da except the (one) `Umra which he performed with his Hajj: His `Umra from Al-hudaibiya, and the one of the following year, and the one from Al-Jr'rana where he distributed the booty (of the battle) of Hunain, and another `Umra with his Hajj. (1780) ☐

702. Narrated Ata: I heard Ibn `Abbas saying, "Allah's Messenger (ﷺ) asked an Ansari woman (Ibn `Abbas named her but `Ata' forgot her name), 'What prevented you from performing Hajj with us?' She replied, 'We have a camel and the father of so-and-so and his son (i.e. her husband and her son) rode it and left one camel for us to use for irrigation.' He said (to her), 'Perform `Umra when Ramadan comes, for `Umra in Ramadan is equal to Hajj (in reward),' or said something similar." (1782) ☐

703. Narrated Jabir bin `Abdullah: Suraqa bin Malik bin Ju'sham met the Prophet (ﷺ) at Al-`Aqaba while the latter was stoning it and said, "O Allah's Messenger (ﷺ)! Is this permissible only for you?" The Prophet replied, "No, it is for ever (i.e. it is permissible for all Muslims to perform `Umra before Hajj." (1785) ☐

704. Narrated Al-Aswad: That `Aisha said, "O Allah's Messenger (ﷺ)! The people are returning after performing the two Nusuks (i.e. Hajj and `Umra) but I am returning with one only?" He said, "Wait till you become clean from your menses and then go to at-Tan`im, assume Ihram (and after performing `Umra) join us at such-andsuch a place. But it (i.e. the reward if `Umra) is according to your expenses or the hardship (which you will undergo while performing it). (1787) ☐

705. Narrated `Abdullah bin `Umar: Whenever Allah's Messenger (ﷺ) returned from a Ghazwa, Hajj or `Umra, he used to say Takbir thrice at every elevation of the ground and then would say,

اَ إِلَهَ إِلاَّ اللَّهُ وَحْدَهُ لاَ شَرِيكَ لَهُ، لَهُ الْمُلْكُ، وَلَهُ الْحَمْدُ، وَهُوَ عَلَى كُلِّ شَيْءٍ قَدِيرٌ، آيِبُونَ تَائِبُونَ عَابِدُونَ سَاجِدُونَ لِرَبِّنَا حَامِدُونَ، صَدَقَ اللَّهُ وَعْدَهُ وَنَصَرَ عَبْدَهُ وَهَزَمَ الأَحْزَابَ وَحْدَهُ

"None has the right to be worshipped but Allah; He is One and has no partner. All the kingdoms is for Him, and all the praises are for Him, and He is Omnipotent. We are returning with repentance, worshipping, prostrating, and praising our Lord. He has kept up His promise and made His slave victorious, and He Alone defeated all the clans of (nonbelievers). (1797) □

706. Narrated Anas: The Prophet (ﷺ) never returned to his family from a journey at night. He used to return either in the morning or in the afternoon. (1800) □

707. Narrated Jabir: The Prophet (ﷺ) forbade going to one's family at night (on arrival from a journey). (1801) □

708. Narrated Abu 'Is-haq: I heard Al-Bara' saying, "The above Verse was revealed regarding us, for the Ansar on returning from Hajj never entered their houses through the proper doors but from behind. One of the Ansar came and entered through the door and he was taunted for it. Therefore, the following was revealed: "It is not righteousness That you enter the houses from the back, But the righteous man is He who fears Allah, Obeys His order and keeps away from What He has forbidden So, enter houses through the proper doors." (2.189) (1803) □

709. Narrated Abu Huraira: The Prophet (ﷺ) said, "Traveling is a kind of torture as it prevents one from eating, drinking and sleeping properly. So, when one's needs are fulfilled, one should return quickly to one's family." (1804) □

28. WHILE ON PILGRIMAGE

710. NARRATED NAFI` (RA): That Ubaidullah bin `Abdullah and Salim bin `Abdullah informed him that they told Ibn `Umar when Ibn Az-Zubair was attacked by the army, saying "There is no harm for you if you did not perform Hajj this year. We are afraid that you may be prevented from reaching the Ka`ba." Ibn `Umar said "We set

out with Allah's Messenger (ﷺ) and the non-believers of Quraish prevented us from reaching the Ka'ba, and so the Prophet (ﷺ) slaughtered his Hadi and got his head shaved." Ibn 'Umar added, "I make you witnesses that I have made 'Umra obligatory for me. And, Allah willing, I will go and then if the way to Ka'ba is clear, I will perform the Tawaf, but if I am prevented from going to the Ka'ba then I will do the same as the Prophet (ﷺ) did while I was in his company." Ibn 'Umar then assumed Ihram for Umra from Dhul-Hulaifa and proceeded for a while and said, "The conditions of 'Umra and Hajj are similar and I make you witnesses that I have made 'Umra and Hajj obligatory for myself." So, he did not finish the Ihram till the day of Nahr (slaughtering) came, and he slaughtered his Hadi. He used to say, "I will not finish the Ihram till I perform the Tawaf, one Tawaf on the day of entering Mecca (i.e. of Safa and Marwa for both 'Umra and Hajj). (1807) ☐

711. Narrated Ibn 'Abbas: Allah's Messenger (ﷺ) was prevented from performing ('Umra) Therefore, he shaved his head and had sexual relations with his wives and slaughtered his Hadi and performed Umra in the following year. (1809) ☐

712. Narrated Salim: (Abdullah) bin 'Umar used to say, "Is not (the following of) the tradition of Allah's Messenger (ﷺ) sufficient for you? If anyone of you is prevented from performing Hajj, he should perform the Tawaf of the Ka'ba and between As-Safa and Al-Marwa and then finish the Ihram and everything will become legal for him which was illegal for him (during the state of Ihram) and he can perform Hajj in a following year and he should slaughter a Hadi or fast in case he cannot afford the Hadi." (1810) ☐

713. Narrated Ka'b bin 'Umra: Allah's Messenger (ﷺ) stood beside me at Al-Hudaibiya and the lice were falling from my head in great number. He asked me, "Have your lice troubled you?" I replied in the affirmative. He ordered me to get my head shaved. Ka'b added, "This Holy Verse: 'And if any of you is ill, or has ailment in his scalp (2.196), etc. was revealed regarding me. "The Prophet (ﷺ) then ordered me either to fast three days, or to feed six poor persons with one Faraq (three Sas) (of dates), or to slaughter a sheep, etc. (sacrifice) whatever was available. (1815) ☐

714. Narrated `Abdullah bin Abu Qatada: That his father had told him that Allah's Messenger (ﷺ) set out for Hajj and so did his companions. He sent a batch of his companions by another route and Abu Qatada was one of them. The Prophet (ﷺ) said to them, "Proceed along the seashore till we meet all together." So, they took the route of the seashore, and when they started all of them assumed Ihram except Abu Qatada. While they were proceeding on, his companions saw a group of onagers (wild ass). Abu Qatada chased the onagers and attacked and wounded a she-onager. They got down and ate some of its meat and said to each other: "How do we eat the meat of the game while we are in a state of Ihram?" So, we (they) carried the rest of the she-onager's meat, and when they met Allah's Messenger (ﷺ) they asked, saying, "O Allah's Messenger (ﷺ)! We assumed Ihram with the exception of Abu Qatada and we saw (a group) of onagers. Abu Qatada attacked them and wounded a she-onager from them. Then we got down and ate from its meat. Later, we said, (to each other), 'How do we eat the meat of the game and we are in a state of Ihram?' So, we carried the rest of its meat. The Prophet asked, "Did anyone of you order Abu Qatada to attack it or point at it?" They replied in the negative. He said, "Then eat what is left of its meat." (1824) ☐

715. Narrated `Abdullah bin `Abbas: From As-Sa'b bin Jath-thama Al-Laithi that the latter presented an onager to Allah's Messenger (ﷺ) while he was at Al-Abwa' or at Waddan, and he refused it. On noticing the signs of some unpleasant feeling of disappointment on his (As-Sab's) face, the Prophet (ﷺ) said to him, "I have only returned it because I am Muhrim." (1825) ☐

716. Narrated Aisha: Allah's Messenger (ﷺ) said, "Five kinds of animals are harmful and could be killed in the Haram (Sanctuary). These are: the crow, the kite, the scorpion, the mouse and the rabid dog." (1829) ☐

717. Narrated `Abdullah: While we were in the company of the Prophet (ﷺ) in a cave at Mina, when Surah-wal-MurSalah were revealed and he recited it and I heard it (directly) from his mouth as soon as he recited its revelation. Suddenly a snake sprang at us and the Prophet (ﷺ) said (ordered us): "Kill it." We ran to kill it but it escaped

quickly. The Prophet (ﷺ) said, "It has escaped your evil and you too have escaped its evil." (1830) □

718. Narrated Ibn `Abbas: "The Prophet (ﷺ) said, 'Allah has made Mecca, a sanctuary, so it was a sanctuary before me and will continue to be a sanctuary after me. It was made legal for me (i.e. I was allowed to fight in it) for a few hours of a day. It is not allowed to uproot its shrubs or to cut its trees, or to chase (or disturb) its game, or to pick up its luqata (fallen things) except by a person who would announce that (what he has found) publicly.' Al-`Abbas said, 'O Allah's Messenger (ﷺ)! Except Al-Idhkhir (a kind of grass) (for it is used) by our goldsmiths and for our graves.' The Prophet (ﷺ) then said, 'Except Al-Idhkhir.'" `Ikrima said, 'Do you know what "chasing or disturbing" the game means? It means driving it out of the shade to occupy its place." (1833) □

719. Narrated Ibn Buhaina: The Prophet, while in the state of Ihram, was cupped at the middle of his head at Liha-Jamal. (1836) □

720. Narrated Ibn `Abbas: The Prophet (ﷺ) married Maimuna while he was in the state of Ihram, (only the ceremonies of marriage were held). (1837) □

721. Narrated `Abdullah bin Hunain: `Abdullah bin Al-Abbas and Al-Miswar bin Makhrama differed at Al-Abwa'; Ibn `Abbas said that a Muhrim could wash his head; while Al-Miswar maintained that he should not do so. `Abdullah bin `Abbas sent me to Abu Aiyub Al-Ansari and I found him bathing between the two wooden posts (of the well) and was screened with a sheet of cloth. I greeted him and he asked who I was. I replied, "I am `Abdullah bin Hunain and I have been sent to you by Ibn `Abbas to ask you how Allah's Messenger (ﷺ) used to wash his head while in the state of Ihram." Abu Aiyub Al-Ansari caught hold of the sheet of cloth and lowered it till his head appeared before me, and then told somebody to pour water on his head. He poured water on his head, and he (Abu Aiyub) rubbed his head with his hands by bringing them from back to front and from front to back and said, "I saw the Prophet (ﷺ) doing like this." (1840) □

722. Narrated Ibn `Abbas: A woman from the tribe of Juhaina came to the Prophet (ﷺ) and said, "My mother had vowed to perform Hajj but she died before performing it. May I perform Hajj on my mother's behalf?" The Prophet (ﷺ) replied, "Perform Hajj on her behalf. Had there been a debt on your mother, would you have paid it or not? So, pay Allah's debt as He has more right to be paid." (1852) □

723. Narrated As-Sa'ib bin Yazid: (With my parents) I was made to perform Hajj with Allah's Messenger (ﷺ) and I was a seven-year-old boy then. (1858) □

724. Narrated Ibn `Abbas: The Prophet (ﷺ) said, "A woman should not travel except with a Dhu-Mahram (her husband or a man with whom that woman cannot marry at all according to the Islamic Jurisprudence), and no man may visit her except in the presence of a Dhu-Mahram." A man got up and said, "O Allah's Messenger (ﷺ)! I intend to go to such and such an army and my wife wants to perform Hajj." The Prophet (ﷺ) said (to him), "Go along with her. (1862) □

725. Narrated Anas: The Prophet (ﷺ) saw an old man walking, supported by his two sons, and asked about him. The people informed him that he had vowed to go on foot (to the Ka`ba). He said, "Allah is not in need of this old man's torturing himself," and ordered him to ride. (1865) □

726. Narrated Ibn `Umar: Fasting for those who perform, Hajj-at-Tamattu` (in lieu of the Hadi which they cannot afford) may be performed up to the day of `Arafat. And if one does not get a Hadi and has not fasted (before the Eid) then one should fast of the days of Mina. (11, 12 and 13th of Dhul Hajja). (1999) □

29. VIRTUES OF MADINAH

727. NARRATED ANAS (RA): The Prophet (ﷺ) said, "Medina is a sanctuary from that place to that. Its trees should not be cut and no heresy should be innovated nor any sin should be committed in it, and whoever innovates in it a heresy (An opinion or a

doctrine at variance with established religious beliefs) or commits sins (bad deeds), then he will incur the curse of Allah, the angels, and all the people." (1867). ☐

728. Narrated Abu Huraira: The Prophet (ﷺ) said, "I have made Medina a sanctuary between its two (Harrat) mountains." The Prophet (ﷺ) went to the tribe of Bani Haritha and said (to them), "I see that you have gone out of the sanctuary," but looking around, he added, "No, you are inside the sanctuary." (1869) ☐

729. Narrated `Ali: We have nothing except the Book of Allah and this written paper from the Prophet (wherein is written :) Medina is a sanctuary from the 'Air Mountain to such and such a place, and whoever innovates in it an heresy or commits a sin, or gives shelter to such an innovator in it will incur the curse of Allah, the angels, and all the people, none of his compulsory or optional good deeds of worship will be accepted. And the asylum (of protection) granted by any Muslim is to be secured (respected) by all the other Muslims; and whoever betrays a Muslim in this respect incurs the curse of Allah, the angels, and all the people, and none of his compulsory or optional good deeds of worship will be accepted, and whoever (freed slave) befriends (take as masters) other than his manumitters without their permission incurs the curse of Allah, the angels, and all the people, and none of his compulsory or optional good deeds of worship will be accepted. (1870) ☐

730. Narrated Abu Huraira: Allah's Messenger (ﷺ) said, "I was ordered to migrate to a town which will swallow (conquer) other towns and is called Yathrib and that is Medina, and it turns out (bad) persons as a furnace removes the impurities of iron. (1871) ☐

731. Narrated Abu Humaid: We came with the Prophet (ﷺ) from Tabuk, and when we reached near Medina, the Prophet (ﷺ) said, "This is Tabah." (1872) ☐

732. Narrated Abu Huraira: If I saw deers grazing in Medina, I would not chase them, for Allah's Messenger (ﷺ) said, "(Medina) is a sanctuary between its two mountains." (1873) ☐

733. Narrated Abu Huraira: I heard Allah's Messenger (ﷺ) saying, "The people will leave Medina in spite of the best state it will have, and none except the wild birds and the beasts of prey will live in it, and the last persons who will die will be two shepherds from the tribe of Muzaina, who will be driving their sheep towards Medina, but will find nobody in it, and when they reach the valley of Thaniyat-al-Wada`, they will fall down on their faces dead." (1874) □

734. Narrated Sufyan b. Abu Zuhair: I heard Allah's Messenger (ﷺ) saying, "Yemen will be conquered and some people will migrate (from Medina) and will urge their families, and those who will obey them to migrate (to Yemen) although Medina will be better for them; if they but knew. Sham will also be conquered and some people will migrate (from Medina) and will urge their families and those who will obey them, to migrate (to Sham) although Medina will be better for them; if they but knew. 'Iraq will be conquered and some people will migrate (from Medina) and will urge their families and those who will obey them to migrate (to 'Iraq) although Medina will be better for them; if they but knew." (1875) □

735. Narrated Abu Huraira: Allah's Messenger (ﷺ) said, "Verily, Belief returns and goes back to Medina as a snake returns and goes back to its hole (when in danger). (1876) □

736. Narrated Sa`d: I heard the Prophet (ﷺ) saying, "None plots against the people of Medina but that he will be dissolved (destroyed) like the salt is dissolved in water." (1877) □

737. Narrated Jabir: A bedouin came to the Prophet (ﷺ) and gave a pledge of allegiance for embracing Islam. The next day he came with fever and said (to the Prophet (ﷺ)), "Please cancel my pledge (of embracing Islam and of immigrating to Medina)." The Prophet (ﷺ) refused (that request) three times and said, "Medina is like a furnace, it expels out the impurities (bad persons) and selects the good ones and makes them perfect." (1883) □

738. Narrated Anas: The Prophet (ﷺ) said, "O Allah! Bestow on Medina twice the

blessings You bestowed on Mecca." (1885) ☐

739. Narrated Anas: Whenever the Prophet (ﷺ) returned from a journey and observed the walls of Medina, he would make his Mount go fast, and if he was on an animal, he would make it gallop because of his love for Medina. (1886) ☐

740. Narrated `Aisha: When Allah's Messenger (ﷺ) reached Medina, Abu Bakr and Bilal became ill. When Abu Bakr's fever got worse, he would recite (this poetic verse): "Everybody is staying alive with his People, yet Death is nearer to him than his shoe laces." And Bilal, when his fever deserted him, would recite: "Would that I could stay overnight in A valley wherein I would be Surrounded by Idhkhir and Jalil (kinds of goodsmelling grass). Would that one day I could Drink the water of the Majanna, and would that (The two mountains) Shama and Tafil would appear to me!" The Prophet (ﷺ) said, "O Allah! Curse Shaiba bin Rabi`a and `Utba bin Rabi`a and Umaiya bin Khalaf as they turned us out of our land to the land of epidemics." Allah's Messenger (ﷺ) then said, "O Allah! Make us love Medina as we love Mecca or even more than that. O Allah! Give blessings in our Sa and our Mudd (measures symbolizing food) and make the climate of Medina suitable for us, and divert its fever towards Aljuhfa." Aisha added: When we reached Medina, it was the most unhealthy of Allah's lands, and the valley of Bathan (the valley of Medina) used to flow with impure colored water. (1889) ☐

741. `Umar said, O Allah! Grant me martyrdom in Your cause, and let my death be in the city of Your Apostle." (1890) ☐

30. FASTING

742. NARRATED TALHA BIN 'UBAIDULLAH (RA): A bedouin with unkempt hair came to Allah's Messenger (ﷺ) and said, "O Allah's Messenger (ﷺ)! Inform me what Allah has made compulsory for me as regards the prayers." He replied: "You have to offer perfectly the five compulsory prayers in a day and night (24 hours), unless you want

to pray Nawafil." The bedouin further asked, "Inform me what Allah has made compulsory for me as regards fasting." He replied, "You have to fast during the whole month of Ramadan, unless you want to fast more as Nawafil." The bedouin further asked, "Tell me how much Zakat Allah has enjoined on me." Thus, Allah's Messenger (ﷺ) informed him about all the rules (i.e. fundamentals) of Islam. The bedouin then said, "By Him Who has honored you, I will neither perform any Nawafil nor will I decrease what Allah has enjoined on me. Allah's Messenger (ﷺ) said, "If he is saying the truth, he will succeed (or he will be granted Paradise). (1891) ☐

743. Narrated `Aisha: (The tribe of) Quraish used to fast on the day of Ashura' in the Pre-Islamic period, and then Allah's Apostle ordered (Muslims) to fast on it till the fasting in the month of Ramadan was prescribed; whereupon the Prophet (ﷺ) said, "He who wants to fast (on 'Ashura') may fast, and he who does not want to fast may not fast." (1893) ☐

744. Narrated Abu Huraira: Allah's Messenger (ﷺ) said, "Fasting is a shield (or a screen or a shelter). So, the person observing fasting should avoid sexual relation with his wife and should not behave foolishly and impudently, and if somebody fights with him or abuses him, he should tell him twice, 'I am fasting." The Prophet (ﷺ) added, "By Him in Whose Hands my soul is, the smell coming out from the mouth of a fasting person is better in the sight of Allah than the smell of musk. (Allah says about the fasting person), 'He has left his food, drink and desires for My sake. The fast is for Me. So I will reward (the fasting person) for it and the reward of good deeds is multiplied ten times." (1894) ☐

745. Narrated Abu Wail from Hudhaifa: `Umar asked the people, "Who remembers the narration of the Prophet (ﷺ) about the affliction?" Hudhaifa said, "I heard the Prophet (ﷺ) saying, 'The affliction of a person in his property, family and neighbors is expiated by his prayers, fasting, and giving in charity." (1895) ☐

746. Narrated Sahl: The Prophet (ﷺ) said, "There is a gate in Paradise called Ar-Raiyan, and those who observe fasts will enter through it on the Day of Resurrection

and none except them will enter through it. It will be said, 'Where are those who used to observe fasts?' They will get up, and none except them will enter through it. After their entry the gate will be closed and nobody will enter through it." (1896) ☐

747. Narrated Abu Huraira: Allah's Messenger (ﷺ) said, "Whoever gives two kinds (of things or property) in charity for Allah's Cause, will be called from the gates of Paradise and will be addressed, 'O slaves of Allah! Here is prosperity.' So, whoever was amongst the people who used to offer their prayers, will be called from the gate of the prayer; and whoever was amongst the people who used to participate in Jihad, will be called from the gate of Jihad; and whoever was amongst those who used to observe fasts, will be called from the gate of Ar-Raiyan; whoever was amongst those who used to give in charity, will be called from the gate of charity." Abu Bakr said, "Let my parents be sacrificed for you, O Allah's Messenger (ﷺ)! No distress or need will befall him who will be called from those gates. Will there be any one who will be called from all these gates?" The Prophet (ﷺ) replied, "Yes, and I hope you will be one of them." (1897) ☐

748. Narrated Abu Huraira: Allah's Messenger (ﷺ) said, "When Ramadan begins, the gates of Paradise are opened." (1898) ☐

749. Narrated Abu Huraira: Allah's Messenger (ﷺ) said, "When the month of Ramadan starts, the gates of the heaven are opened and the gates of Hell are closed and the devils are chained." (1899) ☐

750. Narrated Abu Sa`id: I heard the Prophet (ﷺ) saying, "Indeed, anyone who fasts for one day for Allah's Pleasure, Allah will keep his face away from the (Hell) fire for (a distance covered by a journey of) seventy years." (2840) ☐

751. Narrated Ibn `Umar: I heard Allah's Messenger (ﷺ) saying, "When you see the crescent (of the month of Ramadan), start fasting, and when you see the crescent (of the month of Shawwal), stop fasting; and if the sky is overcast (and you can't see it) then regard the month of Ramadan as of 30 days." (1900) ☐

752. Narrated Abu Huraira: The Prophet (ﷺ) said, "Whoever established prayers on the night of Qadr out of sincere faith and hoping for a reward from Allah, then all his previous sins will be forgiven; and whoever fasts in the month of Ramadan out of sincere faith, and hoping for a reward from Allah, then all his previous sins will be forgiven." (1901) ☐

753. Narrated Ibn `Abbas: The Prophet (ﷺ) was the most generous amongst the people, and he used to be more so in the month of Ramadan when Gabriel visited him, and Gabriel used to meet him on every night of Ramadan till the end of the month. The Prophet (ﷺ) used to recite the Holy Qur'an to Gabriel, and when Gabriel met him, he used to be more generous than a fast wind (which causes rain and welfare). (1902) ☐

754. Narrated Abu Huraira: The Prophet (ﷺ) said, "Whoever does not give up forged speech and evil actions, Allah is not in need of his leaving his food and drink (i.e. Allah will not accept his fasting.)" (1903) ☐

755. Narrated Abu Huraira: Allah's Messenger (ﷺ) said, "Allah said, 'All the deeds of Adam's sons (people) are for them, except fasting which is for Me, and I will give the reward for it.' Fasting is a shield or protection from the fire and from committing sins. If one of you is fasting, he should avoid sexual relation with his wife and quarreling, and if somebody should fight or quarrel with him, he should say, 'I am fasting.' By Him in Whose Hands my soul is' the unpleasant smell coming out from the mouth of a fasting person is better in the sight of Allah than the smell of musk. There are two pleasures for the fasting person, one at the time of breaking his fast, and the other at the time when he will meet his Lord; then he will be pleased because of his fasting." (1904) ☐

756. Narrated Abu Bakra: The Prophet (ﷺ) said, "The two months of Eid i.e. Ramadan and Dhul-Hijja, do not decrease (in superiority). (1912) ☐

757. Narrated Abu Huraira: The Prophet (ﷺ) said, "None of you should fast a day or two before the month of Ramadan unless he has the habit of fasting (Nawafil) (and

if his fasting coincides with that day) then he can fast that day." (1914) ☐

758. Narrated Sahl bin Saud: When the following verses were revealed: 'Eat and drink until the white thread appears to you, distinct from the black thread' and of dawn was not revealed, some people who intended to fast, tied black and white threads to their legs and went on eating till they differentiated between the two. Allah then revealed the words, 'of dawn', and it became clear that meant night and day. (1917) ☐

759. Narrated `Aisha: Bilal used to pronounce the Adhan at night, so Allah's Messenger (ﷺ) said, "Carry on taking your meals till Ibn Um Maktum pronounces the Adhan, for he does not pronounce it till it is dawn. (1918) ☐

760. Narrated Sahl bin Sa`d: I used to take my Suhur meals with my family and then hurry up for presenting myself for the (Fajr) prayer with Allah's Messenger (p.b.u.h). (1920) ☐

761. Narrated Anas: Zaid bin Thabit said, "We took the Suhur with the Prophet (ﷺ). Then he stood for the prayer." I asked, "What was the interval between the Suhur and the Adhan?" He replied, "The interval was sufficient to recite fifty verses of the Qur'an." (1921) ☐

762. Narrated Anas bin Malik: The Prophet (ﷺ) said, "Take Suhur as there is a blessing in it." (1923) ☐

763. Narrated `Aisha and Um Salama: At times Allah's Messenger (ﷺ) used to get up in the morning in the state of Janaba after having sexual relations with his wives. He would then take a bath and fast. (1925) ☐

764. Narrated `Aisha: The Prophet (ﷺ) used to kiss and embrace (his wives) while he was fasting, and he had more power to control his desires than any of you. Said Jabir, "The person who gets discharge after casting a look (on his wife) should complete his fast." (1927) ☐

765. Narrated `Aisha: (At times) in Ramadan the Prophet (ﷺ) used to take a bath in

the morning not because of a wet dream and would continue his fast. (1930) ☐

766. Narrated Abu Huraira: The Prophet (ﷺ) said, "If somebody eats or drinks forgetfully then he should complete his fast, for what he has eaten or drunk, has been given to him by Allah." (1933) ☐

767. Narrated Abu Huraira: While we were sitting with the Prophet (ﷺ) a man came and said, "O Allah's Messenger (ﷺ)! I have been ruined." Allah's Messenger (ﷺ) asked what was the matter with him? He replied "I had sexual intercourse with my wife while I was fasting." Allah's Messenger (ﷺ) asked him, "Can you afford to manumit (set free) a slave?" He replied in the negative. Allah's Messenger (ﷺ) asked him, "Can you fast for two successive months?" He replied in the negative. The Prophet (ﷺ) asked him, "Can you afford to feed sixty poor persons?" He replied in the negative. The Prophet (ﷺ) kept silent and while we were in that state, a big basket full of dates was brought to the Prophet (ﷺ). He asked, "Where is the questioner?" He replied, "I (am here)." The Prophet (ﷺ) said (to him), "Take this (basket of dates) and give it in charity." The man said, "Should I give it to a person poorer than I? By Allah; there is no family between it's (i.e. Medina's) two mountains who are poorer than I." The Prophet (ﷺ) smiled till his premolar teeth became visible and then said, 'Feed your family with it." (1936) ☐

768. Narrated Ibn `Abbas: The Prophet (ﷺ) was cupped while he was in the state of lhram, and also while he was observing a fast. (1938) ☐

769. Narrated Ibn Abi `Aufa: We were in the company of Allah's Messenger (ﷺ) on a journey. He said to a man, "Get down and mix Sawiq (powdered barley) with water for me." The man said, "The sun (has not set yet), O Allah's Messenger (ﷺ)." The Prophet (ﷺ) again said to him, "Get down and mix Sawiq with water for me." The man again said, "O Allah's Messenger (ﷺ)! The sun!" The Prophet (ﷺ) said to him (for the third time) "Get down and mix Sawiq with water for me." The man dismounted and mixed Sawiq with water for him. The Prophet (ﷺ) drank it and then beckoned with his hand (towards the East) and said, "When you see the night falling

from this side, then a fasting person should break his fast." (1941) □

770. Narrated `Aisha: Hamza bin `Amr Al-Aslami asked the Prophet, "Should I fast while traveling?" The Prophet (ﷺ) replied, "You may fast if you wish, and you may not fast if you wish." (1943) □

771. Narrated Abu Ad-Darda: We set out with Allah's Messenger (ﷺ) on one of his journeys on a very hot day, and it was so hot that one had to put his hand over his head because of the severity of heat. None of us was fasting except the Prophet and Ibn Rawaha. (1945) □

772. Narrated Jabir bin `Abdullah: Allah's Messenger (ﷺ) was on a journey and saw a crowd of people, and a man was being shaded (by them). He asked, "What is the matter?" They said, "He (the man) is fasting." The Prophet (ﷺ) said, "It is not righteousness that you fast on a journey." (1946) □

773. Narrated Anas bin Malik: We used to travel with the Prophet (ﷺ) and neither did the fasting persons criticize those who were not fasting, nor did those who were not fasting criticize the fasting ones. (1947) □

774.Narrated Tawus: Ibn `Abbas said, "Allah's Messenger (ﷺ) set out from Medina to Mecca and he fasted till he reached 'Usfan, where he asked for water and raised his hand to let the people see him, and then broke the fast, and did not fast after that till he reached Mecca, and that happened in Ramadan." Ibn `Abbas used to say, "Allah's Messenger (ﷺ) (sometimes) fasted and (sometimes) did not fast during the journeys so whoever wished to fast could fast, and whoever wished not to fast, could do so." (1948) □

775. Narrated Ibrahim Abu Isma`il As-Saksaki: I heard Abu Burda who accompanied Yazid bin Abi Kabsha on a journey. Yazid used to observe fasting on journeys. Abu Burda said to him, "I heard Abu Musa several times saying that Allah's Apostle said, 'When a slave falls ill or travels, then he will get reward similar to that he gets for good deeds practiced at home when in good health." (2996) □

776. Narrated `Aisha: Sometimes I missed some days of Ramadan, but could not fast in lieu of them except in the month of Sha'ban." Said Yahya, a sub-narrator, "She used to be busy serving the Prophet (p.b.u.h)." (1950) □

777. Narrated `Aisha: Allah's Messenger (ﷺ) said, "Whoever died and he ought to have fasted (the missed days of Ramadan) then his guardians must fast on his behalf." (1952) □

778. Narrated Ibn `Abbas: A man came to the Prophet (ﷺ) and said, "O Allah's Messenger (ﷺ)! My mother died and she ought to have fasted one month (for her missed Ramadan). Shall I fast on her behalf?" The Prophet (ﷺ) replied in the affirmative and said, "Allah's debts have more right to be paid." (1953) □

779. Narrated `Umar bin Al-Khattab: Allah's Messenger (ﷺ) said, "When night falls from this side and the day vanishes from this side and the sun sets, then the fasting person should break his fast." (1954) □

780. Narrated Sahl bin Sa`d: Allah's Messenger (ﷺ) said, "The people will remain on the right path as long as they hasten the breaking of the fast." (1957) □

781. Narrated Abu Usama from Hisham bin 'Urwa from Fatima: Asma bint Abi Bakr said, "We broke our fast during the lifetime of the Prophet (ﷺ) on a cloudy day and then the sun appeared." Hisham was asked, "Were they ordered to fast in lieu (instead) of that day?" He replied, "It had to be made up for." Ma`mar said, "I heard Hisham saying, "I don't know whether they fasted in lieu of that day or not." (1959) □

782. Narrated Ar-Rubi' bint Mu'awadh: "The Prophet (ﷺ) sent a messenger to the village of the Ansar in the morning of the day of 'Ashura' (10th of Muharram) to announce: 'Whoever has eaten something should not eat but complete the fast, and whoever is observing the fast should complete it.' "She further said, "Since then we used to fast on that day regularly and also make our boys fast. We used to make toys of wool for the boys and if anyone of them cried for, he was given those toys till it was

the time of the breaking of the fast." (1960) □

783. Narrated Abu Huraira: Allah's Messenger (ﷺ) forbade Al-Wisal in fasting (fasting two days continuously without taking any food or drink). So, one of the Muslims said to him, "But you practice Al-Wisal. O Allah's Messenger (ﷺ)!" The Prophet (ﷺ) replied, "Who amongst you is similar to me? I am given food and drink during my sleep by my Lord." So, when the people refused to stop Al-Wisal (fasting continuously), the Prophet (ﷺ) fasted day and night continuously along with them for a day and then another day and then they saw the crescent moon (of the month of Shawwal). The Prophet (ﷺ) said to them (angrily), "If it (the crescent) had not appeared, I would have made you fast for a longer period." That was as a punishment for them when they refused to stop (practicing Al-Wisal). (1965) □

784. Narrated Abu Sa`id Al-Khudri: Allah's Messenger (ﷺ) said, "Do not fast continuously day and night (practice Al-Wisal) and if anyone of you intends to fast continuously day and night, he should continue till the Suhur time." They said, "But you practice Al-Wisal, O Allah's Messenger (ﷺ)!" The Prophet (ﷺ) said, "I am not similar to you. During my sleep I have One Who makes me eat and drink." (1967) □

785. Narrated Abu Juhaifa: The Prophet (ﷺ) made a bond of brotherhood between Salman and Abu Ad-Darda.' Salman paid a visit to Abu Ad-Darda' and found Um Ad-Darda' dressed in shabby clothes and asked her why she was in that state. She replied, "Your brother Abu Ad-Darda' is not interested in (the luxuries of) this world." In the meantime Abu Ad-Darda' came and prepared a meal for Salman. Salman requested Abu Ad-Darda' to eat (with him), but Abu Ad-Darda' said, "I am fasting." Salman said, "I am not going to eat unless you eat." So, Abu Ad-Darda' ate (with Salman). When it was night and (a part of the night passed), Abu Ad-Darda' got up (to offer the night prayer), but Salman told him to sleep and Abu Ad-Darda' slept. After sometime Abu Ad-Darda' again got up but Salman told him to sleep. When it was the last hours of the night, Salman told him to get up then, and both of them offered the prayer. Salman told Abu Ad-Darda', "Your Lord has a right on you, your soul has a right on you, and your family has a right on you; so you should give

the rights of all those who has a right on you." Abu Ad- Darda' came to the Prophet (ﷺ) and narrated the whole story. The Prophet (ﷺ) said, "Salman has spoken the truth." (1968) ☐

786. Narrated `Aisha: Allah's Messenger (ﷺ) used to fast till one would say that he would never stop fasting, and he would abandon fasting till one would say that he would never fast. I never saw Allah's Messenger (ﷺ) fasting for a whole month except the month of Ramadan, and did not see him fasting in any month more than in the month of Sha'ban. (1969) ☐

787. Narrated `Aisha: The Prophet (ﷺ) never fasted in any month more than in the month of Sha'ban. He used to say, "Do those deeds which you can do easily, as Allah will not get tired (of giving rewards) till you get bored and tired (of performing religious deeds)." The most beloved prayer to the Prophet (ﷺ) was the one that was done regularly (throughout the life) even if it were little. And whenever the Prophet (ﷺ) offered a prayer he used to offer it regularly. (1970) ☐

788. Narrated Humaid: I asked Anas about the fasting of the Prophet. He said "Whenever I liked to see the Prophet (ﷺ) fasting in any month, I could see that, and whenever I liked to see him not fasting, I could see that too, and if I liked to see him praying in any night, I could see that, and if I liked to see him sleeping, I could see that, too." Anas further said, "I never touched silk or velvet softer than the hand of Allah's Messenger (ﷺ) and never smelled musk or perfumeed smoke more pleasant than the smell of Allah's Messenger (p.b.u.h)." (1973) ☐

789. Narrated `Abdullah bin `Amr: Allah's Messenger (ﷺ) was informed that I had taken an oath to fast daily and to pray (every night) all the night throughout my life (so Allah's Messenger (ﷺ) came to me and asked whether it was correct): I replied, "Let my parents be sacrificed for you! I said so." The Prophet (ﷺ) said, "You can not do that. So, fast for few days and give it up for few days, offer Salah (prayer) and sleep. Fast three days a month as the reward of good deeds is multiplied ten times and that will be equal to one year of fasting." The Prophet (ﷺ) said to me, "Fast one day and

give up fasting for two days." I replied, "I can do better than that." The Prophet (ﷺ) said to me, "Fast one day and give up fasting for a day and that is the fasting of Prophet David and that is the best fasting." I said, "I have the power to fast better (more) than that." The Prophet (ﷺ) said, "There is no better fasting than that." (1976) ☐

790. Narrated Mujahid from `Abdullah bin `Amr: Prophet (ﷺ) said, "Recite the whole Qur'an once a month." `Abdullah said, "I can recite more (in a month)," and the argument went on till the Prophet (ﷺ) said, "Recite the Qur'an once each three days." (i.e. you must not recite the whole Qur'an in less than three days). (1978) ☐

791. Narrated `Abdullah bin `Amr bin Al-`As: The Prophet (ﷺ) said to me, "You fast daily all the year and pray every night all the night?" I replied in the affirmative. The Prophet (ﷺ) said, "If you keep on doing this, your eyes will become weak and your body will get tired. He who fasts all the year is as he who did not fast at all. The fasting of three days (a month) will be equal to the fasting of the whole year." I replied, "I have the power for more than this." The Prophet (ﷺ) said, "Then fast like the fasting of David who used to fast on alternate days and would never flee from the battle field, on meeting the enemy." (1979) ☐

792. Narrated Abu Huraira: I heard the Prophet (ﷺ) saying, "None of you should fast on Friday unless he fasts a day before or after it." (1985) ☐

793. Narrated Abu `Ubaid: I witnessed the Eid with `Umar bin Al-Khattab who said, Allah's Messenger (ﷺ) has forbidden people to fast on the day on which you break fasting (the fasts of Ramadan) and the day on which you eat the meat of your sacrifices (the first day of Eid ul Fitr and Eid ul-Adha). (1990) ☐

794. Narrated `Aisha and Ibn `Umar: Nobody was allowed to fast on the days of Tashriq except those who could not afford the Hadi (Sacrifice). (1997) ☐

795. Narrated 'Ata: That he heard Ibn `Abbas reciting the Divine Verse: -- "And for those who can fast they had a choice either fast, or feed a poor for every day..." (2.184) Ibn `Abbas said, "This Verse is not abrogated, but it is meant for old men and old

women who have no strength to fast, so they should feed one poor person for each day of fasting (instead of fasting). (4505) □

31. TARAWEEH

796. NARRATED ABU HURAIRA: Allah's Messenger (ﷺ) said, "Whoever prayed at night the whole month of Ramadan out of sincere Faith and hoping for a reward from Allah, then all his previous sins will be forgiven." Ibn Shihab (a sub-narrator) said, "Allah's Messenger (ﷺ) died and the people continued observing that (i.e. Nawafil offered individually, not in congregation), and it remained as it was during the Caliphate of Abu Bakr and in the early days of 'Umar's Caliphate." (2009) □

797. 'Abdur Rahman bin 'Abdul Qari said, "I went out in the company of 'Umar bin Al-Khattab one night in Ramadan to the mosque and found the people praying in different groups. A man praying alone or a man praying with a little group behind him. So, 'Umar said, 'in my opinion I would better collect these (people) under the leadership of one Qari (Reciter) (i.e. let them pray in congregation!)'. So, he made up his mind to congregate them behind Ubai bin Ka'b. Then on another night I went again in his company and the people were praying behind their reciter. On that, 'Umar remarked, 'what an excellent Bid'a (i.e. innovation in religion) this is; but the prayer which they do not perform, but sleep at its time is better than the one they are offering.' He meant the prayer in the last part of the night. (In those days) people used to pray in the early part of the night." (2010) □

798. Narrated Abu Salama bin `Abdur Rahman: that he asked `Aisha "How was the prayer of Allah's Messenger (ﷺ) in Ramadan?" She replied, "He did not pray more than eleven rak`at in Ramadan or in any other month. He used to pray four rak`at --- let alone their beauty and length----and then he would pray four ----let alone their beauty and length ---- and then he would pray three rak`at (witr)." She added, "I asked, 'O Allah's Messenger (ﷺ)! Do you sleep before praying the witr?' He replied,

'O `Aisha! My eyes sleep but my heart does not sleep." (2013) ☐

32. Virtues of the Night of Qadr

799. NARRATED ABU HURAIRA (RA): The Prophet (ﷺ) said, "Whoever fasted the month of Ramadan out of sincere Faith (i.e. belief) and hoping for a reward from Allah, then all his past sins will be forgiven, and whoever stood for the prayers in the night of Qadr out of sincere Faith and hoping for a reward from Allah, then all his previous sins will be forgiven." (2014) ☐

800. Narrated Ibn `Umar: Some men amongst the companions of the Prophet (ﷺ) were shown in their dreams that the night of Qadr was in the last seven nights of Ramadan. Allah's Messenger (ﷺ) said, "It seems that all your dreams agree that (the Night of Qadr) is in the last seven nights, and whoever wants to search for it, should search in the last seven (nights of Ramadan). (2015) ☐

801. Narrated `Aisha: Allah's Messenger (ﷺ) said, "Search for the Night of Qadr in the odd nights of the last ten days of Ramadan." (2017) ☐

802. Narrated Abu Sa`id Al-Khudri: Allah's Messenger (ﷺ) used to practice I`tikaf (in the mosque) in the middle third of Ramadan and after passing the twenty nights he used to go back to his house on the 21st, and the people who were in I`tikaf with him also used to go back to their houses. Once in Ramadan, in which he practiced I`tikaf, he established the night prayers at the night in which he used to return home, and then he addressed the people and ordered them whatever Allah wished him to order and said, "I used to practice I`tikaf for these ten days (i.e. the middle third but now I intend to stay in I`tikaf for the last ten days (of the month); so whoever was in I`tikaf with me should stay at his place of seclusion. I have verily been shown (the date of) this Night (of Qadr) but I have forgotten it. So search for it in the odd nights of the last ten days (of this month). I also saw myself (in the dream) prostrating in mud and water." On the night of the 21st, the sky was covered with clouds and it

rained, and the rainwater started leaking through the roof of the mosque at the praying place of the Prophet (ﷺ). I saw with my own eyes the Prophet at the completion of the Morning Prayer leaving with his face covered with mud and water. (2018) ☐

803. Narrated 'Ubada bin As-Samit: The Prophet (ﷺ) came out to inform us about the Night of Qadr but two Muslims were quarreling with each other. So, the Prophet (ﷺ) said, "I came out to inform you about the Night of Qadr but such-and-such persons were quarreling, so the news about it had been taken away; yet that might be for your own good, so search for it on the 29th, 27th and 25th (of Ramadan). (2023) ☐

804. Narrated 'Ubada bin As-Samit: The Prophet (ﷺ) came out to inform us about the Night of Qadr but two Muslims were quarreling with each other. So, the Prophet (ﷺ) said, "I came out to inform you about the Night of Qadr but such-and-such persons were quarreling, so the news about it had been taken away; yet that might be for your own good, so search for it on the 29th, 27th and 25th (of Ramadan). (2024) ☐

33. I'TIKAF

805. NARRATED `AISHA (RA): the Prophet (ﷺ) used to practice I`tikaf in the last ten days of Ramadan till he died and then his wives used to practice I`tikaf after him. (2026) ☐

806. Narrated `Aisha: The Prophet (ﷺ) used to (put) bend his head (out) to me while he was in I`tikaf in the mosque during my monthly periods and I would comb and oil his hair. (2028) ☐

807. Narrated `Amra: Aisha said, "the Prophet (ﷺ) used to practice I`tikaf in the last ten days of Ramadan and I used to pitch a tent for him, and after offering the Morning Prayer, he used to enter the tent." Hafsa asked the permission of `Aisha to pitch a

tent for her and she allowed her and she pitched her tent. When Zainab bint Jahsh saw it, she pitched another tent. In the morning the Prophet (ﷺ) noticed the tents. He said, 'What is this?" He was told of the whole situation. Then the Prophet (ﷺ) said, "Do you think that they intended to do righteousness by doing this?" He therefore abandoned the I`tikaf in that month and practiced I`tikaf for ten days in the month of Shawwal." (2033) □

808. Narrated `Ali bin Al-Husain: Safiya, the wife of the Prophet (ﷺ) told me that she went to Allah's Messenger (ﷺ) to visit him in the mosque while he was in I`tikaf in the last ten days of Ramadan. She had a talk with him for a while, then she got up in order to return home. The Prophet (ﷺ) accompanied her. When they reached the gate of the mosque, opposite the door of Um-Salama, two Ansari men were passing by and they greeted Allah's Apostle. He told them: Do not run away! And said, "She is (my wife) Safiya bint Huyai." Both of them said, "Subhan Allah, (How dare we think of any evil) O Allah's Messenger (ﷺ)!" And they felt it. The Prophet said (to them), "Satan reaches everywhere in the human body as blood reaches in it, (everywhere in one's body). I was afraid lest Satan might insert an evil thought in your minds." (2035) □

809. Narrated `Aisha: One of the wives of Allah's Messenger (ﷺ) practiced I`tikaf with him while she had bleeding in between her periods and she would see red (blood) or yellowish traces, and sometimes we put a tray beneath her when she offered the prayer. (2037) □

34. SALES AND TRADE

810. NARRATED ABU HURAIRA (RA): The Prophet (ﷺ) said, "A time will come when one will not care how one gains one's money, legally or illegally." (2059) □

811. Narrated Abu Al-Minhal: I used to practice money exchange, and I asked Zaid bin 'Arqam about it, and he narrated what the Prophet said in the following: Abu Al-

Minhal said, "I asked Al-Bara' bin `Azib and Zaid bin Arqam about practicing money exchange. They replied, 'We were traders in the time of Allah's Messenger (ﷺ) and I asked Allah's Messenger (ﷺ) about money exchange. He replied, 'If it is from hand to hand, there is no harm in it; otherwise it is not permissible." (2060) □

812. Narrated Al-Miqdam: The Prophet (ﷺ) said, "Nobody has ever eaten a better meal than that which one has earned by working with one's own hands. The Prophet (ﷺ) of Allah, David used to eat from the earnings of his manual labor." (2072) □

813. Narrated Jabir bin `Abdullah: Allah's Messenger (ﷺ) said, "May Allah's mercy be on him who is lenient in his buying, selling, and in demanding back his money." (2076) □

814. Narrated Hudhaifa: The Prophet (ﷺ) said, "Before your time the angels received the soul of a man and asked him, 'did you do any good deeds (in your life)?' He replied, 'I used to order my employees to grant time to the rich person to pay his debts at his convenience.' So Allah said to the angels; "Excuse him." Rabi said that (the dead man said), 'I used to be easy to the rich and grant time to the poor.' Or, in another narration, 'grant time to the well-off and forgive the needy,' or, 'accept from the well-off and forgive the needy.' (2077) □

815. Narrated Hakim bin Hizam: Allah's Messenger (ﷺ) said, "The seller and the buyer have the right to keep or return goods as long as they have not parted or till they part; and if both the parties spoke the truth and described the defects and qualities, then they would be blessed in their transaction, and if they told lies or hid something, then the blessings of their transaction would be lost." (2079) □

816. Narrated Aisha: When the last Verses of Surah al- Baqara were revealed, the Prophet (ﷺ) recited them in the mosque and proclaimed the trade of alcohol as illegal. (2084) □

817. Narrated Abu Huraira: I heard Allah's Messenger (ﷺ) saying, "The swearing (by the seller) may persuade the buyer to purchase the goods but that will be deprived of

Allah's blessing." (2087) ☐

818. Narrated `Abdullah bin Abu `Aufa: A man displayed some goods in the market and swore by Allah that he had been offered so much for that, that which was not offered, and he said so, so as to cheat a Muslim. On that occasion the following Verse was revealed: "Indeed, those who exchange the covenant of Allah and their [own] oaths for a small price will have no share in the Hereafter, and Allah will not speak to them or look at them on the Day of Resurrection, nor will He purify them; and they will have a painful punishment." (3.77) (2088) ☐

819. Narrated `Abdullah bin Abu `Aufa: A man displayed some goods in the market and took a false oath that he had been offered so much for them though he was not offered that amount Then the following Divine Verse was revealed 'See the hadith above (3.77)'. Ibn Abu `Aufa added, "Such person as described above is a treacherous Riba eater (i.e. eater of usury). (2675) ☐

820. Narrated `Abdullah bin `Umar: `Umar saw a silk suit being sold, so he said, "O Allah's Messenger (ﷺ)! Why don't you buy it so that you may wear it when delegates come to you, and also on Fridays?" The Prophet (ﷺ) said, "This is worn only by him who has no share in the Hereafter." Afterwards the Prophet (ﷺ) sent to `Umar a silk suit suitable for wearing. `Umar said to the Prophet, "You have given it to me to wear, yet I have heard you saying about it what you said?" The Prophet (ﷺ) said, "I sent it to you so that you might either sell it or give it to somebody else to wear." (5841) ☐

821. Narrated Ibn `Umar: Once the Prophet (ﷺ) went to the house of Fatima but did not enter it. `Ali came and she told him about that. When 'Ali asked the Prophet (ﷺ) about it, he said, "I saw a (multicolored) decorated curtain on her door. I am not interested in worldly things." `Ali went to Fatima and told her about it. Fatima said, "I am ready to dispense with it in the way he suggests." The Prophet (ﷺ) ordered her to send it to such-and such needy people." (2613) ☐

822. Narrated Abu Musa: Allah's Messenger (ﷺ) said, "The example of a good companion (who sits with you) in comparison with a bad one, is like that of the musk

seller and the blacksmith's bellows (or furnace); from the first you would either buy musk or enjoy its good smell while the bellows would either burn your clothes or your house, or you get a bad nasty smell thereof." (2101) □

823. Narrated Anas: The Prophet (ﷺ) said, "O Bani Najjar! Suggest a price for your garden." Part of it was a ruin and it contained some date palms. (2106) □

824. Narrated Ibn `Umar: The Prophet (ﷺ) said, "The buyer and the seller have the option to cancel or confirm the bargain before they separate from each other or if the sale is optional." Nafi` said, "Ibn `Umar used to separate quickly from the seller if he had bought a thing which he liked." (2107) □

825. Narrated `Abdullah bin `Umar: A person came to the Prophet (ﷺ) and told him that he was always betrayed in purchasing. The Prophet (ﷺ) told him to say at the time of buying, "No cheating." (2117) □

826. Narrated Al-Miqdam bin Ma'diyakrib: The Prophet (ﷺ) said, "Measure your foodstuff and you will be blessed." (2128) □

827. Narrated Tawus: Ibn `Abbas said, "Allah's Messenger (ﷺ) forbade the selling of foodstuff before its measuring and transferring into one's possession." I asked Ibn `Abbas, "How is that?" Ibn `Abbas replied, "It will be just like selling money for money, as the foodstuff has not been handed over to the first purchaser who is the present seller." (2132) □

828. Narrated Ibn `Umar: I saw the people buy foodstuff randomly (i.e. blindly without measuring it) in the lifetime of Allah's Apostle and they were punished (by beating), if they tried to sell it before carrying it to their own houses. (2137) □

829. Narrated Abu Huraira: Allah's Messenger (ﷺ) forbade the selling of things by a town dweller on behalf of a desert dweller; and similarly Najsh was forbidden. And one should not urge somebody to return the goods to the seller so as to sell him his own goods; nor should one demand the hand of a girl who has already been engaged to someone else; and a woman should not try to cause some other woman to be

divorced in order to take her place. (2140) ☐

830. Narrated 'Abdullah bin 'Umar: Allah's Messenger (ﷺ) forbade the sale called 'Habal-al-Habala which was a kind of sale practiced in the Pre- Islamic Period of ignorance. One would pay the price of a she-camel which was not born yet would be born by the immediate offspring of an extant she-camel. (2143) ☐

831. Narrated Abu Sa'id: Allah's Messenger (ﷺ) forbade the selling by Munabadha, i.e. to sell one's garment by casting it to the buyer not allowing him to examine or see it. Similarly he forbade the selling by Mulamasa. Mulamasa is to buy a garment, for example, by merely touching it, not looking at it. (2144) ☐

832. Narrated Abu Huraira: The Prophet (ﷺ) said, "Don't keep camels and sheep unmilked for a long time, for whoever buys such an animal has the option to milk it and then either to keep it or return it to the owner along with one Sa of dates." Some narrated from Ibn Seereen (that the Prophet (ﷺ) had said), "One Sa of wheat, and he has the option for three days." And some narrated from Ibn Seereen, "... a Sa of dates," not mentioning the option for three days. But a Sa of dates is mentioned in most narrations. (2148) ☐

833. Narrated 'Abdullah: Some people used to buy foodstuff at the head of the market and used to sell it on the spot. Allah's Apostle forbade them to sell it till they brought it to (their) places. (2167) ☐

834. Narrated Ibn 'Umar: The Prophet (ﷺ) said, "The selling of wheat for wheat is Riba (usury) except if it is handed from hand to hand and equal in amount. Similarly the selling of barley for barley, is Riba except if it is from hand to hand and equal in amount, and dates for dates is usury except if it is from hand to hand and equal in amount. (See Riba-Fadl in the glossary). (2170) ☐

835. Narrated Abu Bakra: Allah's Messenger (ﷺ) said, "Don't sell gold for gold unless equal in weight, nor silver for silver unless equal in weight, but you could sell gold for silver or silver for gold as you like." (2175) ☐

836. Narrated Abu Sa`id Al-Khudri: Allah's Messenger (ﷺ) said, "Do not sell gold for gold unless equivalent in weight, and do not sell less amount for greater amount or vice versa; and do not sell silver for silver unless equivalent in weight, and do not sell less amount for greater amount or vice versa and do not sell gold or silver that is not present at the moment of exchange for gold or silver that is present. (2177) ☐

837. Narrated Abu Salih Az-Zaiyat: I heard Abu Sa`id Al-Khudri saying, "The selling of a Dinar for a Dinar, and a Dirham for a Dirham (is permissible)." I said to him, "Ibn `Abbas does not say the same." Abu Sa`id replied, "I asked Ibn `Abbas whether he had heard it from the Prophet (ﷺ) s or seen it in the Holy Book. Ibn `Abbas replied, "I do not claim that, and you know Allah's Messenger (ﷺ) better than I, but Usama informed me that the Prophet had said, 'There is no Riba (in money exchange) except when it is not done from hand to hand (i.e. when there is delay in payment).'" (2178) ☐

838. Narrated Sahl bin Abu Hathma: Allah's Messenger (ﷺ) forbade the selling of fruits (fresh dates) for dried dates but allowed the sale of fruits on the 'Araya by estimation and their new owners might eat their dates fresh. Sufyan (in another narration) said, "I told Yahya (a sub-narrator) when I was a mere boy, 'Meccans say that the Prophet (ﷺ) allowed them the sale of the fruits on 'Araya by estimation.' Yahya asked, 'How do the Meccans know about it?' I replied, 'They narrated it through Jabir.' On that, Yahya kept quiet." Sufyan said, "I meant that Jabir belonged to Medina." Sufyan was asked whether in Jabir's narration there was any prohibition of selling fruits before their benefit is evident (i.e. no dangers of being spoilt or blighted). He replied that there was none. (2191) ☐

839. Zaid bin Thabit (ra) said, "In the lifetime of Allah's Messenger (ﷺ), the people used to trade with fruits. When they cut their date-fruits and the purchasers came to recieve their rights, the seller would say, 'My dates have got rotten, they are blighted with disease, they are afflicted with Qusham (a disease which causes the fruit to fall before ripening).' They would go on complaining of defects in their purchases. Allah's Messenger (ﷺ) said, "Do not sell the fruits before their benefit is evident (i.e. free

from all the dangers of being spoiled or blighted), by way of advice for they quarrelled too much." Kharija bin Zaid bin Thabit said that Zaid bin Thabit (ra) used not to sell the fruits of his land till Pleiades appeared and one could distinguish the yellow fruits from the red (ripe) ones. (2193) □

840. Narrated Anas bin Malik: Allah's Messenger (ﷺ) forbade the sale of fruits till they are almost ripe. He was asked what is meant by 'are almost ripe.' He replied, "Till they become red." Allah's Messenger (ﷺ) further said, "If Allah spoiled the fruits, what right would one have to take the money of one's brother (i.e. other people)?" (2198) □

841. Narrated Ibn Shihab: If somebody bought fruits before their benefit is evident and then the fruits were spoiled with blights, the loss would be suffered by the owner (not the buyer). (2199) □

842. Narrated Abu Sa`id Al-Khudri and Abu Huraira: Allah's Messenger (ﷺ) appointed somebody as a governor of Khaibar. That governor brought to him an excellent kind of dates (from Khaibar). The Prophet (ﷺ) asked, "Are all the dates of Khaibar like this?" He replied, "By Allah, no, O Allah's Messenger (ﷺ)! But we barter (exchange goods for other goods) one Sa of this (type of dates) for two Sas of dates of ours and two Sas of it for three of ours." Allah's Messenger (ﷺ) said, "Do not do so (as that is a kind of usury) but sell the mixed dates (of inferior quality) for money, and then buy good dates with that money." (2201) □

843. Narrated `Abdullah bin `Umar: Allah's Messenger (ﷺ) said, "If somebody sells pollinated date palms, the fruits will be for the seller unless the buyer stipulates that they will be for himself (and the seller agrees). (2204) □

844. Narrated Ibn `Abbas: Once `Umar was informed that a certain man sold alcohol. `Umar said, "May Allah curse him! Doesn't he know that Allah's Messenger (ﷺ) said, 'May Allah curse the Jews, for Allah had forbidden them to eat the fat of animals but they melted it and sold it." (2223) □

845. Narrated Abu Huraira: The Prophet (ﷺ) said, "Allah says, 'I will be against three persons on the Day of Resurrection: -1. One who makes a covenant in My Name, but he proves treacherous. -2. One who sells a free person (as a slave) and eats the price, -3. And one who employs a laborer and gets the full work done by him but does not pay him his wages.'" (2227) □

846. Narrated Jabir bin `Abdullah: I heard Allah's Messenger (ﷺ), in the year of the Conquest of Mecca, saying, "Allah and His Apostle made illegal the trade of alcohol, dead animals, pigs and idols." The people asked, "O Allah's Messenger (ﷺ)! What about the fat of dead animals, for it was used for greasing the boats and the hides; and people use it for lights?" He said, "No, it is illegal." Allah's Messenger (ﷺ) further said, "May Allah curse the Jews, for Allah made the fat (of animals) illegal for them, yet they melted the fat and sold it and ate its price." (2236) □

847. Narrated Abu Mas`ud Al-Ansari: Allah's Messenger (ﷺ) forbade taking the price of a dog, money earned by prostitution and the earnings of a soothsayer (fortune-teller). (2237) □

848. Narrated `Aun bin Abu Juhaifa: I saw my father buying a slave whose profession was cupping, and ordered that his instruments (of cupping) be broken. I asked him the reason for doing so. He replied, "Allah's Messenger (ﷺ) prohibited taking money for blood, the price of a dog, and the earnings of a slave-girl by prostitution; he cursed her who tattoos and her who gets tattooed, the eater of Riba (usury), and the maker of pictures." (2238) □

849. Narrated Ibn `Abbas: Allah's Messenger (ﷺ) came to Medina and the people used to pay in advance the price of fruits to be delivered within one or two years. (The sub-narrator is in doubt whether it was 1 to 2 years or 2 to 3 years.) The Prophet (ﷺ) said, "Whoever pays money in advance for dates (to be delivered later) should pay it for known specified weight and measure (of the dates). (2239) □

850. Narrated Al-A`mash: We argued at Ibrahim's dwelling place about mortgaging in Salam. He said, "Aisha said, 'The Prophet (ﷺ) bought some foodstuff from a Jew

on credit and the payment was to be made by a definite period, and he mortgaged his iron armor to him." (2252) □

851. Narrated Muhammad bin Abi Al-Mujalid: Abu Burda and `Abdullah bin Shaddad sent me to `Abdur Rahman bin Abza and `Abdullah bin Abi `Aufa to ask them about the Salaf (Salam-pay in advance). They said, "We used to get war booty while we were with Allah's Messenger (ﷺ) and when the peasants of Sham came to us we used to pay them in advance for wheat, barley, and oil to be delivered within a fixed period." I asked them, "Did the peasants own standing crops or not?" They replied, "We never asked them about it." (2254) □

852. Narrated Khabbab: I was a blacksmith and did some work for Al-`As bin Wail. When he owed me some money for my work, I went to him to ask for that amount. He said, "I will not pay you unless you disbelieve in Muhammad." I said, "By Allah! I will never do that till you die and be resurrected." He said, "Will I be dead and then resurrected after my death?" I said, "Yes." He said, "There I will have property and offspring and then I will pay you your due." Then Allah revealed. 'Have you seen him who disbelieved in Our signs, and yet says: I will be given property and offspring?' (19.77) (2275) □

35. AGRICULTURAL LEASE

853. NARRATED IBN `UMAR (RA): `Umar expelled the Jews and the Christians from Hijaz. When Allah's Messenger (ﷺ) had conquered Khaibar, he wanted to expel the Jews from it as its land became the property of Allah, His Apostle, and the Muslims. Allah's Messenger (ﷺ) intended to expel the Jews but they requested him to let them stay there on the condition that they would do the labor and get half of the fruits. Allah's Messenger (ﷺ) told them, "We will let you stay on thus condition, as long as we wish." So, they (i.e. Jews) kept on living there until `Umar forced them to go towards Taima' and Ariha'. (2338) □

854. Narrated `Abdullah bin `Umar: "Allah's Messenger (ﷺ) gave the land of Khaibar to the Jews to work on and cultivate and take half of its yield. Ibn `Umar added, "The land used to be rented for a certain portion (of its yield)." Nafi` mentioned the amount of the portion but I forgot it. (2285) □

855. Narrated `Abdullah bin `Umar: The Prophet (ﷺ) concluded a contract with the people of Khaibar to utilize the land on the condition that half the products of fruits or vegetation would be their share. The Prophet (ﷺ) used to give his wives one hundred Wasqs each, eighty Wasqs of dates and twenty Wasqs of barley. (When `Umar became the Caliph) he gave the wives of the Prophet (ﷺ) the option of either having the land and water as their shares, or carrying on the previous practice. Some of them chose the land and some chose the Wasqs, and `Aisha chose the land. (2328) □

856. Rafi` bin Khadij said, "The Prophet (ﷺ) forbade renting farms." Narrated 'Ubaidullah Nafi` said: Ibn `Umar said: (The contract of Khaibar continued) till `Umar evacuated the Jews (from Khaibar). (2286) □

857. Narrated Rafi` bin Khadij: My uncle Zuhair said, "Allah's Messenger (ﷺ) forbade us to do a thing which was a source of help to us." I said, "Whatever Allah's Messenger (ﷺ) said was right." He said, "Allah's Messenger (ﷺ) sent for me and asked, 'What are you doing with your farms?' I replied, 'We give our farms on rent on the basis that we get the yield produced at the banks of the water streams (rivers) for the rent, or rent it for some Wasqs of barley and dates.' Allah's Messenger (ﷺ) said, 'Do not do so, but cultivate (the land) yourselves or let it be cultivated by others gratis (given or done for nothing; free), or keep it uncultivated.' I said, 'We hear and obey.' (2339) □

858. Narrated Rafi` bin Khadij: We worked on farms more than anybody else in Medina. We used to rent the land at the yield of specific delimited portion of it to be given to the landlord. Sometimes the vegetation of that portion was affected by blights etc., while the rest remained safe and vice versa, so the Prophet (ﷺ) forbade this

practice. At that time gold or silver were not used (for renting the land). If they provided the seeds, they would get so-and-so much. (2327) □

859. Narrated `Amr: I said to Tawus, "I wish you would give up Mukhabara (Sharecropping), for the people say that the Prophet forbade it." On that Tawus replied, "O `Amr! I give the land to sharecroppers and help them. No doubt; the most learned man, namely Ibn `Abbas told me that the Prophet (ﷺ) had not forbidden it but said, 'It is more beneficial for one to give his land free to one's brother than to charge him a fixed rental." (2330) □

860. Narrated Abu Huraira: The Ansar said to the Prophet (ﷺ) "Distribute the date palm trees between us and our emigrant brothers." He replied, "No." The Ansar said (to the emigrants), "Look after the trees (water and watch them) and share the fruits with us." The emigrants said, "We listen and obey." (2325) □

861. Narrated Abu Huraira: Allah's Messenger (ﷺ) said, "Whoever has land should cultivate it himself or give it to his (Muslim) brother gratis; otherwise he should keep it uncultivated." (2341) □

862. Narrated `Amr: When I mentioned it to Tawus, he said, "It is permissible to rent the land for cultivation, for Ibn `Abbas said, 'The Prophet (ﷺ) did not forbid that, but said: One had better give the land to one's brother gratis rather than charge a certain amount for it.'" (2342) □

863. Narrated Nafi`: Ibn `Umar used to rent his farms in the time of Abu Bakr, `Umar, `Uthman, and in the early days of Muawiya. (2343) □

36. Transference of a Debt

864. Narrated Abu Huraira: The Prophet (ﷺ) said, "Whoever takes the money of the people with the intention of repaying it, Allah will repay it on his behalf, and whoever takes it in order to spoil it, then Allah will spoil him." (2387) □

865. Narrated Abu Huraira (ra): Allah's Messenger (ﷺ) said, "If I had gold equal to the mountain of Uhud, it would not please me that it should remain with me for more than three days, except an amount which I would keep for repaying debts." (2389) □

866. Narrated Abu Huraira: The Prophet (ﷺ) said, "Procrastination (delay) in paying debts by a wealthy man is injustice. So, if your debt is transferred from your debtor to a rich debtor, you should agree." (2287) □

867. Narrated Salama bin Al-Akwa: Once, while we were sitting in the company of Prophet, a dead man was brought. The Prophet (ﷺ) was requested to lead the funeral prayer for the deceased. He said, "Is he in debt?" The people replied in the negative. He said, "Has he left any wealth?" They said, "No." So, he led his funeral prayer. Another dead man was brought and the people said, "O Allah's Messenger (ﷺ)! Lead his funeral prayer." The Prophet (ﷺ) said, "Is he in debt?" They said, "Yes." He said, "Has he left any wealth?" They said, "Three Dinars." So, he led the prayer. Then a third dead man was brought and the people said (to the Prophet (ﷺ)), please lead his funeral prayer." He said, "Has he left any wealth?" They said, "No." He asked, "Is he in debt?" They said, ("Yes! He has to pay) three Diners.' He (refused to pray and) said, "Then pray for your (dead) companion." Abu Qatada said, "O Allah's Messenger (ﷺ)! Lead his funeral prayer, and I will pay his debt." So, he led the prayer. (2289) □

868. Narrated Muhammad bin 'Amr Al-Aslami that his father Hamza said: 'Umar (ra) sent him (i.e. Hamza) as a Sadaqa / Zakat collector. A man had committed illegal sexual intercourse with the slave girl of his wife. Hamza took (personal) sureties (a person who takes responsibility for another's performance of an undertaking) for the adulterer till they came to 'Umar. 'Umar had lashed the adulterer one hundred lashes. 'Umar confirmed their claim (that the adulterer had already been punished) and excused him because of being Ignorant. Jarir Al-Ash'ath said to Ibn Mas'ud regarding renegades (i.e., those who became infidels after embracing Islam), "Let them repent and take (personal) sureties for them." They repented and their relatives stood sureties for them. According to Hammad, if somebody stands surety for another person and that person dies, the person giving surety will be released from responsibility.

According to Al-Hakam, his responsibilities continues. (2290) ☐

869. Narrated Abu Huraira: The Prophet (ﷺ) said, "An Israeli man asked another Israeli to lend him one thousand Dinars. The second man required witnesses. The former replied, 'Allah is sufficient as a witness.' The second said, 'I want a surety.' The former replied, 'Allah is sufficient as a surety.' The second said, 'You are right,' and lent him the money for a certain period. The debtor went across the sea. When he finished his job, he searched for a conveyance so that he might reach in time for the repayment of the debt, but he could not find any. So, he took a piece of wood and made a hole in it, inserted in it one thousand Dinars and a letter to the lender and then closed (i.e. sealed) the hole tightly. He took the piece of wood to the sea and said. 'O Allah! You know well that I took a loan of one thousand Dinars from so-and-so. He demanded a surety from me but I told him that Allah's Guarantee was sufficient and he accepted Your guarantee. He then asked for a witness and I told him that Allah was sufficient as a Witness, and he accepted You as a Witness. No doubt, I tried hard to find a conveyance so that I could pay his money but could not find, so I hand over this money to You.' Saying that, he threw the piece of wood into the sea till it went out far into it, and then he went away. Meanwhile he started searching for a conveyance in order to reach the creditor's country.

One day the lender came out of his house to see whether a ship had arrived bringing his money, and all of a sudden he saw the piece of wood in which his money had been deposited. He took it home to use for fire. When he sawed it, he found his money and the letter inside it. Shortly after that, the debtor came bringing one thousand Dinars to him and said, 'By Allah, I had been trying hard to get a boat so that I could bring you your money, but failed to get one before the one I have come by.' The lender asked, 'Have you sent something to me?' The debtor replied, 'I have told you I could not get a boat other than the one I have come by.' The lender said, 'Allah has delivered on your behalf the money you sent in the piece of wood. So, you may keep your one thousand Dinars and depart guided on the right path.'" (2291) ☐

870. Narrated Abu Huraira: Whenever a dead man in debt was brought to Allah's

Messenger (ﷺ) he would ask, "Has he left anything to repay his debt?" If he was informed that he had left something to repay his debts, he would offer his funeral prayer, otherwise he would tell the Muslims to offer their friend's funeral prayer. When Allah made the Prophet (ﷺ) wealthy through conquests, he said, "I am more rightful than other believers to be the guardian of the believers, so if a Muslim dies while in debt, I am responsible for the repayment of his debt, and whoever leaves wealth (after his death) it will belong to his heirs. " (2298) ☐

871. Narrated Abu Huraira: The Prophet (ﷺ) owed somebody a camel of a certain age. When he came to demand it back, the Prophet (ﷺ) said (to some people), "Give him (his due)." When the people searched for a camel of that age, they found none, but found a camel one year older. The Prophet (ﷺ) said, "Give (it to) him." On that, the man remarked, "You have given me my right in full. May Allah give you in full." The Prophet (ﷺ) said, "The best amongst you is the one who pays the rights of others generously." (2305) ☐

872. Narrated Abu Huraira: A man came to the Prophet (ﷺ) demanding his debts and behaved rudely. The companions of the Prophet (ﷺ) intended to harm him, but Allah's Messenger (ﷺ) said (to them), "Leave him, for the creditor (i.e. owner of a right) has the right to speak." Allah's Messenger (ﷺ) then said, "Give him a camel of the same age as that of his." The people said, "O Allah's Messenger (ﷺ)! There is only a camel that is older than his." Allah's Messenger (ﷺ) said, "Give (it to) him, for the best amongst you is he who pays the rights of others handsomely." (2306) ☐

873. Narrated Hudhaifa: I heard the Prophet (ﷺ) saying, "Once a man died and was asked, 'What did you use to say (or do) (in your life time)?' He replied, 'I was a businessman and used to give time to the rich to repay his debt and (used to) deduct part of the debt of the poor.' So he was forgiven (his sins). (2391) ☐

874. Narrated Abu Huraira: The Prophet (ﷺ) said, "There was a merchant who used to lend the people, and whenever his debtor was in straitened circumstances, he would say to his employees, 'Forgive him so that Allah may forgive us.' So, Allah forgave

him." (2078) ☐

875. Narrated Abu Huraira: Allah's Messenger (ﷺ) said, "If a man finds his very things with a bankrupt, he has more right to take them back than anyone else." (2402) ☐

876. Narrated Abu Huraira: Allah's Messenger (ﷺ) mentioned a person who asked an Israeli man to lend him one-thousand Dinars, and the Israeli lent him the sum for a certain fixed period. (2734) ☐

37. AGRICULTURE

877. NARRATED ANAS BIN MALIK: Allah's Messenger (ﷺ) said, "There is none amongst the Muslims who plants a tree or sows seeds, and then a bird, or a person or an animal eats from it, but is regarded as a charitable gift for him." (2320) ☐

878. Narrated Abu Umama al-Bahili (ra): I saw some agricultural equipment and said: "I heard the Prophet (ﷺ) saying: "There is no house in which these equipment enters except that Allah will cause humiliation to enter it." (2321) ☐ (if a person is preoccupied by sowing/farming to the extent that he does not fulfil other obligations and rights on him)

879. Narrated Abu Huraira: Allah's Messenger (ﷺ) said, "Whoever keeps a dog, one Qirat of the reward of his good deeds is deducted daily, unless the dog is used for guarding a farm or cattle." Abu Huraira (in another narration) said from the Prophet, "Unless it is used for guarding sheep or farms, or for hunting." Narrated Abu Hazim from Abu Huraira: The Prophet (ﷺ) said, "A dog for guarding cattle or for hunting." (2322) ☐

880. Narrated Abu Huraira: The Prophet (ﷺ) said, "While a man was riding a cow, it turned towards him and said, 'I have not been created for this purpose, I have been created for ploughing." The Prophet (ﷺ) added, "I, Abu Bakr and `Umar believe in

the story." The Prophet (ﷺ) went on, "A wolf caught a sheep, and when the shepherd chased it, the wolf said, 'who will be its guard on the day of wild beasts, when there will be no shepherd for it except me?' "After narrating it, the Prophet (ﷺ) said, "I, Abu Bakr and `Umar too believe it." Abu Salama (a sub-narrator) said, "Abu Bakr and `Umar were not present then." (2324) ☐

881. Narrated Abu Huraira: Allah's Messenger (ﷺ) said, "Do not withhold the superfluous water, for that will prevent people from grazing their cattle." (2353) ☐

882. Narrated Abu Huraira: Allah's Messenger (ﷺ) said, "No bloodmoney will be charged if somebody dies in a mine or in a well or is killed by an animal; and if somebody finds a treasure in his land he has to give one-fifth of it to the Government." (2355) ☐

883. Narrated Abu Huraira: The Prophet (ﷺ) said, "Allah did not send any prophet but shepherded sheep." His companions asked him, "Did you do the same?" The Prophet (ﷺ) replied, "Yes, I used to shepherd the sheep of the people of Mecca for some Qirats." (2262) ☐

884. Narrated Ibn `Umar: The Prophet (ﷺ) forbade taking a price for animal copulation. (2284) ☐

885. Narrated `Aisha: The Prophet (ﷺ) said, "He who cultivates land that does not belong to anybody is more rightful (to own it)." `Urwa said, "`Umar gave the same verdict in his Caliphate." (2335) ☐

886. Narrated Abu Huraira: Once the Prophet (ﷺ) was narrating (a story), while a bedouin was sitting with him. "One of the inhabitants of Paradise will ask Allah to allow him to cultivate the land. Allah will ask him, 'Are you not living in the pleasures you like?' He will say, 'Yes, but I like to cultivate the land.' " The Prophet (ﷺ) added, "When the man (will be permitted he) will sow the seeds and the plants will grow up and get ripe, ready for reaping and so on till it will be as huge as mountains within a wink. Allah will then say to him, 'O son of Adam! Take here you are, gather (the

yield); nothing satisfies you.' "On that, the bedouin said, "The man must be either from Quraish (i.e. an emigrant) or an Ansari, for they are farmers, whereas we are not farmers." The Prophet (ﷺ) smiled (at this). (2348) □

887. Narrated Abu Huraira: Allah's Messenger (ﷺ) said, "There are three persons whom Allah will not look at on the Day of Resurrection, nor will he purify them and theirs shall be a severe punishment. They are: -1. A man possessed superfluous water, on a way and he withheld it from travelers. -2. A man who gave a pledge of allegiance to a ruler and he gave it only for worldly benefits. If the ruler gives him something he gets satisfied, and if the ruler withholds something from him, he gets dissatisfied. -3. And man displayed his goods for sale after the `Asr prayer and he said, 'By Allah, except Whom None has the right to be worshipped, I have been given so much for my goods,' and somebody believes him (and buys them). The Prophet (ﷺ) then recited: "Verily! Those who purchase a little gain at the cost of Allah's Covenant and their oaths." (3.77) (2358) □

888. Narrated `Abdullah bin Az-Zubair: An Ansari man quarreled with Az-Zubair in the presence of the Prophet (ﷺ) about the Harra Canals which were used for irrigating the date-palms. The Ansari man said to Az-Zubair, "Let the water pass' but Az-Zubair refused to do so. So, the case was brought before the Prophet (ﷺ) who said to Az-Zubair, "O Zubair! Irrigate (your land) and then let the water pass to your neighbor." On that the Ansari got angry and said to the Prophet, "Is it because he (i.e. Zubair) is your aunt's son?" On that the color of the face of Allah's Messenger (ﷺ) changed (because of anger) and he said, "O Zubair! Irrigate (your land) and then withhold the water till it reaches the walls between the pits round the trees." Zubair said, "By Allah, I think that the following verse was revealed on this occasion": "But no, by your Lord they can have No faith Until they make you judge In all disputes between them." (4.65) (2359) □

38. QUARRELS

889. NARRATED `ABDULLAH (RA): I heard a man reciting a verse (of the Holy Qur'an) but I had heard the Prophet (ﷺ) reciting it differently. So, I caught hold of the man by the hand and took him to Allah's Messenger (ﷺ) who said, "Both of you are right." Shu`ba, the sub-narrator said, "I think he said to them, "Don't differ, for the nations before you differed and perished (because of their differences)." (2410) □

890. Narrated `Abdullah bin Mas`ud: Allah's Messenger (ﷺ) said, "Whoever takes a false oath so as to take the property of a Muslim (illegally) will meet Allah while He will be angry with him." Al-Ash'ath said: By Allah, that saying concerned me. I had common land with a Jew, and the Jew later on denied my ownership, so I took him to the Prophet who asked me whether I had a proof of my ownership. When I replied in the negative, the Prophet asked the Jew to take an oath. I said, "O Allah's Messenger (ﷺ)! He will take an oath and deprive me of my property." So, Allah revealed the following verse: "Indeed, those who exchange the covenant of Allah and their [own] oaths for a small price will have no share in the Hereafter, and Allah will not speak to them or look at them on the Day of Resurrection, nor will He purify them; and they will have a painful punishment." (3.77) (2416) □

891. Narrated `Abdullah bin Ka`b bin Malik: Ka`b demanded his debt back from Ibn Abi Hadrad in the Mosque and their voices grew louder till Allah's Messenger (ﷺ) heard them while he was in his house. He came out to them raising the curtain of his room and addressed Ka`b, "O Ka`b!" Ka`b replied, "Labaik, O Allah's Messenger (ﷺ)." (He said to him), "Reduce your debt to one half," gesturing with his hand. Ka`b said, "I have done so, O Allah's Apostle!" On that the Prophet (ﷺ) said to Ibn Abi Hadrad, "Get up and repay the debt, to him." (2418) □

892. Narrated Khabbab: I was a blacksmith In the Pre-Islamic period of ignorance, and 'Asi bin Wail owed me some money. I went to him to demand it, but he said to me, "I will not pay you unless you reject faith in Muhammad." I replied, "By Allah, I

will never disbelieve Muhammad till Allah let you die and then resurrect you." He said, "Then wait till I die and come to life again, for then I will be given property and offspring and will pay your right." So, thus revelation came: "Have you seen him who disbelieved in Our signs and yet says, 'I will be given property and offspring?'" (19.77) (2425) □

39. LOST THINGS

893. NARRATED UBAI BIN KA`B: I found a purse containing one hundred Diners. So I went to the Prophet, he said, "Make public announcement about it for one year" I did so, but nobody turned up to claim it, so I again went to the Prophet (ﷺ) who said, "Make public announcement for another year." I did, but none turned up to claim it. I went to him for the third time and he said, "Keep the container and the string which is used for its tying and count the money it contains and if its owner comes, give it to him; otherwise, utilize it." The sub-narrator Salama said, "I met him (Suwaid, another sub-narrator) in Mecca and he said, 'I don't know whether Ubai made the announcement for three years or just one year.'" (2426) □

894. Narrated Anas (ra): The Prophet (ﷺ) passed a date fallen on the way and said, "Were I not afraid that it may be from a Sadaqa, I would have eaten it." (2431) □

895. Narrated Ibn `Umar: Allah's Messenger (ﷺ) said, "An animal should not be milked without the permission of its owner. Does any of you like that somebody comes to his store and breaks his container and takes away his food? The udders of the animals are the stores of their owners where their provision is kept, so nobody should milk the animals of somebody else, without the permission of its owner." (2435) □

896. Narrated Zaid bin Khalid: A bedouin asked the Prophet (ﷺ) about the Luqata. The Prophet (ﷺ) said, "Make public announcement about it for one year and if then somebody comes and describes the container of the Luqata and the string it was tied

with, (give it to him); otherwise, spend it." He then asked the Prophet (ﷺ) about a lost camel. The face of the Prophet (ﷺ) become red and he said, "You have no concern with it as it has its water reservoir and feet and it will reach water and drink and eat trees. Leave it till its owner finds it." He then asked the Prophet (ﷺ) about a lost sheep. The Prophet (ﷺ) said, "It is for you, for your brother, or for the wolf." (2438) ☐

40. OPPRESSIONS

897. NARRATED ABU SA`ID AL-KHUDRI (RA): Allah's Messenger (ﷺ) said, "When the believers pass safely over (the bridge across) Hell, they will be stopped at a bridge in between Hell and Paradise where they will retaliate upon each other for the injustices done among them in the world, and when they get purified of all their sins, they will be admitted into Paradise. By Him in Whose Hands the life of Muhammad is everybody will recognize his dwelling in Paradise better than he recognizes his dwelling in this world." (2440) ☐

898. Narrated `Abdullah bin `Umar: Allah's Messenger (ﷺ) said, "A Muslim is a brother of another Muslim, so he should not oppress him, nor should he hand him over to an oppressor. Whoever fulfilled the needs of his brother, Allah will fulfill his needs; whoever brought his (Muslim) brother out of a discomfort, Allah will bring him out of the discomforts of the Day of Resurrection, and whoever screened a Muslim, Allah will screen him on the Day of Resurrection." (2442) ☐

899. Narrated Anas: Allah's Messenger (ﷺ) said, "Help your brother, whether he is an oppressor or he is an oppressed one. People asked, "O Allah's Messenger (ﷺ)! It is all right to help him if he is oppressed, but how should we help him if he is an oppressor?" The Prophet (ﷺ) said, "By preventing him from oppressing others." (2444) ☐

900. Narrated An-Nu`man bin Bashir: The Prophet (ﷺ) said, "The example of the

person abiding by Allah's order and restrictions in comparison to those who violate them is like the example of those persons who drew lots for their seats in a boat. Some of them got seats in the upper part, and the others in the lower. When the latter needed water, they had to go up to bring water (and that troubled the others), so they said, 'Let us make a hole in our share of the ship (and get water) saving those who are above us from troubling them. So, if the people in the upper part left the others do what they had suggested, all the people of the ship would be destroyed, but if they prevented them, both parties would be safe." (2493) □

901. Narrated Abu Musa: The Prophet (ﷺ) said, "A believer to another believer is like a building whose different parts enforce each other." The Prophet (ﷺ) then clasped his hands with the fingers interlaced (while saying that). (2446) □

902. Narrated Ibn `Umar: The Prophet (ﷺ) said, "Oppression will be a darkness on the Day of Resurrection." (2447) □

903. Narrated Ibn `Abbas: The Prophet (ﷺ) sent Mu`adh to Yemen and said, "Be afraid, from the curse of the oppressed as there is no screen between his invocation and Allah." (2448) □

904. Narrated Abu Huraira: Allah's Messenger (ﷺ) said, "Whoever has oppressed another person concerning his reputation or anything else, he should beg him to forgive him before the Day of Resurrection when there will be no money (to compensate for wrong deeds), but if he has good deeds, those good deeds will be taken from him according to his oppression which he has done, and if he has no good deeds, the sins of the oppressed person will be loaded on him." (2449) □

905. Narrated Abu Salama: That there was a dispute between him and some people (about a piece of land). When he told `Aisha about it, she said, "O Abu Salama! Avoid taking the land unjustly, for the Prophet (ﷺ) said, 'Whoever usurps even one span of the land of somebody, his neck will be encircled with it down the seven earths." (2453) □

906. Narrated Salim's father (i.e. `Abdullah): The Prophet (ﷺ) said, "Whoever takes a piece of the land of others unjustly, he will sink down the seven earths on the Day of Resurrection." (2454) ☐

907. Narrated `Aisha: The Prophet (ﷺ) said, "The most hated person in the sight of Allah is the most quarrelsome person." (2457) ☐

908. Narrated Abu Huraira: Allah's Messenger (ﷺ) said, "While a man was on the way, he found a thorny branch of a tree there on the way and removed it. Allah thanked him for that deed and forgave him." (2472) ☐

909. Narrated Abu Huraira: The Prophet (ﷺ) judged that seven cubits should be left as a public way when there was a dispute about the land. (2473) ☐

910. Narrated Abu Huraira: The Prophet (ﷺ) said, "When an adulterer commits illegal sexual intercourse, then he is not a believer at the time, he is doing it, and when a drinker of an alcoholic liquor drinks it, then he is not a believer at the time of drinking it, and when a thief steals, then he is not a believer at the time of stealing, and when a robber robs, and the people look at him, then he is not a believer at the time of doing robbery. (2475) ☐

911. 'Narrated `Abdullah bin `Amr bin Al-`As: I heard the Prophet (ﷺ) saying, "Whoever is killed while protecting his property then he is a martyr." (2480) ☐

41. PARTNERSHIP

912. NARRATED ABU MUSA (RA): The Prophet (ﷺ) said, "When the people of Ash`ari tribe ran short of food during the holy battles, or the food of their families in Medina ran short, they would collect all their remaining food in one sheet and then distribute it among themselves equally by measuring it with a bowl. So, these people are from me, and I am from them." (2486) ☐

913. Narrated Anas: that Abu Bakr As-Siddiq wrote to him the law of Zakat which was made obligatory by Allah's Apostle. He wrote: 'Partners possessing joint property (sheep) have to pay its Zakat equally. (2487) □

914. Narrated Ibn `Umar: The Prophet (ﷺ) decreed that one should not eat two dates together at a time unless he gets the permission from his companions (sharing the meal with him). (2489) □

915. Narrated Jabir bin `Abdullah: The Prophet (ﷺ) established the right of Shu'fa (i.e. Preemption) in joint properties; but when the land is divided and the ways are demarcated, then there is no pre-emption. (2495) □

916. Narrated `Abdullah bin Hisham: that his mother Zainab bint Humaid took him to the Prophet (ﷺ) and said, "O Allah's Messenger (ﷺ)! Take the pledge of allegiance from him." But he said, "He is still too young for the pledge," and passed his hand on his (i.e. `Abdullah's) head and invoked for Allah's blessing for him. Zuhra bin Ma`bad stated that he used to go with his grandfather, `Abdullah bin Hisham, to the market to buy foodstuff. Ibn `Umar and Ibn Az-Zubair would meet him and say to him, "Be our partner, as the Prophet (ﷺ) invoked Allah to bless you." So, he would be their partner, and very often he would win a camel's load and send it home. (2501) □

42. MORTGAGING

917. NARRATED `AISHA (RA): The Prophet (ﷺ) bought some foodstuff on credit for a limited period and mortgaged his armor for it. (2509) □

918. Narrated Abu Huraira: Allah's Messenger (ﷺ) said, "The mortgaged animal can be used for riding as long as it is fed and the milk of the milch animal can be drunk according to what one spend on it. The one who rides the animal or drinks its milk should provide the expenditures." (2512) □

43. GIFTS

919. NARRATED ABU HURAIRA (RA): The Prophet (ﷺ) said, "O Muslim women! None of you should look down upon the gift sent by her female neighbor even if it were the trotters of the sheep (fleshless part of legs). (2566) □

920. Narrated `Urwa: Aisha said to me, "O my nephew! We used to see the crescent, and then the crescent and then the crescent in this way we saw three crescents in two months and no fire (for cooking) used to be made in the houses of Allah's Messenger (ﷺ). I said, "O my aunt! Then what use to sustain you?" `Aisha said, "The two black things: dates and water, our neighbors from Ansar had some Manarh and they used to present Allah's Messenger (ﷺ) some of their milk and he used to make us drink." (2567) □

921. Narrated Abu Huraira: The Prophet (ﷺ) said, "I shall accept the invitation even if I were invited to a meal of a sheep's trotter, and I shall accept the gift even if it were an arm or a trotter of a sheep." (2568) □

922. Narrated Abu Huraira: Whenever a meal was brought to Allah's Messenger (ﷺ), he would ask whether it was a gift or Sadaqa (something given in charity). If he was told that it was Sadaqa, he would tell his companions to eat it, but if it was a gift, he would hurry to share it with them. (2576) □

923. Narrated Anas bin Malik: Some meat was brought to the Prophet (ﷺ) and it was said that the meat had been given in charity to Buraira. He said, "It was Sadaqa for Buraira but a gift for us." (2577) □

924. Narrated `Urwa from `Aisha: The wives of Allah's Messenger (ﷺ) were in two groups. One group consisted of `Aisha, Hafsa, Safiyya and Sauda; and the other group consisted of Um Salama and the other wives of Allah's Messenger (ﷺ). The Muslims knew that Allah's Messenger (ﷺ) loved `Aisha, so if any of them had a gift and wished to give to Allah's Messenger (ﷺ), he would delay it, till Allah's Messenger (ﷺ) had

come to `Aisha's home and then he would send his gift to Allah's Messenger (ﷺ) in her home. The group of Um Salama discussed the matter together and decided that Um Salama should request Allah's Messenger (ﷺ) to tell the people to send their gifts to him in whatever wife's house he was. Um Salama told Allah's Messenger (ﷺ) of what they had said, but he did not reply. Then they (those wives) asked Um Salama about it. She said, "He did not say anything to me." They asked her to talk to him again. She talked to him again when she met him on her day, but he gave no reply. When they asked her, she replied that he had given no reply. They said to her, "Talk to him till he gives you a reply." When it was her turn, she talked to him again. He then said to her, "Do not hurt me regarding Aisha, as the Divine Inspirations do not come to me on any of the beds except that of Aisha." On that Um Salama said, "I repent to Allah for hurting you." Then the group of Um Salama called Fatima, the daughter of Allah's Messenger (ﷺ) and sent her to Allah's Messenger (ﷺ) to say to him, "Your wives request to treat them and the daughter of Abu Bakr on equal terms." Then Fatima conveyed the message to him. The Prophet (ﷺ) said, "O my daughter! Don't you love whom I love?" She replied in the affirmative and returned and told them of the situation. They requested her to go to him again but she refused. They then sent Zainab bint Jahsh who went to him and used harsh words saying, "Your wives request you to treat them and the daughter of Ibn Abu Quhafa on equal terms." On that she raised her voice and abused `Aisha to her face so much so that Allah's Messenger (ﷺ) looked at `Aisha to see whether she would retort. `Aisha started replying to Zainab till she silenced her. The Prophet (ﷺ) then looked at `Aisha and said, "She is really the daughter of Abu Bakr." (2581) □

925. Narrated 'Azra bin Thabit Al-Ansari: When I went to Thumama bin `Abdullah, he gave me some perfume and said that Anas would not reject the gifts of perfume. Anas said: The Prophet (ﷺ) used not to reject the gifts of perfume. (2582) □

926. Narrated `Aisha: Allah's Messenger (ﷺ) used to accept gifts and used to give something in return. (2585) □

927. Narrated 'Amir: I heard An-Nu`man bin Bashir on the pulpit saying, "My father

gave me a gift but `Amra bint Rawaha (my mother) said that she would not agree to it unless he made Allah's Messenger (ﷺ) as a witness to it. So, my father went to Allah's Messenger (ﷺ) and said, 'I have given a gift to my son from `Amra bint Rawaha, but she ordered me to make you as a witness to it, O Allah's Messenger (ﷺ)!' Allah's Messenger (ﷺ) asked, 'Have you given (the like of it) to everyone of your sons?' He replied in the negative. Allah's Messenger (ﷺ) said, 'Be afraid of Allah, and be just to your children.' My father then returned and took back his gift." (2587) □

928. Narrated Aisha: I said, "O Allah's Messenger (ﷺ)! I have two neighbors; which of them should I give a gift to?" The Prophet (ﷺ) said, "(Give) to the one whose door is nearer to you." (2595) □

929. Narrated Al-Miswar bin Makhrama: Allah's Messenger (ﷺ) distributed some cloaks but did not give anything thereof to Makhrama. Makhrama said (to me), "O son! Accompany me to Allah's Messenger (ﷺ)." When I went with him, he said, "Call him to me." I called him (i.e. the Prophet (ﷺ)) for my father. He came out wearing one of those cloaks and said, "We kept this (cloak) for you, (Makhrama)." Makhrama looked at the cloak and said, "Makhrama is pleased," (or the Prophet (ﷺ) said), "Is Makhrama pleased?" (2599) □

930. Narrated Ibn `Umar: That he was in the company of the Prophet (ﷺ) on a journey, riding a troublesome camel belonging to `Umar. The camel used to go ahead of the Prophet, so Ibn `Umar's father would say, "O `Abdullah! No one should go ahead of the Prophet." The Prophet (ﷺ) said to him, "Sell it to me." `Umar said to the Prophet "It is for you." So, he bought it and said, "O `Abdullah! It is for you, and you can do with it what you like." (2610) □

931. Narrated Anas: A Jubba (i.e. cloak) made of thick silken cloth was presented to the Prophet. The Prophet (ﷺ) used to forbid people to wear silk. So, the people were pleased to see it. The Prophet (ﷺ) said, "By Him in Whose Hands Muhammad's soul is, the handkerchiefs of Sa`d bin Mu`adh in Paradise are better than this." Anas added, "The present was sent to the Prophet (ﷺ) by Ukaidir (a Christian) from

Dauma." (2616) ☐

932. Narrated Ibn `Abbas: The Prophet (ﷺ) said, "The bad example is not for us. He who takes back his present is like a dog that swallows back its vomit." (2622)

933. Narrated Jabir: The Prophet (ﷺ) gave the verdict that `Umra is for the one to whom it is presented. (2625) ☐

934. Narrated Abu Huraira: Allah's Messenger (ﷺ) said, "What a good Maniha (the she-camel which has recently given birth and which gives profuse milk) is, and (what a good Maniha) (the sheep which gives profuse milk, a bowl in the morning and another in the evening) is!"

Narrated Malik: Maniha is a good deed of charity. (2629) ☐

935. Narrated `Abdullah bin `Amr: That Allah's Messenger (ﷺ) said, "There are forty virtuous deeds and the best of them is the Maniha of a she-goat, and anyone who does one of these virtuous deeds hoping for Allah's reward with firm confidence that he will get it, then Allah will make him enter Paradise because of Hassan (a subnarrator) said, "We tried to count those good deeds below the Maniha; we mentioned replying to the sneezer, removing harmful things from the road, etc., but we failed to count even fifteen." (2631) ☐

44. WITNESSES

936. NARRATED ASMA' BINT ABU BAKR (RA): My mother came to me during the lifetime of Allah's Messenger (ﷺ) and she was a Mushrikah (polytheist, idolatress, pagan). I said to Allah's Messenger (ﷺ) (seeking his verdict), "My mother has come to and she desires to recieve a reward from me, shall I keep good relations with her?" The Prophet (ﷺ) said, "Yes, keep good relation with her." (2624) ☐

937. Narrated `Abdullah bin Abu Mulaika from `Uqba bin Al-Harith: `Uqba married the daughter of Abu Ihab bin `Aziz, and then a woman came and said, "I suckled

`Uqba and his wife." `Uqba said to her, "I do not know that you have suckled me, and you did not inform me." He then sent someone to the house of Abu Ihab to inquire about that but they did not know that she had suckled their daughter. Then `Uqba went to the Prophet (ﷺ) in Medina and asked him about it. The Prophet (ﷺ) said to him, "How (can you keep your wife) after it has been said (that both of you were suckled by the same woman)?" So, he divorced her and she was married to another (husband). (2640) ☐

938. Narrated `Umar bin Al-Khattab: People were (sometimes) judged by the revealing of a Divine Inspiration during the lifetime of Allah's Apostle but now there is no longer any more. Now we judge you by the deeds you practice publicly, so we will trust and favor the one who does good deeds in front of us, and we will not call him to account about what he is really doing in secret, for Allah will judge him for that; but we will not trust or believe the one who presents to us with an evil deed even if he claims that his intentions were good. (2641) ☐

939. Narrated Abu Bakra: The Prophet (ﷺ) said thrice, "Should I inform you out the greatest of the great sins?" They said, "Yes, O Allah's Messenger (ﷺ)!" He said, "To join others in worship with Allah and to be undutiful to one's parents." The Prophet (ﷺ) then sat up after he had been reclining (on a pillow) and said, "And I warn you against giving a false witness, and he kept on saying that warning till we thought he would not stop. (2654) ☐

940. Narrated Abu Sa`id Al-Khudri: The Prophet (ﷺ) said, "Isn't the witness of a woman equal to half of that of a man?" The women said, "Yes." He said, "This is because of the deficiency of a woman's mind." (2658) ☐

941. Narrated Ibn `Umar: Allah's Messenger (ﷺ) called me to present myself in front of him or the eve of the battle of Uhud, while I was fourteen years of age at that time, and he did not allow me to take part in that battle, but he called me in front of him on the eve of the battle of the Trench when I was fifteen years old, and he allowed me (to join the battle)." Nafi` said, "I went to `Umar bin `Abdul `Aziz who was Caliph

at that time and related the above narration to him, He said, "This age (fifteen) is the limit between childhood and manhood," and wrote to his governors to give salaries to those who reached the age of fifteen. (2664) ☐

942. Narrated Ibn Abu Mulaika: Ibn `Abbas wrote that the Prophet (ﷺ) gave his verdict on the basis of the defendant's oath. (2668) ☐

943. Narrated Ibn `Abbas: Hilal bin Umaiya accused his wife before the Prophet (ﷺ) of committing illegal sexual intercourse with Sharik bin Sahma.' The Prophet (ﷺ) said, "Produce a proof, or else you would get the legal punishment (by being lashed) on your back." Hilal said, "O Allah's Messenger (ﷺ)! If anyone of us saw another man over his wife, would he go to search for a proof?" The Prophet (ﷺ) went on saying, "Produce a proof or else you would get the legal punishment (by being lashed) on your back." The Prophet (ﷺ) then mentioned the narration of Lian (as in the Holy Book). (Surah-al-Nur: 24) (2671) ☐

944. Narrated Ibn `Abbas: Hilal bin Umaiyya accused his wife of illegal sexual intercourse and came to the Prophet (ﷺ) to bear witness (against her), (taking the oath of Lian). The Prophet (ﷺ) was saying, "Allah knows that either of you is a liar. Will anyone of you repent (to Allah)?" Then the lady got up and gave her witness. (5307) ☐

945. Narrated Ibn Mas`ud: The Prophet (ﷺ) said, "Whoever takes a (false) oath in order to grab (others) property, then Allah will be angry with him when he will meet Him." (2673) ☐

946. Narrated Abu Huraira: The Prophet (ﷺ) asked some people to take an oath, and they hurried for it. The Prophet (ﷺ) ordered that lots should be drawn amongst them as to who would take an oath first. (2674) ☐

947. Narrated `Abdullah: The Prophet (ﷺ) said, "Whoever has to take an oath should swear by Allah or remain silent." (2679) ☐

948. Narrated Abu Huraira: Allah's Messenger (ﷺ) said, "The signs of a hypocrite are

three: (1) whenever he speaks, he tells a lie, (2) whenever he is entrusted, he proves to be dishonest, (3) whenever he promises, he breaks his promise. (2682) □

949. Ibn 'Abbas (ra) said, "A man from the tribe of Bani Sahm went out in the company of Tamim Ad-Dari and 'Adi bin Badda'. The man of Bani Sahm died in a land where there was no Muslim. When Tamim and 'Adi returned conveying the property of the deceased, they claimed that they had lost a silver bowl with gold engraving. Allah's Messenger (ﷺ) made them take an oath (to confirm their claim), and then the bowl was found in Makkah with some people who claimed that they had bought it from Tamim and 'Adu, Then two witnesses from the relatives of the deceased got up and swore that their witnesses were more valid than the witnesses of 'Adi and Tamim, and that the bowl belonged to their deceased fellow. So, this verse was revealed in connection with this case; "106) O you who have believed, testimony [should be taken] among you when death approaches one of you at the time of bequest - [that of] two just men from among you or two others from outside if you are traveling through the land and the disaster of death should strike you. Detain them after the prayer and let them both swear by Allah if you doubt [their testimony, saying], "We will not exchange our oath for a price, even if he should be a near relative, and we will not withhold the testimony of Allah. Indeed, we would then be of the sinful." (5: 106) (2780) □

45. PEACEMAKING

950. NARRATED SAHL BIN SA`D (RA): There was a dispute amongst the people of the tribe of Bani `Amr bin `Auf. The Prophet (ﷺ) went to them along with some of his companions in order to make peace between them. (2690) □

951. Narrated Anas: It was said to the Prophet (ﷺ) "Would that you see `Abdullah bin Ubai." So, the Prophet (ﷺ) went to him, riding a donkey, and the Muslims accompanied him, walking on salty barren land. When the Prophet (ﷺ) reached

`Abdullah bin Ubai, the latter said, "Keep away from me! By Allah, the bad smell of your donkey has harmed me." On that an Ansari man said (to `Abdullah), "By Allah! The smell of the donkey of Allah's Messenger (ﷺ) is better than your smell." On that a man from `Abdullah's tribe got angry for `Abdullah's sake, and the two men abused each other which caused the friends of the two men to get angry, and the two groups started fighting with sticks, shoes and hands. We were informed that the following Divine Verse was revealed (in this concern): "And if two groups of Believers fall to fighting then, make peace between them." (49.9) (2691) □

952. Narrated Um Kulthum bint `Uqba: That she heard Allah's Messenger (ﷺ) saying, "He who makes peace between the people by inventing good information or saying good things, is not a liar." (2692) □

953. Narrated `Abdur Rahman bin Abi Bakra: Abu Bakra wrote to his son who was in Sijistan: 'Do not judge between two persons when you are angry, for I heard the Prophet (ﷺ) saying, "A judge should not judge between two persons while he is in an angry mood." (7158) □

954. Narrated Sahl bin Sa`d: Once the people of Quba fought with each other till they threw stones on each other. When Allah's Apostle was informed about it, he said, "Let us go to bring about a reconciliation between them." (2693) □

955. Narrated Al-Bara: Prophet (ﷺ) went out of Mecca. The daughter of Hamza ran after them (i.e. the Prophet (ﷺ) and his companions), calling, "O Uncle! O Uncle!" `Ali received her and led her by the hand and said to Fatima, "Take your uncle's daughter." Zaid and Ja`far quarreled about her. `Ali said, "I have more right to her as she is my uncle's daughter." Ja`far said, "She is my uncle's daughter, and her aunt is my wife." Zaid said, "She is my brother's daughter." The Prophet (ﷺ) judged that she should be given to her aunt, and said that the aunt was like the mother. He then said to 'All, "You are from me and I am from you", and said to Ja`far, "You resemble me both in character and appearance", and said to Zaid, "You are our brother (in faith) and our freed slave." (2699) □

956. Narrated Al-Hasan Al-Basri: By Allah, Al-Hasan bin `Ali led large battalions like mountains against Muawiya. `Amr bin Al-As said (to Muawiya), "I surely see battalions which will not turn back before killing their opponents." Muawiya who was really the best of the two men said to him, "O `Amr! If these killed those and those killed these, who would be left with me for the jobs of the public, who would be left with me for their women, who would be left with me for their children?" Then Muawiya sent two Quraishi men from the tribe of `Abd-i-Shams called `Abdur Rahman bin Sumura and `Abdullah bin 'Amir bin Kuraiz to Al-Hasan saying to them, "Go to this man (i.e. Al-Hasan) and negotiate peace with him and talk and appeal to him." So, they went to Al-Hasan and talked and appealed to him to accept peace. Al-Hasan said, "We, the offspring of `Abdul Muttalib, have got wealth and people have indulged in killing and corruption (and money only will appease them)." They said to Al-Hasan, "Muawiya offers you so and so, and appeals to you and entreats you to accept peace." Al-Hasan said to them, "But who will be responsible for what you have said?" They said, "We will be responsible for it." So, whatever Al-Hasan asked they said, "We will be responsible for it for you." So, Al-Hasan concluded a peace treaty with Muawiya. Al-Hasan (Al-Basri) said: I heard Abu Bakr saying, "I saw Allah's Messenger (ﷺ) on the pulpit and Al-Hasan bin `Ali was by his side. The Prophet (ﷺ) was looking once at the people and once at Al-Hasan bin `Ali saying, 'This son of mine is a Saiyid (i.e. a noble) and may Allah make peace between two big groups of Muslims through him." (2704) ☐

957. Narrated Abu Huraira: Allah's Messenger (ﷺ) said, "There is a Sadaqa to be given for every joint of the human body; and for every day on which the sun rises there is a reward of a Sadaqa (i.e. charitable gift) for the one who establishes justice among people." (2707) ☐

958. Narrated `Urwa bin Az-Zubair: A lady committed theft during the lifetime of Allah's Messenger (ﷺ) in the Ghazwa of Al-Fath, ((i.e. Conquest of Mecca). Her folk went to Usama bin Zaid to intercede for her (with the Prophet). When Usama interceded for her with Allah's Messenger (ﷺ), the color of the face of Allah's

Messenger (ﷺ) changed and he said, "Do you intercede with me in a matter involving one of the legal punishments prescribed by Allah?" Usama said, "O Allah's Messenger (ﷺ)! Ask Allah's Forgiveness for me." So in the afternoon, Allah's Apostle got up and addressed the people. He praised Allah as He deserved and then said, "Amma ba'du! The nations prior to you were destroyed because if a noble amongst them stole, they used to excuse him, and if a poor person amongst them stole, they would apply (Allah's) Legal Punishment to him. By Him in Whose Hand Muhammad's soul is, if Fatima, the daughter of Muhammad stole, I would cut her hand." Then Allah's Messenger (ﷺ) gave his order in the case of that woman and her hand was cut off. Afterwards her repentance proved sincere and she got married. `Aisha said, "That lady used to visit me and I used to convey her demands to Allah's Messenger (p.b.u.h). (4304) ☐

959. Narrated Um Salama: Allah's Messenger (ﷺ) heard some people quarreling at the door of his dwelling. He came out and said, "I am only a human being, and opponents come to me (to settle their problems); maybe someone amongst you can present his case more eloquently than the other, whereby I may consider him true and give a verdict in his favor. So, if I give the right of a Muslim to another by mistake, then it is really a portion of (Hell) Fire, he has the option to take or give up (before the Day of Resurrection). (2458) ☐

46. Conditions

960. Narrated Az-Zuhri (ra): `Urwa said, "Aisha told me that Allah's Messenger (ﷺ) used to examine the women emigrants. We have been told also that when Allah revealed the order that the Muslims should return to the pagans what they had spent on their wives who emigrated (after embracing Islam) and that the Muslims should not keep unbelieving women as their wives, `Umar divorced two of his wives, Qariba, the daughter of Abu Umayyah and the daughter of Jarwal Al-Khuza`i. Later on Mu`awiya married Qariba and Abu Jahm married the other." When the pagans

refused to pay what the Muslims had spent on their wives, Allah revealed: "And if any of your wives have gone from you to the unbelievers and you have an accession (by the coming over of a woman from the other side) (then pay to those whose wives have gone) the equivalent of what they had spent (on their Mahr)." (60.11) So, Allah ordered that the Muslim whose wife has gone, should be given, as a compensation of the Mahr he had given to his wife, from the Mahr of the wives of the pagans who had emigrated deserting their husbands. We do not know any of the women emigrants who deserted Islam after embracing it. We have also been told that Abu Basir bin Asid Ath-Thaqafi came to the Prophet (ﷺ) as a Muslim emigrant during the truce. Al-Akhnas bin Shariq wrote to the Prophet (ﷺ) requesting him to return Abu Basir. (2733) □

961. Narrated `Amra: Aisha said that Buraira came to seek her help in the writing of her emancipation (the freeing of someone from slavery). `Aisha said to her, "If you wish, I will pay your masters (your price) and the wala' will be for me." When Allah's Messenger (ﷺ) came, she told him about it. The Prophet (ﷺ) said to her, "Buy her (i.e. Buraira) and manumit her, for the Wala is for the one who manumits." Then Allah's Messenger (ﷺ) ascended the pulpit and said, "What about those people who stipulate conditions which are not in Allah's Laws? Whoever stipulates such conditions as are not in Allah's Laws, then those conditions are invalid even if he stipulated a hundred such conditions." (2735) □

962. Narrated Abu Huraira: Allah's Messenger (ﷺ) said, "Allah has ninety-nine names, and whoever knows them will go to Paradise." (2736) □

963. Narrated Ibn `Umar: Umar bin Khattab got some land in Khaibar and he went to the Prophet (ﷺ) to consult him about it saying, "O Allah's Messenger (ﷺ) I got some land in Khaibar better than which I have never had, what do you suggest that I do with it?" The Prophet (ﷺ) said, "If you like you can give the land as endowment and give its fruits in charity." So `Umar gave it in charity as an endowment on the condition that would not be sold nor given to anybody as a present and not to be inherited, but its yield would be given in charity to the poor people, to the Kith and

kin, for freeing slaves, for Allah's Cause, to the travelers and guests; and that there would be no harm if the guardian of the endowment ate from it according to his need with good intention, and fed others without storing it for the future." (2737) ☐

47. WILLS AND TESTAMENTS

964. NARRATED `ABDULLAH BIN `UMAR (RA): Allah's Messenger (ﷺ) said, "It is not permissible for any Muslim who has something to will to stay for two nights without having his last will and testament written and kept ready with him." (2738) ☐

965. Narrated Talha bin Musarrif: I asked `Abdullah bin Abu `Aufa "Did the Prophet (ﷺ) make a will?" He replied, "No," I asked him, "How is it then that the making of a will has been enjoined on people, (or that they are ordered to make a will)?" He replied, "The Prophet (ﷺ) bequeathed Allah's Book. (2740) ☐

966. Narrated Al-Aswad: In the presence of `Aisha some people mentioned that the Prophet (ﷺ) had appointed `Ali by will as his successor. `Aisha said, "When did he appoint him by will? Verily when he died he was resting against my chest (or said: in my lap) and he asked for a wash-basin and then collapsed while in that state, and I could not even perceive that he had died, so when did he appoint him by will?" (2741) ☐

967. Narrated Sa`d: I fell sick and the Prophet (ﷺ) paid me a visit. I said to him, "O Allah's Messenger (ﷺ)! I invoke Allah that He may not let me expire in the land where I migrated (i.e. Mecca)." He said, "May Allah give you health and let the people benefit by you." I said, "I want to will my property, and I have only one daughter and I want to will half of my property (to be given in charity)." He said," Half is too much." I said, "Then I will one third." He said, "One-third, yet even one-third is too much." (The narrator added, "So the people started to will one third of their property and that was permitted for them.") (2744) ☐

968. Narrated `Aisha: `Utba bin Abi Waqqas entrusted (his son) to his brother Sa`d

bin Abi Waqqas saying, "The son of the slave-girl of Zam`a is my (illegal) son, take him into your custody." So during the year of the Conquest (of Mecca) Sa`d took the boy and said, "This is my brother's son whom my brother entrusted to me." 'Abu bin Zam's got up and said, "He is my brother and the son of the slave girl of my father and was born on my father's bed." Then both of them came to Allah's Apostle and Sa`d said, "O Allah's Messenger (ﷺ)! This is my brother's son whom my brother entrusted to me." Then 'Abu bin Zam`a got up and said, "This is my brother and the son of the slave-girl of my father." Allah's Messenger (ﷺ) said, "O Abu bin Zam`a! This boy is for you as the boy belongs to the bed (where he was born), and for the adulterer is the stone (i.e. deprivation)." Then the Prophet (ﷺ) said to his wife Sauda bint Zam`a, "Screen yourself from this boy," when he saw the boy's resemblance to `Utba. Since then the boy did not see Sauda till he died. (2745) □

969. Narrated Abu Huraira: A man asked the Prophet, "O Allah's Messenger (ﷺ)! What kind of charity is the best?" He replied. "To give in charity when you are healthy and greedy hoping to be wealthy and afraid of becoming poor. Don't delay giving in charity till the time when you are on the death bed when you say, 'Give so much to so and- so and so much to so-and so,' and at that time the property is not yours but it belongs to so-and-so (i.e. your inheritors). (2748) □

"Never will you attain the good [reward] until you spend [in the way of Allah] from that which you love. And whatever you spend - indeed, Allah is Knowing of it." (3:92)

970. Narrated Ibn `Abbas: Some people claim that the order in the above Verse is cancelled, by Allah, it is not cancelled, but the people have stopped acting on it. There are two kinds of guardians (who are in charge of the inheritance): One is that who inherits; such a person should give (of what he inherits to the relatives, the orphans and the needy, etc.), the other is that who does not inherit (e.g. the guardian of the orphans): such a person should speak kindly and say (to those who are present at the time of distribution), "I can not give it to you (as the wealth belongs to the orphans). (2759) □

971. Nafi' said: "Ibn 'Umar never refused to be appointed as guardian." The most beloved thing to Ibn Sirin concerning an orphan's wealth was that the orphan's advisor and guardians would assemble to decide what is best for him. When Tawus was asked about something concerning an orphan's affairs, he would recite: '...And Allah knows him who means mischief from him who means good...' (V 2:220). 'Ata said concerning some orphans, "The guardian is to provide for the young and the old orphans according to their needs from their shares." (2767) □

972. Narrated Abu Huraira: Allah's Messenger (ﷺ) said, "My heirs will not inherit a Dinar or a Dirham (money), for whatever I leave (excluding the adequate support of my wives and the wages of my employees) is given in charity." (2776) □

973. Abu 'Abdur-Rahman narrated: When 'Uthman (ra) was circled (by the rebels), he looked upon them from above and said, "I ask you by Allah, I ask nobody but the Companions of the Prophet (ﷺ), dont you know that Allah's Messenger (ﷺ) said, 'Whoever will (buy and) dig the well of Ruma will be granted Paradise,' and I (bought and) dug it? Don't you know that he said? 'Whoever equip the army of 'Usra (i.e., Tabuk's Ghazwa) will be granted Paradise,' and I equipped it?" They attested whatever he said. When 'Umar founded his endowment he said, "Its administrator can eat from it." The management of the endowment can be taken over by the founder himself or any other person, for both cases are permissible. (2778) □

974. Narrated Jabir bin `Abdullah: I became sick so Allah's Messenger (ﷺ) and Abu Bakr came on foot to pay me a visit. When they came, I was unconscious. Allah's Messenger (ﷺ) performed ablution and he poured over me the water (of his ablution) and I came to my senses and said, "O Allah's Messenger (ﷺ)! What shall I do regarding my property? How shall I distribute it?" The Prophet (ﷺ) did not reply till the Divine Verses of inheritance were revealed. (6723) □

(Holy Quran 4:11) "Allah instructs you concerning your children: for the male, what is equal to the share of two females. But if there are [only] daughters, two or more, for them is two thirds of one's estate. And if there is only one, for her is half. And for one's parents, to each one of them is a sixth of his estate if he left children. But if he had no children and the parents [alone] inherit from him, then for his mother is one third. And if he had brothers [or sisters], for his mother is a sixth, after any bequest he [may have] made or debt. Your parents or your children - you know not which of them are nearest to you in benefit. [These shares are] an obligation [imposed] by Allah. Indeed, Allah is ever Knowing and Wise. 12. And for you is half of what your wives leave if they have no child. But if they have a child, for you is one fourth of what they leave, after any bequest they [may have] made or debt. And for the wives is one fourth if you leave no child. But if you leave a child, then for them is an eighth of what you leave, after any bequest you [may have] made or debt. And if a man or woman leaves neither ascendants nor descendants but has a brother or a sister, then for each one of them is a sixth. But if they are more than two, they share a third, after any bequest which was made or debt, as long as there is no detriment [caused]. [This is] an ordinance from Allah, and Allah is Knowing and Forbearing." (4; 11-12)

975. Narrated Ibn `Abbas: Allah's Messenger (صلى الله عليه وسلم) said, "Give the Fara'id (shares prescribed in the Qur'an) to those who are entitled to receive it; and whatever remains, should be given to the closest male relative of the deceased.' (6735) □

976. Narrated Huzail bin Shirahbil: Abu Musa was asked regarding (the inheritance of) a daughter, a son's daughter, and a sister. He said, "The daughter will take one-half and the sister will take one-half. If you go to Ibn Mas`ud, he will tell you the same." Ibn Mas`ud was asked and was told of Abu Musa's verdict. Ibn Mas`ud then said, "If I give the same verdict, I would stray and would not be of the rightly-guided. The verdict I will give in this case, will be the same as the Prophet (صلى الله عليه وسلم) did, i.e. one-half is for daughter, and one-sixth for the son's daughter, i.e. both shares make two-thirds of the total property; and the rest is for the sister." Afterwards we came to Abu Musa and informed him of Ibn Mas`ud's verdict, whereupon he said, "So, do not ask me for verdicts, as long as this learned man is among you." (6736) □

977. Narrated Ibn `Abbas: (During the early days of Islam), the inheritance used to be given to one's offspring and legacy used to be bequeathed to the parents, then Allah

cancelled what He wished from that order and decreed that the male should be given the equivalent of the portion of two females, and for the parents one-sixth for each of them, and for one's wife one-eighth (if the deceased has children) and one-fourth (if he has no children), for one's husband one-half (if the deceased has no children) and one-fourth (if she has children). (6739) ☐

978. Narrated Al-Aswad: Mu`adh bin Jabal gave this verdict for us in the lifetime of Allah's Messenger (ﷺ). One-half of the inheritance is to be given to the daughter and the other half to the sister. Sulaiman said: Mu`adh gave a verdict for us, but he did not mention that it was so in the lifetime of Allah's Messenger. (6741) ☐

979. Narrated Al-Bara: The last Qur'anic Verse that was revealed (to the Prophet) was the final Verse of Surah-an-Nisa: "They request from you a [legal] ruling. Say, "Allah gives you a ruling concerning one having neither descendants nor ascendants [as heirs]." If a man dies, leaving no child but [only] a sister, she will have half of what he left. And he inherits from her if she [dies and] has no child. But if there are two sisters [or more], they will have two-thirds of what he left. If there are both brothers and sisters, the male will have the share of two females. Allah makes clear to you [His law], lest you go astray. And Allah is Knowing of all things." (4.176) (6744) ☐

980. Narrated Ibn `Umar: A man and his wife had a case of Lian (or Mula'ana) during the lifetime of the Prophet (ﷺ) and the man denied the paternity of her child. The Prophet (ﷺ) gave his verdict for their separation (divorce) and then the child was regarded as belonging to the wife only. (6748) ☐

981. Narrated Usama bin Zaid: the Prophet (ﷺ) said, "A Muslim cannot be the heir of a disbeliever, nor can a disbeliever be the heir of a Muslim." (6764) ☐

48. JIHAAD

982. NARRATED IBN `ABBAS (RA): Allah's Messenger (ﷺ) said, "There is no Hijra (i.e. migration) (from Mecca to Medina) after the Conquest (of Mecca), but Jihad and good intention remain; and if you are called (by the Muslim ruler) for fighting, go forth immediately. (2783) ☐

983. Narrated Abu Huraira: A man came to Allah's Messenger (ﷺ) and said, "Instruct me as to such a deed as equals Jihad (in reward)." He replied, "I do not find such a deed." Then he added, "Can you, while the Muslim fighter is in the battle-field, enter your mosque to perform prayers without cease and fast and never break your fast?" The man said, "But who can do that?" Abu- Huraira added, "The Mujahid (i.e. Muslim fighter) is rewarded even for the footsteps of his horse while it wanders about (for grazing) tied in a long rope." (2785) ☐

984. Narrated Abu Sa`id Al-Khudri: Somebody asked, "O Allah's Messenger (ﷺ)! Who is the best among the people?" Allah's Messenger (ﷺ) replied "A believer who strives his utmost in Allah's Cause with his life and property." They asked, "Who is next?" He replied, "A believer who stays in one of the mountain paths worshipping Allah and leaving the people secure from his mischief." (2786) ☐

985. Narrated Abu Huraira: I heard Allah's Messenger (ﷺ) saying, "The example of a Mujahid in Allah's Cause-- and Allah knows better who really strives in His Cause----is like a person who fasts and prays continuously. Allah guarantees that He will admit the Mujahid in His Cause into Paradise if he is killed, otherwise He will return him to his home safely with rewards and war booty." (2787) ☐

986. Narrated Al-Mughira: Our Prophet (s) has informed us our Lord's Message that whoever of us is martyred, will go to Paradise. (7530) ☐

987. Narrated Abu Huraira: The Prophet (ﷺ) said, "Whoever believes in Allah and His Apostle, offer prayer perfectly and fasts the month of Ramadan, will rightfully be

granted Paradise by Allah, no matter whether he fights in Allah's Cause or remains in the land where he is born." The people said, "O Allah's Messenger (ﷺ)! Shall we acquaint the people with the good news?" He said, "Paradise has one-hundred grades which Allah has reserved for the Mujahidin who fight in His Cause, and the distance between each of two grades is like the distance between the Heaven and the Earth. So, when you ask Allah (for something), ask for Al-firdaus which is the best and highest part of Paradise." (i.e. The sub-narrator added, "I think the Prophet also said, 'Above it (i.e. Al-Firdaus) is the Throne of Beneficent (i.e. Allah), and from it originate the rivers of Paradise.") (2790) □

988. Narrated Anas bin Malik: The Prophet (ﷺ) said, "A single endeavor (of fighting) in Allah's Cause in the forenoon or in the afternoon is better than the world and whatever is in it." (2792) □

989. Narrated Anas bin Malik: The Prophet (ﷺ) said, "Nobody who dies and finds good from Allah (in the Hereafter) would wish to come back to this world even if he were given the whole world and whatever is in it, except the martyr who, on seeing the superiority of martyrdom, would like to come back to the world and get killed again (in Allah's Cause)." (2795) □

990. Narrated Abu Huraira: The Prophet (ﷺ) said, "By Him in Whose Hands my life is! Were it not for some men amongst the believers who dislike to be left behind me and whom I cannot provide with means of conveyance, I would certainly never remain behind any Sariya' (army-unit) setting out in Allah's Cause. By Him in Whose Hands my life is! I would love to be martyred in Allah's Cause and then get resurrected and then get martyred, and then get resurrected again and then get martyred and then get resurrected again and then get martyred. (2797) □

991. Narrated Jundab bin Sufyan: In one of the holy Battles a finger of Allah's Messenger (ﷺ) (got wounded and) bled. He said, "You are just a finger that bled, and what you got is in Allah's Cause." (2802) □

992. Narrated Abu Huraira: Allah's Messenger (ﷺ) said, "By Him in Whose Hands

my soul is! Whoever is wounded in Allah's Cause....and Allah knows well who gets wounded in His Cause....will come on the Day of Resurrection with his wound having the color of blood but the scent of musk." (2803) □

993. Narrated Anas: My uncle Anas bin An-Nadr was absent from the Battle of Badr. He said, "O Allah's Messenger (ﷺ)! I was absent from the first battle you fought against the pagans. (By Allah) if Allah gives me a chance to fight the pagans, no doubt. Allah will see how (bravely) I will fight." On the day of Uhud when the Muslims turned their backs and fled, he said, "O Allah! I apologize to You for what these (i.e. his companions) have done, and I denounce what these (i.e. the pagans) have done." Then he advanced and Sa`d bin Mu`adh met him. He said "O Sa`d bin Mu`adh ! By the Lord of An-Nadr, Paradise! I am smelling its aroma coming from before (the mountain of) Uhud," Later on Sa`d said, "O Allah's Apostle! I cannot achieve or do what he (i.e. Anas bin An-Nadr) did. We found more than eighty wounds by swords and arrows on his body. We found him dead and his body was mutilated so badly that none except his sister could recognize him by his fingers." We used to think that the following Verse was revealed concerning him and other men of his sort: "Among the believers are men who have been true to their covenant with Allah........." (33.23) His sister Ar-Rubbaya' broke a front tooth of a woman and Allah's Messenger (ﷺ) ordered for retaliation. On that Anas (bin An-Nadr) said, "O Allah's Messenger (ﷺ)! By Him Who has sent you with the Truth, my sister's tooth shall not be broken." Then the opponents of Anas's sister accepted the compensation and gave up the claim of retaliation. So Allah's Messenger (ﷺ) said, "There are some people amongst Allah's slaves whose oaths are fulfilled by Allah when they take them." (2805) □

994. Narrated Al-Bara: A man whose face was covered with an iron mask (i.e. clad in armor) came to the Prophet (ﷺ) and said, "O Allah's Messenger (ﷺ)! Shall I fight or embrace Islam first? "The Prophet (ﷺ) said, "Embrace Islam first and then fight." So he embraced Islam, and was martyred. Allah's Messenger (ﷺ) said, A Little work, but a great reward. "(He did very little (after embracing Islam), but he will be rewarded

in abundance). (2808) □

995. Narrated Anas bin Malik: Um Ar-Rubai 'bint Al-Bara', the mother of Hartha bin Suraqa came to the Prophet (ﷺ) and said, "O Allah's Prophet! Will you tell me about Hartha?" Hartha has been killed (i.e. martyred) on the day of Badr with an arrow thrown by an unidentified person. She added, "If he is in Paradise, I will be patient; otherwise, I will weep bitterly for him." He said, "O mother of Hartha! There are Gardens in Paradise and your son got the Firdausal-ala (i.e. the best place in Paradise). (2809) □

996. Narrated Abu Musa: A man came to the Prophet (ﷺ) and asked, "A man fights for war booty; another fights for fame and a third fights for showing off; which of them fights in Allah's Cause?" The Prophet (ﷺ) said, "He who fights that Allah's Word (i.e. Islam) should be superior, fights in Allah's Cause." (2810) □

997. Narrated Abu `Abs: (who is `Abdur-Rahman bin Jabir) Allah's Messenger (ﷺ) said," Anyone whose both feet get covered with dust in Allah's Cause will not be touched by the (Hell) fire." (2811) □

998. Narrated Abu Huraira: Allah's Messenger (ﷺ) said, "Allah welcomes two men with a smile; one of whom kills the other and both of them enter Paradise. One fights in Allah's Cause and gets killed. Later on Allah forgives the 'killer who also get martyred (In Allah's Cause)." (2826) □

999. Narrated Abu Huraira: Allah's Messenger (ﷺ) said, "Five are regarded as martyrs: They are those who die because of plague, Abdominal disease, drowning or a falling building etc., and the martyrs in Allah's Cause." (2829) □

1000. Narrated Sahl bin Sa`d As-Sa`idi: I saw Marwan bin Al-Hakam sitting in the Mosque. So I came forward and sat by his side. He told us that Zaid bin Thabit had told him that Allah's Messenger (ﷺ) had dictated to him the Divine Verse: "Not equal are those believers who sit (at home) and those who strive hard and fight in the Cause of Allah with their wealth and lives.' (4.95) Zaid said, "Ibn-Maktum came to the

Prophet (ﷺ) while he was dictating to me that very Verse. On that Ibn Um Maktum said, "O Allah's Messenger (ﷺ)! If I had power, I would surely take part in Jihad." He was a blind man. So Allah sent down revelation to His Apostle while his thigh was on mine and it became so heavy for me that I feared that my thigh would be broken. Then that state of the Prophet (ﷺ) was over after Allah revealed "...except those who are disabled (by injury or are blind or lame etc.) (4.95) (2832) ☐

1001. Narrated Salim Abu-An-Nadr: `Abdullah bin Abi `Aufa wrote and I read what he wrote that Allah's Messenger (ﷺ) said, "When you face them (i.e. your enemy) then be patient." (2833) ☐

1002. Narrated Anas: While the Prophet (ﷺ) was in a Ghazwa he said, "Some people have remained behind us in Medina and we never crossed a mountain path or a valley, but they were with us (i.e. sharing the reward with us), as they have been held back by a (legal) excuse." (2839) ☐

1003. Narrated Zaid bin Khalid: Allah's Messenger (ﷺ) said, " He who prepares a Ghazi going in Allah's Cause is given a reward equal to that of) a Ghazi; and he who looks after properly the dependents of a Ghazi going in Allah's Cause is (given a reward equal to that of) Ghazi." (2843) ☐

1004. Narrated Anas: The Prophet (ﷺ) used not to enter any house in Medina except the house of Um Sulaim besides those of his wives when he was asked why, he said, "I take pity on her as her brother was killed in my company. " (2844) ☐

1005. Narrated `Urwa Al-Bariqi: The Prophet (ﷺ) said, "Good will remain (as a permanent quality) in the foreheads of horses (for Jihad) till the Day of Resurrection, for they bring about either a reward (in the Hereafter) or (war) booty (in this world)."(2852) ☐

1006. Narrated Abu Huraira: The Prophet (ﷺ) said, "If somebody keeps a horse in Allah's Cause motivated by his faith in Allah and his belief in His Promise, then he will be rewarded on the Day of Resurrection for what the horse has eaten or drunk and for its dung and urine." (2853) ☐

1007. Narrated Abu Huraira: Allah's Messenger (ﷺ) said, "Horses are kept for one of three purposes; for some people they are a source of reward, for some others they are a means of shelter and for some others they are a source of sins. The one for whom they are a source of reward, is he who keeps a horse for Allah's Cause (i.e. Jihad) tying it with a long tether on a meadow or in a garden with the result that whatever it eats from the area of the meadow or the garden where it is tied will be counted as good deeds for his benefit, and if it should break its rope and jump over one or two hillocks then all its dung and its foot marks will be written as good deeds for him; and if it passes by a river and drinks water from it even though he had no intention of watering it, even then he will get the reward for its drinking. As for the man for whom horses are a source of sins, he is the one who keeps a horse for the sake of pride and pretense and showing enmity for Muslims: such a horse will be a source of sins for him. When Allah's Messenger (ﷺ) was asked about donkeys, he replied, "Nothing has been revealed to me about them except this unique, comprehensive Verse: "Then anyone who does an atom's (or a small ant's) weight of good shall see it; and anyone who does an atom's (or a small ant's) weight of evil, shall see it.' (101:7-8) (2860) ☐

1008. Narrated Anas: The Prophet (ﷺ) met them (i.e. the people) while he was riding an unsaddled horse with his sword slung over his shoulder. (2866) ☐

1009. Narrated (`Abdullah) bin `Umar: The Prophet (ﷺ) arranged for a horse race amongst the horses that had been made lean to take place between Al-Hafya" and Thaniyat Al-Wada` (i.e. names of two places) and the horses which had not been mad? Lean from Ath-Thaniyat to the mosque of Bani Zuraiq. I was also amongst those who took part in that horse race. Sufyan, a sub-narrator, said, "The distance between Al-Hafya and Thaniya Al- Wada` is five or six miles; and between Thaniya and the mosque of Bani Zuraiq is one mile." (2868) ☐

1010. Narrated Anas: The Prophet (ﷺ) had a she camel called Al Adba which could not be excelled in a race. (Humaid, a subnarrator said, "Or could hardly be excelled.")

Once a bedouin came riding a camel below six years of age which surpasses it (i.e. Al-`Adba') in the race. The Muslims felt it so much that the Prophet (ﷺ) noticed their distress. He then said, "It is Allah's Law that He brings down whatever rises high in the world." (2872) ☐

1011. Narrated Ar-Rubayyi 'bint Mu'auwidh: We were in the company of the Prophet (ﷺ) providing the wounded with water and treating them and bringing the killed to Medina (from the battle field) (2882) ☐

1012. Narrated `Aisha: The Prophet (ﷺ) was vigilant one night and when he reached Medina, he said, "Would that a pious man from my companions guard me tonight!" Suddenly we heard the clatter of arms. He said, "Who is that?" He (The new comer) replied, " I am Sa`d bin Abi Waqqas and have come to guard you." So, the Prophet (ﷺ) slept (that night). (2885) ☐

1013. Narrated Abu Huraira: The Prophet (ﷺ) said, "Let the slave of Dinar and Dirham, of Quantify and Khamisa perish as he is pleased if these things are given to him, and if not, he is displeased. Let such a person perish and relapse, and if he is pierced with a thorn, let him not find anyone to take it out for him. Paradise is for him who holds the reins of his horse to strive in Allah's Cause, with his hair unkempt and feet covered with dust: if he is appointed in the vanguard, he is perfectly satisfied with his post of guarding, and if he is appointed in the rearward, he accepts his post with satisfaction; (he is so simple and unambiguous that) if he asks for permission he is not permitted, and if he intercedes, his intercession is not accepted." (2887) ☐

1014. Narrated Anas: We were with the Prophet (on a journey) and the only shade one could have was the shade made by one's own garment. Those who fasted did not do any work and those who did not fast served the camels and brought the water on them and treated the sick and (wounded). So, the Prophet (ﷺ) said, "Today, those who were not fasting took (all) the reward." (2890) ☐

1015. Narrated Abu Huraira: The Prophet (ﷺ) said, "Charity is obligatory everyday on every joint of a human being. If one helps a person in matters concerning his riding animal by helping him to ride it or by lifting his luggage on to it, all this will be regarded charity. A good word, and every step one takes to offer the compulsory Congregational prayer, is regarded as charity; and guiding somebody on the road is regarded as charity." (2891) □

1016. Narrated Sahl bin Sa`d As-Sa'di: Allah's Messenger (ﷺ) said, "To guard Muslims from infidels in Allah's Cause for one day is better than the world and whatever is on its surface, and a place in Paradise as small as that occupied by the whip of one of you is better than the world and whatever is on its surface; and a morning's or an evening's journey which a slave (person) travels in Allah's Cause is better than the world and whatever is on its surface." (2892) □

1017. Narrated Mus`ab bin Sa`d: Once Sa`d (bin Abi Waqqas) thought that he was superior to those who were below him in rank. On that the Prophet (ﷺ) said, "You gain no victory or livelihood except through (the blessings and invocations of) the poor amongst you." (2896) □

1018. Narrated Sahl bin Sa`d As-Sa`idi: Allah's Messenger (ﷺ) and the pagans faced each other and started fighting. When Allah's Messenger (ﷺ) returned to his camp and when the pagans returned to their camp, somebody talked about a man amongst the companions of Allah's Messenger (ﷺ) who would follow and kill with his sword any pagan going alone. He said, "Nobody did his job (i.e. fighting) so properly today as that man." Allah's Messenger (ﷺ) said, "Indeed, he is amongst the people of the (Hell) Fire." A man amongst the people said, "I shall accompany him" Thus he accompanied him, and wherever he stood, he would stand with him, and wherever he ran, he would run with him. Then the (brave) man got wounded seriously and he decided to bring about his death quickly. He planted the blade of the sword in the ground directing its sharp end towards his chest between his two breasts. Then he leaned on the sword and killed himself. The other man came to Allah's Messenger (ﷺ) and said, "I testify that you are Allah's Messenger (ﷺ)." The Prophet (ﷺ) asked, "What has happened?" He replied, "(It is about) the man whom you had described as one of the people of the (Hell) Fire. The people were greatly surprised at what you said, and I said, 'I will find out his reality for you.' So, I came out seeking him. He got severely wounded, and hastened to die by slanting the blade of his sword in the ground directing its sharp end towards his chest between his two breasts. Then he eased on his sword and killed himself." when Allah's Messenger (ﷺ) said, "A man may seem to the people as if he were practising the deeds of the people of Paradise while in fact he is from the people of the (Hell) Fire, another may seem to the people as if he were practicing the deeds of the people of Hell (Fire), while in fact he is from the people of Paradise." (2898) □

1019. Narrated Abu Huraira: Tufail bin `Amr Ad-Dausi and his companions came to the Prophet (ﷺ) and said, "O Allah's Messenger (ﷺ)! The people of the tribe of Daus disobeyed and refused to follow you; so invoke Allah against them." The people said, "The tribe of Daus is ruined." The Prophet (ﷺ) said, "O Allah! Give guidance to the people of Daus, and let them embrace Islam." (2937) □

1020. Narrated Anas: When the Prophet (ﷺ) intended to write a letter to the ruler of the Byzantines, he was told that those people did not read any letter unless it was stamped with a seal. So, the Prophet (ﷺ) got a silver ring-- as if I were just looking at its white glitter on his hand ---- and stamped on it the expression "Muhammad, Apostle of Allah". (2938) □

1021. Narrated `Abdullah bin `Abbas: Allah's Messenger (ﷺ) sent his letter to Khusrau and ordered his messenger to hand it over to the Governor of Bahrain who was to hand it over to Khusrau. So, when Khusrau read the letter he tore it. Sa`id bin Al- Musaiyab said, "The Prophet (ﷺ) then invoked Allah to disperse them with full dispersion, (destroy them (i.e. Khusrau and his followers) severely)". (2939) □

1022. Narrated `Abdullah bin `Abbas: Allah's Messenger (ﷺ) wrote to Caesar and invited him to Islam and sent him his letter with Dihya Al-Kalbi whom Allah's Messenger (ﷺ) ordered to hand it over to the Governor of Busra who would forward it to Caesar. Caesar as a sign of gratitude to Allah, had walked from Hims to Ilya (i.e. Jerusalem) when Allah had granted Him victory over the Persian forces. So, when the letter of Allah's Messenger (ﷺ) reached Caesar, he said after reading it, 'Seek for me any one of his people! (Arabs of Quraish tribe) if present here, in order to ask him about Allah's Messenger (ﷺ). At that time Abu Sufyan bin Harb was in Sham with some men frown Quraish who had come (to Sham) as merchants during the truce that had been concluded between Allah's Messenger (ﷺ); and the infidels of Quraish. Abu Sufyan said, Caesar's messenger found us somewhere in Sham so he took me and my companions to Ilya and we were admitted into Ceasar's court to find him sitting in his royal court wearing a crown and surrounded by the senior dignitaries of the Byzantine. He said to his translator. 'Ask them who amongst them is a close relation to the man who claims to be a prophet." Abu Sufyan added, "I replied, 'I am the nearest relative to him.' He asked, 'What degree of relationship do you have with him?' I replied, 'He is my cousin,' and there was none of Bani Abu Manaf in the caravan except myself. Caesar said, 'Let him come nearer.' He then ordered that my companions stand behind me near my shoulder and said to his translator, 'Tell his companions that I am going to ask this man about the man who claims to be a prophet. If he tells a lie, they should contradict him immediately." Abu Sufyan added, "By Allah! Had it not been shameful that my companions label me a liar, I would not have spoken the truth about him when he asked me. But I considered it shameful to be called a liar by my companions. So I told the truth. He then said to his translator, 'Ask him what kind of family does he belong to.' I replied, 'He belongs to a noble family amongst us.' He said, 'Have anybody else amongst you ever claimed the same before him? 'I replied, 'No.' He said, 'Had you ever blamed him for telling lies before he claimed what he claimed? 'I replied, 'No.' He said, 'Was anybody amongst his ancestors a king?' I replied, 'No.' He said, "do the noble or the poor follow him?' I replied, 'It is the poor who follow him.' He said, 'Are they increasing or decreasing (day by day)?' I replied,' they are increasing.' He said, 'Does anybody amongst those who embrace his (the Prophet's) Religion become displeased and then discard his Religion?' I replied, 'No.' He said, 'Does he break his promises? I replied, 'No, but we are now at truce with him and we are afraid that he may betray us." Abu Sufyan added, "Other than the last sentence, I could not say anything against him. Caesar then asked, 'Have you ever had a war with him?' I replied, 'Yes.' He said, 'What was the outcome of your battles with him?' I replied, 'the result was unstable; sometimes he was victorious and sometimes we.' He said, 'What does he order you to do?' I said, 'He tells us to worship Allah alone, and not to worship others along with Him, and to leave all that our fore-fathers used to worship. He orders us to pray, give in charity, be chaste, keep promises and return what is entrusted to us.' When I had said that, Caesar said to his translator, 'Say to him: I ask you about his lineage and your reply was that he belonged to a noble family. In fact, all the apostles came from the noblest lineage of their nations. Then I questioned you whether anybody else amongst you had claimed such a thing, and your reply was in the negative. If the answer had been in the affirmative, I would have thought that this man was following a claim that had been said before him. When I asked you whether he was ever blamed for telling lies, your reply was in the negative, so I took it for granted that a person who did not tell a lie about (others) the people could never tell a lie about Allah. Then I asked you whether any of his ancestors was a king. Your reply was in the negative, and if it had been in the affirmative, I would have thought that this man wanted to take back his ancestral kingdom. When I asked you whether the rich or the poor people followed him, you replied that it was the poor who followed him. In fact, such are the followers of the apostles. Then I asked you whether his followers were increasing or decreasing. You replied that they were increasing. In fact, this is the result of true faith till it is complete (in all respects). I asked you whether there was anybody who, after embracing his religion, became displeased and discarded his religion; your reply was in the negative. In fact, this is the sign of true faith, for when its cheerfulness enters and mixes in the hearts completely, nobody will be displeased with it. I asked you whether he had ever broken his promise. You replied in the negative. And such are the apostles; they never break their promises. When I asked you whether you fought with him and he fought with you, you replied that he did, and that sometimes he was victorious and sometimes you. Indeed, such are the apostles; they are put to trials and the final victory is always theirs. Then I asked you what he ordered you. You replied that he ordered you to worship Allah alone and not to worship others along with

Him, to leave all that your fore-fathers used to worship, to offer prayers, to speak the truth, to be chaste, to keep promises, and to return what is entrusted to you. These are really the qualities of a prophet who, I knew (from the previous Scriptures) would appear, but I did not know that he would be from amongst you. If what you say should be true, he will very soon occupy the earth under my feet, and if I knew that I would reach him definitely, I would go immediately to meet Him; and were I with him, then I would certainly wash his feet.'" Abu Sufyan added, "Caesar then asked for the letter of Allah's Messenger (ﷺ) and it was read. Its contents were: "In the name of Allah, the most Beneficent, the most Merciful (This letter is) from Muhammad, the slave of Allah, and His Apostle, to Heraculius, the Ruler of the Byzantine. Peace be upon the followers of guidance. Now then, I invite you to Islam (i.e. surrender to Allah), embrace Islam and you will be safe; embrace Islam and Allah will bestow on you a double reward. But if you reject this invitation of Islam, you shall be responsible for misguiding the peasants (i.e. your nation). O people of the Scriptures! Come to a word common to you and us and you, that we worship. None but Allah, and that we associate nothing in worship with Him; and that none of us shall take others as Lords besides Allah. Then if they turn away, say: Bear witness that we are (they who have surrendered (unto Him). (3.64) Abu Sufyan added, "When Heraclius had finished his speech, there was a great hue and cry caused by the Byzantine Royalties surrounding him, and there was so much noise that I did not understand what they said. So, we were turned out of the court. When I went out with my companions and we were alone, I said to them, 'Verily, Ibn Abi Kabsha's (i.e. the Prophet's) affair has gained power. This is the King of Bani Al-Asfar fearing him." Abu Sufyan added, "By Allah, I remained low and was sure that his religion would be victorious till Allah converted me to Islam, though I disliked it." (2940) □

1023. Narrated Anas: Whenever Allah's Messenger (ﷺ) attacked some people, he would never attack them till it was dawn. If he heard the Adhan (i.e. call for prayer) he would delay the fight, and if he did not hear the Adhan, he would attack them immediately after dawn. We reached Khaibar at night. (2943) □

1024. An-Nu' man said to Al-Mughira, "If you had participated in a similar battle, in the company of Allah's Messenger (ﷺ) he would not have blamed you for waiting, nor would he have disgraced you. But I accompanied Allah's Apostle in many battles and it was his custom that if he did not fight early by daytime, he would wait till the wind had started blowing and the time for the prayer was due (i.e. after midday). (3160) □

1025. Narrated Abu Huraira: Allah's Apostle said, " I have been ordered to fight with the people till they say, 'None has the right to be worshipped but Allah,' and whoever says, 'None has the right to be worshipped but Allah,' his life and property will be saved by me except for Islamic law, and his accounts will be with Allah, (either to punish him or to forgive him.)" (2946) □

1026. Narrated Ka`b bin Malik: Whenever Allah's Messenger (ﷺ) intended to carry out a Ghazwa, he would use an equivocation to conceal his real destination till it was the Ghazwa of Tabuk which Allah's Messenger (ﷺ) carried out in very hot weather. As he was going to face a very long journey through a wasteland and was to meet and attack a large number of enemies. So, he made the situation clear to the Muslims so that they might prepare themselves accordingly and get ready to conquer their enemy. The Prophet (ﷺ) informed them of the destination he was heading for. (2948) □

1027. Ka`b bin Malik used to say: "Scarcely did Allah's Messenger (ﷺ) set out for a journey on a day other than Thursday." (2949) □

1028. Narrated Abu Hurairah (ra): Allah's Messenger (ﷺ) sent us on military expedition telling us, "If you find such and such persons (he named two men from Quraish), burn them fire." Then we came to bid him farewell, when we wanted to set out, he said: "Previously I ordered you to burn so-and-so and so-and-so with fire, but as punishment with fire is done by none except Allah, if you capture them, kill them, (instead)." (2954) □

1029. Narrated Salim Abu An-Nadr: The freed slave of `Umar bin 'Ubaidullah who was `Umar's clerk: `Abdullah bin Abi `Aufa wrote him (i.e. `Umar) a letter that contained the following: -- "Once Allah's Messenger (ﷺ) (during a holy battle), waited till the sun had declined and then he got up among the people and said, "O people! Do not wish to face the enemy (in a battle) and ask Allah to save you (from calamities) but if you should face the enemy, then be patient and let it be known to you that Paradise is under the shades of swords." He then said, "O Allah! The Revealer of the (Holy) Book, the Mover of the clouds, and Defeater of Al-Ahzab (i.e. the clans of infidels), defeat them infidels and bestow victory upon us." (2965) ☐

1030. Narrated `Abdullah bin `Umar: Allah's Messenger (ﷺ) forbade the people to travel to a hostile country carrying (copies of) the Qur'an. (2990) ☐

1031. Narrated Jabir bin `Abdullah: Whenever we went up a place we would say, "Allahu--Akbar (i.e. Allah is Greater)", and whenever we went down a place we would say, "Subhan Allah." (2993) ☐

1032. Narrated `Abdullah bin `Amr: A man came to the Prophet (ﷺ) asking his permission to take part in Jihad. The Prophet (ﷺ) asked him, "Are your parents alive?" He replied in the affirmative. The Prophet (ﷺ) said to him, "Then exert yourself in their service." (3004) ☐

1033. Narrated Abu Bashir Al-Ansari: That he was in the company of Allah's Messenger (ﷺ) on some of his journeys. (The sub-narrator adds, "I think that Abu Bashir also said, 'And the people were at their sleeping places.") Allah's Apostle sent a messenger ordering: "There shall not remain any necklace of string or any other kind of necklace round the necks of camels except it is cut off." (3005) ☐

1034. Narrated Abu Huraira: The Prophet (ﷺ) said, "Allah wonders at those people who will enter Paradise in chains." (3010) ☐

1035. Narrated As-Sab bin Jaththama: The Prophet (ﷺ) passed by me at a place called Al-Abwa or Waddan, and was asked whether it was permissible to attack the pagan warriors at night with the probability of exposing their women and children to danger. The Prophet (ﷺ) replied, "They (i.e. women and children) are from them (i.e.

pagans)." I also heard the Prophet (ﷺ) saying, "The institution of Hima (reserved pastures) invalid except for Allah and His Apostle." (3012) ☐

1036. Narrated `Abdullah: During some of the Ghazawat of the Prophet (ﷺ) a woman was found killed. Allah's Messenger (ﷺ) disapproved the killing of women and children. (3014) ☐

1037. Narrated Ibn `Umar: During some of the Ghazawat of Allah's Messenger (ﷺ) a woman was found killed, so Allah's Messenger (ﷺ) forbade the killing of women and children. (3015) ☐

1038. Narrated Abu Hurairah (ra): I heard Allah's Messenger (ﷺ) saying, "An ant bit a Prophet amongst the Prophets, and he ordered that the place of the ants be burnt. So, Allah inspired to him, 'It is because one ant bit you that you burnt a nation amongst the nations that glorify Allah?" (3019) ☐

1039. Narrated Jabir bin `Abdullah: The Prophet (ﷺ) said, "War is deceit." (3030) ☐

1040. Narrated Abu Juhaifa: I asked `Ali, "Do you have the knowledge of any Divine Inspiration besides what is in Allah's Book?" `Ali replied, "No, by Him Who splits the grain of corn and creates the soul. I don't think we have such knowledge, but we have the ability of understanding which Allah may endow a person with, so that he may understand the Qur'an, and we have what is written in this paper as well." I asked, "What is written in this paper?" He replied, "(The regulations of) blood-money, the freeing of captives, and the judgment that no Muslim should be killed for killing an infidel." (3047) ☐

1041. Narrated Anas bin Malik: Some Ansari men asked permission from Allah's Messenger (ﷺ) saying, "O Allah's Messenger (ﷺ)! Allow us not to take the ransom of our nephew Al `Abbas. The Prophet (ﷺ) replied, "Do not leave a single Dirham thereof." (3048) ☐

1042. Narrated Salama bin Al-Akwa`: "An infidel spy came to the Prophet (ﷺ) while he was on a journey. The spy sat with the companions of the Prophet (ﷺ) and started talking and then went away. The Prophet (ﷺ) said (to his companions), 'Chase and kill him.' So, I killed him." The Prophet (ﷺ) then gave him the belongings of the killed spy (in addition to his share of the war booty). (3051) □

1043. Narrated `Amr bin Maimun: `Umar (after he was stabbed), instructed (his would-be-successor) saying, "I urge him to take care of those non-Muslims who are under the protection of Allah and His Apostle in that he should observe the convention agreed upon with them, and fight on their behalf (to secure their safety) and he should not over-tax them beyond their capability." (3052) □

1044. Narrated Aslam: `Umar bin Al-Khattab appointed a freed slave of his, called Hunai, manager of the Hima (i.e. a pasture devoted for grazing the animals of the Zakat or other specified animals). He said to him, "O Hunai! Don't oppress the Muslims and ward off their curse (invocations against you) for the invocation of the oppressed is responded to (by Allah); and allow the shepherd having a few camels and those having a few sheep (to graze their animals), and take care not to allow the livestock of `Abdur-Rahman bin `Auf and the livestock of (`Uthman) bin `Affan, for if their livestock should perish, then they have their farms and gardens, while those who own a few camels and those who own a few sheep, if their livestock should perish, would bring their dependents to me and appeal for help saying, 'O chief of the believers! O chief of the believers!' Would I then neglect them? (No, of course). So, I find it easier to let them have water and grass rather than to give them gold and silver (from the Muslims' treasury). By Allah, these people think that I have been unjust to them. This is their land, and during the pre-lslamic period, they fought for it and they embraced Islam (willingly) while it was in their possession. By Him in Whose Hand my life is! Were it not for the animals (in my custody) which I give to be ridden for striving in Allah's Cause, I would not have turned even a span of their land into a Hima." (3059) □

1045. Narrated Hudhaifa: The Prophet (ﷺ) said (to us), "List the names of those people who have announced that they are Muslims." So, we listed one thousand and five hundred men. Then we wondered, "Should we be afraid (of infidels) although we are one thousand and five hundred in number?" No doubt, we witnessed ourselves being afflicted with such bad trials that one would have to offer the prayer alone in fear. (3060) ☐

1046. Narrated Anas bin Malik: Allah's Messenger (ﷺ) delivered a sermon and said, "Zaid received the flag and was martyred, then Ja`far took it and was martyred, then `Abdullah bin Rawaha took it and was martyred, and then Khalid bin Al-Walid took it without being appointed, and Allah gave him victory." The Prophet (ﷺ) added, "I am not pleased (or they will not be pleased) that they should remain (alive) with us," while his eyes were shedding tears. (3063) ☐

1047. Narrated Abu Talha: Whenever the Prophet (ﷺ) conquered some people, he would stay in their town for three days. (3065) ☐

1048. Narrated Nafi' (ra): A horse of Ibn 'Umar fled and the enemy took it. Then the Muslims conquered the enemy and the horse was returned to him during the lifetime of Allah's Messenger (ﷺ). And also, once a slave of Ibn 'Umar (ra) fled and joined the Byzantines, and when the Muslims conquered them, Khalid bin Al-Walid returned the slave to him after the death of the Prophet (ﷺ). (3067) ☐

1049. Narrated Muharib bin Dithar: Jabir bin `Abdullah said, "When Allah's Messenger (ﷺ) arrived at Medina, he slaughtered a camel or a cow." Jabir added, "The Prophet (ﷺ) bought a camel from me for two Uqiyas (of gold) and one or two Dirhams. When he reached Sirar, he ordered that a cow be slaughtered and they ate its meat. When he arrived at Medina, he ordered me to go to the Mosque and offer two rak`at, and weighed (and gave) me the price of the camel." (3089) ☐

49. WAR BOOTY

1050. NARRATED `ALI (RA): I had a she-camel which I got in my share from the booty of the battle of Badr, and the Prophet (ﷺ) had given me another she camel from the

Khumus which Allah had bestowed on him that day. And when I intended to celebrate my marriage to Fatima, the daughter of the Prophet, I made an arrangement with a goldsmith from Bani Qainuqa 'that he should go with me to bring Idhkhir (i.e. a kind of grass used) which I intended to sell to gold-smiths in order to spend its price on the marriage banquet. While I was collecting ropes and sacks of pack saddles for my two she-camels which were kneeling down beside an Ansari's dwelling and after collecting what I needed, I suddenly found that the humps of the two she-camels had been cut off and their flanks had been cut open and portions of their livers had been taken out. On seeing that, I could not help weeping. I asked, "Who has done that?" They (i.e. the people) said, "Hamza bin `Abdul Muttalib has done it. He is present in this house with some Ansari drinkers, a girl singer, and his friends. The singer said in her song, "O Hamza, get at the fat she-camels!" On hearing this, Hamza rushed to his sword and cut of the camels' humps and cut their flanks open and took out portions from their livers." Then I came to the Prophet, with whom Zaid bin Haritha was present. The Prophet (ﷺ) noticed my state and asked, "What is the matter?" I said, "O Allah's Messenger (ﷺ), I have never experienced such a day as today! Hamza attacked my two she-camels, cut off their humps and cut their flanks open, and he is still present in a house along some drinkers." The Prophet (ﷺ) asked for his cloak, put it on, and proceeded, followed by Zaid bin Haritha and myself, till he reached the house where Hamza was. He asked the permission to enter, and he was permitted. The Prophet (ﷺ) started blaming Hamza for what he had done. Hamza was drunk and his eyes were red. He looked at the Prophet (ﷺ) then raised his eyes to look at his knees and raised his eves more to look at his face and then said, "You are not but my father's slaves." When the Prophet (ﷺ) understood that Hamza was drunk, he retreated, walking backwards went out and we left with him. (4003) □

1051. Narrated `Aisha: Fatima the daughter of the Prophet (ﷺ) sent someone to Abu Bakr (when he was a caliph), asking for her inheritance of what Allah's Messenger (ﷺ) had left of the property bestowed on him by Allah from the Fai (i.e. booty gained without fighting) in Medina, and Fadak, and what remained of the Khumus of the Khaibar booty. On that, Abu Bakr said, "Allah's Messenger (ﷺ) said, "Our property is not inherited. Whatever we leave, is Sadaqa, but the family of (the Prophet) Muhammad can eat of this property.' By Allah, I will not make any change in the state of the Sadaqa of Allah's Messenger (ﷺ) and will leave it as it was during the lifetime of Allah's Messenger (ﷺ), and will dispose of it as Allah's Messenger (ﷺ) used to do." So Abu Bakr refused to give anything of that to Fatima. So she became angry with Abu Bakr and kept away from him, and did not task to him till she died. She remained alive for six months after the death of the Prophet. When she died, her husband `Ali, buried her at night without informing Abu Bakr and he said the funeral prayer by himself. When Fatima was alive, the people used to respect `Ali much, but after her death, `Ali noticed a change in the people's attitude towards him. So `Ali sought reconciliation with Abu Bakr and gave him an oath of allegiance. `Ali had not given the oath of allegiance during those months (i.e. the period between the Prophet's death and Fatima's death). `Ali sent someone to Abu Bakr saying, "Come to us, but let nobody come with you," as he disliked that `Umar should come, `Umar said (to Abu Bakr), "No, by Allah, you shall not enter upon them alone " Abu Bakr said, "What do you think they will do to me? By Allah, I will go to them' So Abu Bakr entered upon them, and then `Ali uttered Tashah-hud and said (to Abu Bakr), "We know well your superiority and what Allah has given you, and we are not jealous of the good what Allah has bestowed upon you, but you did not consult us in the question of the rule and we thought that we have got a right in it because of our near relationship to Allah's Messenger (ﷺ) ." Thereupon Abu Bakr's eyes flowed with tears. And when Abu Bakr spoke, he said, "By Him in Whose Hand my soul is to keep good relations with the relatives of Allah's Messenger (ﷺ) is dearer to me than to keep good relations with my own relatives. But as for the trouble which arose between me and you about his property, I will do my best to spend it according to what is good, and will not leave any rule or regulation which I saw Allah's Messenger (ﷺ) following, in disposing of it, but I will follow." On that `Ali said to Abu Bakr, "I promise to give you the oath of allegiance in this after noon." So when Abu Bakr had offered the Zuhr prayer, he ascended the pulpit and uttered the Tashah-hud and then mentioned the story of `Ali and his failure to give the oath of allegiance, and excused him, accepting what excuses he had offered; Then `Ali (got up) and praying (to Allah) for forgiveness, he uttered Tashah-hud, praised Abu Bakr's right, and said, that he had not done what he had done because of jealousy of Abu Bakr or as a protest of that Allah had favored him with. `Ali added, "But we used to consider that we too had some right in this affair (of rulership) and that he (i.e. Abu Bakr) did not consult us in this matter, and therefore caused us to feel sorry." On that all the Muslims became happy and said, "You have done the right thing." The Muslims then became friendly with `Ali as he returned to what the people had done (i.e. giving the oath of allegiance to Abu Bakr). (4240) □

1052. Narrated Malik bin Aus: While I was at home, the sun rose high and it got hot. Suddenly the messenger of `Umar bin Al-Khattab came to me and said, "The chief of the believers has sent for you." So, I went along with him till I entered the place where `Umar was sitting on a bedstead made of date-palm leaves and covered with no mattress, and he was leaning over a leather pillow. I greeted him and sat down. He said, "O Mali! Some persons of your people who have families came to me and I have ordered that a gift should be given to them, so take it and distribute it among them." I said, "O chief of the believers! I wish that you order someone else to do it." He said, "O man! Take it." While I was sitting there with him, his doorman Yarfa' came saying, "`Uthman, `Abdur-Rahman bin `Auf, Az-Zubair and Sa`d bin Abi Waqqas are asking your permission (to see you); may I admit them?" `Umar said, "Yes", so they were admitted and they came in, greeted him, and sat down. After a while Yarfa' came again and said, "May I admit `Ali and `Abbas?" `Umar said, "Yes." So, they were admitted and they came in and greeted (him) and sat down. Then `Abbas said, "O chief of the believers! Judge between me and this (i.e. `Ali)." They had a dispute regarding the property of Bani An-Nadir which Allah had given to His Apostle as Fai. The group (i.e. `Uthman and his companions) said, "O chief of the believers! Judge between them and relieve both of them front each other." `Umar said, "Be patient! I beseech you by Allah by Whose Permission the Heaven and the Earth exist, do you know that Allah's Messenger (ﷺ) said, 'Our (i.e. prophets') property will not be inherited, and whatever we leave, is Sadaqa (to be used for charity),' and Allah's

Messenger (ﷺ) meant himself (by saying "we")?" The group said, "He said so." `Umar then turned to `Ali and `Abbas and said, "I beseech you by Allah, do you know that Allah's Messenger (ﷺ) said so?" They replied, "He said so." `Umar then said, "So, I will talk to you about this matter. Allah bestowed on His Apostle with a special favor of something of this Fai (booty) which he gave to nobody else." `Umar then recited the Holy Verses: "What Allah bestowed as (Fai) Booty on his Apostle (Muhammad) from them --- for this you made no expedition with either cavalry or camelry: But Allah gives power to His Apostles over whomever He will 'And Allah is able to do all things." 9:6) `Umar added "So this property was especially given to Allah's Messenger (ﷺ), but, by Allah, neither did he take possession of it and leave your, nor did he favor himself with it to your exclusion, but he gave it to all of you and distributed it amongst you till this property remained out of it. Allah's Messenger (ﷺ) used to spend the yearly expenses of his family out of this property and used to keep the rest of its revenue to be spent on Allah's Cause. Allah's Apostle kept on doing this during all his lifetime. I ask you by Allah do you know this?" They replies in the affirmative. `Umar then said to `Ali and `Abbas. "I ask you by Allah, do you know this?" `Umar added, "When Allah had taken His Prophet unto Him, 'Abu Bakr said, 'I am the successor of Allah's Messenger (ﷺ) so, Abu Bakr took over that property and managed it in the same way as Allah's Messenger (ﷺ) used to do, and Allah knows that he was true, pious and rightlyguided, and he was a follower of what was right. Then Allah took Abu Bakr unto Him and I became Abu Bakr's successor, and I kept that property in my possession for the first two years of my Caliphate, managing it in the same way as Allah's Messenger (ﷺ) used to do and as Abu Bakr used to do, and Allah knows that I have been true, pious, rightly guided, and a follower of what is right. Now you both (i.e. 'Ah and `Abbas) came to talk to me, bearing the same claim and presenting the same case; you, `Abbas, came to me asking for your share from your nephew's property, and this man, i.e. `Ali, came to me asking for his wife's share from her father's property. I told you both that Allah's Messenger (ﷺ) said, 'Our (prophets') properties are not to be inherited, but what we leave is Sadaqa (to be used for charity).' When I thought it right that I should hand over this property to you, I said to you, 'I am ready to hand over this property to you if you wish, on the condition that you would take Allah's Pledge and Convention that you would manage it in the same way as Allah's Messenger (ﷺ) used to, and as Abu Bakr used to do, and as I have done since I was in charge of it.' So, both of you said (to me), 'Hand it over to us,' and on that condition I handed it over to you. So, I ask you by Allah, did I hand it over to them on this condition?" The group aid, "Yes." Then `Umar faced `Ali and `Abbas saying, "I ask you by Allah, did I hand it over to you on this condition?" They said, "Yes." He said, "Do you want now to give a different decision? By Allah, by Whose Leave both the Heaven and the Earth exist, I will never give any decision other than that (I have already given). And if you are unable to manage it, then return it to me, and I will do the job on your behalf." (3094) □

1053. Abu Bakr said to her, "Allah's Apostle said, 'our property will not be inherited, whatever we (i.e. prophets) leave is Sadaqa (to be used for charity)." Fatima, the daughter of Allah's Messenger (ﷺ) got angry and stopped speaking to Abu Bakr, and continued assuming that attitude till she died. Fatima remained alive for six months after the death of Allah's Messenger (ﷺ). She used to ask Abu Bakr for her share from the property of Allah's Messenger (ﷺ) which he left at Khaibar, and Fadak, and his property at Medina (devoted for charity). Abu Bakr refused to give her that property and said, "I will not leave anything Allah's Messenger (ﷺ) used to do, because I am afraid that if I left something from the Prophet's tradition, then I would go astray." (Later on) `Umar gave the Prophet's property (of Sadaqa) at Medina to `Ali and `Abbas, but he withheld the properties of Khaibar and Fadak in his custody and said, "These two properties are the Sadaqa which Allah's Apostle used to use for his expenditures and urgent needs. Now their management is to be entrusted to the ruler." (Az-Zuhri said, "They have been managed in this way till today.") (3093) □

1054. The sub-narrator said, "I told `Urwa bin Az-Zubair of this Hadith and he said, 'Malik bin Aus has told the truth" I heard `Aisha, the wife of the Prophet (ﷺ) saying, 'The wives of the Prophet (ﷺ) sent `Uthman to Abu Bakr demanding from him their 1/8 of the Fai which Allah had granted to his Apostle. But I used to oppose them and say to them: Will you not fear Allah? Don't you know that the Prophet used to say: Our property is not inherited, but whatever we leave is to be given in charity? The Prophet (ﷺ) mentioned that regarding himself. He added: 'The family of Muhammad can take their sustenance from this property. So the wives of the Prophet (ﷺ) stopped demanding it when I told them of that.' So, this property (of Sadaqa) was in the hands of ʾAli who withheld it from ʾAbbas and overpowered him. Then it came in the hands of Hasan bin ʾAli, then in the hands of Husain bin ʾAli, and then in the hands of ʾAli bin Husain and Hasan bin Hasan, and each of the last two used to manage it in turn, then it came in the hands of Zaid bin Hasan, and it was truly the Sadaqa of Allah's Apostle. (4034) ☐

1055. Narrated Abu Huraira: Allah's Messenger (ﷺ) said, "My heirs should not take even a single Dinar (i.e. anything from my property), and whatever I leave, excluding the expenditure of my wives and my laborers, will be Sadaqa (i.e. be used for charity)." (3096) ☐

1056. Narrated ʾAmr bin Al-Harith: The Prophet (ﷺ) did not leave anything (after his death) except his arms, a white mule, and a (piece of) land which he had given as Sadaqa. (3098)

1057. Narrated Khaula Al-Ansariya: I heard Allah's Messenger (ﷺ) saying, "Some people spend Allah's Wealth (i.e. Muslim's wealth) in an unjust manner; such people will be put in the (Hell) Fire on the Day of Resurrection." (3118) ☐

1058. Narrated Abu Huraira: Allah's Messenger (ﷺ) said, "When Khosrau is ruined, there will be no Khosrau after him; and when Caesar is ruined, there will be no Caesar after him. By Him in Whose Hands my life is, you will spend their treasures in Allah's Cause." (3120) ☐

1059. Narrated Abu Huraira: Allah's Messenger (ﷺ) said, "Allah guarantees him who strives in His Cause and whose motivation for going out is nothing but Jihad in His Cause and belief in His Word, that He will admit him into Paradise (if martyred) or bring him back to his dwelling place, where he has come out, with what he gains of reward and booty." (3123) ☐

1060. Narrated Abu Huraira: The Prophet (ﷺ) said, "A prophet amongst the prophets carried out a holy military expedition, so he said to his followers, 'Anyone who has married a woman and wants to consummate the marriage, and has not done so yet, should not accompany me; nor should a man who has built a house but has not completed its roof; nor a man who has sheep or she-camels and is waiting for the birth of their young ones.' So, the prophet carried out the expedition and when he reached that town at the time or nearly at the time of the `Asr prayer, he said to the sun, 'O sun! You are under Allah's Order and I am under Allah's Order O Allah! Stop it (i.e. the sun) from setting.' It was stopped till Allah made him victorious. Then he collected the booty and the fire came to burn it, but it did not burn it. He said (to his men), 'Some of you have stolen something from the booty. So one man from every tribe should give me a pledge of allegiance by shaking hands with me.' (They did so and) the hand of a man got stuck over the hand of their prophet. Then that prophet said (to the man), 'The theft has been committed by your people. So all the persons of your tribe should give me the pledge of allegiance by shaking hands with me.' The hands of two or three men got stuck over the hand of their prophet and he said, "you have committed the theft.' Then they brought a head of gold like the head of a cow and put it there, and the fire came and consumed the booty. The Prophet (ﷺ) added: Then Allah saw our weakness and disability, so he made booty legal for us." (3124) ☐

1061. Narrated `Abdullah bin Az-Zubair: When Az-Zubair got up during the battle of Al-Jamal, he called me and I stood up beside him, and he said to me, "O my son! Today one will be killed either as an oppressor or as an oppressed one. I see that I will be killed as an oppressed one. My biggest worry is my debts. Do you think, if we pay the debts, there will be something left for us from our money?" Az-Zubair added, "O my son! Sell our property and pay my debts." Az-Zubair then willed one-third of his property and willed one-third of that portion to his sons; namely, `Abdullah's sons. He said, "One-third of the one third. If any property is left after the payment of the debts, one-third (of the one-third of what is left) is to be given to your sons." (Hisham, a sub-narrator added, "Some of the sons of `Abdullah were equal in age to the sons of Az-Zubair e.g. Khubaib and `Abbas. `Abdullah had nine sons and nine daughters at that time." (The narrator `Abdullah added :) My father (Az-Zubair) went on drawing my attention to his debts saying, "If you should fail to pay part of the debts, appeal to my Master to help you." By Allah! I could not understand what he meant till I asked, "O father! Who is your Master?" He replied, "Allah (is my Master)." By Allah, whenever I had any difficulty regarding his debts, I would say, "Master of Az-Zubair! Pay his debts on his behalf." and Allah would (help me to) pay it. Az-Zubair was martyred leaving no Dinar or Dirham but two pieces of land, one of which was (called) Al-Ghaba, and eleven houses in Medina, two in Basra, one in Kufa and one in Egypt. In fact, the source of the debt which he owed was, that if somebody brought some money to deposit with him. Az-Zubair would say, "No, (i won't keep it as a trust), but I take it as a debt, for I am afraid it might be lost." Az-Zubair was never appointed governor or collector of the tax of Kharaj or any other similar thing, but he collected his wealth (from the war booty he gained) during the holy battles he took part in, in the company of the Prophet, Abu Bakr, `Umar, and `Uthman. (`Abdullah bin Az-Zubair added :) When I counted his debt, it turned to be two million and two hundred thousand. (The sub-narrator added :) Hakim bin Hizam met `Abdullah bin Zubair and asked, "O my nephew! How much is the debt of my brother?" `Abdullah kept it as a secret and said, "One hundred thousand," Hakim said, "By Allah! I don't think your property will cover it." On that `Abdullah said to him, "What if it is two million and two hundred thousand?" Hakim said, "I don't think you can pay it; so if you are unable to pay all of it, I will help you." Az- Zubair had already bought Al-Ghaba for one hundred and seventy thousand. `Abdullah sold it for one million and six hundred thousand. Then he called the people saying, "Any person who has any money claim on Az-Zubair should come to us in Al-Ghaba." There came to him `Abdullah bin Ja`far whom Az-Zubair owed four hundred thousand. He said to `Abdullah bin Az-Zubair, "If you wish I will forgive you the debt." `Abdullah (bin Az-Zubair) said, "No." Then Ibn Ja`far said, "If you wish you can defer the payment if you should defer the payment of any debt." Ibn Az-Zubair said, "No." `Abdullah bin Ja`far said, "Give me a piece of the land." `Abdullah bin AzZubair said (to him), "Yours is the land extending from this place to this place." So, `Abdullah bin Az-Zubair sold some of the property (including the houses) and paid his debt perfectly, retaining four and a half shares from the land (i.e. Al-Ghaba). He then went to Mu'awlya while `Amr bin `Uthman, Al-Mundhir bin Az- Zubair and Ibn Zam`a were sitting with him. Mu'awiya asked, "At what price have you appraised Al-Ghaba?" He said, "One hundred thousand for each share," Muawiya asked, "How many shares have been left?" `Abdullah replied, "Four and a half shares." Al-Mundhir bin Az-Zubair said, "I would like to buy one share for one hundred thousand." `Amr bin `Uthman said, "I would like to buy one share for one hundred thousand." Ibn Zam`a said, "I would like to buy one share for one hundred thousand." Muawiya said, "How much is left now?" `Abdullah replied, "One share and a half." Muawiya said, "I would like to buy it for one hundred and fifty thousand." `Abdullah also sold his part to Muawiya six hundred thousand. When Ibn AzZubair had paid all the debts. Az-Zubair's sons said to him, "Distribute our inheritance among us." He said, "No, by Allah, I will not distribute it among you till I announce in four successive Hajj seasons, 'Would those who have money claims on Az-Zubair come so that we may pay them their debt." So, he started to announce that in public in every Hajj season, and when four years had elapsed, he distributed the inheritance among the inheritors. Az-Zubair had four wives, and after the one-third of his property was excluded (according to the will), each of his wives received one million and two hundred thousand. So the total amount of his property was fifty million and two hundred thousand. (3129) □

1062. Narrated Ibn `Umar: `Uthman did not join the Badr battle because he was married to one of the daughters of Allah's Apostle and she was ill. So, the Prophet (ﷺ) said to him. "You will get a reward and a share (from the war booty) similar to the reward and the share of one who has taken part in the Badr battle." (3130) □

1063. Narrated Marwan bin Al-Hakim and Miswar bin Makhrama: When the

Hawazin delegation came to Allah's Messenger (ﷺ) after they had embraced Islam and requested him to return their properties and war prisoners to them, Allah's Messenger (ﷺ) said, "To me the best talk is the truest, so you may choose either of two things; the war prisoners or the wealth, for I have delayed their distribution." Allah's Messenger (ﷺ) had waited for them for over ten days when he returned from Ta'if. So, when those people came to know that Allah's Messenger (ﷺ) was not going to return to them except one of the two things the said, "We choose our war Prisoners 'Allah's Messenger (ﷺ) stood up amongst the Muslims, and after glorifying Allah as He deserved, he said, "Now then, these brothers of yours have come to us with repentance, and I see it logical that I should return their captives to them, so whoever of you likes to do that as a favor then he can do it, and whoever amongst you likes to stick to his share, let him give up his prisoners and we will compensate him from the very first Fai' (i.e. war booty received without fight) which Allah will give us." On that, all the people said. 'O Allah's Messenger (ﷺ) We have agreed willingly to do so (return the captives)" Then Allah's Messenger (ﷺ) said to them "I do not know who amongst you has agreed to this and who has not. You should return and let your leaders inform me of your agreement." The people returned and their leaders spoke to them, and then came to Allah's Apostle and said, "All the people have agreed willingly to do so and have given the permission to return the war prisoners (without Compensation)" (Az-Zuhri, the sub-narrator states) this is what has been related to us about the captives of Hawazin. (3131) ☐

1064. Narrated Nafi` from Ibn `Umar: Allah's Messenger (ﷺ) sent a Sariya (an expedition that the Prophet (s) ordered but didn't personally participate in it) towards Najd, and `Abdullah bin `Umar was in the Sariya. They gained a great number of camels as war booty. The share of each one of them was twelve or eleven camels, and they were given an extra camel each. (3134) ☐

1065. Narrated Ibn `Umar: Allah's Messenger (ﷺ) used to give extra share to some of the members of the Sariya he used to send, in addition to the shares they shared with the army in general. (3135) ☐

1066. Narrated Abu Musa: We got the news of the migration of the Prophet (ﷺ) while we were in Yemen, so we set out migrating to him. We were, I and my two brothers, I being the youngest, and one of my brothers was Abu Burda and the other was Abu Ruhm. We were over fifty (or fifty-three or fifty two) men from our people. We got on board a ship which took us to An-Najashi in Ethiopia, and there we found Ja`far bin Abu Talib and his companions with An-Najaishi. Ja`far said (to us), "Allah's Messenger (ﷺ) has sent us here and ordered us to stay here, so you too, stay with us." We stayed with him till we all left (Ethiopia) and met the Prophet (ﷺ) at the time when he had conquered Khaibar. He gave us a share from its booty (or gave us from its booty). He gave only to those who had taken part in the Ghazwa with him. But he did not give any share to any person who had not participated in Khaibar's conquest except the people of our ship, besides Ja`far and his companions, whom he gave a share as he did them (i.e. the people of the ship). (3136) □

1067. Narrated Abu Musa: The news of the migration of the Prophet (from Mecca to Medina) reached us while we were in Yemen. So we set out as emigrants towards him. We were (three) I and my two brothers. I was the youngest of them, and one of the two was Abu Burda, and the other, Abu Ruhm, and our total number was either 53 or 52 men from my people. We got on board a boat and our boat took us to Negus in Ethiopia. There we met Ja`far bin Abi Talib and stayed with him. Then we all came (to Medina) and met the Prophet (ﷺ) at the time of the conquest of Khaibar. Some of the people used to say to us, namely the people of the ship, "We have migrated before you." Asma' bint 'Umais who was one of those who had come with us, came as a visitor to Hafsa, the wife the Prophet (ﷺ). She had migrated along with those other Muslims who migrated to Negus. `Umar came to Hafsa while Asma' bint 'Umais was with her. `Umar, on seeing Asma,' said, "Who is this?" She said, "Asma' bint 'Umais," `Umar said, "Is she the Ethiopian? Is she the sea-faring lady?" Asma' replied, "Yes." `Umar said, "We have migrated before you (people of the boat), so we have got more right than you over Allah's Messenger (ﷺ) " On that Asma' became angry and said, "No, by Allah, while you were with Allah's Messenger (ﷺ) who was feeding the hungry ones amongst you, and advised the ignorant ones amongst you, we were in the far-off hated land of Ethiopia, and all that was for the sake of Allah's Messenger (ﷺ) . By Allah, I will neither eat any food nor drink anything till I inform Allah's Messenger (ﷺ) of all that you have said. There we were harmed and frightened. I will mention this to the Prophet (ﷺ) and will not tell a lie or curtail your saying or add something to it." (4230) ☐

1068. So when the Prophet (ﷺ) came, she said, "O Allah's Prophet `Umar has said so-and-so." He said (to Asma'), "What did you say to him?" Asma's aid, "I told him so-and-so." The Prophet (ﷺ) said, "He (i.e. `Umar) has not got more right than you people over me, as he and his companions have (the reward of) only one migration, and you, the people of the boat, have (the reward of) two migrations." Asma' later on said, "I saw Abu Musa and the other people of the boat coming to me in successive groups, asking me about this narration,, and to them nothing in the world was more cheerful and greater than what the Prophet (ﷺ) had said about them." Narrated Abu Burda: Asma' said, "I saw Abu Musa requesting me to repeat this narration again and again." (4231) ☐

1069. Narrated Abu Burda: Abu Musa said, "The Prophet (ﷺ) said, "I recognize the voice of the group of Al- Ashariyun, when they recite the Qur'an, when they enter their homes at night, and I recognize their houses by (listening) to their voices when they are reciting the Qur'an at night although I have not seen their houses when they came to them during the day time. Amongst them is Hakim who, on meeting the cavalry or the enemy, used to say to them (i.e. the enemy). My companions order you to wait for them.'" (4232) ☐

1070. Narrated `Umar bin Al-Khattab: By Him in Whose Hand my soul is, were I not afraid that the other Muslims might be left in poverty, I would divide (the land of) whatever village I may conquer (among the fighters), as the Prophet (ﷺ) divided the land of Khaibar. But I prefer to leave it as a (source of) a common treasury for them to distribute it revenue amongst themselves. (4235) ☐

1071. Narrated Abu Huraira: Allah's Messenger (ﷺ) sent Aban from Medina to Najd as the commander of a Sariya. Aban and his companions came to the Prophet (ﷺ) at Khaibar after the Prophet (ﷺ) had conquered it, and the reins of their horses were made of the fire of date palm trees. I said, "O Allah's Messenger (ﷺ)! Do not give them a share of the booty." on, that, Aban said (to me), "Strange! You suggest such a thing though you are what you are, O guinea pig coming down from the top of Ad-Dal (a lotus tree)! "On that the Prophet said, "O Aban, sit down!" and did not give them any share. (4238) □

1072. Narrated Abu Huraira: The Prophet (ﷺ) got up amongst us and mentioned Al Ghulul (Stealing from out of booty), emphasized its magnitude and declared that it was a great sin saying, "Don't commit Ghulul for I should not like to see anyone amongst you on the Day of Ressurection, carrying over his neck a sheep that will be bleating, or carrying over his neck a horse that will be neighing. Such a man will be saying: 'O Allah's Messenger (ﷺ)! Intercede with Allah for me,' and I will reply, 'I can't help you, for I have conveyed Allah's Message to you nor should I like to see a man carrying over his neck, a camel that will be grunting. Such a man will say, 'O Allah's Apostle! Intercede with Allah for me, and I will say, 'I can't help you for I have conveyed Allah's Message to you,' or one carrying over his neck gold and silver and saying, 'O Allah's Messenger (ﷺ)! Intercede with Allah for me,' and I will say, 'I can't help you for I have conveyed Allah's Message to you,' or one carrying clothes that will be fluttering, and the man will say, 'O Allah's Messenger (ﷺ)! Intercede with Allah for me.' And I will say, 'I can't help you, for I have conveyed Allah's Message to you." (3073) □

1073. Narrated `Abdullah bin `Amr: There was a man who looked after the family and the belongings of the Prophet (ﷺ) and he was called Karkara. The man died and Allah's Messenger (ﷺ) said, "He is in the Fire." The people then went to look at him and found in his place, a cloak he had stolen from the war booty. (3074) □

1074. Narrated Abu Huraira: When we conquered Khaibar, we gained neither gold nor silver as booty, but we gained cows, camels, goods and gardens. Then we departed with Allah's Messenger (ﷺ) to the valley of Al-Qira, and at that time Allah's

Messenger (ﷺ) had a slave called Mid`am who had been presented to him by one of Banu Ad-Dibbab. While the slave was dismounting the saddle of Allah's Messenger (ﷺ) an arrow the thrower of which was unknown, came and hit him. The people said, "Congratulations to him for the martyrdom." Allah's Apostle said, "No, by Him in Whose Hand my soul is, the sheet (of cloth) which he had taken (illegally) on the day of Khaibar from the booty before the distribution of the booty, has become a flame of Fire burning him." On hearing that, a man brought one or two leather straps of shoes to the Prophet and said, "These are things I took (illegally)." On that Allah's Messenger (ﷺ) said, "This is a strap, or these are two straps of Fire." (4234) □

1075. Narrated Jabir: Allah's Messenger (ﷺ) said (to me), "If the property of Bahrain had come to us, I would have given you so much and so much." But the Bahrain property did not come till the Prophet (ﷺ) had died. When the Bahrain property came. Abu Bakr ordered somebody to announce, "Any person who has money claim on Allah's Messenger (ﷺ) or whom Allah's Messenger (ﷺ) had promised something, should come to us." So, I went to him and said, "Allah's Messenger (ﷺ) had promised to give me so much and so much." Abu Bakr scooped up money with both hands thrice for me." (The sub-narrator Sufyan illustrated this action by scooping up with both hands and said, "Ibn Munkadir, another sub-narrator, used to illustrate it in this way.") Narrated Jabir: Once I went to Abu Bakr and asked for the money but he did not give me, and I went to him again, but he did not give me, so I went to him for the third time and said, "I asked you, but you did not give me; then I asked you (for the second time) and you did not give me; then I asked you (for the third time) but you did not give me. You should either give me or allow yourself to be considered a miser regarding my case." Abu Bakr said, "You tell me that I am a miser with regard to you. But really, whenever I rejected your request, I had the inclination to give you." (In another narration Jabir added :) So, Abu Bakr scooped up money with both hands for me and asked me to count it. I found out that it was five hundred. Abu Bakr told me to take twice that amount. (3137) □

1076. Narrated Jabir bin `Abdullah: While Allah's Messenger (ﷺ) was distributing the booty at Al-Ja'rana, somebody said to him "Be just (in your distribution)." The Prophet (ﷺ) replied, "Verily I would be miserable if I did not act justly." (3138) □

1077. Narrated Jubair bin Mut'im: The Prophet (ﷺ) talked about war prisoners of Badr saying, "Had Al-Mut'im bin Adi been alive and interceded with me for these mean people, I would have freed them for his sake." (3139) □

1078. Narrated Jubair bin Mut'im: I and `Uthman bin `Affan went to Allah's Messenger (ﷺ) and said, "O Allah's Messenger (ﷺ)! You have given to Bani Al-Muttalib and left us although they and we are of the same kinship to you." Allah's Messenger (ﷺ) said, "Bani Muttalib and Bani Hashim are one and the same." The Prophet (ﷺ) did not give a share to Bani `Abd Shams and Bani Naufai. (Ibn 'Is-haq said, "Abd Shams and Hashim and Al-Muttalib were maternal brothers and their mother was 'Atika bint Murra and Naufal was their paternal brother.) (3140) □

1079. Narrated Abu Qatada: We set out in the company of Allah's Messenger (ﷺ) on the day (of the battle) of Hunain. When we faced the enemy, the Muslims retreated and I saw a pagan throwing himself over a Muslim. I turned around and came upon him from behind and hit him on the shoulder with the sword He (i.e. the pagan) came towards me and seized me so violently that I felt as if it were death itself, but death overtook him and he released me. I followed `Umar bin Al Khattab and asked (him), "What is wrong with the people (fleeing)?" He replied, "This is the Will of Allah," After the people returned, the Prophet (ﷺ) sat and said, "Anyone who has killed an enemy and has a proof of that, will posses his spoils." I got up and said, "Who will be a witness for me?" and then sat down. The Prophet (ﷺ) again said, "Anyone who has killed an enemy and has proof of that, will possess his spoils." I (again) got up and said, "Who will be a witness for me?" and sat down. Then the Prophet (ﷺ) said the same for the third time. I again got up, and Allah's Messenger (ﷺ) said, "O Abu Qatada! What is your story?" Then I narrated the whole story to him. A man (got up and) said, "O Allah's Messenger (ﷺ)! He is speaking the truth, and the spoils of the killed man are with me. So please compensate him on my behalf." On that Abu Bakr As-Siddiq said, "No, by Allah, he (i.e. Allah's Messenger (ﷺ)) will not agree to give you the spoils gained by one of Allah's Lions who fights on the behalf of Allah and His Apostle." The Prophet (ﷺ) said, "Abu Bakr has spoken the truth." So, Allah's Messenger (ﷺ) gave the spoils to me. I sold that armor (i.e. the spoils) and with its price I bought a garden at Bani Salima, and this was my first property which I gained after my conversion to Islam. (3142) □

1080. Narrated Nafi`:`Umar bin Al-Khattab said, "O Allah's Messenger (ﷺ)! I vowed to observe I`tikaf for one day during the PreIslamic period." The Prophet (ﷺ) ordered him to fulfill his vow. `Umar gained two lady captives from the war prisoners of Hunain and he left them in some of the houses at Mecca. When Allah's Messenger (ﷺ) freed the captives of Hunain without ransom, they came out walking in the streets. `Umar said (to his son), "O `Abdullah! See what is the matter." `Abdullah replied, "Allah's Messenger (ﷺ) has freed the captives without ransom." He said (to him), "Go and set free those two slave girls." (Nafi` added :) Allah's Apostle did not perform the `Umra from Al-Jarana, and if he had performed the `Umra, it would not have been hidden from `Abdullah. (3144) □

1081. Narrated `Amr bin Taghlib: Allah's Messenger (ﷺ) gave (gifts) to some people to the exclusion of some others. The latter seemed to be displeased by that. The Prophet (ﷺ) said, "I give to some people, lest they should deviate from True Faith or lose patience, while I refer other people to the goodness and contentment which Allah has put in their hearts, and `Amr bin Taghlib is amongst them." `Amr bin Taghlib said, "The statement of Allah's Apostle is dearer to me than red camels." Narrated Al-Hasan: `Amr bin Taghlib told us that Allah's Messenger (ﷺ) got some property or some war prisoners and he distributed them in the above way (i.e. giving to some people to the exclusion of others). (3145) □

1082. Narrated Anas: The Prophet (ﷺ) said, "I give to Quraish people in order to let them adhere to Islam, for they are near to their life of Ignorance (i.e. they have newly embraced Islam and it is still not strong in their hearts." (3146) □

1083. Narrated Anas bin Malik: When Allah favored His Apostle with the properties of Hawazin tribe as Fai (booty), he started giving to some Quarries men even up to one-hundred camels each, whereupon some Ansari men said about Allah's Messenger (ﷺ), "May Allah forgive His Apostle! He is giving to (men of) Quraish and leaves us, in spite of the fact that our swords are still dropping blood (of the infidels)" When Allah's Messenger (ﷺ) was informed of what they had said, he called the Ansar and gathered them in a leather tent and did not call anybody else along, with them. When they gathered, Allah's Messenger (ﷺ) came to them and said, "What is the statement which, I have been informed, and that which you have said?" The learned ones among them replied," O Allah's Messenger (ﷺ)! The wise ones amongst us did not say anything, but the youngsters amongst us said, 'May Allah forgive His Apostle; he gives the Quarish and leaves the Ansar, in spite of the fact that our swords are still dribbling (wet) with the blood of the infidels.' "Allah's Messenger (ﷺ) replied, I give to such people as are still close to the period of Infidelity (i.e. they have recently embraced Islam and Faith is still weak in their hearts). Won't you be pleased to see people go with fortune, while you return with Allah's Messenger (ﷺ) to your houses? By Allah, what you will return with, is better than what they are returning with." The Ansar replied, "Yes, O Allah's Messenger (ﷺ), we are satisfied' Then the Prophet (ﷺ) said to them." You will find after me, others being preferred to you. Then be patient till you meet Allah and meet His Apostle at Al-Kauthar (i.e. a fount in Paradise)." (Anas added :) But we did not remain patient. (3147) □

1084. Narrated Abu Sa`id Al-Khudri:`Ali bin Abi Talib sent a piece of gold not yet taken out of its ore, in a tanned leather container to Allah's Messenger (ﷺ) . Allah's Messenger (ﷺ) distributed that amongst four Persons: 'Uyaina bin Badr, Aqra bin H`Abis, Zaid Al-Khail and the fourth was either Alqama or Amir bin at-Tufail. On that, one of his companions said, "We are more deserving of this (gold) than these (persons)." When that news reached the Prophet (ﷺ), he said, "Don't you trust me though I am the truth worthy man of the One in the Heavens, and I receive the news of Heaven (i.e. Divine Inspiration) both in the morning and in the evening?" There got up a man with sunken eyes, raised cheek bones, raised forehead, a thick beard, a shaven head and a waist sheet that was tucked up and he said, "O Allah's Messenger

(🕮)! Be afraid of Allah." The Prophet (🕮) said, "Woe to you! Am I not of all the people of the earth the most entitled to fear Allah?" Then that man went away. Khalid bin Al-Wahd said, "O Allah's Messenger (🕮)! Shall I chop his neck off?" The Prophet (🕮) said, "No, for he may offer prayers." Khalid said, "Numerous are those who offer prayers and say by their tongues (i.e. mouths) what is not in their hearts." Allah's Messenger (🕮) said, "I have not been ordered (by Allah) to search the hearts of the people or cut open their bellies." Then the Prophet looked at him (i.e. that man) while the latter was going away and said, "From the offspring of this (man there will come out (people) who will recite the Qur'an continuously and elegantly but it will not exceed their throats. (They will neither understand it nor act upon it). They would go out of the religion (i.e. Islam) as an arrow goes through a game's body." I think he also said, "If I should be present at their time I would kill them as the nations a Thamud were killed." (4351) □

1085. Narrated Jubair bin Mut`im: That while he was with Allah's Messenger (🕮) who was accompanied by the people on their way back from Hunain, the bedouins started begging things of Allah's Messenger (🕮) so much so that they forced him to go under a Samura tree where his loose outer garment was snatched away. On that, Allah's Messenger (🕮) stood up and said to them, "Return my garment to me. If I had as many camels as these trees, I would have distributed them amongst you; and you will not find me a miser or a liar or a coward." (3148) □

1086. Narrated Anas bin Malik: While I was walking with the Prophet (🕮) who was wearing a Najrani outer garment with a thick hem, a bedouin came upon the Prophet (🕮) and pulled his garment so violently that I could recognize the impress of the hem of the garment on his shoulder, caused by the violence of his pull. Then the bedouin said, "Order for me something from Allah's Fortune which you have." The Prophet (🕮) turned to him and smiled, and ordered that a gift be given to him. (3149) □

1087. Narrated `Abdullah: On the day (of the battle) of Hunain, Allah's Messenger (🕮) favored some people in the distribution of the booty (to the exclusion of others); he gave Al-Aqra' bin H`Abis one-hundred camels and he gave 'Uyaina the same amount, and also gave to some of the eminent Arabs, giving them preference in this regard. Then a person came and said, "By Allah, in this distribution justice has not been observed, nor has Allah's Pleasure been aimed at." I said (to him), "By Allah, I will inform the Prophet (of what you have said), "I went and informed him, and he said, "If Allah and His Apostle did not act justly, who else would act justly. May Allah be merciful to Moses, for he was harmed with more than this, yet he kept patient." (3150) □

1088. Narrated Ibn `Umar: In our holy battles, we used to get honey and grapes, as war booty which we would eat and would not store. (3154) □

1089. Narrated Aslam: Once I went with `Umar bin Al-Khattab to the market. A young woman followed `Umar and said, "O chief of the believers! My husband has died, leaving little children. By Allah, they have not even a sheep's trotter to cook; they have no farms or animals. I am afraid that they may die because of hunger, and I am the daughter of Khufaf bin Ima Al-Ghafari, and my father witnessed the Pledge of allegiance) of Al-Hudaibiya with the Prophet.' `Umar stopped and did not proceed, and said, "I welcome my near relative." Then he went towards a strong camel which was tied in the house, and carried on to it, two sacks he had loaded with food grains and put between them money and clothes and gave her its rope to hold and said, "Lead it, and this provision will not finish till Allah gives you a good supply." A man said, "O chief of the believers! You have given her too much." "`Umar said disapprovingly. "May your mother be bereaved of you! By Allah, I have seen her father and brother besieging a fort for a long time and conquering it, and then we were discussing what their shares they would have from that war booty." (4160) □

1090. Narrated Ibn `Umar: On the day of Khaibar, Allah's Messenger (ﷺ) divided (the war booty of Khaibar) with the ratio of two shares for the horse and one-share for the foot soldier. (The sub-narrator, Nafi` explained this, saying, "If a man had a horse, he was given three shares and if he had no horse, then he was given one share.") (4228) □

50. JIZYAH AND MAWAADA'AH

1091. NARRATED `AMR BIN DINAR (RA): I was sitting with Jabir bin Zaid and `Amr bin Aus, and Bjalla was narrating to them in 70 A.H. the year when Mus`ab bin Az-Zubair was the leader of the pilgrims of Basra. We were sitting at the steps of Zamzam well and Bajala said, "I was the clerk of Juz bin Muawiya, Al-Ahnaf's paternal uncle. A letter came from `Umar bin Al-Khattab one year before his death; and it was read: -- "Cancel every marriage contracted among the Magians between relatives of close kinship (marriages that are regarded illegal in Islam: a relative of this sort being called Dhu-Mahram.)" `Umar did not take the Jizya from the Magian infidels till `Abdur-Rahman bin `Auf testified that Allah's Messenger (ﷺ) had taken the Jizya from the Magians of Hajar. (3156) □

1092. Narrated `Amr bin `Auf Al-Ansari: (who was an ally of Bam `Amr bin Lu'ai and one of those who had taken part in (the Ghazwa of) Badr): Allah's Messenger (ﷺ) sent Abu 'Ubaida bin Al-Jarreh to Bahrain to collect the Jizya. Allah's Messenger (ﷺ) had established peace with the people of Bahrain and appointed Al-`Ala' bin Al-Hadrami as their governor. When Abu 'Ubaida came from Bahrain with the money, the Ansar heard of Abu 'Ubaida's arrival which coincided with the time of the Morning Prayer with the Prophet. When Allah's Messenger (ﷺ) led them in the morning prayer and finished, the Ansar approached him, and he looked at them and smiled on seeing them and said, "I feel that you have heard that Abu. 'Ubaida has brought something?" They said, "Yes, O Allah's Messenger (ﷺ)' He said, "Rejoice and hope for what will please you! By Allah, I am not afraid of your poverty but I am afraid that you will lead a life of luxury as past nations did, whereupon you will compete with each other for it, as they competed for it, and it will destroy you as it destroyed them." (3158) □

1093. Narrated Jubair bin Haiya: `Umar sent the Muslims to the great countries to fight the pagans. When Al-Hurmuzan embraced Islam, `Umar said to him. "I would like to consult you regarding these countries which I intend to invade." Al-Hurmuzan said, "Yes, the example of these countries and their inhabitants who are the enemies. of the Muslims, is like a bird with a head, two wings and two legs; If one of its wings got broken, it would get up over its two legs, with one wing and the head; and if the other wing got broken, it would get up with two legs and a head, but if its head got destroyed, then the two legs, two wings and the head would become useless. The head stands for Khosrau, and one wing stands for Caesar and the other wing stands for Faris. So, order the Muslims to go towards Khosrau." So, `Umar sent us (to Khosrau) appointing An-Nu`man bin Muqrin as our commander. When we reached the land of the enemy, the representative of Khosrau came out with forty-thousand warriors, and an interpreter got up saying, "Let one of you talk to me!" Al-Mughira replied, "Ask whatever you wish." The other asked, "Who are you?" Al-Mughira replied, "We are some people from the Arabs; we led a hard, miserable, disastrous life: we used to suck the hides and the date stones from hunger; we used to wear clothes made up of fur of camels and hair of goats, and to worship trees and stones. While we were in this state, the Lord of the Heavens and the Earths, Elevated is His Remembrance and Majestic is His Highness, sent to us from among ourselves a Prophet whose father and mother are known to us. Our Prophet, the Messenger of our Lord, has ordered us to fight you till you worship Allah Alone or give Jizya (i.e. tribute); and our Prophet has informed us that our Lord says: -- "Whoever amongst us is killed (i.e. martyred), shall go to Paradise to lead such a luxurious life as he has never seen, and whoever amongst us remain alive, shall become your master." (Al-Mughira, then blamed An-Nu`man for delaying the attack and) An-Nu' man said to Al-Mughira, "If you had participated in a similar battle, in the company of Allah's Messenger (ﷺ) he would not have blamed you for waiting, nor would he have disgraced you. But I accompanied Allah's Apostle in many battles and it was his custom that if he did not fight early by daytime, he would wait till the wind had started blowing and the time for the prayer was due (i.e. after midday) (3159) □

1094. Narrated Abu Humaid As-Saidi: We accompanied the Prophet (ﷺ) in the Ghazwa of Tabuk and the king of 'Aila presented a white mule and a cloak as a gift to the Prophet. And the Prophet (ﷺ) wrote to him a peace treaty allowing him to keep authority over his country. (3161) ☐

1095. Narrated Juwairiya bin Qudama at-Tamimi: We said to `Umar bin Al-Khattab, O Chief of the believers! Advise us." He said, "I advise you to fulfill Allah's Convention (made with the Dhimmis) as it is the convention of your Prophet and the source of the livelihood of your dependents (i.e. the taxes from the Dhimmis.)" (3162) ☐

1096. Narrated `Abdullah bin `Amr: The Prophet (ﷺ) said, "Whoever killed a person having a treaty with the Muslims, shall not smell the smell of Paradise though its smell is perceived from a distance of forty years." (3166) ☐

1097. Narrated Ibrahim at-Tamimi's father: `Ali delivered a sermon saying, "We have no book to read except the Book of Allah and what is written in this paper which contains verdicts regarding (retaliation for) wounds, the ages of the camels (given as Zakat) and the fact that Medina is a sanctuary in between Air mountain to so-and-so (mountain). So, whoever innovates in it a heresy or commits a sin or gives shelter in it, to such an innovator will incur the Curse of Allah, the angels and all the people, and none of his compulsory or optional good deeds of worship will be accepted. And whoever (freed slave) takes as his master (i.e. befriends) other than his real masters will incur the same (Curse). And the asylum granted by any Muslim is to be secured by all the other Muslims, and whoever betrays a Muslim in this respect will incur the same (Curse). (3172) ☐

1098. Narrated ' `Abdullah bin `Abbas: That Abu Sufyan bin Harb Informed him that Heraclius called him and the members of a caravan from Quraish who had gone to Sham as traders, during the truce which Allah's Messenger (ﷺ) had concluded with Abu Sufyan and the Quraish infidels. (3174) ☐

1099. Narrated Abu Huraira: Abu Bakr, on the day of Nahr (i.e. slaughtering of animals for sacrifice), sent me in the company of others to make this announcement: "After this year, no pagan will be allowed to perform the Hajj, and none will be allowed to perform the Tawaf of the Ka`ba undressed." And the day of Al-Hajj-ul-

Akbar is the day of Nahr, and it called Al-Akbar because the people call the `Umra Al-Hajj-ul-Asghar (i.e. the minor Hajj). Abu Bakr threw back the pagans' covenant that year, and therefore, no pagan performed the Hajj in the year of Hajj-ul-Wada` of the Prophets (s). (3177) □

1100. Narrated Sa`id:Abu Huraira once said (to the people), "What will your state be when you can get no Dinar or Dirhan (i.e. taxes from the Dhimmis)?" on that someone asked him, "What makes you know that this state will take place, O Abu-Huraira?" He said, "By Him in Whose Hands Abu Huraira's life is, I know it through the statement of the true and truly inspired one (the Prophet)." The people asked, "What does the Statement say?" He replied, "Allah and His Apostle's asylum granted to Dhimmis, (i.e. non-Muslims living in a Muslim territory) will be outraged, and so Allah will make the hearts of these Dhimmis so daring that they will refuse to pay the Jizya they will be supposed to pay." (3180) □

1101. Narrated Asma 'bint Abi Bakr: During the period of the peace treaty of Quraish with Allah's Messenger (ﷺ), my mother, accompanied by her father, came to visit me, and she was a pagan. I consulted Allah's Messenger (ﷺ), "O Allah's Messenger (ﷺ)! My mother has come to me and she desires to receive a reward from me, shall I keep good relation with her?" He said, "Yes, keep good relation with her." (3183) □

1102. Narrated Anas: The Prophet (ﷺ) said, "Every betrayer will have a flag on the Day of Resurrection" One of the two subnarrators said that the flag would be fixed, and the other said that it would be shown on the Day of Resurrection, so that the betrayer might be recognized by it. (3186) □

51. BEGINNING OF CREATION

1103. NARRATED IMRAN BIN HUSAIN (RA): I went to the Prophet (ﷺ) and tied my she-camel at the gate. The people of Bani Tamim came to the Prophet (ﷺ) who said "O Bani Tamim! Accept the good tidings." They said twice, 'You have given us the good tidings, now give us something" Then some Yemenites came to him and he said, "Accept the good tidings, O people of Yemem, for Bani Tamim refused them." They said, "We accept it, O Allah's Messenger (ﷺ)! We have come to ask you about this matter (i.e. the start of creations)." He said, "First of all, there was nothing but Allah, and (then He created His Throne). His throne was over the water, and He wrote everything in the Book and created the Heavens and the Earth." Then a man shouted, "O Ibn Husain! Your she-camel has gone away!" So, I went away and could not see the she-camel because of the mirage. By Allah, I wished I had left that she-camel (but not that gathering). (3191) ☐

1104. Narrated Abu Huraira: Allah's Messenger (ﷺ) said, "Allah the Most Superior said, "The son of Adam slights Me, and he should not slight Me, and he disbelieves in Me, and he ought not to do so. As for his slighting Me, it is that he says that I have a son; and his disbelief in Me is his statement that I shall not recreate him as I have created (him) before." (3193) ☐

1105. Narrated Abu Bakra: The Prophet (ﷺ) said. "(The division of time has turned to its original form which was current when Allah created the Heavens and the Earths. The year is of twelve months, out of which four months are sacred: Three are in succession Dhul-Qa' da, Dhul-Hijja and Muharram, and (the fourth is) Rajab of (the tribe of) Mudar which comes between Jumadi-ath-Thaniyah and Sha ban." (3197) ☐

1106. Narrated Abu Dhar: The Prophet (ﷺ) asked me at sunset, "Do you know where the sun goes (at the time of sunset)?" I replied, "Allah and His Apostle know better." He said, "It goes (i.e. travels) till it prostrates Itself underneath the Throne and takes the permission to rise again, and it is permitted and then (a time will come when) it will be about to prostrate itself but its prostration will not be accepted, and it will ask permission to go on its course but it will not be permitted, but it will be ordered to return where it has come and so it will rise in the west. And that is the interpretation of the Statement of Allah: "And the sun runs its fixed course for a term (decreed). That is The Decree of (Allah) The Exalted in Might, The All- Knowing." (36.38)

(3199) □

1107. Narrated Malik bin Sasaa: The Prophet (ﷺ) said, "While I was at the House in a state midway between sleep and wakefulness, (an angel recognized me) as the man lying between two men. A golden tray full of wisdom and belief was brought to me and my body was cut open from the throat to the lower part of the `Abdomen and then my `Abdomen was washed with Zamzam water and (my heart was) filled with wisdom and belief. Al- Buraq, a white animal, smaller than a mule and bigger than a donkey was brought to me and I set out with Gabriel. When I reached the nearest heaven. Gabriel said to the heaven gate-keeper, 'Open the gate.' The gatekeeper asked, 'Who is it?' He said, 'Gabriel.' The gate-keeper,' who is accompanying you?' Gabriel said, 'Muhammad.' The gate-keeper said, 'Has he been called?' Gabriel said, 'Yes.' Then it was said, 'He is welcomed. What a wonderful visit his is!' Then I met Adam and greeted him and he said, 'You are welcomed O son and a Prophet.' Then we ascended to the second heaven. It was asked, 'Who is it?' Gabriel said, 'Gabriel.' It was said, 'Who is with you?' He said, 'Muhammad' It was asked, 'has he been sent for?' He said, 'Yes.' It was said, 'He is welcomed. What a wonderful visit his is!" Then I met Jesus and Yahya (John) who said, 'You are welcomed, O brother and a Prophet.' Then we ascended to the third heaven. It was asked, 'Who is it?' Gabriel said, 'Gabriel.' It was asked, 'Who is with you? Gabriel said, 'Muhammad.' It was asked, 'Has he been sent for?' 'Yes,' said Gabriel. 'He is welcomed. What a wonderful visit his is!' (The Prophet (ﷺ) added :). There I met Joseph and greeted him, and he replied, 'You are welcomed, O brother and a Prophet!' Then we ascended to the 4th heaven and again the same questions and answers were exchanged as in the previous heavens. There I met Idris and greeted him. He said, 'You are welcomed O brother and Prophet.' Then we ascended to the 5th heaven and again the same questions and answers were exchanged as in previous heavens. There I met and greeted Aaron who said, 'You are welcomed O brother and a Prophet". Then we ascended to the 6th heaven and again the same questions and answers were exchanged as in the previous heavens. There I met and greeted Moses who said, 'You are welcomed O brother and. a Prophet.' When I proceeded on, he started weeping and on being asked why he was weeping, he said, 'O Lord! Followers of this youth who was sent after me will enter Paradise in greater number than my followers.' Then we ascended to the seventh heaven and again the same questions and answers were exchanged as in the previous heavens. There I met and greeted Abraham who said, 'You are welcomed o son and a Prophet.' Then I was shown Al-Bait-al-Ma'mur (i.e. Allah's House). I asked Gabriel about it and he said, This is Al Bait-ul-Ma'mur where 70,000 angels perform prayers daily and when they leave they never return to it (but always a fresh batch comes into it daily).' Then I was shown Sidrat-ul-Muntaha (i.e. a tree in the seventh heaven) and I saw its Nabk fruits which resembled the clay jugs of Hajr (i.e. a town in Arabia), and its leaves were like the ears of elephants, and four rivers originated at its root, two of them were apparent and two were hidden. I asked Gabriel about those rivers and he said, 'The two hidden rivers are in Paradise, and the apparent ones are the Nile and the Euphrates.' Then fifty prayers were enjoined on me. I descended till I met Moses who asked me, 'What have you done?' I said, 'Fifty prayers have been enjoined on me.' He said, 'I know the people better than you, because I had the hardest experience to bring Bani Israel to obedience. Your followers cannot put up with such obligation. So, return to your Lord and request Him (to reduce the number of prayers.' I returned and requested Allah (for reduction) and He made it forty. I returned and (met Moses) and had a similar discussion, and then returned again to Allah for reduction and He made it thirty, then twenty, then ten, and then I came to Moses who repeated the same advice. Ultimately Allah reduced it to five. When I came to Moses again, he said, 'What have you done?' I said, 'Allah has made it five only.' He repeated the same advice but I said that I surrendered (to Allah's Final Order)'" Allah's Messenger (ﷺ) was addressed by Allah, "I have decreed My Obligation and have reduced the burden on My slaves, and I shall reward a single good deed as if it were ten good deeds." (3207) □

1108. Narrated Abu Huraira: The Prophet (ﷺ) said, "If Allah loves a person, He calls Gabriel saying, 'Allah loves so and-so; O Gabriel! Love him.' Gabriel would love him and make an announcement amongst the inhabitants of the Heaven. 'Allah loves so-and-so, therefore you should love him also,' and so all the inhabitants of the Heaven

would love him, and then he is granted the pleasure of the people on the earth." (3209)
□

1109. Narrated Abu Huraira: The Prophet (ﷺ) said, "When Allah ordains something on the Heaven the angels beat with their wings in obedience to His Statement which sounds like that of a chain dragged over a rock. His Statement: "Until when the fear is banished from their hearts, the Angels say, 'what was it that your Lord said?' 'They reply, '(He has said) the Truth. And He is the Most High, The Great." (34.23) (7481)
□

1110. Narrated `Aisha: I heard Allah's Messenger (ﷺ) saying, "The angels descend, the clouds and mention this or that matter decreed in the Heaven. The devils listen stealthily to such a matter, come down to inspire the soothsayers (fortune-teller) with it, and the latter would add to it one-hundred lies of their own." (3210) □

1111. Narrated Sa`id bin Al-Musaiyab: `Umar came to the Mosque while Hassan was reciting a poem. (`Umar disapproved of that). On that Hassan said, "I used to recite poetry in this very Mosque in the presence of one (i.e. the Prophet (ﷺ)) who was better than you." Then he turned towards Abu Huraira and said (to him), "I ask you by Allah, did you hear Allah's Messenger (ﷺ) saying (to me), "Retort (reply) on my behalf. O Allah! Support him (i.e. Hassan) with the Holy Spirit?" Abu Huraira said, "Yes." (3212) □

1112. Narrated Ibn `Abbas: Allah's Messenger (ﷺ) asked Gabriel, "Why don't you visit us more often than you do?" Then the following Holy Verse was revealed (in this respect):-- "And we (angels) descend not but by the order of your Lord. To Him belong what is before us and what is behind us, and what is between those two and your Lord was never forgetful." (19.64) (3218) □

1113. Narrated Abu Talha: I heard Allah's Messenger (ﷺ) saying; "Angels (of Mercy) do not enter a house wherein there is a dog or a picture of a living creature (a human being or an animal). (3225) □

1114. Narrated `Aisha: That she asked the Prophet (ﷺ), 'Have you encountered a day harder than the day of the battle) of Uhud?" The Prophet (ﷺ) replied, "Your tribes have troubled me a lot, and the worse trouble was the trouble on the day of 'Aqaba when I presented myself to Ibn `Abd-Yalail bin `Abd-Kulal and he did not respond to my demand. So I departed, overwhelmed with excessive sorrow, and proceeded on, and could not relax till I found myself at Qarnath-Tha-alib where I lifted my head towards the sky to see a cloud shading me unexpectedly. I looked up and saw Gabriel in it. He called me saying, 'Allah has heard your people's saying to you, and what they have replied back to you, Allah has sent the Angel of the Mountains to you so that you may order him to do whatever you wish to these people.' The Angel of the Mountains called and greeted me, and then said, "O Muhammad! Order what you wish. If you like, I will let Al-Akh-Shabain (i.e. two mountains) fall on them." The Prophet (ﷺ) said, "No but I hope that Allah will let them beget (to produce) children who will worship Allah Alone, and will worship None besides Him." (3231) ☐

1115. Narrated Abu 'Is-haq-Ash-Shaibani: I asked Zir bin Hubaish regarding the Statement of Allah: " And was at a distance of two bow lengths or nearer; So did (Allah) convey The Inspiration to His slave (Gabriel) and then he (Gabriel) Conveyed (that to Muhammad). (53.9-10) On that, Zir said, "Ibn Mas`ud informed us that the Prophet (ﷺ) had seen Gabriel having 600 wings." (3232) ☐

1116. Narrated `Abdullah: Regarding the Verse: "Indeed he (Muhammad) did see. Of the Signs of his Lord, The Greatest!" (53.18) That the Prophet (ﷺ) had seen a green carpet spread all over the horizon of the sky. (3233) ☐

1117. Narrated Aisha: Whoever claimed that (the Prophet) Muhammad saw his Lord, is committing a great fault, for he only saw Gabriel in his genuine shape in which he was created covering the whole horizon. (3234) ☐

1118. Narrated `Aisha: Magic was worked on the Prophet (ﷺ) so that he began to fancy that he was doing a thing which he was not actually doing. One day he invoked (Allah) for a long period and then said, "I feel that Allah has inspired me as how to cure myself. Two persons came to me (in my dream) and sat, one by my head and the other by my feet. One of them asked the other, "What is the ailment of this man?" The other replied, 'He has been bewitched" The first asked, 'Who has bewitched him?' The other replied, 'Lubaid bin Al-A'sam.' The first one asked, 'What material has he used?' The other replied, 'A comb, the hair gathered on it, and the outer skin of the pollen of the male date-palm.' The first asked, 'Where is that?' The other replied, 'It is in the well of Dharwan.' "So, the Prophet (ﷺ) went out towards the well and then returned and said to me on his return, "Its date-palms (the date-palms near the well) are like the heads of the devils." I asked, "Did you take out those things with which the magic was worked?" He said, "No, for I have been cured by Allah and I am afraid that this action may spread evil amongst the people." Later on the well was filled up with earth. (3268)

1119. Narrated Abu Huraira: Allah's Messenger (ﷺ) said, "During your sleep, Satan knots three knots at the back of the head of each of you, and he breathes the following words at each knot, 'The night is, long, so keep on sleeping,' If that person wakes up and celebrates the praises of Allah, then one knot is undone, and when he performs ablution the second knot is undone, and when he prays, all the knots are undone, and he gets up in the morning lively and in good spirits, otherwise he gets up in low spirits and lethargic (lack of energy)." (3269) ☐

1120. Narrated Abu Huraira: Allah's Messenger (ﷺ) said, "Satan comes to one of you and says, 'Who created so-and-so?' till he says, 'Who has created your Lord?' So, when he inspires such a question, one should seek refuge with Allah and give up such thoughts." (3276) ☐

1121. Narrated Abu Huraira: Allah's Messenger (ﷺ) said, "If one says one-hundred times in one day:

لَا إِلَهَ إِلَّا اللهُ وَحْدَهُ لَا شَرِيكَ لَهُ، لَهُ الْمُلْكُ وَلَهُ الْحَمْدُ، وَهُوَ عَلَى كُلِّ شَيْءٍ قَدِيرٌ

"Laa 'ilaaha 'illallaahu wahdahu laa shareeka lahu, lahul-mulku wa lahul-hamdu, wa Huwa 'alaa kulli shay'in Qadeer." (None has the right to be worshipped but Allah, the Alone Who has no partners, to Him belongs Dominion and to Him belong all the Praises, and He has power over all things (i.e. Omnipotent)), one will get the reward of manumitting ten slaves, and one-hundred good deeds will be written in his account, and one-hundred bad deeds will be wiped off or erased from his account, and on that day he will be protected from the morning till evening from Satan, and nobody will be superior to him except one who has done more than that which he has done." (3293) □

1122. Narrated Ibn `Umar: That he heard the Prophet (ﷺ) delivering a sermon on the pulpit saying, "Kill snakes and kill Dhu-at-Tufyatain (i.e. a snake with two white lines on its back) and ALBATROSS (i.e. a snake with short or mutilated tail) for they destroy the sight of one's eyes and bring about abortion." (Ibn Umar further added): Once while I was chasing a snake in order, to kill it, Abu Lubaba called me saying: "Don't kill it," I said. "Allah's Messenger (ﷺ) ordered us to kill snakes." He said, "But later on he prohibited the killing of snakes living in the houses." (Az-Zuhri said. "Such snakes are called Al-Awamir.") (3297) □

1123. Narrated Abu Huraira: The Prophet (ﷺ) said, "When you hear the crowing of cocks, ask for Allah's Blessings for (their crowing indicates that) they have seen an angel. And when you hear the braying of donkeys, seek Refuge with Allah from Satan for (their braying indicates) that they have seen a Satan." (3303) □

1124. Narrated Jabir bin `Abdullah: Allah's Messenger (ﷺ) said, "When night falls (or it is evening), keep your children close to you for the devils spread out at that time. But when an hour of the night elapses, you can let them free. Close the doors and mention the Name of Allah, for Satan does not open a closed door." (3304) □

1125. Narrated Abu Huraira: The Prophet (ﷺ) said, "A group of Israelites were lost. Nobody knows what they did. But I do not see them except that they were cursed and changed into rats, for if you put the milk of a she-camel in front of a rat, it will not drink it, but if the milk of a sheep is put in front of it, it will drink it." I told this to Ka`b who asked me, "Did you hear it from the Prophet (ﷺ)?" I said, "Yes." Ka`b asked me the same question several times. I said to Ka`b. "Do I read the Torah? (i.e. I tell you this from the Prophet.)" (3305) ☐

1126. Narrated Aisha: The Prophet (ﷺ) called the Salamander, a mischief-doer. I have not heard him ordering that it should be killed. Sa`d bin Waqqas claims that the Prophet (ﷺ) ordered that it should be killed. (3306) ☐

1127. Narrated Um Sharik: That the Prophet (ﷺ) ordered her to kill Salamanders. (3307) ☐

1128. Narrated Abu Mulaika: Ibn `Umar used to kill snakes, but afterwards he forbade their killing and said, "Once the Prophet (ﷺ) pulled down a wall and saw a cast-off skin of a snake in it. He said, 'Look for the snake. 'They found it and the Prophet (ﷺ) said, "Kill it." For this reason I used to kill snakes. Later on I met Abu Lubaba who told me the Prophet (ﷺ) said, 'Do not kill snakes except the short-tailed or mutilated-tailed snake with two white lines on its back, for it causes abortion and makes one blind. So kill it.'" (3310) ☐

1129. Narrated Nafi`: Ibn `Umar used to kill snakes but when Abu Lubaba informed him that the Prophet (ﷺ) had forbidden the killing of snakes living in houses, he gave up killing them. (3313) ☐

1130. Narrated `Abdullah bin `Umar: Allah's Messenger (ﷺ) said, "It is not sinful of a person in the state of Ihram to kill any of these five animals: The scorpion, the rat, the rabid dog, the crow and the kite." (3315) ☐

1131. Narrated Jabir bin `Abdullah: The Prophet (ﷺ) said, "Cover your utensils and tie your water skins, and close your doors and keep your children close to you at night, as the Jinns spread out at such time and snatch things away. When you go to bed, put out your lights, for the mischief-doer (i.e. the rat) may drag away the wick of the candle and burn the dwellers of the house." Ata said, "The devils." (instead of the Jinns). (3316) ☐

1132. Narrated Abu Huraira: Allah's Messenger (ﷺ) said, "A prostitute was forgiven by Allah, because, passing by a panting dog near a well and seeing that the dog was about to die of thirst, she took off her shoe, and tying it with her head-cover she drew out some water for it. So, Allah forgave her because of that." (3321) □

52. PROPHETS

1133. NARRATED ABU HURAIRA (RA): The Prophet (ﷺ) said, "Allah created Adam, making him 60 cubits tall. When He created him, He said to him, "Go and greet that group of angels, and listen to their reply, for it will be your greeting (salutation) and the greeting (salutations of your offspring." So, Adam said (to the angels), As-Salamu Alaikum (i.e. Peace be upon you). The angels said, "As-salamu Alaika wa Rahmatu-l-lahi" (i.e. Peace and Allah's Mercy be upon you). Thus the angels added to Adam's salutation the expression, 'Wa Rahmatu-l-lahi,' any person who will enter Paradise will resemble Adam (in appearance and figure). People have been decreasing in stature since Adam's creation. (3326) □

1134. Narrated `Abdullah: Allah's Messenger (ﷺ) said, "Whenever a person is murdered unjustly, there is a share from the burden of the crime on the first son of Adam for he was the first to start the tradition of murdering." (3335) □

1135. Narrated Abu Huraira: The Prophet (ﷺ) said, "On the Day of Resurrection Abraham will meet his father Azar whose face will be dark and covered with dust. (Abraham will say to him): 'Didn't I tell you not to disobey me?' His father will reply: 'Today I will not disobey you.' 'Abraham will say: 'O Lord! You promised me not to disgrace me on the Day of Resurrection; and what will be more disgraceful to me than cursing and dishonoring my father?' Then Allah will say (to him):' 'I have forbidden Paradise for the disbelievers." Then he will be addressed, 'O Abraham! Look! What is underneath your feet?' He will look and there he will see a Dhabh (an animal,) blood-stained, which will be caught by the legs and thrown in the (Hell) Fire." (3350) □

1136. Narrated Ibn `Abbas: The Prophet (ﷺ) entered the Ka`ba and found in it the pictures of (Prophet) Abraham and Mary. On that he said' "What is the matter with them (i.e. Quraish)? They have already heard that angels do not enter a house in which there are pictures; yet this is the picture of Abraham. And why is he depicted as practicing divination by arrows?" (3351) □

1137. Narrated Ibn `Abbas: When the Prophet (ﷺ) saw pictures in the Ka`ba, he did not enter it till he ordered them to be erased. When he saw (the pictures of Abraham and Ishmael carrying the arrows of divination (the practice that seeks to foresee future events), he said, "May Allah curse them (i.e. the Quraish)! By Allah, neither Abraham nor Ishmael practiced divination by arrows." (3352) □

1138. Narrated Abu Huraira: The people said, "O Allah's Messenger (ﷺ)! Who is the most honorable amongst the people (in Allah's Sight)?" He said, "The most righteous amongst them." They said, "We do not ask you, about this." He said, "Then Joseph (Yusuf), Allah's Prophet, the son of Allah's Prophet (Yakub), the son of Allah's Prophet (Ishaq), the son of Allah's Khalil (i.e. Abraham)." They said, "We do not want to ask about this," He said' "Then you want to ask about the descent of the Arabs. Those who were the best in the pre-lslamic period of ignorance will be the best in Islam provided they comprehend the religious knowledge." (3353) □

1139. Narrated Samura: Allah's Messenger (ﷺ) said, "Two persons came to me at night (in dream) (and took me with them). We passed by a tall man who was so tall that I was not able to see his head and that person was Abraham." (3354) □

1140. Narrated Mujahid: That when the people mentioned before Ibn `Abbas that the Dajjal would have the word Kafir, (i.e. unbeliever) or the letters Kafir (the root of the Arabic verb 'disbelieve') written on his forehead, I heard Ibn `Abbas saying, "I did not hear this, but the Prophet (ﷺ) said, 'If you want to see Abraham, then look at your companion (i.e. the Prophet) but Moses was a curly-haired, brown man (who used to ride) a red camel, the reins of which was made of fires of date-palms. As if I were now looking down a valley." (3355) □

1141. Narrated Abu Huraira: Allah's Messenger (ﷺ) said, "Abraham did his circumcision with an adze (a cutting tool) at the age of eighty." (3356) □

1142. Narrated Abu Huraira: Abraham did not tell a lie except on three occasions. Twice for the Sake of Allah when he said, "I am sick," and he said, "(I have not done this but) the big idol has done it." The (third was) that while Abraham and Sarah (his wife) were going (on a journey) they passed by (the territory of) a tyrant. Someone said to the tyrant, "This man (i.e. Abraham) is accompanied by a very charming lady." So, he sent for Abraham and asked him about Sarah saying, "Who is this lady?" Abraham said, "She is my sister." Abraham went to Sarah and said, "O Sarah! There are no believers on the surface of the earth except you and me. This man asked me about you and I have told him that you are my sister, so don't contradict my statement." The tyrant then called Sarah and when she went to him, he tried to take hold of her with his hand, but (his hand got stiff and) he was confounded. He asked Sarah. "Pray to Allah for me, and I shall not harm you." So Sarah asked Allah to cure him and he got cured. He tried to take hold of her for the second time, but (his hand got as stiff as or stiffer than before and) was more confounded. He again requested Sarah, "Pray to Allah for me, and I will not harm you." Sarah asked Allah again and he became alright. He then called one of his guards (who had brought her) and said, "You have not brought me a human being but have brought me a devil." The tyrant then gave Hajar as a girl-servant to Sarah. Sarah came back (to Abraham) while he was praying. Abraham, gesturing with his hand, asked, "What has happened?" She replied, "Allah has spoiled the evil plot of the infidel (or immoral person) and gave me Hajar for service." (Abu Huraira then addressed his listeners saying, "That (Hajar) was your mother, O Bani Ma-is-Sama (i.e. the Arabs, the descendants of Ishmael, Hajar's son). (3358) □

1143. Narrated Um Sharik: Allah's Messenger (ﷺ) ordered that the salamander should be killed and said, "It (i.e. the salamander) blew (the fire) on Abraham." (3359) □

1144. Narrated Ibn `Abbas: The first lady to use a girdle was the mother of Ishmael. She used a girdle so that she might hide her tracks from Sarah. Abraham brought her and her son Ishmael while she was suckling him, to a place near the Ka`ba under a tree on the spot of Zamzam, at the highest place in the mosque. During those days there was nobody in Mecca, nor was there any water so he made them sit over there and placed near them a leather bag containing some dates, and a small water-skin containing some water, and set out homeward. Ishmael's mother followed him saying, "O Abraham! Where are you going, leaving us in this valley where there is no person whose company we may enjoy, nor is there anything (to enjoy)?" She repeated that to him many times, but he did not look back at her then she asked him, "Has Allah ordered you to do so?" He said, "Yes." She said, "Then He will not neglect us," and returned while Abraham proceeded onwards, and on reaching the Thaniya where they could not see him, he faced the Ka`ba, and raising both hands, invoked Allah saying the following prayers: 'O our Lord! I have made some of my offspring dwell in a valley without cultivation, by Your Sacred House (Ka`ba at Mecca) in order, O our Lord, that they may offer prayer perfectly. So fill some hearts among men with love towards them, and (O Allah) provide them with fruits, so that they may give thanks.' (14.37) Ishmael's mother went on suckling Ishmael and drinking from the water (she had). When the water in the water-skin had all been used up, she became thirsty and her child also became thirsty. She started looking at him (i.e. Ishmael) tossing in agony; She left him, for she could not endure looking at him, and found that the mountain of Safa was the nearest mountain to her on that land. She stood on it and started looking at the valley keenly so that she might see somebody, but she could not see anybody. Then she descended from Safa and when she reached the valley, she tucked up her robe and ran in the valley like a person in distress and trouble, till she crossed the valley and reached the Marwa mountain where she stood and started looking, expecting to see somebody, but she could not see anybody. She repeated that (running between Safa and Marwa) seven times." The Prophet (ﷺ) said, "This is the source of the tradition of the walking of people between them (i.e. Safa and Marwa). When she reached the Marwa (for the last time) she heard a voice and she asked herself to be quiet and listened attentively. She heard the voice again and said, 'O, (whoever you may be)! You have made me hear your voice; have you got something to help me?"

And behold! She saw an angel at the place of Zamzam, digging the earth with his heel (or his wing), till water flowed from that place. She started to make something like a basin around it, using her hand in this way, and started filling her water-skin with water with her hands, and the water was flowing out after she had scooped some of it." The Prophet (ﷺ) added, "May Allah bestow Mercy on Ishmael's mother! Had she let the Zamzam (flow without trying to control it) (or had she not scooped from that water) (to fill her water-skin), Zamzam would have been a stream flowing on the surface of the earth." The Prophet (ﷺ) further added, "Then she drank (water) and suckled her child. The angel said to her, 'Don't be afraid of being neglected, for this is the House of Allah which will be built by this boy and his father, and Allah never neglects His people.' The House (i.e. Ka`ba) at that time was on a high place resembling a hillock, and when torrents came, they flowed to its right and left. She lived in that way till some people from the tribe of Jurhum or a family from Jurhum passed by her and her child, as they (i.e. the Jurhum people) were coming through the way of Kada'. They landed in the lower part of Mecca where they saw a bird that had the habit of flying around water and not leaving it. They said, 'This bird must be flying around water, though we know that there is no water in this valley.' They sent one or two messengers who discovered the source of water, and returned to inform them of the water. So, they all came (towards the water)." The Prophet (ﷺ) added, "Ishmael's mother was sitting near the water. They asked her, 'Do you allow us to stay with you?' She replied, 'Yes, but you will have no right to possess the water.' They agreed to that." The Prophet (ﷺ) further said, "Ishmael's mother was pleased with the whole situation as she used to love to enjoy the company of the people. So, they settled there, and later on they sent for their families who came and settled with them so that some families became permanent residents there. The child (i.e. Ishmael) grew up and learnt Arabic from them and (his virtues) caused them to love and admire him as he grew up, and when he reached the age of puberty they made him marry a woman from amongst them. After Ishmael's mother had died, Abraham came after Ishmael's marriage in order to see his family that he had left before, but he did not find Ishmael there. When he asked Ishmael's wife about him, she replied, 'He has gone in search of our livelihood.' Then he asked her about their way of living and their condition, and she replied, 'We are living in misery; we are living in hardship and destitution,' complaining to him. He said, 'When your husband returns, convey my salutation to him and tell him to change the threshold of the gate (of his house).' When Ishmael came, he seemed to have felt something unusual, so he asked his wife, 'Has anyone visited you?' She replied, 'Yes, an old man of so-and-so description came and asked me about you and I informed him, and he asked about our state of living, and I told him that we were living in a hardship and poverty.' On that Ishmael said, 'Did he advise you anything?' She replied, 'Yes, he told me to convey his salutation to you and to tell you to change the threshold of your gate.' Ishmael said, 'It was my father, and he has ordered me to divorce you. Go back to your family.' So, Ishmael divorced her and married another woman from amongst them (i.e. Jurhum). Then Abraham stayed away from them for a period as long as Allah wished and called on them again but did not find Ishmael. So he came to Ishmael's wife and asked her about Ishmael. She said, 'He has gone in search of our livelihood.' Abraham asked her, 'How are you getting on?' asking her about their sustenance and living. She replied, 'We are prosperous and well-off (i.e. we have everything in abundance).' Then she thanked Allah' Abraham said, 'What kind of food do you eat?' She said. 'Meat.' He said, 'What do you drink?' She said, 'Water." He said, "O Allah! Bless their meat and water." The Prophet added, "At that time they did not have grain, and if they had grain, he would have also invoked Allah to bless it." The Prophet (ﷺ) added, "If somebody has only these two things as his sustenance, his health and disposition will be badly affected, unless he lives in Mecca." The Prophet (ﷺ) added," Then Abraham said Ishmael's wife, "when your husband comes, give my regards to him and tell him that he should keep firm the threshold of his gate.' When Ishmael came back, he asked his wife, 'Did anyone call on you?' She replied, 'Yes, a good-looking old man came to me,' so she praised him and added. 'He asked about you, and I informed him, and he asked about our livelihood and I told him that we were in a good condition.' Ishmael asked her, 'Did he give you any piece of advice?' She said, 'Yes, he told me to give his regards to you and ordered that you should keep firm the threshold of your gate.' On that

Ishmael said, 'It was my father, and you are the threshold (of the gate). He has ordered me to keep you with me.' Then Abraham stayed away from them for a period as long as Allah wished, and called on them afterwards. He saw Ishmael under a tree near Zamzam, sharpening his arrows. When he saw Abraham, he rose up to welcome him (and they greeted each other as a father does with his son or a son does with his father). Abraham said, 'O Ishmael! Allah has given me an order.' Ishmael said, 'Do what your Lord has ordered you to do.' Abraham asked, 'Will you help me?' Ishmael said, 'I will help you.' Abraham said, Allah has ordered me to build a house here,' pointing to a hillock higher than the land surrounding it." The Prophet (ﷺ) added, "Then they raised the foundations of the House (i.e. the Ka`ba). Ishmael brought the stones and Abraham was building, and when the walls became high, Ishmael brought this stone and put it for Abraham who stood over it and carried on building, while Ishmael was handing him the stones, and both of them were saying, 'O our Lord! Accept (this service) from us, Verily, You are the All-Hearing, the All-Knowing.' The Prophet (ﷺ) added, "Then both of them went on building and going round the Ka`ba saying: O our Lord! Accept (this service) from us, Verily, You are the All-Hearing, the All-Knowing." (2.127) (3364) □

1145. Narrated Ibn `Abbas: When Abraham had differences with his wife), (because of her jealousy of Hajar, Ishmael's mother), he took Ishmael and his mother and went away. They had a water-skin with them containing some water, Ishmael's mother used to drink water from the water-skin so that her milk would increase for her child. When Abraham reached Mecca, he made her sit under a tree and afterwards returned home. Ishmael's mother followed him, and when they reached Kada', she called him from behind, 'O Abraham! To whom are you leaving us?' He replied, '(I am leaving you) to Allah's (Care).' She said, 'I am satisfied to be with Allah.' She returned to her place and started drinking water from the water-skin, and her milk increased for her child. When the water had all been used up, she said to herself, 'I'd better go and look so that I may see somebody.' She ascended the Safa Mountain and looked, hoping to see somebody, but in vain. When she came down to the valley, she ran till she reached the Marwa Mountain. She ran to and fro (between the two mountains) many times.

They she said to herself, 'i'd better go and see the state of the child,' she went and found it in a state of one on the point of dying. She could not endure to watch it dying and said (to herself), 'If I go and look, I may find somebody.' She went and ascended the Safa Mountain and looked for a long while but could not find anybody. Thus she completed seven rounds (of running) between Safa and Marwa. Again she said (to herself), 'I'd better go back and see the state of the child.' But suddenly she heard a voice, and she said to that strange voice, 'Help us if you can offer any help.' Lo! It was Gabriel (who had made the voice). Gabriel hit the earth with his heel like this (Ibn `Abbas hit the earth with his heel to Illustrate it), and so the water gushed out. Ishmael's mother was astonished and started digging. (Abu Al-Qasim) (i.e. the Prophet) said, "If she had left the water, (flow naturally without her intervention), it would have been flowing on the surface of the earth.") Ishmael's mother started drinking from the water and her milk increased for her child. Afterwards some people of the tribe of Jurhum, while passing through the bottom of the valley, saw some birds, and that astonished them, and they said, 'Birds can only be found at a place where there is water.' They sent a messenger who searched the place and found the water, and returned to inform them about it. Then they all went to her and said, 'O ishmael's mother! Will you allow us to be with you (or dwell with you)?' (And thus they stayed there.) Later on her boy reached the age of puberty and married a lady from them. Then an idea occurred to Abraham which he disclosed to his wife (Sarah), 'I want to call on my dependents I left (at Mecca).' When he went there, he greeted (Ishmael's wife) and said, 'Where is Ishmael?' She replied, 'He has gone out hunting.' Abraham said (to her), 'When he comes, tell him to change the threshold of his gate.' When he came, she told him the same whereupon Ishmael said to her, 'You are the threshold, so go to your family (i.e. you are divorced).' Again Abraham thought of visiting his dependents whom he had left (at Mecca), and he told his wife (Sarah) of his intentions. Abraham came to Ishmael's house and asked. "Where is Ishmael?" Ishmael's wife replied, "He has gone out hunting," and added, "Will you stay (for some time) and have something to eat and drink?' Abraham asked, 'What is your food and what is your drink?' She replied, 'Our food is meat and our drink is water.' He said, 'O Allah! Bless their meals and their drink." Abu Al-Qa-sim (i.e. Prophet) said, "Because of Abraham's invocation there are blessings (in Mecca)." Once more Abraham thought of visiting his family he had left (at Mecca), so he told his wife (Sarah) of his decision. He went and found Ishmael behind the Zamzam well, mending his arrows. He said, "O Ishmael, Your Lord has ordered me to build a house for Him." Ishmael said, "Obey (the order of) your Lord." Abraham said, "Allah has also ordered me that you should help me therein." Ishmael said, "Then I will do." So, both of them rose and Abraham started building (the Ka`ba) while Ishmael went on handing him the stones, and both of them were saying, "O our Lord! Accept (this service) from us, Verily, You are the All-Hearing, the All-Knowing." (2.127). When the building became high and the old man (i.e. Abraham) could no longer lift the stones (to such a high position), he stood over the stone of Al- Maqam and Ishmael carried on handing him the stones, and both of them were saying, 'O our Lord! Accept (this service) from us, Verily You are All-Hearing, All-Knowing." (2.127) (3365) □

1146. Narrated Abu Dhar: I said, "O Allah's Messenger (ﷺ)! Which mosque was first built on the surface of the earth?" He said, "Al- Masjid-ul-, Haram (in Mecca)." I said, "Which was built next?" He replied "The mosque of Al-Aqsa (in Jerusalem)." I said, "What was the period of construction between the two?" He said, "Forty years." He added, "Wherever (you may be, and) the prayer time becomes due, perform the prayer there, for the best thing is to do so (i.e. to offer the prayers in time). (3366) □

1147. Narrated Abu Huraira: Allah's Messenger (ﷺ) said, "We are more liable to be in doubt than Abraham when he said, 'My Lord! Show me how You give life to the dead." He (i.e. Allah) slid: 'Don't you believe then?' He (i.e. Abraham) said: "Yes, but (I ask) in order to be stronger in Faith." (2.260) And may Allah send His Mercy on Lot! He wished to have a powerful support. If I were to stay in prison for such a long time as Joseph did I would have accepted the offer (of freedom without insisting on having my guiltless declared). (3372) □

1148. Narrated Salama bin Al-Akwa`: The Prophet (ﷺ) passed by some people of the tribe of Bani Aslam who were practicing archery. The Prophet said, "O Bani Isma`il!

Practice archery as your father Isma`il was a great archer. Keep on throwing arrows and I am with Bani so-and-so." So one of the parties ceased throwing. Allah's Apostle said, "Why do you not throw?" They replied, "How should we throw while you are with them (i.e. on their side)?" On that the Prophet (ﷺ) said, "Throw, and I am with all of you." (2899) ☐

1149. Narrated `Abdullah bin Zam`a: I heard the Prophet (s) while referring to the person who had cut the legs of the she-camel (of the Prophet Salih), saying, "The man who was appointed for doing this job, was a man of honor and power in his nation like Abu Zam`a." (3377) ☐

1150. Narrated `Abdullah bin `Umar: The people landed at the land of Thamud called Al-Hijr along with Allah's Messenger (ﷺ) and they took water from its well for drinking and kneading the dough with it as well. (When Allah's Messenger (s) heard about it) he ordered them to pour out the water they had taken from its wells and feed the camels with the dough, and ordered them to take water from the well where the she-camel (of Prophet Salih) used to drink. (3379) ☐

1151. Narrated `Abdullah bin `Umar: When the Prophet (ﷺ) passed by (a place called) Al Hijr, he said, "Do not enter the house of those who were unjust to themselves, unless (you enter) weeping, lest you should suffer the same punishment as was inflicted upon them." After that he covered his face with his sheet cloth while he was on the camel-saddle. (3380) ☐

1152. Narrated Abu Huraira: The Prophet (ﷺ) said, "While Job (Ayyub) was naked, taking a bath, a swarm of gold locusts fell on him and he started collecting them in his garment. His Lord called him, 'O Job! Have I not made you rich enough to need what you see? He said, 'Yes, O Lord! But I cannot dispense with your Blessing.'" (3391) ☐

1153. Narrated Ibn `Abbas: The Prophet (ﷺ) said, "On the night of my Ascent to the Heaven, I saw Moses who was a tall brown curly haired man as if he was one of the men of Shan'awa tribe, and I saw Jesus, a man of medium height and moderate complexion inclined to the red and white colors and of lank hair. I also saw Malik, the gate-keeper of the (Hell) Fire and Ad-Dajjal amongst the signs which Allah showed me." (The Prophet then recited the Holy Verse): "So be not you in doubt of meeting him' when you met Moses during the night of Mi'raj over the heavens" (32.23) Narrated Anas and Abu Bakra: "The Prophet (ﷺ) said, "The angels will guard Medina from Ad-Dajjal. (3239) ☐

1154. Narrated Ibn `Abbas: When the Prophet (ﷺ) came to Medina, he found (the Jews) fasting on the day of 'Ashura' (i.e. 10th of Muharram). They used to say: "This is a great day on which Allah saved Moses and drowned the folk of Pharaoh. Moses observed the fast on this day, as a sign of gratitude to Allah." The Prophet (ﷺ) said, "I am closer to Moses than they." So, he observed the fast (on that day) and ordered the Muslims to fast on it. (3397) ☐

1155. Narrated Abu Huraira: The Prophet (ﷺ) said, "Were it not for Bani Israel, meat would not decay; and were it not for Eve, no woman would ever betray her husband." (3399) ☐

1156. Narrated Sa`id bin Jubair: I said to Ibn `Abbas, "Nauf-Al-Bakali claims that Moses (the companion of Khadir) was not the Moses of Bani Israel but he was another Moses." Ibn `Abbas remarked that the enemy of Allah (Nauf) was a liar. Narrated Ubai bin Ka`b: The Prophet (ﷺ) said, "Once the Prophet (ﷺ) Moses stood up and addressed Bani Israel. He was asked, "Who is the most learned man amongst the people. He said, "I am the most learned." Allah admonished Moses as he did not attribute absolute knowledge to Him (Allah). So Allah inspired to him "At the junction of the two seas there is a slave amongst my slaves who is more learned than you." Moses said, "O my Lord! How can I meet him?" Allah said: Take a fish in a large basket (and proceed) and you will find him at the place where you will lose the fish. So Moses set out along with his (servant) boy, Yusha` bin Noon and carried a fish in a large basket till they reached a rock, where they laid their heads (i.e. lay down) and slept. The fish came out of the basket and it took its way into the sea as in a tunnel. So it was an amazing thing for both Moses and his (servant) boy. They proceeded for the rest of that night and the following day. When the day broke, Moses said to his (servant) boy: "Bring us our early meal. No doubt, we have suffered much fatigue in this journey." Moses did not get tired till he passed the place about which he was told. There the (servant) boy told Moses, "Do you remember when we betook ourselves to the rock, I indeed forgot the fish." Moses remarked, "That is what we have been seeking. So they went back retracing their footsteps, till they reached the rock. There they saw a man covered with a garment (or covering himself with his own garment). Moses greeted him. Al-Khadir replied saying, "How do people greet each other in your land?" Moses said, "I am Moses." He asked, "The Moses of Bani Israel?" Moses replied in the affirmative and added, "May I follow you so that you teach me of that knowledge which you have been taught." Al-Khadir replied, "Verily! You will not be able to remain patient with me, O Moses! I have some of the knowledge of Allah which He has taught me and which you do not know, while you have some knowledge which Allah has taught you which I do not know." Moses said, "Allah willing, you will find me patient and I will disobey no order of yours. So both of them set out walking along the seashore, as they did not have a boat. In the meantime a boat passed by them and they requested the crew of the boat to take them on board. The crew recognized Al-Khadir and took them on board without fare. Then a sparrow came and stood on the edge of the boat and dipped its beak once or twice in the sea. Al-Khadir said: "O Moses! My knowledge and your knowledge have not decreased Allah's knowledge except as much as this sparrow has decreased the water of the sea with its beak." Al-Khadir went to one of the planks of the boat and plucked it out. Moses said, "These people gave us a free lift but you have broken their boat and scuttled it so as to drown its people." Al-Khadir replied, "Didn't I tell you that you will not be able to remain patient with me." Moses said, "Call me not to account for what I forgot." The first (excuse) of Moses was that he had forgotten. Then they proceeded further and found a boy playing with other boys. Al-Khadir took hold of the boy's head from the top and plucked it out with his hands (i.e. killed him). Moses said, "Have you killed an innocent soul who has killed none." Al-Khadir replied, "Did I not tell you that you cannot remain patient with me?" Then they both proceeded till when they came to the people of a town, they asked them for food, but they refused to entertain them. Then they found there a wall on the point of collapsing. Al-Khadir repaired it with his own hands. Moses said, "If you had wished, surely you could have taken wages for it." Al-Khadir replied, "This is the parting between you and me." The Prophet added, "May Allah be Merciful to Moses! Would that he could have been more patient to learn more about his story with Al-Khadir. (122) ☐

1157. Narrated Abu Huraira: The Prophet (ﷺ) said, "Al-Khadir was named so because he sat over a barren white land, it turned green with plantation after (his sitting over it." (3402) ☐

1158. Narrated Abu Huraira: Allah's Messenger (ﷺ) said, "It was said to Bani Israel, Enter the gate (of the town) with humility (prostrating yourselves) and saying: "Repentance", but they changed the word and entered the town crawling on their buttocks and saying: "A wheat grain in the hair." (3403) ☐

1159. Narrated Abu Huraira: Allah's Messenger (ﷺ) said, "(The Prophet) Moses was a shy person and used to cover his body completely because of his extensive shyness. One of the children of Israel hurt him by saying, 'He covers his body in this way only because of some defect in his skin, either leprosy or scrotal hernia, or he has some other defect.' Allah wished to clear Moses of what they said about him, so one day while Moses was in seclusion, he took off his clothes and put them on a stone and started taking a bath. When he had finished the bath, he moved towards his clothes so as to take them, but the stone took his clothes and fled; Moses picked up his stick and ran after the stone saying, 'O stone! Give me my garment!' Till he reached a group of Bani Israel who saw him naked then, and found him the best of what Allah had created, and Allah cleared him of what they had accused him of. The stone stopped there and Moses took and put his garment on and started hitting the stone with his stick. By Allah, the stone still has some traces of the hitting, three, four or five marks. This was what Allah refers to in His Saying: -- "O you who believe! Be you not like those who annoyed Moses, But Allah proved his innocence of that which they alleged, and he was honorable In Allah's Sight." (33.69) (3404) ☐

1160. Narrated Abu Huraira: The Angel of Death was sent to Moses when he came to Moses, Moses slapped him on the eye. The angel returned to his Lord and said, "You have sent me to a Slave who does not want to die." Allah said, "Return to him and tell him to put his hand on the back of an ox and for every hair that will come under it, he will be granted one year of life." Moses said, "O Lord! What will happen after that?" Allah replied, "Then death." Moses said, "Let it come now." Moses then requested Allah to let him die close to the Sacred Land so much so that he would be at a distance of a stone's throw from it." Abu Huraira added, "Allah's Messenger (ﷺ) said, 'If I were there, I would show you his grave below the red sand hill on the side of the road." (3407) ☐

1161. Narrated Abu Huraira: Allah's Messenger (ﷺ) said, "Adam and Moses argued with each other. Moses said to Adam. 'You are Adam whose mistake expelled you from Paradise.' Adam said to him, 'You are Moses whom Allah selected as His Messenger and as the one to whom He spoke directly; yet you blame me for a thing which had already been written in my fate before my creation?'" Allah's Messenger (ﷺ) said twice, "So, Adam overpowered Moses." (3409) ⊔

1162. Narrated Abu Huraira: The Prophet (ﷺ) said, "The reciting of the Zabur (i.e. Psalms) was made easy for David. He used to order that his riding animals be saddled, and would finish reciting the Zabur before they were saddled. And he would never eat except from the earnings of his manual work." (3417) ☐

1163. Narrated Mujahid: I asked Ibn `Abbas, "Should we perform a prostration on reciting Surah-Sa`d?" He recited (the Sura) including: 'And among his progeny, David, Solomon..(up to)...so follow their guidance (6.84-91) And then he said, "Your Prophet is amongst those people who have been ordered to follow them (i.e. the preceding apostles). (3421) ☐

1164. Narrated Abu Huraira: The Prophet (ﷺ) said, "A strong demon from the Jinns came to me yesterday suddenly, so as to spoil my prayer, but Allah enabled me to overpower him, and so I caught him and intended to tie him to one of the pillars of the Mosque so that all of you might see him, but I remembered the invocation of my brother Solomon: 'And grant me a kingdom such as shall not belong to any other after me.' (38.35) so I let him go cursed." (3423) ☐

1165. Narrated Abu Huraira: The Prophet (ﷺ) said, "Solomon (the son of) David said, 'Tonight I will sleep with seventy ladies each of whom will conceive a child who will be a knight fighting for "Allah's Cause.' His companion said, 'If Allah will.' But Solomon did not say so; therefore none of those women got pregnant except one who gave birth to a half child." The Prophet (ﷺ) further said, "If the Prophet (ﷺ) Solomon had said it (i.e. 'If Allah will') he would have begotten children who would have fought in Allah's Cause." Shuaib and Ibn Abi Az-Zinad said, "Ninety (women) is more correct (than seventy). (3424) ☐

1166. Narrated Abu Huraira: Allah's Messenger (ﷺ) said, "My example and the example o the people is like that of a person who lit a fire and let the moths, butterflies and these insects fall in it." He also said, "There were two women, each of whom had a child with her. A wolf came and took away the child of one of them, whereupon the other said, 'It has taken your child.' The first said, 'But it has taken your child.' So they both carried the case before David who judged that the living child be given to the elder lady. So both of them went to Solomon bin David and informed him (of the case). He said, 'Bring me a knife so as to cut the child into two pieces and distribute it between them.' The younger lady said, 'May Allah be merciful to you! Don't do that, for it is her (i.e. the other lady's) child.' So he gave the child to the younger lady." (3427) ☐

1167. Narrated Sa`id bin Al-Musaiyab: Abu Huraira said, "I heard Allah's Messenger (ﷺ) saying, 'There is none born among the off-spring of Adam, but Satan touches it. A child therefore, cries loudly at the time of birth because of the touch of Satan, except Mary and her child." Then Abu Huraira recited: "And I seek refuge with You for her and for her offspring from the outcast Satan" (3.36) (3431) ☐

1168. Narrated `Ali: I heard the Prophet (ﷺ) saying, "Mary, the daughter of `Imran, was the best among the women (of the world of her time) and Khadija is the best amongst the women. (of this nation). (3432) □

1169. Narrated Abu Musa Al-Ash`ari: The Prophet (ﷺ) said, "The superiority of `Aisha to other ladies is like the superiority of Tharid (i.e. meat and bread dish) to other meals. Many men reached the level of perfection, but no woman reached such a level except Mary, the daughter of `Imran and Asia, the wife of Pharaoh." (3433) □

1170. Narrated 'Ubada: The Prophet (ﷺ) said, "If anyone testifies that None has the right to be worshipped but Allah Alone Who has no partners, and that Muhammad is His Slave and His Apostle, and that Jesus is Allah's Slave and His Apostle and His Word which He bestowed on Mary and a Spirit created by Him, and that Paradise is true, and Hell is true, Allah will admit him into Paradise with the deeds which he had done even if those deeds were few." (Junada, the sub-narrator said, " 'Ubada added, 'such a person can enter Paradise through any of its eight gates he likes.") (3435) □

1171. Narrated Abu Huraira: The Prophet (ﷺ) said, "None spoke in cradle but three: (The first was) Jesus, (the second was), there a man from Bani Israel called Juraij. While he was offering his prayers, his mother came and called him. He said (to himself), 'Shall I answer her or keep on praying?" (He went on praying) and did not answer her, his mother said, "O Allah! Do not let him die till he sees the faces of prostitutes." So while he was in his hermitage, a lady came and sought to seduce him, but he refused. So she went to a shepherd and presented herself to him to commit illegal sexual intercourse with her and then later she gave birth to a child and claimed that it belonged to Juraij. The people, therefore, came to him and dismantled his hermitage and expelled him out of it and abused him. Juraij performed the ablution and offered prayer, and then came to the child and said, 'O child! Who is your father?' The child replied, 'The shepherd.' (After hearing this) the people said, 'We shall rebuild your hermitage of gold,' but he said, 'No, of nothing but mud.'(The third was the hero of the following story) A lady from Bani Israel was nursing her child at her breast when a handsome rider passed by her. She said, 'O Allah! Make my child like him.' On that the child left her breast, and facing the rider said, 'O Allah! Do not make me like him.' The child then started to suck her breast again. (Abu Huraira further said, "As if I were now looking at the Prophet (ﷺ) sucking his finger (in way of demonstration.") After a while the people passed by, with a lady slave and she (i.e. the child's mother) said, 'O Allah! Do not make my child like this (slave girl)! On that the child left her breast and said, 'O Allah! Make me like her.' When she asked why, the child replied, 'The rider is one of the tyrants while this slave girl is falsely accused of theft and illegal sexual intercourse." (3436) □

1172. Narrated Ibn `Abbas: The Prophet (ﷺ) said, "I saw Moses, Jesus and Abraham (on the night of my Ascension to the heavens). Jesus was of red complexion, curly hair and a broad chest. Moses was of brown complexion, straight hair and tall stature as if he was from the people of Az-Zutt." (3438) □

1173. Narrated Salim from his father: No, By Allah, the Prophet (ﷺ) did not tell that Jesus was of red complexion but said, "While I was asleep circumambulating the Ka`ba (in my dream), suddenly I saw a man of brown complexion and lank hair walking between two men, and water was dropping from his head. I asked, 'Who is this?' The people said, 'He is the son of Mary.' Then I looked behind and I saw a red-complexioned, fat, curly-haired man, blind in the right eye which looked like a bulging out grape. I asked, 'Who is this?' They replied, 'He is Ad-Dajjal.' The one who resembled to him among the people, was Ibn Qatar." (Az-Zuhri said, "He (i.e. Ibn Qatan) was a man from the tribe Khuza`a who died in the pre-lslamic period.") (3441) □

1174. Narrated Abu Huraira: Allah's Messenger (ﷺ) said, "Both in this world and in the Hereafter, I am the nearest of all the people to Jesus. The prophets are paternal brothers; their mothers are different, but their religion is one." (3443) □

1175. Narrated Abu Huraira: The Prophet (ﷺ) said, "Jesus, seeing a man stealing, asked him, 'Did you steal? He said, 'No, by Allah, except Whom there is None who has the right to be worshipped' Jesus said, 'I believe in Allah and suspect my eyes."

(3444) ☐

1176. Narrated `Umar: I heard the Prophet (ﷺ) saying, "Do not exaggerate in praising me as the Christians praised the son of Mary, for I am only a Slave. So, call me the Slave of Allah and His Apostle." (3445) ☐

1177. Narrted Ibn `Abbas: Allah's Messenger (ﷺ) said, "You will be resurrected (and assembled) bare-footed, naked and uncircumcised." The Prophet (ﷺ) then recited the Divine Verse: -- "As We began the first creation, We shall repeat it: A promise We have undertaken. Truly we shall do it." (21.104) He added, "The first to be dressed will be Abraham. Then some of my companions will take to the right and to the left. I will say: 'My companions! 'It will be said, 'They had been renegades since you left them.' I will then say what the Pious Slave Jesus, the son of Mary said: 'And I was a witness over them while I dwelt amongst them; when You did take me up, You were the Watcher over them, and You are a Witness to all things. If You punish them, they are Your slaves, and if you forgive them, You, only You are the All-Mighty the All-Wise.'" (5.117-118) Narrated Quaggas, "Those were the apostates who renegade from Islam during the Caliphate of Abu Bakr who fought them". (3447) ☐

1178. Narrated Abu Huraira: Allah's Messenger (ﷺ) said, "By Him in Whose Hands my soul is, surely (Jesus,) the son of Mary will soon descend amongst you and will judge mankind justly (as a Just Ruler); he will break the Cross and kill the pigs and there will be no Jizya (i.e. taxation taken from non Muslims). Money will be in abundance so that nobody will accept it, and a single prostration to Allah (in prayer) will be better than the whole world and whatever is in it." Abu Huraira added "If you wish, you can recite (this verse of the Holy Book): -- 'And there is none Of the people of the Scriptures (Jews and Christians) But must believe in him (i.e Jesus as an Apostle of Allah and a human being) Before his death. And on the Day of Judgment He will be a witness against them." (4.159) (3448) ☐

1179. Narrated Abu Huraira: Allah's Messenger (ﷺ) said "How will you be when the son of Mary (Jesus) descends amongst you and your imam is among you." (3449) ☐

53. STORY OF AHL AL-KITAB

1180. NARRATED RABI BIN HIRASH (RA): `Uqba bin `Amr said to Hudhaifa, "Won't you relate to us of what you have heard from Allah's Apostle?" He said, "I heard him saying, "When Ad-Dajjal appears, he will have fire and water along with him. What the people will consider as cold water, will be fire that will burn (things). So, if anyone of you comes across this, he should fall in the thing which will appear to him as fire, for in reality, it will be fresh cold water." Hudhaifa added, "I also heard him saying, 'From among the people preceding your generation, there was a man whom the angel of death visited to capture his soul. (So his soul was captured) and he was asked if he had done any good deed.' He replied, 'I don't remember any good deed.' He was asked to think it over. He said, 'I do not remember, except that I used to trade with the people in the world and I used to give a respite to the rich and forgive the poor (among my debtors). So Allah made him enter Paradise." Hudhaifa further said, "I also heard him saying, 'once there was a man on his death-bed, who, losing every hope of surviving said to his family: When I die, gather for me a large heap of wood and make a fire (to burn me). When the fire eats my meat and reaches my bones, and when the bones burn, take and crush them into powder and wait for a windy day to throw it (i.e. the powder) over the sea. They did so, but Allah collected his particles and asked him: Why did you do so? He replied: For fear of You. So Allah forgave him." `Uqba bin `Amr said, "I heard him saying that the Israeli used to dig the grave of the dead (to steal their shrouds). (3452) □

1181. Narrated `Aisha and Ibn `Abbas: On his death-bed Allah's Messenger (ﷺ) put a sheet over his-face and when he felt hot, he would remove it from his face. When in that state (of putting and removing the sheet) he said, "May Allah's Curse be on the Jews and the Christians for they build places of worship at the graves of their prophets." (By that) he intended to warn (the Muslim) from what they (i.e. Jews and Christians) had done. (3453) □

1182. Narrated Ibn `Umar: Allah's Messenger (ﷺ) said, "Your period (i.e. the

Muslims period) in comparison to the periods of the previous nations, is like the period between the `Asr prayer and sunset. And your example in comparison to the Jews and the Christians is like the example of a person who employed some laborers and asked them, 'Who will work for me till midday for one Qirat each?' The Jews worked for half a day for one Qirat each. The person asked, 'Who will do the work for me from midday to the time of the `Asr (prayer) for one Qirat each?' The Christians worked from midday till the `Asr prayer for one Qirat. Then the person asked, 'Who will do the work for me from the `Asr till sunset for two Qirats each?'" The Prophet (صلى الله عليه وسلم) added, "It is you (i.e. Muslims) who are doing the work from the `Asr till sunset, so you will have a double reward. The Jews and the Christians got angry and said, 'We have done more work but got less wages.' Allah said, 'Have I been unjust to you as regards your rights?' They said, 'No.' So Allah said, 'Then it is My Blessing which I bestow on whomever I like." (3459) □

1183. Narrated `Abdullah bin `Amr: The Prophet (صلى الله عليه وسلم) said, "Convey (my teachings) to the people even if it were a single sentence, and tell others the stories of Bani Israel (which have been taught to you), for it is not sinful to do so. And whoever tells a lie on me intentionally, will surely take his place in the (Hell) Fire." (3461) □

1184. Narrated Jundub: Allah's Messenger (صلى الله عليه وسلم) said, "Amongst the nations before you there was a man who got a wound, and growing impatient (with its pain), he took a knife and cut his hand with it and the blood did not stop till he died. Allah said, 'My Slave hurried to bring death upon himself so I have forbidden him (to enter) Paradise.'" (3463) □

1185. Narrated Abu Huraira: that he heard Allah's Messenger (صلى الله عليه وسلم) saying, "Allah willed to test three Israelis who were a Leper, a blind man and a bald-headed man. So, he sent them an angel who came to the leper and said, 'What thing do you like most?' He replied, 'Good color and good skin, for the people have a strong aversion to me.' The angel touched him and his illness was cured, and he was given a good color and beautiful skin. The angel asked him, 'What kind of property do you like best?' He replied, 'Camels (or cows).' (The narrator is in doubt, for either the leper or the bald-headed man demanded camels and the other demanded cows). So he (i.e. the leper) was given a pregnant she-camel, and the angel said (to him), 'May Allah bless you in it.' The angel then went to the bald-headed man and said, 'What thing do you like most?' He said, 'I like good hair and wish to be cured of this disease, for the people feel repulsion for me.' The angel touched him and his illness was cured, and he was given good hair. The angel asked (him), 'What kind of property do you like best?' He replied, 'Cows.' The angel gave him a pregnant cow and said, 'May Allah bless you in it.' The angel went to the blind man and asked, 'What thing do you like best?' He said, '(I like) that Allah may restore my eye-sight to me so that I may see the people.' The angel touched his eyes and Allah gave him back his eye-sight. The angel asked him, 'What kind of property do you like best?' He replied, 'Sheep.' The angel gave him a pregnant sheep. Afterwards, all the three pregnant animals gave birth to young ones, and multiplied and brought forth so much that one of the (three) men had a herd of camels filling a valley, and one had a herd of cows filling a valley, and one had a flock of sheep filling a valley. Then the angel, disguised in the shape and appearance of a leper, went to the leper and said, I am a poor man, who has lost all means of livelihood while on a journey. So none will satisfy my need except Allah and then you. In the Name of Him Who has given you such nice color and beautiful skin, and so much property, I ask you to give me a camel so that I may reach my destination. The man replied, 'I have many obligations (so I cannot give you).' The angel said, 'I think I know you; were you not a leper to whom the people had a strong aversion? Weren't you a poor man, and then Allah gave you (all this property)?' He replied, '(This is all wrong), I got this property through inheritance from my fore-fathers.' The angel said, 'If you are telling a lie, then let Allah make you as you were before. ' Then the angel, disguised in the shape and appearance of a bald man, went to the bald man and said to him the same as he told the first one, and he too answered the same as the first one did. The angel said, 'If you are telling a lie, then let Allah make you as you were before.' The angel, disguised in the shape of a blind man, went to the blind man and said, 'I am a poor man and a traveler, whose means of livelihood have been exhausted while on a journey. I have nobody to help me except Allah, and after Him, you yourself. I ask you in the Name of Him Who has given you back your eye-sight to give me a sheep, so that with its help, I may complete my journey.' The man said, 'No doubt, I was blind and Allah gave me back my eye-sight; I was poor and Allah made me rich; so take anything you wish from my property. By Allah, I will not stop you for taking anything (you need) of my property which you may take for Allah's sake.' The angel replied, 'Keep your property with you. You (i.e the three men) have been tested, and Allah is pleased with you and is angry with your two companions." (3464) □

1186. Narrated Ibn `Umar: Allah's Messenger (ﷺ) said, "Once three persons (from the previous nations) were traveling, and suddenly it started raining and they took shelter in a cave. The entrance of the cave got closed while they were inside. They said to each other, 'O you! Nothing can save you except the truth, so each of you should ask Allah's Help by referring to such a deed as he thinks he did sincerely (i.e. just for gaining Allah's Pleasure).' So one of them said, 'O Allah! You know that I had a laborer who worked for me for one Faraq (i.e. three Sas) of rice, but he departed, leaving it (i.e. his wages). I sowed that Faraq of rice and with its yield I bought cows (for him). Later on when he came to me asking for his wages, I said (to him), 'Go to those cows and drive them away.' He said to me, 'But you have to pay me only a Faraq of rice,' I said to him, 'Go to those cows and take them, for they are the product of that Faraq (of rice).' So he drove them. O Allah! If you consider that I did that for fear of You, then please remove the rock.' The rock shifted a bit from the mouth of the cave. The second one said, 'O Allah, You know that I had old parents whom I used to provide with the milk of my sheep every night. One night I was delayed and when I came, they had slept, while my wife and children were crying with hunger. I used not to let them (i.e. my family) drink unless my parents had drunk first. So I disliked to wake them up and also disliked that they should sleep without drinking it, I kept on waiting (for them to wake) till it dawned. O Allah! If You consider that I did that for fear of you, then please remove the rock.' So the rock shifted and they could see the sky through it. The (third) one said, 'O Allah! You know that I had a cousin (i.e. my paternal uncle's daughter) who was most beloved to me and I sought to seduce her, but she refused, unless I paid her one-hundred Dinars (i.e. gold pieces). So I collected the amount and brought it to her, and she allowed me to sleep with her. But when I sat between her legs, she said, 'Be afraid of Allah, and do not deflower me but legally. 'I got up and left the hundred Dinars (for her). O Allah! If You consider that I did that for fear of you than please remove the rock. So Allah saved them and they came out (of the cave)." (3465) □

1187. Narrated Humaid bin `Abdur-Rahman: That he heard Muawiya bin Abi Sufyan (talking) on the pulpit in the year when he performed the Hajj. He took a tuft of hair that was in the hand of an orderly and said, "O people of Medina! Where are your learned men? I heard the Prophet (ﷺ) forbidding such a thing as this (i.e. false hair) and he used to say, 'The Israelis were destroyed when their ladies practiced this habit (of using false hair to lengthen their locks). (3468) □

1188. Narrated Abu Sa`id Al-Khudri: The Prophet (ﷺ) said, "Amongst the men of Bani Israel there was a man who had murdered ninety-nine persons. Then he set out asking (whether his repentance could be accepted or not). He came upon a monk and asked him if his repentance could be accepted. The monk replied in the negative and so the man killed him. He kept on asking till a man advised to go to such and such village. (So he left for it) but death overtook him on the way. While dying, he turned his chest towards that village (where he had hoped his repentance would be accepted), and so the angels of mercy and the angels of punishment quarrelled amongst themselves regarding him. Allah ordered the village (towards which he was going) to come closer to him, and ordered the village (where he had come), to go far away, and then He ordered the angels to measure the distances between his body and the two villages. So he was found to be one span closer to the village (he was going to). So he was forgiven." (3470) □

1189. Narrated Abu Huraira: Allah's Messenger (ﷺ) said, "A man bought a piece of and from another man, and the buyer found an earthenware jar filled with gold in the land. The buyer said to the seller. 'Take your gold, as I have bought only the land from you, but I have not bought the gold from you.' The (former) owner of the land said, "I have sold you the land with everything in it.' So both of them took their case before a man who asked, 'Do you have children?' One of them said, "I have a boy.' The other said, "I have a girl.' The man said, 'Marry the girl to the boy and spend the money on both of them and give the rest of it in charity.'" (3472) □

1190. Narrated `Abdullah: As if I saw the Prophet (ﷺ) talking about one of the prophets whose nation had beaten him and caused him to bleed, while he was cleaning the blood off his face and saying, "O Allah! Forgive my nation, for they have no knowledge." (3477) □

54. MERITS OF THE PROPHET (ﷺ)

1191. NARRATED KULAIB BIN WAIL (RA): I asked Zainab bint Abi Salama (i.e. daughter of the wife of the Prophet,) "Tell me about the Prophet (ﷺ). Did he belong to the tribe of Mudar?" She replied, "Yes, he belonged to the tribe of Mudar and was from the offspring of An-Nadr bin Kinana." (3491) □

1192. Narrated Abu Huraira: The Prophet (ﷺ) said, "The tribe of Quraish has precedence over the people in this connection (i.e the right of ruling). The Muslims follow the Muslims amongst them, and the infidels follow the infidels amongst them. People are of different natures: The best amongst them in the pre-lslamic period are the best in Islam provided they comprehend the religious knowledge. You will find that the best amongst the people in this respect (of ruling) is he who hates it (the idea of ruling) most, till he is given the pledge of allegiance."(3495) □

1193. Narrated Tawus: Ibn `Abbas recited the Qur'anic Verse: "It is that of which Allah gives good tidings to His servants who believe and do righteous deeds. Say, [O Muhammad], "I do not ask you for this message any payment [but] only good will through kinship." And whoever commits a good deed - We will increase for him good therein. Indeed, Allah is Forgiving and Appreciative." (42.23) Sa`id bin Jubair said, "(The Verse implies) the kinship of Muhammad." Ibn `Abbas said, "There was not a single house (i.e. sub-tribe) of Quraish but had a kinship to the Prophet (ﷺ) and so the above Verse was revealed in this connection, and its interpretation is: 'O Quraish! You should keep good relation between me (i.e. Muhammad) and you." (3497) □

1194. Narrated Muhammad bin Jubair bin Mut`im: That while he was with a delegation from Quraish to Muawiya, the latter heard the news that `Abdullah bin `Amr bin Al-`As said that there would be a king from the tribe of Qahtan. On that Muawiya became angry, got up and then praised Allah as He deserved, and said, "Now then, I have heard that some men amongst you narrate things which are neither in the Holy Book, nor have been told by Allah's Messenger (ﷺ). Those men are the ignorant amongst you. Beware of such hopes as make the people go astray, for I heard Allah's Messenger (ﷺ) saying, 'Authority of ruling will remain with Quraish, and whoever bears hostility to them, Allah will destroy him as long as they abide by the laws of the religion.'" (3500) □

1195. Narrated Ibn `Umar: The Prophet (ﷺ) said, "Authority of ruling will remain with Quraish, even if only two of them remained." (3501) □

1196. Narrated `Urwa bin Az-Zubair: `Abdullah bin Az-Zubair went with some women of the tribe of Bani Zuhra to `Aisha who used to treat them nicely because of their relation to Allah's Messenger (p.b.u.h). (3503) □

1197. Narrated `Urwa bin Az-Zubair:`Abdullah bin Az-Zubair was the most beloved person to `Aisha excluding the Prophet (ﷺ) and Abu Bakr, and he in his turn, was the most devoted to her, `Aisha used not to withhold the money given to her by Allah, but she used to spend it in charity. (`Abdullah) bin Az-Zubair said, "`Aisha should be stopped from doing so." (When `Aisha heard this), she said protestingly, "Shall I be stopped from doing so? I vow that I will never talk to `Abdullah bin Az-Zubair." On that, Ibn Az-Zubair asked some people from Quraish and particularly the two uncles of Allah's Messenger (ﷺ) to intercede with her, but she refused (to talk to him). Az-Zuhriyun, the uncles of the Prophet, including `Abdur-Rahman bin Al-Aswad bin `Abd Yaghuth and Al-Miswar bin Makhrama said to him, "When we ask for the permission to visit her, enter her house along with us (without taking her leave)." He did accordingly (and she accepted their intercession). He sent her ten slaves whom she manumitted as an expiation for (not keeping) her vow. `Aisha manumitted more slaves for the same purpose till she manumitted forty slaves. She said, "I wish I had specified what I would have done in case of not fulfilling my vow when I made the vow, so that I might have done it easily." (3505) ☐

1198. Narrated Ibn `Umar: While Allah's Messenger (ﷺ) was on the pulpit, he said, "May Allah forgive the tribe of Ghifar! And may Allah save the tribe of Aslam! The tribe of `Usaiya have disobeyed Allah and His Apostle." (3513) ☐

1199. Narrated Ibn `Abbas: When the Verse: 'And warn your tribe of near kindred.' (26.214) was revealed, the Prophet (ﷺ) started calling (the 'Arab tribes), "O Bani Fihr, O Bani `Adi" mentioning first the various branch tribes of Quraish. (3525) ☐

1200. Narrated Abu Huraira: The Prophet (ﷺ) said, "O Bani `Abd Munaf! Buy yourselves from Allah; O Bani `Abdul-Muttalib! Buy yourselves from Allah; O mother of Az-Zubair bin Al-Awwam, the aunt of Allah's Messenger (ﷺ), and O Fatima bint Muhammad! Buy yourselves from Allah, for I cannot defend you before Allah. You (both) can ask me from my property as much as you like." (3527) ☐

1201. Narrated Anas: The Prophet (ﷺ) sent for the Ansar (and when they came), he asked, 'Is there any stranger amongst you?" They said, "No except the son of our sister." Allah's Messenger (ﷺ) said, "The son of the sister of some people belongs to them." (3528) ☐

1202. Narrated `Aisha: Once Hassan bin Thabit asked the permission of the Prophet (ﷺ) to lampoon (i.e. compose satirical poetry defaming) the infidels. The Prophet (ﷺ) said, "What about the fact that I have common descent with them?" Hassan replied, "I shall take you out of them as a hair is taken out of dough." Narrated `Urwa: I started abusing Hassan in front of `Aisha, whereupon she said. "Don't abuse him, for he used to defend the Prophet (with his poetry). (3531) ☐

1203. Narrated Jubair bin Mut`im: Allah's Messenger (ﷺ) said, "I have five names: I am Muhammad and Ahmad; I am Al-Mahi through whom Allah will eliminate infidelity; I am Al-Hashir who will be the first to be resurrected, the people being resurrected there after; and I am also Al-`Aqib (i.e. There will be no prophet after me). (3532) ☐

1204. Narrated Abu Huraira: Allah's Messenger (ﷺ) said, "Doesn't it astonish you how Allah protects me from the Quraish's abusing and cursing? They abuse Mudhammam and curse Mudhammam while I am Muhammad (and not Mudhammam). (3533) ☐

1205. Narrated Jabir bin `Abdullah: The Prophet (ﷺ) said, "My similitude (likeness) in comparison with the other prophets is that of a man who has built a house completely and excellently except for a place of one brick. When the people enter the house, they admire its beauty and say: 'But for the place of this brick (how splendid the house will be)!" (3534) ☐

1206. Narrated As- Scab bin Yazid: My aunt took me to Allah's Messenger (ﷺ) and said, "O Allah's Messenger (ﷺ)! My nephew is sick"' The Prophet (ﷺ) passed his hands over my head and blessed me. Then he performed ablution and I drank the remaining water, and standing behind him. A saw the seal in between his shoulders." (3541) ☐

1207. Narrated `Uqba bin Al-Harith: (Once) Abu Bakr offered the `Asr prayer and then went out walking and saw Al-Hasan playing with the boys. He lifted him on to his shoulders and said, "Let my parents be sacrificed for your sake! (You) resemble the Prophet (ﷺ) and not `Ali," while `Ali was smiling. (3542) ☐

1208. Narrated Isma`il bin Abi Khalid: I heard Abii Juhaifa saying, "I saw the Prophet, and Al-Hasan bin `Ali resembled him." I said to Abu- Juhaifa, "Describe him for me." He said, "He was white and his beard was black with some white hair. He promised to give us 13 young she-camels, but he expired before we could get them." (3544) ☐

1209. Narrated Hariz bin `Uthman: That he asked `Abdullah bin Busr (i.e. the companion of the Prophet), "Did you see the Prophet (ﷺ) when he was old?" He said, "He had a few white hairs between the lower lip and the chin." (3546) ☐

1210. Narrated Rabi`a bin Abi `Abdur-Rahman: I heard Anas bin Malik describing the Prophet (ﷺ) saying, "He was of medium height amongst the people, neither tall nor short; he had a rosy color, neither absolutely white nor deep brown; his hair was neither completely curly nor quite lank (hanging straight). Divine Inspiration was revealed to him when he was forty years old. He stayed ten years in Mecca receiving the Divine Inspiration, and stayed in Medina for ten more years. When he expired, he had scarcely twenty white hairs in his head and beard." Rabi`a said, "I saw some of his hairs and it was red. When I asked about that, I was told that it turned red because of scent." (3547) ☐

1211. Narrated Al-Bara: Allah's Messenger (ﷺ) was the handsomest of all the people, and had the best appearance. He was neither very tall nor short. (3549) ☐

1212. Narrated Qatada: I asked Anas, "Did the Prophet (ﷺ) use to dye (his) hair?" He said, "No, for there were only a few white hairs on his temples." (3550) ☐

1213. Narrated Al-Bara: The Prophet (ﷺ) was of moderate height having broad shoulders (long) hair reaching his ear-lobes. Once I saw him in a red cloak and I had never seen a more handsome than him." (3551) ☐

1214. Narrated Anas: The Prophet (ﷺ) had big hands and feet, and I have not seen anybody like him, neither before nor after him, and his palms were soft. (5907) ☐

1215. Narrated Anas: The Prophet (ﷺ) had big feet and hands. (5910) ☐

1216. Narrated Abu 'Is-haq: Al-Bara' was asked, "Was the face of the Prophet (as bright) as a sword?" He said, "No, but (as bright) as a moon." (3552) ☐

1217. Narrated `Abdullah bin Ka`b: I heard Ka`b bin Malik talking after his failure to join (the Ghazwa of) Tabuk. He said, "When I greeted Allah's Messenger (ﷺ)

whose face was glittering with happiness, for whenever Allah's Messenger (ﷺ) was happy, his face used to glitter, as if it was a piece of the moon, and we used to recognize it (i.e. his happiness) from his face." (3556) □

1218. Narrated Abu Huraira: Allah's Messenger (ﷺ) said, "I have been sent (as an Apostle) in the best of all the generations of Adam's offspring since their Creation." (3557) □

1219. Narrated `Aisha: Whenever Allah's Messenger (ﷺ) was given the choice of one of two matters, he would choose the easier of the two, as long as it was not sinful to do so, but if it was sinful to do so, he would not approach it. Allah's Messenger (ﷺ) never took revenge (over anybody) for his own sake but (he did) only when Allah's Legal Bindings were outraged in which case he would take revenge for Allah's Sake. (3560) □

1220. Narrated Anas: I have never touched silk or Dibaj (i.e. thick silk) softer than the palm of the Prophet (ﷺ) nor have I smelt a perfume nicer than the sweat of the Prophet. (3561) □

1221. Narrated Abu Sa`id Al-Khudri: The Prophet (ﷺ) was shier than a veiled virgin girl. (3562) □

1223. Narrated `Aisha: The Prophet (ﷺ) used to talk so clearly that if somebody wanted to count the number of his words, he could do so. (3567) □

1224. Narrated Sharik bin `Abdullah bin Abi Namr: I heard Anas bin Malik telling us about the night when the Prophet (ﷺ) was made to travel from the Ka`ba Mosque. Three persons (i.e. angels) came to the Prophet (ﷺ) before he was divinely inspired was an Aspostle), while he was sleeping in Al Masjid-ul-Haram. The first (of the three angels) said, "Which of them is he?" The second said, "He is the best of them." That was all that happened then, and he did not see them till they came at another night and he perceived their presence with his heart, for the eyes of the Prophet (ﷺ) were closed when he was asleep, but his heart was not asleep (not unconscious). This is characteristic of all the prophets: Their eyes sleep but their hearts do not sleep. Then Gabriel took charge of the Prophet (ﷺ) and ascended along with him to the Heaven. (3570) □

55. MIRACLES OF PROPHET (ﷺ)

1225. NARRATED ABU HURAIRA (RA): The Prophet (ﷺ) said, "Every Prophet was given miracles because of which people believed, but what I have been given, is Divine Inspiration which Allah has revealed to me. So I hope that my followers will outnumber the followers of the other Prophets on the Day of Resurrection." (4981) □

1226. Narrated Anas bin Malik: The people of Mecca asked Allah's Messenger (ﷺ) to show them a miracle. So he showed them the moon split in two halves between which they saw the Hira' mountain. (3868) □

1227. Narrated 'Abdullah: The moon was split (into two pieces) while we were with the Prophet (ﷺ) in Mina. He said, "Be witnesses." Then a Piece of the moon went towards the mountain. (3869) □

1228. Narrated 'Imran bin Husain: That they were with the Prophet (ﷺ) on a journey. They travelled the whole night, and when dawn approached, they took a rest and sleep overwhelmed them till the sun rose high in the sky. The first to get up was Abu Bakr. Allah's Messenger (ﷺ) used not to be awakened from his sleep, but he would wake up by himself. 'Umar woke up and then Abu Bakr sat by the side of the Prophet's head and started saying: Allahu-Akbar raising his voice till the Prophet (ﷺ) woke up, (and after traveling for a while) he dismounted and led us in the Morning Prayer. A man amongst the people failed to join us in the prayer. When the Prophet (ﷺ) had finished the prayer, he asked (the man), "O so-and-so! What prevented you from offering the prayer with us?" He replied, "I am Junub," Alllah's Apostle ordered him to perform Tayammam with clean earth. The man then offered the prayer.

Allah's Messenger (ﷺ) ordered me and a few others to go ahead of him. We had become very thirsty. While we were on our way (looking for water), we came across a lady (riding an animal), hanging her legs between two water-skins. We asked her, "Where can we get water?" She replied, "Oh! There is no water." We asked, "how far is your house from the water?" She replied, "A distance of a day and a night travel." We said, "Come on to Allah's Messenger (ﷺ), "She asked, "What is Allah's Messenger (ﷺ)?" So we brought her to Allah's Messenger (ﷺ) against her will, and she told him what she had told us before and added that she was the mother of orphans. So the Prophet (ﷺ) ordered that her two water-skins be brought and he rubbed the mouths of the water-skins. As we were thirsty, we drank till we quenched our thirst and we were forty men. We also filled all our waterskins and other utensils with water, but we did not water the camels. The waterskin was so full that it was almost about to burst. The Prophet (ﷺ) then said, "Bring what you have." So some dates and pieces of bread were collected for the lady, and when she went to her people, she said, "I have met either the greatest magician or a prophet as the people claim." So Allah guided the people of that village through that lady. She embraced Islam and they all embraced Islam. (3571) ☐

1229. Narrated Jabir bin `Abdullah: I was accompanying the Prophet (ﷺ) on a journey and was riding a slow camel that was lagging behind the others. The Prophet (ﷺ) passed by me and asked, "Who is this?" I replied, "Jabir bin `Abdullah." He asked, "What is the matter, (why are you late)?" I replied, "I am riding a slow camel." He asked, "Do you have a stick?" I replied in the affirmative. He said, "Give it to me." When I gave it to him, he beat the camel and rebuked it. Then that camel surpassed the others thenceforth. (2309) ☐

1230. Narrated `Urwa: That the Prophet (ﷺ) gave him one Dinar so as to buy a sheep for him. `Urwa bought two sheep for him with the money. Then he sold one of the sheep for one Dinar, and brought one Dinar and a sheep to the Prophet. On that, the Prophet (ﷺ) invoked Allah to bless him in his deals. So `Urwa used to gain (from any deal) even if he bought dust. (3642) ☐

1231. Narrated Jabir bin `Abdullah: My father died and was in debt. I suggested that his creditors take the fruits (i.e. dates) of my garden in lieu of the debt of my father, but they refused the offer, as they thought that it would not cover the full debt. So, I went to the Prophet (ﷺ) and told him about it. He said (to me), "When you pluck the dates and collect them in the Mirbad (i.e. a place where dates are dried), call me (Allah's Messenger (ﷺ))." Finally he came accompanied by Abu Bakr and `Umar and sat on the dates and invoked Allah to bless them. Then he said, "Call your creditors and give them their full rights." So, I paid all my father's creditors in full and yet thirteen extra Wasqs of dates remained, seven of which were 'Ajwa and six were Laun or six of which were Ajwa and seven were Laun. I met Allah's Messenger (ﷺ) at sunset and informed him about it. On that he smiled and said, "Go to Abu Bakr and `Umar and tell them about it." They said, "We perceived that was going to happen, as Allah's Messenger (ﷺ) did what he did." (2709) ☐

1232. Narrated Salama: Once (on a journey) our provisions diminished and the people were reduced to poverty. They went to the Prophet (ﷺ) and asked his permission to slaughter their camels, and he agreed. `Umar met them and they told him about it, and he said, "How would you survive after slaughtering your camels?" Then he went to the Prophet and said, "O Allah's Messenger (ﷺ)! How would they survive after slaughtering their camels?" Allah's Messenger (ﷺ) ordered `Umar, "Call upon the people to bring what has remained of their food." A leather sheet was spread and all the food was collected and heaped over it. Allah's Messenger (ﷺ) stood up and invoked Allah to bless it, and then directed all the people to come with their utensils, and they started taking from it till all of them got what was sufficient for them. Allah's Messenger (ﷺ) then said, "I testify that None has the right to be worshipped but Allah, and I am His Messenger." (2484) ☐

1233. Narrated `Abdur-Rahman bin Abu Bakr: We were one-hundred and thirty persons accompanying the Prophet (ﷺ) who asked us whether anyone of us had food. There was a man who had about a Sa of wheat which was mixed with water then. A very tall pagan came driving sheep. The Prophet (ﷺ) asked him, "Will you sell us (a sheep) or give it as a present?" He said, "I will sell you (a sheep)." The Prophet (ﷺ) bought a sheep and it was slaughtered. The Prophet ordered that its liver and other abdominal organs be roasted. By Allah, the Prophet (ﷺ) gave every person of the one-hundred-and-thirty a piece of that; he gave all those of them who were present; and kept the shares of those who were absent. The Prophet (ﷺ) then put its meat in two huge basins and all of them ate to their fill, and even then more food was left in the two basins which were carried on the camel (or said something like it). (2618) □

1234. Narrated Jabir bin `Abdullah: When the Trench was dug, I saw the Prophet (ﷺ) in the state of severe hunger. So I returned to my wife and said, "Have you got anything (to eat), for I have seen Allah's Messenger (ﷺ) in a state of severe hunger." She brought out for me, a bag containing one Sa of barley, and we had a domestic she animal (i.e. a kid) which I slaughtered then, and my wife ground the barley and she finished at the time I finished my job (i.e. slaughtering the animal). Then I cut the meat into pieces and put it in an earthenware (cooking) pot, and returned to Allah's Messenger (ﷺ). My wife said, "Do not disgrace me in front of Allah's Apostle and those who are with him." So I went to him and said to him secretly, "O Allah's Messenger (ﷺ)! I have slaughtered a she-animal (i.e. kid) of ours, and we have ground a Sa of barley which was with us. So please come, you and another person along with you." The Prophet (ﷺ) raised his voice and said, "O people of Trench! Jabir has prepared a meal so let us go." Allah's Messenger (ﷺ) said to me, "Don't put down your earthenware meat pot (from the fireplace) or bake your dough till I come." So I came (to my house) and Allah's Messenger (ﷺ) too, came, proceeding before the people. When I came to my wife, she said, "May Allah do so-and-so to you." I said, "I have told the Prophet (ﷺ) of what you said." Then she brought out to him (i.e. the Prophet (ﷺ) the dough, and he spat in it and invoked for Allah's Blessings in it. Then he proceeded towards our earthenware meat-pot and spat in it and invoked for Allah's Blessings in it. Then he said (to my wife). Call a lady-baker to bake along with you and keep on taking out scoops from your earthenware meat-pot, and do not put it down from its fireplace." They were onethousand (who took their meals), and by Allah they all ate, and when they left the food and went away, our earthenware pot was still bubbling (full of meat) as if it had not decreased, and our dough was still being baked as if nothing had been taken from it. (4102) □

1235. Narrated Al-Bara: Do you (people) consider the conquest of Mecca, the Victory (referred to in the Qur'an 48:1). Was the conquest of Mecca a victory? We really consider that the actual Victory was the Ar-Ridwan Pledge of allegiance which we gave on the day of Al-Hudaibiya (to the Prophet). On the day of Al-Hudaibiya we were fourteen hundred men along with the Prophet (ﷺ) Al-Hudaibiya was a well, the water of which we used up leaving not a single drop of water in it. When the Prophet (ﷺ) was informed of that, he came and sat on its edge. Then he asked for a utensil of water, performed ablution from it, rinsed (his mouth), invoked (Allah), and poured the remaining water into the well. We stayed there for a while and then the well brought forth what we required of water for ourselves and our riding animals. (4150) □

1236. Narrated Salim: Jabir said "On the day of Al-Hudaibiya, the people felt thirsty and Allah's Messenger (ﷺ) had a utensil containing water. He performe ablution from it and then the people came towards him. Allah's Apostle said, 'What is wrong with you?' The people said, 'O Allah's Messenger (ﷺ)! We haven't got any water to perform ablution with or to drink, except what you have in your utensil.' So the Prophet (ﷺ) put his hand in the utensil and the water started spouting out between his fingers like springs. So we drank and performed ablution." I said to Jabir, "What was your number on that day?" He replied, "Even if we had been one hundred thousand, that water would have been sufficient for us. Anyhow, we were 1500.' (4152) □

1237. Narrated Abu Huraira: By Allah except Whom none has the right to- be worshipped, (sometimes) I used to lay (sleep) on the ground on my liver (abdomen) because of hunger, and (sometimes) I used to bind a stone over my belly because of hunger. One day I sat by the way from where they (the Prophet (ﷺ) and his companions) used to come out. When Abu Bakr passed by, I asked him about a Verse from Allah's Book and I asked him only that he might satisfy my hunger, but he passed by and did not do so. Then `Umar passed by me and I asked him about a Verse from Allah's Book, and I asked him only that he might satisfy my hunger, but he passed by without doing so. Finally Abu-1-Qasim (the Prophet (ﷺ)) passed by me and he smiled when he saw me, for he knew what was in my heart and on my face. He said, "O Aba Hirr (Abu Huraira)!" I replied, "Labbaik, O Allah's Messenger (ﷺ)!" He said to me, "Follow me." He left and I followed him. Then he entered the house and I asked permission to enter and was admitted. He found milk in a bowl and said, "From where is this milk?" They said, "It has been presented to you by such-and-such man (or by such and such woman)." He said, "O Aba Hirr!" I said, "Labbaik, O Allah's Messenger (ﷺ)!" He said, "Go and call the people of Suffa to me." These people of Suffa were the guests of Islam who had no families, nor money, nor anybody to depend upon, and whenever an object of charity was brought to the Prophet (ﷺ), he would send it to them and would not take anything from it, and whenever any present was given to him, he used to send some for them and take some of it for himself. The order off the Prophet upset me, and I said to myself, "How will this little milk be enough for the people of As- Suffa?" thought I was more entitled to drink from that milk in order to strengthen myself, but behold! The Prophet (ﷺ) came to order me to give that milk to them. I wondered what will remain of that milk for me, but anyway, I could not but obey Allah and His Apostle so I went to the people of As-Suffa and called them, and they came and asked the Prophet's permission to enter. They were admitted and took their seats in the house. The Prophet (ﷺ) said, "O Aba-Hirr!" I said, "Labbaik, O Allah's Messenger (ﷺ)!" He said, "Take it and give it to them." So I took the bowl (of Milk) and started giving it to one man who would drink his fill and return it to me, whereupon I would give it to another man who, in his turn, would drink his fill and return it to me, and I would then offer it to another man who would drink his fill and return it to me. Finally, after the whole group had drunk their fill, I reached the Prophet (ﷺ) who took the bowl and put it on his hand, looked at me and smiled and said. "O Aba Hirr!" I replied, "Labbaik, O Allah's Messenger (ﷺ)!" He said, "There remain you and I." I said, "You have said the truth, O Allah's Messenger (ﷺ)!" He said, "Sit down and drink." I sat down and drank. He said, "Drink," and I drank. He kept on telling me repeatedly to drink, till I said, "No. by

Allah Who sent you with the Truth, I have no space for it (in my stomach)." He said, "Hand it over to me." When I gave him the bowl, he praised Allah and pronounced Allah's Name on it and drank the remaining milk. (6452) □

1238. Narrated Yazid bin Abi Ubaid: I saw the trace of a wound in Salama's leg. I said to him, "O Abu Muslim! What is this wound?" He said, "This was inflicted on me on the day of Khaibar and the people said, 'Salama has been wounded.' Then I went to the Prophet (ﷺ) and he puffed his saliva in it (i.e. the wound) thrice. And since then I have not had any pain in it till this hour." (4206) □

56. COMPANIONS

1239. NARRATED ANAS BIN MALIK (RA): The Prophet (ﷺ) noticed the absence of Thabit bin Qais. A man said, "O Allah's Messenger (ﷺ)! I shall bring you his news." So he went to him and saw him sitting in his house drooping his head (sadly). He asked Thabit, "What's the matter?" Thabit replied, "An evil situation: A man used to raise his voice over the voice of the Prophet (ﷺ) and so all his good deeds have been annulled and he is from the people of Hell." The man went back and told the Prophet (ﷺ) that Thabit had said so-and-so. (The sub-narrator, Musa bin Anas said, "The man went to Thabit again with glad tidings). The Prophet (ﷺ) said to him, "Go and say to Thabit: 'You are not from the people of Fire, but from the people of Paradise." (3613) □

1240. Narrated Abu Sa'id Al-Khudri: "Allah's Messenger (ﷺ) said, "A time will come upon the people, when a group of people will wage a holy war and it will be said, 'Is there amongst you anyone who has accompanied Allah's Messenger (ﷺ)?' They will say, 'Yes.' And so victory will be bestowed on them. Then a time will come upon the people when a group of people will wage a holy war, and it will be said, "Is there amongst you anynone who has accompanied the companions of Allah's Messenger (ﷺ)?' They will say, 'Yes.' And so victory will be bestowed on them. Then a time will come upon the people when a group of people will wage a holy war, and it will be said, "Is there amongst you anyone who has been in the company of the companions of the companions of Allah's Messenger (ﷺ)?' They will say, 'Yes.' And victory will be bestowed on them." (3649) ☐

1241. Narrated Abu Sa`id Al-Khudri: Allah's Messenger (ﷺ) addressed the people saying, "Allah has given option to a slave to choose this world or what is with Him. The slave has chosen what is with Allah." Abu Bakr wept, and we were astonished at his weeping caused by what the Prophet (ﷺ) mentioned as to a Slave (of Allah) who had been offered a choice, (we learned later on) that Allah's Messenger (ﷺ) himself was the person who was given the choice, and that Abu Bakr knew best of all of us. Allah's Messenger (ﷺ) added, "The person who has favored me most of all both with his company and wealth, is Abu Bakr. If I were to take a Khalil other than my Lord, I would have taken Abu Bakr as such, but (what relates us) is the Islamic brotherhood and friendliness. All the gates of the Mosque should be closed except the gate of Abu Bakr." (3654) ☐

1242. Narrated Ibn `Umar: We used to compare the people as to who was better during the lifetime of Allah's Messenger (ﷺ). We used to regard Abu Bakr as the best, then `Umar, and then `Uthman. (3655) ☐

1243. Narrated Aiyub: The Prophet (ﷺ) said, "If I were to take a Khalil, I would have taken him (i.e. Abu Bakr) as a Khalil, but the Islamic brotherhood is better." (3657) ☐

1244. Narrated Jubair bin Mut`im: A woman came to the Prophet (ﷺ) who ordered her to return to him again. She said, "What if I came and did not find you?" as if she wanted to say, "If I found you dead?" The Prophet (ﷺ) said, "If you should not find me, go to Abu Bakr." (3659) ☐

1245. Narrated `Ammar: I saw Allah's Messenger (ﷺ) and there was none with him but five slaves, two women and Abu Bakr (i.e. those were the only converts to Islam then). (3660) ☐

1246. Narrated Abu Ad-Darda: While I was sitting with the Prophet, Abu Bakr came, lifting up one corner of his garment uncovering his knee. The Prophet (ﷺ) said, "Your companion has had a quarrel." Abu Bakr greeted (the Prophet (ﷺ)) and said, "O Allah's Messenger (ﷺ)! There was something (i.e. quarrel) between me and the Son of Al-Khattab. I talked to him harshly and then regretted that, and requested him to forgive me, but he refused. This is why I have come to you." The Prophet (ﷺ) said thrice, "O Abu Bakr! May Allah forgive you." In the meanwhile, `Umar regretted (his refusal of Abu Bakr's excuse) and went to Abu Bakr's house and asked if Abu Bakr was there. They replied in the negative. So he came to the Prophet (ﷺ) and greeted him, but signs of displeasure appeared on the face of the Prophet (ﷺ) till Abu Bakr pitied (`Umar), so he knelt and said twice, "O Allah's Messenger (ﷺ)! By Allah! I was more unjust to him (than he to me)." The Prophet (ﷺ) said, "Allah sent me (as a Prophet) to you (people) but you said (to me), 'You are telling a lie,' while Abu Bakr said, 'He has said the truth,' and consoled me with himself and his money." He then said twice, "Won't you then give up harming my companion?" After that nobody harmed Abu Bakr. (3661) □

1247. Narrated `Amr bin Al-As: The Prophet (ﷺ) deputed me to read the Army of Dhat-as-Salasil. I came to him and said, "Who is the most beloved person to you?" He said, "`Aisha." I asked, "Among the men?" He said, "Her father." I said, "Who then?" He said, "Then `Umar bin Al-Khattab." He then named other men. (3662) □

1248. Narrated Abu Sa`id: The Prophet (ﷺ) said, "Do not abuse my companions for if any one of you spent gold equal to Uhud (in Allah's Cause) it would not be equal to a Mud or even a half Mud spent by one of them." (3673) □

1249. Narrated Abu Musa Al-Ash`ari: I performed ablution in my house and then went out and said, "Today I shall stick to Allah's Messenger (ﷺ) and stay with him all this day of mine (in his service)." I went to the Mosque and asked about the Prophet. They said, "He had gone in this direction." So I followed his way, asking about him till he entered a place called Bir Aris. I sat at its gate that was made of date-palm leaves till the Prophet (ﷺ) finished answering the call of nature and performed ablution. Then I went up to him to see him sitting at the well of Aris at the middle of its edge with his legs uncovered, hanging in the well. I greeted him and went back and sat at the gate. I said, "Today I will be the gatekeeper of the Prophet." Abu Bakr came and pushed the gate. I asked, "Who is it?" He said, "Abu Bakr." I told him to wait, went in and said, "O Allah's Messenger (ﷺ)! Abu Bakr asks for permission to enter." He said, "Admit him and give him the glad tidings that he will be in Paradise." So I went out and said to Abu Bakr, "Come in, and Allah's Messenger (ﷺ) gives you the glad tidings that you will be in Paradise" Abu Bakr entered and sat on the right side of Allah's Messenger (ﷺ) on the built edge of the well and hung his legs n the well as the Prophet (ﷺ) did and uncovered his legs. I then returned and sat (at the gate). I had left my brother performing ablution and he intended to follow me. So I said (to myself). "If Allah wants good for so-and-so (i.e. my brother) He will bring him here." Suddenly somebody moved the door. I asked, "Who is it?" He said, "`Umar bin Al-Khattab." I asked him to wait, went to Allah's Messenger (ﷺ), greeted him and said, `Umar bin Al-Khattab asks the permission to enter." He said, "Admit him, and give him the glad tidings that he will be in Paradise." I went to "`Umar and said "Come in, and Allah's Messenger (ﷺ), gives you the glad tidings that you will be in Paradise." So he entered and sat beside Allah's Messenger (ﷺ) on the built edge of the well on the left side and hung his legs in the well. I returned and sat (at the gate) and said, (to myself), "If Allah wants good for so-and-so, He will bring him here." Somebody came and moved the door. I asked "Who is it?" He replied, "Uthman bin `Affan." I asked him to wait and went to the Prophet (ﷺ) and informed him. He said, "Admit him, and give him the glad tidings of entering Paradise, I asked him to wait and went to the Prophet (ﷺ) and informed him. He said, "Adult him, and give him the glad tidings of entering Paradise after a calamity that will befall him." So I went up to him and said to him, "Come in; Allah's Apostle gives you the glad tidings of entering Paradise after a calamity that will befall you." Uthman then came in and found that the built edge of the well was occupied, so he sat opposite to the Prophet (ﷺ) on the other side. Sa`id bin Al-Musaiyab said, "I interpret this (narration) in terms of their graves." (3674) □

1250. Narrated Anas bin Malik: The Prophet (ﷺ) once climbed the mountain of Uhud with Abu Bakr, `Umar and `Uthman. The mountain shook with them. The Prophet (ﷺ) said (to the mountain), "Be firm, O Uhud! For on you there are no more than a Prophet, a Siddiq and two martyrs. (3675) □

1251. Narrated `Abdullah bin `Umar: Allah's Messenger (ﷺ) said. "While (in a dream), I was standing by a well, drawing water from it. Abu Bakr and `Umar came to me. Abu Bakr took the bucket (from me) and drew one or two buckets of water, and there was some weakness in his drawing. May Allah forgive him. Then Ibn Al-Khattab took the bucket from Abu Bakr, and the bucket turned into a very large one in his hands. I had never seen such a mighty person amongst the people as him in performing such hard work. He drew so much water that the people drank to their satisfaction and watered their camels." (Wahab, a sub-narrator said, "till their camels drank and knelt down.") (3676) □

1252. Narrated Abu `Uthman:`Abdur Rahman bin Abi Bakr said, "The Suffa Companions were poor people and the Prophet (ﷺ) said, 'Whoever has food for two persons should take a third one from them (Suffa companions). And whosoever has food for four persons he should take one or two from them' Abu Bakr took three men and the Prophet (ﷺ) took ten of them." `Abdur Rahman added, my father my mother and I were there (in the house). (The sub-narrator is in doubt whether `Abdur Rahman also said, 'My wife and our servant who was common for both my house and Abu Bakr's house). Abu Bakr took his supper with the Prophet (ﷺ) and remained there till the `Isha' prayer was offered. Abu Bakr went back and stayed with the Prophet (ﷺ) till the Prophet (ﷺ) took his meal and then Abu Bakr returned to his house after a long portion of the night had passed. Abu Bakr's wife said, 'What detained you from your guests (or guest)?' He said, 'Have you not served them yet?' She said, 'They refused to eat until you come. The food was served for them but they refused." `Abdur Rahman added, "I went away and hid myself (being afraid of Abu Bakr) and in the meantime he (Abu Bakr) called me, 'O Ghunthar (a harsh word)!'

and also called me bad names and abused me and then said (to his family), 'Eat. No welcome for you.' Then (the supper was served). Abu Bakr took an oath that he would not eat that food. The narrator added: By Allah, whenever any one of us (myself and the guests of Suffa companions) took anything from the food, it increased from underneath. We all ate to our fill and the food was more than it was before its serving. Abu Bakr looked at it (the food) and found it as it was before serving or even more than that. He addressed his wife (saying) 'O the sister of Bani Firas! What is this?' She said, 'O the pleasure of my eyes! The food is now three times more than it was before.' Abu Bakr ate from it, and said, 'That (oath) was from Satan' meaning his oath (not to eat). Then he again took a morsel (mouthful) from it and then took the rest of it to the Prophet. So that meal was with the Prophet. There was a treaty between us and some people, and when the period of that treaty had elapsed the Prophet (ﷺ) divided us into twelve (groups) (the Prophet's companions) each being headed by a man. Allah knows how many men were under the command of each (leader). So all of them (12 groups of men) ate of that meal." (602) □

1253. Narrated Jabir bin `Abdullah: The Prophet (ﷺ) said, "I saw myself (in a dream) entering Paradise, and behold! I saw Ar-Rumaisa', Abu Talha's wife. I heard footsteps. I asked, who is it? Somebody said, 'It is Bilal ' Then I saw a palace and a lady sitting in its courtyard. I asked, 'For whom is this palace?' Somebody replied, 'It is for `Umar.' I intended to enter it and see it, but I thought of your (`Umar's) Ghira (and gave up the attempt)." `Umar said, "Let my parents be sacrificed for you, O Allah's Messenger (ﷺ)! How dare I think of my Ghira (self-respect) being offended by you? (3679) □

1254. Narrated Hamza's father: Allah's Messenger (ﷺ) said, "While I was sleeping, I saw myself drinking (i.e. milk), and I was so contented that I saw the milk flowing through my nails. Then I gave (the milk) to `Umar." They (i.e. the companions of the Prophet) asked, "What do you interpret it?" He said, "Knowledge." (3681) □

1255. Narrated Sa`d bin Abi Waqqas:`Umar bin Al-Khattab asked the permission of Allah's Messenger (ﷺ) to see him while some Quraishi women were sitting with him, talking to him and asking him for more expenses, raising their voices above the voice of Allah's Messenger (ﷺ). When `Umar asked for the permission to enter, the women quickly put on their veils. Allah'sf Apostle allowed him to enter and `Umar came in while Allah's Messenger (ﷺ) was smiling, `Umar said "O Allah's Apostle! May Allah always keep you smiling." The Prophet (ﷺ) said, "These women who have been here, roused my wonder, for as soon as they heard your voice, they quickly put on their veils." `Umar said, "O Allah's Messenger (ﷺ)! You have more right to be feared by them than I." Then `Umar addressed the women saying, "O enemies of yourselves! You fear me more than you do Allah's Messenger (ﷺ)?" They said, "Yes, for you are harsher and sterner than Allah's Messenger (ﷺ)." Then Allah's Messenger (ﷺ) said, "O Ibn Al-Khattab! By Him in Whose Hands my life is! Never does Satan find you going on a way, but he takes another way other than yours." (3683) □

1256. Narrated `Abdullah: We have been powerful since `Umar embraced Islam. (3684) □

1257. Narrated Aslam: Ibn `Umar asked me about some matters concerning `Umar. He said, "Since Allah's Messenger (ﷺ) died. I have never seen anybody more serious, hard working and generous than `Umar bin Al-Khattab (till the end of his life." (3687) □

1258. Narrated Abu Huraira: Allah's Messenger (ﷺ) said, "Among the nations before you there used to be people who were inspired (though they were not prophets). And if there is any of such a persons amongst my followers, it is 'Umar." (3689) □

1259. Narrated Abu Huraira: The Prophet (ﷺ) said, "Among the nation of Bani Israel who lived before you, there were men who used to be inspired with guidance though they were not prophets, and if there is any of such persons amongst my followers, it is 'Umar." (3689) □

1260. Narrated Abu Sa`id Al-Khudri: I heard Allah's Messenger (ﷺ) saying, "While I was sleeping, the people were presented to me (in a dream). They were wearing shirts, some of which were merely covering their (chests). And some were a bit longer.

`Umar was presented before me and his shirt was so long that he was dragging it."
They asked, "How have you interpreted it, O Allah's Messenger (ﷺ)?" He said,
"Religion." (3691) ☐

1261. Narrated Al-Miswar bin Makhrama: When `Umar was stabbed, he showed
signs of agony. Ibn `Abbas, as if intending to encourage `Umar, said to him, "O Chief
of the believers! Never mind what has happened to you, for you have been in the
company of Allah's Messenger (ﷺ) and you kept good relations with him and you
parted with him while he was pleased with you. Then you were in the company of
Abu Bakr and kept good relations with him and you parted with him (i.e. he died)
while he was pleased with you. Then you were in the company of the Muslims, and
you kept good relations with them, and if you leave them, you will leave them while
they are pleased with you." `Umar said, (to Ibn "Abbas), "As for what you have said
about the company of Allah's Messenger (ﷺ) and his being pleased with me, it is a
favor, Allah did to me; and as for what you have said about the company of Abu Bakr
and his being pleased with me, it is a favor Allah did to me; and concerning my
impatience which you see, is because of you and your companions. By Allah! If I had
gold equal to the earth, I would have ransomed myself with it from the Punishment
of Allah before I meet Him." (3692) ☐

1262. Narrated 'Ubaidullah bin `Adi bin Al-Khiyar: Al-Miswar bin Makhrama and
`Abdur-Rahman bin Al-Aswad bin 'Abu Yaghuth said (to me), "What forbids you to
talk to `Uthman about his brother Al-Walid because people have talked much about
him?" So I went to `Uthman and when he went out for prayer I said (to him), "I have
something to say to you and it is a piece of advice for you " `Uthman said, "O man,
from you." (`Umar said: I see that he said, "I seek Refuge with Allah from you.") So
I left him and went to them. Then the messenger of `Uthman came and I went to
him (i.e. `Uthman), `Uthman asked, "What is your advice?" I replied, "Allah sent
Muhammad with the Truth, and revealed the Divine Book (i.e. Qur'an) to him; and
you were amongst those who followed Allah and His Apostle, and you participated
in the two migrations (to Ethiopia and to Medina) and enjoyed the company of

Allah's Messenger (ﷺ) and saw his way. No doubt, the people are talking much about Al-Walid." `Uthman said, "Did you receive your knowledge directly from Allah's Messenger (ﷺ)?" I said, "No, but his knowledge did reach me and it reached (even) to a virgin in her seclusion." `Uthman said, "And then Allah sent Muhammad with the Truth and I was amongst those who followed Allah and His Apostle and I believed in what ever he (i.e. the Prophet) was sent with, and participated in two migrations, as you have said, and I enjoyed the company of Allah's Messenger (ﷺ) and gave the pledge of allegiance him. By Allah! I never disobeyed him, nor did I cheat him till Allah took him unto Him. Then I treated Abu Bakr and then `Umar similarly and then I was made Caliph. So, don't I have rights similar to theirs?" I said, "Yes." He said, "Then what are these talks reaching me from you people? Now, concerning what you mentioned about the question of Al-Walid, Allah willing, I shall deal with him according to what is right." Then he called `Ali and ordered him to flog him, and `Ali flogged him (i.e. Al-Walid) eighty lashes. (3696) □

1263. Narrated `Uthman: (the son of Muhib) An Egyptian who came and performed the Hajj to the Ka`ba saw some people sitting. He enquire, "Who are these people?" Somebody said, "They are the tribe of Quraish." He said, "Who is the old man sitting amongst them?" The people replied, "He is `Abdullah bin `Umar." He said, "O Ibn `Umar! I want to ask you about something; please tell me about it. Do you know that `Uthman fled away on the day (of the battle) of Uhud?" Ibn `Umar said, "Yes." The (Egyptian) man said, "Do you know that `Uthman was absent on the day (of the battle) of Badr and did not join it?" Ibn `Umar said, "Yes." The man said, "Do you know that he failed to attend the Ar Ridwan pledge and did not witness it (i.e. Hudaibiya pledge of allegiance)?" Ibn `Umar said, "Yes." The man said, "Allahu Akbar!" Ibn `Umar said, "Let me explain to you (all these three things). As for his flight on the day of Uhud, I testify that Allah has excused him and forgiven him; and as for his absence from the battle of Badr, it was due to the fact that the daughter of Allah's Messenger (ﷺ) was his wife and she was sick then. Allah's Messenger (ﷺ) said to him, "You will receive the same reward and share (of the booty) as anyone of those who participated in the battle of Badr (if you stay with her).' As for his absence from the Ar-Ridwan pledge of allegiance, had there been any person in Mecca more respectable than `Uthman (to be sent as a representative). Allah's Messenger (ﷺ) would have sent him instead of him. No doubt, Allah's Messenger (ﷺ) had sent him, and the incident of the Ar-Ridwan pledge of Allegiance happened after `Uthman had gone to Mecca. Allah's Messenger (ﷺ) held out his right hand saying, 'This is `Uthman's hand.' He stroke his (other) hand with it saying, 'This (pledge of allegiance) is on the behalf of `Uthman.' Then Ibn `Umar said to the man, 'Bear (these) excuses in mind with you.' (3698) □

1264. Narrated Anas: The Prophet (ﷺ) ascended the mountain of Uhud and Abu Bakr, `Umar and `Uthman were accompanying him. The mountain gave a shake (i.e. trembled underneath them). The Prophet (ﷺ) said, "O Uhud! Be calm." I think that the Prophet (ﷺ) hit it with his foot, adding, "For upon you there are none but a Prophet, a Siddiq and two martyrs." (3699) □

1265. Narrated `Amr bin Maimun: I saw `Umar bin Al-Khattab a few days before he was stabbed in Medina. He was standing with Hudhaifa bin Al-Yaman and `Uthman bin Hunaif to whom he said, "What have you done? Do you think that you have imposed more taxation on the land (of As-Swad i.e. 'Iraq) than it can bear?" They replied, "We have imposed on it what it can bear because of its great yield." `Umar again said, "Check whether you have imposed on the land what it can not bear." They said, "No, (we haven't)." `Umar added, "If Allah should keep me alive I will let the widows of Iraq need no men to support them after me." But only four days had elapsed when he was stabbed (to death). The day he was stabbed, I was standing and there was nobody between me and him (i.e. `Umar) except `Abdullah bin `Abbas. Whenever `Umar passed between the two rows, he would say, "Stand in straight lines." When he saw no defect (in the rows), he would go forward and start the prayer with Takbir. He would recite Surah Yusuf or An-Nahl or the like in the first rak`a so that the people may have the time to Join the prayer. As soon as he said Takbir, I heard him saying, "The dog has killed or eaten me," at the time he (i.e. the murderer) stabbed him. A non-Arab infidel proceeded on carrying a double-edged knife and stabbing all the persons he passed by on the right and left (till) he stabbed thirteen persons out of whom seven died. When one of the Muslims saw that, he threw a cloak on him. Realizing that he had been captured, the non-Arab infidel killed himself, `Umar held the hand of `Abdur-Rahman bin `Auf and let him lead the prayer. Those who were standing by the side of `Umar saw what I saw, but the people who were in the other parts of the Mosque did not see anything, but they lost the voice of `Umar and they were saying, "Subhan Allah! Subhan Allah! (i.e. Glorified be Allah)." `Abdur-Rahman bin `Auf led the people a short prayer. When they finished the prayer, `Umar said, "O Ibn `Abbas! Find out who attacked me." Ibn `Abbas kept on looking here and there for a short time and came to say. "The slave of Al Mughira." On that `Umar said, "The craftsman?" Ibn `Abbas said, "Yes." `Umar said, "May Allah curse him. I did not treat him unjustly. All the Praises are for Allah Who has not caused me to die at the hand of a man who claims himself to be a Muslim. No doubt, you and your father (Abbas) used to love to have more non-Arab infidels in Medina." Al-Abbas had the greatest number of slaves. Ibn `Abbas said to `Umar. "If you wish, we will do." He meant, "If you wish we will kill them." `Umar said, "You are mistaken (for you can't kill them) after they have spoken your language, prayed towards your Qibla, and performed Hajj like yours." Then `Umar was carried to his house, and we went along with him, and the people were as if they had never suffered a calamity before. Some said, "Do not worry (he will be alright soon)." Some said, "We are afraid (that he will die)." Then an infusion of dates was brought to him and he drank it but it came out (of the wound) of his belly. Then milk was brought to him and he drank it, and it also came out of his belly. The people realized that he would die. We went to him, and the people came, praising him. A young man came saying, "O chief of the believers! Receive the glad tidings from Allah to you due to your company with Allah's Messenger (ﷺ) and your superiority in Islam which you know. Then you became the ruler (i.e. Caliph) and you ruled with justice and finally you have been martyred." `Umar said, "I wish that all these privileges will counterbalance (my shortcomings) so that I will neither lose nor gain anything." When the young man turned back to leave, his clothes seemed to be touching the ground. `Umar said,

"Call the young man back to me." (When he came back) `Umar said, "O son of my brother! Lift your clothes, for this will keep your clothes clean and save you from the Punishment of your Lord." `Umar further said, "O `Abdullah bin `Umar! See how much I am in debt to others." When the debt was checked, it amounted to approximately eighty-six thousand. `Umar said, "If the property of `Umar's family covers the debt, then pay the debt thereof; otherwise request it from Bani `Adi bin Ka`b, and if that too is not sufficient, ask for it from Quraish tribe, and do not ask for it from any one else, and pay this debt on my behalf." `Umar then said (to `Abdullah), "Go to `Aisha (the mother of the believers) and say: "`Umar is paying his salutation to you. But don't say: 'The chief of the believers,' because today I am not the chief of the believers. And say: "`Umar bin Al-Khattab asks the permission to be buried with his two companions (i.e. the Prophet, and Abu Bakr)." `Abdullah greeted `Aisha and asked for the permission for entering, and then entered to her and found her sitting and weeping. He said to her, "`Umar bin Al-Khattab is paying his salutations to you, and asks the permission to be buried with his two companions." She said, "I had the idea of having this place for myself, but today I prefer `Umar to myself." When he returned it was said (to `Umar), "`Abdullah bin `Umar has come." `Umar said, "Make me sit up." Somebody supported him against his body and `Umar asked (`Abdullah), "What news do you have?" He said, "O chief of the believers! It is as you wish. She has given the permission." `Umar said, "Praise be to Allah, there was nothing more important to me than this. So when I die, take me, and greet `Aisha and say: "`Umar bin Al-Khattab asks the permission (to be buried with the Prophet (ﷺ)), and if she gives the permission, bury me there, and if she refuses, then take me to the grave-yard of the Muslims." Then Hafsa (the mother of the believers) came with many other women walking with her. When we saw her, we went away. She went in (to `Umar) and wept there for sometime. When the men asked for permission to enter, she went into another place, and we heard her weeping inside. The people said (to `Umar), "O chief of the believers! Appoint a successor." `Umar said, "I do not find anyone more suitable for the job than the following persons or group whom Allah's Messenger (ﷺ) had been pleased with before he died." Then `Umar mentioned `Ali, `Uthman,

AzZubair, Talha, Sa`d and `Abdur-Rahman (bin `Auf) and said, "Abdullah bin `Umar will be a witness to you, but he will have no share in the rule. His being a witness will compensate him for not sharing the right of ruling. If Sa`d becomes the ruler, it will be alright: otherwise, whoever becomes the ruler should seek his help, as I have not dismissed him because of disability or dishonesty." `Umar added, "I recommend that my successor takes care of the early emigrants; to know their rights and protect their honor and sacred things. I also recommend that he be kind to the Ansar who had lived in Medina before the emigrants and Belief had entered their hearts before them. I recommend that the (ruler) should accept the good of the righteous among them and excuse their wrong-doers, and I recommend that he should do good to all the people of the towns (Al-Ansar), as they are the protectors of Islam and the source of wealth and the source of annoyance to the enemy. I also recommend that nothing be taken from them except from their surplus with their consent. I also recommend that he do good to the 'Arab bedouin, as they are the origin of the 'Arabs and the material of Islam. He should take from what is inferior, amongst their properties and distribute that to the poor amongst them. I also recommend him concerning Allah's and His Apostle's protectees (i.e. Dhimmis) to fulfill their contracts and to fight for them and not to overburden them with what is beyond their ability." So when `Umar expired, we carried him out and set out walking. `Abdullah bin `Umar greeted (`Aisha) and said, "`Umar bin Al-Khattab asks for the permission." `Aisha said, "Bring him in." He was brought in and buried beside his two companions. When he was buried, the group (recommended by `Umar) held a meeting. Then `Abdur-Rahman said, "Reduce the candidates for rulership to three of you." Az-Zubair said, "I give up my right to `Ali." Talha said, "I give up my right to `Uthman," Sa`d, 'I give up my right to `Abdur-Rahman bin `Auf." `Abdur-Rahman then said (to `Uthman and `Ali), "Now which of you is willing to give up his right of candidacy to that he may choose the better of the (remaining) two, bearing in mind that Allah and Islam will be his witnesses." So both the sheiks (i.e. `Uthman and `Ali) kept silent. `Abdur-Rahman said, "Will you both leave this matter to me, and I take Allah as my Witness that I will not choose but the better of you?" They said, "Yes." So `Abdur-Rahman took the hand of one of them (i.e. `Ali) and said, "You are related to Allah's Messenger (ﷺ) and one of the earliest Muslims as you know well. So I ask you by Allah to promise that if I select you as a ruler you will do justice, and if I select `Uthman as a ruler you will listen to him and obey him." Then he took the other (i.e. `Uthman) aside and said the same to him. When `Abdur-Rahman secured (their agreement to) this covenant, he said, "O `Uthman! Raise your hand." So he (i.e. `Abdur-Rahman) gave him (i.e. `Uthman) the solemn pledge, and then `Ali gave him the pledge of allegiance and then all the (Medina) people gave him the pledge of allegiance. (3700) □

1266. Narrated Abu Hazim: A man came to Sahl bin Sa`d and said, "This is so-and-so," meaning the Governor of Medina, "He is calling `Ali bad names near the pulpit." Sahl asked, "What is he saying?" He (i.e. the man) replied, "He calls him (i.e. `Ali) Abu Turab." Sahl laughed and said, "By Allah, none but the Prophet (ﷺ) called him by this name and no name was dearer to `Ali than this." So I asked Sahl to tell me more, saying, "O Abu `Abbas! How (was this name given to `Ali)?" Sahl said, "`Ali went to Fatima and then came out and slept in the Mosque. The Prophet (ﷺ) asked Fatima, "Where is your cousin?" She said, "In the Mosque." The Prophet (ﷺ) went to him and found that his (i.e. `Ali's) covering sheet had slipped of his back and dust had soiled his back. The Prophet (ﷺ) started wiping the dust off his back and said twice, "Get up! O Abu Turab (i.e. O. man with the dust). (3703) □

1267. And narrated Sad that the Prophet (ﷺ) said to 'Ali, "Will you not be pleased from this that you are to me like Aaron was to Moses?" (3706) □

1268. Narrated Abu Huraira: The people used to say, "Abu Huraira narrates too many narrations." In fact I used to keep close to Allah's Messenger (ﷺ) and was satisfied with what filled my stomach. I ate no leavened bread and dressed no decorated striped clothes, and never did a man or a woman serve me, and I often used to press my belly against gravel because of hunger, and I used to ask a man to recite a Qur'anic Verse to me although I knew it, so that he would take me to his home and feed me. And the most generous of all the people to the poor was Ja`far bin Abi Talib. He used to take us to his home and offer us what was available therein. He would even offer us an empty folded leather container (of butter) which we would split and lick whatever was in it. (3708) □

1269. Narrated Marwan bin Al-Hakam: `Uthman bin `Affan was afflicted with severe nose-bleeding in the year when such illness was prevelant and that prevented him from performing Hajj, and (because of it) he made his will. A man from Quraish came to him and said, "Appoint your successor." `Uthman asked, "Did the people name him? The man said, "Yes." `Uthman asked, "Who is that?" The man remained silent. Another man came to `Uthman and I think it was Al-Harith. He also said, "Appoint your successor." `Uthman asked, "Did the people name him?" The man replied "Yes." `Uthman said, "Who is that?" The man remained silent. `Uthman said, "Perhaps they have mentioned Az-Zubair?" The man said, "Yes." `Uthman said, "By Him in Whose Hands my life is, he is the best of them as I know, and the dearest of them to Allah's Messenger (p.b.u.h)." (3717) □

1270. Narrated `Abdullah bin Az-Zubair: During the battle of Al-Ahzab, I and `Umar bin Abi-Salama were kept behind with the women. Behold! I saw (my father) Az-Zubair riding his horse, going to and coming from Bani Quraiza twice or thrice. So when I came back I said, "O my father! I saw you going to and coming from Bani Quraiza?" He said, "Did you really see me, O my son?" I said, "Yes." He said, "Allah's Messenger (ﷺ) said, 'Who will go to Bani Quraiza and bring me their news?' So I went, and when I came back, Allah's Apostle mentioned for me both his parents saying, "Let my father and mother be sacrificed for you."(3720)□

1271. Narrated `Urwa: On the day of the battle of Al-Yarmuk, the companions of the Prophet (ﷺ) said to Az-Zubair, "Will you attack the enemy vigorously so that we may attack them along with you?" So Az-Zubair attacked them, and they inflicted two wounds over his shoulder, and in between these two wounds there was an old scar he had received on the day of the battle of Badr When I was a child, I used to insert my fingers into those scars in play. (3721) □

1272. Narrated Qais bin Abi Hazim: I saw Talha's paralyzed hand with which he had protected the Prophet (from an arrow). (3724) ☐

1273. Narrated Sa`d bin Abi Waqqas: No man embraced Islam before the day on which I embraced Islam, and no doubt, I remained for seven days as one third of the then extant Muslims. (3727) ☐

1274. Narrated Qais: I heard Sa`d saying, "I was the first amongst the 'Arabs who shot an arrow for Allah's Cause. We used to fight along with the Prophets, while we had nothing to eat except the leaves of trees so that one's excrete would look like the excrete balls of camel or a sheep, containing nothing to mix them together. Today Banu Asad tribe blame me for not having understood Islam. I would be a loser if my deeds were in vain." Those people complained about Sa`d to `Umar, claiming that he did not offer his prayers perfectly. (3728) ☐

1275. Narrated Al-Miswar bin Makhrama: `Ali demanded the hand of the daughter of Abu Jahl. Fatima heard of this and went to Allah's Messenger (ﷺ) saying, "Your people think that you do not become angry for the sake of your daughters as `Ali is now going to marry the daughter of Abu Jahl. "On that Allah's Messenger (ﷺ) got up and after his recitation of Tashah-hud. I heard him saying, "Then after! I married one of my daughters to Abu Al-`As bin Al- Rabi` (the husband of Zainab) before Islam and he proved truthful in whatever he said to me. No doubt, Fatima is a part of me, I hate to see her being troubled. By Allah, the daughter of Allah's Messenger (ﷺ) and the daughter of Allah's Enemy cannot be the wives of one man." So `Ali gave up that engagement. 'Al-Miswar further said: I heard the Prophet (ﷺ) talking and he mentioned a son-in-law of his belonging to the tribe of Bani `Abd-Shams. He highly praised him concerning that relationship and said (whenever) he spoke to me, he spoke the truth, and whenever he promised me, he fulfilled his promise." (3729) ☐

1276. Narrated `Abdullah bin `Umar: The Prophet (ﷺ) sent an army under the command of Usama bin Zaid. When some people criticized his leadership, the Prophet (ﷺ) said, "If you are criticizing Usama's leadership, you used to criticize his father's leadership before. By Allah! He was worthy of leadership and was one of the dearest persons to me, and (now) this (i.e. Usama) is one of the dearest to me after him (i.e. Zaid). (3730) □

1277. Narrated `Urwa: Aisha said, "A Qaif (one skilled in recognizing the lineage of a person through Physiognomy and through examining the body parts of an infant) came to me while the Prophet (ﷺ) was present, and Usama bin Zaid and Zaid bin Haritha were Lying asleep. The Qa'if said. These feet (of Usama and his father) are of persons belonging to the same lineage.' "The Prophet (ﷺ) was pleased with that saying which won his admiration, and he told `Aisha of it. (3731) □

1278. Narrated Usama bin Zaid: That the Prophet (ﷺ) used to take him (i.e. Usama) and Al-Hassan (in his lap) and say: "O Allah! Love them, as I love them." (3735) □

1279. Narrated Anas bin Malik: Allah's Messenger (ﷺ) said, "Every nation has an extremely trustworthy man, and the trustworthy man of this (i.e. Muslim) nation is Abu 'Ubaida bin Al-Jarrah." (3744) □

1280. Narrated Muhammad: Anas bin Malik said, "The head of Al-Husain was brought to 'Ubaidullah bin Ziyad and was put in a tray, and then Ibn Ziyad started playing with a stick at the nose and mouth of Al-Husain's head and saying something about his handsome features." Anas then said (to him), "Al-Husain resembled the Prophet more than the others did." Anas added, "His (i.e. Al-Husain's) hair was dyed with Wasma (i.e. a kind of plant used as a dye). (3748) □

1281. Narrated Al-Bara: I saw the Prophet (ﷺ) carrying Al-Hasan on his shoulder and saying, "O Allah! I love him, so please love him." (3749) □

1282. Narrated Ibn Abi Nu'm: A person asked `Abdullah bin `Umar whether a Muslim could kill flies. I heard him saying (in reply). "The people of Iraq are asking about the killing of flies while they themselves murdered the son of the daughter of Allah's Messenger (ﷺ). The Prophet (ﷺ) said, they (i.e. Hasan and Husain) are my two sweet basils in this world." (3753) □

1283. Narrated Qais: Bilal said to Abu Bakr, "If you have bought me for yourself then keep me (for yourself), but if you have bought me for Allah's Sake, then leave me for Allah's Work." (3755) □

1284. Narrated Ibn `Abbas: Once the Prophet (ﷺ) embraced me (pressed me to his chest) and said, "O Allah, teach him wisdom (i.e. the understanding of the knowledge of Qur'an). (3756) □

1285. Narrated Alqama: I went to Sham and was offering a two-rak`at prayer; I said, "O Allah! Bless me with a (pious) companion." Then I saw an old man coming towards me, and when he came near I said, (to myself), "I hope Allah has given me my request." The man asked (me), "Where are you from?" I replied, "I am from the people of Kufa." He said, "Weren't there amongst you the Carrier of the (Prophet's) shoes, Siwak and the ablution water container (Abdullah ibn Masud)? Weren't there amongst you the man who was given Allah's Refuge from the Satan (Ammar bin Yasir)? And weren't there amongst you the man who used to keep the (Prophet's) secrets which nobody else knew (Huzaifah)? How did Ibn Um `Abd (i.e. `Abdullah bin Mas`ud) use to recite Surah-al-lail (the Night: 92)?" I recited: -- "By the Night as it envelops By the Day as it appears in brightness. And by male and female." (92.1-3) On that, Abu Darda said, "By Allah, the Prophet (ﷺ) made me read the Verse in this way after listening to him, but these people (of Sham) tried their best to let me say something different." (3761) □

1286. Narrated `Abdur-Rahman bin Yazid: We asked Hudhaifa to tell us of a person resembling (to some extent) the Prophet (ﷺ) in good appearance and straight forward behavior so that we may learn from him (good manners and acceptable conduct). Hudhaifa replied, "I do not know anybody resembling the Prophet (to some extent) in appearance and conduct more than Ibn Um `Abd. (3762) □

1287. Narrated Abu Musa Al-Ash`ari: My brother and I came from Yemen, and for some time we continued to consider `Abdullah bin Mas`ud as one of the members of the family of the Prophet (ﷺ) because we used to see him and his mother going in the house of the Prophet (ﷺ) very often. (3763) ☐

1288. Narrated Ibn Abi Mulaika: Somebody said to Ibn `Abbas, "Can you speak to the chief of the believers Mu`awiyah, as he does not pray except one rak`a as witr?" Ibn `Abbas replied, "He is a Faqih (i.e. a learned man who can give religious verdicts)." (3765) ☐

1289. Narrated Abu Salama: `Aisha said, "Once Allah's Messenger (ﷺ) said (to me), 'O Aish (`Aisha)! This is Gabriel greeting you.' I said, 'Peace and Allah's Mercy and Blessings be on him, you see what I don't see' "She was addressing Allah's Apostle. (3768) ☐

1290. Narrated Abu Musa Al-Ash`ari: Allah's Messenger (ﷺ) said, "Many amongst men attained perfection but amongst women none attained the perfection except Mary, the daughter of `Imran and Asiya, the wife of Pharaoh. And the superiority of `Aisha to other women is like the superiority of Tharid (i.e. an Arabic dish) to other meals." (3769) ☐

1291. Narrated Hisham's father: When Allah's Messenger (ﷺ) was in his fatal illness, he started visiting his wives and saying, "Where will I be tomorrow?" He was anxious to be in `Aisha's home. `Aisha said, "So when it was my day, the Prophet became silent (no longer asked the question). (3774) ☐

1292. Narrated Hisham's father: The people used to send presents to the Prophet (ﷺ) on the day of `Aisha's turn. `Aisha said, "My companions (i.e. the other wives of the Prophet) gathered in the house of Um Salama and said, "O Um Salama! By Allah, the people choose to send presents on the day of `Aisha's turn and we too, love the good (i.e. presents etc.) as `Aisha does. You should tell Allah's Messenger (ﷺ) to tell the people to send their presents to him wherever he may be, or wherever his turn may be." Um Salama said that to the Prophet and he turned away from her, and when the Prophet (ﷺ) returned to her (i.e. Um Salama), she repeated the same, and the Prophet (ﷺ) again turned away, and when she told him the same for the third time, the Prophet (ﷺ) said, "O Um Salama! Don't trouble me by harming `Aisha, for by

Allah, the Divine Inspiration never came to me while I was under the blanket of any woman amongst you except her." (3775) □

1293. Narrated Abu Huraira: The Prophet (ﷺ) said, "The best women are the riders of the camels and the righteous among the women of Quraish. They are the kindest women to their children in their childhood and the more careful women of the property of their husbands." (5082) □

57. MERITS OF ANSAAR

1294. NARRATED GHAILAN BIN JARIR: I asked Anas, "Tell me about the name." Al-Ansar, Did you call yourselves by it or did Allah call you by it?" He said, "Allah called us by it." We used to visit Anas and he used to narrate to us the virtues and deeds of the Ansar, and he used to address me or a person from the tribe of Al-Azd and say, "Your tribe did so-and-so on such-and-such a day." (3776) □

1295. Narrated `Aisha (ra): The day of Bu'ath (i.e. Day of fighting between the two tribes of the Ansar, the Aus and Khazraj) was brought about by Allah for the good of His Apostle so that when Allah's Messenger (ﷺ) reached (Medina), the tribes of Medina had already divided and their chiefs had been killed and wounded. So Allah had brought about the battle for the good of H is Apostle in order that they (i.e. the Ansar) might embrace Islam. (3777) □

1296. Narrated Anas: On the day of the Conquest of Mecca, when the Prophet (ﷺ) had given (from the booty) the Quraish, the Ansar said, "By Allah, this is indeed very strange: While our swords are still dribbling with the blood of Quraish, our war booty are distributed amongst them." When this news reached the Prophet (ﷺ) he called the Ansar and said, "What is this news that has reached me from you?" They used not to tell lies, so they replied, "What has reached you is true." He said, "Doesn't it please you that the people take the booty to their homes and you take Allah's Messenger (ﷺ) to your homes? If the Ansar took their way through a valley or a mountain pass, I would take the Ansar's valley or a mountain pass." (3778) □

1297. Narrated Abu Huraira: The Prophet (ﷺ), "If the Ansar took their way through a valley or a mountain pass, I would take Ansar's valley. And but for the migration, I would have been one of the Ansar." Abu Huraira used to say, "The Prophet (ﷺ) is not unjust (by saying so). May my parents be sacrificed for him, for the Ansar sheltered and helped him," or said a similar sentence. (3779) □

1298. Narrated Sa`d's father: When the emigrants reached Medina. Allah's Messenger (ﷺ) established the bond of fraternity between `Abdur-Rahman and Sa`d bin Ar-Rabi. Sa`d said to `Abdur-Rahman, "I am the richest of all the Ansar, so I want to divide my property (between us), and I have two wives, so see which of the two you like and tell me, so that I may divorce her, and when she finishes her prescribed period (i.e. 'Idda) of divorce, then marry her." `Abdur-Rahman said, "May Allah bless your family and property for you; where is your market?" So they showed him the Qainuqa' market. (He went there and) returned with a profit in the form of dried yogurt and butter. He continued going (to the market) till one day he came, bearing the traces of yellow scent. The Prophet (ﷺ) asked, "What is this (scent)?" He replied, "I got married." The Prophet (ﷺ) asked, "How much Mahr did you give her?" He replied, "I gave her a datestone of gold or a gold piece equal to the weight of a date-stone." (The narrator, Ibrahim, is in doubt as to which is correct.) (3780) □

1299. Narrated Al-Bara: I heard the Prophet (ﷺ) said, "None loves the Ansar but a believer, and none hates them but a hypocrite. So Allah will love him who loves them, and He will hate him who hates them." (3783) □

1300. Narrated Anas bin Malik: Once an Ansari woman, accompanied by a son of her, came to Allah's Messenger (ﷺ). Allah's Messenger (ﷺ) spoke to her and said twice, "By Him in Whose Hand my life is, you are the most beloved people to me." (3786) □

1301. Narrated Abu Hamza: A man from the Ansar, "Every nation has followers and (O Prophet) we have followed you, so invoke Allah to let our followers be considered from us (as Ansar like ourselves)." So the Prophet (ﷺ) said, "O Allah! Let their followers be considered as Ansar like themselves." (3788) □

1302. Narrated Abu Humaid: The Prophet (ﷺ) said, "The best of the Ansar families are the families of Banu An- Najjar, and then that of Banu `Abdul Ash-hal, and then that of Banu Al-Harith, and then that of Banu Saida; and there is good in all the families (homes) of the Ansar." Sa`d bin 'Ubada followed us and said, "O Abu Usaid! Don't you see that the Prophet (ﷺ) compared the Ansar and made us the last of them in superiority? Then Sa`d met the Prophet (ﷺ) and said, "O Allah's Messenger (ﷺ)! In comparing the Ansar's families (homes) as to the degree of superiority, you have made us the last of them." Allah's Messenger (ﷺ) replied, "Isn't it sufficient that you are regarded amongst the best?" (3791) □

1303. Narrated Yahya bin Sa`id: That he heard Anas bin Malik when he went with him to Al-Walid, saying, "Once the Prophet (ﷺ) called the Ansar in order to give them the territory of Bahrain they said, 'No, unless you give to our emigrant brethren a similar share.' On that he said 'If you do not agree to it, then be patient till you meet me, for after me others will be given preference to you.'" (3794) □

1304. Narrated Abu Huraira: A man came to the Prophet. The Prophet (ﷺ) sent a messenger to his wives (for food) but they said that they had nothing except water. Then Allah's Messenger (ﷺ) said, "Who will take this (person) or entertain him as a guest?" An Ansar man said, "I." So he took him to his wife and said to her, "Entertain generously the guest of Allah's Messenger (ﷺ)" She said, "We have got nothing except the meals of my children." He said, "Prepare your meal, light your lamp and let your children sleep if they ask for supper." So she prepared her meal, lighted her lamp and made her children sleep, and then stood up pretending to mend her lamp, but she put it off. Then both of them pretended to be eating, but they really went to bed hungry. In the morning the Ansari went to Allah's Messenger (ﷺ) who said, "Tonight Allah laughed or wondered at your action." Then Allah revealed: "But give them (emigrants) preference over themselves even though they were in need of that And whosoever is saved from the covetousness such are they who will be successful." (59.9)

(3798) □

1305. Narrated Anas bin Malik: Abu Bakr and Al-`Abbas passed by one of the gatherings of the Ansar who were weeping then. He (i.e. Abu Bakr or Al-`Abbas) asked, "Why are you weeping?" They replied, "We are weeping because we remember the gathering of the Prophet (ﷺ) with us." So Abu Bakr went to the Prophet (ﷺ) and told him of that. The Prophet (ﷺ) came out, tying his head with a piece of the hem of a sheet. He ascended the pulpit which he never ascended after that day. He glorified and praised Allah and then said, "I request you to take care of the Ansar as they are my near companions to whom I confided my private secrets. They have fulfilled their obligations and rights which were enjoined on them but there remains what is for them. So, accept the good of the good-doers amongst them and excuse the wrongdoers amongst them." (3799) □

1306. Narrated Jabir: I heard the Prophet (ﷺ) saying, "The Throne (of Allah) shook at the death of Sa`d bin Mu`adh." Through another group of narrators, Jabir added, "I heard the Prophet (ﷺ): saying, 'The Throne of the Beneficent shook because of the death of Sa`d bin Mu`adh." (3803) □

1307. Narrated Anas bin Malik: The Prophet (ﷺ) said to Ubai, "Allah has ordered me to recite to you: 'Those who disbelieve (Surah-al- Bayina 98).' "Ubai said, "Has He mentioned my name?" The Prophet (ﷺ) said, "Yes." On hearing this, Ubai started weeping. (3809) □

1308. Narrated Sa`d bin Abi Waqqas: I have never heard the Prophet (ﷺ) saying about anybody walking on the earth that he is from the people of Paradise except `Abdullah bin Salam. The Verse was revealed concerning him: "And a witness from the children of Israel testifies that this Qur'an is true" (46.10) (3812) □

1309. Narrated Qatada: We do not know of any tribe amongst the 'Arab tribes who lost more martyrs than Al-Ansar, and they will have superiority on the Day of Resurrection. Anas bin Malik told us that seventy from the Ansar were martyred on the day of Uhud, and seventy on the day (of the battle of) Bir Ma'una, and seventy on

the day of Al-Yamama. Anas added, "The battle of Bir Ma'una took place during the lifetime of Allah's Messenger (ﷺ) and the battle of Al-Yamama, during the caliphate of Abu Bakr, and it was the day when Musailamah Al-Kadhdhab was killed." (4078)
☐

58. Pre-Migration Period

1310. Narrated Jabir bin `Abdullah (ra): When the Ka`ba was built, the Prophet (ﷺ) and `Abbas went to bring stones (for its construction). Al `Abbas said to the Prophet, "Take off your waist sheet and put it on your neck." (When the Prophet (ﷺ) took it off) he fell on the ground with his eyes open towards the sky and said, "Give me my waist sheet." And he covered himself with it. (1582) ☐

1311. Narrated Abu Huraira: Gabriel came to the Prophet (ﷺ) and said, "O Allah's Messenger (ﷺ)! This is Khadija coming to you with a dish having meat soup (or some food or drink). When she reaches you, greet her on behalf of her Lord (i.e. Allah) and on my behalf, and give her the glad tidings of having a Qasab palace in Paradise wherein there will be neither any noise nor any fatigue (trouble)." (3820) ☐

1312. Narrated 'Aisha: Once Hala bint Khuwailid, Khadija's sister, asked the permission of the Prophet (ﷺ) to enter. On that, the Prophet (ﷺ) remembered the way Khadija used to ask permission, and that upset him. He said, "O Allah! Hala!" So I became jealous and said, "What makes you remember an old woman amongst the old women of Quraish an old woman (with a teethless mouth) of red gums who died long ago, and in whose place Allah has given you somebody better than her?" (3821) ☐

1313. Narrated Jarir bin 'Abdullah: Allah's Messenger (ﷺ) has never refused to admit me since I embraced Islam, and whenever he saw me, he would smile. (3822) ☐

1314. Narrated Ibn 'Umar: Zaid bin 'Amr bin Nufail went to Sham, inquiring about a true religion to follow. He met a Jewish religious scholar and asked him about their religion. He said, "I intend to embrace your religion, so tell me some thing about it." The Jew said, "You will not embrace our religion unless you receive your share of Allah's Anger." Zaid said, "'I do not run except from Allah's Anger, and I will never bear a bit of it if I have the power to avoid it. Can you tell me of some other religion?" He said, "I do not know any other religion except the Hanif." Zaid enquired, "What is Hanif?" He said, "Hanif is the religion of (the prophet) Abraham who was neither a Jew nor a Christian, and he used to worship None but Allah (Alone)" Then Zaid went out and met a Christian religious scholar and told him the same as before. The Christian said, "You will not embrace our religion unless you get a share of Allah's Curse." Zaid replied, "I do not run except from Allah's Curse, and I will never bear any of Allah's Curse and His Anger if I have the power to avoid them. Will you tell me of some other religion?" He replied, "I do not know any other religion except Hanif." Zaid enquired, "What is Hanif?" He replied, Hanif is the religion of (the prophet) Abraham who was neither a Jew nor a Christian and he used to worship None but Allah (Alone)" When Zaid heard their Statement about (the religion of) Abraham, he left that place, and when he came out, he raised both his hands and said, "O Allah! I make You my Witness that I am on the religion of Abraham." (3827) □

1315. Narrated Sa`id bin Al-Musaiyab's grand-father: In the pre-lslamic period of ignorance a flood of rain came and filled the valley in between the two mountains (around the Ka`ba). (3833) □

1316. Ibn `Abbas said: "In the pre-lslamic period of ignorance I heard my father saying, "Provide us with Kasan Dihaqa (glass full (of alcohol))." (3840) □

1317. Narrated Abu Huraira: The Prophet (ﷺ) said, "The most true words said by a poet was the words of Labid." He said, Verily, Everything except Allah is perishable and Umaiya bin As-Salt was about to be a Muslim (but he did not embrace Islam). (3841) □

1318. Narrated Ibn `Abbas: The first event of Qasama in the pre-lslamic period of ignorance was practiced by us (i.e. Banu Hashim). A man from Banu Hashim was employed by a Quraishi man from another branch-family. The (Hashimi) laborer set out with the Quraishi driving his camels. There passed by him another man from Banu Hashim. The leather rope of the latter's bag had broken so he said to the laborer, "Will you help me by giving me a rope in order to tie the handle of my bag lest the camels should run away from me?" The laborer gave him a rope and the latter tied his bag with it. When the caravan halted, all the camels' legs were tied with their fetters except one camel. The employer asked the laborer, "Why, from among all the camels has this camel not been fettered?" He replied, "There is no fetter for it." The Quraishi asked, "Where is its fetter?" and hit the laborer with a stick that caused his death (later on Just before his death) a man from Yemen passed by him. The laborer asked (him), "Will you go for the pilgrimage?" He replied, "I do not think I will attend it, but perhaps I will attend it." The (Hashimi) laborer said, "Will you please convey a message for me once in your life?" The other man said, "yes." The laborer wrote: 'When you attend the pilgrimage, call the family of Quraish, and if they respond to you, call the family of Banu Hashim, and if they respond to you, ask about Abu Talib and tell him that so-and-so has killed me for a fetter." Then the laborer expired. When the employer reached (Mecca), Abu Talib visited him and asked, "What has happened to our companion?" He said, "He became ill and I looked after him nicely (but he died) and I buried him." Then Abu Talib said, "The deceased deserved this from you." After some time, the messenger whom the laborer has asked to convey the message, reached during the pilgrimage season. He called, "O the family of Quraish!" The people replied, "This is Quraish." Then he called, "O the family of Banu Hashim!" Again the people replied, "This is Banu Hashim." He asked, "Who is Abu Talib?" The people replied, "This is Abu Talib." He said, "'So-and-so has asked me to convey a message to you that so-and-so has killed him for a fetter (of a camel)." Then Abu Talib went to the (Quraishi) killer and said to him, "Choose one of three alternatives: (i) If you wish, give us one-hundred camels because you have murdered our companion, (ii) or if you wish, fifty of your men should take an oath that you have not murdered our companion, and if you do not accept this, (iii) we will kill you in Qisas." The killer went to his people and they said, "We will take an oath." Then a woman from Banu Hashim who was married to one of them (i.e.the Quraishis) and had given birth to a child from him, came to Abu Talib and said, "O Abu Talib! I wish that my son from among the fifty men, should be excused from this oath, and that he should not take the oath where the oathtaking is carried on." Abu Talib excused him. Then another man from them came (to Abu Talib) and said, "O Abu Talib! You want fifty persons to take an oath instead of giving a hundred camels, and that means each man has to give two camels (in case he does not take an oath). So there are two camels I would like you to accept from me and excuse me from taking an oath where the oaths are taken. Abu Talib accepted them from him. Then 48 men came and took the oath. Ibn `Abbas further said:) By Him in Whose Hand my life is, before the end of that year, none of those 48 persons remained alive. (3845) □

1319. Narrated Abu As-Safar: I heard Ibn `Abbas saying, "O people! Listen to what I say to you, and let me hear whatever you say, and don't go (without understanding), and start saying, 'Ibn `Abbas said so-and-so, Ibn `Abbas said so and- so, Ibn `Abbas said so-and-so.' He who wants to perform the Tawaf around the Ka`ba should go behind Al-Hijr (i.e. a portion of the Ka`ba left out unroofed) and do not call it Al-Hatim, for in the pre-Islamic period of ignorance if any man took an oath, he used to throw his whip, shoes or bow in it. (3848) □

1320. Narrated Sufyan:'Ubaidullah said: "I heard Ibn `Abbas saying, "Following are some traits of the people of the pre-Islamic period of ignorance to defame the ancestry of other families, and to wail over the dead." 'Ubaidullah forgot the third trait. Sufyan said, "They say it (i.e. the third trait) was to believe that rain was caused by the influence of stars (i.e. if a special star appears it will rain). (3850) □

1321. Narrated `Abdullah bin Mas`ud: Once the Prophet (ﷺ) was offering prayers at the Ka`ba. Abu Jahl was sitting with some of his companions. One of them said to the others, "Who amongst you will bring the Abdominal contents of a camel of Bani so and so and put it on the back of Muhammad, when he prostrates?" The most unfortunate of them got up and brought it. He waited till the Prophet (ﷺ) prostrated and then placed it on his back between his shoulders. I was watching but could not do any thing. I wish I had some people with me to hold out against them. They started laughing and falling on one another. Allah's Messenger (ﷺ) was in prostration and he did not lift his head up till Fatima (Prophet's daughter) came and threw that (camel's Abdominal contents) away from his back. He raised his head and said thrice, "O Allah! Punish Quraish." So it was hard for Abu Jahl and his companions when the Prophet invoked Allah against them as they had a conviction that the prayers and invocations were accepted in this city (Mecca). The Prophet (ﷺ) said, "O Allah! Punish Abu Jahl, `Utba bin Rabi`a, Shaiba bin Rabi`a, Al-Walid bin `Utba, Umaiya bin Khalaf, and `Uqba bin Al Mu'it (and he mentioned the seventh whose name I cannot recall). By Allah in Whose Hands my life is, I saw the dead bodies of those persons who were counted by Allah's Messenger (ﷺ) in the Qalib (one of the wells) of Badr. (240) ☐

1322. Narrated `Urwa bin Az-Zubair: I asked Ibn `Amr bin Al-As, "Tell me of the worst thing which the pagans did to the Prophet." He said, "While the Prophet (ﷺ) was praying in the Hijr of the Ka`ba; `Uqba bin Abi Mu'ait came and put his garment around the Prophet's neck and throttled him violently. Abu Bakr came and caught him by his shoulder and pushed him away from the Prophet (ﷺ) and said, "Do you want to kill a man just because he says, 'My Lord is Allah?'" (3856) ☐

1323. Narrated `Abdur-Rahman: "I asked Masruq, 'who informed the Prophet (ﷺ) about the Jinns at the night when they heard the Qur'an?' He said, 'your father `Abdullah informed me that a tree informed the Prophet (ﷺ) about them.'" (3859) ☐

1324. Narrated `Abdullah bin `Umar: While `Umar was at home in a state of fear, there came Al-`As bin Wail As-Sahmi Abu `Amr, wearing an embroidered cloak and a shirt having silk hems. He was from the tribe of Bani Sahm who were our allies during the pre-Islamic period of ignorance. Al-`As said to `Umar "What is wrong with you?" He said, "Your people claim that they would kill me if I become a Muslim." Al-`As said, "Nobody will harm you after I have given protection to you." So Al-`As went out and met the people streaming in the whole valley. He said, "Where are you going?" They said, "We want Ibn Al-Khattab who has embraced Islam." Al-`As said,

"There is no way for anybody to touch him." So the people retreated. (3864) ☐

1325. Narrated `Abdullah bin `Umar: When `Umar embraced Islam, all the (disbelieving) people gathered around his home and said, "`Umar has embraced Islam." At that time I was still a boy and was on the roof of my house. There came a man wearing a cloak of Dibaj (i.e. a kind of silk), and said, "`Umar has embraced Islam. Nobody can harm him for I am his protector." I then saw the people going away from `Umar and asked who the man was, and they said, "Al-`As bin Wail." (3865) ☐

1326. Narrated Ibn `Abbas: If you wish to know about the ignorance of the Arabs, refer to Surah-al-Anam after Verse No. 130:-- Indeed lost are those who have killed their children from folly without knowledge and have forbidden that which Allah has provided for them, inventing a lie against Allah. They have indeed gone astray and were not guided.' (6.14) (3524) ☐

1327. Narrated Abu Huraira: The Prophet (ﷺ) said, "Neither Fara' nor 'Atira is permissible." Al-Fara' was the first offspring (they got of camels or sheep) which they (pagans) used to offer (as a sacrifice) to their idols. 'Atira was (a sheep which used to be slaughtered) during the month of Rajab. (5474) ☐

1328. Narrated Abu Raja Al-Utaridi: We used to worship stones, and when we found a better stone than the first one, we would throw the first one and take the latter, but if we could not get a stone then we would collect some earth (i.e. soil) and then bring a sheep and milk that sheep over it, and perform the Tawaf around it. When the month of Rajab came, we used (to stop the military actions), calling this month the iron remover, for we used to remove and throw away the iron parts of every spear and arrow in the month of Rajab. (4376) ☐

1329. Narrated Sa`id bin Al-Musaiyab: Bahira is a she-camel whose milk is kept for the idols and nobody is allowed to milk it; Sa'iba was the she-camel which they used to set free for their gods and nothing was allowed to be carried on it. Abu Huraira said: Allah's Messenger (ﷺ) said, "I saw `Amr bin 'Amir Al-Khuza`i (in a dream) dragging his intestines in the Fire, and he was the first person to establish the tradition of setting free the animals (for the sake of their deities)," Wasila is the she-camel which gives birth to a she-camel as its first delivery, and then gives birth to another she-camel as its second delivery. People (in the Pre-lslamic periods of ignorance) used to let that she camel loose for their idols if it gave birth to two she-camels successively without giving birth to a male camel in between. 'Ham' was the male camel which was used for copulation. When it had finished the number of copulations assigned for it, they would let it loose for their idols and excuse it from burdens so that nothing would be carried on it, and they called it the 'Hami.' Abu Huraira said, "I heard the Prophet (ﷺ) saying so." (4623) □

1330. Narrated Ibn `Abbas: All the idols which were worshipped by the people of Noah were worshipped by the Arabs later on. As for the idol Wadd, it was worshipped by the tribe of Kalb at Daumat-al-Jandal; Suwa' was the idol of (the tribe of) Murad and then by Ban, Ghutaif at Al-Jurf near Saba; Yauq was the idol of Hamdan, and Nasr was the idol of Himyr, the branch of Dhi-al-Kala.' The names (of the idols) formerly belonged to some pious men of the people of Noah, and when they died Satan inspired their people to (prepare and place idols at the places where they used to sit, and to call those idols by their names. The people did so, but the idols were not worshipped till those people (who initiated them) had died and the origin of the idols had become obscure, whereupon people began worshipping them. (4920) □

1331. Narrated 'Urwa bin Az-Zubair: 'Aishah, the wife of the Prophet (ﷺ) told him that there were four types of marriage during Pre-Islamic period of Ignorance. One type was similar to that of the present day i.e. a man used to ask somebody else for the hand of a girl under his guardianship or for his daughter's hand, and give her Mahr and then marry her. The second type was that a man would say to his wife after she had become clean from her period. "Send for so-and-so and have sexual intercourse with him." Her husband would then keep away from her and would never sleep with her till she got pregnant from the other man with whom she was sleeping. When her pregnancy became evident, he husband would sleep with her if he wished.

Her husband did so (i.e. let his wife sleep with some other man) so that he might have a child of noble breed. Such marriage was called as Al-Istibda'. Another type of marriage was that a group of less than ten men would assemble and enter upon a woman, and all of them would have sexual relation with her. If she became pregnant and delivered a child and some days had passed after delivery, she would sent for all of them and none of them would refuse to come, and when they all gathered before her, she would say to them, "You (all) know waht you have done, and now I have given birth to a child. So, it is your child so-and-so!" naming whoever she liked, and her child would follow him and he could not refuse to take him. The fourth type of marriage was that many people would enter upon a lady and she would never refuse anyone who came to her. Those were the prostitutes who used to fix flags at their doors as sign, and he who would wished, could have sexual intercourse with them. If anyone of them got pregnant and delivered a child, then all those men would be gathered for her and they would call the Qa'if (persons skilled in recognizing the likeness of a child to his father) to them and would let the child follow the man (whom they recognized as his father) and she would let him adhere to him and be called his son. The man would not refuse all that. But when Muhammad (ﷺ) was sent with the Truth, he abolished all the types of marriages observed in pre-Islamic period of Ignorance except the type of marriage the people recognize today. (5127) □

1332. Narrated `Abdullah bin `Umar: I never heard `Umar saying about something that he thought it would be so-and-so, but he was quite right. Once, while `Umar was sitting, a handsome man passed by him, `Umar said, "If I am not wrong, this person is still on his religion of the pre-lslamic period of ignorance or he was their foreteller. Call the man to me." When the man was called to him, he told him of his thought. The man said, "I have never seen such a day on which a Muslim is faced with such an accusation." `Umar said, "I am determined that you should tell me the truth." He said, "I was a foreteller in the pre-lslamic period of ignorance." Then `Umar said, "Tell me the most astonishing thing your female Jinn has told you of." He said, "One-day while I was in the market, she came to me scared and said, 'Haven't you seen the Jinns and their despair and they were overthrown after their defeat (and prevented from listening to the news of the heaven) so that they (stopped going to the sky and) kept following camel-riders (i.e. 'Arabs)?" `Umar said, "He is right." and added, "One day while I was near their idols, there came a man with a calf and slaughtered it as a sacrifice (for the idols). An (unseen) creature shouted at him, and I have never heard harsher than his voice. He was crying, 'O you bold evil-doer! A matter of success! An eloquent man is saying: None has the right to be worshipped except you (O Allah).' On that the people fled, but I said, 'I shall not go away till I know what is behind this.' Then the cry came again: 'O you bold evil-doer! A matter of success! An eloquent man is saying: None has the right to be worshipped except Allah.' I then went away and a few days later it was said, "A prophet has appeared." (3866) ☐

1333. Narrated Qais: I heard Sa`id bin Zaid saying to the people, "If you but saw me and `Umar's sister tied and forced by `Umar to leave Islam while he was not yet a Muslim. And if the mountain of Uhud could move from its place for the evil which you people have done to `Uthman, it would have the right to do that." (3867) ☐

1334. Narrated Al-Abbas bin `Abdul Muttalib: That he said to the Prophet (ﷺ) "You have not been of any avail to your uncle (Abu Talib) (though) by Allah, he used to protect you and used to become angry on your behalf." The Prophet (ﷺ) said, "He is in a shallow fire, and had it not been for me, he would have been in the bottom of the (Hell) Fire." (3883) ☐

1335. Narrated Al-Musaiyab: When Abu Talib was in his death bed, the Prophet (ﷺ) went to him while Abu Jahl was sitting beside him. The Prophet (ﷺ) said, "O my uncle! Say: None has the right to be worshipped except Allah, an expression I will defend your case with, before Allah." Abu Jahl and `Abdullah bin Umaiya said, "O Abu Talib! Will you leave the religion of `Abdul Muttalib?" So they kept on saying this to him so that the last statement he said to them (before he died) was: "I am on the religion of `Abdul Muttalib." Then the Prophet said, "I will keep on asking for Allah's Forgiveness for you unless I am forbidden to do so." Then the following Verse was revealed: "It is not fitting for the Prophet (ﷺ) and the believers to ask Allah's

Forgiveness for the pagans, even if they were their near relatives, after it has become clear to them that they are the dwellers of the (Hell) Fire." (9.113) The other Verse was also revealed: "(O Prophet!) Verily, you guide not whom you like, but Allah guides whom He will ...." (28.56) (3884) □

1336. Narrated Abu Sa`id Al-Khudri: That he heard the Prophet (ﷺ) when somebody mentioned his uncle (i.e. Abu Talib), saying, "Perhaps my intercession will be helpful to him on the Day of Resurrection so that he may be put in a shallow fire reaching only up to his ankles. His brain will boil from it."

Narrated Yazid: "will make his brain boil." (3885) □

1337. Narrated Jabir bin `Abdullah: That he heard Allah's Messenger (ﷺ) saying, "When the people of Quraish did not believe me (i.e. the story of my Night Journey), I stood up in Al-Hijr and Allah displayed Jerusalem in front of me, and I began describing it to them while I was looking at it." (3886) □

1338. Narrated Ibn `Abbas: The Prophet (ﷺ) went out towards Al-Batha' and ascended the mountain and shouted, "O Sabahah!" So the Quraish people gathered around him. He said, "Do you see? If I tell you that an enemy is going to attack you in the morning or in the evening, will you believe me?" They replied, "Yes." He said, "Then I am a plain warner to you of a coming severe punishment." Abu Lahab said, "Is it for this reason that you have gathered us? May you perish! " Then Allah revealed: 'Perish the hands of Abu Lahab!' (4972) □

1339. Narrated Hisham's father: Khadija died three years before the Prophet (ﷺ) departed to Medina. He stayed there for two years or so and then he married `Aisha when she was a girl of six years of age, and he consumed that marriage when she was nine years old. (3896) □

59. PROPHET'S MIGRATION

1340. NARRATED IBN `ABBAS: Allah's Messenger (ﷺ) started receiving the Divine Inspiration at the age of forty. Then he stayed in Mecca for thirteen years, receiving the Divine Revelation. Then he was ordered to migrate and he lived as an Emigrant for ten years and then died at the age of sixty-three (years). (3902) ☐

1341. Narrated Abu Musa (ra): The Prophet (ﷺ) said, "I saw in a dream that I was migrating from Mecca to a land where there were date palm trees. I thought that it might be the land of Al-Yamama or Hajar, but behold, it turned out to be Yathrib (i.e. Medina). (7035) ☐

1342. Narrated 'Aisha: I never remembered my parents believing in any religion other than the true religion (i.e. Islam), and (I don't remember) a single day passing without our being visited by Allah's Messenger (ﷺ) in the morning and in the evening. When the Muslims were put to test (i.e. troubled by the pagans), Abu Bakr set out migrating to the land of Ethiopia, and when he reached Bark-al-Ghimad, Ibn Ad-Daghina, the chief of the tribe of Qara, met him and said, "O Abu Bakr! Where are you going?" Abu Bakr replied, "My people have turned me out (of my country), so I want to wander on the earth and worship my Lord." Ibn Ad-Daghina said, "O Abu Bakr! A man like you should not leave his home-land, nor should he be driven out, because you help the destitute, earn their livings, and you keep good relations with your Kith and kin, help the weak and poor, entertain guests generously, and help the calamity-stricken persons. Therefore I am your protector. Go back and worship your Lord in your town."

So Abu Bakr returned and Ibn Ad-Daghina accompanied him. In the evening Ibn Ad-Daghina visited the nobles of Quraish and said to them. "A man like Abu Bakr should not leave his homeland, nor should he be driven out. Do you (i.e. Quraish) drive out a man who helps the destitute, earns their living, keeps good relations with his Kith and kin, helps the weak and poor, entertains guests generously and helps the calamity-stricken persons?" So the people of Quraish could not refuse Ibn Ad-Daghina's protection, and they said to Ibn Ad-Daghina, "Let Abu Bakr worship his Lord in his house. He can pray and recite there whatever he likes, but he should not hurt us with it, and should not do it publicly, because we are afraid that he may affect our women and children." Ibn Ad-Daghina told Abu Bakr of all that. Abu Bakr stayed in that state, worshipping his Lord in his house. He did not pray publicly, nor did he recite Quran outside his house.

Then a thought occurred to Abu Bakr to build a mosque in front of his house, and there he used to pray and recite the Quran. The women and children of the pagans began to gather around him in great number. They used to wonder at him and look at him. Abu Bakr was a man who used to weep too much, and he could not help weeping on reciting the Quran. That situation scared the nobles of the pagans of Quraish, so they sent for Ibn Ad-Daghina. When he came to them, they said, "We accepted your protection of Abu Bakr on condition that he should worship his Lord in his house, but he has violated the conditions and he has built a mosque in front of his house where he prays and recites the Quran publicly. We are now afraid that he may affect our women and children unfavorably. So, prevent him from that. If he likes to confine the worship of his Lord to his house, he may do so, but if he insists on doing that openly, ask him to release you from your obligation to protect him, for we dislike to break our pact with you, but we deny Abu Bakr the right to announce his act publicly." Ibn Ad-Daghina went to Abu- Bakr and said, ("O Abu Bakr!) You know well what contract I have made on your behalf; now, you are either to abide by it, or else release me from my obligation of protecting you, because I do not want the 'Arabs hear that my people have dishonored a contract I have made on behalf of another man." Abu Bakr replied, "I release you from your pact to protect me, and am pleased with the protection from Allah."

At that time the Prophet (ﷺ) was in Mecca, and he said to the Muslims, "In a dream I have been shown your migration place, a land of date palm trees, between two mountains, the two stony tracts." So, some people migrated to Medina, and most of those people who had previously migrated to the land of Ethiopia, returned to Medina. Abu Bakr also prepared to leave for Medina, but Allah's Messenger (ﷺ) said to him, "Wait for a while, because I hope that I will be allowed to migrate also." Abu Bakr said, "Do you indeed expect this? Let my father be sacrificed for you!" The Prophet (ﷺ) said, "Yes." So Abu Bakr did not migrate for the sake of Allah's Messenger (ﷺ) in order to accompany him. He fed two she-camels he possessed with the leaves of As-Samur tree that fell on being struck by a stick for four months.

One day, while we were sitting in Abu Bakr's house at noon, someone said to Abu Bakr, "This is Allah's Messenger (ﷺ) with his head covered coming at a time at which he never used to visit us before." Abu Bakr said, "May my parents be sacrificed for him. By Allah, he has not come at this hour except for a great necessity." So Allah's Messenger (ﷺ) came and asked permission to enter, and he was allowed to enter. When he entered, he said to Abu Bakr. "Tell everyone who is present with you to go away." Abu Bakr replied, "There are none but your family. May my father be sacrificed for you, O Allah's Messenger (ﷺ)!" The Prophet (ﷺ) said, "i have been given permission to migrate." Abu Bakr said, "Shall I accompany you? May my father be sacrificed for you, O Allah's Messenger (ﷺ)!" Allah's Messenger (ﷺ) said, "Yes." Abu Bakr said, "O Allah's Messenger (ﷺ)! May my father be sacrificed for you, take one of these two she-camels of mine." Allah's Messenger (ﷺ) replied, "(I will accept it) with payment." So we prepared the baggage quickly and put some journey food in a leather bag for them. Asma, Abu Bakr's daughter, cut a piece from her waist belt and tied the mouth of the leather bag with it, and for that reason she was named Dhat-un-Nitaqain (i.e. the owner of two belts).

Then Allah's Messenger (ﷺ) and Abu Bakr reached a cave on the mountain of Thaur and stayed there for three nights. 'Abdullah bin Abi Bakr who was intelligent and a sagacious youth, used to stay (with them) aver night. He used to leave them before day break so that in the morning he would be with Quraish as if he had spent the night in Mecca. He would keep in mind any plot made against them, and when it became dark he would (go and) inform them of it. 'Amir bin Fuhaira, the freed slave of Abu Bakr, used to bring the milch sheep (of his master, Abu Bakr) to them a little while after nightfall in order to rest the sheep there. So they always had fresh milk at night, the milk of their sheep, and the milk which they warmed by throwing heated stones in it. 'Amir bin Fuhaira would then call the herd away when it was still dark (before daybreak). He did the same in each of those three nights. Allah's Messenger (ﷺ) and Abu Bakr had hired a man from the tribe of Bani Ad-Dail from the family of Bani Abd bin Adi as an expert guide, and he was in alliance with the family of Al-'As bin Wail As-Sahmi and he was on the religion of the infidels of Quraish. The Prophet (ﷺ) and Abu Bakr trusted him and gave him their two she-camels and took his promise to bring their two she camels to the cave of the mountain of Thaur in the morning after three nights later. And (when they set out), 'Amir bin Fuhaira and the guide went along with them and the guide led them along the sea-shore. (3905) □

1343. Narrated Al-Bara': Abu Bakr bought a (camel) saddle from `Azib for thirteen Dirhams. Abu Bakr said to `Azib, "Tell Al-Bara' to carry the saddle for me." `Azib said, "No, unless you relate to me what happened to you and Allah's Messenger (ﷺ) when you left Mecca while the pagans were in search of you." Abu Bakr said, "We left Mecca and we traveled continuously for that night and the following day till it was midday. I looked (around) searching for shade to take as shelter, and suddenly I came across a rock, and found a little shade there. So I cleaned the place and spread a bed for the Prophet (ﷺ) in the shade and said to him, 'Lie down, O Allah's Messenger (ﷺ).' So the Prophet (ﷺ) lay down and I went out, looking around to see if there was any person pursuing us. Suddenly I saw a shepherd driving his sheep towards the rock, seeking what we had already sought from it. I asked him, 'To whom do you belong, O boy?' He said, 'I belong to a man from Quraish.' He named the man and I recognized him. I asked him, 'Is there any milk with your sheep?' He said, 'Yes.' I said, 'Will you then milk (some) for us?' He said, 'Yes.' Then I asked him to tie the legs of one of the sheep and clean its udder, and then ordered him to clean his hands from dust. Then the shepherd cleaned his hands by striking his hands against one another. After doing so, he milked a small amount of milk. I used to keep for Allah's Messenger (ﷺ) a leather water-container, the mouth of which was covered with a piece of cloth. I poured water on the milk container till its lower part was cold. Then I took the milk to the Prophet (ﷺ) whom I found awake. I said to him, 'Drink, O Allah's Messenger (ﷺ).' So he drank till I became pleased. Then I said, 'It is time for us to move, O Allah's Apostle!' He said, 'Yes.' So we set out while the people (i.e. Quraish pagans) were searching for us, but none found us except Suraqah bin Malik bin Ju`shum who was riding his horse. I said, 'These are our pursuers who have found us. O Allah's Messenger (ﷺ)!' He said, 'Do not grieve, for Allah is with us." (3652) □

The nephew of Suraqa bin Ju'sham said that his father informed him that he heard Suraqa bin Ju'sham saying, "The messengers of the heathens of Quraish came to us declaring that they had assigned for the persons why would kill or arrest Allah's Messenger (ﷺ) and Abu Bakr, a reward equal to their bloodmoney. While I was sitting in one of the gatherings of my tribe. Bani Mudlij, a man from them came to us and stood up while we were sitting, and said, "O Suraqa! No doubt, I have just seen some people far away on the seashore, and I think they are Muhammad and his companions." Suraqa added, "I too realized that it must have been they. But I said 'No, it is not they, but you have seen so-and-so, and so-and-so whom we saw set out.' I stayed in the gathering for a while and then got up and left for my home. And ordered my slave-girl to get my horse which was behind a hillock, and keep it ready for me.

Then I took my spear and left by the back door of my house dragging the lower end of the spear on the ground and keeping it low. Then I reached my horse, mounted it and made it gallop. When I approached them (i.e. Muhammad and Abu Bakr), my horse stumbled and I fell down from it, Then I stood up, got hold of my quiver and took out the divining arrows and drew lots as to whether I should harm them (i.e. the Prophet (ﷺ) and Abu Bakr) or not, and the lot which I disliked came out. But I remounted my horse and let it gallop, giving no importance to the divining arrows. When I heard the recitation of the Quran by Allah's Messenger (ﷺ) who did not look hither and thither while Abu Bakr was doing it often, suddenly the forelegs of my horse sank into the ground up to the knees, and I fell down from it. Then I rebuked it and it got up but could hardly take out its forelegs from the ground, and when it stood up straight again, its fore-legs caused dust to rise up in the sky like smoke. Then again I drew lots with the divining arrows, and the lot which I disliked, came out. So I called upon them to feel secure. They stopped, and I remounted my horse and went to them. When I saw how I had been hampered from harming them, it came to my mind that the cause of Allah's Messenger (ﷺ) (i.e. Islam) will become victorious. So I said to him, "Your people have assigned a reward equal to the bloodmoney for your head." Then I told them all the plans the people of Mecca had made concerning them. Then I offered them some journey food and goods but they refused to take anything and did not ask for anything, but the Prophet (ﷺ) said, "Do not tell others about us." Then I requested him to write for me a statement of security and peace. He ordered 'Amr bin Fuhaira who wrote it for me on a parchment, and then Allah's Messenger (ﷺ) proceeded on his way.

1344. Narrated 'Urwa bin Az-Zubair: Allah's Messenger (ﷺ) met Az-Zubair in a caravan of Muslim merchants who were returning from Sham. Az-Zubair provided Allah's Messenger (ﷺ) and Abu Bakr with white clothes to wear. When the Muslims of Medina heard the news of the departure of Allah's Messenger (ﷺ) from Mecca (towards Medina), they started going to the Harra every morning. They would wait for him till the heat of the noon forced them to return. One day, after waiting for a long while, they returned home, and when they went into their houses, a Jew climbed up the roof of one of the forts of his people to look for some thing, and he saw Allah's Messenger (ﷺ) and his companions dressed in white clothes, emerging out of the desert mirage.

The Jew could not help shouting at the top of his voice, "O you 'Arabs! Here is your great man whom you have been waiting for!" So all the Muslims rushed to their arms and received Allah's Messenger (ﷺ) on the summit of Harra. The Prophet (ﷺ) turned with them to the right and alighted at the quarters of Bani 'Amr bin 'Auf, and this was on Monday in the month of Rabi-ul-Awal. Abu Bakr stood up, receiving the people while Allah's Messenger (ﷺ) sat down and kept silent. Some of the Ansar who came and had not seen Allah's Messenger (ﷺ) before, began greeting Abu Bakr, but when the sunshine fell on Allah's Messenger (ﷺ) and Abu Bakr came forward and shaded him with his sheet only then the people came to know Allah's Messenger (ﷺ). Allah's Messenger (ﷺ) stayed with Bani 'Amr bin 'Auf for ten nights and established the mosque (mosque of Quba) which was founded on piety. Allah's Messenger (ﷺ) prayed in it and then mounted his she-camel and proceeded on, accompanied by the people till his she-camel knelt down at (the place of) the Mosque of Allah's Messenger (ﷺ) at Medina. Some Muslims used to pray there in those days, and that place was a yard for drying dates belonging to Suhail and Sahl, the orphan boys who were under the guardianship of 'Asad bin Zurara. When his she-camel knelt down, Allah's Messenger (ﷺ) said, "This place, Allah willing, will be our abiding place." Allah's Messenger (ﷺ) then called the two boys and told them to suggest a price for that yard so that he might take it as a mosque. The two boys said, "No, but we will give it as a gift, O Allah's Messenger (ﷺ)!" Allah's Messenger (ﷺ) then built a mosque there. The Prophet (ﷺ) himself started carrying unburnt bricks for its building and while doing so, he was saying "This load is better than the load of Khaibar, for it is more pious in the Sight of Allah and purer and better rewardable." He was also saying, "O Allah! The actual reward is the reward in the Hereafter, so bestow Your Mercy on the Ansar and the Emigrants." Thus the Prophet (ﷺ) recited (by way of proverb) the poem of some Muslim poet whose name is unknown to me. (Ibn Shibab said, "In the Hadiths it does not occur that Allah's Apostle recited a complete poetic verse other than this one.") (3906) □

1345. Narrated Anas bin Malik: Allah's Messenger (ﷺ) arrived at Medina with Abu Bakr, riding behind him on the same camel. Abu Bakr was an elderly man known to the people, while Allah's Messenger (ﷺ) was a youth that was unknown. Thus, if a man met Abu Bakr, he would say, "O Abu Bakr! Who is this man in front of you?" Abu Bakr would say, "This man shows me the Way," One would think that Abu Bakr meant the road, while in fact, Abu Bakr meant the way of virtue and good. Then Abu Bakr looked behind and saw a horse-rider pursuing them. He said, "O Allah's

Messenger (ﷺ)! This is a horse-rider pursuing us." The Prophet (ﷺ) looked behind and said, "O Allah! Cause him to fall down." So the horse threw him down and got up neighing. After that the rider, Suraqa said, "O Allah's Prophet! Order me whatever you want." The Prophet said, "Stay where you are and do not allow anybody to reach us." So, in the first part of the day Suraqa was an enemy of Allah's Prophet and in the last part of it, he was a protector. Then Allah's Apostle alighted by the side of the Al-Harra and sent a message to the Ansar, and they came to Allah's Prophet and Abu Bakr, and having greeted them, they said, "Ride (your she-camels) safe and obeyed." Allah's Messenger (ﷺ) and Abu Bakr rode and the Ansar, carrying their arms, surrounded them. The news that Allah's Prophet had come circulated in Medina. The people came out and were eagerly looking and saying "Allah's Prophet has come! Allah's Prophet has come! So the Prophet (ﷺ) went on till he alighted near the house of Abu Ayub. While the Prophet (ﷺ) was speaking with the family members of Abu Ayub, `Abdullah bin Salam heard the news of his arrival while he himself was picking the dates for his family from his family garden. He hurried to the Prophet (ﷺ) carrying the dates which he had collected for his family from the garden. He listened to Allah's Prophet and then went home. Then Allah's Prophet said, "Which is the nearest of the houses of our kith and kin?" Abu Ayub replied, "Mine, O Allah's Prophet! This is my house and this is my gate." The Prophet (ﷺ) said, "Go and prepare a place for our midday rest." Abu Ayub said, "Get up (both of you) with Allah's Blessings." So when Allah's Prophet went into the house, `Abdullah bin Salam came and said "I testify that you (i.e. Muhammad) are Apostle of Allah and that you have come with the Truth. The Jews know well that I am their chief and the son of their chief and the most learned amongst them and the son of the most learned amongst them. So send for them (i.e. Jews) and ask them about me before they know that I have embraced Islam, for if they know that they will say about me things which are not correct." So Allah's Messenger (ﷺ) sent for them, and they came and entered. Allah's Messenger (ﷺ) said to them, "O (the group of) Jews! Woe to you: be afraid of Allah. By Allah except Whom none has the right to be worshipped, you people know for certain, that I am Apostle of Allah and that I have come to you with the Truth, so embrace Islam."

The Jews replied, "We do not know this." So they said this to the Prophet and he repeated it thrice. Then he said, "What sort of a man is `Abdullah bin Salam amongst you?" They said, "He is our chief and the son of our chief and the most learned man, and the son of the most learned amongst us." He said, "What would you think if he should embrace Islam?" They said, "Allah forbid! He can not embrace Islam." He said, "What would you think if he should embrace Islam?" They said, "Allah forbid! He can not embrace Islam." He said, "What would you think if he should embrace Islam?" They said, "Allah forbid! He can not embrace Islam." He said, "O Ibn Salam! Come out to them." He came out and said, "O (the group of) Jews! Be afraid of Allah except Whom none has the right to be worshipped. You know for certain that he is Apostle of Allah and that he has brought a True Religion!' They said, "You tell a lie." On that Allah's Messenger (ﷺ) turned them out. (3911) ☐

1346. Narrated Abu Bakr: I was with the Prophet (ﷺ) in the Cave. When I raised my head, I saw the feet of the people. I said, "O Allah's Messenger (ﷺ)! If some of them should look down, they will see us." The Prophet (ﷺ) said, "O Abu Bakr, be quiet! (For we are) two and Allah is the Third of us." (3922) ☐

1347. Narrated Al-Bara bin Azib: The first people who came to us (in Medina) were Mus`ab bin `Umar and Ibn Um Maktum who were teaching Qur'an to the people. Then their came Bilal. Sa`d and `Ammar bin Yasir. After that `Umar bin Al-Khattab came along with twenty other companions of the Prophet. Later on the Prophet (ﷺ) himself (to Medina) and I had never seen the people of Medina so joyful as they were on the arrival of Allah's Apostle, for even the slave girls were saying, "Allah's Messenger (ﷺ) has arrived!" And before his arrival I had read the Sura starting with: -- "Glorify the Name of your Lord, the Most High" (87.1) together with other Suras of Al-Mufassal. (3925) ☐

1348. Narrated Sahl bin Sa`d: The Prophet's companions did not take as a starting date for the Muslim calendar, the day, the Prophet (ﷺ) had been sent as an Apostle or the day of his death, but the day of his arrival at Medina. (3934) ☐

1349. Narrated Anas: When the news of the arrival of the Prophet (ﷺ) at Medina reached `Abdullah bin Salam, he went to him to ask him about certain things, He said, "I am going to ask you about three things which only a Prophet can answer: What is the first sign of The Hour? What is the first food which the people of Paradise will eat? Why does a child attract the similarity to his father or to his mother?" The Prophet (ﷺ) replied, "Gabriel has just now informed me of that." Ibn Salam said, "He (i.e. Gabriel) is the enemy of the Jews amongst the angels. The Prophet (ﷺ) said, "As for the first sign of The Hour, it will be a fire that will collect the people from the East to the West. As for the first meal which the people of Paradise will eat, it will be the caudate (extra) lobe of the fish-liver. As for the child, if the man's discharge proceeds the woman's discharge, the child attracts the similarity to the man, and if the woman's discharge proceeds the man's, then the child attracts the similarity to the woman." On this, `Abdullah bin Salam said, "I testify that None has the right to be worshipped except Allah, and that you are the Messenger of Allah." and added, "O Allah's Messenger (ﷺ)! Jews invent such lies as make one astonished, so please ask them about me before they know about my conversion to I slam . "The Jews came, and the Prophet (ﷺ) said, "What kind of man is `Abdullah bin Salam among you?" They replied, "The best of us and the son of the best of us and the most superior among us, and the son of the most superior among us."The Prophet (ﷺ) said, "What would you think if `Abdullah bin Salam should embrace Islam?" They said, "May Allah protect him from that." The Prophet (ﷺ) repeated his question and they gave the same answer. Then `Abdullah came out to them and said, "I testify that None has the right to be worshipped except Allah and that Muhammad is the Messenger of Allah!" On this, the Jews said, "He is the most wicked among us and the son of the most wicked among us." So they degraded him. On this, he (i.e. `Abdullah bin Salam) said, "It is this that I was afraid of, O Allah's Messenger (p.b.u.h). (3938) □

1350. Narrated Abu Huraira: The Prophet (ﷺ) said, "Had only ten Jews (amongst their chiefs) believe me, all the Jews would definitely have believed me." (3941) □

1351. Narrated Salman: The interval between Jesus and Muhammad was six hundred years. (3948) □

60. MILITARY EXPEDITIONS

1352. NARRATED ABU 'IS-HAQ (RA): Once, while I was sitting beside Zaid bin Al-Arqam, he was asked, "How many Ghazwat did the Prophet undertake?" Zaid replied, "Nineteen." They said, "In how many Ghazwat did you join him?" He replied, "Seventeen." I asked, "Which of these was the first?" He replied, "Al-`Ashira or Al-`Ashiru." (3949) □

1353. Narrated `Abdullah bin Mas`ud: From Sa`d bin Mu`adh: Sa`d bin Mu`adh was an intimate friend of Umaiya bin Khalaf and whenever Umaiya passed through Medina, he used to stay with Sa`d, and whenever Sa`d went to Mecca, he used to stay with Umaiya. When Allah's Messenger (ﷺ) arrived at Medina, Sa`d went to perform `Umra and stayed at Umaiya's home in Mecca. He said to Umaiya, "Tell me of a time when (the Mosque) is empty so that I may be able to perform Tawaf around the Ka`ba." So Umaiya went with him about midday. Abu Jahl met them and said, "O Abu Safwan! Who is this man accompanying you?" He said, "He is Sa`d." Abu Jahl addressed Sa`d saying, "I see you wandering about safely in Mecca inspite of the fact that you have given shelter to the people who have changed their religion (i.e. became Muslims) and have claimed that you will help them and support them. By Allah, if you were not in the company of Abu Safwan, you would not be able to go your family safely." Sa`d, raising his voice, said to him, "By Allah, if you should stop me from doing this (i.e. performing Tawaf) I would certainly prevent you from something which is more valuable for you, that is, your passage through Medina." On this, Umaiya said to him, "O Sa`d do not raise your voice before Abu-l-Hakam, the chief of the people of the Valley (of Mecca)." Sa`d said, "O Umaiya, stop that! By Allah, I have heard Allah's Messenger (ﷺ) predicting that the Muslim will kill you." Umaiya asked, "In Mecca?" Sa`d said, "I do not know." Umaiya was greatly scared by that news. When Umaiya returned to his family, he said to his wife, "O Um Safwan! Don't you know what Sa`d told me? "She said, "What has he told you?" He replied, "He claims that Muhammad has informed them (i.e. companions that they will kill me. I asked him, 'In Mecca?' He replied, 'I do not know." Then Umaiya added, "By Allah, I will never go out of Mecca." But when the day of (the Ghazwa of) Badr came, Abu Jahl called the people to war, saying, "Go and protect your caravan." But Umaiya disliked to go out (of Mecca). Abu Jahl came to him and said, "O Abu Safwan! If the people see you staying behind though you are the chief of the people of the Valley, then they will remain behind with you." Abu Jahl kept on urging him to go until he (i.e. Umaiya) said, "As you have forced me to change my mind, by Allah, I will buy the best camel in Mecca. Then Umaiya said (to his wife). "O Um Safwan, prepare what I need (for the journey)." She said to him, "O Abu Safwan! Have you forgotten what your Yathribi brother told you?" He said, "No, but I do not want to go with them but for a short distance." So when Umaiya went out, he used to tie his camel wherever he camped. He kept on doing that till Allah caused him to be killed at Badr. (3950) □

1354. Narrated Ka`b bin Malik: I never failed to join Allah's Messenger (ﷺ) in any of his Ghazawat except in the Ghazwa of Tabuk. However, I did not take part in the Ghazwa of Badr, but none who failed to take part in it, was blamed, for Allah's Messenger (ﷺ) had gone out to meet the caravans of (Quraish, but Allah caused them (i.e. Muslims) to meet their enemy unexpectedly (with no previous intention). (3951) □

1355. Narrated Ibn Masud: I witnessed Al-Miqdad bin Al-Aswad in a scene which would have been dearer to me than anything had I been the hero of that scene. He (i.e. Al-Miqdad) came to the Prophet (ﷺ) while the Prophet (ﷺ) was urging the Muslims to fight with the pagans. Al-Miqdad said, "We will not say as the People of Moses said: Go you and your Lord and fight you two. (5.27). But we shall fight on your right and on your left and in front of you and behind you." I saw the face of the Prophet (ﷺ) getting bright with happiness, for that saying delighted him. (3952) □

1356. Narrated Ibn `Abbas: On the day of the battle of Badr, the Prophet (ﷺ) said, "O Allah! I appeal to You (to fulfill) Your Covenant and Promise. O Allah! If Your Will is that none should worship You (then give victory to the pagans)." Then Abu Bakr took hold of him by the hand and said, "This is sufficient for you." The Prophet came out saying, "Their multitude will be put to flight and they will show their backs." (54.45) (3953) ☐

1357. Narrated Ibn `Abbas: The believers who failed to join the Ghazwa of Badr and those who took part in it are not equal (in reward). (3954) ☐

1358. Narrated Al-Bara: I and Ibn `Umar were considered too young (to take part) in the battle of Badr, and the number of the Emigrant warriors were over sixty (men) and the Ansar were over 249. (3956) ☐

1359. Narrated Al-Bara: The companions of (the Prophet) Muhammad who took part in Badr, told me that their number was that of Saul's (i.e. Talut's) companions who crossed the river (of Jordan) with him and they were over three-hundred-and-ten men. By Allah, none crossed the river with him but a believer. (See Qur'an 2:249) (3957) ☐

1360. Narrated Abu Talha: On the day of Badr, the Prophet (ﷺ) ordered that the corpses of twenty four leaders of Quraish should be thrown into one of the dirty dry wells of Badr. (It was a habit of the Prophet (ﷺ) that whenever he conquered some people, he used to stay at the battle-field for three nights. So, on the third day of the battle of Badr, he ordered that his she-camel be saddled, then he set out, and his companions followed him saying among themselves." "Definitely he (i.e. the Prophet) is proceeding for some great purpose." When he halted at the edge of the well, he addressed the corpses of the Quraish infidels by their names and their fathers' names, "O so-and-so, son of so-and-so and O so-and-so, son of so-and-so! Would it have pleased you if you had obeyed Allah and His Apostle? We have found true what our Lord promised us. Have you too found true what your Lord promised you?" `Umar said, "O Allah's Messenger (ﷺ)! You are speaking to bodies that have no souls!"

Allah's Messenger (ﷺ) said, "By Him in Whose Hand Muhammad's soul is, you do not hear, what I say better than they do." (Qatada said, "Allah brought them to life (again) to let them hear him, to reprimand them and slight them and take revenge over them and caused them to feel remorseful and regretful.") (3976) □

1361. Narrated `Ali: Allah's Messenger (ﷺ) sent me, Abu Marthad and Az-Zubair, and all of us were riding horses, and said, "Go till you reach Raudat-Khakh where there is a pagan woman carrying a letter from Hatib bin Abi Balta' a to the pagans of Mecca." So we found her riding her camel at the place which Allah's Messenger (ﷺ) had mentioned. We said (to her),"(Give us) the letter." She said, "I have no letter." Then we made her camel kneel down and we searched her, but we found no letter. Then we said, "Allah's Messenger (ﷺ) had not told us a lie, certainly. Take out the letter, otherwise we will strip you naked." When she saw that we were determined, she put her hand below her waist belt, for she had tied her cloak round her waist, and she took out the letter, and we brought her to Allah's Messenger (ﷺ) then `Umar said, "O Allah's Apostle! (This Hatib) has betrayed Allah, His Apostle and the believers! Let me cut off his neck!" The Prophet asked Hatib, "What made you do this?" Hatib said, "By Allah, I did not intend to give up my belief in Allah and His Apostle but I wanted to have some influence among the (Mecca) people so that through it, Allah might protect my family and property. There is none of your companions but has some of his relatives there through whom Allah protects his family and property." The Prophet (ﷺ) said, "He has spoken the truth; do no say to him but good." `Umar said, "He as betrayed Allah, His Apostle and the faithful believers. Let me cut off his neck!" The Prophet (ﷺ) said, "Is he not one of the Badr warriors? May be Allah looked at the Badr warriors and said, 'Do whatever you like, as I have granted Paradise to you, or said, 'I have forgiven you.'" On this, tears came out of `Umar's eyes, and he said, "Allah and His Apostle know better." (3983) □

1362. Narrated Usaid: On the day of Badr, Allah's Messenger (ﷺ) said to us, "When the enemy comes near to you, shoot at them but use your arrows sparingly (so that your arrows should not be wasted). (3984) □

1363. Narrated `Abdur-Rahman bin `Auf: While I was fighting in the front file on the day (of the battle) of Badr, suddenly I looked behind and saw on my right and left two young boys and did not feel safe by standing between them. Then one of them asked me secretly so that his companion may not hear, "O Uncle! Show me Abu Jahl." I said, "O nephew! What will you do to him?" He said, "I have promised Allah that if I see him (i.e. Abu Jahl), I will either kill him or be killed before I kill him." Then the other said the same to me secretly so that his companion should not hear. I would not have been pleased to be in between two other men instead of them. Then I pointed him (i.e. Abu Jahl) out to them. Both of them attacked him like two hawks till they knocked him down. Those two boys were the sons of 'Afra' (i.e. an Ansari woman). (3988) □

1364. Narrated Rifaa: (who was one of the Badr warriors) Gabriel came to the Prophet (ﷺ) and said, "How do you look upon the warriors of Badr among yourselves?" The Prophet (ﷺ) said, "As the best of the Muslims." or said a similar statement. On that, Gabriel said, "And so are the Angels who participated in the Badr (battle). (3992) □

1365. Narrated Ibn `Abbas: The Prophet (ﷺ) said on the day (of the battle) of Badr, "This is Gabriel holding the head of his horse and equipped with arms for the battle. (3995) □

1366. Narrated `Urwa: Az-Zubair said, "I met Ubaida bin Sa`id bin Al-As on the day (of the battle) of Badr and he was covered with armor; so much that only his eyes were visible. He was surnamed Abu Dhat-al-Karish. He said (proudly), 'I am Abu-al-Karish.' I attacked him with the spear and pierced his eye and he died. I put my foot over his body to pull (that spear) out, but even then I had to use a great force to take it out as its both ends were bent." `Urwa said, "Later on Allah's Messenger (ﷺ) asked Az-Zubair for the spear and he gave it to him. When Allah's Messenger (ﷺ) died, Az-Zubair took it back. After that Abu Bakr demanded it and he gave it to him, and when Abu Bakr died, Az-Zubair took it back. `Umar then demanded it from him and he gave it to him. When `Umar died, Az-Zubair took it back, and then `Uthman demanded it from him and he gave it to him. When `Uthman was martyred, the spear remained with `Ali's offspring. Then `Abdullah bin Az-Zubair demanded it back, and it remained with him till he was martyred. (3998) ☐

1367. Narrated Anas: Allah's Messenger (ﷺ) said on the day of Badr, "Who will go and see what has happened to Abu Jahl?" Ibn Mas`ud went and saw him struck by the two sons of 'Afra and was on the point of death. Ibn Mas`ud said, "Are you Abu Jahl?" Abu Jahl replied, "Can there be a man more superior to the one whom you have killed (or as Sulaiman said, or his own folk have killed.)?" Abu Jahl added, "Would that I had been killed by other than a mere farmer." (4020) ☐

1368. Narrated Qais: The Badr warriors were given five thousand (Dirhams) each, yearly. `Umar said, "I will surely give them more than what I will give to others." (4022) ☐

1369. Narrated Ibn Shihab: `Abdullah said, the total number of Muslim fighters from Quraish who fought in the battle of Badr and were given their share of the booty, were 81 men." Az-Zubair said, "When their shares were distributed, their number was 101 men. But Allah knows it better." (4026) ☐

1370. Narrated Az-Zubair: On the day of Badr, (Quraishi) Emigrants received 100 shares of the war booty." (4027) ☐

1371. Narrated Ibn `Umar: Bani An-Nadir and Bani Quraiza fought (against the Prophet (ﷺ) violating their peace treaty), so the Prophet exiled Bani An-Nadir and allowed Bani Quraiza to remain at their places (in Medina) taking nothing from them till they fought against the Prophet (ﷺ) again). He then killed their men and distributed their women, children and property among the Muslims, but some of them came to the Prophet (ﷺ) and he granted them safety, and they embraced Islam. He exiled all the Jews from Medina. They were the Jews of Bani Qainuqa', the tribe of `Abdullah bin Salam and the Jews of Bani Haritha and all the other Jews of Medina. (4028) ☐

1372. Narrated Anas bin Malik: Some people used to allot some date palm trees to the Prophet (ﷺ) as gift till he conquered Banu Quraiza and Bani An-Nadir, where upon he started returning their date palms to them. (4030) □

1373. Narrated Ibn `Umar: Allah's Messenger (ﷺ) had the date-palm trees of Bani Al-Nadir burnt and cut down at a place called Al- Buwaira. Allah then revealed: "What you cut down of the date-palm trees (of the enemy) or you left them standing on their stems. It was by Allah's Permission." (59.5) (4031) □

1374. Narrated Jabir bin `Abdullah: Allah's Messenger (ﷺ) said, "Who is willing to kill Ka`b bin Al-Ashraf who has hurt Allah and His Apostle?" Thereupon Muhammad bin Maslama got up saying, "O Allah's Messenger (ﷺ)! Would you like that I kill him?" The Prophet (ﷺ) said, "Yes," Muhammad bin Maslama said, "Then allow me to say a (false) thing (i.e. to deceive Ka`b)."The Prophet (ﷺ) said, "You may say it." Then Muhammad bin Maslama went to Ka`b and said, "That man (i.e. Muhammad demands Sadaqa (i.e. Zakat) from us, and he has troubled us, and I have come to borrow something from you." On that, Ka`b said, "By Allah, you will get tired of him!" Muhammad bin Maslama said, "Now as we have followed him, we do not want to leave him unless and until we see how his end is going to be. Now we want you to lend us a camel load or two of food." (Some difference between narrators about a camel load or two.) Ka`b said, "Yes, (I will lend you), but you should mortgage something to me." Muhammad bin Mas-lama and his companion said, "What do you want?" Ka`b replied, "Mortgage your women to me." They said, "How can we mortgage our women to you and you are the most handsome of the 'Arabs?" Ka`b said, "Then mortgage your sons to me." They said, "How can we mortgage our sons to you? Later they would be abused by the people's saying that so-and-so has been mortgaged for a camel load of food. That would cause us great disgrace, but we will mortgage our arms to you." Muhammad bin Maslama and his companion promised Ka`b that Muhammad would return to him. He came to Ka`b at night along with Ka`b's foster brother, Abu Na'ila. Ka`b invited them to come into his fort, and then he went down to them. His wife asked him, "Where are you going at this time?" Ka`b replied, "None but Muhammad bin Maslama and my (foster) brother Abu Na'ila have come." His wife said, "I hear a voice as if dropping blood is from him, Ka`b said."They are none but my brother Muhammad bin Maslama and my foster brother Abu Naila. A generous man should respond to a call at night even if invited to be killed." Muhammad bin Maslama went with two men. (Some narrators mention the men as 'Abu bin Jabr. Al Harith bin Aus and `Abbad bin Bishr). So Muhammad bin Maslama went in together with two men, and sail to them, "When Ka`b comes, I will touch his hair and smell it, and when you see that I have got hold of his head, strip him. I will let you smell his head." Ka`b bin Al-Ashraf came down to them wrapped in his clothes, and diffusing perfume. Muhammad bin Maslama said, "Have never smelt a better scent than this. Ka`b replied. "I have got the best 'Arab women who know how to use the high class of perfume." Muhammad bin Maslama requested Ka`b "Will you allow me to smell your head?" Ka`b said, "Yes." Muhammad smelt it and made his companions smell it as well. Then he requested Ka`b again, "Will you let me (smell your head)?" Ka`b said, "Yes." When Muhammad got a strong hold of him, he said (to his companions), "Get at him!" So they killed him and went to the Prophet (ﷺ) and informed him. (Abu Rafi`) was killed after Ka`b bin Al-Ashraf." (4037) □

1375. Narrated Al-Bara: Allah's Messenger (ﷺ) sent `Abdullah bin 'Atik and `Abdullah bin `Utba with a group of men to Abu Rafi` (to kill him). They proceeded till they approached his castle, whereupon `Abdullah bin Atik said to them, "Wait (here), and in the meantime I will go and see." `Abdullah said later on, "I played a trick in order to enter the castle. By chance, they lost a donkey of theirs and came out carrying a flaming light to search for it. I was afraid that they would recognize me, so I covered my head and legs and pretended to answer the call to nature. The gatekeeper called, 'Whoever wants to come in, should come in before I close the gate.' So I went in and hid myself in a stall of a donkey near the gate of the castle. They took their supper with Abu Rafi` and had a chat till late at night. Then they went back to their homes. When the voices vanished and I no longer detected any movement, I came out. I had seen where the gate-keeper had kept the key of the castle in a hole in the wall. I took it and unlocked the gate of the castle, saying to myself, 'If these people should notice me, I will run away easily.' Then I locked all the doors of their houses from outside while they were inside, and ascended to Abu Rafi` by a staircase. I saw the house in complete darkness with its light off, and I could not know where the man was. So I called, 'O Abu Rafi`!' He replied, 'Who is it?' I proceeded towards the voice and hit him. He cried loudly but my blow was futile. Then I came to him, pretending to help him, saying with a different tone of my voice, ' What is wrong with you, O Abu Rafi`?' He said, 'Are you not surprised? Woe on your mother! A man has come to me and hit me with a sword!' So again I aimed at him and hit him, but the blow proved futile again, and on that Abu Rafi` cried loudly and his wife got up. I came again and changed my voice as if I were a helper, and found Abu Rafi` lying straight on his back, so I drove the sword into his belly and bent on it till I heard the sound of a bone break. Then I came out, filled with astonishment and went to the staircase to descend, but I fell down from it and got my leg dislocated. I bandaged it and went to my companions limping. I said (to them), 'Go and tell Allah's Messenger (ﷺ) of this good news, but I will not leave (this place) till I hear the news of his death.' When dawn broke, an announcer of death got over the wall and announced, 'I convey to you the news of Abu Rafi`'s death.' I got up and proceeded without feeling any pain till I caught up with my companions before they reached the Prophet (ﷺ) to whom I conveyed the good news." (4040) □

1376. Narrated `Uqba bin Amir: Allah's Messenger (ﷺ) offered the funeral prayers of the martyrs of Uhud eight years after (their death), as if bidding farewell to the living and the dead, then he ascended the pulpit and said, "I am your predecessor before you, and I am a witness on you, and your promised place to meet me will be Al- Haud (i.e. the Tank) (on the Day of Resurrection), and I am (now) looking at it from this place of mine. I am not afraid that you will worship others besides Allah, but I am afraid that worldly life will tempt you and cause you to compete with each other for it." That was the last look which I cast on Allah's Messenger (peace be upon him). (4042) □

1377. Narrated Al-Bara: We faced the pagans on that day (of the battle of Uhud) and the Prophet (ﷺ) placed a batch of archers (at a special place) and appointed `Abdullah (bin Jubair) as their commander and said, "Do not leave this place; if you should see us conquering the enemy, do not leave this place, and if you should see them conquering us, do not (come to) help us," So, when we faced the enemy, they took to their heels till I saw their women running towards the mountain, lifting up their clothes from their legs, revealing their leg-bangles. The Muslims started saying, "The booty, the booty!" `Abdullah bin Jubair said, "The Prophet (ﷺ) had taken a firm promise from me not to leave this place." But his companions refused (to stay). So when they refused (to stay there), (Allah) confused them so that they could not know where to go, and they suffered seventy casualties. Abu Sufyan ascended a high place and said, "Is Muhammad present amongst the people?" The Prophet (ﷺ) said, "Do not answer him." Abu Sufyan said, "Is the son of Abu Quhafa present among the people?" The Prophet (ﷺ) said, "Do not answer him." `Abu Sufyan said, "Is the son of Al-Khattab amongst the people?" He then added, "All these people have been killed, for, were they alive, they would have replied." On that, `Umar could not help saying, "You are a liar, O enemy of Allah! Allah has kept what will make you unhappy." Abu Sufyan said, "Superior may be Hubal!" On that the Prophet said (to his companions), "Reply to him." They asked, "What may we say?" He said, "Say: Allah is More Elevated and More Majestic!" Abu Sufyan said, "We have (the idol) Al-`Uzza, whereas you have no `Uzza!" The Prophet (ﷺ) said (to his companions), "Reply to him." They said, "What may we say?" The Prophet (ﷺ) said, "Say: Allah is our Helper and you have no helper." Abu Sufyan said, "(This) day compensates for our loss at Badr and (in) the battle (the victory) is always undecided and shared in turns by the belligerents. You will see some of your dead men mutilated, but neither did I urge this action, nor am I sorry for it." Narrated Jabir: Some people took wine in the morning of the day of Uhud and were then killed as martyrs. (4043) □

1378. Narrated Jabir bin `Abdullah: On the day of the battle of Uhud, a man came to the Prophet (ﷺ) and said, "Can you tell me where I will be if I should get martyred?" The Prophet (ﷺ) replied, "In Paradise." The man threw away some dates he was carrying in his hand, and fought till he was martyred. (4046) ☐

1379. Narrated Zaid bin Thabit: When the Prophet (ﷺ) set out for (the battle of) Uhud, some of those who had gone out with him, returned. The companions of the Prophet (ﷺ) were divided into two groups. One group said, "We will fight them (i.e. the enemy)," and the other group said, "We will not fight them." So there came the Divine Revelation: -- '(O Muslims!) Then what is the matter within you that you are divided. Into two parties about the hypocrites? Allah has cast them back (to disbelief) Because of what they have earned.' (4.88) On that, the Prophet (ﷺ) said, "That is Taiba (i.e. the city of Medina) which clears one from one's sins as the fire expels the impurities of silver." (4050) ☐

1380. Narrated Sa`d bin Abi Waqqas: I saw Allah's Messenger (ﷺ) on the day of the battle of Uhud accompanied by two men fighting on his behalf. They were dressed in white and were fighting as bravely as possible. I had never seen them before, nor did I see them later on. (4054) ☐

1381. Narrated Sa`d bin Abi Waqqas: The Prophet (ﷺ) took out a quiver (of arrows) for me on the day of Uhud and said, "Throw (arrows); let my father and mother be sacrificed for you." (4055) ☐

1382. Narrated Anas: When it was the day of Uhud, the people left the Prophet (ﷺ) while Abu Talha was in front of the Prophet (ﷺ) shielding him with his leather shield. Abu Talha was a skillful archer who used to shoot violently. He broke two or three arrow bows on that day. If a man carrying a quiver full of arrows passed by, the Prophet would say (to him), put (scatter) its contents for Abu Talha." The Prophet (ﷺ) would raise his head to look at the enemy, whereupon Abu Talha would say, "Let my father and mother be sacrificed for you! Do not raise your head, lest an arrow of the enemy should hit you. (Let) my neck (be struck) rather than your neck." I saw `Aisha, the daughter of Abu Bakr, and Um Sulaim rolling up their dresses so that I saw their leg-bangles while they were carrying water skins on their backs and emptying them in the mouths of the (wounded) people. They would return to refill them and again empty them in the mouths of the (wounded) people. The sword fell from Abu Talha's hand twice or thrice (on that day). (4064) □

1383. Narrated `Aisha: When it was the day of Uhud, the pagans were defeated. Then Satan, Allah's Curse be upon him, cried loudly, "O Allah's Worshippers, beware of what is behind!" On that, the front files of the (Muslim) forces turned their backs and started fighting with the back files. Hudhaifa looked, and on seeing his father Al-Yaman, he shouted, "O Allah's Worshippers, my father, my father!" But by Allah, they did not stop till they killed him. Hudhaifa said, "May Allah forgive you." (The sub-narrator, `Urwa, said, "By Allah, Hudhaifa continued asking Allah's Forgiveness for the killers of his father till he departed to Allah (i.e. died).") (4065) □

1384. Narrated Al-Bara' bin `Azib: The Prophet (ﷺ) appointed `Abdullah bin Jubair as the commander of the cavalry archers on the day of the battle of Uhud. Then they returned defeated, and that what is referred to by Allah's Statement: "And the Apostle (Muhammad) was in your rear calling you back." (3.153) (4067) □

1385. Abu Talha (ra) said: I was amongst those who were overtaken by slumber until my sword fell from my hand on several occasions. The sword fell and I picked it up, and it fell again, and I picked it up." (4068) □

1386. Narrated Tha`laba bin Abi Malik: `Umar bin Al-Khattab distributed woolen clothes amongst some women of Medina, and a nice woolen garment remained. Some of those who were sitting with him, said, "O chief of the believers! Give it to the daughter of Allah's Messenger (ﷺ) who is with you," and by that, they meant Um Kulthum, the daughter of `Ali. `Umar said, "Um Salit has got more right than she." Um Salit was amongst those Ansari women who had given the pledge of allegiance to Allah's Messenger (ﷺ). `Umar added, "She (i.e. Um Salit) used to carry the filled water skins for us on the day of the battle of Uhud." (4071) □

1387. Narrated Jafar bin `Amr bin Umaiya: I went out with 'Ubaidullah bin `Adi Al-Khaiyar. When we reached Hims (i.e. a town in Syria), 'Ubaidullah bin `Adi said (to me), "Would you like to see Wahshi so that we may ask him about the killing of

Hamza?" I replied, "Yes." Wahshi used to live in Hims. We enquired about him and somebody said to us, "He is that in the shade of his palace, as if he were a full water skin." So we went up to him, and when we were at a short distance from him, we greeted him and he greeted us in return. 'Ubaidullah was wearing his turban and Wahshi could not see except his eyes and feet. 'Ubaidullah said, "O Wahshi! Do you know me?" Wahshi looked at him and then said, "No, by Allah! But I know that `Adi bin Al-Khiyar married a woman called Um Qital, the daughter of Abu Al-Is, and she delivered a boy for him at Mecca, and I looked for a wet nurse for that child. (Once) I carried that child along with his mother and then I handed him over to her, and your feet resemble that child's feet." Then 'Ubaidullah uncovered his face and said (to Wahshi), "Will you tell us (the story of) the killing of Hamza?" Wahshi replied "Yes, Hamza killed Tuaima bin `Adi bin Al-Khaiyar at Badr (battle) so my master, Jubair bin Mut`im said to me, 'If you kill Hamza in revenge for my uncle, then you will be set free." When the people set out (for the battle of Uhud) in the year of 'Ainain ...'Ainain is a mountain near the mountain of Uhud, and between it and Uhud there is a valley.. I went out with the people for the battle. When the army aligned for the fight, Siba' came out and said, 'Is there any (Muslim) to accept my challenge to a duel?' Hamza bin `Abdul Muttalib came out and said, 'O Siba'. O Ibn Um Anmar, the one who circumcises other ladies! Do you challenge Allah and His Apostle?' Then Hamza attacked and killed him, causing him to be non-extant like the bygone yesterday. I hid myself under a rock, and when he (i.e. Hamza) came near me, I threw my spear at him, driving it into his umbilicus so that it came out through his buttocks, causing him to die. When all the people returned to Mecca, I too returned with them. I stayed in (Mecca) till Islam spread in it (i.e. Mecca). Then I left for Taif, and when the people (of Taif) sent their messengers to Allah's Messenger (ﷺ), I was told that the Prophet (ﷺ) did not harm the messengers; so I too went out with them till I reached Allah's Messenger (ﷺ). When he saw me, he said, 'Are you Wahshi?' I said, 'Yes.' He said, 'was it you who killed Hamza?' I replied, 'What happened is what you have been told of.' He said, 'Can you hide your face from me?' So I went out when Allah's Messenger (ﷺ) died, and Musailamah Al-Kadhdhab appeared (claiming to be a prophet). I said, 'I will go out to Musailamah so that I may kill him, and make amends for killing Hamza. So I went out with the people (to fight Musailamah and his followers) and then famous events took place concerning that battle. Suddenly I saw a man (i.e. Musailamah) standing near a gap in a wall. He looked like an ash-colored camel and his hair was dishevelled. So I threw my spear at him, driving it into his chest in between his breasts till it passed out through his shoulders, and then an Ansari man attacked him and struck him on the head with a sword. `Abdullah bin `Umar said, 'A slave girl on the roof of a house said: Alas! The chief of the believers (i.e. Musailamah) has been killed by a black slave." (4072) □

1388. Narrated Abu Huraira: Allah's Messenger (ﷺ) (pointing to his broken canine tooth) said, "Allah's Wrath has become severe on the people who harmed His Prophet. Allah's Wrath has become severe on the man who is killed by the Apostle of Allah in Allah's Cause." (4073) □

1389. Narrated Abu Hazim: That he heard Sahl bin Sa`d being asked about the wounds of Allah's Messenger (ﷺ) saying, "By Allah, I know who washed the wounds of Allah's Messenger (ﷺ) and who poured water (for washing them), and with what he was treated." Sahl added, "Fatima, the daughter of Allah's Messenger (ﷺ) used to wash the wounds, and `Ali bin Abi Talib used to pour water from a shield. When Fatima saw that the water aggravated the bleeding, she took a piece of a mat, burnt it, and inserted its ashes into the wound so that the blood was congealed (and bleeding stopped). His canine tooth got broken on that day, and face was wounded, and his helmet was broken on his head." (4075) □

1390. Narrated Ibn `Abbas: Allah's Wrath gets severe on a person killed by a prophet, and Allah's Wrath became severe on him who had caused the face of Allah's Messenger (ﷺ) to bleed. (4076) □

1391. Narrated `Aisha: Regarding the Holy Verse: "Those who responded (To the call) of Allah and the Apostle (Muhammad), after being wounded, For those of them Who did good deeds And refrained from wrong, there is a great reward." (3.172) She said to `Urwa, "O my nephew! Your father, Az-Zubair and Abu Bakr were amongst them (i.e. those who responded to the call of Allah and the Apostle on the day (of the battle of Uhud). When Allah's Messenger (ﷺ), suffered what he suffered on the day of Uhud and the pagans left, the Prophet (ﷺ) was afraid that they might return. So he said, 'who will go on their (i.e. pagans') track?' He then selected seventy men from amongst them (for this purpose)." (The sub-narrator added, "Abu Bakr and Az-Zubair were amongst them.") (4077) □

1392. Narrated Jabir bin `Abdullah: Allah's Messenger (ﷺ) used to shroud two martyrs of Uhud in one sheet and then say, "Which of them knew Qur'an more?" When one of the two was pointed out, he would put him first in the grave. Then he said, "I will be a witness for them on the Day of Resurrection." He ordered them to be buried with their blood (on their bodies). Neither was the funeral prayer offered for them, nor were they washed. Jabir added, "When my father was martyred, I started weeping and uncovering his face. The companions of the Prophet (ﷺ) stopped me from doing so but the Prophet (ﷺ) did not stop me. Then the Prophet said, '(O Jabir.) don't weep over him, for the angels kept on covering him with their wings till his body was carried away (for burial). (4079) □

1393. Narrated Al-Bara' bin `Azib: On the day of Uhud the Prophet (ﷺ) appointed `Abdullah bin Jubair as chief of the archers, and seventy among us were injured and martyred. On the day (of the battle) of Badr, the Prophet (ﷺ) and his companions had inflicted 140 casualties on the pagans, 70 were taken prisoners, and 70 were killed. Abu Sufyan said, "This is a day of (revenge) for the day of Badr and the issue of war is undecided." (3986) □

1394. Narrated Abu Musa: The Prophet (ﷺ) said, "I saw in a dream that I moved a sword and its blade got broken, and that symbolized the casualties which the believers suffered on the day of Uhud. Then I moved it again, and it became as perfect as it had been, and that symbolized the Conquest (of Mecca) which Allah helped us to achieve, and the union of all the believers. I (also) saw cows in the dream, and what Allah does is always beneficial. Those cows appeared to symbolize the faithful believers (who were martyred) on the day of Uhud." (4081) ☐

1395. Narrated Abu Huraira: The Prophet (ﷺ) sent a Sariya of spies and appointed `Asim bin Thabit, the grandfather of `Asim bin `Umar bin Al-Khattab, as their leader. So they set out, and when they reached (a place) between 'Usfan and Mecca, they were mentioned to one of the branch tribes of Bani Hudhail called Lihyan. So, about one-hundred archers followed their traces till they (i.e. the archers) came to a journey station where they (i.e. `Asim and his companions) had encamped and found stones of dates they had brought as journey food from Medina. The archers said, "These are the dates of Medina," and followed their traces till they took them over. When `Asim and his companions were not able to go ahead, they went up a high place, and their pursuers encircled them and said, "You have a covenant and a promise that if you come down to us, we will not kill anyone of you." `Asim said, "As for me, I will never come down on the security of an infidel. O Allah! Inform Your Prophet about us." So they fought with them till they killed `Asim along with seven of his companions with arrows, and there remained Khubaib, Zaid and another man to whom they gave a promise and a covenant. So when the infidels gave them the covenant and promise, they came down. When they captured them, they opened the strings of their arrow bows and tied them with it. The third man who was with them said, "This is the first breach in the covenant," and refused to accompany them. They dragged him and tried to make him accompany them, but he refused, and they killed him. Then they proceeded on taking Khubaib and Zaid till they sold them in Mecca. The sons of Al-Harith bin `Amr bin Naufal bought Khubaib. It was Khubaib who had killed Al-Harith bin `Amr on the day of Badr. Khubaib stayed with them for a while as a captive till they decided unanimously to kill him. (At that time) Khubaib borrowed a razor from one of the daughters of Al- Harith to shave his pubic hair. She gave it to him. She said later on, "I was heedless of a little baby of mine, who moved towards Khubaib, and when it reached him, he put it on his thigh. When I saw it, I got scared so much that Khubaib noticed my distress while he was carrying the razor in his hand. He said 'Are you afraid that I will kill it? Allah willing, I will never do that,' " Later on she used to say, "I have never seen a captive better than Khubaib

Once I saw him eating from a bunch of grapes although at that time no fruits were available at Mecca, and he was fettered with iron chains, and in fact, it was nothing but food bestowed upon him by Allah." So they took him out of the Sanctuary (of Mecca) to kill him. He said, "Allow me to offer a two-rak`at prayer." Then he went to them and said, "Had I not been afraid that you would think I was afraid of death, I would have prayed for a longer time." So it was Khubaib who first set the tradition of praying two rak`at before being executed. He then said, "O Allah! Count them one by one," and added, 'When I am being martyred as a Muslim, I do not care in what way I receive my death for Allah's Sake, because this death is in Allah's Cause. If He wishes, He will bless the cut limbs." Then `Uqba bin Al-Harith got up and martyred him. The narrator added: The Quraish (infidels) sent some people to `Asim in order to bring a part of his body so that his death might be known for certain, for `Asim had killed one of their chiefs on the day of Badr. But Allah sent a cloud of wasps which protected his body from their messengers who could not harm his body consequently. (4086) □

1396. Narrated Anas: Allah's Messenger (ﷺ) said Al-Qunut for one month after the posture of Bowing, invoking evil upon some 'Arab tribes. (4089) □

1397. Narrated Anas bin Malik: (The tribes of) Ril, Dhakwan, 'Usaiya and Bani Lihyan asked Allah's Messenger (ﷺ) to provide them with some men to support them against their enemy. He therefore provided them with seventy men from the Ansar whom we used to call Al-Qurra' in their lifetime. They used to collect wood by daytime and pray at night. When they were at the well of Ma'una, the infidels killed them by betraying them. When this news reached the Prophet (ﷺ), he said Al-Qunut for one month in the Morning Prayer, invoking evil upon some of the 'Arab tribes, upon Ril, Dhakwan, 'Usaiya and Bani Libyan. We used to read a verse of the Qur'an revealed in their connection, but later the verse was cancelled. It was: "convey to our people on our behalf the information that we have met our Lord, and He is pleased with us, and has made us pleased." (Anas bin Malik added :) Allah's Prophet said Qunut for one month in the Morning Prayer, invoking evil upon some of the 'Arab tribes (namely), Ril, Dhakwan, Usaiya, and Bani Libyan. Those seventy Ansari men were killed at the well of Mauna. (4090) ☐

1398. Narrated Anas: That the Prophet (ﷺ) sent his uncle, the brother of Um Sulaim at the head of seventy riders. The chief of the pagans, 'Amir bin at-Tufail proposed three suggestions (to the Prophet (ﷺ)) saying, "Choose one of three alternatives: (1) that the bedouins will be under your command and the townspeople will be under my command; (2) or that I will be your successor, (3) or otherwise I will attack you with two thousand from Bani Ghatafan." But 'Amir was infected with plague in the House of Um so-and-so. He said, "Shall I stay in the house of a lady from the family of so-and-so after having a (swelled) gland like that she-camel? Get me my horse." So he died on the back of his horse. Then Haram, the brother of Um Sulaim and a lame man along with another man from so-and-so (tribe) went towards the pagans (i.e. the tribe of 'Amir). Haram said (to his companions), "Stay near to me, for I will go to them. If they (i.e. infidels) should give me protection, you will be near to me, and if they should kill me, then you should go back to your companions. Then Haram went to them and said, "Will you give me protection so as to convey the message of Allah's Messenger (ﷺ)?" So, he started talking to them' but they signalled to a man (to kill him) and he went behind him and stabbed him (with a spear). He (i.e. Haram) said, "Allahu Akbar! I have succeeded, by the Lord of the Ka`ba!" The companion of Haram was pursued by the infidels, and then they (i.e. Haram's companions) were all killed except the lame man who was at the top of a mountain. Then Allah revealed to us a verse that was among the cancelled ones later on. It was: 'We have met our Lord and He is pleased with us and has made us pleased.' (After this event) the Prophet (ﷺ) invoked evil on the infidels every morning for 30 days. He invoked evil upon the (tribes of) Ril, Dhakwan, Bani Lihyan and Usaiya who disobeyed Allah and His Apostle. (4091) ☐

1399. Narrated `Aisha: Abu Bakr asked the Prophet (ﷺ) to allow him to go out (of Mecca) when he was greatly annoyed (by the infidels). But the Prophet (ﷺ) said to him, "Wait." Abu Bakr said, O Allah's Messenger (ﷺ)! Do you hope that you will be allowed (to migrate)?" Allah's Messenger (ﷺ) replied, "I hope so." So Abu Bakr waited for him till one day Allah's Messenger (ﷺ) came at noon time and addressed him saying "Let whoever is present with you, now leave you." Abu Bakr said, "None is present but my two daughters." The Prophet (ﷺ) said, "Have you noticed that I have been allowed to go out (to migrate)?" Abu Bakr said, "O Allah's Apostle, I would like to accompany you." The Prophet (ﷺ) said, "You will accompany me." Abu Bakr said, "O Allah's Messenger (ﷺ)! I have got two she-camels which I had prepared and kept ready for (our) going out." So he gave one of the two (she-camels) to the Prophet (ﷺ) and it was Al-Jad`a. They both rode and proceeded till they reached the Cave at the mountain of Thaur where they hid themselves. Amir bin Fuhaira was the slave of `Abdullah bin at-Tufail bin Sakhbara `Aisha's brother from her mother's side. Abu Bakr had a milch she-camel. Amir used to go with it (i.e. the milch she-camel) in the afternoon and come back to them before noon by setting out towards them in the early morning when it was still dark and then he would take it to the pasture so that none of the shepherds would be aware of his job. When the Prophet (and Abu Bakr) went away (from the Cave), he (i.e. 'Amir) too went along with them and they both used to make him ride at the back of their camels in turns till they reached Medina. 'Amir bin Fuhaira was martyred on the day of Bir Ma'una. Narrated `Urwa: When those (Muslims) at Bir Ma'una were martyred and `Amr bin Umaiya Ad- Damri was taken prisoner, 'Amir bin at-Tufail, pointing at a killed person, asked `Amr, "Who is this?" `Amr bin Umaiya said to him, "He is 'Amir bin Fuhaira." 'Amir bin at-Tufail said, "I saw him lifted to the sky after he was killed till I saw the sky between him and the earth, and then he was brought down upon the earth. Then the news of the killed Muslims reached the Prophet (ﷺ) and he announced the news of their death saying, "Your companions (of Bir Ma'una) have been killed, and they have asked their Lord saying, 'O our Lord! Inform our brothers about us as we are pleased with You and You are pleased with us." So Allah informed them (i.e. the Prophet (ﷺ) and his companions) about them (i.e. martyrs of Bir Mauna). On that day, `Urwa bin Asma bin As-Salt who was one of them, was killed, and `Urwa (bin Az- Zubair) was named after `Urwa bin Asma and Mundhir (bin AzZubair) was named after Mundhir bin

`Amr (who had also been martyred on that day). (4093) □

1400. Narrated Anas: Allah's Messenger (ﷺ) went out towards the Khandaq (i.e. Trench) and saw the Emigrants and the Ansar digging the trench in the cold morning. They had no slaves to do that (work) for them. When the Prophet saw their hardship and hunger, he said, 'O Allah! The real life is the life of the Hereafter, so please forgive Ansar and the Emigrants." They said in reply to him, "We are those who have given the Pledge of allegiances to Muhammad for to observe Jihad as long as we live." (4099) □

1401. Narrated Jabir: We were digging (the trench) on the day of (Al-Khandaq (i.e. Trench)) and we came across a big solid rock. We went to the Prophet (ﷺ) and said, "Here is a rock appearing across the trench." He said, "I am coming down." Then he got up, and a stone was tied to his belly for we had not eaten anything for three days. So the Prophet (ﷺ) took the spade and struck the big solid rock and it became like sand. I said, "O Allah's Messenger (ﷺ)! Allow me to go home." (When the Prophet (ﷺ) allowed me) I said to my wife, "I saw the Prophet (ﷺ) in a state that I cannot treat lightly. Have you got something (for him to eat?" She replied, "I have barley and a she goat." So I slaughtered the she-kid and she ground the barley; then we put the meat in the earthenware cooking pot. Then I came to the Prophet (ﷺ) when the dough had become soft and fermented and (the meat in) the pot over the stone trivet had nearly been well-cooked, and said, "I have got a little food prepared, so get up O Allah's Messenger (ﷺ), you and one or two men along with you (for the food)." The Prophet (ﷺ) asked, "How much is that food?" I told him about it. He said, "It is abundant and good. Tell your wife not to remove the earthenware pot from the fire and not to take out any bread from the oven till I reach there." Then he said (to all his companions), "Get up." So the Muhajirn (i.e. Emigrants) and the Ansar got up. When I came to my wife, I said, "Allah's Mercy be upon you! The Prophet came along with the Muhajirin and the Ansar and those who were present with them." She said, "Did the Prophet (ﷺ) ask you (how much food you had)?" I replied, "Yes." Then the Prophet (ﷺ) said, "Enter and do not throng." The Prophet (ﷺ) started cutting the bread (into pieces) and put the cooked meat over it. He covered the earthenware pot and the oven whenever he took something out of them. He would give the food to his companions and take the meat out of the pot. He went on cutting the bread and scooping the meat (for his companions) till they all ate their fill, and even then, some food remained. Then the Prophet (ﷺ) said (to my wife), "Eat and present to others as the people are struck with hunger." (4101) □

1402. Narrated `Aisha: As regards the following Qur'anic Verse:-- "When they came on you from above and from below you (from east and west of the valley) and when the eyes grew wild and the hearts reached up to the throats....." (33.10) That happened on the day of Al-Khandaq (i.e. Trench). (4103) □

1403. Narrated Al-Bara: The Prophet (ﷺ) was carrying earth on the day of Al-Khandaq till his `Abdomen was fully covered with dust, and he was saying, "By Allah, without Allah we would not have been guided, neither would we have given in charity, nor would we have prayed. So (O Allah), please send Sakina (i.e. calmness) upon us, and make our feet firm if we meet the enemy as the enemy have rebelled against us, and if they intended affliction, (i.e. want to frighten us and fight against us then we would not flee but withstand them)." The Prophet (ﷺ) used to raise his voice saying, "Abaina! Abaina! (i.e. would not, we would not). (4104) □

1404. Narrated Sulaiman bin Surd: When the clans were driven away, I heard the Prophet (ﷺ) saying, "From now onwards we will go to attack them (i.e. the infidels) and they will not come to attack us, but we will go to them." (4110) □

1405. Narrated `Ali: On the day of Al-Khandaq, the Prophet (ﷺ) said '(Let) Allah fill their (the infidels') houses and graves with fire just as they have prevented us from offering the Middle Prayer (i.e. `Asr prayer) till the sun had set." (4111) □

1406. Narrated Jabir: On the day of Al-Ahzab (clans), Allah's Messenger (ﷺ) said, 'Who will bring us the news of the people (the clans of Quraish infidels)?" Az-Zubair said, "I." The Prophet (ﷺ) again said, "Who will bring us the news of the people?" Az-Zubair said, "I." The Prophet (ﷺ) again said, "Who will bring us the news of the people?" Az-Zubair said, "I." The Prophet (ﷺ) then said, "Every prophet has his Hawari (disciplespecial helper); my disciple is Az-Zubair. (4113) □

1407. Narrated `Abdullah bin Abi `Aufa: Allah's Messenger (ﷺ) invoked evil upon the clans saying, "Allah, the Revealer of the Holy Book (i.e. the Qur'an), the Quick Taker of the accounts! Please defeat the clans. O Allah! Defeat them and shake them." (4115) □

1408. Narrated `Aisha: When the Prophet (ﷺ) returned from Al-Khandaq (i.e. Trench) and laid down his arms and took a bath, Gabriel came and said (to the Prophet (ﷺ)), You have laid down your arms? By Allah, we angels have not laid them down yet. So set out for them." The Prophet (ﷺ) said, "Where to go?" Gabriel said, "Towards this side," pointing towards Banu Quraiza. So the Prophet (ﷺ) went out towards them. (4117) □

1409. Narrated Ibn `Umar: On the day of Al-Ahzab (i.e. Clans) the Prophet (ﷺ) said, "None of you Muslims) should offer the `Asr prayer but at Banu Quraiza's place." The `Asr prayer became due for some of them on the way. Some of those said, "We will not offer it till we reach it, the place of Banu Quraiza," while some others said, "No, we will pray at this spot, for the Prophet (ﷺ) did not mean that for us." Later on it was mentioned to the Prophet (ﷺ) and he did not berate any of the two groups. (4119) □

1410. Narrated Abu Sa`id Al-Khudri: The people of (Banu) Quraiza agreed to accept the verdict of Sa`d bin Mu`adh. So the Prophet (ﷺ) sent for Sa`d, and the latter came (riding) a donkey and when he approached the Mosque, the Prophet (ﷺ) said to the Ansar, "Get up for your chief or for the best among you." Then the Prophet (ﷺ) said (to Sa`d)." These (i.e. Banu Quraiza) have agreed to accept your verdict." Sa`d said, "Kill their (men) warriors and take their offspring as captives, "On that the Prophet (ﷺ) said, "You have judged according to Allah's Judgment," or said, "according to the King's judgment." (4121) □

1411. Narrated `Aisha: Sa`d was wounded on the day of Khandaq (i.e. Trench) when a man from Quraish, called Hibban bin Al-`Araqa hit him (with an arrow). The man was Hibban bin Qais from (the tribe of) Bani Mais bin 'Amir bin Lu'ai who shot an arrow at Sa`d's medial arm vein (or main artery of the arm). The Prophet (ﷺ) pitched a tent (for Sa`d) in the Mosque so that he might be near to the Prophet (ﷺ) to visit. When the Prophet returned from the (battle) of Al-Khandaq (i.e. Trench) and laid down his arms and took a bath Gabriel came to him while he (i.e. Gabriel) was shaking the dust off his head, and said, "You have laid down the arms?" By Allah, I have not laid them down. Go out to them (to attack them)." The Prophet (ﷺ) said, "Where?" Gabriel pointed towards Bani Quraiza. So Allah's Messenger (ﷺ) went to them (i.e. Banu Quraiza) (i.e. besieged them). They then surrendered to the Prophet's judgment but he directed them to Sa`d to give his verdict concerning them. Sa`d said, "I give my judgment that their warriors should be killed, their women and children should be taken as captives, and their properties distributed." Narrated Hisham: My father informed me that `Aisha said, "Sa`d said, "O Allah! You know that there is nothing more beloved to me than to fight in Your Cause against those who disbelieved Your Apostle and turned him out (of Mecca). O Allah! I think you have put to an end the fight between us and them (i.e. Quraish infidels). And if there still remains any fight with the Quraish (infidels), then keep me alive till I fight against them for Your Sake. But if you have brought the war to an end, then let this wound burst and cause my death thereby.' So blood gushed from the wound. There was a tent in the Mosque belonging to Banu Ghifar who were surprised by the blood flowing towards them. They said, 'O people of the tent! What is this thing which is coming to us from your side?' Behold! Blood was flowing profusely out of Sa`d's wound. Sa`d then died because of that." (4122) □

1412. Al-Bara' bin `Azib said (through another chain of sub-narrators):"On the day of Quraiza's (siege), Allah's Messenger (ﷺ) said to Hassan bin Thabit, 'Abuse them (with your poems), and Jibril is with you.'" (4124) □

1413. Jabir added:"The Prophet (ﷺ) set out for the battle of Dhat-ur-Riqa' at a place called Nakhl and he met a group of people from Ghatafan, but there was no clash (between them); the people were afraid of each other and the Prophet (ﷺ) offered the two raka'at of the Fear prayer." (4127) □

1414. Narrated Abu Burda: Abu Musa said, "We went out in the company of the Prophet (ﷺ) for a Ghazwa and we were six persons having one camel which we rode in rotation. So, (due to excessive walking) our feet became thin and my feet became thin and my nail dropped, and we used to wrap our feet with the pieces of cloth, and for this reason, the Ghazwa was named Dhat-ur-Riqa as we wrapped our feet with rags." When Abu- Musa narrated this (Hadith), he felt regretful to do so and said, as if he disliked to have disclosed a good deed of his. (4128) □

1415. Narrated Salih bin Khawwat: Concerning those who witnessed the Fear Prayer that was performed in the battle of Dhat-ur-Riqa' in the company of Allah's Messenger (ﷺ); One batch lined up behind him while another batch (lined up) facing the enemy. The Prophet (ﷺ) led the batch that was with him in one rak`a, and he stayed in the standing posture while that batch completed their (two rak`at) prayer by themselves and went away, lining in the face of the enemy, while the other batch came and he (i.e. the Prophet) offered his remaining rak`a with them, and then, kept on sitting till they completed their prayer by themselves, and he then finished his prayer with Taslim along with them. (4129) □

1416. Narrated Ibn `Umar: I took part in a Ghazwa towards Najd along with Allah's Messenger (ﷺ) and we clashed with the enemy, and we lined up for them. (4132) □

1417. Narrated Jabir bin `Abdullah: We took part in the Ghazwa of Najd along with Allah's Messenger (ﷺ) and when the time for the afternoon rest approached while he was in a valley with plenty of thorny trees, he dismounted under a tree and rested in its shade and hung his sword (on it). The people dispersed amongst the trees in order to have shade. While we were in this state, Allah's Messenger (ﷺ) called us and we came and found a bedouin sitting in front of him. The Prophet (ﷺ) said, "This (Bedouin) came to me while I was asleep, and he took my sword stealthily. I woke up while he was standing by my head, holding my sword without its sheath. He said,

'Who will save you from me?' I replied, 'Allah.' So he sheathed it (i.e. the sword) and sat down, and here he is." But Allah's Messenger (ﷺ) did not punish him. (4139) □

1418. Narrated `Aisha: Whenever Allah's Messenger (ﷺ) intended to go on a journey, he used to draw lots amongst his wives, and Allah's Messenger (ﷺ) used to take with him the one on whom lot fell. He drew lots amongst us during one of the Ghazwat which he fought. The lot fell on me and so I proceeded with Allah's Messenger (ﷺ) after Allah's order of veiling (the women) had been revealed. I was carried (on the back of a camel) in my howdah and carried down while still in it (when we came to a halt). So we went on till Allah's Messenger (ﷺ) had finished from that Ghazwa of his and returned. When we approached the city of Medina he announced at night that it was time for departure. So when they announced the news of departure, I got up and went away from the army camps, and after finishing from the call of nature, I came back to my riding animal. I touched my chest to find that my necklace which was made of Zifar beads (i.e. Yemenite beads partly black and partly white) was missing. So I returned to look for my necklace and my search for it detained me. (In the meanwhile) the people who used to carry me on my camel, came and took my howdah and put it on the back of my camel on which I used to ride, as they considered that I was in it. In those days women were light in weight for they did not get fat, and flesh did not cover their bodies in abundance as they used to eat only a little food. Those people therefore, disregarded the lightness of the howdah while lifting and carrying it; and at that time I was still a young girl. They made the camel rise and all of them left (along with it). I found my necklace after the army had gone. Then I came to their camping place to find no call maker of them, nor one who would respond to the call. So I intended to go to the place where I used to stay, thinking that they would miss me and come back to me (in my search). While I was sitting in my resting place, I was overwhelmed by sleep and slept. Safwan bin Al-Muattal As-Sulami Adh-Dhakwani was behind the army. When he reached my place in the morning, he saw the figure of a sleeping person and he recognized me on seeing me as he had seen me before the order of compulsory veiling (was prescribed). So I woke up when he recited Istirja' (i.e. "Inna li l-lahi wa inna llaihi raji'un") as soon as he recognized me. I veiled my face with my head cover at once, and by Allah, we did not speak a single word, and I did not hear him saying any word besides his Istirja'. He dismounted from his camel and made it kneel down, putting his leg on its front legs and then I got up and rode on it. Then he set out leading the camel that was carrying me till we overtook the army in the extreme heat of midday while they were at a halt (taking a rest). (Because of the event) some people brought destruction upon themselves and the one who spread the Ifk (i.e. slander) more, was `Abdullah bin Ubai Ibn Salul." (Urwa said, "The people propagated the slander and talked about it in his (i.e. `Abdullah's) presence and he confirmed it and listened to it and asked about it to let it prevail." `Urwa also added, "None was mentioned as members of the slanderous group besides (`Abdullah) except Hassan bin Thabit and Mistah bin Uthatha and Hamna bint Jahsh along with others about whom I have no knowledge, but they were a group as Allah said. It is said that the one who carried most of the slander was `Abdullah bin Ubai bin Salul." `Urwa added, "`Aisha disliked to have Hassan abused in her presence and she used to say, 'It was he who said: My father and his (i.e. my father's) father and my honor are all for the protection of Muhammad's honor from you."). `Aisha added, "After we returned to Medina, I became ill for a month. The people were propagating the forged statements of the slanderers while I was unaware of anything of all that, but I felt that in my present ailment, I was not receiving the same kindness from Allah's Messenger (ﷺ) as I used to receive when I got sick. (But now) Allah's Messenger (ﷺ) would only come, greet me and say,' How is that (lady)?' and leave. That roused my doubts, but I did not discover the evil (i.e. slander) till I went out after my convalescence, I went out with Um Mistah to Al-Manasi' where we used to answer the call of nature and we used not to go out (to answer the call of nature) except at night, and that was before we had latrines near our houses. And this habit of our concerning evacuating the bowels, was similar to the habits of the old 'Arabs living in the deserts, for it would be troublesome for us to take latrines near our houses. So I and Um Mistah who was the daughter of Abu Ruhm bin Al-Muttalib bin `Abd Manaf, whose mother was the daughter of Sakhr bin 'Amir and the aunt of Abu Bakr As-Siddiq and whose son was Mistah bin Uthatha bin `Abbas bin Al-Muttalib, went out. I and Um Mistah returned to my house after we finished answering the call of nature. Um Mistah stumbled by getting her foot entangled in her covering sheet and on that she said, 'Let Mistah be ruined!' I said, 'What a hard word you have said. Do you abuse a man who took part in the battle of Badr?' On that she said, 'O you Hantah! Didn't you hear what he (i.e. Mistah) said? 'I said, 'What did he say?' Then she told me the slander of the people of Ifk. So my ailment was aggravated, and when I reached my home, Allah's Messenger (ﷺ) came to me, and after greeting me, said, 'How is that (lady)?' I said, 'Will you allow me to go to my parents?' as I wanted to be sure about the news through them. Allah's Apostle allowed me (and I went to my parents) and asked my mother, 'O mother! What are the people talking about?' She said, 'O my daughter! Don't worry, for scarcely is there a charming woman who is loved by her husband and whose husband has other wives besides herself that they (i.e. women) would find faults with her.' I said, 'Subhan-Allah! (I testify the uniqueness of Allah). Are the people really talking in this way?' I kept on weeping that night till dawn I could neither stop weeping nor sleep then in the morning again, I kept on weeping. When the Divine Inspiration was delayed. Allah's Messenger (ﷺ) called `Ali bin Abi Talib and Usama bin Zaid to ask and consult them about divorcing me. Usama bin Zaid said what he knew of my innocence, and the respect he preserved in himself for me. Usama said, '(O Allah's Messenger (ﷺ)!) She is your wife and we do not know anything except good about her.' `Ali bin Abi Talib said, 'O Allah's Messenger (ﷺ)! Allah does not put you in difficulty and there are plenty of women other than her, yet, ask the maid-servant who will tell you the truth.' On that Allah's Messenger (ﷺ) called Barira (i.e. the maid-servant) and said, 'O Barira! Did you ever see anything which aroused your suspicion?' Barira said to him, 'By Him Who has sent you with the Truth. I have never seen anything in her (i.e. Aisha) which I would conceal, except that she is a young girl who sleeps leaving the dough of her family exposed so that the domestic goats come and eat it.' So, on that day, Allah's Messenger (ﷺ) got up on the pulpit and complained about `Abdullah bin Ubai (bin Salul) before his companions, saying, 'O you Muslims! Who will relieve me from that man who has hurt me with his evil statement about my family? By Allah, I know nothing except good about my family and they have blamed a man about whom I know nothing except good and he used never to enter my home except with me.' Sa`d bin Mu`adh the brother of Banu `Abd Al-Ashhal got up and said, 'O Allah's Messenger (ﷺ)! I will relieve you from him; if he is from the tribe of Al-Aus, then I will chop his head off, and if he is from our brothers, i.e. Al-Khazraj, then order us, and we will fulfill your order.' On that, a man from Al-Khazraj got up. Um Hassan, his cousin, was from his branch tribe, and he was Sa`d bin Ubada, chief of Al-Khazraj. Before this incident, he was a pious man, but his love for his tribe goaded him into saying to Sa`d (bin Mu`adh). 'By Allah, you have told a lie; you shall not and cannot kill him. If he belonged to your people, you would not wish him to be killed.' On that, Usaid bin Hudair who was the cousin of Sa`d (bin Mu`adh) got up and said to Sa`d bin 'Ubada, 'By Allah! You are a liar! We will surely kill him, and you are a hypocrite arguing on the behalf of hypocrites.' On this, the two tribes of Al-Aus and Al Khazraj got so much excited that they were about to fight while Allah's Messenger (ﷺ) was standing on the pulpit. Allah's Messenger (ﷺ) kept on quietening them till they became silent and so did he. All that day I kept on weeping with my tears never ceasing, and I could never sleep. In the morning my parents were with me and I wept for two nights and a day with my tears never ceasing and I could never sleep till I thought that my liver would burst from weeping. So, while my parents were sitting with me and I was weeping, an Ansari woman asked me to grant her admittance. I allowed her to come in, and when she came in, she sat down and started weeping with me. While we were in this state, Allah's Messenger (ﷺ) came, greeted us and sat down. He had never sat with me since that day of the slander. A month had elapsed and no Divine Inspiration came to him about my case. Allah's Apostle then recited Tashah-hud and then said, 'Amma Badu, O `Aisha! I have been informed so-andso about you; if you are innocent, then soon Allah will reveal your innocence, and if you have committed a sin, then repent to Allah and ask Him for forgiveness for when a slave confesses his sins and asks Allah for forgiveness, Allah accepts his repentance.' (continued...) (continuing... 1): -5.462:... ... When Allah's Messenger (ﷺ) finished his speech, my tears ceased flowing completely that I no longer felt a single drop of tear flowing. I said to my father, 'Reply to Allah's Messenger (ﷺ) on my behalf concerning what he has said.' My father said, 'By Allah, I do not know what to say to Allah's Messenger (ﷺ).' Then I said to my mother, 'Reply to Allah's Messenger (ﷺ) on my behalf concerning what he has said.' She said, 'By Allah, I do not know what to say to Allah's Messenger (ﷺ).' In spite of the fact that I was a young girl and had a little knowledge of Qur'an, I said, 'By Allah, no doubt I know that you heard this (slanderous) speech so that it has been planted in your hearts (i.e. minds) and you have taken it as a truth. Now if I tell you that I am innocent, you will not believe me, and if confess to you about it, and Allah knows that I am innocent, you will surely believe me. By Allah, I find no similitude for me and you except that of Joseph's father when he said, '(For me) patience in the most fitting against that which you assert; it is Allah (Alone) Whose Help can be sought.' Then I turned to the other side and lay on my bed; and Allah knew then that I was innocent and hoped that Allah would reveal my innocence. But, by Allah, I never thought that Allah would reveal about my case, Divine Inspiration, that would be recited (forever) as I considered myself too unworthy to be talked of by Allah with something of my concern, but I hoped that Allah's Messenger (ﷺ) might have a dream in which Allah would prove my innocence. But, by Allah, before Allah's Messenger (ﷺ) left his seat and before any of the household left, the Divine inspiration came to Allah's Messenger (ﷺ). So there overtook him the same hard condition which used to overtake him, (when he used to be inspired Divinely). The sweat was dropping from his body like pearls though it was a wintry day and that was because of the weighty statement which was being revealed to him. When that state of Allah's Messenger (ﷺ) was over, he got up smiling, and the first word he said was, 'O `Aisha! Allah has declared your innocence!' Then my Mother said to me, 'Get up and go to him (i.e. Allah's Messenger (ﷺ)). I replied, 'By Allah, I will not go to him, and I praise none but Allah. So Allah revealed the ten Verses: -- "Verily! They who spread the slander Are a gang, among you............." (24.11-20) Allah revealed those Qur'anic Verses to declare my innocence. Abu Bakr As-Siddiq who used to disburse money for Mistah bin Uthatha because of his relationship to him and his poverty, said, 'By Allah, I will never give to Mistah bin

Uthatha anything after what he has said about Aisha.' Then Allah revealed:-- "And let not those among you who are good and wealthy swear not to give (any sort of help) to their kinsmen, those in need, and those who have left their homes for Allah's cause, let them pardon and forgive. Do you not love that Allah should forgive you? And Allah is oft-Forgiving Most Merciful." (24.22) Abu Bakr As-Siddiq said, 'Yes, by Allah, I would like that Allah forgive me.' and went on giving Mistah the money he used to give him before. He also added, 'By Allah, I will never deprive him of it at all.' Aisha further said:." Allah's Messenger (ﷺ) also asked Zainab bint Jahsh (i.e. his wife) about my case. He said to Zainab, 'What do you know and what did you see?" She replied, "O Allah's Messenger (ﷺ)! I refrain from claiming falsely that I have heard or seen anything. By Allah, I know nothing except good (about `Aisha).' From amongst the wives of the Prophet (ﷺ) Zainab was my peer (in beauty and in the love she received from the Prophet) but Allah saved her from that evil because of her piety. Her sister Hamna, started struggling on her behalf and she was destroyed along with those who were destroyed. The man who was blamed said, 'Subhan-Allah! By Him in Whose Hand my soul is, I have never uncovered the cover (i.e. veil) of any female.' Later on the man was martyred in Allah's Cause." (4141) □

1419. Narrated Az-Zuhri: Al-Walid bin `Abdul Malik said to me, "Have you heard that `Ali' was one of those who slandered `Aisha?" I replied, "No, but two men from your people (named) Abu Salama bin `Abdur-Rahman and Abu Bakr bin `Abdur-Rahman bin Al-Harith have informed me that Aisha told them that `Ali remained silent about her case." (4142) □

1420. Narrated Hisham's father: I started abusing Hassan (bin Thabit) in front of `Aisha. She said, "Do not abuse him as he used to defend Allah's Apostle (against the infidels). `Aisha added, "Once Hassan took the permission from the Prophet (ﷺ) to say poetic verses against the infidels. On that the Prophet (ﷺ) said, 'How will you exclude my forefathers (from that)? Hassan replied, 'I will take you out of them as one takes a hair out of the dough." Hisham's father added, "I abused Hassan as he was one of those who spoke against `Aisha." (4145) □

1421. Narrated Masruq: We went to `Aisha while Hassan bin Thabit was with her reciting poetry to her from some of his poetic verses, saying "A chaste wise lady about whom nobody can have suspicion. She gets up with an empty stomach because she never eats the flesh of indiscreet (ladies)." `Aisha said to him, "But you are not like that." I said to her, "Why do you grant him admittance, though Allah said: -- "and as for him among them, who had the greater share therein, his will be a severe torment." (24.11) On that, `Aisha said, "And what punishment is more than blinding?" She, added, "Hassan used to defend or say poetry on behalf of Allah's Messenger (ﷺ) (against the infidels). (4146) □

1422. Narrated Qatada: I said to Sa`id bin Al-Musaiyab, "I have been informed that Jabir bin `Abdullah said that the number (of Al-Hudaibiya Muslim warriors) was 1400." Sa`id said to me, "Jabir narrated to me that they were 1500 who gave the Pledge of allegiance to the Prophet (ﷺ) on the day of Al-Hudaibiya.' (4153) □

1423. Narrated Jabir bin `Abdullah: On the day of Al-Hudaibiya, Allah's Messenger (ﷺ) said to us' "You are the best people on the earth!" We were 1400 then. If I could see now, I would have shown you the place of the Tree (beneath which we gave the Pledge of Allegiance)." Salim said, "Our number was 1400." (4154) □

1424. Narrated Yazid bin Abi Ubaid: I said to Salama bin Al-Akwa`, "For what did you give the Pledge of allegiance to Allah's Messenger (ﷺ) on the day of Al-Hudaibiya?" He replied, "For death (in the Cause of Islam.). (4169) □

1425. Narrated Habib bin Abi Thabit: I went to Abu Wail to ask him (about those who had rebelled against `Ali). On that Abu Wail said, "We were at Siffin (a city on the bank of the Euphrates, the place where me battle took place between `Ali and Muawiya) A man said, "Will you be on the side of those who are called to consult Allah's Book (to settle the dispute)?" `Ali said, 'Yes (I agree that we should settle the matter in the light of the Qur'an)." 'Some people objected to `Ali's agreement and wanted to fight. On that Sahl bin Hunaif said, 'Blame yourselves! I remember how, on the day of Al-Hudaibiya (i.e. the peace treaty between the Prophet (ﷺ) and the

Quraish pagans), if we had been allowed to choose fighting, we would have fought (the pagans). At that time `Umar came (to the Prophet) and said, "Aren't we on the right (path) and they (pagans) in the wrong? Won't our killed persons go to Paradise, and theirs in the Fire?" The Prophet replied, "Yes." `Umar further said, "Then why should we let our religion be degraded and return before Allah has settled the matter between us?" The Prophet (ﷺ) said, "O the son of Al-Khattab! No doubt, I am Allah's Messenger (ﷺ) and Allah will never neglect me." So `Umar left the place angrily and he was so impatient that he went to Abu Bakr and said, "O Abu Bakr! Aren't we on the right (path) and they (pagans) on the wrong?" Abu Bakr said, "O the son of Al-Khattab! He is Allah's Messenger (ﷺ), and Allah will never neglect him." Then Sura Al-Fath (The Victory) was revealed." (4844) □

1426. Narrated Al-Miswar bin Makhrama and Marwan bin Al-Hakam: (one of them said more than his friend): The Prophet (ﷺ) set out in the company of more than one thousand of his companions in the year of Al-Hudaibiya, and when he reached Dhul-Hulaifa, he garlanded his Hadi (i.e. sacrificing animal), assumed the state of Ihram for `Umra from that place and sent a spy of his from Khuzi'a (tribe). The Prophet (ﷺ) proceeded on till he reached (a village called) Ghadir-al-Ashtat. There his spy came and said, "The Quraish (infidels) have collected a great number of people against you, and they have collected against you the Ethiopians, and they will fight with you, and will stop you from entering the Ka`ba and prevent you." The Prophet (ﷺ) said, "O people! Give me your opinion. Do you recommend that I should destroy the families and offspring of those who want to stop us from the Ka`ba? If they should come to us (for peace) then Allah will destroy a spy from the pagans, or otherwise we will leave them in a miserable state." On that Abu Bakr said, "O Allah Apostle! You have come with the intention of visiting this House (i.e. Ka`ba) and you do not want to kill or fight anybody. So proceed to it, and whoever should stop us from it, we will fight him." On that the Prophet (ﷺ) said, "Proceed on, in the Name of Allah!" (4178) □

1427. Narrated Al-Miswar bin Makhrama and Marwan: (whose narrations attest each other) Allah's Messenger (ﷺ) set out at the time of Al-Hudaibiya (treaty), and when they proceeded for a distance, he said, "Khalid bin Al-Walid leading the cavalry of Quraish constituting the front of the army, is at a place called Al-Ghamim, so take the way on the right." By Allah, Khalid did not perceive the arrival of the Muslims till the dust arising from the march of the Muslim army reached him, and then he turned back hurriedly to inform Quraish. The Prophet (ﷺ) went on advancing till he reached the Thaniya (i.e. a mountainous way) through which one would go to them (i.e. people of Quraish). The she-camel of the Prophet (ﷺ) sat down. The people tried their best to cause the she-camel to get up but in vain, so they said, "Al-Qaswa' (i.e. the she-camel's name) has become stubborn! Al-Qaswa' has become stubborn!" The Prophet (ﷺ) said, "Al-Qaswa' has not become stubborn, for stubbornness is not her habit, but she was stopped by Him Who stopped the elephant." Then he said, "By the Name of Him in Whose Hands my soul is, if they (i.e. the Quraish infidels) ask me anything which will respect the ordinances of Allah, I will grant it to them." The Prophet (ﷺ) then rebuked the she-camel and she got up. The Prophet (ﷺ) changed his way till he dismounted at the farthest end of Al-Hudaibiya at a pit (i.e. well) containing a little water which the people used in small amounts, and in a short while the people used up all its water and complained to Allah's Messenger (ﷺ); of thirst. The Prophet (ﷺ) took an arrow out of his arrow-case and ordered them to put the arrow in that pit. By Allah, the water started and continued sprouting out till all the people quenched their thirst and returned with satisfaction. While they were still in that state, Budail bin Warqa-al- Khuza`i came with some persons from his tribe Khuza`a and they were the advisers of Allah's Messenger (ﷺ) who would keep no secret from him and were from the people of Tihama. Budail said, "I left Ka`b bin Luai and 'Amir bin Luai residing at the profuse water of Al-Hudaibiya and they had milch camels (or their women and children) with them, and will wage war against you, and will prevent you from visiting the Ka`ba." Allah's Messenger (ﷺ) said, "We have not come to fight anyone, but to perform the `Umra. No doubt, the war has weakened Quraish and they have suffered great losses, so if they wish, I will conclude a truce with them, during which they should refrain from interfering between me and the people (i.e. the 'Arab infidels other than Quraish), and if I have victory over those infidels, Quraish will have the option to embrace Islam as the other people do, if they wish; they will at least get strong enough to fight. But if they do not accept the truce, by Allah in Whose Hands my life is, I will fight with them defending my Cause till I get killed, but (I am sure) Allah will definitely make His Cause victorious." Budail said, "I will inform them of what you have said." So, he set off till he reached Quraish and said, "We have come from that man (i.e. Muhammad) whom we heard saying something which we will disclose to you if you should like." Some of the fools among Quraish shouted that they were not in need of this information, but the wiser among them said, "Relate what you heard him saying." Budail said, "I heard him saying so-and-so," relating what the Prophet (ﷺ) had told him. `Urwa bin Mas`ud got up and said, "O people! Aren't you the sons? They said, "Yes." He added, "Am I not the father?" They said, "Yes." He said, "Do you mistrust me?" They said, "No." He said, "Don't you know that I invited the people of `Ukaz for your help, and when they refused I brought my relatives and children and those who obeyed me (to help you)?" They said, "Yes." He said, "Well, this man (i.e. the Prophet) has offered you a reasonable proposal, you'd better accept it and allow me to meet him." They said, "You may meet him." So, he went to the Prophet (ﷺ) and started talking to him. The Prophet (ﷺ) told him almost the same as he had told Budail. Then `Urwa said, "O Muhammad! Won't you feel any scruple in extirpating your relations? Have you ever heard of anyone amongst the Arabs extirpating his relatives before you? On the other hand, if the reverse should happen, (nobody will aid you, for) by Allah, I do not see (with you) dignified people, but people from various tribes who would run away leaving you alone." Hearing that, Abu Bakr abused him and said, "Do you say we would run and leave the Prophet (ﷺ) alone?" `Urwa said, "Who is that man?" They said, "He is Abu Bakr." `Urwa said to Abu Bakr, "By Him in Whose Hands my life is, were it not for the favor which you did to me and which I did not compensate, I would retort on you." `Urwa kept on talking to the Prophet (ﷺ) and seizing the Prophet's beard as he was talking while Al-Mughira bin Shu`ba was standing near the head of the Prophet, holding a sword and wearing a helmet. Whenever `Urwa stretched his hand towards the beard of the Prophet, Al-Mughira would hit his hand with the handle of the sword and say (to `Urwa), "Remove your hand from the beard of Allah's Messenger (ﷺ)." `Urwa raised his head and asked, "Who is that?" The people said, "He is Al-Mughira bin Shu`ba." `Urwa said, "O treacherous! Am I not doing my best to prevent evil consequences of your treachery?" Before embracing Islam Al-Mughira was in the company of some people. He killed them and took their property and came (to Medina) to embrace Islam. The Prophet (ﷺ) said (to him, "As regards your Islam, I accept it, but as for the property I do not take anything of it. (As it was taken through treason). `Urwa then started looking at the Companions of the Prophet. By Allah, whenever Allah's Messenger (ﷺ) spat, the spittle would fall in the hand of one of them (i.e. the Prophet's companions) who would rub it on his face and skin; if he ordered them they would carry his orders immediately; if he performed ablution, they would struggle to take the remaining water; and when they spoke to him, they would lower their voices and would not look at his face constantly out of respect. `Urwa returned to his people and said, "O people! By Allah, I have been to the kings and to Caesar, Khosrau and An- Najashi, yet I have never seen any of them respected by his courtiers as much as Muhammad is respected by his companions. By Allah, if he spat, the spittle would fall in the hand of one of them (i.e. the Prophet's companions) who would rub it on his face and skin; if he ordered them, they would carry out his order immediately; if he performed ablution, they would struggle to take the remaining water; and when they spoke, they would lower their voices and would not look at his face constantly out of respect." `Urwa added, "No doubt, he has presented to you a good reasonable offer, so please accept it." A man from the tribe of Bani Kinana said, "Allow me to go to him," and they allowed him, and when he approached the Prophet and his companions, Allah's Messenger (ﷺ) said, "He is so-and-so who belongs to the tribe that respects the Budn (i.e. camels of the sacrifice). So, bring the Budn in front of him." So, the Budn were brought before him and the people received him while they were reciting Talbiya. When he saw that scene, he said, "Glorified be Allah! It is not fair to prevent these people from visiting the Ka`ba." When he returned to his people, he said, 'I saw the Budn garlanded (with colored knotted ropes) and marked (with stabs on their backs). I do not think it is advisable to prevent them from visiting the Ka`ba." Another person called Mikraz bin Hafs got up and sought their permission to go to Muhammad, and they allowed him, too. When he approached the Muslims, the Prophet (ﷺ) said, "Here is Mikraz and he is a vicious man." Mikraz started talking to the Prophet and as he was talking, Suhail bin `Amr came. When Suhail bin `Amr came, the Prophet (ﷺ) said, "Now the matter has become easy." Suhail said to the Prophet "Please conclude a peace treaty with us." So, the Prophet (ﷺ) called the clerk and said to him, "Write: By the Name of Allah, the most Beneficent, the most Merciful." Suhail said, "As for 'Beneficent,' by Allah, I do not know what it means. So write: By Your Name O Allah, as you used to write previously." The Muslims said, "By Allah, we will not write except: By the Name of Allah, the most Beneficent, the most Merciful." The Prophet (ﷺ) said, "Write: By Your Name O Allah." Then he dictated, "This is the peace treaty which Muhammad, Allah's Messenger (ﷺ) has concluded." Suhail said, "By Allah, if we knew that you are Allah's Messenger (ﷺ) we would not prevent you from visiting the Ka`ba, and would not fight with you. So, write: "Muhammad bin `Abdullah." The Prophet (ﷺ) said, "By Allah! I am Apostle of Allah even if you people do not believe me. Write: Muhammad bin `Abdullah." (Az-Zuhri said, "The Prophet (ﷺ) accepted all those things, as he had already said that he would accept everything they would demand if it respects the ordinance of Allah, (i.e. by letting him and his companions perform `Umra.)" The Prophet (ﷺ) said to Suhail, "On the condition that you allow us to visit the House (i.e. Ka`ba) so that we may perform Tawaf around it." Suhail said, "By Allah, we will not (allow you this year) so as not to give chance to the 'Arabs to say that we have yielded to you, but we will allow you next year." So, the Prophet (ﷺ) got that written. Then Suhail said, "We also stipulate that you should return to us whoever comes to you from us, even if he embraced your religion." The Muslims said, "Glorified be Allah! How will such a person be returned to the pagans after he has become a Muslim? While they were in this state Abu- Jandal bin Suhail bin `Amr came from the valley of Mecca staggering with his fetters and fell down amongst the Muslims. Suhail said, "O Muhammad! This is the very first term with which we make peace with you, i.e. you shall return Abu Jandal to me." The Prophet (ﷺ) said, "The peace treaty has not been written yet." Suhail said, "I will never allow you to keep him." The Prophet (ﷺ) said, "Yes, do." He said, "I won't do.: Mikraz said, "We allow you (to keep him)." Abu Jandal said, "O Muslims! Will I be returned to the pagans though I have come as a Muslim? Don't you see how much I have suffered?" (continued...) (continuing... 1): -3.891:... ... Abu Jandal had been tortured severely for the Cause of Allah. `Umar bin Al-Khattab said, "I went to the Prophet (ﷺ) and said, 'Aren't you truly the Messenger of Allah?' The Prophet (ﷺ) said, 'Yes, indeed.' I said, 'isn't our Cause just and the cause of the enemy unjust?' He said, 'Yes.' I said, 'Then why should we be humble in our religion?' He said, 'I am Allah's Messenger (ﷺ) and I do not disobey Him, and He will make me victorious.' I said, 'Didn't you tell us that we would go to the Ka`ba and perform Tawaf around it?' He said, 'Yes, but did I tell you that we would visit the Ka`ba this year?' I said, 'No.' He said, 'So you will visit it and perform Tawaf around it?' "`Umar further said, "I went to Abu Bakr and said, 'O Abu Bakr! Isn't he truly Allah's Prophet?' He replied, 'Yes.' I said, 'Then why should we be humble in our religion?' He said, 'Indeed, he is Allah's Messenger (ﷺ) and he does not disobey his Lord, and He will make him victorious. Adhere to him as, by Allah, he is on the right.' I said, 'Was he not telling us that we would go to the Ka`ba and perform Tawaf around it?' He said, 'Yes, but did he tell you that you would go to the Ka`ba this year?' I said, 'No.' He said, "You will go to Ka`ba and perform Tawaf around it." (Az-Zuhri said, "`Umar said, 'I performed many good deeds as expiation for the improper questions I asked them.' ") When the writing of the peace treaty was concluded, Allah's Messenger (ﷺ) said to his companions, "Get up and' slaughter your sacrifices and get your head shaved." By Allah none of them got up, and the Prophet repeated his order thrice. When none of them got up, he left them and went to Um Salama and told her of the people's attitudes towards him. Um Salama said, "O the Prophet (ﷺ) of Allah! Do you want your order to be carried out? Go out and don't say a word to anybody till you have slaughtered your sacrifice and call your barber to shave your head." So, the Prophet (ﷺ) went out and did not talk to anyone of them till he did that, i.e. slaughtered the sacrifice and called his barber who shaved his head. Seeing that, the companions of the Prophet (ﷺ) got up, slaughtered their sacrifices, and started shaving the heads of one another, and there was so much rush that there was a danger of killing each other. Then some believing women came (to the Prophet (ﷺ)); and Allah revealed the following Divine Verses:-- "O you who believe, when the believing women come to you as emigrants examine them . . ." (60.10) `Umar then divorced two wives of his who were infidels. Later on Muawiya bin Abu Sufyan married one of them, and Safwan bin Umaiya married the other. When the Prophet (ﷺ) returned to Medina, Abu Basir, a new Muslim convert from Quraish came to him. The Infidels sent in his pursuit two men who said (to the Prophet (ﷺ)), "Abide by the promise you gave us." So, the Prophet (ﷺ) handed him over to them. They took him out (of the City) till they reached Dhul-Hulaifa where they dismounted to eat some dates they had with them. Abu Basir said to one of them, "By Allah, O so-and-so, I see you have a fine sword." The other drew it out (of the scabbard) and said, "By Allah, it is very fine and I have tried it many times." Abu Basir said, "Let me have a look at it." When the other gave it to him, he hit him with it till he died, and his companion ran away till he came to Medina and entered the Mosque running. When Allah's Messenger (ﷺ) saw him he said, "This man appears to have been frightened." When he reached the Prophet (ﷺ) he said, "My companion has been murdered and I would have been murdered too." Abu Basir came and said, "O Allah's Messenger (ﷺ), by Allah, Allah has made you fulfill your obligations by your returning me to them (i.e. the Infidels), but Allah has saved me from them." The Prophet (ﷺ) said, "Woe to his mother! What excellent war kindler he would be, should he only have supporters." When Abu Basir heard that he understood that the Prophet (ﷺ) would return him to them again, so he set off till he reached the seashore. Abu Jandal bin Suhail got himself released from them (i.e. infidels) and joined Abu Basir. So, whenever a man from Quraish embraced Islam he would follow Abu Basir till they formed a strong group. By Allah, whenever they heard about a caravan of Quraish heading towards Sham, they stopped it and attacked and killed them (i.e. infidels) and took their properties. The people of Quraish sent a message to the Prophet (ﷺ) requesting him for the Sake of Allah and Kith and kin to send for (i.e. Abu Basir and his companions) promising that whoever (amongst them) came to the Prophet (ﷺ)

would be secure. So the Prophet (ﷺ) sent for them (i.e. Abu Basir's companions) and Allah I revealed the following Divine Verses: "And it is He Who Has withheld their hands from you and your hands from them in the midst of Mecca, After He made you the victorious over them. ... the unbelievers had pride and haughtiness, in their hearts ... the pride and haughtiness of the time of ignorance." (48.24-26) And their pride and haughtiness was that they did not confess (write in the treaty) that he (i.e. Muhammad) was the Prophet of Allah and refused to write: "In the Name of Allah, the most Beneficent, the Most Merciful," and they (the mushriks) prevented them (the Muslims) from visiting the House (the Ka`bah). (2731) □

1428. Narrated `Urwa bin Az-Zubair: That he heard Marwan bin Al-Hakam and Al-Miswar bin Makhrama relating one of the events that happened to Allah's Messenger (ﷺ) in the `Umra of Al-Hudaibiya. They said, "When Allah's Messenger (ﷺ) concluded the truce with Suhail bin `Amr on the day of Al-Hudaibiya, one of the conditions which Suhail bin `Amr stipulated, was his saying (to the Prophet), "If anyone from us (i.e. infidels) ever comes to you, though he has embraced your religion, you should return him to us, and should not interfere between us and him." Suhail refused to conclude the truce with Allah's Messenger (ﷺ) except on this condition. The believers disliked this condition and got disgusted with it and argued about it. But when Suhail refused to conclude the truce with Allah's Messenger (ﷺ) except on that condition, Allah's Apostle concluded it. Accordingly, Allah's Messenger (ﷺ) then returned Abu Jandal bin Suhail to his father, Suhail bin `Amr, and returned every man coming to him from them during that period even if he was a Muslim. The believing women Emigrants came and Um Kulthum, the daughter of `Uqba bin Abi Mu'ait was one of those who came to Allah's Messenger (ﷺ) and she was an adult at that time. Her relatives came, asking Allah's Messenger (ﷺ) to return her to them, and in this connection, Allah revealed the Verses dealing with the believing (women). (4180) □

1429. Aisha said, "Allah's Messenger (ﷺ) used to test all the believing women who migrated to him, with the following Verse: -- "O Prophet! When the believing

Women come to you, to give the pledge of allegiance to you." (60.12) `Urwa's uncle said, "We were informed when Allah ordered His Apostle to return to the pagans what they had given to their wives who lately migrated (to Medina) and we were informed that Abu Basir..." relating the whole narration. (4182) □

1430. Narrated Nafi`: The people used to say that Ibn `Umar had embraced Islam before `Umar. This is not true. What happened is that `Umar sent `Abdullah to bring his horse from an Ansari man so as to fight on it. At that time the people were giving the Pledge of allegiance to Allah's Messenger (ﷺ) near the Tree, and `Umar was not aware of that. So `Abdullah gave the Pledge of Allegiance (to the Prophet) and went to take the horse and brought it to `Umar. While `Umar was putting on the armor to get ready for fighting, `Abdullah informed him that the people were giving the Pledge of allegiance to Allah's Apostle beneath the Tree. So `Umar set out and `Abdullah accompanied him till he gave the Pledge of allegiance to Allah's Messenger (ﷺ), and it was this event that made people say that Ibn `Umar had embraced Islam before `Umar. (4186) □

1431. Narrated Abu Wail: When Sahl bin Hunaif returned from (the battle of) Siffin, we went to ask him (as to why he had come back). He replied, "(You should not consider me a coward) but blame your opinions. I saw myself on the day of Abu Jandal (inclined to fight), and if I had the power of refusing the order of Allah's Apostle then, I would have refused it (and fought the infidels bravely). Allah and His Apostle know (what is convenient) better. Whenever we put our swords on our shoulders for any matter that terrified us, our swords led us to an easy agreeable solution before the present situation (of disagreement and dispute between the Muslims). When we mend the breach in one side, it opened in another, and we do not know what to do about it." (4189) □

1432. Narrated Salama bin Al-Akwa`: Once I went (from Medina) towards (Al-Ghaba) before the first Adhan of the Fajr Prayer. The she-camels of Allah's Messenger (ﷺ) used to graze at a place called Dhi-Qarad. A slave of `Abdur-Rahman bin `Auf met me (on the way) and said, "The she-camels of Allah's Messenger (ﷺ)

had been taken away by force." I asked, "Who had taken them?" He replied "(The people of) Ghatafan." I made three loud cries (to the people of Medina) saying, "O Sabahah!" I made the people between the two mountains of Medina hear me. Then I rushed onward and caught up with the robbers while they were watering the camels. I started throwing arrows at them as I was a good archer and I was saying, "I am the son of Al-Akwa`, and today will perish the wicked people." I kept on saying like that till I restored the she-camels (of the Prophet), I also snatched thirty Burda (i.e. garments) from them. Then the Prophet (ﷺ) and the other people came there, and I said, "O Allah's Prophet! I have stopped the people (of Ghatafan) from taking water and they are thirsty now. So send (some people) after them now." On that the Prophet said, "O the son of Al-Akwa`! You have over-powered them, so forgive them." Then we all came back and Allah's Messenger (ﷺ) seated me behind him on his she-camel till we entered Medina. (4194) □

1433. Narrated Salama bin Al-Akwa`: We went out to Khaibar in the company of the Prophet. While we were proceeding at night, a man from the group said to 'Amir, "O 'Amir! Won't you let us hear your poetry?" 'Amir was a poet, so he got down and started reciting for the people poetry that kept pace with the camels' footsteps, saying:-- "O Allah! Without You we Would not have been guided On the right path Neither would be have given In charity, nor would We have prayed. So please forgive us, what we have committed (i.e. our defects); let all of us Be sacrificed for Your Cause And send Sakina (i.e. calmness) Upon us to make our feet firm When we meet our enemy, and If they will call us towards An unjust thing, We will refuse. The infidels have made a hue and Cry to ask others' help against us." The Prophet (ﷺ) on that, asked, "Who is that (camel) driver (reciting poetry)?" The people said, "He is 'Amir bin Al-Akwa`." Then the Prophet (ﷺ) said, "May Allah bestow His Mercy on him." A man amongst the people said, "O Allah's Prophet! Has (martyrdom) been granted to him? Would that you let us enjoy his company longer." Then we reached and besieged Khaibar till we were afflicted with severe hunger. Then Allah helped the Muslims conquer it (i.e. Khaibar). In the evening of the day of the conquest of the city, the Muslims made huge fires. The Prophet (ﷺ) said, "What are these fires? For cooking what, are you making the fire?" The people replied, "(For cooking) meat." He asked, "What kind of meat?" They (i.e. people) said, "The meat of donkeys." The Prophet (ﷺ) said, "Throw away the meat and break the pots!" Some man said, "O Allah's Messenger (ﷺ)! Shall we throw away the meat and wash the pots instead?" He said, "(Yes, you can do) that too." So when the army files were arranged in rows (for the clash), 'Amir's sword was short and he aimed at the leg of a Jew to strike it, but the sharp blade of the sword returned to him and injured his own knee, and that caused him to die. When they returned from the battle, Allah's Messenger (ﷺ) saw me (in a sad mood). He took my hand and said, "What is bothering you?" I replied, "Let my father and mother be sacrificed for you! The people say that the deeds of 'Amir are lost." The Prophet (ﷺ) said, "Whoever says so, is mistaken, for 'Amir has got a double reward." The Prophet raised two fingers and added, "He (i.e. Amir) was a persevering struggler in the Cause of Allah and there are few 'Arabs who achieved the like of (good deeds) 'Amir had done." (4196) ☐

1434. Narrated Anas: Allah's Messenger (ﷺ) reached Khaibar at night and it was his habit that, whenever he reached the enemy at night, he will not attack them till it was morning. When it was morning, the Jews came out with their spades and baskets, and when they saw him (i.e. the Prophet (ﷺ)), they said, "Muhammad! By Allah! Muhammad and his army!" The Prophet (ﷺ) said, "Khaibar is destroyed, for whenever we approach a (hostile) nation (to fight), then evil will be the morning for those who have been warned." (4197) ☐

1435. Narrated Anas bin Malik: Someone came to Allah's Messenger (ﷺ) and said, "The donkeys have been eaten (by the Muslims)." The Prophet kept quiet. Then the man came again and said, "The donkeys have been eaten." The Prophet (ﷺ) kept quiet. The man came to him the third time and said, "The donkeys have been consumed." On that the Prophet (ﷺ) ordered an announcer to announce to the people, "Allah and His Apostle forbid you to eat the meat of donkeys." Then the cooking pots were upset while the meat was still boiling in them. (4199) ☐

1436. Narrated Sahl bin Sa`d As Saidi: Allah's Messenger (ﷺ) (and his army) encountered the pagans and the two armies fought and then Allah's Apostle returned to his army camps and the others (i.e. the enemy) returned to their army camps. Amongst the companions of the Prophet (ﷺ) there was a man who could not help pursuing any single isolated pagan to strike him with his sword. Somebody said, "None has benefited the Muslims today more than so-and-so." On that Allah's Messenger (ﷺ) said, "He is from the people of the Hell-Fire certainly." A man amongst the people (i.e. Muslims) said, "I will accompany him (to know the fact)." So he went along with him, and whenever he stopped he stopped with him, and whenever he hastened, he hastened with him. The (brave) man then got wounded severely, and seeking to die at once, he planted his sword into the ground and put its point against his chest in between his breasts, and then threw himself on it and committed suicide. On that the person (who was accompanying the deceased all the time) came to Allah's Messenger (ﷺ) and said, "I testify that you are the Messenger of Allah." The Prophet (ﷺ) said, "Why is that (what makes you say so)?" He said "It is concerning the man whom you have already mentioned as one of the dwellers of the Hell-Fire. The people were surprised by your statement, and I said to them, "I will try to find out the truth about him for you." So I went out after him and he was then inflicted with a severe wound and because of that, he hurried to bring death upon himself by planting the handle of his sword into the ground and directing its tip towards his chest between his breasts, and then he threw himself over it and committed suicide." Allah's Messenger (ﷺ) then said, "A man may do what seem to the people as the deeds of the dwellers of Paradise but he is from the dwellers of the Hell-Fire and another may do what seem to the people as the deeds of the dwellers of the Hell- Fire, but he is from the dwellers of Paradise." (4202) □

1437. Narrated Sahl bin Sa`d: On the day of Khaibar, Allah's Messenger (ﷺ) said, "Tomorrow I will give this flag to a man through whose hands Allah will give us victory. He loves Allah and His Apostle, and he is loved by Allah and His Apostle." The people remained that night, wondering as to who would be given it. In the morning the people went to Allah's Messenger (ﷺ) and every one of them was hopeful to receive it (i.e. the flag). The Prophet said, "Where is `Ali bin Abi Talib?" It was

said, "He is suffering from eye trouble O Allah's Apostle." He said, "Send for him."
`Ali was brought and Allah's Messenger (ﷺ) spat in his eye and invoked good upon
him. So `Ali was cured as if he never had any trouble. Then the Prophet (ﷺ) gave him
the flag. `Ali said "O Allah's Messenger (ﷺ)! I will fight with them till they become
like us." Allah's Messenger (ﷺ) said, "Proceed and do not hurry. When you enter their
territory, call them to embrace Islam and inform them of Allah's Rights which they
should observe, for by Allah, even if a single man is led on the right path (of Islam)
by Allah through you, then that will be better for you than the nice red camels. (4210)
□

1438. Narrated Ibn Abi `Aufa: We where afflicted with severe hunger on the day of
Khaibar. While the cooking pots were boiling and some of the food was well-cooked,
the announcer of the Prophet (ﷺ) came to say, "Do not eat anything the donkey-meat
and upset the cooking pots." We then thought that the Prophet (ﷺ) had prohibited
such food because the Khumus had not been taken out of it. Some others said, "He
prohibited the meat of donkeys from the point of view of principle, because donkeys
used to eat dirty things." (4220) □

1439. Narrated Al-Bara Bin Azib: During the Ghazwa of Khaibar, the Prophet (ﷺ)
ordered us to throw away the meat of the donkeys whether it was still raw or cooked.
He did not allow us to eat it later on. (4226) □

1440. Narrated Ibn `Umar: We did not eat our fill except after we had conquered
Khaibar. (4243) □

1441. Narrated Al-Bara: When the Prophet (ﷺ) went out for the `Umra in the month
of Dhal-Qa'da, the people of Mecca did not allow him to enter Mecca till he agreed
to conclude a peace treaty with them by virtue of which he would stay in Mecca for
three days only (in the following year). When the agreement was being written, the
Muslims wrote: "This is the peace treaty, which Muhammad, Apostle of Allah has
concluded." The infidels said (to the Prophet), "We do not agree with you on this,
for if we knew that you are Apostle of Allah we would not have prevented you for

anything (i.e. entering Mecca, etc.), but you are Muhammad, the son of `Abdullah." Then he said to `Ali, "Erase (the name of) 'Apostle of Allah'." `Ali said, "No, by Allah, I will never erase you (i.e. your name)." Then Allah's Messenger (ﷺ) took the writing sheet...and he did not know a better writing...and he wrote or got it the following written! "This is the peace treaty which Muhammad, the son of `Abdullah, has concluded: "Muhammad should not bring arms into Mecca except sheathed swords, and should not take with him any person of the people of Mecca even if such a person wanted to follow him, and if any of his companions wants to stay in Mecca, he should not forbid him." (In the next year) when the Prophet (ﷺ) entered Mecca and the allowed period of stay elapsed, the infidels came to `Ali and said "Tell your companion (Muhammad) to go out, as the allowed period of his stay has finished." So the Prophet (ﷺ) departed (from Mecca) and the daughter of Hamza followed him shouting "O Uncle, O Uncle!" `Ali took her by the hand and said to Fatima, "Take the daughter of your uncle." So she made her ride (on her horse). (When they reached Medina) `Ali, Zaid and Ja`far quarreled about her. `Ali said, "I took her for she is the daughter of my uncle." Ja`far said, "She is the daughter of my uncle and her aunt is my wife." Zaid said, "She is the daughter of my brother." On that, the Prophet (ﷺ) gave her to her aunt and said, "The aunt is of the same status as the mother." He then said to `Ali, "You are from me, and I am from you," and said to Ja`far, "You resemble me in appearance and character," and said to Zaid, "You are our brother and our freed slave." `Ali said to the Prophet 'Won't you marry the daughter of Hamza?" The Prophet (ﷺ) said, "She is the daughter of my foster brother." (4251) □

1442. Narrated Ibn `Umar: Allah's Messenger (ﷺ) set out with the intention of performing `Umra, but the infidels of Quraish intervened between him and the Ka`ba, so the Prophet (ﷺ) slaughtered his Hadi (i.e. sacrificing animals and shaved his head at Al-Hudaibiya and concluded a peace treaty with them (the infidels) on condition that he would perform the `Umra the next year and that he would not carry arms against them except swords, and would not stay (in Mecca) more than what they would allow. So the Prophet (ﷺ) performed the `Umra in the following year and according to the peace treaty, he entered Mecca, and when he had stayed there for three days, the infidels ordered him to leave, and he left. (4252) □

1443. Narrated Ibn `Umar: When we reached (Hudaibiya) in the next year (of the treaty of Hudaibiya), not even two men amongst us agreed unanimously as to which was the tree under which we had given the pledge of allegiance, and that was out of Allah's Mercy. (The sub narrator asked Naf'i, "For what did the Prophet (ﷺ) take their pledge of allegiance, was it for death?" Naf'i replied "No, but he took their pledge of allegiance for patience.") (2958) □

1444. Narrated Nafi`: Ibn `Umar informed me that on the day (of Mu'tah) he stood beside Ja`far who was dead (i.e. killed in the battle), and he counted fifty wounds in his body, caused by stabs or strokes, and none of those wounds was in his back. (4260) □

1445.`Abdullah bin `Umar said:"Allah's Messenger (ﷺ) appointed Zaid bin Haritha as the commander of the army during the Ghazwa of Mu'tah and said, "If Zaid is martyred, Ja`far should take over his position, and if Ja`far is martyred, `Abdullah bin Rawaha should take over his position." Abdulla-h bin `Umar further said, "I was present amongst them in that battle and we searched for Ja`far bin Abi Talib and found his body amongst the bodies of the martyred ones, and found over ninety wounds over his body, caused by stabs or shots (of arrows). (4261) □

1446. Narrated Anas: The Prophet (ﷺ) had informed the people of the martyrdom of Zaid, Ja`far and Ibn Rawaha before the news of their death reached. The Prophet (ﷺ) said, "Zaid took the flag (as the commander of the army) and was martyred, then Ja`far took it and was martyred, and then Ibn Rawaha took it and was martyred." At that time the Prophet's eyes were shedding tears. He added, "Then the flag was taken by a Sword amongst the Swords of Allah (i.e. Khalid) and Allah made them (i.e. the Muslims) victorious." (4262) □

1447. Narrated `Amra: I heard `Aisha saying, "When the news of the martyrdom of Ibn Haritha, Ja`far bin Abi Talib and `Abdullah bin Rawaka reached, Allah's Messenger (ﷺ) sat with sorrow explicit on his face." `Aisha added, "I was then peeping through a chink in the door. A man came to him and said, "O Allah's Messenger (ﷺ)! The women of Ja`far are crying.' Thereupon the Prophet (ﷺ) told him to forbid them to do so. So the man went away and returned saying, "I forbade them but they did not listen to me." The Prophet (ﷺ) ordered him again to go (and forbid them). He went again and came saying, 'By Allah, they overpowered me (i.e. did not listen to me)." `Aisha said that Allah's Messenger (ﷺ) said (to him), "Go and throw dust into their mouths." Aisha added, "I said, May Allah put your nose in the dust! By Allah, neither have you done what you have been ordered, nor have you relieved Allah's Messenger (ﷺ) from trouble." (4263) ☐

1448. Narrated 'Amir: Whenever Ibn `Umar greeted the son of Ja`far, he used to say (to him), "Assalam 'Alaika (i.e. peace be on you) O the son of two-winged person." (4264) ☐

1449. Narrated Khalid bin Al-Walid: On the day of Mu'tah, nine swords were broken in my hand and only a Yemenite sword of mine remained in my hand. (4266) ☐

1450. Narrated An-Nu`man bin Bashir: `Abdullah bin Rawaha fell down unconscious and his sister `Amra started crying and was saying loudly, "O Jabala! Oh so-and-so! Oh so-and-so! and went on calling him by his (good) qualities one by one). When he came to his senses, he said (to his sister), "When-ever you said something, I was asked, 'Are you really so (i.e. as she says)?" (4267) ☐

1451. Narrated Ash Shabi: An Nu`man bin Bashir said, "Abdullah bin Rawaha fell down unconscious…"(And mentioned the above Hadith adding, "Thereupon, when he died she (i.e. his sister) did not weep over him." (4268) ☐

1452. Narrated Ibn `Abbas: The Prophet (ﷺ) left Medina (for Mecca) in the company of ten-thousand (Muslim warriors) in (the month of) Ramadan, and that was eight and a half years after his migration to Medina. He and the Muslims who were with him, proceeded on their way to Mecca. He was fasting and they were fasting, but when they reached a place called Al-Kadid which was a place of water between 'Usfan and Kudaid, he broke his fast and so did they. (Az-Zuhri said, "One should take the last action of Allah's Messenger (ﷺ) and leave his early action (while taking a verdict.") (4276) □

1453. Narrated Ibn `Abbas: Allah's Messenger (ﷺ) set out towards Hunain in the month of Ramadan and some of the people were fasting while some others were not fasting, and when the Prophet (ﷺ) mounted his she-camel, he asked for a tumbler of milk or water and put it on the palm of his hand or on his she-camel and then the people looked at him; and those who were not fasting told those who were fasting, to break their fast (i.e. as the Prophet (ﷺ) had done so). (4277) □

1454. Narrated Hisham's father: When Allah's Messenger (ﷺ) set out (towards Mecca) during the year of the Conquest (of Mecca) and this news reached (the infidels of Quraish), Abu Sufyan, Hakim bin Hizam and Budail bin Warqa came out to gather information about Allah's Messenger (ﷺ), They proceeded on their way till they reached a place called Marr-az-Zahran (which is near Mecca). Behold! There they saw many fires as if they were the fires of `Arafat. Abu Sufyan said, "What is this? It looked like the fires of `Arafat." Budail bin Warqa' said, "Banu `Amr are less in number than that." Some of the guards of Allah's Messenger (ﷺ) saw them and took them over, caught them and brought them to Allah's Messenger (ﷺ). Abu Sufyan embraced Islam. When the Prophet (ﷺ) proceeded, he said to Al-Abbas, "Keep Abu Sufyan standing at the top of the mountain so that he would look at the Muslims. So Al-`Abbas kept him standing (at that place) and the tribes with the Prophet (ﷺ) started passing in front of Abu Sufyan in military batches. A batch passed and Abu Sufyan said, "O `Abbas who are these?" `Abbas said, "They are (Banu) Ghifar." Abu Sufyan said, I have got nothing to do with Ghifar." Then (a batch of the tribe of) Juhaina passed by and he said similarly as above. Then (a batch of the tribe of) Sa`d bin Huzaim passed by and he said similarly as above. Then (Banu) Sulaim passed by and he said similarly as above. Then came a batch, the like of which Abu Sufyan had not seen. He said, "Who are these?" `Abbas said, "They are the Ansar headed by Sa`d bin Ubada, the one holding the flag." Sa`d bin Ubada said, "O Abu Sufyan! Today is the day of a great battle and today (what is prohibited in) the Ka`ba will be permissible." Abu Sufyan said, "O `Abbas! How excellent the day of destruction is! "Then came another batch (of warriors) which was the smallest of all the batches, and in it there was Allah's Messenger (ﷺ) and his companions and the flag of the Prophet (ﷺ) was carried by Az-Zubair bin Al Awwam. When Allah's Messenger (ﷺ) passed by Abu Sufyan, the latter said, (to the Prophet), "Do you know what Sa`d bin 'Ubada said?" The Prophet (ﷺ) said, "What did he say?" Abu Sufyan said, "He said so-and-so." The Prophet (ﷺ) said, "Sa`d told a lie, but today Allah will give superiority to the Ka`ba and today the Ka`ba will be covered with a (cloth) covering." Allah's Messenger (ﷺ) ordered that his flag be fixed at Al-Hajun. Narrated `Urwa: Nafi` bin Jubair bin Mut`im said, "I heard Al-Abbas saying to Az-Zubair bin Al- `Awwam, 'O Abu `Abdullah ! Did Allah's Messenger (ﷺ) order you to fix the flag here?'" Allah's Messenger (ﷺ) ordered Khalid bin Al-Walid to enter Mecca from its upper part from Ka'da while the Prophet (ﷺ) himself entered from Kuda. Two men from the cavalry of Khalid bin Al-Wahd named Hubaish bin Al-Ash'ar and Kurz bin Jabir Al-Fihri were martyred on that day. (4280) □

1455. Narrated Abu Huraira: Allah's Messenger (ﷺ) said, "If Allah makes us victorious, our encamping place will be Al-Khaif, the place where the infidels took an oath to be loyal to Heathenism (by boycotting Banu Hashim, the Prophet's folk). (4284) □

1456. Narrated Anas bin Malik: On the day of the Conquest, the Prophet (ﷺ) entered Mecca, wearing a helmet on his head. When he took it off, a man came and said, "Ibn Khatal is clinging to the curtain of the Ka`ba." The Prophet (ﷺ) said, "Kill him." (Malik a sub-narrator said, "On that day the Prophet (ﷺ) was not in a state of Ihram as it appeared to us, and Allah knows better.") (4286) □

1457. Narrated `Abdullah: When the Prophet (ﷺ) entered Mecca on the day of the Conquest, there were 360 idols around the Ka`ba. The Prophet (ﷺ) started striking them with a stick he had in his hand and was saying, "Truth has come and Falsehood will neither start nor will it reappear. (4287) □

1458. Narrated Ibn `Abbas: When Allah's Messenger (ﷺ) arrived in Mecca, he refused to enter the Ka`ba while there were idols in it. So he ordered that they be taken out. The pictures of the (Prophets) Abraham and Ishmael, holding arrows of divination in their hands, were carried out. The Prophet (ﷺ) said, "May Allah ruin them (i.e. the infidels) for they knew very well that they (i.e. Abraham and Ishmael) never drew lots by these (divination arrows). Then the Prophet (ﷺ) entered the Ka`ba and said. "Allahu Akbar" in all its directions and came out and not offer any prayer therein. (4288) □

1459. Narrated 'Abdullāh bin 'Umar (ra): Allah's Messenger (ﷺ) entered Makkah through its upper part and he was riding his she-camel. Usāma bin Zaid was his Companion-rider behind him (on the same she-camel). In his company were Bilāl and 'Uthmān bin Talha, who was one of the Al-Hajabah (who keep the key of the gate of the Ka'bah). When he made his she-camel kneel down in the Mosque (i.e., Al-Masjid al-Haram), he ordered him (i.e., 'Uthman) to bring the key of the Ka'bah. Then Allah's Messenger (ﷺ) entered the Ka'bah along with 'Usāma bin Zaid, Bilāl and 'Uthmān bin Talha, and he stayed in it for a long period and then came out. The people rushed (to get in) and `Abdullāh bin 'Umar was the first to enter and he found Bilāl standing behind the door. Ibn `Umar asked Bilāl, "Where did Allah's Messenger (ﷺ) offer the Salah (prayer)?" Bilāl showed him the place where he (ﷺ) had offered Salah (prayer). `Abdullah later on said, "I forgot to ask Bilāl how many prostrations (i.e., Rak'a) the Prophet offered." (4289) □

1460. Narrated `Amr bin Salama: We were at a place which was a thoroughfare for the people, and the caravans used to pass by us and we would ask them, "What is wrong with the people? What is wrong with the people? Who is that man? They would say, "That man claims that Allah has sent him (as an Apostle), that he has been divinely inspired, that Allah has revealed to him such-and-such." I used to memorize that (Divine) Talk, and feel as if it was inculcated in my chest (i.e. mind) And the 'Arabs (other than Quraish) delayed their conversion to Islam till the Conquest (of Mecca). They used to say." "Leave him (i.e. Muhammad) and his people Quraish: if he overpowers them then he is a true Prophet. So, when Mecca was conquered, then every tribe rushed to embrace Islam, and my father hurried to embrace Islam before (the other members of) my tribe. When my father returned to his tribe, he said, "By Allah, I have come to you from the Prophet (ﷺ) for sure!" The Prophet (ﷺ) afterwards said to them, 'Offer such-and-such prayer at such-and-such time, and when the time for the prayer becomes due, then one of you should pronounce the Adhan (for the prayer), and let the one amongst you who knows Qur'an most should, lead the prayer." So they looked for such a person and found none who knew more Qur'an than I because of the Qur'anic material which I used to learn from the caravans. They therefore made me their Imam ((to lead the prayer) and at that time I was a boy of six or seven years, wearing a Burda (i.e. a black square garment) proved to be very short for me (and my body became partly naked). A lady from the tribe said, "Won't you cover the anus of your reciter for us?" So they bought (a piece of cloth) and made a shirt for me. I had never been so happy with anything before as I was with that shirt. (4302) □

1461. Narrated Majashi: I took my brother to the Prophet (ﷺ) after the Conquest (of Mecca) and said, "O Allah's Messenger (ﷺ)! I have come to you with my brother so that you may take a pledge of allegiance from him for migration." The Prophet (ﷺ) said, the people of migration (i.e. those who migrated to Medina before the Conquest) enjoyed the privileges of migration (i.e. there is no need for migration anymore)." I said to the Prophet, "For what will you take his pledge of allegiance?" The Prophet (ﷺ) said, "I will take his pledge of allegiance for Islam, Belief, and for Jihad (i.e. fighting in Allah's Cause). (4305) □

1462. Narrated `Ata' bin Abi Rabah: `Ubaid bin `Umar and I visited `Aisha, and he asked her about the migration. She said, "There is no migration today. A believer used to flee with his religion to Allah and His Prophet for fear that he might be put to trial as regards his religion. Today Allah has rendered Islam victorious; therefore a believing one can worship one's Lord wherever one wishes. But there is Jihad (for Allah's Cause) and intentions." (4312) □

1463. Narrated Abu Musa: When the Prophet (ﷺ) had finished from the battle of Hunain, he sent Abu Amir at the head of an army to Autas He (i.e. Abu Amir) met Duraid bin As Summa and Duraid was killed and Allah defeated his companions. The Prophet (ﷺ) sent me with Abu 'Amir. Abu Amir was shot at his knee with an arrow which a man from Jushm had shot and fixed into his knee. I went to him and said, "O Uncle! Who shot you?" He pointed me out (his killer) saying, "That is my killer who shot me (with an arrow)." So I headed towards him and overtook him, and when he saw me, he fled, and I followed him and started saying to him, "Won't you be ashamed? Won't you stop?" So that person stopped, and we exchanged two hits with the swords and I killed him. Then I said to Abu 'Amir. "Allah has killed your killer." He said, "Take out this arrow" So I removed it, and water oozed out of the wound. He then said, "O son of my brother! Convey my compliments to the Prophet (ﷺ) and request him to ask Allah's Forgiveness for me." Abu Amir made me his successor in commanding the people (i.e. troops). He survived for a short while and then died. (Later) I returned and entered upon the Prophet (ﷺ) at his house, and found him lying in a bed made of stalks of date-palm leaves knitted with ropes, and on it there was bedding. The strings of the bed had their traces over his back and sides. Then I told the Prophet (ﷺ) about our and Abu Amir's news and how he had said "Tell him to ask for Allah's Forgiveness for me." The Prophet (ﷺ) asked for water, performed ablution and then raised hands, saying, "O Allah's Forgive `Ubaid, Abu Amir." At that time I saw the whiteness of the Prophet's armpits. The Prophet (ﷺ) then said, "O Allah, make him (i.e. Abu Amir) on the Day of Resurrection, superior to many of Your human creatures." I said, "Will you ask Allah's Forgiveness for me?" (On that) the Prophet (ﷺ) said, "O Allah, forgive the sins of `Abdullah bin Qais and admit him to a nice entrance (i.e. paradise) on the Day of Resurrection." Abu Burda said, "One of the prayers was for Abu 'Amir and the other was for Abu Musa (Abdullah bin Qais).(4323)☐

1464. Narrated `Abdullah bin `Amr: When Allah's Messenger (ﷺ) besieged Taif and could not conquer its people, he said, "We will return (to Medina) if Allah wills." That distressed the Companions (of the Prophet (ﷺ) and they said, "Shall we go away without conquering it (i.e. the Fort of Taif)?" Once the Prophet (ﷺ) said, "Let us return." Then the Prophet said (to them), "Fight tomorrow." They fought and (many of them) got wounded, whereupon the Prophet (ﷺ) said, "We will return (to Medina) tomorrow if Allah wills." That delighted them, whereupon the Prophet (ﷺ) smiled. The sub-narrator, Sufyan said once, "(The Prophet) smiled." (4325) □

1465. Narrated Abu Burda: Abu Musa said, "I was with the Prophet (ﷺ) when he was encamping at Al-Jarana (a place) between Mecca and Medina and Bilal was with him. A bedouin came to the Prophet (ﷺ) and said, "Won't you fulfill what you have promised me?" The Prophet (ﷺ) said, 'Rejoice (at what I will do for you).' The bedouin said, "(You have said to me) rejoice too often." Then the Prophet (ﷺ) turned to me (i.e. Abu Musa) and Bilal in an angry mood and said, 'The bedouin has refused the good tidings, so you both accept them.' Bilal and I said, 'We accept them.' Then the Prophet (ﷺ) asked for a drinking bowl containing water and washed his hands and face in it, and then took a mouthful of water and threw it therein saying (to us), "Drink (some of) it and pour (some) over your faces and chests and be happy at the good tidings." So they both took the drinking bowl and did as instructed. Um Salama called from behind a screen, "Keep something (of the water) for your mother." So they left some of it for her. (4328) □

1466. Narrated Abu 'Is-haq: I heard Al-Bara' narrating when a man came and said to him, "O Abu ʿUmara! Did you flee on the day (of the battle) of Hunain?" Al-Bara' replied, "I testify that the Prophet (ﷺ) did not flee, but the hasty people hurried away and the people of Hawazin threw arrows at them. At that time, Abu Sufyan bin Al-Harith was holding the white mule of the Prophet (ﷺ) by the head, and the Prophet (ﷺ) was saying, "I am the Prophet (ﷺ) undoubtedly: I am the son of ʿAbdul-Muttalib." (4315) □

1467. Narrated Abu Musa: My Companions sent me to Allah's Messenger (ﷺ) to ask him for some animals to ride on as they were accompanying him in the army of Al-Usra, and that was the Ghazwa (Battle) of Tabuk, I said, "O Allah's Prophet! My companions have sent me to you to provide them with means of transportation." He said, "By Allah! I will not make you ride anything." It happened that when I reached him, he was in an angry mood, and I didn't notice it. So I returned in a sad mood because of the refusal the Prophet (ﷺ) and for the fear that the Prophet (ﷺ) might have become 'angry with me. So I returned to my companions and informed them of what the Prophet (ﷺ) had said. Only a short while had passed when I heard Bilal calling, "O `Abdullah bin Qais!" I replied to his call. Bilal said, "Respond to Allah's Messenger (ﷺ) who is calling you." When I went to him. He said, "Take these two camels tied together and also these two camels tied together,'" referring to six camels he had brought them from Sa`d at that time. The Prophet (ﷺ) added, "Take them to your companions and say, 'Allah (or Allah's Messenger (ﷺ)) allows you to ride on these,' so ride on them." So I took those camels to them and said, "The Prophet (ﷺ) allows you to ride on these (camels) but by Allah, I will not leave you till some of you proceed with me to somebody who heard the statement of Allah's Messenger (ﷺ). Do not think that I narrate to you a thing which Allah's Messenger (ﷺ) has not said." They said to me, "We consider you truthful, and we will do what you like." The sub-narrator added: So Abu Musa proceeded along with some of them till they came to those who have heard the statement of Allah's Messenger (ﷺ) wherein he denied them (some animals to ride on) and (his statement) whereby he gave them the same. So these people told them the same information as Abu Musa had told them. (4415) □

1468. Narrated Sa`d: Allah's Messenger (ﷺ) set out for Tabuk. Appointing `Ali as his deputy (in Medina). `Ali said, "Do you want to leave me with the children and women?" The Prophet (ﷺ) said, "Will you not be pleased that you will be to me like Aaron to Moses? But there will be no prophet after me." (4416) □

1469. Narrated `Abdullah bin Ka`b bin Malik: Who, from among Ka`b's sons, was the guide of Ka`b when he became blind: I heard Ka`b bin Malik narrating the story of (the Ghazwa of) Tabuk in which he failed to take part. Ka`b said, "I did not remain behind Allah's Messenger (ﷺ) in any Ghazwa that he fought except the Ghazwa of Tabuk, and I failed to take part in the Ghazwa of Badr, but Allah did not admonish anyone who had not participated in it, for in fact, Allah's Messenger (ﷺ) had gone out in search of the caravan of Quraish till Allah made them (i.e. the Muslims) and their enemy meet without any appointment. I witnessed the night of Al-`Aqaba (pledge) with Allah's Messenger (ﷺ) when we pledged for Islam, and I would not exchange it for the Badr battle although the Badr battle is more popular amongst the people than it (i.e. Al-`Aqaba pledge). As for my news (in this battle of Tabuk), I had never been stronger or wealthier than I was when I remained behind the Prophet (ﷺ) in that Ghazwa. By Allah, never had I two she-camels before, but I had then at the time of this Ghazwa. Whenever Allah's Messenger (ﷺ) wanted to make a Ghazwa, he used to hide his intention by apparently referring to different Ghazwa till it was the time of that Ghazwa (of Tabuk) which Allah's Messenger (ﷺ) fought in severe heat, facing, a long journey, desert, and the great number of enemy. So the Prophet (ﷺ) announced to the Muslims clearly (their destination) so that they might get prepared for their Ghazwa. So he informed them clearly of the destination he was going to. Allah's Messenger (ﷺ) was accompanied by a large number of Muslims who could not be listed in a book namely, a register." Ka`b added, "Any man who intended to be absent would think that the matter would remain hidden unless Allah revealed it through Divine Revelation. So Allah's Messenger (ﷺ) fought that Ghazwa at the time when the fruits had ripened and the shade looked pleasant. Allah's Messenger (ﷺ) and his companions prepared for the battle and I started to go out in order to get myself ready along with them, but I returned without doing anything. I would say to myself, 'I can do that.' So I kept on delaying it every now and then till the people got ready and Allah's Messenger (ﷺ) and the Muslims along with him departed, and I had not prepared anything for my departure, and I said, I will prepare myself (for departure) one or two days after him, and then join them.' In the morning following their departure, I went out to get myself ready but returned having done nothing. Then again in the next morning, I went out to get ready but returned without doing anything. Such was the case with me till they hurried away and the battle was missed (by me). Even then I intended to depart to take them over. I wish I had done so! But it was not in my luck. So, after the departure of Allah's Messenger (ﷺ), whenever I went out and walked amongst the people (i.e, the remaining persons), it grieved me that I could see none around me, but one accused of hypocrisy or one of those weak men whom Allah had excused. Allah's Messenger (ﷺ) did not remember me till he reached Tabuk. So while he was sitting amongst the people in Tabuk, he said, 'What did Ka`b do?' A man from Banu Salama said, 'O Allah's Messenger (ﷺ)! He has been stopped by his two Burdas (i.e. garments) and his looking at his own flanks with pride.' Then Mu`adh bin Jabal said, 'What a bad thing you have said! By Allah! O Allahs Apostle! We know nothing about him but good.' Allah's Messenger (ﷺ) kept silent." Ka`b bin Malik added, "When I heard that he (i.e. the Prophet (ﷺ)) was on his way back to Medina. I got dipped in my concern, and began to think of false excuses, saying to myself, 'How can I avoid his anger tomorrow?' And I took the advice of wise member of my family in this matter. When it was said that Allah's Messenger (ﷺ), had come near all the evil false excuses abandoned from my mind and I knew well that I could never come out of this problem by forging a false statement. Then I decided firmly to speak the truth. So Allah's Messenger (ﷺ) arrived in the morning, and whenever he returned from a journey., he used to visit the Mosque first of all and offer a two-rak`at prayer therein and then sit for the people. So when he had done all that (this time), those who had failed to join the battle (of Tabuk) came and started offering (false) excuses and taking oaths before him. They were something over eighty men; Allah's Messenger (ﷺ) accepted the excuses they had expressed, took their pledge of allegiance asked for Allah's Forgiveness for them, and left the secrets of their hearts for Allah to judge. Then I came to him, and when I greeted him, he smiled a smile of an angry person and then said, 'Come on.' So I came walking till I sat before him. He said to me, 'What stopped you from joining us. Had you not purchased an animal for carrying you?' I answered, "Yes, O Allah's Messenger (ﷺ)! But by Allah, if I were sitting before any person from among the people of the world other than you, I would have avoided his anger with an excuse. By Allah, I have been bestowed with the power of speaking fluently and eloquently, but by Allah, I knew well that if today I tell you a lie to seek your favor, Allah would surely make you angry with me in the near future, but if I tell you the truth, though you will get angry because of it, I hope for Allah's Forgiveness. Really, by Allah, there was no excuse for me. By

Allah, I had never been stronger or wealthier than I was when I remained behind you.' Then Allah's Messenger (ﷺ) said, 'As regards this man, he has surely told the truth. So get up till Allah decides your case.' I got up, and many men of Banu Salama followed me and said to me. 'By Allah, we never witnessed you doing any sin before this. Surely, you failed to offer excuse to Allah's Messenger (ﷺ) as the others who did not join him, have offered. The prayer of Allah's Messenger (ﷺ) to Allah to forgive you would have been sufficient for you.' By Allah, they continued blaming me so much that I intended to return (to the Prophet) and accuse myself of having told a lie, but I said to them, 'Is there anybody else who has met the same fate as I have?' They replied, 'Yes, there are two men who have said the same thing as you have, and to both of them was given the same order as given to you.' I said, 'Who are they?' They replied, Murara bin Ar-Rabi Al- Amri and Hilal bin Umaiya Al-Waqifi.' By that they mentioned to me two pious men who had attended the Ghazwa (Battle) of Badr, and in whom there was an example for me. So I did not change my mind when they mentioned them to me. Allah's Messenger (ﷺ) forbade all the Muslims to talk to us, the three aforesaid persons out of all those who had remained behind in that Ghazwa. So we kept away from the people and they changed their attitude towards us till the very land (where I lived) appeared strange to me as if I did not know it. We remained in that condition for fifty nights. As regards my two fellows, they remained in their houses and kept on weeping, but I was the youngest of them and the firmest of them, so I used to go out and witness the prayers along with the Muslims and roam about in the markets, but none would talk to me, and I would come to Allah's Messenger (ﷺ) and greet him while he was sitting In his gathering after the prayer, and I would wonder whether the Prophet (ﷺ) did move his lips in return to my greetings or not. Then I would offer my prayer near to him and look at him stealthily. When I was busy with my prayer, he would turn his face towards me, but when I turned my face to him, he would turn his face away from me. When this harsh attitude of the people lasted long, I walked till I scaled the wall of the garden of Abu Qatada who was my cousin and dearest person to me, and I offered my greetings to him. By Allah, he did not return my greetings. I said, 'O Abu Qatada! I beseech you by Allah!

Do you know that I love Allah and His Apostle?' He kept quiet. I asked him again, beseeching him by Allah, but he remained silent. Then I asked him again in the Name of Allah. He said, "Allah and His Apostle know it better.' Thereupon my eyes flowed with tears and I returned and jumped over the wall." Ka`b added, "While I was walking in the market of Medina, suddenly I saw a Nabati (i.e. a Christian farmer) from the Nabatis of Sham who came to sell his grains in Medina, saying, 'Who will lead me to Ka`b bin Malik?' The people began to point (me) out for him till he came to me and handed me a letter from the king of Ghassan in which the following was written: "To proceed, I have been informed that your friend (i.e. the Prophet (ﷺ)) has treated you harshly. Anyhow, Allah does not let you live at a place where you feel inferior and your right is lost. So join us, and we will console you." When I read it, I said to myself, 'This is also a sort of a test.' Then I took the letter to the oven and made a fire therein by burning it. When forty out of the fifty nights elapsed, behold! There came to me the messenger of Allah's Messenger (ﷺ) and said, 'Allah's Messenger (ﷺ) orders you to keep away from your wife,' I said, 'should I divorce her; or else! what should I do?' He said, 'No, only keep aloof from her and do not cohabit her.' The Prophet (ﷺ) sent the same message to my two fellows. Then I said to my wife. 'Go to your parents and remain with them till Allah gives His Verdict in this matter." Ka`b added, "The wife of Hilal bin Umaiya came to Apostle and said, 'O Allah's Messenger (ﷺ)! Hilal bin Umaiya is a helpless old man who has no servant to attend on him. Do you dislike that I should serve him?' He said, 'No (you can serve him) but he should not come near you.' She said, 'By Allah, he has no desire for anything. By, Allah, he has never ceased weeping till his case began till this day of his.' (continued...) (continuing... 1): -5.702:... ... On that, some of my family members said to me, 'Will you also ask Allah's Messenger (ﷺ) to permit your wife (to serve you) as he has permitted the wife of Hilal bin Umaiya to serve him?' I said, 'By Allah, I will not ask the permission of Allah's Messenger (ﷺ) regarding her, for I do not know What Allah's Messenger (ﷺ) would say if I asked him to permit her (to serve me) while I am a young man.' Then I remained in that state for ten more nights after that till the period of fifty nights was completed starting from the time when Allah's

Messenger (ﷺ) prohibited the people from talking to us. When I had offered the Fajr prayer on the 50th morning on the roof of one of our houses and while I was sitting in the condition which Allah described (in the Qur'an) i.e. my very soul seemed straitened to me and even the earth seemed narrow to me for all its spaciousness, there I heard the voice of one who had ascended the mountain of Sala' calling with his loudest voice, 'O Ka`b bin Malik! Be happy (by receiving good tidings).' I fell down in prostration before Allah, realizing that relief has come. Allah's Messenger (ﷺ) had announced the acceptance of our repentance by Allah when he had offered the Fajr prayer. The people then went out to congratulate us. Some bringers of good tidings went out to my two fellows, and a horseman came to me in haste, and a man of Banu Aslam came running and ascended the mountain and his voice was swifter than the horse. When he (i.e. the man) whose voice I had heard, came to me conveying the good tidings, I took off my garments and dressed him with them; and by Allah, I owned no other garments than them on that day. Then I borrowed two garments and wore them and went to Allah's Apostle. The people started receiving me in batches, congratulating me on Allah's Acceptance of my repentance, saying, 'We congratulate you on Allah's Acceptance of your repentance." Ka`b further said, "When I entered the Mosque. I saw Allah's Messenger (ﷺ) sitting with the people around him. Talha bin Ubaidullah swiftly came to me, shook hands with me and congratulated me. By Allah, none of the Muhajirin (i.e. Emigrants) got up for me except him (i.e. Talha), and I will never forget this for Talha." Ka`b added, "When I greeted Allah's Messenger (ﷺ) he, his face being bright with joy, said "Be happy with the best day that you have got ever since your mother delivered you." Ka`b added, "I said to the Prophet (ﷺ) 'Is this forgiveness from you or from Allah?' He said, 'No, it is from Allah.' Whenever Allah's Messenger (ﷺ) became happy, his face would shine as if it were a piece of moon, and we all knew that characteristic of him. When I sat before him, I said, 'O Allah's Messenger (ﷺ)! Because of the acceptance of my repentance I will give up all my wealth as alms for the Sake of Allah and His Apostle. Allah's Apostle said, 'Keep some of your wealth, as it will be better for you.' I said, 'So I will keep my share from Khaibar with me,' and added, 'O Allah's Messenger (ﷺ)! Allah has saved me for telling the truth; so it is a part of my repentance not to tell but the truth as long as I am alive. By Allah, I do not know anyone of the Muslims whom Allah has helped fortelling the truth more than me. Since I have mentioned that truth to Allah's Messenger (ﷺ) till today, I have never intended to tell a lie. I hope that Allah will also save me (from telling lies) the rest of my life. So Allah revealed to His Apostle the Verse: -- "Verily, Allah has forgiven the Prophet, the Muhajirin (i.e. Emigrants (up to His Saying) And be with those who are true (in word and deed)." (9.117-119) By Allah, Allah has never bestowed upon me, apart from His guiding me to Islam, a Greater blessing than the fact that I did not tell a lie to Allah's Messenger (ﷺ) which would have caused me to perish as those who have told a lie perished, for Allah described those who told lies with the worst description He ever attributed to anybody else. Allah said:-- "They (i.e. the hypocrites) will swear by Allah to you when you return to them (up to His Saying) Certainly Allah is not pleased with the rebellious people-- " (9.95-96) Ka`b added, "We, the three persons, differed altogether from those whose excuses Allah's Apostle accepted when they swore to him. He took their pledge of allegiance and asked Allah to forgive them, but Allah's Messenger (ﷺ) left our case pending till Allah gave His Judgment about it. As for that Allah said):-- And to the three (He did for give also) who remained behind." (9.118) What Allah said (in this Verse) does not indicate our failure to take part in the Ghazwa, but it refers to the deferment of making a decision by the Prophet (ﷺ) about our case in contrast to the case of those who had taken an oath before him and he excused them by accepting their excuses. (4418) □

1470. Narrated Salim's father: The Prophet (ﷺ) sent Khalid bin Al-Walid to the tribe of Jadhima and Khalid invited them to Islam but they could not express themselves by saying, "Aslamna (i.e. we have embraced Islam)," but they started saying "Saba'na! Saba'na (i.e. we have come out of one religion to another)." Khalid kept on killing (some of) them and taking (some of) them as captives and gave every one of us his Captive. When there came the day then Khalid ordered that each man should kill his captive, I said, "By Allah, I will not kill my captive, and none of my companions will kill his captive." When we reached the Prophet, we mentioned to him the whole story.

On that, the Prophet (ﷺ) raised both his hands and said twice, "O Allah! I am free from what Khalid has done." (4339) □

1471. Narrated Al-Bara: Allah's Messenger (ﷺ) sent us to Yemen along with Khalid bin Al-Walid. Later on he sent `Ali bin Abi Talib in his place. The Prophet (ﷺ) said to `Ali, "Give Khalid's companions the choice of either staying with you (in Yemen) or returning to Medina." I was one of those who stayed with him (i.e. `Ali) and got several Awaq (of gold from the war booty. (4349) □

1472. Narrated Qais: Jarir said "Allah's Messenger (ﷺ) said to me, "Won't you relieve me from Dhul-Khalasa?" I replied, "Yes, (I will relieve you)." So I proceeded along with one-hundred and fifty cavalry from Ahmas tribe who were skillful in riding horses. I used not to sit firm over horses, so I informed the Prophet (ﷺ) of that, and he stroke my chest with his hand till I saw the marks of his hand over my chest and he said, O Allah! Make him firm and one who guides others and is guided (on the right path).' Since then I have never fallen from a horse. Dhul-l-Khulasa was a house in Yemen belonging to the tribe of Khatham and Bajaila, and in it there were idols which were worshipped, and it was called Al-Ka`ba." Jarir went there, burnt it with fire and dismantled it. When Jarir reached Yemen, there was a man who used to foretell and give good omens by casting arrows of divination. Someone said to him. "The messenger of Allah's Messenger (ﷺ) is present here and if he should get hold of you, he would chop off your neck." One day while he was using them (i.e. arrows of divination), Jarir stopped there and said to him, "Break them (i.e. the arrows) and testify that None has the right to be worshipped except Allah, or else I will chop off your neck." So the man broke those arrows and testified that none has the right to be worshipped except Allah. Then Jarir sent a man called Abu Artata from the tribe of Ahmas to the Prophet to convey the good news (of destroying Dhu-l-Khalasa). So when the messenger reached the Prophet, he said, "O Allah's Messenger (ﷺ)! By Him Who sent you with the Truth, I did not leave it till it was like a scabby camel." Then the Prophet (ﷺ) blessed the horses of Ahmas and their men five times. (4357) □

1473. Narrated Jabir bin `Abdullah: Allah's Messenger (ﷺ) sent us who were three-hundred riders under the command of Abu Ubaida bin Al- Jarrah in order to watch the caravan of the Quraish pagans. We stayed at the seashore for half a month and were struck with such severe hunger that we ate even the Khabt (i.e. the leaves of the Salam, a thorny desert tree), and because of that, the army was known as Jaish-ul-Khabt. Then the sea threw out, an animal (i.e. a fish) called Al-`Anbar and we ate of that for half a month, and rubbed its fat on our bodies till our bodies returned to their original state (i.e. became strong and healthy). Abu Ubaida took one of its ribs, fixed it on the ground; then he went to the tallest man of his companions (to let him pass under the rib). Once Sufyan said, "He took a rib from its parts and fixed it, and then took a man and camel and they passed from underneath it (without touching it)." Jabir added: There was a man amongst the people who slaughtered three camels and then slaughtered another three camels and then slaughtered other three camels, and then Abu 'Ubaida forbade him to do so. Narrated Abu Salih: Qais bin Sa`d said to his father. "I was present in the army and the people were struck with severe hunger." He said, "You should have slaughtered (camels) (for them)." Qais said, "I did slaughter camels but they were hungry again. He said, "You should have slaughtered (camels) again." Qais said, "I did slaughter (camels) again but the people felt hungry again." He said, "You should have slaughtered (camels) again." Qais said, "I did slaughter (camels) again, but the people again felt hungry." He said, "You should have slaughtered (camels) again." Qais said, "But I was forbidden (by Abu 'Ubaida this time). (4361) □

1474. Narrated Jabir: We set out in the army of Al-Khabt and Abu Ubaida was the commander of the troops. We were struck with severe hunger and the sea threw out a dead fish the like of which we had never seen, and it was called Al-`Anbar. We ate of it for half a month. Abu Ubaida took (and fixed) one of its bones and a rider passed underneath it (without touching it). (Jabir added :) Abu 'Ubaida said (to us), "Eat (of that fish)." When we arrived at Medina, we informed the Prophet (ﷺ) about that, and he said, "Eat, for it is food Allah has brought out for you, and feed us if you have some of it." So some of them gave him (of that fish) and he ate it. (4362) □

1475. Narrated Abu Huraira: I have not ceased to like Banu Tamim ever since I heard of three qualities attributed to them by Allah's Messenger (ﷺ) (He said): They, out of all my followers, will be the strongest opponent of Ad-Dajjal; `Aisha had a slave-girl from them, and the Prophet (ﷺ) told her to manumit her as she was from the descendants of (the Prophet) Ishmael; and, when their Zakat was brought, the Prophet (ﷺ) said, "This is the Zakat of my people." (4366) ☐

1476. Narrated Abu Huraira: The Prophet (ﷺ) sent some cavalry towards Najd and they brought a man from the tribe of Banu Hanifa who was called Thumama bin Uthal. They fastened him to one of the pillars of the Mosque. The Prophet went to him and said, "What have you got, O Thumama?" He replied," I have got a good thought, O Muhammad! If you should kill me, you would kill a person who has already killed somebody, and if you should set me free, you would do a favor to one who is grateful, and if you want property, then ask me whatever wealth you want." He was left till the next day when the Prophet (ﷺ) said to him, "What have you got, Thumama? He said, "What I told you, i.e. if you set me free, you would do a favor to one who is grateful." The Prophet (ﷺ) left him till the day after, when he said, "What have you got, O Thumama?" He said, "I have got what I told you."On that the Prophet (ﷺ) said, "Release Thumama." So he (i.e. Thumama) went to a garden of date-palm trees near to the Mosque, took a bath and then entered the Mosque and said, "I testify that None has the right to be worshipped except Allah, and also testify that Muhammad is His Apostle! By Allah, O Muhammad! There was no face on the surface of the earth most disliked by me than yours, but now your face has become the most beloved face to me. By Allah, there was no religion most disliked by me than yours, but now it is the most beloved religion to me. By Allah, there was no town most disliked by me than your town, but now it is the most beloved town to me. Your cavalry arrested me (at the time) when I was intending to perform the `Umra. And now what do you think?" The Prophet (ﷺ) gave him good tidings (congratulated him) and ordered him to perform the `Umra. So when he came to Mecca, someone said to him, "You have become a Sabian?" Thumama replied, "No! By Allah, I have embraced Islam with Muhammad, Apostle of Allah. No, by Allah! Not a single grain of wheat will come to you from Yamamah unless the Prophet gives his permission." (4372) □

1477. Narrated Ibn `Abbas: Musailima Al-Kadhdhab came during the lifetime of the Prophet (ﷺ) and started saying, "If Muhammad gives me the rule after him, I will follow him." And he came to Medina with a great number of the people of his tribe. Allah's Messenger (ﷺ) went to him in the company of Thabit bin Qais bin Shammas, and at that time, Allah's Messenger (ﷺ) had a stick of a date-palm tree in his hand. When he (i.e. the Prophet (ﷺ)) stopped near Musailima while the latter was amidst his companions, he said to him, "If you ask me for this piece (of stick), I will not give it to you, and Allah's Order you cannot avoid, (but you will be destroyed), and if you turn your back from this religion, then Allah will destroy you. And I think you are the same person who was shown to me in my dream, and this is Thabit bin Qais who will answer your questions on my behalf." Then the Prophet (ﷺ) went away from him. I asked about the statement of Allah's Messenger (ﷺ): "You seem to be the same person who was shown to me in my dream," and Abu Huraira informed me that Allah's Messenger (ﷺ) said, "When I was sleeping, I saw (in a dream) two bangles of gold on my hands and that worried me. And then I was inspired Divinely in the dream that I should blow on them, so I blew on them and both the bangles flew away. And I interpreted it that two liars (who would claim to be prophets) would appear after me. One of them has proved to be Al Ansi and the other, Musailima." (4373) □

1478. Narrated Abu Huraira: Allah's Messenger (ﷺ) said, "While I was sleeping, I was given the treasures of the earth and two gold bangles were put in my hands, and I did not like that, but I received the inspiration that I should blow on them, and I did so, and both of them vanished. I interpreted it as referring to the two liars between whom I am present; the ruler of Sana and the Ruler of Yamaha." (4375) □

1479. Narrated Abu Raja Al-Utaridi: We used to worship stones, and when we found a better stone than the first one, we would throw the first one and take the latter, but if we could not get a stone then we would collect some earth (i.e. soil) and then bring a sheep and milk that sheep over it, and perform the Tawaf around it. When the month of Rajab came, we used (to stop the military actions), calling this month the iron remover, for we used to remove and throw away the iron parts of every spear and arrow in the month of Rajab. Abu Raja' added: When the Prophet (ﷺ) sent with (Allah's) Message, I was a boy working as a shepherd of my family camels. When we heard the news about the appearance of the Prophet, we ran to the fire, i.e. to Musailima al-Kadhdhab. (4377) ☐

1480. Narrated Hudhaifa: Al-`Aqib and Saiyid, the rulers of Najran, came to Allah's Messenger (ﷺ) with the intention of doing Lian one of them said to the other, "Do not do (this Lian) for, by Allah, if he is a Prophet and we do this Lian, neither we, nor our offspring after us will be successful." Then both of them said (to the Prophet (ﷺ)), "We will give what you should ask but you should send a trustworthy man with us, and do not send any person with us but an honest one." The Prophet (ﷺ) said, "I will send an honest man who is really trustworthy." Then every one of the companions of Allah's Messenger (ﷺ) wished to be that one. Then the Prophet said, "Get up, O Abu 'Ubaida bin Al-Jarrah." When he got up, Allah's Messenger (ﷺ) said, "This is the Trustworthy man of this (Muslim) nation." (4380) ☐

1481. Narrated Tariq bin Shibab: Some Jews said, "Had this Verse been revealed to us, we would have taken that day as `Id (festival)." `Umar said, "What Verse?" They said: "This day I have Perfected your religion for you, Completed My Favor upon you And have chosen for you Islam as your religion" (5.3) `Umar said, "I know the place where it was revealed; It was revealed while Allah's Messenger (ﷺ) was staying at `Arafat." (4407) ☐

1482. Narrated Usama bin Zaid: Allah's Messenger (ﷺ) sent us towards Al-Huruqa, and in the morning we attacked them and defeated them. I and an Ansari man followed a man from among them and when we took him over, he said, "La ilaha illal-Lah." On hearing that, the Ansari man stopped, but I killed him by stabbing him with my spear. When we returned, the Prophet (ﷺ) came to know about that and he said, "O Usama! Did you kill him after he had said "La ilaha ilal-Lah?" I said, "But he said so only to save himself." The Prophet (ﷺ) kept on repeating that so often that I wished I had not embraced Islam before that day. (4269) ☐

61. DEATH OF THE PROPHET (ﷺ)

1483. NARRATED IBN `ABBAS (RA): `Umar used to admit me (into his house) along with the old men who had fought in the Badr battle. Some of them said (to `Umar), "Why do you allow this young man to enter with us, while we have sons of his own age?" `Umar said, "You know what person he is." One day `Umar called them and called me along with them, I had thought he called me on that day to show them something about me (i.e. my knowledge). `Umar asked them, "What do you say about (the Sura): "When comes the help of Allah and the Conquest (of Mecca) and you see mankind entering the Religion of Allah (i.e. Islam) in crowds. 'So celebrate the Praises Of your Lord and ask for His forgiveness, Truly, He is the One Who accepts repentance and forgives." (110.1-3) some of them replied, "We are ordered to praise Allah and repent to Him if we are helped and granted victory." Some said, "We do not know." Others kept quiet. `Umar then said to me, "Do you say similarly?" I said, "No." `Umar said "What do you say then?" I said, "This Verse indicates the approaching of the death of Allah's Messenger (ﷺ) of which Allah informed him. When comes the help of Allah and the Conquest, (i.e. the Conquest of Mecca, that will be the sign of your Prophet's) approaching death, so testify the uniqueness of your Lord (i.e. Allah) and praise Him and repent to Him as He is ready to forgive." On that, `Umar said, "I do not know about it anything other than what you know." (4294) □

1484. Narrated `Aisha: Once Fatima came walking and her gait (manner of walking) resembled the gait of the Prophet (ﷺ). The Prophet (ﷺ) said, "Welcome, O my daughter!" Then he made her sit on his right or on his left side, and then he told her a secret and she started weeping. I asked her, "Why are you weeping?" He again told her a secret and she started laughing. I said, "I never saw happiness so near to sadness as I saw today." I asked her what the Prophet (ﷺ) had told her. She said, "I would never disclose the secret of Allah's Messenger (ﷺ)." When the Prophet (ﷺ) died, I asked her about it. (3623) □

1485. She replied. "The Prophet (ﷺ) said: 'Every year Gabriel used to revise the Qur'an with me once only, but this year he has done so twice. I think this portends my death, and you will be the first of my family to follow me.' So I started weeping. Then he said. 'Don't you like to be the chief of all the ladies of Paradise or the chief of the believing women? So I laughed for that." (3624) □

1486. Narrated `Aisha: The Prophet (ﷺ) in his ailment in which he died, used to say, "O `Aisha! I still feel the pain caused by the food I ate at Khaibar, and at this time, I feel as if my aorta is being cut from that poison." (4428) □

1487. Narrated `Aisha: I heard the Prophet (ﷺ) and listened to him before his death while he was leaning his back on me and saying, "O Allah! Forgive me, and bestow Your Mercy on me, and let me meet the (highest) companions (of the Hereafter)." (4440) □

1488. Narrated Aisha: "When the ailment of Allah's Messenger (ﷺ) became aggravated, he requested his wives to permit him to be (treated) nursed in my house, and they gave him permission. He came out (to my house), walking between two men with his feet dragging on the ground, between `Abbas bin `Abdul--Muttalib and another man" `Ubaidullah said, "I told `Abdullah of what `Aisha had said, `Abdullah bin `Abbas said to me, 'Do you know who is the other man whom `Aisha did not name?' I said, 'No.' Ibn `Abbas said, 'It was `Ali bin Abu Talib." `Aisha, the wife of the Prophet (ﷺ) used to narrate saying, "When Allah's Messenger (ﷺ) entered my house and his disease became aggravated, he said, " Pour on me the water of seven water skins, the mouths of which have not been untied, so that I may give advice to the people.' So we let him sit in a big basin belonging to Hafsa, the wife of the Prophet (ﷺ) and then started to pour water on him from these water skins till he started pointing to us with his hands intending to say, 'You have done your job." `Aisha added, "Then he went out to the people and led them in prayer and preached to them." (4442) □

1489. Narrated 'Ubaidullah Ibn `Abdullah bin `Utba: I went to `Aisha and asked her to describe to me the illness of Allah's Messenger (ﷺ). `Aisha said, "Yes. The Prophet became seriously ill and asked whether the people had prayed. We replied, 'No. O Allah's Apostle! They are waiting for you.' He added, 'Put water for me in a trough." `Aisha added, "We did so. He took a bath and tried to get up but fainted. When he recovered, he again asked whether the people had prayed. We said, 'No, they are waiting for you. O Allah's Messenger (ﷺ),' He again said, 'Put water in a trough for me.' He sat down and took a bath and tried to get up but fainted again. Then he recovered and said, 'Have the people prayed?' We replied, 'No, they are waiting for you. O Allah's Apostle.' He said, 'Put water for me in the trough.' Then he sat down and washed himself and tried to get up but he fainted. When he recovered, he asked, 'Have the people prayed?' We said, 'No, they are waiting for you. O Allah's Messenger (ﷺ)! The people were in the mosque waiting for the Prophet (ﷺ) for the `Isha prayer. The Prophet (ﷺ) sent for Abu Bakr to lead the people in the prayer. The messenger went to Abu Bakr and said, 'Allah's Messenger (ﷺ) orders you to lead the people in the prayer.' Abu Bakr was a softhearted man, so he asked `Umar to lead the prayer but `Umar replied, 'You are more rightful.' So Abu Bakr led the prayer in those days. When the Prophet (ﷺ) felt a bit better, he came out for the Zuhr prayer with the help of two persons one of whom was Al-`Abbas. While Abu Bakr was leading the people in the prayer. When Abu Bakr saw him he wanted to retreat but the Prophet (ﷺ) beckoned him not to do so and asked them to make him sit beside Abu Bakr and they did so. Abu Bakr was following the Prophet (in the prayer) and the people were following Abu Bakr. The Prophet (prayed) sitting." 'Ubaidullah added "I went to `Abdullah bin `Abbas and asked him, Shall I tell you what Aisha has told me about the fatal illness of the Prophet?' Ibn `Abbas said, 'Go ahead. I told him her narration and he did not deny anything of it but asked whether `Aisha told me the name of the second person (who helped the Prophet (ﷺ)) along with Al-Abbas. I said. 'No.' He said, 'He was `Ali (Ibn Abi Talib). (687) □

1490. `Aisha and `Abdullah bin `Abbas said, "When Allah's Messenger (ﷺ) became ill seriously, he started covering his face with his woolen sheet, and when he felt short of breath, he removed it from his face and said, 'That is so! Allah's curse be on the

Jews and the Christians, as they took the graves of their prophets as (places of worship),' intending to warn (the Muslims) of what they had done." (4444) ☐

1491. `Aisha added, "I argued with Allah's Messenger (ﷺ) repeatedly about that matter (i.e. his order that Abu Bakr should lead the people in prayer in his place when he was ill), and what made me argue so much, was, that it never occurred to my mind that after the Prophet, the people would ever love a man who had taken his place, and I felt that anybody standing in his place, would be a bad omen to the people, so I wanted Allah's Messenger (ﷺ) to give up the idea of choosing Abu Bakr (to lead the people in prayer). (4445) ☐

1492. Narrated `Aisha: The Prophet (ﷺ) died while he was between my chest and chin, so I never dislike the death agony for anyone after the Prophet. (4446) ☐

1493. Narrated `Abdullah bin `Abbas: `Ali bin Abu Talib came out of the house of Allah's Messenger (ﷺ) during his fatal illness. The people asked, "O Abu Hasan (i.e. `Ali)! How is the health of Allah's Messenger (ﷺ) this morning?" `Ali replied, "He has recovered with the Grace of Allah." `Abbas bin `Abdul Muttalib held him by the hand and said to him, "In three days you, by Allah, will be ruled (by somebody else), and by Allah, I feel that Allah's Apostle will die from this ailment of his, for I know how the faces of the offspring of `Abdul Muttalib look at the time of their death. So let us go to Allah's Messenger (ﷺ) and ask him who will take over the Caliphate. If it is given to us we will know as to it, and if it is given to somebody else, we will inform him so that he may tell the new ruler to take care of us." `Ali said, "By Allah, if we asked Allah's Apostle for it (i.e. the Caliphate) and he denied it us, the people will never give it to us after that. And by Allah, I will not ask Allah's Messenger (ﷺ) for it." (4447) ☐

1494. Narrated Anas bin Malik: While the Muslims were offering the Fajr prayer on Monday and Abu Bakr was leading them in prayer, suddenly Allah's Messenger (ﷺ) lifted the curtain of `Aisha's dwelling and looked at them while they were in the rows of the prayers and smiled. Abu Bakr retreated to join the row, thinking that Allah's

Apostle wanted to come out for the prayer. The Muslims were about to be put to trial in their prayer (i.e. were about to give up praying) because of being overjoyed at seeing Allah's Messenger (ﷺ). But Allah's Apostle beckoned them with his hand to complete their prayer and then entered the dwelling and let fall the curtain. (4448) □

1495. Narrated Aisha: It was one of the favors of Allah towards me that Allah's Messenger (ﷺ) expired in my house on the day of my turn while he was leaning against my chest and Allah made my saliva mix with his saliva at his death. `Abdur-Rahman entered upon me with a Siwak in his hand and I was supporting (the back of) Allah's Messenger (ﷺ) (against my chest). I saw the Prophet (ﷺ) looking at it (i.e. Siwak) and I knew that he loved the Siwak, so I said (to him), "Shall I take it for you?" He nodded in agreement. So I took it and it was too stiff for him to use, so I said, "Shall I soften it for you?" He nodded his approval. So I softened it and he cleaned his teeth with it. In front of him there was a jug or a tin, (The sub-narrator, `Umar is in doubt as to which was right) containing water. He started dipping his hand in the water and rubbing his face with it, he said, "None has the right to be worshipped except Allah. Death has its agonies." He then lifted his hands (towards the sky) and started saying, "With the highest companion," till he expired and his hand dropped down. (4449) □

1496. Narrated `Aisha: The Prophet (ﷺ) expired in my house and on the day of my turn, leaning against my chest. One of us (i.e. the Prophet's wives) used to recite a prayer asking Allah to protect him from all evils when he became sick. So I started asking Allah to protect him from all evils (by reciting a prayer). He raised his head towards the sky and said, "With the highest companions, with the highest companions." `Abdur- Rahman bin Abu Bakr passed carrying a fresh leaf-stalk of a date-palm and the Prophet (ﷺ) looked at it and I thought that the Prophet (ﷺ) was in need of it (for cleaning his teeth). So I took it (from `Abdur Rahman) and chewed its head and shook it and gave it to the Prophet (ﷺ) who cleaned his teeth with it, in the best way he had ever cleaned his teeth, and then he gave it to me, and suddenly his hand dropped down or it fell from his hand (i.e. he expired). So Allah made my saliva mix with his saliva on his last day on earth and his first day in the Hereafter.

(4451) ☐

1497. Narrated 'Aisha: Allah's Messenger (ﷺ) died while Abu Bakr was at a place called As-Sunah (Al-'Aliya) 'Umar stood up and said, "By Allah! Allah's Messenger (ﷺ) is not dead!" 'Umar (later on) said, "By Allah! Nothing occurred to my mind except that." He said, "Verily! Allah will resurrect him and he will cut the hands and legs of some men." Then Abu Bakr came and uncovered the face of Allah's Messenger (ﷺ), kissed him and said, "Let my mother and father be sacrificed for you, (O Allah's Messenger (ﷺ)), you are good in life and in death. By Allah in Whose Hands my life is, Allah will never make you taste death twice." Then he went out and said, "O oath-taker! Don't be hasty." When Abu Bakr spoke, 'Umar sat down. (3667) ☐

1498. Narrated Ibn `Abbas: Abu Bakr went out while `Umar bin Al-Khattab was talking to the people. Abu Bakr said, "Sit down, O `Umar!" But `Umar refused to sit down. So the people came to Abu Bakr and left `Umar. Abu Bakr said, "To proceed, if anyone amongst you used to worship Muhammad, then Muhammad is dead, but if (anyone of) you used to worship Allah, then Allah is Alive and shall never die. Allah said: "Muhammad is not but a messenger. [Other] messengers have passed on before him. So if he was to die or be killed, would you turn back on your heels [to unbelief]? And he who turns back on his heels will never harm Allah at all; but Allah will reward the grateful." (3.144) By Allah, it was as if the people never knew that Allah had revealed this Verse before till Abu Bakr recited it and all the people received it from him, and I heard everybody reciting it (then). Narrated Az-Zuhri: Sa`id bin Al-Musaiyab told me that `Umar said, "By Allah, when I heard Abu Bakr reciting it, my legs could not support me and I fell down at the very moment of hearing him reciting it, declaring that the Prophet (ﷺ) had died." (4454) ☐

1499. Abu Bakr praised and glorified Allah and said, No doubt! Whoever worshipped Muhammad, then Muhammad is dead, but whoever worshipped Allah, then Allah is Alive and shall never die." Then he recited Allah's Statement: "(O Muhammad) Verily you will die, and they also will die." (39.30) He also recited: "Muhammad is no more than an Apostle; and indeed many Apostles have passed away, before him,

If he dies Or is killed, will you then Turn back on your heels? And he who turns back On his heels, not the least Harm will he do to Allah And Allah will give reward to those Who are grateful." (3.144) □

The people wept loudly, and the Ansar were assembled with Sad bin 'Ubada in the shed of Bani Saida. They said (to the emigrants). "There should be one 'Amir from us and one from you." Then Abu Bakr, Umar bin Al-Khattab and Abu 'baida bin Al-Jarrah went to them. 'Umar wanted to speak but Abu Bakr stopped him. 'Umar later on used to say, "By Allah, I intended only to say something that appealed to me and I was afraid that Abu Bakr would not speak so well. Then Abu Bakr spoke and his speech was very eloquent. He said in his statement, "We are the rulers and you (Ansars) are the ministers (i.e. advisers)," Hubab bin Al-Mundhir said, "No, by Allah we won't accept this. But there must be a ruler from us and a ruler from you." Abu Bakr said, "No, we will be the rulers and you will be the ministers, for they (i.e. Quarish) are the best family amongst the 'Arabs and of best origin. So you should elect either 'Umar or Abu 'Ubaida bin Al-Jarrah as your ruler." 'Umar said (to Abu Bakr), "No but we elect you, for you are our chief and the best amongst us and the most beloved of all of us to Allah's Messenger (ﷺ)." So 'Umar took Abu Bakr's hand and gave the pledge of allegiance and the people too gave the pledge of allegiance to Abu Bakr. Someone said, "You have killed Sad bin Ubada." 'Umar said, "Allah has killed him." (3668) □

1500. Narrated Anas: When the ailment of the Prophet (ﷺ) got aggravated, he became unconscious whereupon Fatima said, "Oh, how distressed my father is!" He said, "Your father will have no more distress after today." When he expired, she said, "O Father! Who has responded to the call of the Lord Who has invited him! O Father, whose dwelling place is the Garden of Paradise (i.e. Al-Firdaus)! O Father! We convey this news (of your death) to Gabriel." When he was buried, Fatima said, "O Anas! Do you feel pleased to throw earth over Allah's Messenger (p.b.u.h)?" (4462) □

1501. Narrated `Aisha: When the Prophet (ﷺ) was healthy, he used to say, "No soul of a prophet is captured till he is shown his place in Paradise and then he is given the option." When death approached him while his head was on my thigh, he became unconscious and then recovered his consciousness. He then looked at the ceiling of the house and said, "O Allah! (with) the highest companions." I said (to myself), "Hence, he is not going to choose us." Then I realized that what he had said was the application of the narration which he used to mention to us when he was healthy. The last word he spoke was, "O Allah! (with) the highest companion." (4463) ☐

1502. Narrated `Aisha: When Allah's Messenger (ﷺ) died, he was covered with a Hibra Burd (green square decorated garment). (5814) ☐

1503. Narrated Abu Burda: Aisha brought out to us a Kisa and an Izar and said, "The Prophet (ﷺ) died while wearing these two." (Kisa, a square black piece of woolen cloth. Izar, a sheet cloth garment covering the lower half of the body). (5818) ☐

1504. Narrated `Aisha: There was a leather or wood container full of water in front of Allah's Messenger (ﷺ) (at the time of his death). He would put his hand into the water and rub his face with it, saying, "None has the right to be worshipped but Allah! No doubt, death has its stupors." Then he raised his hand and started saying, "(O Allah!) with the highest companions." (See Qur'an 4:69) (and kept on saying it) till he expired and his hand dropped." (6510) ☐

1505. Narrated `Aisha: The Prophet (ﷺ) died while his armor was mortgaged to a Jew for thirty Sa's of barley. (4467) ☐

62. TAFSEER

1506. NARRATED IBN ABU MULAIKA (RA): Ibn `Abbas recited: "(Respite will be granted) until when the Apostles gave up hope (of their people) and thought that they were denied (by their people). There came to them Our Help ...." (12.110) reading Kudhibu without doubling the sound 'dh', and that was what he understood of the

Verse. Then he went on reciting: "...even the Apostle and those who believed along with him said: When (will come) Allah's Help? Yes, verily, Allah's Help is near." (2.214) Then I met `Urwa bin Az-Zubair and I mentioned that to him. He said, "Aisha said, 'Allah forbid! By Allah, Allah never promised His Apostle anything but he knew that it would certainly happen before he died. But trials were continuously presented before the Apostles till they were afraid that their followers would accuse them of telling lies. So I used to recite: -- "Till they (come to) think that they were treated as liars." reading 'Kudh-dhibu with double 'dh.' (4524) □

1507. Narrated Nafi`: Whenever Ibn `Umar recited the Qur'an, he would not speak to anyone till he had finished his recitation. Once I held the Qur'an and he recited Surah-al-Baqara from his memory and then stopped at a certain Verse and said, "Do you know in what connection this Verse was revealed?" I replied, "No." He said, "It was revealed in such-and-such connection." Ibn `Umar then resumed his recitation. Nafi` added regarding the Verse:--"So go to your tilth when or how you will" Ibn `Umar said, "It means one should approach his wife in..." (4526)

1508. Narrated Jabir: Jews used to say: "If one has sexual intercourse with his wife from the back, then she will deliver a squint-eyed child." So this Verse was revealed: -- "Your wives are a tilth unto you; so go to your tilth when or how you will." (2.223) (4528) □

* Some people imagine that it is permissible to have intercourse with one's wife in her back passage. But this is a misunderstanding of the verse. Allaah says "so go to your tilth when or how you will" which means that all variations of intercourse are permitted, so long as it is in the place of tilth, i.e., the vagina, not the back passage. So it is permissible for a man to have intercourse with his wife from behind or from in front or lying on their sides so long as it is in the place of tilth and not the back passage. The vagina and penis were made for each other. But the tongue and lips were not made to contact the vagina nor the anus or rectum. Also, the penis and anus were not made for each other. The anus is different from the vagina in the following points:

1- The vagina is self-lubricating to allow for tense sex and back and forth strokes by the penis. The anus does not have this.

2- The vagina is stretchable that even a baby can come out of it. The anus is not.

3- The vagina has a clitorous and a G-spot (about 2 inches inside the vagina), which allow for sensational feelings for the woman to occur during sex. The anus and rectum have none.

4- Anal sex weakens the anus' muscles that hold the feces from coming out on their own. One would eventually need to wear adult diapers during his/her young years if they regularly practice anal sex.

1509. Narrated Ibn Az-Zubair: I said to `Uthman, "This Verse which is in Surah-al-Baqara: "Those of you who die and leave widows behind...without turning them out." has been abrogated by another Verse. Why then do you write it (in the Qur'an)?" `Uthman said. "Leave it (where it is), O the son of my brother, for I will not shift anything of it (i.e. the Qur'an) from its original position." (4536) □

1510. Narrated Ubaid bin Umair: Once `Umar (bin Al-Khattab) said to the companions of the Prophet (ﷺ) "What do you think about this Verse:--"Does any of you wish that he should have a garden?" They replied, "Allah knows best." `Umar became angry and said, "Either say that you know or say that you do not know!" On that Ibn `Abbas said, "O chief of the believers! I have something in my mind to say about it." `Umar said, "O son of my brother! Say, and do not under estimate yourself." Ibn `Abbas said, "This Verse has been set up as an example for deeds." `Umar said, "What kind of deeds?" Ibn `Abbas said, "For deeds." `Umar said, "This is an example for a rich man who does goods out of obedience of Allah and then Allah sends him Satan whereupon he commits sins till all his good deeds are lost." (4538) □

1511. Narrated Ibn `Umar: This Verse:--"Whether you show what is in your minds or conceal it..." (2.284) was abrogated. (4545) □

1512. Narrated `Aisha: Allah's Messenger (ﷺ) recited the Verse: "It is He who has sent down to you the Book. In it are Verses that are entirely clear, they are the foundation of the Book, others not entirely clear. So as for those in whose hearts there is a deviation (from the Truth). Follow thereof that is not entirely clear seeking affliction and searching for its hidden meanings; but no one knows its hidden meanings but Allah. And those who are firmly grounded in knowledge say: "We believe in it (i.e. in the Qur'an) the whole of it (i.e. its clear and unclear Verses) are from our Lord. And none receive admonition except men of understanding." (3.7) Then Allah's Messenger (ﷺ) said, "If you see those who follow thereof that is not entirely clear, then they are those whom Allah has named [as having deviation (from the Truth)] 'So beware of them." (4547) □

1513. Narrated Abu Huraira: The Verse: "You (true Muslims) are the best of peoples ever raised up for mankind." means, the best of peoples for the people, as you bring them with chains on their necks till they embrace Islam. (4557) □

1514. Narrated Jabir bin `Abdullah: The Verse: "When two parties from among you were about to lose heart, but Allah was their Protector," (3.122) was revealed concerning us, and we were the two parties, i.e. Banu Haritha and Banu Salama, and we do not wish (that it had not been revealed) or I would not have been pleased (if it had not been revealed), for Allah says: ".Allah was their Protector." (4558) □

1515. Narrated Salim's father: That he heard Allah's Messenger (ﷺ) on raising his head from the bowing in the last rak`a in the Fajr prayer, saying, "O Allah, curse such-and-such person and such-and-such person, and such-and-such person," after saying, "Allah hears him who sends his praises to Him, O our Lord, all praise is for you." So Allah revealed: "Not for you (O Muhammad) (but for Allah) is the decision, verily they are indeed wrongdoers." (3.128) (4559) □

1516. Narrated Ibn `Abbas: 'Allah is Sufficient for us and He Is the Best Disposer of affairs," was said by Abraham when he was thrown into the fire; and it was said by Muhammad when they (hypocrites) said, "A great army is gathering against you, therefore, fear them," but it only increased their faith and they said: "Allah is

Sufficient for us, and He is the Best Disposer (of affairs, for us)." (3.173)(4563)☐

1517. Narrated Ibn `Abbas: The last statement of Abraham when he was thrown into the fire was: "Allah is Sufficient for us and He is the Best Disposer (of affairs for us)." (3.173) (4564) ☐

1518. Narrated Abu Sa`id Al-Khudri: During the lifetime of Allah's Messenger (ﷺ), some men among the hypocrites used to remain behind him (i.e. did not accompany him) when he went out for a Ghazwa and they would be pleased to stay at home behind Allah's Messenger (ﷺ) When Allah's Messenger (ﷺ) returned (from the battle) they would put forward (false) excuses and take oaths, wishing to be praised for what they had not done. So there was revealed: -- "Think not that those who rejoice in what they have done, and love to be praised for what they have not done..." (3.188) (4567) ☐

1519. Narrated Alqama bin Waqqas: Marwan said to his gatekeeper, "Go to Ibn `Abbas, O Rafi`, and say, 'If everybody who rejoices in what he has done, and likes to be praised for what he has not done, will be punished, then all of us will be punished." Ibn `Abbas said, "What connection have you with this case? It was only that the Prophet (ﷺ) called the Jews and asked them about something, and they hid the truth and told him something else, and showed him that they deserved praise for the favor of telling him the answer to his question, and they became happy with what they had concealed. Then Ibn `Abbas recited: -- "(And remember) when Allah took a Covenant (an agreement) from those who were given the Scripture...and those who rejoice in what they have done and love to be praised for what they have not done.'" (3.187-188) (4568) ☐

1520. Narrated Ibn `Abbas: The Verse: "Obey Allah and Obey the Apostle and those of you (Muslims) who are in authority." (4.59) was revealed in connection with `Abdullah bin Hudhafa bin Qais bin `Adi' when the Prophet (ﷺ) appointed him as the commander of a Sariyya (army detachment). (4584) ☐

1521. Narrated Ibn `Abbas: Regarding the Verse: "And say not to anyone who offers you peace (by accepting Islam), you are not a believer." There was a man amidst his sheep. The Muslims pursued him, and he said (to them) "Peace be on you." But they killed him and took over his sheep. Thereupon Allah revealed in that concern, the above Verse up to: -- "...seeking the perishable good of this life." (4.94) i.e. those sheep. (4591) ☐

1522. Narrated Muhammad bin `Abdur-Rahman Abu Al-Aswad: The people of Medina were forced to prepare an army (to fight against Sham during the caliphate of `Abdullah bin Az-Zubair at Mecca), and I was enlisted in it; Then I met `Ikrima, the freed slave of Ibn `Abbas, and informed him (about it), and he forbade me strongly to do so (to enlist in that army), and then said, "Ibn `Abbas informed me that some Muslim people were with the pagans, increasing the number of the pagans against Allah's Messenger (ﷺ). An arrow used to be shot which would hit one of them (the Muslims in the company of the pagans) and kill him, or he would be struck and killed (with a sword)." Then Allah revealed: "Verily! as for those whom the angels take (in death) while they are wronging themselves (by staying among the disbelievers)" (4.97) Abu Al-Aswad also narrated it. (4596) ☐

1523. Narrated Al-Aswad: While we were sitting in a circle in `Abdullah's gathering, Hudhaifa came and stopped before us, and greeted us and then said, "People better than you became hypocrites." Al-Aswad said: I testify the uniqueness of Allah! Allah says: "Verily! The hypocrites will be in the lowest depths of the Fire." (4.145) On that `Abdullah smiled and Hudhaifa sat somewhere in the Mosque. `Abdullah then got up and his companions (sitting around him) dispersed. Hudhaifa then threw a pebble at me (to attract my attention). I went to him and he said, "I was surprised at `Abdullah's smile though he understood what I said. Verily, people better than you became hypocrite and then repented and Allah forgave them." (4602) ☐

1524. Narrated Abu Qilaba: That he was sitting behind `Umar bin `Abdul `Aziz and the people mentioned and mentioned (about at-Qasama) and they said (various things), and said that the Caliphs had permitted it. `Umar bin `Abdul `Aziz turned towards Abu Qilaba who was behind him and said. "What do you say, O `Abdullah bin Zaid?" or said, "What do you say, O Abu Qilaba?" Abu Qilaba said, "I do not know that killing a person is lawful in Islam except in three cases: a married person committing illegal sexual intercourse, one who has murdered somebody unlawfully, or one who wages war against Allah and His Apostle." 'Anbasa said, "Anas narrated to us such-and-such." Abu Qilaba said, "Anas narrated to me in this concern, saying, some people came to the Prophet (ﷺ) and they spoke to him saying, 'The climate of this land does not suit us.' The Prophet (ﷺ) said, 'These are camels belonging to us, and they are to be taken out to the pasture. So take them out and drink of their milk and urine.' So they took them and set out and drank of their urine and milk, and having recovered, they attacked the shepherd, killed him and drove away the camels.' Why should there be any delay in punishing them as they murdered (a person) and waged war against Allah and His Apostle and frightened Allah's Messenger (ﷺ)?" 'Anbasa said, "I testify the uniqueness of Allah!" Abu Qilaba said, "Do you suspect me?" 'Anbasa said, "No, Anas narrated that (Hadith) to us." Then 'Anbasa added, "O the people of such-and-such (country), you will remain in good state as long as Allah keeps this (man) and the like of this (man) amongst you." (4610) □

1525. Narrated `Aisha: Whoever tells that Muhammad concealed part of what was revealed to him, is a liar, for Allah says: "O Apostle (Muhammad)! Proclaim (the Message) which has been sent down to you from your Lord." (5.67) (4612) □

1526. Narrated Abu Wail: `Abdullah (bin Mas`ud) said, "None has more sense of ghaira than Allah therefore - He prohibits shameful sins (illegal sexual intercourse, etc.) whether committed openly or secretly. And none loves to be praised more than Allah does, and for this reason He praises Himself." I asked Abu Wali, "Did you hear it from `Abdullah?" He said, "Yes," I said, "Did `Abdullah ascribe it to Allah's Messenger (ﷺ)?" He said, "Yes." (4634) □

1527. Narrated Abu Huraira: Allah's Messenger (ﷺ) said, "The Hour will not be established until the sun rises from the West: and when the people see it, then whoever will be living on the surface of the earth will have faith, and that is (the time) when no good will it do to a soul to believe then, if it believed not before." (6.158)

(4635) ☐

1528. `Abdullah bin Az-Zubair said: Allah ordered His Prophet to forgive the people their misbehavior (towards him). (4644) ☐

1529. Narrated Sa`id bin Jubair: I asked Ibn `Abbas regarding Surah-al-Anfal. He said, "It was revealed in connection with the Battle of Badr." (4645) ☐

1530. Narrated Ibn `Abbas: Regarding the Verse: "Verily! The worst of beasts in the Sight of Allah are the deaf and the dumb---- those who understand not." (8.22) (The people referred to here) were some persons from the tribe of Bani `Abd-Addar. (4646) ☐

1531. Narrated Anas bin Malik: Abu Jahl said, "O Allah! If this (Qur'an) is indeed the Truth from You, then rain down on us a shower of stones from the sky or bring on us a painful torment." So Allah revealed: "But Allah would not punish them while you were amongst them, nor He will punish them while they seek (Allah's) forgiveness..." (8.33) And why Allah should not punish them while they turn away (men) from Al- Masjid-al-Haram..." (8.33-34) (4648) ☐

1532. Narrated Ibn `Abbas: When the Verse: "If there are twenty steadfast amongst you, they will overcome two hundred." (8.65) was revealed, then it became obligatory for the Muslims that one (Muslim) should not flee from ten (non-Muslims). Sufyan (the sub-narrator) once said, "Twenty (Muslims) should not flee before two hundred (non Muslims)." Then there was revealed: 'But now Allah has lightened your (task)...' (8.66) So it became obligatory that one-hundred (Muslims) should not flee before two hundred (non-muslims). (Once Sufyan said extra, "The Verse: 'Urge the believers to the fight. If there are twenty steadfast amongst you (Muslims)...' was revealed.) Sufyan said, "Ibn Shabrama said, "I see that this order is applicable to the obligation of enjoining good and forbidding evil." (4652) ☐

1533. Narrated Abu Huraira: Allah's Messenger (ﷺ) said, "The Kanz (money, the Zakat of which is not paid) of anyone of you will appear in the form of bald-headed poisonous male snake on the Day of Resurrection." (4659) □

1534. Narrated Samura bin Jundab: Allah's Messenger (ﷺ) said, "Tonight two (visitors) came to me (in my dream) and took me to a town built with gold bricks and silver bricks. There we met men who, half of their bodies, look like the most handsome human beings you have ever seen, and the other half, the ugliest human beings you have ever seen. Those two visitors said to those men, 'Go and dip yourselves in that river. So they dipped themselves therein and then came to us, their ugliness having disappeared and they were in the most handsome shape. The visitors said, 'The first is the Garden of Eden and that is your dwelling place.' Then they added, 'As for those people who were half ugly and half handsome, they were those who mixed good deeds and bad deeds, but Allah forgave them." (4674) □

1535. Narrated Muhammad bin `Abbas bin Ja`far: That he heard Ibn `Abbas reciting: "No doubt! They fold up their breasts." (11.5) and asked him about its explanation. He said, "Some people used to hide themselves while answering the call of nature in an open space lest they be exposed to the sky, and also when they had sexual relation with their wives in an open space lest they be exposed to the sky, so the above revelation was sent down regarding them." (4681) □

1536. Narrated Abu Musa: Allah's Messenger (ﷺ) said, "Allah gives respite to the oppressor, but when He takes him over, He never releases him." Then he recited: "such is the seizure of your Lord when He seizes (population of) towns in the midst of their wrong: Painful indeed, and severe is His seizure.' (11.102) (4686) □

1537. Narrated Abu Wail: `Abdullah bin Mas`ud recited "Haita laka (Come you)," and added, "We recite it as we were taught it." (4692) □

1538. Narrated `Urwa bin Az-Zubair: That when he asked `Aisha about the statement of Allah "Until when the Apostles gave up hope (of their people)." (12.110) she told him (its meaning), `Urwa added, "I said, 'Did they (Apostles) suspect that they were betrayed (by Allah) or that they were treated as liars by (their people)?' `Aisha said, '(They suspected) that they were treated as liars by (their people),' I said,

'But they were sure that their people treated them as liars and it was not a matter of suspicion.' She said, 'Yes, upon my life they were sure about it.' I said to her. 'So they (Apostles) suspected that they were betrayed (by Allah).' She said, "Allah forbid! The Apostles never suspected their Lord of such a thing.' I said, 'What about this Verse then?' She said, 'It is about the Apostles' followers who believed in their Lord and trusted their Apostles, but the period of trials was prolonged and victory was delayed till the Apostles gave up all hope of converting those of the people who disbelieved them and the Apostles thought that their followers treated them as liars; thereupon Allah's help came to them. (4695) □

1539. Narrated Abu Huraira: The Prophet (ﷺ) said, "When Allah has ordained some affair in the Heaven, the angels beat with their wings in obedience to His statement, which sounds like a chain dragged over a rock." (`Ali and other sub-narrators said, "The sound reaches them.") "Until when fear is banished from their (angels) hearts, they (angels) say, 'What was it that your Lord said? They say, 'The truth; And He is the Most High, the Most Great.' (34.23) Then those who gain a hearing by stealing (i.e. devils) will hear Allah's Statement: 'Those who gain a hearing by stealing, (stand one over the other like this). (Sufyan, to illustrate this, spread the fingers of his right hand and placed them one over the other horizontally.) A flame may overtake and burn the eavesdropper before conveying the news to the one below him; or it may not overtake him till he has conveyed it to the one below him, who in his turn, conveys it to the one below him, and so on till they convey the news to the earth. (Or probably Sufyan said, "Till the news reaches the earth.") Then the news is inspired to a sorcerer who would add a hundred lies to it. His prophecy will prove true (as far as the heavenly news is concerned). The people will say. 'Didn't he tell us that on such-and-such a day, such-and-such a thing will happen? We have found that is true because of the true news heard from heaven." (4701) □

1540. Narrated Ibn `Abbas: Those who have made their Scripture into parts are the people of the Scripture who divided it into portions and believed in a part of it and disbelieved the other. (4705) □

1541. Narrated `Abdullah: Regarding the Verse: 'Those whom they call upon (worship) (like Jesus the Son of Mary or angels etc.) desire (for themselves) means of access, to their Lord....' (17.57) (It was revealed regarding) some Jinns who used to be worshipped (by human beings). They later embraced Islam (while those people kept on worshipping them). (4715) ☐

1542. Narrated Ibn `Abbas: Regarding: 'And We granted the vision (Ascension to the Heaven "Miraj") which We showed you (O Muhammad as an actual eye witness) but as a trial for mankind.' (17.60) It was an actual eyewitness which was shown to Allah's Messenger (ﷺ) during the night he was taken on a journey (through the heavens). And the cursed tree is the tree of Az-Zaqqum (a bitter pungent tree which grows at the bottom of Hell). (4716) ☐

1543. Narrated Ibn `Umar: On the Day of Resurrection the people will fall on their knees and every nation will follow their prophet and they will say, "O so-and-so! Intercede (for us with Allah), "till (the right) intercession is given to the Prophet (Muhammad) and that will be the day when Allah will raise him into a station of praise and glory (i.e. Al-Maqam -al-Mahmud). (4718) ☐

1544. Narrated `Abdullah: While I was in the company of the Prophet (ﷺ) on a farm and he was reclining on a palm leave stalk, some Jews passed by. Some of them said to the others. "Ask him about the spirit." Some of them said, "What urges you to ask him about it" Others said, "(Don't) lest he should give you a reply which you dislike." But they said, "Ask him." So they asked him about the Spirit. The Prophet (ﷺ) kept quiet and did not give them any answer. I knew that he was being divinely inspired so I stayed at my place. When the divine inspiration had been revealed, the Prophet (ﷺ) said. "They ask you (O, Muhammad) concerning the Spirit, Say: "The spirit," its knowledge is with my Lord; and of knowledge you (mankind) have been given only a Little." (17.85) (4721) ☐

1545. Narrated Ibn `Abbas: (regarding): 'Neither say your, prayer aloud, nor say it in a low tone.' (17.110) This Verse was revealed while Allah's Messenger (ﷺ) was hiding himself in Mecca. When he prayed with his companions, he used to raise his voice with the recitation of Qur'an, and if the pagans happened to hear him, they would abuse the Qur'an, the One who revealed it and the one who brought it. Therefore Allah said to His Prophet: 'Neither say your prayer aloud.' (17.110) i.e. do not recite aloud lest the pagans should hear you, but follow a way between. (4722) □

1546. Narrated Mus`ab: I asked my father, "Was the Verse: 'Say: (O Muhammad) Shall We tell you the greatest losers in respect of their deeds?'(18.103) revealed regarding Al-Haruriyya?" He said, "No, but regarding the Jews and the Christians, for the Jews disbelieved Muhammad and the Christians disbelieved in Paradise and say that there are neither meals nor drinks therein. Al- Hururiyya are those people who break their pledge to Allah after they have confirmed that they will fulfill it, and Sa`d used to call them 'Al-Fasiqin (evildoers who forsake Allah's obedience). (4728) □

1547. Narrated Abu Huraira: Allah's Messenger (ﷺ) said, "On the Day of Resurrection, a huge fat man will come who will not weigh, the weight of the wing of a mosquito in Allah's Sight." and then the Prophet (ﷺ) added, 'We shall not give them any weight on the Day of Resurrection ' (18.105) (4729) □

1548: Narrated Ibn `Abbas: Regarding the Verse: "And among men is he who worships Allah's as it were on the very edge." (22.11). A man used to come to Medina as if his wife brought a son and his mares produces offspring. He would say, "This religion (Islam) is good," but if his wife did not give birth to a child and his mares produced no offspring, he would say, "This religion is bad." (4742) □

1549. Narrated Safiya bint Shaiba: `Aisha used to say: "When (the Verse): "They should draw their veils over their necks and bosoms," was revealed, (the ladies) cut their waist sheets at the edges and covered their heads and faces with those cut pieces of cloth." (4758) □

1550. Narrated Anas bin Malik: A man said, "O Allah's Prophet! Will Allah gather the non-believers on their faces on the Day of Resurrection?" He said, "Will not the

One Who made him walk on his feet in this world, be able to make him walk on his face on the Day of Resurrection?" (Qatada, a subnarrator, said: Yes, By the Power of Our Lord!) (4760) ☐

1551. Narrated Sa`id bin Jubair: I asked Ibn `Abbas about Allah's saying: '... this reward is Hell Fire.' (4.93) He said, "No repentance is accepted from him (i.e. the murderer of a believer)." I asked him regarding the saying of Allah: 'Those who invoke not with Allah any other god.'... (25.68) He said, "This Verse was revealed concerning the pagans of the pre-lslamic period." (4764) ☐

1552. Narrated `Aisha: Allah's Messenger (ﷺ) came to me when Allah ordered him to give option to his wives. So Allah's Messenger (ﷺ) started with me, saying, "I am going to mention to you something but you should not hasten (to give your reply) unless you consult your parents.' He knew that my parents would not order me to leave him. Then he said, "Allah says: "O Prophet! Say to your wives..." (33.28-29) On that I said to him, "Then why should I consult my parents? Verily, I seek Allah, His Apostle and the Home of the Hereafter." (4785) ☐

1553. Narrated Aisha: Sauda went out to answer the call of nature after it was made obligatory (for all the Muslims ladies) to observe the veil. She had a large frame and everybody who knew her before could recognize her. So `Umar bin Al-Khattab saw her and said, "O Sauda! By Allah, you cannot hide yourself from us, so think of a way by which you should not be recognized on going out. Sauda returned while Allah's Messenger (ﷺ) was in my house taking his supper and a bone covered with meat was in his hand. She entered and said, "O Allah's Messenger (ﷺ)! I went out to answer the call of nature and `Umar said to me so-and-so." Then Allah inspired him (the Prophet) and when the state of inspiration was over and the bone was still in his hand as he had not put it down, he said (to Sauda), "You (women) have been allowed to go out for your needs." (4795) ☐

1554. Narrated Masruq: We came upon `Abdullah bin Mas`ud and he said "O people! If somebody knows something, he can say it, but if he does not know it, he should say, "Allah knows better,' for it is a sign of having knowledge to say about something which one does not know, 'Allah knows better.' Allah said to His Prophet: 'Say (O Muhammad!) No wage do I ask of You for this (Qur'an) nor am I one of the pretenders (a person who pretends things which do not exist).' (38.86) (4809) □

1555. Narrated Ibn `Abbas: Some pagans who committed murders in great number and committed illegal sexual intercourse excessively, came to Muhammad and said, "O Muhammad! Whatever you say and invite people to, is good: but we wish if you could inform us whether we can make an expiration for our (past evil) deeds." So the Divine Verses came: 'Those who invoke not with Allah any other god, not kill such life as Allah has forbidden except for just cause, nor commit illegal sexual intercourse.' (25.68) And there was also revealed: -- 'Say: O My slaves who have transgressed against their souls! Despair not of the Mercy of Allah.' (39.53) (4810) □

1556. Narrated Ibn Abi Mulaika: The two righteous persons were about to be ruined. They were Abu Bakr and `Umar who raised their voices in the presence of the Prophet (ﷺ) when a mission from Bani Tamim came to him. One of the two recommended Al-Aqra' bin Habeas, the brother of Bani Mujashi (to be their governor) while the other recommended somebody else. (Nafi`, the sub-narrator said, I do not remember his name). Abu Bakr said to `Umar, "You wanted nothing but to oppose me!" `Umar said, "I did not intend to oppose you." Their voices grew loud in that argument, so Allah revealed: 'O you who believe! Raise not your voices above the voice of the Prophet.' (49.2) Ibn Az-Zubair said, "Since the revelation of this Verse, `Umar used to speak in such a low tone that the Prophet (ﷺ) had to ask him to repeat his statements." But Ibn Az-Zubair did not mention the same about his (maternal) grandfather (i.e. Abu Bakr). (4845) □

1557. Narrated Masruq: I said to `Aisha, "O Mother! Did Prophet Muhammad see his Lord?" Aisha said, "What you have said makes my hair stand on end! Know that if somebody tells you one of the following three things, he is a liar: Whoever tells you that Muhammad saw his Lord, is a liar." Then Aisha recited the Verse: 'No vision can grasp Him, but His grasp is over all vision. He is the Most Courteous Well-

Acquainted with all things.' (6.103) 'It is not fitting for a human being that Allah should speak to him except by inspiration or from behind a veil.' (42.51) `Aisha further said, "And whoever tells you that the Prophet knows what is going to happen tomorrow, is a liar." She then recited: 'No soul can know what it will earn tomorrow.' (31.34) She added: "And whoever tell you that he concealed (some of Allah's orders), is a liar." Then she recited: 'O Apostle! Proclaim (the Message) which has been sent down to you from your Lord...' (5.67) `Aisha added. "But the Prophet (ﷺ) saw Gabriel in his true form twice." (4855) ☐

1558. Narrated Sa`id bin Jubair: I asked Ibn `Abbas about Surah Al-Tauba, and he said, "Surah Al-Tauba? It is exposure (of all the evils of the infidels and the hypocrites). And it continued revealing (that the oft-repeated expression): '...and of them ...and of them.' till they started thinking that none would be left unmentioned therein." I said, "(What about) Surah Al-Anfal?" He replied, "Surah Al-Anfal was revealed in connection with the Badr Battle." I said, "(What about) Surah Al-Hashr?" He replied, "It was revealed in connection with Bani an-Nadir." (4882) ☐

1559. Narrated Abu Huraira: While we were sitting with the Prophet (ﷺ) Surah Al-Jumu'a was revealed to him, and when the Verse, "And He (Allah) has sent him (Muhammad) also to other (Muslims).....' (62.3) was recited by the Prophet, I said, "Who are they, O Allah's Messenger (ﷺ)?" The Prophet (ﷺ) did not reply till I repeated my question thrice. At that time, Salman Al-Farisi was with us. So Allah's Messenger (ﷺ) put his hand on Salman, saying, "If Faith were at (the place of) Ath-Thuraiya (pleiades, the highest star), even then (some men or man from these people (i.e. Salman's folk) would attain it." (4897) ☐

1560. Narrated Zaid bin Arqam: While I was taking part in a Ghazwa. I heard `Abdullah bin Ubai (bin Abi Salul) saying. "Don't spend on those who are with Allah's Messenger (ﷺ), that they may disperse and go away from him. If we return (to Medina), surely, the more honorable will expel the meaner amongst them." I reported that (saying) to my uncle or to `Umar who, in his turn, informed the Prophet (ﷺ) of it. The Prophet (ﷺ) called me and I narrated to him the whole story. Then

Allah's Messenger (ﷺ) sent for `Abdullah bin Ubai and his companions, and they took an oath that they did not say that. So Allah's Messenger (ﷺ) disbelieved my saying and believed his. I was distressed as I never was before. I stayed at home and my uncle said to me. "You just wanted Allah's Messenger (ﷺ) to disbelieve your statement and hate you." So Allah revealed (the Sura beginning with) 'When the hypocrites come to you.' (63.1) The Prophet (ﷺ) then sent for me and recited it and said, "O Zaid! Allah confirmed your statement." (4900) □

1561. Narrated Jabir bin `Abdullah: We were in a Ghazwa (Sufyan once said, in an army) and a man from the emigrants kicked an Ansari man (on the buttocks with his foot). The Ansari man said, "O the Ansar! (Help!)" and the emigrant said. "O the emigrants! (Help!) Allah's Messenger (ﷺ) heard that and said, "What is this call for, which is characteristic of the period of ignorance?" They said, "O Allah's Messenger (ﷺ)! A man from the emigrants kicked one of the Ansar (on the buttocks with his foot)." Allah's Messenger (ﷺ) said, "Leave it (that call) as is a detestable thing." `Abdullah bin Ubai heard that and said, 'Have they (the emigrants) done so? By Allah, if we return Medina, surely, the more honorable will expel therefrom the meaner." When this statement reached the Prophet. `Umar got up an, said, "O Allah's Messenger (ﷺ)! Let me chop off the head of this hypocrite (`Abdullah bin Ubai)!" The Prophet (ﷺ) said "Leave him, lest the people say that Muhammad kills his companions." The Ansar were then more in number than the emigrants when the latter came to Medina, but later on the emigrant increased. (4905) □

1562. Narrated Ibn `Abbas: If someone says to his wife, "You are unlawful to me." he must make an expiation (for his oath). Ibn `Abbas added: There is for you in Allah's Messenger (ﷺ), an excellent example to follow. (4911) □

1563. Narrated `Aisha: Allah's Messenger (ﷺ) used to drink honey in the house of Zainab, the daughter of Jahsh, and would stay there with her. So Hafsa and I agreed secretly that, if he come to either of us, she would say to him. "It seems you have eaten Maghafir (a kind of bad-smelling resin), for I smell in you the smell of Maghafir," (We did so) and he replied. "No, but I was drinking honey in the house of Zainab, the daughter of Jahsh, and I shall never take it again. I have taken an oath as to that, and you should not tell anybody about it." (4912) □

1564. Narrated Ibn `Abbas: For the whole year I had the desire to ask `Umar bin Al-Khattab regarding the explanation of a Verse (in Surah Al-Tahrim) but I could not ask him because I respected him very much. When he went to perform the Hajj, I too went along with him. On our return, while we were still on the way home. `Umar went aside to answer the call of nature by the Arak trees. I waited till he finished and then I proceeded with him and asked him. "O chief of the Believers! Who were the two wives of the Prophet (ﷺ) who aided one another against him?" He said, "They were Hafsa and `Aisha." Then I said to him, "By Allah, I wanted to ask you about this a year ago, but I could not do so owing to my respect for you." `Umar said, "Do not refrain from asking me. If you think that I have knowledge (about a certain matter), ask me; and if I know (something about it), I will tell you." Then `Umar added, "By Allah, in the Pre-lslamic Period of Ignorance we did not pay attention to women until Allah revealed regarding them what He revealed regarding them and assigned for them what He has assigned. Once while I was thinking over a certain matter, my wife said, "I recommend that you do so-and-so." I said to her, "What have you got to do with this matter? Why do you poke your nose in a matter which I want to see fulfilled?" She said, how strange you are, O son of Al-Khattab! You don't want to be argued with whereas your daughter, Hafsa surely, argues with Allah's Messenger (ﷺ) so much that he remains angry for a full day!" `Umar then reported; how he at once put on his outer garment and went to Hafsa and said to her, "O my daughter! Do you argue with Allah's Messenger (ﷺ) so that he remains angry the whole day?" H. afsa said, "By Allah, we argue with him." `Umar said, "Know that I warn you of Allah's punishment and the anger of Allah's Messenger (ﷺ) . . . O my daughter! Don't be betrayed by the one who is proud of her beauty because of the love of Allah's Messenger (ﷺ) for her (Aisha)." `Umar addled, "Then I went out to Um Salama's house who was one of my relatives, and I talked to her. She said, O son of Al-Khattab! It is rather astonishing that you interfere in everything; you even want to interfere between Allah's Apostle and his wives!' By Allah, by her talk she influenced me so much that I lost some of my anger. I left her (and went home). At that time I had a friend from the Ansar who used to bring news (from the Prophet) in case of my absence, and I used to bring him the news if he was absent. In those days we were afraid of one of the kings of Ghassan tribe. We heard that he intended to move and attack us, so fear filled our hearts because of that. (One day) my Ansari friend unexpectedly knocked at my door, and said, "Open Open!' I said, 'Has the king of Ghassan come?' He said, 'No, but something worse; Allah's Messenger (﷽) has isolated himself from his wives.' I said, 'Let the nose of `Aisha and Hafsa be stuck to dust (humiliated)!' Then I put on my clothes and went to Allah's Messenger (﷽)'s residence, and behold, he was staying in an upper room of his to which he ascended by a ladder, and a black slave of Allah's Messenger (﷽) was (sitting) on the first step. I said to him, 'Say `Umar bin Al-Khattab is here.' Then the Prophet (﷽) admitted me and I narrated the story to Allah's Messenger (﷽). When I reached the story of Um Salama, Allah's Messenger (﷽) smiled while he was lying on a mat made of palm tree leaves with nothing between him and the mat. Underneath his head there was a leather pillow stuffed with palm fibres, and leaves of a saut tree were piled at his feet, and above his head hung a few water skins. On seeing the marks of the mat imprinted on his side, I wept. He said.' 'Why are you weeping?' I replied, "O Allah's Messenger (﷽)! Caesar and Khosrau are leading the life (Luxurious life) while you, Allah's Messenger (﷽) though you are, is living in destitute". The Prophet (﷽) then replied. 'Won't you be satisfied that they enjoy this world and we the Hereafter?'" (4913) □

1565. Narrated Ibn `Abbas: (regarding the Verse):-- 'Cruel after all that, base-born (of illegitimate birth).' (68.13) It was revealed in connection with a man from Quaraish who had a notable sign (Zanamah) similar to the notable sign which usually-hung on the neck of a sheep (to recognize it). (4917) □

1566. Narrated Abu Sa`id: I heard the Prophet (﷽) saying, "Allah will bring forth the severest Hour, and then all the Believers, men and women, will prostrate themselves before Him, but there will remain those who used to prostrate in the world for showing off and for gaining good reputation. Such people will try to prostrate (on the

Day of Judgment) but their backswill be as stiff as if it is one bone (a single vertebra). (4919) □

1567. Narrated Ibn `Abbas: Allah's Messenger (ﷺ) went out along with a group of his companions towards `Ukaz Market. At that time something intervened between the devils and the news of the Heaven, and flames were sent down upon them, so the devils returned. Their fellow-devils said, "What is wrong with you?" They said, "Something has intervened between us and the news of the Heaven, and fires (flames) have been shot at us." Their fellow-devils said, "Nothing has intervened between you and the news of the Heaven, but an important event has happened. Therefore, travel all over the world, east and west, and try to find out what has happened." And so they set out and travelled all over the world, east and west, looking for that thing which intervened between them and the news of the Heaven. Those of the devils who had set out towards Tihama, went to Allah's Messenger (ﷺ) at Nakhla (a place between Mecca and Taif) while he was on his way to `Ukaz Market while he was offering the Fajr prayer with his companions. When they heard the Holy Qur'an being recited (by Allah's Messenger (ﷺ)), they listened to it and said (to each other). This is the thing which has intervened between you and the news of the Heavens." Then they returned to their people and said, "O our people! We have really heard a wonderful recital (Qur'an). It gives guidance to the right, and we have believed therein. We shall not join in worship, anybody with our Lord." (See 72.1-2) Then Allah revealed to His Prophet (Surah al- Jinn): 'Say: It has been revealed to me that a group (3 to 9) of Jinns listened (to the Qur'an).' (72.1) The statement of the Jinns was revealed to him. (4921) □

1568. Narrated Yahya bin Abi Kathir: I asked Aba Salama bin `Abdur-Rahman about the first Surah revealed of the Qur'an. He replied "O you, wrapped-up (i.e. Al Muddaththir)." I said, "They say it was, 'Read, in the Name of your Lord Who created,' (i.e. Surah Al-`Alaq (the Clot)." On that, Abu Salama said, "I asked Jabir bin `Abdullah about that, saying the same as you have said, whereupon he said, 'I will not tell you except what Allah's Messenger (ﷺ) had told us. Allah's Messenger (ﷺ)

said, "I was in seclusion in the cave of Hira', and after I completed the limited period of my seclusion. I came down (from the cave) and heard a voice calling me. I looked to my right, but saw nothing. Then I looked up and saw something. So I went to Khadija (the Prophet's wife) and told her to wrap me up and pour cold water on me. So they wrapped me up and poured cold water on me." Then, 'O you, (Muhammad) wrapped up! Arise and warn,' (Surah Al Muddaththir) was revealed." (74.1) (4922) □

1569. Narrated Ibn `Abbas: The Prophet (ﷺ) used to move his tongue when the divine Inspiration was being revealed to him. (Sufyan, a subnarrator, demonstrated (how the Prophet (ﷺ) used to move his lips)) and added. "In order to memorize it." So Allah revealed: "Move not your tongue concerning (the Qur'an) to make haste therewith." (75.16) (4927) □

1570. Narrated Ibn `Abbas: (as regards) Allah's Statement: "Move not your tongue concerning (the Qur'an) to make haste therewith." (75.16) When Gabriel revealed the Divine Inspiration in Allah's Messenger (ﷺ) , he (Allah's Messenger (ﷺ)) moved his tongue and lips, and that state used to be very hard for him, and that movement indicated that revelation was taking place. So Allah revealed in Surah Al-Qiyama which begins: 'I do swear by the Day of Resurrection...' (75) the Verses:-- 'Move not your tongue concerning (the Qur'an) to make haste therewith. It is for Us to collect it (Qur'an) in your mind, and give you the ability to recite it by heart. (75.16-17) Ibn `Abbas added: It is for Us to collect it (Qur'an) (in your mind), and give you the ability to recite it by heart means, "When We reveal it, listen. Then it is for Us to explain it," means, 'It is for us to explain it through your tongue.' So whenever Gabriel came to Allah's Messenger (ﷺ) ' he would keep quiet (and listen), and when the Angel left, the Prophet (ﷺ) would recite that revelation as Allah promised him. (4929) □

1571. Narrated `Abdullah: While we were with Allah's Messenger (ﷺ) in a cave, Surah "Wal MurSalah" was revealed to him and we received it directly from his mouth as soon as he had received the revelation. Suddenly a snake came out and Allah's Messenger (ﷺ) said, "Get at it and kill it!" We ran to kill it but it outstripped us.

Allah's Apostle said, "It has escaped your evil, as you too, have escaped its." (4931) ☐

1572. Narrated Al-Bara: The first of the companions of the Prophet (ﷺ) who came to us (in Medina), were Mus`ab bin `Umar and Ibn Um Maktum, and they started teaching us the Qur'an. Then came `Ammar, Bilal and Sa`d. Afterwards `Umar bin Al-Kkattab came along with a batch of twenty (men): and after that the Prophet (ﷺ) came. I never saw the people of Medina so pleased with anything as they were with his arrival, so that even the little boys and girls were saying, "This is Allah's Messenger (ﷺ) who has come." He (the Prophet (ﷺ)) did not come (to Medina) till I had learnt Surah Al-Ala and also other similar Suras. (4941) ☐

1573. Narrated Aisha: The commencement of the Divine Inspiration to Allah's Messenger (ﷺ) was in the form of true dreams. The Angel came to him and said, "Read, in the Name of your Lord Who has created (all that exists), has created man a clot. Read! And your Lord is Most Generous..." (96.1,2,3) (4955) ☐

1574. Narrated Ibn `Abbas: Abu Jahl said, "If I see Muhammad praying at the Ka`ba, I will tread on his neck." When the Prophet (ﷺ) heard of that, he said, "If he does so, the Angels will snatch him away." (4958) ☐

1575. Narrated Anas: When the Prophet (ﷺ) was made to ascend to the Heavens, he said (after his return), "I came upon a river the banks of which were made of tents of hollow pearls. I asked Gabriel. What is this (river?) He replied, 'This is the Kauthar.' (4964) ☐

1576. Narrated Abu Ubaida: I asked `Aisha 'regarding the verse: 'Verily we have granted you the Kauthar.' She replied, "The Kauthar is a river which has been given to your Prophet on the banks of which there are (tents of) hollow pearls and its utensils are as numberless as the stars." (4965) ☐

1577. Narrated Abu Bishr: Sa`id bin Jubair said that Ibn `Abbas said about Al-Kauthar. "That is the good which Allah has bestowed upon His Apostle." I said to Sa`id bin Jubair. "But the people claim that it is a river in Paradise." Sa`id said, "The river in Paradise is part of the good which Allah has bestowed on His Apostle." (4966)

□

63. COMPILATION OF THE QURAN

1578. NARRATED ANAS BIN MALIK (RA): Allah sent down His Divine Inspiration to His Apostle continuously and abundantly during the period preceding his death till He took him unto Him. That was the period of the greatest part of revelation; and Allah's Messenger (ﷺ) died after that. (4982) □

1579. Narrated Zaid bin Thabit: Abu Bakr As-Siddiq sent for me when the people of Yamama had been killed (i.e., a number of the Prophet's Companions who fought against Musailima). (I went to him) and found `Umar bin Al- Khattab sitting with him. Abu Bakr then said (to me), "`Umar has come to me and said: "Casualties were heavy among the Qurra' of the Qur'an (i.e. those who knew the Qur'an by heart) on the day of the Battle of Yamama, and I am afraid that more heavy casualties may take place among the Qurra' on other battlefields, whereby a large part of the Qur'an may be lost. Therefore I suggest, you (Abu Bakr) order that the Qur'an be collected." I said to `Umar, "How can you do something which Allah's Apostle did not do?" `Umar said, "By Allah, that is a good project." `Umar kept on urging me to accept his proposal till Allah opened my chest for it and I began to realize the good in the idea which `Umar had realized." Then Abu Bakr said (to me). 'You are a wise young man and we do not have any suspicion about you, and you used to write the Divine Inspiration for Allah's Messenger (ﷺ). So you should search for (the fragmentary scripts of) the Qur'an and collect it in one book." By Allah if they had ordered me to shift one of the mountains, it would not have been heavier for me than this ordering me to collect the Qur'an. Then I said to Abu Bakr, "How will you do something which Allah's Messenger (ﷺ) did not do?" Abu Bakr replied, "By Allah, it is a good project." Abu Bakr kept on urging me to accept his idea until Allah opened my chest for what He had opened the chests of Abu Bakr and `Umar. So I started looking for the Qur'an and collecting it from (what was written on) palme stalks, thin white stones and also from the men who knew it by heart, till I found the last Verse of Surah at-Tauba (Repentance) with Abi Khuzaima Al-Ansari, and I did not find it with anybody other than him. The Verse is: 'Verily there has come unto you an Apostle (Muhammad) from amongst yourselves. It grieves him that you should receive any injury or difficulty..(till the end of Surah-Baraa' (at-Tauba) (9.128-129). Then the complete manuscripts (copy) of the Qur'an remained with Abu Bakr till he died, then with `Umar till the end of his life, and then with Hafsa, the daughter of `Umar. (4986) □

1580. Narrated Anas bin Malik: Hudhaifa bin Al-Yaman came to `Uthman at the time when the people of Sham and the people of Iraq were waging war to conquer Arminya and Adharbijan. Hudhaifa was afraid of their (the people of Sham and Iraq) differences in the recitation of the Qur'an, so he said to `Uthman, "O chief of the Believers! Save this nation before they differ about the Book (Qur'an) as Jews and the Christians did before." So `Uthman sent a message to Hafsa saying, "Send us the manuscripts of the Qur'an so that we may compile the Qur'anic materials in perfect copies and return the manuscripts to you." Hafsa sent it to `Uthman. `Uthman then ordered Zaid bin Thabit, `Abdullah bin AzZubair, Sa`id bin Al-As and `AbdurRahman bin Harith bin Hisham to rewrite the manuscripts in perfect copies. `Uthman said to the three Quraishi men, "In case you disagree with Zaid bin Thabit on any point in the Qur'an, then write it in the dialect of Quraish, the Qur'an was revealed in their tongue." They did so, and when they had written many copies, `Uthman returned the original manuscripts to Hafsa. `Uthman sent to every Muslim province one copy of what they had copied, and ordered that all the other Qur'anic materials, whether written in fragmentary manuscripts or whole copies, be burnt. (4987) □

1581. Zaid bin Thabit added, "A verse from Surah Ahzab was missed by me when we copied the Qur'an and I used to hear Allah's Messenger (ﷺ) reciting it. So we searched for it and found it with Khuza`ima bin Thabit Al-Ansari. (That Verse was):'Among the Believers are men who have been true in their covenant with Allah.' (33.23) (4988) ☐

1582. Narrated `Abdullah bin `Abbas: Allah's Messenger (ﷺ) said, "Gabriel recited the Qur'an to me in one way. Then I requested him (to read it in another way), and continued asking him to recite it in other ways, and he recited it in several ways till he ultimately recited it in seven different ways." (4991) ☐

1583. Narrated `Umar bin Al-Khattab: I heard Hisham bin Hakim reciting Surah Al-Furqan during the lifetime of Allah's Messenger (ﷺ) and I listened to his recitation and noticed that he recited in several different ways which Allah's Messenger (ﷺ) had not taught me. I was about to jump over him during his prayer, but I controlled my temper, and when he had completed his prayer, I put his upper garment around his neck and seized him by it and said, "Who taught you this Sura which I heard you reciting?" He replied, "Allah's Messenger (ﷺ) taught it to me." I said, "You have told a lie, for Allah's Messenger (ﷺ) has taught it to me in a different way from yours." So I dragged him to Allah's Messenger (ﷺ) and said (to Allah's Messenger (ﷺ)), "I heard this person reciting Surah Al-Furqan in a way which you haven't taught me!" On that Allah's Apostle said, "Release him, (O `Umar!) Recite, O Hisham!" Then he recited in the same way as I heard him reciting. Then Allah's Messenger (ﷺ) said, "It was revealed in this way," and added, "Recite, O `Umar!" I recited it as he had taught me. Allah's Messenger (ﷺ) then said, "It was revealed in this way. This Qur'an has been revealed to be recited in seven different ways, so recite of it whichever (way) is easier for you (or read as much of it as may be easy for you). (4992) ☐

1584. Narrated Yusuf bin Mahk: While I was with Aisha, the mother of the Believers, a person from Iraq came and asked, "What type of shroud is the best?" `Aisha said, "May Allah be merciful to you! What does it matter?" He said, "O mother of the Believers! Show me (the copy of) your Qur'an," She said, "Why?" He said, "In order to compile and arrange the Qur'an according to it, for people recite it with its Suras not in proper order." `Aisha said, "What does it matter which part of it you read first? (Be informed) that the first thing that was revealed thereof was a Sura from Al-

Mufassal, and in it was mentioned Paradise and the Fire. When the people embraced Islam, the Verses regarding legal and illegal things were revealed. If the first thing to be revealed was: 'Do not drink alcoholic drinks.' people would have said, 'We will never leave alcoholic drinks,' and if there had been revealed, 'Do not commit illegal sexual intercourse, 'they would have said, 'We will never give up illegal sexual intercourse.' While I was a young girl of playing age, the following Verse was revealed in Mecca to Muhammad: 'Nay! But the Hour is their appointed time (for their full recompense), and the Hour will be more grievous and more bitter.' (54.46) Sura Al-Baqara (The Cow) and Surah An-Nisa (The Women) were revealed while I was with him." Then `Aisha took out the copy of the Qur'an for the man and dictated to him the Verses of the Suras (in their proper order). (4993) ☐

1585. Narrated `Abdullah bin Mas`ud: Surah Bani-Israel, Al-Kahf (The Cave), Maryam, Taha, Al-Anbiya' (The prophets) are amongst my first earnings and my old property, and (in fact) they are my old property. (4994) ☐

1686. Narrated Shaqiq: `Abdullah said, "I learnt An-Naza'ir which the Prophet (ﷺ) used to recite in pairs in each rak`a." Then `Abdullah got up and Alqama accompanied him to his house, and when Alqama came out, we asked him (about those Suras). He said, "They are twenty Suras that start from the beginning of Al-Mufassal, according to the arrangement done by Ibn Mas`ud, and end with the Suras starting with Ha Mim, e.g. Ha Mim (the Smoke), and "About what they question one another?" (78.1) (4996) ☐

1587. Narrated Abu-Huraira: Gabriel used to repeat the recitation of the Qur'an with the Prophet (ﷺ) once a year, but he repeated it twice with him in the year he died. The Prophet (ﷺ) used to stay in I`tikaf for ten days every year (in the month of Ramadan), but in the year of his death, he stayed in I`tikaf for twenty days. (4998) ☐

1588. Narrated Masriq: `Abdullah bin `Amr mentioned `Abdullah bin Masud and said, "I shall ever love that man, for I heard the Prophet (ﷺ) saying, 'take (learn) the Qur'an from four: `Abdullah bin Masud, Salim, Mu`adh and Ubai bin Ka`b.'" (4999)

□

1589. Narrated Shaqiq bin Salama: Once `Abdullah bin Mas`ud delivered a sermon before us and said, "By Allah, I learnt over seventy Suras direct from Allah's Messenger (ﷺ). By Allah, the companions of the Prophet (ﷺ) came to know that I am one of those who know Allah's Book best of all of them, yet I am not the best of them." Shaqiq added: I sat in his religious gathering and I did not hear anybody opposing him (in his speech). (5000) □

1590. Narrated `Abdullah (bin Mas`ud): By Allah other than Whom none has the right to be worshipped! There is no Surah revealed in Allah's Book but I know at what place it was revealed; and there is no Verse revealed in Allah's Book but I know about whom it was revealed. And if I know that there is somebody who knows Allah's Book better than I, and he is at a place that camels can reach, I would go to him. (5002) □

1591. Narrated Qatada: I asked Anas bin Malik: "Who collected the Qur'an at the time of the Prophet (ﷺ)?" He replied, "Four, all of whom were from the Ansar: Ubai bin Ka`b, Mu`adh bin Jabal, Zaid bin Thabit and Abu Zaid." (5003) □

1592. Narrated Ibn `Abbas: `Umar said, Ubai was the best of us in the recitation (of the Qur'an) yet we leave some of what he recites.' Ubai says, 'PI have taken it from the mouth of Allah's Messenger (ﷺ) and will not leave for anything whatever." But Allah said "None of Our Revelations do We abrogate or cause to be forgotten but We substitute something better or similar." ((2.106). (5005) □

1593. Narrated Anas: There was a Christian who embraced Islam and read Surah-al-Baqara and Al-`Imran, and he used to write (the revelations) for the Prophet. Later on he returned to Christianity again and he used to say: "Muhammad knows nothing but what I have written for him." Then Allah caused him to die, and the people buried him, but in the morning they saw that the earth had thrown his body out. They said, "This is the act of Muhammad and his companions. They dug the grave of our companion and took his body out of it because he had run away from them." They again dug the grave deeply for him, but in the morning they again saw that the earth had thrown his body out. They said, "This is an act of Muhammad and his companions. They dug the grave of our companion and threw his body outside it, for he had run away from them." They dug the grave for him as deep as they could, but in the morning they again saw that the earth had thrown his body out. So they believed that what had befallen him was not done by human beings and had to leave him thrown (on the ground). (3617) □

64. Virtues of the Qur'an

1594. Narrated Abu Sa`id Al-Mu'alla (ra): While I was praying, the Prophet (ﷺ) called me but I did not respond to his call. Later I said, "O Allah's Apostle! I was praying." He said, "Didn't Allah say: 'O you who believe! Give your response to Allah (by obeying Him) and to His Apostle when he calls you'?" (8.24) He then said, "Shall I not teach you the most superior Surah in the Qur'an?" He said, '(It is), 'Praise be to Allah, the Lord of the worlds.' (i.e., Surah Al-Fatiha) which consists of seven repeatedly recited Verses and the Magnificent Qur'an which was given to me." (5006) □

1595. Narrated Abu Sa`id: Some of the companions of the Prophet (ﷺ) went on a journey till they reached some of the 'Arab tribes (at night). They asked the latter to treat them as their guests but they refused. The chief of that tribe was then bitten by a snake (or stung by a scorpion) and they tried their best to cure him but in vain. Some of them said (to the others), "Nothing has benefited him, will you go to the people who resided here at night, it may be that some of them might possess something (as treatment)," They went to the group of the companions (of the Prophet (ﷺ)) and said, "Our chief has been bitten by a snake (or stung by a scorpion) and we have tried everything but he has not benefited. Have you got anything (useful)?" One of them replied, "Yes, by Allah! I can recite a Ruqya, but as you have refused to accept us as your guests, I will not recite the Ruqya for you unless you fix for us some wages for it." They agrees to pay them a flock of sheep. One of them then went and recited (Surah-ul-Fatiha): 'All the praises are for the Lord of the Worlds' and puffed over the chief who became all right as if he was released from a chain, and got up and started walking, showing no signs of sickness. They paid them what they agreed to pay. Some of them (i.e. the companions) then suggested to divide their earnings among themselves, but the one who performed the recitation said, "Do not divide them till we go to the Prophet (ﷺ) and narrate the whole story to him, and wait for his order." So, they went to Allah's Messenger (ﷺ) and narrated the story. Allah's Messenger (ﷺ) asked, "How did you come to know that Surahul- Fatiha was recited as Ruqya?" Then he added, "You have done the right thing. Divide (what you have earned) and assign a share for me as well." The Prophet (ﷺ) smiled thereupon. (2276) □

1596. Narrated Abu Mas'ud: The Prophet (ﷺ) said, "If somebody recited the last two Verses of Surah Al-Baqara at night that will be sufficient for him." (5009) □

1597. Narrated Abu Huraira: Allah's Messenger (ﷺ) deputed me to keep Sadaqat (al-Fitr) of Ramadan. A comer came and started taking handfuls of the foodstuff (of the Sadaqa) (stealthily). I took hold of him and said, "By Allah, I will take you to Allah's Messenger (ﷺ)." He said, "I am needy and have many dependents, and I am in great need." I released him, and in the morning Allah's Messenger (ﷺ) asked me, "What did your prisoner do yesterday?" I said, "O Allah's Messenger (ﷺ)! The person complained of being needy and of having many dependents, so, I pitied him and let him go." Allah's Messenger (ﷺ) said, "Indeed, he told you a lie and he will be coming again." I believed that he would show up again as Allah's Messenger (ﷺ) had told me that he would return. So, I waited for him watchfully. When he (showed up and) started stealing handfuls of foodstuff, I caught hold of him again and said, "I will definitely take you to Allah's Messenger (ﷺ). He said, "Leave me, for I am very needy and have many dependents. I promise I will not come back again." I pitied him and let him go.

In the morning Allah's Messenger (ﷺ) asked me, "What did your prisoner do." I replied, "O Allah's Messenger (ﷺ)! He complained of his great need and of too many dependents, so I took pity on him and set him free." Allah's Apostle said, "Verily, he told you a lie and he will return." I waited for him attentively for the third time, and when he (came and) started stealing handfuls of the foodstuff, I caught hold of him and said, "I will surely take you to Allah's Messenger (ﷺ) as it is the third time you promise not to return, yet you break your promise and come." He said, "(Forgive me and) I will teach you some words with which Allah will benefit you." I asked, "What are they?" He replied, "Whenever you go to bed, recite "Ayat-al-Kursi"-- 'Allahu la ilaha illa huwa-l-Haiy-ul Qaiyum' till you finish the whole verse. (If you do so), Allah will appoint a guard for you who will stay with you and no satan will come near you till morning." So, I released him. In the morning, Allah's Apostle asked, "What did your prisoner do yesterday?" I replied, "He claimed that he would teach me some words by which Allah will benefit me, so I let him go." Allah's Messenger (ﷺ) asked, "What are they?" I replied, "He said to me, 'Whenever you go to bed, recite Ayat-al-Kursi from the beginning to the end ---- Allahu la ilaha illa huwa-lHaiy-ul-Qaiyum----.' He further said to me, '(If you do so), Allah will appoint a guard for you who will stay with you, and no satan will come near you till morning.' (Abu Huraira or another sub-narrator) added that they (the companions) were very keen to do good deeds. The Prophet (ﷺ) said, "He really spoke the truth, although he is an absolute liar. Do you know whom you were talking to, these three nights, O Abu Huraira?" Abu Huraira said, "No." He said, "It was Satan." (2311) □

1598. Narrated Al-Bara': A man was reciting Surah Al-Kahf and his horse was tied with two ropes beside him. A cloud came down and spread over that man, and it kept on coming closer and closer to him till his horse started jumping (as if afraid of something). When it was morning, the man came to the Prophet, and told him of that experience. The Prophet (ﷺ) said, "That was As-Sakina (tranquility) which descended because of (the recitation of) the Qur'an." (5011) □

1599. Narrated Aslam: Allah's Messenger (ﷺ) was traveling on one of his journeys, and `Umar bin Al-Khattab was traveling along with him at night. `Umar asked him about something, but Allah's Messenger (ﷺ) did not answer him. He asked again, but he did not answer. He asked for the third time, but he did not answer. On that, `Umar said to himself, "May your mother lose you! You have asked Allah's Messenger (ﷺ) three times, but he did not answer at all!" `Umar said, "So I made my camel go fast till I was ahead of the people, and I was afraid that something might be revealed about me. After a little while I heard a call maker calling me, I said, 'I was afraid that some Qur'anic Verse might be revealed about me.' So I went to Allah's Apostle and greeted him. He said, 'Tonight there has been revealed to me a Surah which is dearer to me than that on which the sun shines (i.e. the world).' Then he recited: 'Verily! We have given you (O Muhammad), a manifest victory.'" (Surah al-Fath) No. (48.1). (5012) □

1600. Narrated Abu Said Al-Khudri: A man heard another man reciting (Surah-Al-Ikhlas) 'Say He is Allah, (the) One.' (112. 1) repeatedly. The next morning he came to Allah's Messenger (ﷺ) and informed him about it as if he thought that it was not enough to recite. On that Allah's Messenger (ﷺ) said, "By Him in Whose Hand my life is, this Surah is equal to one-third of the Qur'an!" (5013) □

1601. Narrated Abu Sa`id Al-Khudri: The Prophet (ﷺ) said to his companions, "Is it difficult for any of you to recite one third of the Qur'an in one night?" This suggestion was difficult for them so they said, "Who among us has the power to do so, O Allah's Messenger (ﷺ)?" Allah Apostle replied: "Allah (the) One, the Self-Sufficient Master Whom all creatures need.' (Surah Al-Ikhlas 112.1--to the End) is equal to one third of the Qur'an." (5015) □

1602. Narrated `Aisha: Whenever Allah's Messenger (ﷺ) became sick, he would recite Mu'awwidhat (Surah Al-Falaq and Surah An- Nas) and then blow his breath over his body. When he became seriously ill, I used to recite (these two Suras) and rub his hands over his body hoping for its blessings. (5016) □

1603. Narrated 'Aisha: Whenever the Prophet (ﷺ) went to bed every night, he used to cup his hands together and blow over it after reciting Surah Al-Ikhlas, Surah Al-Falaq and Surah An-Nas, and then rub his hands over whatever parts of his body he was able to rub, starting with his head, face and front of his body. He used to do that three times. (5017) ☐

1604. Narrated Usaid bin Hudair: That while he was reciting Surah Al-Baqara (The Cow) at night, and his horse was tied beside him, the horse was suddenly startled and troubled. When he stopped reciting, the horse became quiet, and when he started again, the horse was startled again. Then he stopped reciting and the horse became quiet too. He started reciting again and the horse was startled and troubled once again. Then he stopped reciting and his son, Yahya was beside the horse. He was afraid that the horse might trample on him. When he took the boy away and looked towards the sky, he could not see it. The next morning he informed the Prophet who said, "Recite, O Ibn Hudair! Recite, O Ibn Hudair!" Ibn Hudair replied, "O Allah's Messenger (ﷺ)! My son, Yahya was near the horse and I was afraid that it might trample on him, so I looked towards the sky, and went to him. When I looked at the sky, I saw something like a cloud containing what looked like lamps, so I went out in order not to see it." The Prophet (ﷺ) said, "Do you know what that was?" Ibn Hudair replied, "No." The Prophet (ﷺ) said, "Those were Angels who came near to you for your voice and if you had kept on reciting till dawn, it would have remained there till morning when people would have seen it as it would not have disappeared. (5018) ☐

1605. Narrated Abu Musa Al-Ash`ari: The Prophet (ﷺ) said, "The example of him (a believer) who recites the Qur'an is like that of a citron which tastes good and smells good. And he (a believer) who does not recite the Qur'an is like a date which is good in taste but has no smell. And the example of a dissolute wicked person who recites the Qur'an is like the Raihana (sweet basil) which smells good but tastes bitter. And the example of a dissolute wicked person who does not recite the Qur'an is like the colocynth which tastes bitter and has no smell. (5020) ☐

1606. Narrated Abu Huraira: The Prophet (ﷺ) said, "Allah does not listen to a prophet as He listens to a prophet who recites the Qur'an in a loud and pleasant tone." Sufyan said, "This saying means: a prophet who regards the Qur'an as something that makes him dispense with many worldly pleasures." (5024) ☐

1607. Narrated `Abdullah bin `Umar: Allah's Messenger (ﷺ) said, "Not to wish to be the like except of two men. A man whom Allah has given the knowledge of the Book and he recites it during the hours of the night, and a man whom Allah has given wealth, and he spends it in charity during the night and the hours of the day." (5025) ☐

1608. Narrated `Uthman: The Prophet (ﷺ) said, "The best among you (Muslims) are those who learn the Qur'an and teach it." (5027) ☐

1609. Narrated `Abdullah: The Prophet (ﷺ) said, "It is a bad thing that some of you say, 'I have forgotten such-and-such verse of the Qur'an,' for indeed, he has been caused (by Allah) to forget it. So you must keep on reciting the Qur'an because it escapes from the hearts of men faster than camel do." (5032) ☐

1610. Narrated Aisha: Allah's Messenger (ﷺ) heard a man reciting the Qur'an at night, and said, "May Allah bestow His Mercy on him, as he has reminded me of such-and-such Verses of such-and-such Suras, which I was caused to forget." (5038) ☐

1611. Narrated Qatada: Anas was asked, "how was the recitation (of the Qur'an) of the Prophet?' He replied, "It was characterized by the prolongation of certain sounds." He then recited: In the Name of Allah, the Most Beneficent, the Most Merciful prolonging the pronunciation of 'In the Name of Allah, 'the most Beneficent,' and 'the Most Merciful. (5046) ☐

1612. Narrated `Abdullah bin Mughaffal: I saw the Prophet (ﷺ) reciting (Qur'an) while he was riding on his she camel or camel which was moving, carrying him. He was reciting Surah Fath or part of Surah Fath very softly and in an Attractive vibrating tone. (5047) ☐

1613. Narrated Sufyan: Ibn Shubruma said, "I wanted to see how much of the Qur'an can be enough (to recite in prayer) and I could not find a Surah containing less than three Verses, therefore I said to myself, "One ought not to recite less than three (Quranic) Verses (in prayer)." (5051) ☐

1614. Narrated `Abdullah bin `Amr bin Al `As: My father got me married to a lady of a noble family, and often used to ask my wife about me, and she used to reply, "What a wonderful man he is! He never comes to my bed, nor has he approached me since he married me." When this state continued for a long period, my father told the story to the Prophet who said to my father, "Let me meet him." Then I met him and he asked me, "How do you fast?" I replied, "I fast daily," He asked, "How long does it take you to finish the recitation of the whole Qur'an?" I replied, "I finish it every night." On that he said, "Fast for three days every month and recite the Qur'an (and finish it) in one month." I said, "But I have power to do more than that." He said, "Then fast for three days per week." I said, "I have the power to do more than that." He said, "Therefore, fast the most superior type of fasting, (that is, the fasting of (prophet) David who used to fast every alternate day; and finish the recitation of the whole Qur'an In seven days." I wish I had accepted the permission of Allah's Messenger (ﷺ) as I have become a weak old man. It is said that `Abdullah used to recite one-seventh of the Qur'an during the day-time to some of his family members, for he used to check his memorization of what he would recite at night during the daytime so that it would be easier for him to read at night. And whenever he wanted to gain some strength, he used to give up fasting for some days and count those days to fast for a similar period, for he disliked to leave those things which he used to do during the lifetime of the Prophet. (5052) ☐

1615. Narrated `Abdullah (bin Mas`ud): Allah's Messenger (ﷺ) said (to me), "Recite the Qur'an to me." I said, "Shall I recite (it) to you while it has been revealed to you?" He said, "I like to hear it from another person." So I recited Surah An-Nisa (The Women) till I reached the Verse: 'How (will it be) then when We bring from each nation a witness, and We bring you (O Muhammad) as a witness against these people.' (4.41) Then he said to me, "Stop!" Thereupon I saw his eyes overflowing with tears. (5055) ☐

1616. Narrated `Abdullah: The Prophet (ﷺ) said, "Recite (and study) the Qur'an as long as you agree about its interpretation, but if you have any difference of opinion (as regards to its interpretation and meaning) then you should stop reciting it (for the time being). (5060) ☐

1617. Narrated Aisha: The Prophet (ﷺ) said, "Such a person as recites the Qur'an and masters it by heart, will be with the noble righteous scribes (in Heaven). And such a person exerts himself to learn the Qur'an by heart, and recites it with great difficulty, will have a double reward." (4937) ☐

1618. Narrated Abu Salama: Abu Huraira said, "Allah's Messenger (ﷺ) said, 'Whoever does not recite Qur'an in a nice voice is not from us,' and others said extra," (that means) to recite it aloud." (7527) ☐

65. MARRIAGE

1619. NARRATED ANAS BIN MALIK (RA): A group of three men came to the houses of the wives of the Prophet (ﷺ) asking how the Prophet (ﷺ) worshipped (Allah), and when they were informed about that, they considered their worship insufficient and said, "Where are we from the Prophet (ﷺ) as his past and future sins have been forgiven." Then one of them said, "I will offer the prayer throughout the night forever." The other said, "I will fast throughout the year and will not break my fast." The third said, "I will keep away from the women and will not marry forever." Allah's Messenger (ﷺ) came to them and said, "Are you the same people who said so-and-so? By Allah, I am more submissive to Allah and more afraid of Him than you; yet I fast and break my fast, I do sleep and I also marry women. So he who does not follow my tradition in religion, is not from me (not one of my followers). (5063) ☐

1620. Narrated `Abdullah: We were with the Prophet (ﷺ) while we were young and had no wealth whatever. So Allah's Messenger (ﷺ) said, "O young people! Whoever among you can marry, should marry, because it helps him lower his gaze and guard his modesty (i.e. his private parts from committing illegal sexual intercourse etc.), and whoever is not able to marry, should fast, as fasting diminishes his sexual power."

(5066) ☐

1621. Narrated 'Ata: We presented ourselves along with Ibn `Abbas at the funeral procession of Maimuna at a place called Sarif. Ibn `Abbas said, "This is the wife of the Prophet (ﷺ) so when you lift her bier, do not Jerk it or shake it much, but walk smoothly because the Prophet (ﷺ) had nine wives and he used to observe the night turns with eight of them, and for one of them there was no night turn." (5067) ☐

1622. Narrated Anas: The Prophet (ﷺ) used to go round (have sexual relations with) all his wives in one night, and he had nine wives. (5068) ☐

1623. Narrated Sa`d bin Abi Waqqas: Allah's Messenger (ﷺ) forbade `Uthman bin Maz'un to abstain from marrying (and other pleasures) and if he had allowed him, we would have gotten ourselves castrated (remove the testicles). (5073) ☐

1624. Narrated 'Abdullah: We used to participate in the holy battles led by Allah's Messenger (ﷺ) and we had nothing (no wives) with us. So we said, "Shall we get ourselves castrated?" He forbade us that and then allowed us to marry women with a temporary contract and recited to us: -- 'O you who believe! Make not unlawful the good things which Allah has made lawful for you, but commit no transgression.' (5.87) (5075) ☐

1625. Narrated Abu Huraira: I said, "O Allah's Messenger (ﷺ)! I am a young man and I am afraid that I may commit illegal sexual intercourse and I cannot afford to marry." He kept silent, and then repeated my question once again, but he kept silent. I said the same (for the third time) and he remained silent. Then repeated my question (for the fourth time), and only then the Prophet said, "O Abu Huraira! The pen has dried after writing what you are going to confront. So (it does not matter whether you) get yourself castrated or not." (5076) ☐

1626. Narrated `Aisha: I said, "O Allah's Messenger (ﷺ)! Suppose you landed in a valley where there is a tree of which something has been eaten and then you found trees of which nothing has been eaten, of which tree would you let your camel graze?"

He said, "(I will let my camel graze) of the one of which nothing has been eaten before." (The sub-narrator added: `Aisha meant that Allah's Messenger (ﷺ) had not married a virgin besides herself.) (5077) □

1627. Narrated Jabir bin `Abdullah: While we were returning from a Ghazwa (Holy Battle) with the Prophet, I started driving my camel fast, as it was a lazy camel. A rider came behind me and pricked my camel with a spear he had with him, and then my camel started running as fast as the best camel you may see. Behold! The rider was the Prophet (ﷺ) himself. He said, 'What makes you in such a hurry?" I replied, I am newly married." He said, "Did you marry a virgin or a matron? I replied, "A matron." He said, "Why didn't you marry a young girl so that you may play with her and she with you?" When we were about to enter (Medina), the Prophet (ﷺ) said, "Wait so that you may enter (Medina) at night so that the lady of unkempt hair may comb her hair and the one whose husband has been absent may shave her pubic region. (5079) □

1628. Narrated 'Urwa: The Prophet (ﷺ) asked Abu Bakr for `Aisha's hand in marriage. Abu Bakr said "But I am your brother." The Prophet (ﷺ) said, "You are my brother in Allah's religion and His Book, but she (Aisha) is lawful for me to marry." (5081) □

1629. Narrated Anas bin Malik: We arrived at Khaibar, and when Allah helped His Apostle to open the fort, the beauty of Safiya bint Huyai bin Akhtaq whose husband had been killed while she was a bride, was mentioned to Allah's Apostle. The Prophet (ﷺ) selected her for himself, and set out with her, and when we reached a place called Sidd-as-Sahba,' Safiya became clean from her menses then Allah's Messenger (ﷺ) married her. Hais (i.e. an 'Arabian dish) was prepared on a small leather mat. Then the Prophet (ﷺ) said to me, "I invite the people around you." So that was the marriage banquet of the Prophet (ﷺ) and Safiya. Then we proceeded towards Medina, and I saw the Prophet, making for her a kind of cushion with his cloak behind him (on his camel). He then sat beside his camel and put his knee for Safiya to put her foot on, in order to ride (on the camel). (4211) □

1630. Narrated Anas: The Prophet (ﷺ) stayed for three days between Khaibar and Medina, and there he consummated his marriage to Safiyya bint Huyai. I invited the Muslims to the wedding banquet in which neither meat nor bread was offered. He ordered for leather dining-sheets to be spread, and dates, dried yoghurt and butter were laid on it, and that was the Prophet's wedding banquet. The Muslims wondered, "Is she (Saffiyya) considered as his wife or his slave girl?" Then they said, "If he orders her to veil herself, she will be one of the mothers of the Believers; but if he does not order her to veil herself, she will be a slave girl. So when the Prophet (ﷺ) proceeded from there, he spared her a space behind him (on his she-camel) and put a screening veil between her and the people. (5085) □

1631. Narrated Sahl bin Sa`d As-Sa`idi: A woman came to Allah's Messenger (ﷺ) and said, "O Allah's Messenger (ﷺ)! I have come to give you myself in marriage (without Mahr)." Allah's Messenger (ﷺ) looked at her. He looked at her carefully and fixed his glance on her and then lowered his head. When the lady saw that he did not say anything, she sat down. A man from his companions got up and said, "O Allah's Messenger (ﷺ)! If you are not in need of her, then marry her to me." The Prophet (ﷺ) said, "Have you got anything to offer?" The man said, "No, by Allah, O Allah's Messenger (ﷺ)!" The Prophet (ﷺ) said (to him), "Go to your family and see if you have something." The man went and returned, saying, "No, by Allah, I have not found anything." Allah's Apostle said, "(Go again) and look for something, even if it is an iron ring." He went again and returned, saying, "No, by Allah, O Allah's Messenger (ﷺ)! I could not find even an iron ring, but this is my Izar (waist sheet)." He had no rida. He added, "I give half of it to her." Allah's Messenger (ﷺ) said, "What will she do with your Izar? If you wear it, she will be naked, and if she wears it, you will be naked." So that man sat down for a long while and then got up (to depart). When Allah's Messenger (ﷺ) saw him going, he ordered that he be called back. When he came, the Prophet (ﷺ) said, "How much of the Qur'an do you know?" He said, "I know such Sura and such Sura," counting them. The Prophet (ﷺ) said, "Do you know them by heart?" He replied, "Yes." The Prophet (ﷺ) said, "Go, I marry her to you for that much of the Qur'an which you have." (5087) □

1632. Narrated Abu Huraira: The Prophet (ﷺ) said, "A woman is married for four things, i.e., her wealth, her family status, her beauty and her religion. So you should marry the religious woman (otherwise) you will be a losers. (5090) □

1633. Narrated Sahl: A man passed by Allah's Messenger (ﷺ) and Allah s Apostle asked (his companions) "What do you say about this (man)?" They replied "If he asks for a lady's hand, he ought to be given her in marriage; and if he intercedes (for someone) his intercessor should be accepted; and if he speaks, he should be listened to." Allah's Messenger (ﷺ) kept silent, and then a man from among the poor Muslims passed by, an Allah's Apostle asked (them) "What do you say about this man?" They replied, "If he asks for a lady's hand in marriage he does not deserve to be married, and he intercedes (for someone), his intercession should not be accepted; and if he speaks, he should not be listened to.' Allah's Messenger (ﷺ) said, "this poor man is better than so many of the first as filling the earth.' (5091) □

1634. Narrated Usama bin Zaid: The Prophet (ﷺ) said, "After me I have not left any trial more severe to men than women." (5096) □

1635. Narrated `Aisha: that while Allah's Messenger (ﷺ) was with her, she heard a voice of a man asking permission to enter the house of Hafsa. `Aisha added: I said, "O Allah's Messenger (ﷺ)! This man is asking permission to enter your house." The Prophet (ﷺ) said, "I think he is so-and-so," naming the foster-uncle of Hafsa. `Aisha said, "If so-and-so," naming her foster uncle, "were living, could he enter upon me?" The Prophet (ﷺ) said, "Yes, for foster suckling relations make all those things unlawful which are unlawful through corresponding birth (blood) relations." (5099) □

1636. Narrated Um Habiba: (daughter of Abu Sufyan) I said, "O Allah's Messenger (ﷺ)! Marry my sister. The daughter of Abu Sufyan." The Prophet (ﷺ) said, "Do you like that?" I replied, "Yes, for even now I am not your only wife and I like that my sister should share the good with me." The Prophet (ﷺ) said, "But that is not lawful for me." I said, We have heard that you want to marry the daughter of Abu Salama."

He said, "(You mean) the daughter of Um Salama?" I said, "Yes." He said, "Even if she were not my step-daughter, she would be unlawful for me to marry as she is my foster niece. I and Abu Salama were suckled by Thuwaiba. So you should not present to me your daughters or your sisters (in marriage)." Narrated 'Urwa: Thuwaiba was the freed slave girl of Abu Lahb whom he had manumitted, and then she suckled the Prophet. When Abu Lahb died, one of his relatives saw him in a dream in a very bad state and asked him, "What have you encountered?" Abu Lahb said, "I have not found any rest since I left you, except that I have been given water to drink in this (the space between his thumb and other fingers) and that is because of my manumitting Thuwaiba." (5101) ☐

1637. Narrated `Aisha: that the Prophet (ﷺ) entered upon her while a man was sitting with her. Signs of answer seemed to appear on his face as if he disliked that. She said, "Here is my (foster) brother." He said, "Be sure as to who is your foster brother, for foster suckling relationship is established only when milk is the only food of the child." (5102) ☐

1638. Narrated Aisha: that Aflah the brother of Abu Al-Qu'ais, her foster uncle, came, asking permission to enter upon her after the Verse of Al-Hijab (the use of veils by women) was revealed. `Aisha added: I did not allow him to enter, but when Allah's Messenger (ﷺ) came, I told him what I had done, and he ordered me to give him permission. (5103) ☐

1639. Ibn 'Abbas further said, "Seven types of marriages are unlawful because of blood relations, and seven because of marriage relations." Then Ibn 'Abbas recited the Verse: "Forbidden for you (for marriages) are your mothers..." (4:23). 'Abdullah bin Ja'far married the daughter and wife of 'Ali at the same time (they were step-daughter and mother). Ibn Sirin said, "There is no harm in that." But Al-Hasan Al-Basri disapproved of it at first, but then said that there was no harm in it. Al-Hasan bin Al-Hasan bin 'Ali married two of his cousins in one night. Ja'far bin Zaid disapproved of that because of it would bring hatred (between the two cousins), but it is not unlawful, as Allah said, "Lawful to you are all others [beyond those (mentioned)]. (4:24). Ibn

'Abbas said: "If somebody commits illegal sexual intercourse with his wife's sister, his wife does not become unlawful for him." And narrated Abu Ja'far, "If a person commits homosexuality with a boy, then the mother of that boy is unlawful for him to marry." Narrated Ibn 'Abbas, "If one commits illegal sexual intercourse with his mother in law, then his married relation to his wife does not become unlawful." Abu Nasr reported to have said that Ibn 'Abbas in the above case, regarded his marital relation to his wife unlawful, but Abu Nasr is not known well for hearing Hadith from Ibn 'Abbas. Imran bin Hussain, Jabir b. Zaid, Al-Hasan and some other Iraqi's, are reported to have judged that his marital relations to his wife would be unlawful. In the above case Abu Hurairah said, "The marital relation to one's wife does not become unlawful except if one as had sexual intercourse (with her mother)." Ibn Al-Musaiyab, 'Urwa, and Az-Zuhri allows such person to keep his wife. 'Ali said, "His marital relations to his wife does not become unlawful." (5105) □

1640. Narrated Abu Huraira: Allah's Messenger (ﷺ) said, "A woman and her paternal aunt should not be married to the same man; and similarly, a woman and her maternal aunt should not be married to the same man." (5109) □

1641. Narrated Ibn `Umar: Allah's Messenger (ﷺ) forbade Ash-Shighar, which means that somebody marries his daughter to somebody else, and the latter marries his daughter to the former without paying Mahr. (5112) □

1642. Salama bin Al-Akwa` said: Allah's Messenger (ﷺ)'s said, "If a man and a woman agree (to marry temporarily), their marriage should last for three nights, and if they like to continue, they can do so; and if they want to separate, they can do so." I do not know whether that was only for us or for all the people in general. Abu `Abdullah (Al-Bukhari) said: `Ali made it clear that the Prophet said, "The Mut'a marriage has been cancelled (made unlawful). (5119) □

1643. Narrated `Abdullah bin `Umar: `Umar bin Al-Khattab said, "When Hafsa bint `Umar became a widow after the death of (her husband) Khunais bin Hudhafa As-Sahmi who had been one of the companions of the Prophet, and he died at Medina.

I went to `Uthman bin `Affan and presented Hafsa (for marriage) to him. He said, "I will think it over.' I waited for a few days, then he met me and said, 'It seems that it is not possible for me to marry at present.'" `Umar further said, "I met Abu Bakr As-Siddique and said to him, 'If you wish, I will marry my daughter Hafsa to you." Abu Bakr kept quiet and did not say anything to me in reply. I became more angry with him than with `Uthman. I waited for a few days and then Allah's Messenger (ﷺ) asked for her hand, and I gave her in marriage to him. Afterwards I met Abu Bakr who said, 'Perhaps you became angry with me when you presented Hafsa to me and I did not give you a reply?' I said, 'Yes.' Abu Bakr said, 'Nothing stopped me to respond to your offer except that I knew that Allah's Apostle had mentioned her, and I never wanted to let out the secret of Allah's Messenger (ﷺ). And if Allah's Apostle had refused her, I would have accepted her.'" (5122) □

1644. Ibn `Abbas said: "Hint your intention of marrying' is made by saying (to the widow) for example: "I want to marry, and I wish that Allah will make a righteous lady available for me.'" Al-Qasim said: One may say to the widow: 'I hold all respect for you, and I am interested in you; Allah will bring you much good, or something similar 'Ata said: One should hint his intention, and should not declare it openly. One may say: 'I have some need. Have good tidings. Praise be to Allah; you are fit to remarry.' She (the widow) may say in reply: I am listening to what you say,' but she should not make a promise. Her guardian should not make a promise (to somebody to get her married to him) without her knowledge. But if, while still in the Iddat period, she makes a promise to marry somebody, and he ultimately marries her, they are not to be separated by divorce (i.e., the marriage is valid). (5124) □

1645. Narrated `Aisha: that the Prophet (ﷺ) married her when she was six years old and he consummated his marriage when she was nine years old. Hisham said: I have been informed that `Aisha remained with the Prophet (ﷺ) for nine years (i.e. till his death). (5134) □

1646. Narrated Abu Huraira: The Prophet (ﷺ) said, "A matron [who is old or a widow (= a woman whose husband has died)] should not be given in marriage except after consulting her; and a virgin should not be given in marriage except after her permission." The people asked, "O Allah's Messenger (ﷺ)! How can we know her permission?" He said, "Her silence (indicates her permission). (5136) ☐

1647. Narrated Khansa bint Khidam Al-Ansariya: that her father gave her in marriage when she was a matron and she disliked that marriage. So she went to Allah's Messenger (ﷺ) and he declared that marriage invalid. (5138) ☐

1648. Narrated 'Urwa bin Az-Zubair: that he asked `Aisha, saying to her, "O Mother! (In what connection was this Verse revealed): 'If you fear that you shall not be able to deal justly with orphan girls (to the end of the verse) that your right hands possess?" (4.3) Aisha said, "O my nephew! It was about the female orphan under the protection of her guardian who was interested in her beauty and wealth and wanted to marry her with a little or reduced Mahr. So such guardians were forbidden to marry female orphans unless they deal with them justly and give their full Mahr; and they were ordered to marry women other than them."`Aisha added, "(Later) the people asked Allah's Messenger (ﷺ), for instructions, and then Allah revealed: 'They ask your instruction concerning the women . . . And yet whom you desire to marry.' (4.127) So Allah revealed to them in this Verse that–if a female orphan had wealth and beauty, they desired to marry her and were interested in her noble descent and the reduction of her Mahr; but if she was not desired by them because of her lack in fortune and beauty they left her and married some other woman. So, as they used to leave her when they had no interest in her, they had no right to marry her if they had the desire to do so, unless they deal justly with her and gave her a full amount of Mahr." (5140) ☐

1649. Narrated Abu Huraira: The Prophet (ﷺ) said, "Beware of suspicion (about others), as suspicion is the falsest talk, and do not spy upon each other, and do not listen to the evil talk of the people about others' affairs, and do not have enmity with one another, but be brothers. And none should ask for the hand of a girl who is already engaged to his (Muslim) brother, but one should wait till the first suitor marries her or leaves her." (5144) ☐

1650. Narrated Ar-Rabi`: (the daughter of Muawwidh bin Afra) After the consummation of my marriage, the Prophet (ﷺ) came and sat on my bed as far from me as you are sitting now, and our little girls started beating the tambourines and reciting elegiac verses mourning my father who had been killed in the battle of Badr. One of them said, "Among us is a Prophet who knows what will happen tomorrow." On that the Prophet said, "Leave this (saying) and keep on saying the verses which you had been saying before." (5147) ☐

1651. Narrated `Uqba: The Prophet (ﷺ) said: "The stipulations most entitled to be abided by are those with which you are given the right to enjoy the (women's) private parts (i.e. the stipulations of the marriage contract). (5151) ☐

1652. Narrated Abu Huraira: The Prophet (ﷺ) said, "It is not lawful for a woman (at the time of wedding) to ask for the divorce of her sister (i.e. the other wife of her would-be husband) in order to have everything for herself, for she will take only what has been written for her." (5152) ☐

1653. Narrated Anas: The Prophet (ﷺ) saw the traces of Sufra (yellow perfume) on `Abdur-Rahman bin `Auf and said, "What is this?" `Abdur-Rahman, said, "I have married a woman and have paid gold equal to the weight of a datestone (as her Mahr). The Prophet (ﷺ) said to him, "May Allah bless you: Offer a wedding banquet even with one sheep." (5155) ☐

1654. Narrated `Aisha: When the Prophet (ﷺ) married me, my mother came to me and made me enter the house where I saw some women from the Ansar who said, "May you prosper and have blessings and have good omen." (5156) ☐

1655. Narrated Abu Huraira: The Prophet (ﷺ) said, "A prophet among the prophets went for a military expedition and said to his people: "A man who has married a lady and wants to consummate his marriage with her and he has not done so yet, should not accompany me."' (5157) ☐

1656. Narrated Jabir bin `Abdullah: Allah's Messenger (ﷺ) said, "Did you get Anmat (large carpets with fringes)?" I said, 'O Allah's Messenger (ﷺ)! From where can we have Anmat?" The Prophet (ﷺ) said, "Soon you will have them. (5161) □

1657. Narrated 'Aisha: that she prepared a lady for a man from the Ansar as his bride and the Prophet said, "O 'Aisha! Haven't you got any amusement (during the marriage ceremony) as the Ansar like amusement?" (5162) □

1658. Narrated Anas bin Malik: "Whenever the Prophet (ﷺ) passed by (my mother Um-Sulaim) he used to enter her and greet her. Anas further said: Once the Prophet (ﷺ) way a bridegroom during his marriage with Zainab, Um Sulaim said to me, "Let us give a gift to Allah's Messenger (ﷺ)." I said to her, "Do it." So she prepared Haisa (a sweet dish) made from dates, butter and dried yoghurt and she sent it with me to him. I took it to him and he said, "Put it down," and ordered me to call some men whom he named, and to invite whomever I would meet. I did what he ordered me to do, and when I returned, I found the house crowded with people and saw the Prophet (ﷺ) keeping his hand over the Haisa and saying over it whatever Allah wished (him to say). Then he called the men in batches of ten to eat of it, and he said to them, "Mention the Name of Allah, and each man should eat of the dish the nearest to him." When all of them had finished their meals, some of them left and a few remained there talking, over which I felt unhappy. Then the Prophet (ﷺ) went out towards the dwelling places (of his wives) and I too, went out after him and told him that those people had left. Then he returned and entered his dwelling place and let the curtains fall while I was in (his) dwelling place, and he was reciting the Verses: -- 'O you who believe! Enter not the Prophet's house until leave is given you for a meal, (and then) not (as early as) to what for its preparation. But when you are invited, enter, and when you have taken your meals, disperse without sitting for a talk. Verily such (behavior) annoys the Prophet; and he would be shy of (asking) you (to go), but Allah is not shy of (telling you) the Truth.' (33-53) Abu Uthman said: Anas said, "I served the Prophet for ten years." (5163) □

1659. Narrated Ibn `Abbas: The Prophet (ﷺ) said, "If anyone of you, when having sexual intercourse with his wife, says:

بِاسْمِ اللَّهِ، اللَّهُمَّ جَنِّبْنِي الشَّيْطَانَ، وَجَنِّبِ الشَّيْطَانَ مَا رَزَقْتَنَا

Bismillah, Allahumma jannibni-Sh-Shaitan wa jannib-ish-Shaitan ma razaqtana (I am having relations in the name of Allah. O Allah save us from Satan and keep him away from the children You grant us.), and if it is destined that they should have a child, then Satan will never be able to harm him." (5165) □

1660. Narrated Anas: The Prophet (ﷺ) did not give a better wedding banquet on the occasion of marrying any of his wives than the one he gave on marrying Zainab, and that banquet was with (consisted of) one sheep. (5168) □

1661. Narrated Anas: Allah's Messenger (ﷺ) manumitted Safiyya and then married her, and her Mahr was her manumission, and he gave a wedding banquet with Hais (a sort of sweet dish made from butter, cheese and dates). (5169) □

1662. Narrated Safiyya bint Shaiba: The Prophet (ﷺ) gave a banquet with two Mudds of barley on marrying some of his wives. (1 Mudd= 1 3/4 of a kilogram). (5172) □

1663. Narrated `Abdullah bin `Umar: Allah's Messenger (ﷺ) said, "If anyone of you is invited to a wedding banquet, he must go for it (accept the invitation)." (5173) □

1664. Narrated Abu Musa: The Prophet (ﷺ) said, "Set the captives free, accept the invitation (to a wedding banquet), and visit the patients." (5174) □

1665. Narrated Al-Bara' bin `Azib: The Prophet (ﷺ) ordered us to do seven (things) and forbade us from seven. He ordered us to visit the patients, to follow the funeral procession, to reply to the sneezer (i.e., say to him, 'Yarhamuka-l-lah (May Allah bestow His Mercy upon you), if he says 'Al-hamduli l-lah' (Praise be to Allah), to help others to fulfill their oaths, to help the oppressed, to greet (whomever one should meet), and to accept the invitation (to a wedding banquet). He forbade us to wear golden rings, to use silver utensils, to use Maiyathir (cushions of silk stuffed with cotton and placed under the rider on the saddle), the Qasiyya (linen clothes containing silk brought from an Egyptian town), the Istibraq (thick silk) and the Dibaj (another kind of silk). (5175) □

1666. Narrated Abu Huraira: The worst food is that of a wedding banquet to which only the rich are invited while the poor are not invited. And he who refuses an invitation (to a banquet) disobeys Allah and His Apostle. (5177) □

1667. Narrated Nafi`:`Abdullah bin `Umar said, "Allah's Messenger (ﷺ) said, 'Accept the marriage invitation if you are invited to it.'" Ibn `Umar used to accept the invitation whether to a wedding banquet or to any other party, even when he was fasting. (5179) □

1668. Narrated Abu Huraira: Allah's Messenger (ﷺ) said, "A man bought a piece of and from another man, and the buyer found an earthenware jar filled with gold in the land. The buyer said to the seller. 'Take your gold, as I have bought only the land from you, but I have not bought the gold from you.' The owner of the land said, "I have sold you the land with everything in it.' So both of them took their case before a man who asked, 'Do you have children?' One of them said, "I have a boy.' The other said, "I have a girl.' The man said, 'Marry the girl to the boy and spend the money on both of them and give the rest of it in charity.'" (3472) □

66. MARRIED LIFE

1669. NARRATED ABU HURAIRA (RA): Allah's Messenger (ﷺ) said, "The woman is like a rib; if you try to straighten her, she will break. So if you want to get benefit from her, do so while she still has some crookedness." (5184) □

1670. Narrated Abu Huraira: The Prophet (ﷺ) said, "Whoever believes in Allah and the Last Day should not hurt (trouble) his neighbor. And I advise you to take care of the women, for they are created from a rib and the most crooked portion of the rib is its upper part; if you try to straighten it, it will break, and if you leave it, it will remain crooked, so I urge you to take care of the women." (5186) □

1671. Narrated Ibn `Umar: During the lifetime of the Prophet (ﷺ) we used to avoid chatting leisurely and freely with our wives lest some Divine inspiration might be revealed concerning us. But when the Prophet (ﷺ) had died, we started chatting leisurely and freely (with them). (5187) □

1672. Narrated `Abdullah bin `Umar: The Prophet (ﷺ) said, "Every one of you is a guardian and every one of you is responsible (for his wards). A ruler is a guardian and is responsible (for his subjects); a man is a guardian of his family and responsible (for them); a wife is a guardian of her husband's house and she is responsible (for it), a slave is a guardian of his master's property and is responsible (for that). Beware! All of you are guardians and are responsible (for your wards). (5188) □

1673. Narrated 'Urwa: Aisha said, "While the Ethiopians were playing with their small spears, Allah's Messenger (ﷺ) screened me behind him and I watched (that display) and kept on watching till I left on my own." So you may estimate of what age a little girl may listen to amusement. (5190) □

1674. Narrated Ibn `Abbas: I had been eager to ask `Umar bin Al-Khattab about the two ladies from among the wives of the Prophet regarding whom Allah said 'If you two (wives of the Prophet (ﷺ) namely Aisha and Hafsa) turn in repentance to Allah, your hearts are indeed so inclined (to oppose what the Prophet (ﷺ) likes). (66.4) till `Umar performed the Hajj and I too, performed the Hajj along with him. (On the way) `Umar went aside to answer the call of nature, and I also went aside along with him carrying a tumbler full of water, and when `Umar had finished answering the call of nature, I poured water over his hands and he performed the ablution. Then I said to him, "O chief of the Believers! Who were the two ladies from among the wives of the Prophet (ﷺ) regarding whom Allah said: 'If you two (wives of the Prophet) turn in repentance to Allah your hearts are indeed so inclined (to oppose what the Prophet (ﷺ) likes)?" (66.4) He said, "I am astonished at your question, O Ibn `Abbas. They were `Aisha and Hafsa." Then `Umar went on narrating the Hadith and said, "I and an Ansari neighbor of mine from Bani Umaiyya bin Zaid who used to live in `Awali-al-Medina, used to visit the Prophet (ﷺ) in turn. He used to go one day and I another day. When I went, I would bring him the news of what had happened that day regarding the Divine Inspiration and other things, and when he went, he used to do the same for me. We, the people of Quraish used to have the upper hand over our wives, but when we came to the Ansar, we found that their women had the upper hand over their men, so our women also started learning the ways of the Ansari women. I shouted at my wife and she retorted against me and I disliked that she should answer me back. She said to me, 'Why are you so surprised at my answering you back? By Allah, the wives of the Prophet answer him back and some of them may leave (does not speak to) him throughout the day till the night.' The (talk) scared me and I said to her, 'Whoever has done so will be ruined!' Then I proceeded after dressing myself, and entered upon Hafsa and said to her, 'Does anyone of you keep the Prophet (ﷺ) angry till night?' She said, 'Yes.' I said, 'You are a ruined losing person! Don't you fear that Allah may get angry for the anger of Allah's Messenger (ﷺ) and thus you will be ruined? So do not ask more from the Prophet (ﷺ) and do not answer him back and do not give up talking to him. Ask me whatever you need and do not be tempted to imitate your neighbor (i.e., `Aisha) in her manners for she is more charming than you and more beloved to the Prophet (ﷺ)." `Umar added,"At that time a talk was circulating among us that (the tribe of) Ghassan were preparing their horses to invade us. My Ansari companion, on the day of his turn, went (to the town) and returned to us at night and knocked at my door violently and asked if I was there. I became horrified and came out to him. He said, 'Today a great thing has happened.' I asked, 'What is it? Have (the people of) Ghassan come?' He said, 'No, but (What has happened) is greater and more horrifying than that: Allah's Messenger (ﷺ); has divorced his wives. `Umar added, "The Prophet (ﷺ) kept away from his wives and I said "Hafsa is a ruined loser.' I had already thought that most probably this (divorce) would happen in the near future. So I dressed myself and offered the Morning Prayer with the Prophet (ﷺ) and then the Prophet; entered an upper room and stayed there in seclusion. I entered upon Hafsa and saw her weeping. I asked, 'What makes you weep? Did I not warn you about that? Did the Prophet (ﷺ) divorce you all?' She said, 'I do not know. There he is retired alone in the upper room.' I came out and sat near the pulpit and saw a group of people sitting around it and some of them were weeping. I sat with them for a while but could not endure the situation, so I went to the upper room where the Prophet; was and said to a black slave of his, 'Will you get the permission (of the Prophet (ﷺ)) for `Umar (to enter)?' The slave went in, talked to the Prophet (ﷺ) about it and then returned saying, 'I have spoken to the Prophet (ﷺ) and mentioned you but he kept quiet.' Then I returned and sat with the group of people sitting near the pulpit. But I could not bear the situation and once again I said to the slave, 'Will you get the permission for `Umar?' He went in and returned saying, 'I mentioned you to him but he kept quiet.' So I returned again and sat with the group of people sitting near the pulpit, but I could not bear the situation, and so I went to the slave and said, 'Will you get the permission for `Umar?' He went in and returned to me saying, 'I mentioned you to him but he kept quiet.' When I was leaving, behold! The slave called me, saying, 'The Prophet (ﷺ) has given you permission.' Then I entered upon Allah's Messenger (ﷺ) and saw him lying on a bed made of stalks of date palm leaves and there was no bedding between it and him. The stalks left marks on his side and he was leaning on a leather pillow stuffed with date-palm fires. I greeted him and while still standing I said, 'O Allah's Apostle! Have you divorced your wives?' He looked at me and said, 'No.' I said, 'Allah Akbar!' And then, while still standing, I said chatting, 'Will you heed what I say, O Allah's Messenger (ﷺ)? We, the people of Quraish used to have power over our women, but when we arrived at Medina we found that the men (here) were overpowered by their women.' The Prophet (ﷺ) smiled and then I said to him, 'Will you heed what I say, O Allah's Messenger (ﷺ)? I entered upon Hafsa and said to her, "Do not be tempted to imitate your companion (`Aisha), for she is more charming than you and more beloved to the Prophet."' The Prophet (ﷺ) smiled for a second time. When I saw him smiling, I sat down. Then I looked around his house, and by Allah, I could not see anything of importance in his house except three hides, so I said, 'O Allah's Messenger (ﷺ)! Invoke Allah to make your followers rich, for the Persians and the Romans have been made prosperous and they have been given (the pleasures of the world), although they do not worship Allah.' Thereupon the Prophet (ﷺ) sat up as he was reclining. And said, 'Are you of such an opinion, O the son of Al-Khattab? These are the people who have received the rewards for their good deeds in this world.' I said, 'O Allah's Messenger (ﷺ)! Ask Allah to forgive me.' Then the Prophet (ﷺ) kept away from his wives for twenty-nine days because of the story which Hafsa had disclosed to `Aisha. The Prophet (ﷺ) had said, 'I will not enter upon them (my wives) for one month,' because of his anger towards them, when Allah had admonished him. So, when twenty nine days had passed, the Prophet (ﷺ) first entered upon `Aisha. `Aisha said to him, 'O Allah's Messenger (ﷺ)! You had sworn that you would not enter upon us for one month, but now only twenty-nine days have passed, for I have been counting them one by one.' The Prophet (ﷺ) said, 'The (present) month is of twenty nine days.' `Aisha added, 'Then Allah revealed the Verses of the option. (2) And out of all his-wives he asked me first, and I chose him.' Then he gave option to his other wives and they said what `Aisha had said." (1) The Prophet, ' had decided to abstain from eating a certain kind of food because of a certain event, so Allah blamed him for doing so. Some of his wives were the cause of him taking that decision, therefore he deserted them for one month. See Qur'an: (66.4) (5191) ☐

1675. Narrated Abu Huraira: The Prophet (ﷺ) said, "If a man invites his wife to sleep with him and she refuses to come to him, then the angels send their curses on her till morning." (5193) ☐

1676. Narrated Abu Huraira: Allah's Messenger (ﷺ) said, "It is not lawful for a lady to fast (Nawafil) without the permission of her husband when he is at home; and she should not allow anyone to enter his house except with his permission; and if she spends of his wealth (on charitable purposes) without being ordered by him, he will get half of the reward." (5195) ☐

1677. Narrated `Abdullah bin Zam`a: The Prophet (ﷺ) said, "None of you should flog his wife as he flogs a slave and then have sexual intercourse with her in the last part of the day." (5204) ☐

1678. Narrated Aisha: Regarding the Verse: 'If a wife fears cruelty or desertion on her husband's part ...') (4.128) It concerns the woman whose husband does not want to keep her with him any longer, but wants to divorce her and marry some other lady, so she says to him: 'Keep me and do not divorce me, and then marry another woman, and you may neither spend on me, nor sleep with me.' This is indicated by the Statement of Allah: 'There is no blame on them if they arrange an amicable settlement between them both, and (such) settlement is better." (4.128) (5206) ☐

1679. Narrated Jabir: We used to practice coitus interrupt us during the lifetime of Allah's Messenger (p.b.u.h). (5207) ☐

1680. Narrated Abu Sa`id Al-Khudri: We got female captives in the war booty and we used to do coitus interruptus with them. So we asked Allah's Messenger (ﷺ) about it and he said, "Do you really do that?" repeating the question thrice, "There is no soul that is destined to exist but will come into existence, till the Day of Resurrection." (5210) ☐

1681. Narrated al-Qasim: Aisha said that whenever the Prophet (ﷺ) intended to go on a journey, he drew lots among his wives (so as to take one of them along with him). During one of his journeys the lot fell on `Aisha and Hafsa. When night fell the Prophet (ﷺ) would ride beside `Aisha and talk with her. One night Hafsa said to `Aisha, "Won't you ride my camel tonight and I ride yours, so that you may see (me) and I see (you) (in new situation)?" `Aisha said, "Yes, (I agree.)" So `Aisha rode, and then the Prophet (ﷺ) came towards `Aisha's camel on which Hafsa was riding. He greeted Hafsa and then proceeded (beside her) till they dismounted (on the way). `Aisha missed him, and so, when they dismounted, she put her legs in the Idhkhir and said, "O Lord (Allah)! Send a scorpion or a snake to bite me for I am not to blame him (the Prophet (p.b.u.h). (5211) ☐

1682. Narrated Anas: It is the Prophet's tradition that if someone marries a virgin and he has already a matron wife then he should stay for seven days with her (the virgin) and then by turns; and if someone marries a matron and he has already a virgin wife then he should stay with her (the matron) for three days, and then by turns. (5214) ☐

1683. Narrated `Aisha: Whenever Allah's Messenger (ﷺ) finished his `Asr prayer, he would enter upon his wives and stay with one of them. One day he went to Hafsa and stayed with her longer than usual. (5216) □

1684. Narrated Asma: Some lady said, "O Allah's Messenger (ﷺ)! My husband has another wife, so it is sinful of me to claim that he has given me what he has not given me (in order to tease her)?" Allah's Messenger (ﷺ) said, the one who pretends that he has been given what he has not been given, is just like the (false) one who wears two garments of falsehood." (5219) □

1685. Narrated Asma' bint Abu Bakr: When Az-Zubair married me, he had no real property or any slave or anything else except a camel which drew water from the well, and his horse. I used to feed his horse with fodder and drew water and sew the bucket for drawing it, and prepare the dough, but I did not know how to bake bread. So our Ansari neighbors used to bake bread for me, and they were honorable ladies. I used to carry the date stones on my head from Zubair's land given to him by Allah's Messenger (ﷺ) and this land was two third Farsakh (about two miles) from my house. One day, while I was coming with the date stones on my head, I met Allah's Messenger (ﷺ) along with some Ansari people. He called me and then, (directing his camel to kneel down) said, "Ikh! Ikh!" so as to make me ride behind him (on his camel). I felt shy to travel with the men and remembered Az-Zubair and his sense of Ghira, as he was one of those people who had the greatest sense of Ghira. Allah's Messenger (ﷺ) noticed that I felt shy, so he proceeded. I came to Az-Zubair and said, "I met Allah's Messenger (ﷺ) while I was carrying a load of date stones on my head, and he had some companions with him. He made his camel kneel down so that I might ride, but I felt shy in his presence and remembered your sense of Ghira (See the glossary). On that Az-Zubair said, "By Allah, your carrying the date stones (and you being seen by the Prophet (ﷺ) in such a state) is more shameful to me than your riding with him." (I continued serving in this way) till Abu Bakr sent me a servant to look after the horse, whereupon I felt as if he had set me free. (5224) □

1686. Narrated Anas: While the Prophet (ﷺ) was in the house of one of his wives, one of the mothers of the believers sent a meal in a dish. The wife at whose house the Prophet (ﷺ) was, struck the hand of the servant, causing the dish to fall and break. The Prophet (ﷺ) gathered the broken pieces of the dish and then started collecting on them the food which had been in the dish and said, "Your mother (my wife) felt jealous." Then he detained the servant till a (sound) dish was brought from the wife at whose house he was. He gave the sound dish to the wife whose dish had been broken and kept the broken one at the house where it had been broken. (5225) ☐

1687. Narrated Aisha: That Allah's Messenger (ﷺ) said to her, "I know when you are pleased with me or angry with me." I said, "Where do you know that?" He said, "When you are pleased with me, you say, 'No, by the Lord of Muhammad,' but when you are angry with me, then you say, 'No, by the Lord of Abraham.'" Thereupon I said, "Yes (you are right), but by Allah, O Allah's Messenger (ﷺ), I leave nothing but your name." (5228) ☐

1688. Narrated `Aisha: I never felt so jealous of any wife of Allah's Messenger (ﷺ) as I did of Khadija because Allah's Messenger (ﷺ) used to remember and praise her too often and because it was revealed to Allah's Messenger (ﷺ) that he should give her (Khadija) the glad tidings of her having a palace of Qasab in Paradise . (5229) ☐

1689. Narrated Al-Miswar bin Makhrama: I heard Allah's Messenger (ﷺ) who was on the pulpit, saying, "Banu Hisham bin Al-Mughira have requested me to allow them to marry their daughter to `Ali bin Abu Talib, but I don't give permission, and will not give permission unless `Ali bin Abi Talib divorces my daughter in order to marry their daughter, because Fatima is a part of my body, and I hate what she hates to see, and what hurts her, hurts me." (5230) ☐

1690. Narrated `Uqba bin 'Amir: Allah's Messenger (ﷺ) said, "Beware of entering upon the ladies." A man from the Ansar said, "Allah's Apostle! What about Al-Hamu the in-laws of the wife (the brothers of her husband or his nephews etc.)?" The Prophet (ﷺ) replied: The in-laws of the wife are death itself. (5232) ☐

1691. Narrated Um Salama: that while the Prophet (ﷺ) was with her, there was an effeminate (girlish boy) man in the house. The effeminate man said to Um Salama's brother, `Abdullah bin Abi Umaiyya, "If Allah should make you conquer Ta'if tomorrow, I recommend that you take the daughter of Ghailan (in marriage) for (she is so fat) that she shows four folds of flesh when facing you and eight when she turns her back." Thereupon the Prophet (ﷺ) said (to us), "This (effeminate man) should not enter upon you (anymore). (5235) □

1692. Narrated Salim's father: The Prophet (ﷺ) said, "If the wife of anyone of you asks permission to go to the mosque, he should not forbid her." (5238) □

1693. Narrated `Abdullah bin Mas`ud: The Prophet (ﷺ) said, "A woman should not look at or touch another woman to describe her to her husband in such a way as if he was actually looking at her." (5240) □

67. DIVORCE

1694. NARRATED `ABDULLAH BIN `UMAR (RA): that he had divorced his wife while she was menstruating during the lifetime of Allah's Messenger (ﷺ). `Umar bin Al-Khattab asked Allah's Messenger (ﷺ) about that. Allah's Messenger (ﷺ) said, "Order him (your son) to take her back and keep her till she is clean and then to wait till she gets her next period and becomes clean again, whereupon, if he wishes to keep her, he can do so, and if he wishes to divorce her he can divorce her before having sexual intercourse with her; and that is the prescribed period which Allah has fixed for the women meant to be divorced." (5251) □

1695. Narrated Ibn `Umar: (Divorcing my wife during her menses) was counteds one legal divorce. (5253) □

1696. Narrated Abu Usaid: We went out with the Prophet (ﷺ) to a garden called Ash-Shaut till we reached two walls between which we sat down. The Prophet (ﷺ) said, "Sit here," and went in (the garden). The Jauniyya (a lady from Bani Jaun) had been brought and lodged in a house in a date-palm garden in the home of Umaima bint An- Nu`man bin Sharahil, and her wet nurse was with her. When the Prophet (ﷺ) entered upon her, he said to her, "Give me yourself (in marriage) as a gift." She said, "Can a princess give herself in marriage to an ordinary man?" The Prophet (ﷺ) raised his hand to pat her so that she might become tranquil. She said, "I seek refuge with Allah from you." He said, "You have sought refuge with One Who gives refuge. Then the Prophet (ﷺ) came out to us and said, "O Abu Usaid! Give her two white linen dresses to wear and let her go back to her family." (5255) □

1697. Narrated Masruq: I asked `Aisha about the option: She said, "The Prophet (ﷺ) gave us the option. Do you think that option was considered as a divorce?" I said, "It matters little to me if I give my wife the option once or a hundred times after she has chosen me."(5263) □

1698. Narrated `Aisha: A man divorced his wife and she married another man who proved to be impotent and divorced her. She could not get her satisfaction from him, and after a while he divorced her. Then she came to the Prophet and said, "O Allah's Messenger (ﷺ)! My first husband divorced me and then I married another man who entered upon me to consummate his marriage but he proved to be impotent and did not approach me except once during which he benefited nothing from me. Can I remarry my first husband in this case?" Allah's Messenger (ﷺ) said, "It is unlawful to marry your first husband till the other husband consummates his marriage with you." (5265) □

1699. Narrated Sa`id bin Jubair: that he heard Ibn `Abbas saying, "If a man makes his wife unlawful for him, it does not mean that she is divorced." He added, "Indeed in the Messenger of Allah, you have a good example to follow." (5266) □

1700. Narrated Ibn `Abbas: The wife of Thabit bin Qais came to the Prophet (ﷺ) and said, "O Allah's Messenger (ﷺ)! I do not blame Thabit for defects in his character or his religion, but I, being a Muslim, dislike to behave in un-Islamic manner (if I remain with him)." On that Allah's Messenger (ﷺ) said (to her), "Will you give back the garden which your husband has given you (as Mahr)?" She said, "Yes." Then the Prophet (ﷺ) said to Thabit, "O Thabit! Accept your garden, and divorce her once." (5273) □

1701. Narrated Nafi`: Whenever Ibn `Umar was asked about marrying a Christian lady or a Jewess, he would say: "Allah has made it unlawful for the believers to marry ladies who ascribe partners in worship to Allah, and I do not know of a greater thing, as regards to ascribing partners in worship, etc. to Allah, than that a lady should say that Jesus is her Lord although he is just one of Allah's slaves." (5285) □

1702. Narrated Ibn 'Abbas: The pagans were of two kinds as regards their relationship to the Prophet and the Believers. Some of them were those with whom the Prophet was at war and used to fight against, and they used to fight him; the others were those with whom the Prophet (ﷺ) made a treaty, and neither did the Prophet (ﷺ) fight them, nor did they fight him. If a lady from the first group of pagans emigrated towards the Muslims, her hand would not be asked in marriage unless she got the menses and then became clean. When she became clean, it would be lawful for her to get married, and if her husband emigrated too before she got married, then she would be returned to him. If any slave or female slave emigrated from them to the Muslims, then they would be considered free persons (not slaves) and they would have the same rights as given to other emigrants. The narrator then mentioned about the pagans involved with the Muslims in a treaty, the same as occurs in Mujahid's narration. If a male slave or a female slave emigrated from such pagans as had made a treaty with the Muslims, they would not be returned, but their prices would be paid (to the pagans). (5286) □

1703. Narrated Nafi`: Ibn `Umar used to say about the Ila (which Allah defined in the Holy Book), "If the period of Ila expires, then the husband has either to retain his wife in a handsome manner or to divorce her as Allah has ordered." (5290) □

1704. Ibn `Umar added: "When the period of four months has expired, the husband should be put in prison so that he should divorce his wife, but the divorce does not occur unless the husband himself declares it. This has been mentioned by `Uthman, `Ali, Abu Ad-Darda, `Aisha and twelve other companions of the Prophet (p.b.u.h)." (5291) ☐

1705. Narrated Abu Huraira: A man came to the Prophet (ﷺ) and said, "O Allah's Messenger (ﷺ)! A black child has been born for me." The Prophet asked him, "Have you got camels?" The man said, "Yes." The Prophet (ﷺ) asked him, "What color are they?" The man replied, "Red." The Prophet (ﷺ) said, "Is there a grey one among them?' The man replied, "Yes." The Prophet (ﷺ) said, "Where comes that?" He said, "May be it is because of heredity." The Prophet (ﷺ) said, "May be your latest son has this color because of heredity." (5305) ☐

1706. Narrated `Abdullah: An Ansari man accused his wife (of committing illegal sexual intercourse). The Prophet (ﷺ) made both of them takes the oath of Lian, and separated them from each other (by divorce). (5306) ☐

1707. Narrated Ibn Juraij: Ibn Shihab informed me of Lian and the tradition related to it, referring to the narration of Sahl bin Sa`d, the brother of Bani Sa`idi He said, "An Ansari man came to Allah's Messenger (ﷺ) and said, 'O Allah's Apostle! If a man saw another man with his wife, should he kill him, or what should he do?' So Allah revealed concerning his affair what is mentioned in the Holy Qur'an about the affair of those involved in a case of Lian. The Prophet (ﷺ) said, 'Allah has given His verdict regarding you and your wife.' So they carried out Lian in the mosque while I was present there. When they had finished, the man said, "O Allah's Messenger (ﷺ)! If I should now keep her with me as a wife then I have told a lie about her. Then he divorced her thrice before Allah's Messenger (ﷺ) ordered him, when they had finished the Lian process. So he divorced her in front of the Prophet (ﷺ)." Ibn Shihab added, "After their case, it became a tradition that a couple involved in a case of Lian should be separated by divorce. That lady was pregnant then, and later on her son was called by his mother's name. The tradition concerning their inheritance was that she would be his heir and he would inherit of her property the share Allah had prescribed for him." Ibn Shihab said that Sahl bin Sa`d As'Saidi said that the Prophet (ﷺ) said (in the above narration), "If that lady delivers a small red child like a lizard, then the lady has spoken the truth and the man was a liar, but if she delivers a child with black eyes and huge lips, then her husband has spoken the truth." Then she delivered it in the shape one would dislike (as it proved her guilty). (5309) ☐

1708. Narrated Al-Qasim bin Muhammad: Ibn `Abbas; said, "Once Lian was mentioned before the Prophet (ﷺ) whereupon `Asim bin Adi said something and went away. Then a man from his tribe came to him, complaining that he had found a man with his wife. `Asim said, 'I have not been put to task except for my statement (about Lian).' `Asim took the man to the Prophet (ﷺ) and the man told him of the state in which he had found his wife. The man was pale, thin, and of lank hair, while the other man whom he claimed he had seen with his wife, was brown, fat and had much flesh on his calves. The Prophet (ﷺ) invoked, saying, 'O Allah! Reveal the truth.' So that lady delivered a child resembling the man whom her husband had mentioned he had found her with. The Prophet (ﷺ) then made them carry out Lian." Then a man from that gathering asked Ibn `Abbas, "Was she the same lady regarding which the Prophet (ﷺ) had said, 'If I were to stone to death someone without witness, I would have stoned this lady'?" Ibn `Abbas said, "No, that was another lady who, though being a Muslim, used to arouse suspicion by her outright misbehavior." (5310) ☐

1709. Narrated Sa`id bin Jubair: I asked Ibn `Umar, "(What is the verdict if) a man accuses his wife of illegal sexual intercourse?" Ibn `Umar said, "The Prophet (ﷺ) separated (by divorce) the couple of Bani Al-Ajlan, and said, (to them), 'Allah knows that one of you two is a liar; so will one of you repent?' But both of them refused. He again said, 'Allah knows that one of you two is a liar; so will one of you repent?' But both of them refused. So he separated them by divorce." (Aiyub, a sub-narrator said: `Amr bin Dinar said to me, "There is something else in this Hadith which you have not mentioned. It goes thus: The man said, 'What about my money (i.e. the Mahr that I have given to my wife)?' It was said, 'You have no right to restore any money, for if you have spoken the truth (as regards the accusation), you have also consummated your marriage with her; and if you have told a lie, you are less rightful to have your money back.' ") (5311) □

1710. Narrated Ibn `Umar: The Prophet (ﷺ) made a man and his wife carry out Lian, and the husband repudiated her child. So the Prophet got them separated (by divorce) and decided that the child belonged to the mother only. (5315) □

1711. Narrated Um Salama: A lady from Bani Aslam, called Subai'a, become a widow while she was pregnant. Abu As-Sanabil bin Ba'kak demanded her hand in marriage, but she refused to marry him and said, "By Allah, I cannot marry him unless I have completed one of the two prescribed periods." About ten days later (after having delivered her child), she went to the Prophet (ﷺ) and he said (to her), "You can marry now." (5318) □

1712. Narrated Qasim bin Muhammad and Sulaiman bin Yasar: that Yahya bin Sa`id bin Al-`As divorced the daughter of `Abdur-Rahman bin Al-Hakarn. `Abdur-Rahman took her to his house. On that `Aisha sent a message to Marwan bin Al-Hakam who was the ruler of Medina, saying, "Fear Allah, and urge your brother) to return her to her house." Marwan (in Sulaiman's version) said, "Abdur-Rahman bin Al-Hakam did not obey me (or had a convincing argument)." (In Al-Qasim's versions Marwan said, "Have you not heard of the case of Fatima bint Qais?" Aisha said, "The case of Fatima bint Qais is not in your favor.' Marwan bin Al-Hakam said to `Aisha, "The reason that made Fatima bint Qais go to her father's house is just applicable to the daughter of `Abdur-Rahman." (5321) □

1713. Narrated Qasim: Urwa said to Aisha, "Do you know so-and-so, the daughter of Al-Hakam? Her husband divorced her irrevocably and she left (her husband's house)." `Aisha said, "What a bad thing she has done!" 'Urwa said (to `Aisha), "Haven't you heard the statement of Fatima?" `Aisha replied, "It is not in her favor to mention." 'Urwa added, `Aisha reproached (Fatima) severely and said, "Fatima was in a lonely place, and she was prone to danger, so the Prophet (ﷺ) allowed her (to go out of her husband's house). (5325) □

1714. Narrated Al-Hasan: The sister of Ma'qil bin Yasar was married to a man and then that man divorced her and remained away from her till her period of the 'Iddah expired. Then he demanded for her hand in marriage, but Ma'qil got angry out of pride and haughtiness and said, "He kept away from her when he could still retain her, and now he demands her hand again?" So Ma'qil disagreed to remarry her to him. Then Allah revealed: 'When you have divorced women and they have fulfilled the term of their prescribed period, do not prevent them from marrying their (former) husbands.' (2.232) So the Prophet (ﷺ) sent for Ma'qil and recited to him (Allah's order) and consequently Ma'qil gave up his pride and haughtiness and yielded to Allah's order. (5331) ☐

1715. Zainab further said: "I heard my mother, Um Salama saying that a woman came to Allah's Messenger (ﷺ) and said, "O Allah's Messenger (ﷺ)! The husband of my daughter has died and she is suffering from an eye disease, can she apply kohl to her eye?" Allah's Messenger (ﷺ) replied, "No," twice or thrice. (Every time she repeated her question) he said, "No." Then Allah's Messenger (ﷺ) added, "It is just a matter of four months and ten days. In the Pre-Islamic Period of ignorance a widow among you should throw a globe of dung when one year has elapsed." (5336) ☐

1716. I (Humaid) said to Zainab, "What does 'throwing a globe of dung when one year had elapsed' mean?" Zainab said, "When a lady was bereaved of her husband, she would live in a wretched small room and put on the worst clothes she had and would not touch any scent till one year had elapsed. Then she would bring an animal, e.g. a donkey, a sheep or a bird and rub her body against it. The animal against which she would rub her body would scarcely survive. Only then she would come out of her room, whereupon she would be given a globe of dung which she would throw away and then she would use the scent she liked or the like." (5337) ☐

1717. Narrated Mujahid: (regarding the Verse): 'If any of you dies and leaves wives behind,' That was the period of the 'Iddah which the widow was obliged to spend in the house of the late husband. Then Allah revealed: And those of you who die and leave wives should bequeath for their wives a year's maintenance and residence without turning them out, but if they leave, there is no blame on you for what they do of themselves, provided it is honorable (i.e. lawful marriage) (2.240) Mujahid said: Allah has ordered that a widow has the right to stay for seven months and twenty days with her husband's relatives through her husband's will and testament so that she will complete the period of one year (of 'Iddah). But the widow has the right to stay that extra period or go out of her husband's house as is indicated by the statement of Allah: 'But if they leave there is no blame on you,...' (2.240) Ibn `Abbas said: The above Verse has cancelled the order of spending the period of the 'Iddah at her late husband's house, and so she could spend her period of the 'Iddah wherever she likes. And Allah says: 'Without turning them out.' 'Ata said: If she would, she could spend her period of the 'Iddah at her husband's house, and live there according to her (husband's) will and testament, and if she would, she could go out (of her husband's house) as Allah says: 'There is no blame on you for what they do of themselves.' (2.240) 'Ata added: Then the Verses of inheritance were revealed and the order of residence (for the widow) was cancelled, and she could spend her period of the 'Iddah wherever she would like, and she was no longer entitled to be accommodated by her husband's family. (5344) □

68. SUPPORTING THE FAMILY

1718. NARRATED ABU MAS`UD AL-ANSARI (RA): The Prophet (ﷺ) said, "When a Muslim spends something on his family intending to receive Allah's reward it is regarded as Sadaqa for him." (5351) □

1719. Narrated Abu Huraira: Allah's Messenger (ﷺ) said, "Allah said, 'O son of Adam! Spend, and I shall spend on you." (5352) □

1720. Narrated Abu Huraira: The Prophet (ﷺ) said, "The one who looks after a widow or a poor person is like a Mujahid (warrior) who fights for Allah's Cause, or like him who performs prayers all the night and fasts all the day." (5353) □

1721. Narrated Abu Huraira: "The Prophet (ﷺ) said, 'The best alms is that which is given when one is rich, and a giving hand is better than a taking one, and you should start first to support your dependents.' A wife says, 'You should either provide me with food or divorce me.' A slave says, 'Give me food and enjoy my service." A son says, "Give me food; to whom do you leave me?" The people said, "O Abu Huraira! Did you hear that from Allah's Messenger (ﷺ)?" He said, "No, it is from my own self." (5355) □

1722. Narrated `Umar: The Prophet (ﷺ) used to sell the dates of the garden of Bani An-Nadir and store for his family so much food as would cover their needs for a whole year. (5357) □

1723. Narrated `Aisha: Hind bint `Utba said, "O Allah's Messenger (ﷺ)! Abu Sufyan is a miser and he does not give me what is sufficient for me and my children. Can I take of his property without his knowledge?" The Prophet (ﷺ) said, "Take what is sufficient for you and your children, and the amount should be just and reasonable. (5364) □

69. Food, Meals

1724. Narrated Abu Musa Al-Ash`ari (ra): The Prophet (ﷺ) said, "Give food to the hungry, pay a visit to the sick and release (set free) the one in captivity (by paying his ransom). (5373) □

1725. Narrated Abu Huraira: The family of Muhammad did not eat their fill for three successive days till he died. (5374) □

1726. Narrated `Umar bin Abi Salama: I was a boy under the care of Allah's Messenger (ﷺ) and my hand used to go around the dish while I was eating. So Allah's Messenger (ﷺ) said to me, 'O boy! Mention the Name of Allah and eat with your right hand, and eat of the dish what is nearer to you." Since then I have applied those instructions when eating. (5376) ☐

1727. Narrated Anas bin Malik: A tailor invited Allah's Messenger (ﷺ) to a meal which he had prepared. I went along with Allah's Messenger (ﷺ) and saw him seeking to eat the pieces of gourd from the various sides of the dish. Since that day I have liked to eat gourd. `Umar bin Abi Salama said: The Prophet, said to me, "Eat with your right hand." (5379) ☐

1728. Narrated Khalid bin Al-Walid: That he went with Allah's Messenger (ﷺ) to the house of Maimuna, who was his and Ibn `Abbas' aunt. He found with her a roasted mastigure which her sister Hufaida bint Al-Harith had brought from Najd. Maimuna presented the mastigure before Allah's Messenger (ﷺ) who rarely started eating any (unfamiliar) food before it was described and named for him. (But that time) Allah's Messenger (ﷺ) stretched his hand towards the (meat of the) mastigure whereupon a lady from among those who were present, said, "You should inform Allah's Messenger (ﷺ) of what you have presented to him. O Allah's Messenger (ﷺ)! It is the meat of a mastigure." (On learning that) Allah's Messenger (ﷺ) withdrew his hand from the meat of the mastigure. Khalid bin Al-Walid said, "O Allah's Messenger (ﷺ)! Is this unlawful to eat?" Allah's Messenger (ﷺ) replied, "No, but it is not found in the land of my people, so I do not like it." Khalid said, "Then I pulled the mastigure (meat) towards me and ate it while Allah's Messenger (ﷺ) was looking at me. (5391) ☐

1729. Narrated Abu Huraira: Allah's Messenger (ﷺ) said, "The food for two persons is sufficient for three, and the food of three persons is sufficient for four persons." (5392) ☐

1730. Narrated Nafi`: Ibn `Umar never used to take his meal unless a poor man was called to eat with him. One day I brought a poor man to eat with him, the man ate too much, whereupon Ibn `Umar said, "O Nafi`! Don't let this man enter my house, for I heard the Prophet (ﷺ) saying, "A believer eats in one intestine (is satisfied with a little food), and a kafir (unbeliever) eats in seven intestines (eats much food). (5393)

☐

1731. Narrated `Amr: Abu Nahik was avaricious eater. Ibn `Umar said to him, "Allah's Messenger (ﷺ) said, "A Kafir eats in seven intestines (eats much)." On that Abu Nahik said, "But I believe in Allah and His Apostle." (5395) ☐

1732. Narrated Abu Juhaifa: Allah's Messenger (ﷺ) said, "I do not take my meals while leaning (against something). (5398) ☐

1733. Narrated Sahl bin Sa`d: We used to be happy on Fridays, for there was an old lady who used to pull out the roots of Silq and put it in a cooking pot with some barley. When we had finished the prayer, we would visit her and she would present that dish before us. So we used to be happy on Fridays because of that, and we never used to take our meals or have a mid-day nap except after the Friday prayer. By Allah, that meal contained no fat. (5403) ☐

1734. Narrated Abu Huraira: The Prophet (ﷺ) never criticized any food (he was invited to) but he used to eat if he liked the food, and leave it if he disliked it. (5409) ☐

1735. Narrated Abu Huraira: Once the Prophet (ﷺ) distributed dates among his companions and gave each one seven dates. He gave me seven dates too, one of which was dry and hard, but none of the other dates was more liked by me than that one, for it prolonged my chewing it. (5411)

1736. Narrated Abu Hazim: I asked Sahl bin Sa`d, "Did Allah's Messenger (ﷺ) ever eat white flour?" Sahl said, "Allah's Messenger (ﷺ) never saw white flour since Allah sent him as an Apostle till He took him unto Him." I asked, "Did the people have (use) sieves during the lifetime of Allah's Messenger (ﷺ)?" Sahl said, "Allah's Messenger (ﷺ) never saw (used) a sieve (sift) since Allah sent him as an Apostle until He took him unto Him," I said, "How could you eat barley unsifted?" he said, "We used to grind it and then blow off its husk, and after the husk flew away, we used to prepare the dough (bake) and eat it." (5413) ☐

1737. Narrated Abu Huraira: that he passed by a group of people in front of whom there was a roasted sheep. They invited him but he refused to eat and said, "Allah's Messenger (ﷺ) left this world without satisfying his hunger even with barley bread." (5414) ☐

1738. Narrated Anas bin Malik: The Prophet (ﷺ) never took his meals at a dining table, nor in small plates, and he never ate thin wellbaked bread. (The sub-narrator asked Qatada, "Over what did they use to take their meals?" Qatada said, "On leather dining sheets." (5415) ☐

1739. Narrated `Aisha: The family of Muhammad had not eaten wheat bread to their satisfaction for three consecutive days since his arrival at Medina till he died. (5416) ☐

1740. Narrated `Aisha: that whenever one of her relatives died, the women assembled and then dispersed (returned to their houses) except her relatives and close friends. She would order that a pot of Talbina be cooked. Then Tharid (a dish prepared from meat and bread) would be prepared and the Talbina would be poured on it. `Aisha would say (to the women),"Eat of it, for I heard Allah's Messenger (ﷺ) saying, 'The Talbina soothes the heart of the patient and relieves him from some of his sadness.'" (5417) ☐

1741. Narrated `Aisha: Allah's Messenger (ﷺ) used to love sweet edible things and honey. (5431) ☐

1742. Narrated Abu Mas`ud Al-Ansari: There was a man called Abu Shu'aib, and he had a slave who was a butcher. He said (to his slave), "Prepare a meal to which I may invite Allah's Messenger (ﷺ) along with four other men." So he invited Allah's Messenger (ﷺ) and four other men, but another man followed them whereupon the Prophet (ﷺ) said, "You have invited me as one of five guests, but now another man has followed us. If you wish you can admit him, and if you wish you can refuse him." On that the host said, "But I admit him." Narrated Muhammad bin Isma`il: If guests are sitting at a dining table, they do not have the right to carry food from other tables to theirs, but they can pass on food from their own table to each other; otherwise they should leave it. (5434) ☐

1743. Narrated `Abdullah bin Ja`far bin Abi Talib: I saw Allah's Messenger (ﷺ) eating fresh dates with snake cucumber. (5440) ☐

1744. Narrated Jabir bin `Abdullah: The Prophet (ﷺ) said, "Whoever has eaten garlic or onion should keep away from us (or should keep away from our mosque).' (5452) ☐

1745. Narrated Jabir bin `Abdullah: We were with Allah's Messenger (ﷺ) collecting Al-Kabath at Mar-Az-Zahran. The Prophet (ﷺ) said, "Collect the black ones, for they are better." Somebody said, (O Allah's Messenger (ﷺ)!) Have you ever shepherded sheep?" He said, "There has been no prophet but has shepherded them." (5453) ☐

1746. Narrated Ibn `Abbas: The Prophet (ﷺ) said, 'When you eat, do not wipe your hands till you have licked it, or had it licked by somebody else." (5456) ☐

1747. Narrated Abu Umama: Whenever the Prophet (ﷺ) finished his meals (or when his dining sheet was taken away), he used to say. "Praise be to Allah Who has satisfied our needs and quenched our thirst. Your favor cannot by compensated or denied." Once he said, upraise be to You, O our Lord! Your favor cannot be compensated, nor can be left, nor can be dispensed with, O our Lord!" (5459) ☐

1748. Narrated Abu Huraira: The Prophet (ﷺ) said, "When your servant brings your food to you, if you do not ask him to join you, then at least ask him to take one or two handfuls, for he has suffered from its heat (while cooking it) and has taken pains to cook it nicely." (5460) ☐

1749. Narrated Anas bin Malik: The Prophet (ﷺ) said, If supper is served and the Iqama for (Isha) prayer is proclaimed, start with you supper first." (5463) ☐

1750. Narrated Jabala: "We were in Medina with some of the Iraqi people, and we were struck with famine and Ibn Az-Zubair used to give us dates. Ibn `Umar used to pass by and say, "The Prophet (ﷺ) forbade us to eat two dates at a time, unless one takes the permission of one's companions." (2455) ☐

1751. Narrated Anas: No doubt, the Prophet (ﷺ) mortgaged his armor for barley grams. Once I took barley bread with some dissolved fat on it to the Prophet (ﷺ) and I heard him saying, "The household of Muhammad did not possess except a Sa (of food grain, barley, etc.) for both the morning and the evening meals although they were nine houses." (2508) ☐

1752. Narrated `Aisha: Abu Bakr had a slave who used to give him some of his earnings. Abu Bakr used to eat from it. One day he brought something and Abu Bakr ate from it. The slave said to him, "Do you know what this is?" Abu Bakr then enquired, "What is it?" The slave said, "Once, in the pre-Islamic period of ignorance I foretold somebody's future though I did not know this knowledge of foretelling but I, cheated him, and when he met me, he gave me something for that service, and that is what you have eaten from." Then Abu Bakr put his hand in his mouth and vomited whatever was present in his stomach. (3842) ☐

1753. Narrated `Aisha: When the Prophet (ﷺ) died, nothing which can be eaten by a living creature was left on my shelf except some barley grain. I ate of it for a period and when I measured it, it finished. (6451) ☐

1754. Narrated `Aisha: A complete month would pass by during which we would not make a fire (for cooking), and our food used to be only dates and water unless we were given a present of some meat. (6458) ☐

70. Aqiqa

1755. Narrated Abu Musa (ra): A son was born to me and I took him to the Prophet (ﷺ) who named him Ibrahim, did Tahnik (touching the lips of a newborn baby with honey, sweet juice or pressed dates) for him with a date, invoked Allah to bless him and returned him to me. (5467) □

1756. Narrated Asma' bint Abu Bakr: I conceived `Abdullah bin Az-Zubair at Mecca and went out while I was about to give birth. I came to Medina and encamped at Quba', and gave birth at Quba'. Then I brought the child to Allah's Messenger (ﷺ) and placed it (on his lap). He asked for a date, chewed it, and put his saliva in the mouth of the child. So the first thing to enter its stomach was the saliva of Allah's Messenger (ﷺ). Then he did its Tahnik with a date, and invoked Allah to bless him. It was the first child born in the Islamic era, therefore they (Muslims) were very happy with its birth, for it had been said to them that the Jews had bewitched them, and so they would not produce any offspring. (5469) □

1757. Narrated Anas bin Malik: Abu Talha had a child who was sick. Once, while Abu Talha was out, the child died. When Abu Talha returned home, he asked, "How does my son fare?" Um Salaim (his wife) replied, "He is quieter than he has ever been." Then she brought supper for him and he took his supper and slept with her. When he had finished, she said (to him), "Bury the child (as he's dead)." Next morning Abu Talha came to Allah's Messenger (ﷺ) and told him about that. The Prophet (ﷺ) said (to him), "Did you sleep with your wife last night?" Abu Talha said, "Yes". The Prophet (ﷺ) said, "O Allah! Bestow your blessing on them as regards that night of theirs." Um Sulaim gave birth to a boy. Abu Talha told me to take care of the child till it was taken to the Prophet. Then Abu Talha took the child to the Prophet (ﷺ) and Um Sulaim sent some dates along with the child. The Prophet (ﷺ) took the child (on his lap) and asked if there was something with him. The people replied, "Yes, a few dates." The Prophet took a date, chewed it, took some of it out of his mouth, put it into the child's mouth and did Tahnik for him with that, and named him 'Abdullah. (5470) □

1758. Narrated Salman bin 'Amri Ad-Dabbi, the Prophet (ﷺ) said, 'Aqiqa is to be offered for a (newly born) boy. (5471) □

1759. Narrated Wathila bin Al-Asqa: Allah's Messenger (ﷺ) said, "Verily, one of the worst lies is to claim falsely to be the son of someone other than one's real father, or to claim to have had a dream one has not had, or to attribute to me what I have not said." (3509) □

1760. Narrated Said bin Jubair: Ibn 'Abbas was asked, "How old were you when the Prophet (ﷺ) died?" He replied. "At that time I had been circumcised." At that time, people did not circumcise the boys till they attained the age of puberty. Sa'id bin Jubair said, "Ibn 'Abbas said, 'When the Prophet died, I had already been circumcised. (6299) □

71. Hunting, Slaughtering

1761. Narrated `Adi bin Hatim (ra): I asked Allah's Messenger (ﷺ) about the Mi'rad. He said, "If you hit the game with its sharp edge, eat it, but if the Mi'rad hits the game with its shaft with a hit by its broad side do not eat it, for it has been beaten to death with a piece of wood. (i.e. unlawful)." I asked, "If I let loose my trained hound after a game?" He said, "If you let loose your trained hound after game, and mention the name of Allah, then you can eat." I said, "If the hound eats of the game?" He said "Then you should not eat of it, for the hound has hunted the game for itself and not for you." I said, "Some times I send my hound and then I find some other hound with it?" He said "Don't eat the game, as you have mentioned the Name of Allah on your dog only and not on the other." (5476) □

1762. Narrated Abu Tha`laba Al-Khushani: I said, "O Allah's Prophet! We are living in a land ruled by the people of the Scripture; can we take our meals in their utensils? In that land there is plenty of game and I hunt the game with my bow and with my hound that is not trained and with my trained hound. Then what is lawful for me to eat?" He said, "As for what you have mentioned about the people of the Scripture, if you can get utensils other than theirs, do not eat out of theirs, but if you cannot get other than theirs, wash their utensils and eat out of it. If you hunt an animal with your bow after mentioning Allah's Name, eat of it. and if you hunt something with your trained hound after mentioning Allah's Name, eat of it, and if you hunt something with your untrained hound (and get it before it dies) and slaughter it, eat of it." (5478) □

1763. Narrated `Abdullah bin Maghaffal: that he saw a man throwing stones with two fingers (at something) and said to him, "Do not throw stones, for Allah's Messenger (صلى الله عليه وسلم) has forbidden throwing stones, or he used to dislike it." `Abdullah added: Throwing stones will neither hunt the game, nor kill (or hurt) an enemy, but it may break a tooth or gouge out an eye." Afterwards `Abdullah once again saw the man throwing stones. He said to him, "I tell you that Allah's Messenger (صلى الله عليه وسلم) has forbidden or disliked the throwing the stones (in such a way), yet you are throwing stones! I shall not talk to you for such-and-such a period." (5479) □

1764. Narrated `Abdullah bin Mughaffal Al-Muzani: The Prophet (صلى الله عليه وسلم) forbade the throwing of stones (with the thumb and the index or middle finger), and said "It neither hunts a game nor kills (or hurts) an enemy, but it gouges out an eye or breaks a tooth." (6220) □

1765. Narrated Ibn `Umar: The Prophet (صلى الله عليه وسلم) said, "Whoever keeps a (pet) dog which is neither a watch dog nor a hunting dog, will get a daily deduction of two Qirat from his good deeds." (5480) □

1766. Narrated Adi bin Hatim: The Prophet (صلى الله عليه وسلم) said, "If you let loose your hound after a game and mention Allah's Name on sending it, and the hound catches the game and kills it, then you can eat of it. But if the hound eats of it, then you should not eat thereof, for the hound has caught it for itself. And if along with your hound, joined other hounds, and Allah's Name was not mentioned at the time of their sending, and they catch an animal and kill it, you should not eat of it, for you will not know which of them has killed it. And if you have thrown an arrow at the game and then find it (dead) two or three days later and, it bears no mark other than the wound inflicted by your arrow, then you can eat of it. But if the game is found (dead) in water, then do not eat of it." (5484) □

1767. Narrated Anas bin Malik: We provoked a rabbit at Marr Az-Zahran till it started jumping. My companions chased it till they got tired. But I alone ran after it and caught it and brought it to Abu Talha. He sent both its legs to the Prophet who accepted them. (5489) □

1768. Narrated Ibn Abi `Aufa: We participated with the Prophet (ﷺ) in six or seven Ghazawat, and we used to eat locusts with him. (5495) □

1769. Narrated `Abdullah: Allah's Messenger (ﷺ) said that he met Zaid bin `Amr Nufail at a place near Baldah and this had happened before Allah's Messenger (ﷺ) received the Divine Inspiration. Allah's Messenger (ﷺ) presented a dish of meat (that had been offered to him by the pagans) to Zaid bin `Amr, but Zaid refused to eat of it and then said (to the pagans), "I do not eat of what you slaughter on your stonealtars (Ansabs) nor do I eat except that on which Allah's Name has been mentioned on slaughtering." (5499) □

1770. Narrated Ka`b: that a slave girl of theirs used to shepherd some sheep at Si'a (a mountain near Medina). On seeing one of her sheep dying, she broke a stone and slaughtered it. Ka`b said to his family, "Do not eat till I go to the Prophet (ﷺ) and ask him, or, till I send someone to ask him." So he went to the Prophet (ﷺ) or sent someone to him The Prophet (ﷺ) permitted (them) to eat it. (5501) □

1771. Narrated `Aisha: A group of people said to the Prophet, "Some people bring us meat and we do not know whether they have mentioned Allah's Name or not on slaughtering the animal." He said, "Mention Allah's Name on it and eat." Those people had embraced Islam recently. (5507) □

1772. Narrated Ibn `Umar: that he entered upon Yahya bin Sa`id while one of Yahya's sons was aiming at a hen after tying it. Ibn `Umar walked to it and untied it. Then he brought it and the boy and said. "Prevent your boys from tying the birds for the sake of killing them, as I have heard the Prophet (ﷺ) forbidding the killing of an animal or other living thing after tying them." (5514) □

1773. Narrated Sa`id bin Jubair: While I was with Ibn `Umar, we passed by a group of young men who had tied a hen and started shooting at it. When they saw Ibn `Umar, they dispersed, leaving it. On that Ibn `Umar said, "Who has done this? The Prophet (ﷺ) cursed the one who did so." (5515) □

1774. Narrated `Abdullah bin Yazid: The Prophet (ﷺ) forbade An-Nuhba and Al-Muthla (looting and Mutilation). (5516) □

1775. Narrated Jabir bin `Abdullah: On the Day of the battle of Khaibar, Allah's Messenger (ﷺ) made donkey's meat unlawful and allowed the eating of horse flesh. (5520) □

1776. Narrated Abu Tha`laba: Allah's Messenger (ﷺ) forbade the eating of the meat of beasts having fangs (a long, sharp tooth). (5530) □

1777. Narrated `Abdullah bin `Abbas: Once Allah's Messenger (ﷺ) passed by a dead sheep and said (to the people), "Why don't you use its hide (skin)?" They said, "But it is dead," He said, "Only eating it, is prohibited." (5531) □

1778. Narrated Maimuna: A mouse fell into the butter-fat and died. The Prophet (ﷺ) was asked about that. He said, "Throw away the mouse and the butter-fat that surrounded it, and eat the rest of the butter-fat (As-Samn). (5538) □

1779. Narrated Salim: Ibn `Umar disliked the branding of animals on the face. Ibn `Umar said, "The Prophet (ﷺ) forbade beating (animals) on the face." (5541) □

1780. Narrated Anas: I brought a brother of mine to the Prophet (ﷺ) to do Tahnik for him while the Prophet (ﷺ) was in a sheep fold of his, and I saw him branding a sheep. (Sub-narrator said: I think Anas said, branding it on the ear.) (5542) □

1781. Narrated Rafi` bin Khadij: We used to offer the `Asr prayer with the Prophet (ﷺ) and slaughter a camel, the meat of which would be divided in ten parts. We would eat the cooked meat before sunset. (2485) □

72. AL-ADHA FESTIVAL SACRIFICE

1782. THE PROPHET (ﷺ) SAID (on the day of Idal-Adha): The first thing we will do on this day of ours, is to offer the (Eid) prayer and then return to slaughter the sacrifice. Whoever does so, he acted according to our Sunnah (tradition), and whoever slaughtered (the sacrifice) before the prayer, what he offered was just meat he presented to his family, and that will not be considered as Nusak (sacrifice)." (On hearing that) Abu Burda bin Niyar got up, for he had slaughtered the sacrifice before the prayer, and said, "I have got a six month old ram." The Prophet (ﷺ) said, 'Slaughter it (as a sacrifice) but it will not be sufficient for any-one else (as a sacrifice after you). Al-Bara' added: The Prophet (ﷺ) said, "Whoever slaughtered (the sacrifice) after the prayer, he slaughtered it at the right time and followed the tradition of the Muslims." (5545) □

1783. Narrated Anas bin Malik (ra): The Prophet (ﷺ) said on the day of Nahr, "Whoever has slaughtered his sacrifice before the prayer, should repeat it (slaughter another sacrifice)." A man got up and said, "O Allah's Messenger (ﷺ)! This is a day on which meat is desired." He then mentioned his neighbors saying, "I have a six month old ram which is to me better than the meat of two sheep." The Prophet (ﷺ) allowed him to slaughter it as a sacrifice, but I do not know whether this permission was valid for other than that man or not. The Prophet (ﷺ) then went towards two rams and slaughtered them, and then the people went towards some sheep and distributed them among themselves. (5549) □

1784. Ibn 'Umar said, "Allah's Messenger (ﷺ) used to slaughter (camels and sheep, etc.,) as sacrifices at the Musalla (where Eid congregations are held)." (5552) □

1785. Narrated `Uqba bin 'Amir: that the Prophet (ﷺ) gave him some sheep to distribute among his companions to slaughter as sacrifices (Eid--al--Adha). A kid was left and he told the Prophet (ﷺ) of that whereupon he said to him, "Slaughter it as a sacrifice (on your behalf). (5555) ☐

1786. Narrated Anas: The Prophet (ﷺ) slaughtered two rams, black and white in color (as sacrifices), and I saw him putting his foot on their sides and mentioning Allah's Name and Takbir (Allahu Akbar). Then he slaughtered them with his own hands. (5558) ☐

1787. Narrated Salama bin Al-Aqua': The Prophet (ﷺ) said, "Whoever has slaughtered a sacrifice should not keep anything of Its meat after three days." When it was the next year the people said, "O Allah's Messenger (ﷺ)! Shall we do as we did last year?" He said, ' Eat of it and feed of it to others and store of it for in that year the people were having a hard time and I wanted you to help (the needy). (5569) ☐

1789. Narrated Abu `Ubaid: I witnessed the Eid with `Uthman bin `Affan, and that was on a Friday. He offered the prayer before the sermon, saying, " O people! Today you have two 'It's (festivals) together, so whoever of those who live at Al-`Awali (suburbs) would like to wait for the Jumua prayer, he may wait, and whoever would like to return (home) is granted my permission to do so." (5572) ☐

73. DRINKS

1790. NARRATED AZ-ZUHRI: Anas bin Malik said, that once a domestic sheep was milked for Allah's Messenger (ﷺ) while he was in the house of Anas bin Malik. The milk was mixed with water drawn from the well in Anas's house. A tumbler (a glass) of it was presented to Allah's Messenger (ﷺ) who drank from it. Then Abu Bakr was sitting on his left side and a bedouin on his right side. When the Prophet (ﷺ) removed the tumbler from his mouth, Umar was afraid that the Prophet (ﷺ) might give it to the bedouin, so he said. "O Allah's Messenger (ﷺ)! Give it to Abu Bakr who is sitting by your side." But the Prophet (ﷺ) gave it to the bedouin, who was to his right and said, "You should start with the one on your right side." (2352) ☐

1791. Narrated Ibn `Umar: Allah's Messenger (ﷺ) said, "Whoever drinks alcoholic drinks in the world and does not repent (before dying), will be deprived of it in the Hereafter." (5575) □

1792. Narrated Abu Huraira: On the night Allah's Messenger (ﷺ) was taken on a night journey (Miraj) two cups, one containing wine and the other milk, were presented to him at Jerusalem. He looked at it and took the cup of milk. Gabriel said, "Praise be to Allah Who guided you to Al-Fitra (the right path); if you had taken (the cup of) wine, your nation would have gone astray." (5576) □

1793. Narrated Anas: "Alcoholic drinks were prohibited at the time we could rarely find wine made from grapes in Medina, for most of our liquors were made from unripe and ripe dates. (5580) □

1794. Narrated Anas bin Malik: I was serving Abu 'Ubaida, Abu Talha and Ubai bin Ka`b with a drink prepared from ripe and unripe dates. Then somebody came to them and said, "Alcoholic drinks have been prohibited." Abu Talha said, "Get up. O Anas, and pour (throw) it out! So I poured (threw) it out. (5582) □

1795. Narrated `Aisha: Allah's Messenger (ﷺ) was asked about Al-Bit (a kind of intoxicants made from fermented honey and water). He said, "All drinks that intoxicate are unlawful (to drink.) (5585) □

1796. Narrated Ibn `Umar: `Umar delivered a sermon on the pulpit of Allah's Messenger (ﷺ), saying, "Alcoholic drinks were prohibited by Divine Order, and these drinks used to be prepared from five things, i.e., grapes, dates, wheat, barley and honey. Alcoholic drink is that, that disturbs the mind." `Umar added, "I wish Allah's Apostle had not left us before he had given us definite verdicts concerning three matters, i.e., how much a grandfather may inherit (of his grandson), the inheritance of Al-Kalala (the deceased person among whose heirs there is no father or son), and various types of Riba (usury) ." □

1797. Narrated Abu 'Amir or Abu Malik Al-Ash'ari: that he heard the Prophet (ﷺ)

saying, "From among my followers there will be some people who will consider illegal sexual intercourse, the wearing of silk, the drinking of alcoholic drinks and the use of musical instruments, as lawful. And there will be some people who will stay near the side of a mountain and in the evening their shepherd will come to them with their sheep and ask them for something, but they will say to him, 'Return to us tomorrow.' Allah will destroy them during the night and will let the mountain fall on them, and He will transform the rest of them into monkeys and pigs and they will remain so till the Day of Resurrection." (5590) ☐

1798. Narrated `Abdullah bin `Amr: When the Prophet (ﷺ) forbade the use of certain containers (that were used for preparing alcoholic drinks), somebody said to the Prophet (ﷺ). "But not all the people can find skins." So he allowed them to use clay jars not covered with pitch. (5593) ☐

1799. Narrated Sahl bin Sa`d: Abu Usaid As Sa`idi invited the Prophet (ﷺ) to his wedding banquet. At that time his wife was serving them and she was the bride. She said, "Do you know what (kind of syrup) I soaked (made) for Allah's Apostle? I soaked some dates in water in a Tur (bowl) overnight.' (5597) ☐

1800. Narrated Abu Al-Juwairiyya: I asked Ibn `Abbas about Al-Badhaq. He said, "Muhammad prohibited alcoholic drinks before it was called Al-Badhaq (by saying), 'Any drink that intoxicates is unlawful.' I said, 'What about good lawful drinks?' He said,'Apart from what is lawful and good, all other things are unlawful and not good (unclean Al-Khabith). (5598) ☐

1801. Narrated Anas: While I was serving Abu Talha. Abu Dujana and Abu Suhail bin Al-Baida' with a drink made from a mixture of unripe and ripe dates, alcoholic drinks, were made unlawful, whereupon I threw it away, and I was their butler and the youngest of them, and we used to consider that drink as an alcoholic drink in those days. (5600) ☐

1802. Narrated Abu Qatada: The Prophet (ﷺ) forbade the mixing of ripe and unripe dates and also the mixing of dates and raisins (for preparing a syrup) but the syrup of each kind of fruit should be prepared separately. (One may have such drinks as long as it is fresh). (5602) □

1803. Narrated Jabir: Abu Humaid, an Ansari man, came from An-Naqi carrying a cup of milk to the Prophet. The Prophet (ﷺ) said, "Will you not cover it even by placing a stick across it?" (5606) □

1804. Narrated An-Nazzal: Ali came to the gate of the courtyard (of the Mosque) and drank (water) while he was standing and said, "Some people dislike to drink while standing, but I saw the Prophet (ﷺ) doing (drinking water) as you have seen me doing now." (5615) □

1805. Narrated Sahl bin Sa`d: Allah's Messenger (ﷺ) was offered something to drink. He drank of it while on his right was a boy and on his left were some elderly people. He said to the boy, "May I give these (elderly) people first?" The boy said, "By Allah, O Allah's Messenger (ﷺ)! I will not give up my share from you to somebody else." On that Allah's Messenger (ﷺ) placed the cup in the hand of that boy. (5620) □

1806. Narrated Jabir bin `Abdullah: The Prophet (ﷺ) and one of his companions entered upon an Ansari man. The Prophet (ﷺ) and his companion greeted (the man) and he replied, "O Allah's Messenger (ﷺ)! Let my father and mother be sacrificed for you! It is hot," while he was watering his garden. The Prophet (ﷺ) asked him, "If you have water kept overnight in a water skin, (give us), or else we will drink by putting our mouths in the basin." The man was watering the garden. The man said, "O Allah's Messenger (ﷺ)! I have water kept overnight in a water-skin. He went to the shade and poured some water into a bowl and milked some milk from a domestic goat in it. The Prophet (ﷺ) drank and then gave the bowl to the man who had come along with him to drink. (5621) □

1807. Narrated Jabir bin `Abdullah: Allah's Messenger (ﷺ) said, "When night falls (or when it is evening), stop your children from going out, for the devils spread out at that time. But when an hour of the night has passed, release them and close the doors and mention Allah's Name, for Satan does not open a closed door. Tie the mouth of your waterskin and mention Allah's Name; cover your containers and utensils and mention Allah's Name. Cover them even by placing something across it, and extinguish your lamps." (5623) ☐

1808. Narrated Abu Huraira: Allah's Messenger (ﷺ) forbade drinking directly from the mouth of a water skin or other leather containers. And forbade preventing one's neighbor from fixing a peg in (the wall of) one's house. (5627) ☐

1809. Narrated Abu Qatada: Allah's Messenger (ﷺ) said, "When you drink (water), do not breathe in the vessel; and when you urinate, do not touch your penis with your right hand. And when you cleanse yourself after defecation (poo), do not use your right hand." (5630) ☐

1810. Narrated Thumama bin `Abdullah: Anas used to breathe twice or thrice in the vessel (while drinking) and used to say that the Prophet; used to take three breaths while drinking. (5631) ☐

1811. Narrated Ibn Abi Laila: While Hudhaita was at Mada'in, he asked for water. The chief of the village brought him a silver vessel. Hudhaifa threw it away and said, "I have thrown it away because I told him not to use it, but he has not stopped using it. The Prophet (ﷺ) forbade us to wear clothes of silk or Dibaj, and to drink in gold or silver utensils, and said, 'These things are for them (unbelievers) in this world and for you (Muslims) in the Hereafter." (5632) ☐

1812. Narrated Um Salama: Allah's Messenger (ﷺ) said, "He who drinks in silver utensils is only filling his `Abdomen with Hell Fire." (5634) ☐

1813. Narrated Sahl bin Sa`d: An Arab lady was mentioned to the Prophet (ﷺ) so he asked Abu Usaid As-Sa`idi to send for her, and he sent for her and she came and stayed in the castle of Bani Sa`ida. The Prophet (ﷺ) came out and went to her and entered upon her. Behold, it was a lady sitting with a drooping head. When the Prophet (ﷺ) spoke to her, she said, "I seek refuge with Allah from you." He said, "I grant you refuge from me." They said to her, "Do you know who this is?" She said,

"No." They said, "This is Allah's Messenger (ﷺ) who has come to command your hand in marriage." She said, "I am very unlucky to lose this chance." Then the Prophet and his companions went towards the shed of Bani Sa`ida and sat there. Then he said, "Give us water, O Sahl!" So I took out this drinking bowl and gave them water in it. The sub-narrator added: Sahl took out for us that very drinking bowl and we all drank from it. Later on `Umar bin `Abdul `Aziz requested Sahl to give it to him as a present, and he gave it to him as a present. (5637) □

1814. Narrated `Asim al-Ahwal: I saw the drinking bowl of the Prophet (ﷺ) with Anas bin Malik, and it had been broken, and he had mended it with silver plates. That drinking bowl was quite wide and made of Nadar wood, Anas said, "I gave water to the Prophet (ﷺ) in that bowl more than so-and-so (for a long period)." Ibn Seereen said: Around that bowl there was an iron ring, and Anas wanted to replace it with a silver or gold ring, but Abu Talha said to him, "Do not change a thing that Allah's Messenger (ﷺ) has made." So Anas left it as it was. (5638) □

74. SICKNESS

1815. NARRATED ABU SA`ID AL-KHUDRI AND ABU HURAIRA (RA): The Prophet (ﷺ) said, "No fatigue, nor disease, nor sorrow, nor sadness, nor hurt, nor distress befalls a Muslim, even if it were the prick he receives from a thorn, but that Allah expiates some of his sins for that." (5641) □

1816. Narrated Ka`b: The Prophet (ﷺ) said, "The example of a believer is that of a fresh tender plant, which the wind bends it sometimes and some other time it makes it straight. And the example of a hypocrite is that of a pine tree which keeps straight till once it is uprooted suddenly. (5643) □

1817. Narrated Abu Huraira: Allah's Messenger (ﷺ) said, "If Allah wants to do good to somebody, He afflicts him with trials." (5645) □

1818. Narrated Aisha: I never saw anybody suffering so much from sickness as Allah's Messenger (p.b.u.h). (5646) ☐

1819. Narrated `Abdullah: I visited Allah's Messenger (ﷺ) while he was suffering from a high fever. I said, "O Allah's Messenger (ﷺ)! You have a high fever." He said, "Yes, I have as much fever as two men of you." I said, "Is it because you will have a double reward?" He said, "Yes, it is so. No Muslim is afflicted with any harm, even if it were the prick of a thorn, but that Allah expiates his sins because of that, as a tree sheds its leaves." (5648) ☐

1820. Narrated Abu Muisa Al-Ash`ari: The Prophet (ﷺ) said, "Feed the hungry, visit the sick, and set free the captives." (5649) ☐

1821. Narrated Al-Bara bin Azib: Allah's Messenger (ﷺ) ordered us to do seven things and forbade us to do seven other things. He forbade us to wear gold rings, silk, Dibaj, Istabriq, Qissy, and Maithara; and ordered us to accompany funeral processions, visit the sick and greet everybody. (5650) ☐

1822. Narrated 'Ata bin Abi Rabah: Ibn `Abbas said to me, "Shall I show you a woman of the people of Paradise?" I said, "Yes." He said, "This black lady came to the Prophet (ﷺ) and said, 'I get attacks of epilepsy and my body becomes uncovered; please invoke Allah for me.' The Prophet (ﷺ) said (to her), 'If you wish, be patient and you will have (enter) Paradise; and if you wish, I will invoke Allah to cure you.' She said, 'I will remain patient,' and added, 'but I become uncovered, so please invoke Allah for me that I may not become uncovered.' So he invoked Allah for her." (5652) ☐

1823. Narrated Anas bin Malik: I heard Allah's Messenger (ﷺ) saying, "Allah said, 'If I deprive my slave of his two beloved things (i.e., his eyes) and he remains patient, I will let him enter Paradise in compensation for them.'" (5653) ☐

1824. Narrated Jabir: The Prophet (ﷺ) came to visit me (while I was sick) and he was riding neither a mule, nor a horse. (5664) ☐

1825. Narrated Ka`b bin 'Ujara: The Prophet (ﷺ) passed by me while I was kindling a fire under a (cooking) pot. He said, "Do the lice of your head trouble you?" I said, "Yes." So he called a barber to shave my head and ordered me to make expiation for that." (5665) ☐

1826. Narrated Al-Qasim bin Muhammad: `Aisha, (complaining of headache) said, "Oh, my head"! Allah's Messenger (ﷺ) said, "I wish that had happened while I was still living, for then I would ask Allah's Forgiveness for you and invoke Allah for you." Aisha said, "Wa thuklayah! By Allah, I think you want me to die; and If this should happen, you would spend the last part of the day sleeping with one of your wives!" The Prophet (ﷺ) said, "Nay, I should say, 'Oh my head!' I felt like sending for Abu Bakr and his son, and appoint him as my successor lest some people claimed something or some others wished something, but then I said (to myself), 'Allah would not allow it to be otherwise, and the Muslims would prevent it to be otherwise". (5666) ☐

1827. Narrated As-Sa'ib: My aunt took me to Allah's Messenger (ﷺ) and said, "O Allah's Messenger (ﷺ)! My nephew is- ill." The Prophet (ﷺ) touched my head with his hand and invoked Allah to bless me. He then performed ablution and I drank of the remaining water of his ablution and then stood behind his back and saw "Khatam An- Nubuwwa" (The Seal of Prophethood) between his shoulders like a button of a tent. (5670) ☐

1828. Narrated Anas bin Malik: The Prophet (ﷺ) said, "None of you should wish for death because of a calamity befalling him; but if he has to wish for death, he should say: "O Allah! Keep me alive as long as life is better for me, and let me die if death is better for me.'" (5671) ☐

1829. Narrated Abu Huraira: I heard Allah's Messenger (ﷺ) saying, "The good deeds of any person will not make him enter Paradise." (None can enter Paradise through his good deeds.) They (the Prophet's companions) said, 'Not even you, O Allah's Messenger (ﷺ)?' He said, "Not even myself, unless Allah bestows His favor and mercy on me." So be moderate in your religious deeds and do the deeds that are within your ability: and none of you should wish for death, for if he is a good doer, he may increase his good deeds, and if he is an evil doer, he may repent to Allah." (5673) □

1830. Narrated `Aisha: Whenever Allah's Messenger (ﷺ) paid a visit to a patient, or a patient was brought to him, he used to invoke Allah, saying,

اللَّهُمَّ ربَّ النَّاسِ ، أَذْهِب الْبَأْسَ ، واشْفِ ، أَنْتَ الشَّافي لا شِفَاءَ إِلاَّ شِفَاؤُكَ ، شِفَاءً لا يُغَادِرُ سقَماً

"Allahumma Rabban-naas, azhibil-ba's, washfi antash-Shaafi laa shifaa'a illaa shifaa'uka, shifaa'an laa yughaadiru saqamaa."

(Take away the disease, O the Lord of the people! Cure him as You are the One Who cures. There is no cure but Yours, a cure that leaves no disease.) (5675) □

75. MEDICINE

1831. NARRATED ABU HURAIRA (RA): The Prophet (ﷺ) said, "There is no disease that Allah has created, except that He also has created its treatment." (5678) □

1832. Narrated Ibn `Abbas: (The Prophet (ﷺ) said), "Healing is in three things: A gulp of honey, cupping, and branding with fire (cauterizing)." But I forbid my followers to use (cauterization) branding with fire." (5680) □

1833. Narrated Abu Sa`id Al-Khudri: A man came to the Prophet (ﷺ) and said, "My brother has some Abdominal trouble." The Prophet (ﷺ) said to him "Let him drink honey." The man came for the second time and the Prophet (ﷺ) said to him, 'Let him drink honey." He came for the third time and the Prophet (ﷺ) said, "Let him drink honey." He returned again and said, "I have done that ' The Prophet (ﷺ) then said, "Allah has said the truth, but your brother's `Abdomen has told a lie. Let him drink honey." So he made him drink honey and he was cured. (5684)

1834. Narrated Khalid bin Sa`d: We went out and Ghalib bin Abjar was accompanying us. He fell ill on the way and when we arrived at Medina he was still sick. Ibn Abi 'Atiq came to visit him and said to us, "Treat him with black cumin. Take five or seven seeds and crush them (mix the powder with oil) and drop the resulting mixture into both nostrils, for `Aisha has narrated to me that she heard the Prophet (ﷺ) saying, 'This black cumin is healing for all diseases except As-Sam.' Aisha said, 'What is As-Sam?' He said, 'Death." (5687) □

1835. Narrated 'Urwa: Aisha used to recommend at-Talbina for the sick and for such a person as grieved over a dead person. She used to say, "I heard Allah's Messenger (ﷺ) saying, 'at-Talbina gives rest to the heart of the patient and makes it active and relieves some of his sorrow and grief.'" (5689) □

1836. Narrated Hisham's father: `Aisha used to recommend at-Talbina and used to say, "It is disliked (by the patient) although it is beneficial." (5690) □

1837. Narrated Ibn `Abbas: The Prophet (ﷺ) was cupped and he paid the wages to the one who had cupped him and then took Su'ut (Medicine sniffed by nose). (5691) □

1838. Narrated Ibn `Abbas: The Prophet (ﷺ) was cupped while he was fasting. (5694) □

1839. Narrated Anas: that he was asked about the wages of the one who cups others. He said, 'Allah's Messenger (ﷺ) was cupped by `Abd Taiba, to whom he gave two Sa of food and interceded for him with his masters who consequently reduced what they used to charge him daily. Then the Prophet (ﷺ) said, "The best medicines you may treat yourselves with are cupping and sea incense.' He added, "You should not torture your children by treating tonsillitis by pressing the tonsils or the palate with the finger, but use incense." (5696) □

1840. Narrated Ibn `Abbas: The Prophet (ﷺ) was cupped on his head for an ailment he was suffering from while he was in a state of Ihram. At a water place called Lahl Jamal. Ibn `Abbas further said: Allah s Apostle was cupped on his head for unilateral headache while he was in a state of Ihram. (5701) □

1841. Narrated Ibn `Abbas: Allah's Messenger (ﷺ) said, 'Nations were displayed before me; one or two prophets would pass by along with a few followers. A prophet would pass by accompanied by nobody. Then a big crowd of people passed in front of me and I asked, Who are they Are they my followers?" It was said, 'No. It is Moses and his followers It was said to me, 'Look at the horizon." Behold! There was a multitude of people filling the horizon. Then it was said to me, 'Look there and there about the stretching sky! Behold! There was a multitude filling the horizon,' It was said to me, 'This is your nation out of whom seventy thousand shall enter Paradise without reckoning.' "Then the Prophet (ﷺ) entered his house without telling his companions who they (the 70,000) were. So the people started talking about the issue and said, "It is we who have believed in Allah and followed His Apostle; therefore those people are either ourselves or our children who are born m the Islamic era, for we were born in the Pre-lslamic Period of Ignorance." When the Prophet (ﷺ) heard of that, he came out and said. "Those people are those who do not treat themselves with Ruqya, nor do they believe in bad or good omen (from birds etc.) nor do they get themselves branded (Cauterized). But they put their trust (only) in their Lord." On that 'Ukasha bin Muhsin said. "Am I one of them, O Allah's Messenger (ﷺ)?' The Prophet (ﷺ) said, "Yes." Then another person got up and said, "Am I one of them?" The Prophet (ﷺ) said, 'Ukasha has anticipated you." (5705) □

1842. Narrated Abu Huraira: Allah's Messenger (ﷺ) said, '(There is) no 'Adwa (no contagious disease is conveyed without Allah's permission), nor is there any bad omen (from birds), nor is there any Hamah, nor is there any bad omen in the month of Safar, and one should run away from the leper as one runs away from a lion." (5707) □

1843. Narrated Sa`id bin Zaid: I heard the Prophet (ﷺ) saying, "Truffles are like Manna (i.e. they grow naturally without man's care) and their water heals eye diseases." (5708) □

1844. Narrated Usama bin Zaid: Allah's Messenger (ﷺ) said, "Plague was a means of torture sent on a group of Israelis (or on some people before you). So if you hear of its spread in a land, don't approach it, and if a plague should appear in a land where you are present, then don't leave that land in order to run away from it (i.e. plague). (3473) ☐

1845. Narrated Ibn `Abbas and `Aisha: Abu Bakr kissed (the forehead of) the Prophet (ﷺ) when he was dead. `Aisha added: We put medicine in one side of his mouth but he started waving us not to insert the medicine into his mouth. We said, "He dislikes the medicine as a patient usually does." But when he came to his senses he said, "Did I not forbid you to put medicine (by force) in the side of my mouth?" We said, "We thought it was just because a patient usually dislikes medicine." He said, "None of those who are in the house but will be forced to take medicine in the side of his mouth while I am watching, except Abbas, for he had not witnessed your deed." (5712) ☐

1846. Narrated Um Qais: I went to Allah's Messenger (ﷺ) along with a son of mine whose palate and tonsils I had pressed with my finger as a treatment for a (throat and tonsil) disease. The Prophet (ﷺ) said, "Why do you pain your children by pressing their throats! Use Ud Al-Hindi (certain Indian incense) for it cures seven diseases, one of which is pleurisy. It is used as a snuff for treating throat and tonsil disease and it is inserted into one side of the mouth of one suffering from pleurisy." (5713) ☐

1847. Narrated Abu Huraira: Allah's Messenger (ﷺ) said, 'There is no 'Adha (no disease is conveyed from the sick to the healthy without Allah's permission), nor Safar, nor Hama." A bedouin stood up and said, "Then what about my camels? They are like deer on the sand, but when a mangy camel comes and mixes with them, they all get infected with mangy." The Prophet (ﷺ) said, "Then who conveyed the (mange) disease to the first one?" (5717) ☐

1848. Narrated Anas bin Malik: Allah's Messenger (ﷺ) allowed one of the Ansar families to treat persons who have taken poison and also who are suffering from ear ailment with Ruqya. Anas added: I got myself branded (cauterized) for pleurisy, when Allah's Messenger (ﷺ) was still alive. Abu Talha, Anas bin An-Nadr and Zaid bin Thabit witnessed that, and it was Abu Talha who branded me. (5720) ☐

1849. Narrated Sahl bin Saud As-Sa`idi: When the helmet broke on the head of the Prophet (ﷺ) and his face became covered with blood and his incisor tooth broke (i.e. during the battle of Uhud), `Ali used to bring water in his shield while Fatima was washing the blood off his face. When Fatima saw that the bleeding increased because of the water, she took a mat (of palm leaves), burnt it, and stuck it (the burnt ashes) on the wound of Allah's Apostle, whereupon the bleeding stopped. (5722) □

1850. Narrated Nazi':`Abdullah bin `Umar said, "The Prophet (ﷺ) said, 'Fever is from the heat of Hell, so put it out (cool it) with water.'" Nafi` added: `Abdullah used to say, "O Allah! Relieve us from the punishment," (when he suffered from fever). (5723) □

1851. Narrated `Abdullah bin `Abbas: `Umar bin Al-Khattab departed for Sham and when he reached Sargh, the commanders of the (Muslim) army, Abu 'Ubaida bin Al-Jarrah and his companions met him and told him that an epidemic had broken out in Sham. `Umar said, "Call for me the early emigrants." So `Umar called them, consulted them and informed them that an epidemic had broken out in Sham. Those people differed in their opinions. Some of them said, "We have come out for a purpose and we do not think that it is proper to give it up," while others said (to `Umar), "You have along with you. Other people and the companions of Allah's Messenger (ﷺ) so do not advise that we take them to this epidemic." `Umar said to them, "Leave me now." Then he said, "Call the Ansar for me." I called them and he consulted them and they followed the way of the emigrants and differed as they did. He then said to them, Leave me now," and added, "Call for me the old people of Quraish who emigrated in the year of the Conquest of Mecca." I called them and they gave a unanimous opinion saying, "We advise that you should return with the people and do not take them to that (place) of epidemic." So `Umar made an announcement, "I will ride back to Medina in the morning, so you should do the same." Abu 'Ubaida bin Al-Jarrah said (to `Umar), "Are you running away from what Allah had ordained?" `Umar said, "Would that someone else had said such a thing, O Abu 'Ubaida! Yes, we are running from what Allah had ordained to what Allah has ordained. Don't you agree that if you had camels that went down a valley having two places, one green and the other dry, you would graze them on the green one only if Allah had ordained that, and you would graze them on the dry one only if Allah had ordained that?" At that time `Abdur-Rahman bin `Auf, who had been absent because of some job, came and said, "I have some knowledge about this. I have heard Allah's Messenger (ﷺ) saying, 'If you hear about it (an outbreak of plague) in a land, do not go to it; but if plague breaks out in a country where you are staying, do not run away from it.'" `Umar thanked Allah and returned to Medina. (5729) □

1852. Narrated Anas bin Malik: Allah's Messenger (ﷺ) said, "(Death from) plague is martyrdom for every Muslim." (5732) □

1853. Narrated Abu Huraira: The Prophet (ﷺ) said, "He (a Muslim) who dies of an abdominal disease is a martyr, and he who dies of plague is a martyr." (5733) □

1854. Narrated `Aisha: that she asked Allah's Messenger (ﷺ) about plague, and Allah's Messenger (ﷺ) informed her saying, "Plague was a punishment which Allah used to send on whom He wished, but Allah made it a blessing for the believers. None (among the believers) remains patient in a land in which plague has broken out and considers that nothing will befall him except what Allah has ordained for him, but that Allah will grant him a reward similar to that of a martyr." (5734) □

1855. Narrated `Aisha: The Prophet (ﷺ) ordered me or somebody else to do Ruqya (if there was danger) from an evil eye. (5738) □

1856. Narrated Um Salama: that the Prophet (ﷺ) saw in her house a girl whose face had a black spot. He said. "She is under the effect of an evil eye; so treat her with a Ruqya." (5739) □

1857. Narrated Abu Huraira: The Prophet (ﷺ) said, "The effect of an evil eye is a fact." And he prohibited tattooing. (5740) □

1858. Narrated Al-Aswad: I asked `Aisha about treating poisonous stings (a snake-bite or a scorpion sting) with a Ruqya. She said, "The Prophet (ﷺ) allowed the treatment of poisonous sting with Ruqya." (5741) ☐

1859. Narrated `Aisha: The Prophet (ﷺ) used to treat some of his wives by passing his right hand over the place of ailment and used to say,

اللَّهُمَّ رَبَّ النَّاسِ أَذْهِبِ الْبَاسَ، اشْفِهِ وَأَنْتَ الشَّافِي، لاَ شِفَاءَ إِلاَّ شِفَاؤُكَ، شِفَاءً لاَ يُغَادِرُ سَقَمًا

"Allahumma Rabbin Nasi, Adhabal basa, Ashfihi Wa Anta shafee, La shifaaa illa shifauuka, shifa'an La Yugadiru Saqama."

(O Allah, the Lord of the people! Remove the trouble and heal the patient, for You are the Healer. No healing is of any avail but Yours; healing that will leave behind no ailment.) (5743) ☐

1860. Narrated `Aisha: Allah's Messenger (ﷺ) used to treat with a Ruqya saying,

"O the Lord of the people! Remove the trouble The cure is in Your Hands, and there is none except You who can remove it (the disease)." (5744) ☐

1861. Narrated `Aisha: The Prophet (ﷺ) used to say to the patient,

بِسْمِ اللَّهِ، تُرْبَةُ أَرْضِنَا. بِرِيقَةِ بَعْضِنَا، يُشْفَى سَقِيمُنَا بِإِذْنِ رَبِّنَا

"In the Name of Allah The earth of our land and the saliva of some of us cure our patient." (5745) ☐

1862. Narrated `Aisha: Whenever Allah's Messenger (ﷺ) went to bed, he used to recite Surah-al-Ikhlas, Surah-al-Falaq and Surah-an- Nas and then blow on his palms and pass them over his face and those parts of his body that his hands could reach. And when he fell ill, he used to order me to do like that for him. (5748) ☐

1863. Narrated `Aisha: The Prophet, during his fatal ailment used to blow (on his hands and pass them) over his body while reciting the Mu'auwidhat (Surah-an-Nas and Surah-al-Falaq). When his disease got aggravated, I used to recite them for him and blow (on his hands) and let him pass his hands over his body because of its blessing. (Ma`mar asked Ibn Shihab: How did he use to do Nafth? He said: He used to blow on his hands and then pass them over his face.) (5751) ☐

1864. Narrated `Abdullah bin `Umar: Allah's Messenger (ﷺ) said, "There is neither 'Adha (no contagious disease is conveyed to others without Allah's permission) nor Tiyara, but an evil omen may be in three a woman, a house or an animal." (5753) ☐

1865. Narrated Abu Huraira: The Prophet (ﷺ) said, "There is no Tiyara and the best omen is the Fal," Somebody said, "What is the Fal, O Allah's Messenger (ﷺ)?" He said, "A good word that one of you hears (and takes as a good omen). (5755) ☐

1866. Narrated `Aisha: A man called Labid bin al-A'sam from the tribe of Bani Zaraiq worked magic on Allah's Messenger (ﷺ) till Allah's Messenger (ﷺ) started imagining that he had done a thing that he had not really done. One day or one night he was with us, he invoked Allah and invoked for a long period, and then said, "O `Aisha! Do you know that Allah has instructed me concerning the matter I have asked him about? Two men came to me and one of them sat near my head and the other near my feet. One of them said to his companion, "What is the disease of this man?" The other replied, "He is under the effect of magic.' The first one asked, 'Who has worked the magic on him?' The other replied, "Labid bin Al-A'sam.' The first one asked, 'What material did he use?' The other replied, 'A comb and the hairs stuck to it and the skin of pollen of a male date palm.' The first one asked, 'Where is that?' The other replied, '(That is) in the well of Dharwan;' " So Allah's Messenger (ﷺ) along with some of his companions went there and came back saying, "O `Aisha, the color of its water is like the infusion of Henna leaves. The tops of the date-palm trees near it are like the heads of the devils." I asked. "O Allah's Messenger (ﷺ)? Why did you not show it (to the people)?" He said, "Since Allah cured me, I disliked to let evil spread among the people." Then he ordered that the well be filled up with earth. (5763) ☐

1867. Narrated Abu Huraira: The Prophet (ﷺ) said, "Avoid the seven great destructive sins." The people enquire, "O Allah's Messenger (ﷺ)! What are they? "He said, "To join others in worship along with Allah, to practice sorcery, to kill the life which Allah has forbidden except for a just cause, (according to Islamic law), to eat up Riba (usury), to eat up an orphan's wealth, to give back to the enemy and fleeing from the battlefield at the time of fighting, and to accuse, chaste women, who never even think of anything touching chastity and are good believers. (2766) □

1868. Narrated ʿAbdullah bin ʿUmar: Two men came from the East and addressed the people who wondered at their eloquent speeches On that Allah's Messenger (ﷺ) said. Some eloquent speech is as effective as magic.' (5767) □

1869. Narrated Saud: I heard Allah's Messenger (ﷺ) saying, "If Somebody takes seven 'Ajwa dates in the morning, neither magic nor poison will hurt him that day." (5769) □

1870. Narrated ʿAmr: Here (i.e. in Mecca) there was a man called Nawwas and he had camels suffering from the disease of excessive and unquenchable thirst. Ibn ʿUmar went to the partner of Nawwas and bought those camels. The man returned to Nawwas and told him that he had sold those camels. Nawwas asked him, "To whom have you sold them?" He replied, "To such and such Sheikh." Nawwas said, "Woe to you; By Allah, that Sheikh was Ibn ʿUmar." Nawwas then went to Ibn ʿUmar and said to him, "My partner sold you camels suffering from the disease of excessive thirst and he had not known you." Ibn ʿUmar told him to take them back. When Nawwas went to take them, Ibn ʿUmar said to him, "Leave them there as I am happy with the decision of Allah's Messenger (ﷺ) that there is no oppression." (2099) □

1871. Narrated Abu Huraira: Allah's Messenger (ﷺ) said, "No 'Adha." Abu Huraira also said: The Prophet (ﷺ) said, "The cattle suffering from a disease should not be mixed up with healthy cattle (or said "Do not put a patient with a healthy person as a precaution.") Abu Huraira also said: Allah's Messenger (ﷺ) said, "No 'Adha." A bedouin got up and said, "Don't you see how camels on the sand look like deer but when a mangy camel mixes with them, they all get infected with mange?" On that the Prophet (ﷺ) said, "Then who conveyed the (mange) disease to the first camel?" (5774) □

1872. Narrated Abu Tha`laba Al-Khushani: The Prophet (ﷺ) forbade the eating of wild animals having fangs. (Az-Zuhri said: I did not hear this narration except when I went to Sham.) Al-Laith said: Narrated Yunus: I asked Ibn Shihab, "May we perform the ablution with the milk of she-asses or drink it, or drink the bile of wild animals or urine of camels?" He replied, "The Muslims used to treat themselves with that and did not see any harm in it. As for the milk of she-asses, we have learnt that Allah's Messenger (ﷺ) forbade the eating of their meat, but we have not received any information whether drinking of their milk is allowed or forbidden." As for the bile of wild animals, Ibn Shihab said, "Abu Idris Al-Khaulani told me that Allah's Messenger (ﷺ) forbade the eating of the flesh of every wild beast having fangs." (5781) ☐

1873. Narrated Abu Huraira: Allah's Messenger (ﷺ) said, "If a fly falls in the vessel of any of you, let him dip all of it (into the vessel) and then throw it away, for in one of its wings there is a disease and in the other there is healing (antidote for it) i e. the treatment for that disease." (5782) ☐

76. DRESS

1874. NARRATED `ABDULLAH BIN `UMAR (RA): The Prophet (ﷺ) said Allah will not look, on the Day of Resurrection at the person who drags his garment (behind him) out of conceit. On that Abu Bakr said, "O Allah's Messenger (ﷺ)! One side of my Izar hangs low if I do not take care of it." The Prophet (ﷺ) said, 'You are not one of those who do that out of conceit (excessive pride in oneself)." (5784) ☐

1875. Narrated Abu Huraira: The Prophet (ﷺ) said, "The part of an Izar which hangs below the ankles is in the Fire." (5787) ☐

1876. Narrated Ibn `Umar: The Prophet (ﷺ) said, "While a man was walking, dragging his dress with pride, he was caused to be swallowed by the earth and will go on sinking in it till the Day of Resurrection." (3485) ☐

1877. Narrated Qatada: I asked Anas, "What kind of clothes was most beloved to the Prophet?" He replied, "The Hibra (a kind of Yemenese cloth). (5812) ☐

1878. Narrated Abu Sa`id Al-Khudri: Allah's Messenger (ﷺ) forbade Ishtimal-As-Samma' (wrapping one's body with a garment so that one cannot raise its end or take one's hand out of it). He also forbade Al-Ihtiba' (sitting on buttocks with knees close to `Abdomen and feet apart with the hands circling the knees) while wrapping oneself with a single garment, without having a part of it over the private parts. (367) ☐

1879. Narrated Abu Dharr: I came to the Prophet (ﷺ) while he was wearing white clothes and sleeping. (5827) ☐

1880. Narrated Aba `Uthman An-Nahdi: While we were with `Utba bin Farqad at Adharbijan, there came `Umar's letter indicating that Allah's Apostle had forbidden the use of silk except this much, then he pointed with his index and middle fingers. To our knowledge, by that he meant embroidery. (5828) ☐

1881. Narrated Anas bin Malik: The Prophet (ﷺ) said, whoever wears silk in this world shall not wear it in the Hereafter." (5832) ☐

1882. Narrated Hudhaifa: The Prophet (ﷺ) forbade us to drink out of gold and silver vessels, or eat in it, Ann also forbade the wearing of silk and Dibaj or sitting on it. (5837) ☐

1883. Narrated Ibn Azib: The Prophet (ﷺ) forbade us to use the red Mayathir and to use Al-Qassiy. (5838) ☐

1884. Narrated Anas: The Prophet (ﷺ) allowed Az-Zubair and `Abdur-Rahman to wear silk because they were suffering from an itch. (5839) ☐

1885. Narrated `Ali bin Abi Talib: The Prophet (ﷺ) gave me a silk suit. I went out wearing it, but seeing the signs of anger on his face, I tore it and distributed it among my wives. (5840) ☐

1886. Narrated Anas bin Malik: that he had seen Um Kulthum, the daughter of

Allah's Messenger (ﷺ), wearing a red silk garment. (5842) ☐

1887. Narrated Um Khalid bint Khalid: Some clothes were presented to Allah's Messenger (ﷺ) as a gift and there was a black Khamisa with it. The Prophet asked (his companions), "To whom do you suggest we give this Khamisa?" The people kept quiet. Then he said, "Bring me Um Khalid," So I was brought to him and he dressed me with it with his own hands and said twice, "May you live so long that you will wear out many garments." He then started looking at the embroidery of that Khamisa and said, "O Um Khalid! This is Sana!" (Sana in Ethiopian language means beautiful.) 'Is-haq, a sub-narrator, said: A woman of my family had told me that she had seen the Khamisa worn by Um Khalid. (5845) ☐

1888. Narrated Anas: The Prophet (ﷺ) forbade men to use saffron. (5846) ☐

1889. Narrated Al-Bara: The Prophet (ﷺ) was of a modest height. I saw him wearing a red suit, and I did not see anything better than him. (5848) ☐

1890. Narrated Sa`id Al-Maqburi: 'Ubai bin Juraij said to `Abdullah Ben `Umar, "I see you doing four things which are not done by your friends." Ibn `Umar said, "What are they, O Ibn Juraij?" He said, "I see that you do not touch except the two Yemenite corners of the Ka`ba (while performing the Tawaf): and I see you wearing the Sabtiyya shoes; and I see you dyeing (your hair) with Sufra; and I see that when you are in Mecca, the people assume the state of Ihram on seeing the crescent (on the first day of Dhul-Hijja) while you do not assume the state of Ihram till the Day of Tarwiya (8th Dhul Hijja)." `Abdullah bin `Umar said to him, "As for the corners of the Ka`ba, I have not seen Allah's Messenger (ﷺ) touching except the two Yemenite corners, As for the Sabtiyya shoes, I saw Allah's Messenger (ﷺ) wearing leather shoes that had no hair, and he used to perform the ablution while wearing them. Therefore, I like to wear such shoes. As regards dyeing with Sufra, I saw Allah's Messenger (ﷺ) dyeing his hair with it, so I like to dye (my hair) with it. As regards the crescent (of Dhul-Hijja), I have not seen Allah's Messenger (ﷺ) assuming the state of Ihram till his she-camel set out (on the 8th of Dhul-Hijja). (5851) ☐

1891. Narrated Abu Huraira: Allah's Messenger (ﷺ) said, "If you want to put on your shoes, put on the right shoe first; and if you want to take them off, take the left one first. Let the right shoe be the first to be put on and the last to be taken off." (5855) ☐

1892. Narrated Abu Huraira: Allah's Messenger (ﷺ) said, "None of you should walk, wearing one shoe only; he should either put on both shoes or put on no shoes whatsoever." (5856) ☐

1893. Narrated Isaa bin Tahman: Anas bin Malik brought out for us, two sandals having two straps. Thabit Al-Banani said, "These were the sandals of the Prophet (p.b.u.h)." (5858) ☐

1894. Narrated Abu Huraira: The Prophet (ﷺ) forbade the wearing of a gold ring. (5864) ☐

1895. Narrated Ibn. `Umar: Allah's Messenger (ﷺ) wore a gold ring or a silver ring and placed its stone towards the palm of his hand and had the name 'Muhammad, the Messenger of Allah' engraved on it. The people also started wearing gold rings like it, but when the Prophet (ﷺ) saw them wearing such rings, he threw away his own ring and said. "I will never wear it," and then wore a silver ring, whereupon the people too started wearing silver rings. Ibn `Umar added: After the Prophet (ﷺ) Abu Bakr wore the ring, and then `Umar and then `Uthman wore it till it fell in the Aris well from `Uthman. (5866) ☐

1896. Narrated Anas bin Malik: that he saw a silver ring on the hand of Allah's Messenger (ﷺ) for one day only. Then the people had silver rings made for themselves and wore it. On that, Allah's Messenger (ﷺ) threw away their rings as well. (5868) ☐

1897. Narrated Anas: The ring of the Prophet (ﷺ) was of silver, and its stone was of silver too. (5870) ☐

1898. Narrated Anas bin Malik: Allah's Messenger (ﷺ) wanted to write a letter to a group of people or some non-Arabs. It was said to him, "They do not accept any letter unless it is stamped." So the Prophet (ﷺ) had a silver ring made for himself, and on it was engraved: 'Muhammad, the Messenger of Allah'. .. as if I am now looking at the glitter of the ring on the finger (or in the palm) of the Prophet (p.b.u.h). (5872) ☐

1899. Narrated Anas: The Prophet (ﷺ) got a ring made for himself and said, "I have got a ring made (for myself) and engraved a certain engraving on it so none of you should get such an engraving on his ring." I saw the glitter of the ring on his little finger. (5874) ☐

1900. Narrated Anas: that when Abu Bakr became the Caliph, he wrote a letter to him (and stamped it with the Prophet's ring) and the engraving of the ring was in three lines: Muhammad in one line, 'Apostle' in another line, and 'Allah' in a third line. (5878) ☐

1901. Anas added: The ring of the Prophet (ﷺ) was in his hand, and after him, in Abu Bakr's hand, and then in `Umar's hand after Abu Bakr. When `Uthman was the Caliph, once he was sitting at the well of Aris. He removed the ring from his hand and while he was trifling with it, dropped into the well. We kept on going to the well with `Uthman for three days looking for the ring, and finally the well was drained, but the ring was not found. (5879) ☐

1902. Narrated Abu Huraira: I was with Allah's Messenger (ﷺ) in one of the Markets of Medina. He left (the market) and so did I. Then he asked thrice, "Where is the small (child)?" Then he said, "Call Al-Hasan bin `Ali." So Al-Hasan bin `Ali got up and started walking with a necklace (of beads) around his neck. The Prophet (ﷺ) stretched his hand out like this, and Al-Hasan did the same. The Prophet (ﷺ) embraced him and said, "0 Allah! I love him, so please love him and love those who love him." Since Allah's Messenger (ﷺ) said that. Nothing has been dearer to me than Al-Hasan. (5884) ☐

1903. Narrated Ibn `Abbas: Allah's Messenger (ﷺ) cursed those men who are in the similitude (assume the manners) of women and those women who are in the similitude (assume the manners) of men. (5885) ☐

1904. Narrated Ibn `Abbas: The Prophet (ﷺ) cursed effeminate men (those men who are in the similitude (assume the manners of women) and those women who assume the manners of men, and he said, "Turn them out of your houses." The Prophet (ﷺ) turned out such-and-such man, and `Umar turned out such-and-such woman. (5886) □

1905. Narrated Abu Huraira: Allah's Messenger (ﷺ) said, "Five practices are characteristics of the Fitra: circumcision, shaving the pubic region, clipping the nails and cutting the moustaches short." (5889) □

1906. Narrated Nafi`: Ibn `Umar said, The Prophet (ﷺ) said, 'Do the opposite of what the pagans do. Keep the beards and cut the moustaches short.' Whenever Ibn `Umar performed the Hajj or `Umra, he used to hold his beard with his hand and cut whatever remained outside his hold. (5892) □

1907. Narrated Thabit: Anas was asked whether the Prophet (ﷺ) used a hair dye or not. He replied, "The Prophet (ﷺ) did not have enough grey hair to dye, (such that) if I wanted to count the fading hairs in his beard (I could have)." (5895) □

1908. Narrated Abu Huraira: The Prophet (ﷺ) said, "Jews and Christians do not dye their hair so you should do the opposite of what they do. (5899)

1909. Narrated Qatada: 1 asked Anas bin Malik about the hair of Allah's Messenger (ﷺ). He said, "The hair of Allah's Messenger (ﷺ) was neither much straight, nor much curly, and it used to hang down till between his shoulders and his earlobes. (5905)

1910. Narrated `Abdullah bin `Umar: I heard `Umar saying, "Whoever braids his hair should shave it (on finishing lhram). You'd better not do, something like Talbid (Matting The Hair)." Ibn `Umar used to say: "I saw Allah's Messenger (ﷺ) with his hair stuck together with gum." (5914)

1911. Narrated Ibn `Abbas: The Prophet (ﷺ) used to copy the people of the Scriptures in matters in which there was no order from Allah. The people of the Scripture used to let their hair hang down while the pagans used to part their hair. So the Prophet

(ﷺ) let his hair hang down first, but later on he parted it. (5917)

1912. Narrated Ubaidullah bin Hafs: that `Umar bin Nafi` told him that Nafi`, Maula `Abdullah had heard `Umar saying, "I heard Allah's Apostle forbidding Al-Qaza'." 'Ubaidullah added: I said, "What is Al-Qaza'?" 'Ubaidullah pointed (towards his head) to show us and added, "Nafi` said, 'It is when a boy has his head shaved leaving a tuft of hair here and a tuft of hair there." Ubaidullah pointed towards his forehead and the sides of his head. 'Ubaidullah was asked, "Does this apply to both girls and boys?" He said, "I don't know, but Nafi` said, 'The boy.'" 'Ubaidullah added, "I asked Nafi` again, and he said, 'As for leaving hair on the temples and the back part of the boy's head, there is no harm, but Al-Qaza' is to leave a tuft of hair on his forehead unshaved while there is no hair on the rest of his head, and also to leave hair on either side of his head." (5920) ☐

1913. Narrated Aisha: I used to perfume Allah's Messenger (ﷺ) with the best scent available till I saw the shine of the scent on his head and shine beard. (5923) ☐

1914. Narrated `Aisha: The Prophet (ﷺ) used to like to start from the right side as far as possible in combing and in performing ablution. (5926) ☐

1915. Narrated Sa`id bin Al-Musaiyab: Mu'awiya came to Medina for the last time and delivered a sermon. He took out a tuft of hair and said, "I thought that none used to do this (i.e. use false hair) except Jews. The Prophet (ﷺ) labelled such practice, (i.e. the use of false hair), as cheating. (5938) ☐

1916. Narrated 'Alqama:`Abdullah cursed those women who practiced tattooing and those who removed hair from their faces and those who created spaces between their teeth artificially to look beautiful, such ladies as changed what Allah has created. Um Ya'qub said, "What is that?" `Abdullah said, "Why should I not curse those who were cursed by Allah's Messenger (ﷺ) and are referred to in Allah's Book?" She said to him "By Allah, I have read the whole Qur'an but I have not found such a thing. `Abdullah said, "By Allah, if you had read it (carefully) you would have found it. (Allah says :) 'And what the Apostle gives you take it and what he forbids you abstain (from it).'

(59.7) (5939) ☐

1917. Narrated Asma': A woman asked the Prophet (ﷺ) saying, "0 Allah's Messenger (ﷺ)! My daughter got measles and her hair fell out. Now that I got her married, may I let her use false hair?" He said (to her), "Allah has cursed the lady who lengthens hair artificially and the one who gets her hair lengthened artificially." (5941) ☐

1918. Narrated Muslim: We were with Masruq at the house of Yasar bin Numair. Masruq saw pictures on his terrace and said, "I heard `Abdullah saying that he heard the Prophet (ﷺ) saying, "The people who will receive the severest punishment from Allah will be the picture makers.'" (5950) ☐

1919. Narrated `Aisha: I never used to leave in the Prophet (ﷺ) house anything carrying images or crosses but he obliterated it. (5952) ☐

1920. Narrated Abu Zur'a: 1 entered a house in Medina with Abu Huraira, and he saw a man making pictures at the top of the house. Abu Huraira said, "I heard Allah's Messenger (ﷺ) saying that Allah said, 'Who would be more unjust than the one who tries to create the like of My creatures? Let them create a grain: let them create a gnat (a small two-winged fly that resembles a mosquito).' "Abu Huraira then asked for a water container and washed his arms up to his armpits. I said, "0 Abu Huraira! Is this something you have heard I from Allah's Messenger (ﷺ)?" He said, "The limit for ablution is up to the place where the ornaments will reach on the Day of Resurrection.' (5953) ☐

1921. Narrated `Aisha: Allah's Messenger (ﷺ) returned from a journey when I had placed a curtain of mine having pictures over (the door of) a chamber of mine. When Allah's Messenger (ﷺ) saw it, he tore it and said, "The people who will receive the severest punishment on the Day of Resurrection will be those who try to make the like of Allah's creations." So we turned it (i.e., the curtain) into one or two cushions. (5954) ☐

1922. Narrated `Aisha: I purchased a cushion with pictures on it. The Prophet (came and) stood at the door but did not enter. I said (to him), "I repent to Allah for what (the guilt) I have done." He said, "What is this cushion?" I said, "It is for you to sit on and recline on." He said, "The makers of these pictures will be punished on the Day of Resurrection and it will be said to them, 'Make alive what you have created.' Moreover, the angels do not enter a house where there are pictures.'" (5957) ☐

1923. Narrated Abu Talha: Allah's Messenger (ﷺ) said, "Angels (of mercy) do not enter a house where there are pictures.'" The subnarrator Busr added: "Then Zaid fell ill and we paid him a visit. Behold! There was, hanging at his door, a curtain decorated with a picture. I said to 'Ubaidullah Al-Khaulani, the step son of Maimuna, the wife of the Prophet (ﷺ), "Didn't Zaid tell us about the picture the day before yesterday?" 'Ubaidullah said, "Didn't you hear him saying: 'except a design in a garment'?" (5958) ☐

1924. Narrated Salim's father: Once Gabriel promised to visit the Prophet (ﷺ) but he delayed and the Prophet (ﷺ) got worried about that. At last he came out and found Gabriel and complained to him of his grief (for his delay). Gabriel said to him, "We do not enter a place in which there is a picture or a dog." (5960) ☐

1925. Narrated Anas bin Malik: We were coming from Khaibar along with Allah's Messenger (ﷺ) while 1 was riding behind Abu Talha and he was proceeding. While one of the wives of Allah's Messenger (ﷺ) was riding behind Allah's Messenger (ﷺ), suddenly the foot of the camel Slipped and I said, "The woman!" and alighted (hurriedly). Allah's Apostle said, "She is your mother." Sol resaddled the she-camel and Allah's Messenger (ﷺ) mounted it. When he approached or saw Medina, he said, "Ayibun, ta'ibun, 'abidun, li-Rabbina hami-dun." (5968) ☐

1926. Narrated Aiman: I went to `Aisha and she was wearing a coarse dress costing five Dirhams. `Aisha said, "Look up and see my slave-girl who refuses to wear it in the house though during the lifetime of Allah's Messenger (ﷺ) I had a similar dress which no woman desiring to appear elegant (before her husband) failed to borrow from me." (2628) ☐

1927. Narrated `Aisha: The bed mattress of the Prophet (ﷺ) was made of a leather case stuffed with palm fibres. (6456) ☐

77. RIGHTS OF RELATIVES

1928. NARRATED ABU HURAIRA (RA): A man came to Allah's Messenger (ﷺ) and said, "O Allah's Messenger (ﷺ)! Who is more entitled to be treated with the best companionship by me?" The Prophet (ﷺ) said, "Your mother." The man said. "Who is next?" The Prophet said, "Your mother." The man further said, "Who is next?" The Prophet (ﷺ) said, "Your mother." The man asked for the fourth time, "Who is next?" The Prophet (ﷺ) said, "Your father." (5971) ☐

1929. Narrated `Abdullah bin `Amr: Allah's Messenger (ﷺ) said. "It is one of the greatest sins that a man should curse his parents." It was asked (by the people), "O Allah's Messenger (ﷺ)! How does a man curse his parents?" The Prophet (ﷺ) said, "'The man abuses the father of another man and the latter abuses the father of the former and abuses his mother." (5973) ☐

1930. Narrated Al-Mughira: The Prophet (ﷺ) said, "Allah has forbidden you (1) to be undutiful to your mothers (2) to withhold (what you should give) or (3) demand (what you do not deserve), and (4) to bury your daughters alive. And Allah has disliked that (A) you talk too much about others (B), ask too many questions (in religion), or (C) waste your property." (5975) ☐

1931. Narrated Asma' bint Abu Bakr: My mother came to me, hoping (for my favor) during the lifetime of the Prophet. I asked the Prophet, "May I treat her kindly?" He replied, "Yes." Ibn 'Uyaina said, "Then Allah revealed: 'Allah forbids you not with regards to those who fought not against you because of religion, and drove you not out from your homes, that you should show them kindness and deal justly with them.'.......(60.8) (5978) ☐

1932. Narrated Jubair bin Mut`im: That he heard the Prophet (ﷺ) saying, "The person who severs the bond of kinship will not enter Paradise." (5984) □

1933. Narrated Anas bin Malik: I heard Allah's Messenger (ﷺ) saying, "Whoever desires an expansion in his sustenance and age, should keep good relations with his Kith and kin." (2067) □

1934. Narrated Abu Huraira: The Prophet (ﷺ) said, "Allah created the creations, and when He finished from His creations, Ar-Rahm i.e., womb said, "(O Allah) at this place I seek refuge with You from all those who sever me (i.e. sever the ties of Kith and kin). Allah said, 'Yes, won't you be pleased that I will keep good relations with the one who will keep good relations with you, and I will sever the relation with the one who will sever the relations with you.' It said, 'Yes, O my Lord.' Allah said, 'Then that is for you.'" Allah's Messenger (ﷺ) added, "Read (in the Qur'an) if you wish, the Statement of Allah: 'Would you then, if you were given the authority, do mischief in the land and sever your ties of kinship?' (47.22) (5987) □

1935. Narrated Abu Huraira: The Prophet (ﷺ) said, "The word 'Ar-Rahm (womb) derives its name from Ar-Rahman (i.e., one of the names of Allah) and Allah said: 'I will keep good relation with the one who will keep good relation with you, (womb i.e. Kith and Kin) and sever the relation with him who will sever the relation with you, (womb, i.e. Kith and Kin). (5988) □

1936. Narrated `Amr bin Al-`As: I heard the Prophet (ﷺ) saying openly not secretly, "The family of Abu so-and-so (i.e. Talib) are not among my protectors." `Amr said that there was a blank space in the Book of Muhammad bin Ja`far. He added, "My Protector is Allah and the righteous believing people." `Amr bin Al-`As added: I heard the Prophet (ﷺ) saying, 'But they (that family) have kinship (Rahm) with me and I will be good and dutiful to them." (5990) □

1937. Narrated Abdullah bin Amr: The Prophet (ﷺ) said, "Al-Wasil is not the one who recompenses the good done to him by his relatives, but Al-Wasil is the one who keeps good relations with those relatives who had severed the bond of kinship with him." (5991) ☐

1938. Narrated Hakim bin Hizam: That he said, "O Allah's Messenger (ﷺ)! What do you think about my good deeds which I used to do during the period of ignorance (before embracing Islam) like keeping good relations with my Kith and kin, manumitting of slaves and giving alms etc; Shall I receive the reward for that?" Allah's Messenger (ﷺ) said, "You have embraced Islam with all those good deeds which you did. (5992) ☐

1939. Narrated `Aisha: A lady along with her two daughters came to me asking me (for some alms), but she found nothing with me except one date which I gave to her and she divided it between her two daughters, and then she got up and went away. Then the Prophet (ﷺ) came in and I informed him about this story. He said, "Whoever is in charge of (put to test by) these daughters and treats them generously, then they will act as a shield for him from the (Hell) Fire." (5995) ☐

1940. Narrated Abu Huraira: Allah's Messenger (ﷺ) kissed Al-Hasan bin Ali while Al-Aqra' bin H`Abis at-Tamim was sitting beside him. Al-Aqra said, "I have ten children and I have never kissed anyone of them," Allah's Messenger (ﷺ) cast a look at him and said, "Whoever is not merciful to others will not be treated mercifully." (5997) ☐

1941. Narrated `Aisha: A bedouin came to the Prophet (ﷺ) and said, "You (people) kiss the boys! We don't kiss them." The Prophet said, "I cannot put mercy in your heart after Allah has taken it away from it." (5998) ☐

1942. Narrated Umar (RA): Some Sabi (i.e. war prisoners, children and woman) were brought before the Prophet (ﷺ) and behold, a woman amongst them was milking her breasts to feed and whenever she found a child amongst the captives, she took it over her chest and nursed it (she had lost her child but later she found him) the Prophet said to us, "Do you think that this lady can throw her son in the fire?" We replied, "No, if she has the power not to throw it (in the fire)." The Prophet (ﷺ) then said, "Allah is more merciful to His slaves than this lady to her son." (5999) ☐

1943. Narrated Abu Huraira: I heard Allah's Messenger (ﷺ) saying, Allah divided Mercy into one hundred parts. He kept ninety nine parts with Him and sent down one part to the earth, and because of that, its one single part, His Creations are merciful to each other, so that even the mare lifts up its hoofs away from its baby animal, lest it should trample on it." (6000) ☐

1944. Narrated `Abdullah: I said 'O Allah's Messenger (ﷺ)! Which sin is the greatest?" He said, "To set up a rival unto Allah, though He Alone created you." I said, "What next?" He said, "To kill your son lest he should share your food with you." I further asked, "What next?" He said, "To commit illegal sexual intercourse with the wife of your neighbor." And then Allah revealed as proof of the statement of the Prophet: 'Those who invoke not with Allah any other god).... (to end of verse)...' (25.68) (6001) ☐

1945. Narrated Aisha: I never felt so jealous of any woman as I did of Khadija, though she had died three years before the Prophet married me, and that was because I heard him mentioning her too often, and because his Lord had ordered him to give her the glad tidings that she would have a palace in Paradise, made of Qasab and because he used to slaughter a sheep and distribute its meat among her friends. (6004) ☐

1946. Narrated Sahl bin Sa`d: The Prophet (ﷺ) said, "I and the person who looks after an orphan and provides for him, will be in Paradise like this," putting his index and middle fingers together. (6005) ☐

1947. Narrated Abu Huraira: Allah's Messenger (ﷺ) said, "While a man was walking on a road. He became very thirsty. Then he came across a well, got down into it, drank (of its water) and then came out. Meanwhile he saw a dog panting and licking mud because of excessive thirst. The man said to himself "This dog is suffering from the same state of thirst as I did." So he went down the well (again) and filled his shoe (with water) and held it in his mouth and watered the dog. Allah thanked him for that deed and forgave him." The people asked, "O Allah's Messenger (ﷺ)! Is there a reward for us in serving the animals?" He said, "(Yes) There is a reward for serving any animate (living being)." (6009) ☐

1948. Narrated Abu Huraira: Allah's Messenger (ﷺ) stood up for the prayer and we too stood up along with him. Then a bedouin shouted while offering prayer. "O Allah! Bestow Your Mercy on me and Muhammad only and do not bestow it on anybody else along with us." When the Prophet (ﷺ) had finished his prayer with Taslim, he said to the Bedouin, "You have limited (narrowed) a very vast (thing)," meaning Allah's Mercy. (6010) ☐

1949. Narrated An-Nu`man bin Bashir: Allah's Messenger (ﷺ) said, "You see the believers as regards their being merciful among themselves and showing love among themselves and being kind, resembling one body, so that, if any part of the body is not well then the whole body shares the sleeplessness (insomnia) and fever with it." (6011) ☐

1950. Narrated Jarir bin `Abdullah: The Prophet (ﷺ) said, "He who is not merciful to others, will not be treated mercifully. (6013) ☐

1951. Narrated `Aisha: The Prophet (ﷺ) said "Gabriel continued to recommend me about treating the neighbors Kindly and politely so much so that I thought he would order me to make them as my heirs. (6014) ☐

1952. Narrated Abu Shuraih: The Prophet (ﷺ) said, "By Allah, he does not believe! By Allah, he does not believe! By Allah, he does not believe!" It was said, "Who is that, O Allah's Messenger (ﷺ)?" He said, "That person whose neighbor does not feel safe from his evil." (6016) ☐

1953. Narrated Abu Shuraih Al-Adawi: My ears heard and my eyes saw the Prophet (ﷺ) when he spoke, "Anybody who believes in Allah and the Last Day, should serve his neighbor generously, and anybody who believes in Allah and the Last Day should serve his guest generously by giving him his reward." It was asked. "What is his reward, O Allah's Messenger (ﷺ)?" He said, "(To be entertained generously) for a day and a night with high quality of food and the guest has the right to be entertained for three days (with ordinary food) and if he stays longer, what he will be provided with will be regarded as Sadaqa (a charitable gift). And anybody who believes in Allah and the Last Day should talk what is good or keep quiet (i.e. abstain from all kinds of dirty and evil talks). (6019) ☐

78. GOOD MANNERS

1954. NARRATED JABIR BIN `ABDULLAH (RA): The Prophet (ﷺ) said, Enjoining, all that is good is a Sadaqa." (6021) ☐

1955. Narrated Masruq: Abdullah bin 'Amr mentioned Allah's Messenger (ﷺ) saying that he was neither a Fahish (when someone is immoral/one who speaks bad words) nor a Mutafahish (when someone does something immoral/one who speaks obscene evil words to make people laugh). Abdullah bin 'Amr added, Allah's Messenger (ﷺ) said, 'The best among you are those who have the best manners and character.' (6029) ☐

1956. Narrated `Abdullah bin Mulaika: `Aisha said that the Jews came to the Prophet (ﷺ) and said, "As-Samu 'Alaikum" (death be on you). `Aisha said, "(Death) be on you, and may Allah curse you and shower His wrath upon you!" The Prophet (ﷺ) said, "Be calm, O `Aisha! You should be kind and lenient, and beware of harshness and Fuhsh (i.e. bad words)." She said (to the Prophet), "Haven't you heard what they (Jews) have said?" He said, "Haven't you heard what I have said (to them)? I said the same to them, and my invocation against them will be accepted while theirs against me will be rejected (by Allah)." (6030) ☐

1957. Narrated Anas bin Malik: The Prophet (ﷺ) was not one who would abuse (others) or say obscene words, or curse (others), and if he wanted to admonish anyone of us, he used to say: "What is wrong with him, his forehead be dusted!" (6031) ☐

1958. Narrated 'Aisha: A man asked permission to enter upon the Prophet. When the Prophet (ﷺ) saw him, he said, "What an evil brother of his tribe! And what an evil son of his tribe!" When that man sat down, the Prophet (ﷺ) behaved with him in a nice and polite manner and was completely at ease with him. When that person had left, 'Aisha said (to the Prophet). "O Allah's Apostle! When you saw that man, you said so-and-so about him, then you showed him a kind and polite behavior, and you enjoyed his company?" Allah's Messenger (ﷺ) said, "O 'Aisha! Have you ever seen me speaking a bad and dirty language? (Remember that) the worst people in Allah's sight on the Day of Resurrection will be those whom the people leave (undisturbed) to be away from their evil (deeds)." (6032) ☐

1959. Narrated Jabir: Never was the Prophet (ﷺ) asked for a thing to be given for which his answer was 'no'. (6034) ☐

1960. Narrated Anas: I served the Prophet (ﷺ) for ten years, and he never said to me, "Uf" (a minor harsh word denoting impatience) and never blamed me by saying, "Why did you do so or why didn't you do so?" (6038) ☐

1961. Narrated Abu Dhar: That he heard the Prophet (ﷺ) saying, "If somebody accuses another of Fusuq (by calling him 'Fasiq' i.e. a wicked person) or accuses him of Kufr, such an accusation will revert to him (i.e. the accuser) if his companion (the accused) is innocent." (6045) ☐

1962. Narrated Thabit bin Ad-Dahhak: Allah's Messenger (ﷺ) said, "Whoever swears by a religion other than Islam (i.e. if somebody swears by saying that he is a non-Muslim e.g., a Jew or a Christian, etc.) in case he is telling a lie, he is really so if his oath is false, and a person is not bound to fulfill a vow about a thing which he does not possess. And if somebody commits suicide with anything in this world, he will be tortured with that very thing on the Day of Resurrection; and if somebody curses a believer, then his sin will be as if he murdered him; and whoever accuses a believer of Kufr (disbelief), then it is as if he killed him." (6047) ☐

1963. Narrated Hudhaifa: I heard the Prophet (ﷺ) saying, "A Qattat [a slanderer, a tale bearer (someone who reports the words that he has heard from others)] will not enter Paradise." (6056) ☐

1964. Narrated Abu Huraira: The Prophet (ﷺ) said, "The worst people in the Sight of Allah on the Day of Resurrection will be the double faced people who appear to some people with one face and to other people with another face." (6058) ☐

1965. Narrated Anas bin Malik: Allah's Messenger (ﷺ) said, "Do not hate one another, and do not be jealous of one another, and do not desert each other, and O, Allah's worshipers! Be brothers. Lo! It is not permissible for any Muslim to desert (not talk to) his brother (Muslim) for more than three days." (6065) ☐

1966. Narrated Abu Huraira: Allah's Messenger (ﷺ) said, "Beware of suspicion, for suspicion is the worst of false tales. and do not look for the others' faults, and do not do spying on one another, and do not practice Najsh, and do not be jealous of one another and do not hate one another, and do not desert (stop talking to) one another. And O, Allah's worshipers! Be brothers!" (6066) ☐

1967. Narrated `Aisha: The Prophet (ﷺ) said, "I do not think that so-and-so and so-and-so know anything of our religion." (And Al-Laith said, "These two persons were among the hypocrites.") (6067) ☐

1968. Narrated Abu Huraira: I heard Allah's Messenger (ﷺ) saying. "All the sins of my followers will be forgiven except those of the Mujahirin (those who commit a sin openly or disclose their sins to the people). An example of such disclosure is that a person commits a sin at night and though Allah screens it from the public, then he comes in the morning, and says, 'O so-and-so, I did such-and-such (evil) deed yesterday,' though he spent his night screened by his Lord (none knowing about his sin) and in the morning he removes Allah's screen from himself." (6069) ☐

1969. Anas bin Malik said, "Any of the female slaves of Medina could take hold of the hand of Allah's Messenger (ﷺ) and take him wherever she wished. (6072)

1970. Narrated Abu Aiyub Al-Ansari: Allah's Messenger (ﷺ) said, "It is not lawful for a man to desert his brother Muslim for more than three nights. (It is unlawful for them that) when they meet, one of them turns his face away from the other, and the other turns his face from the former, and the better of the two will be the one who greets the other first." (6077) ☐

1971. Narrated `Asim: I said to Anas bin Malik, "Did it reach you that the Prophet (ﷺ) said, "There is no treaty of brotherhood in Islam'?" Anas said, "The Prophet (ﷺ) made a treaty (of brotherhood) between the Ansar and the Quraish in my home." (6083) ☐

1072. Narrated Jarir: The Prophet (ﷺ) did not screen himself from me (had never prevented me from entering upon him) since I embraced Islam, and whenever he saw me, he would receive me with a smile. Once I told him that I could not sit firm on horses. He stroked me on the chest with his hand, and said, "O Allah! Make him firm and make him a guiding and a rightly guided man. (6089) ☐

1973. Narrated `Aisha: I never saw the Prophet (ﷺ) laughing to an extent that one could see his palate, but he always used to smile only. (6092) ☐

1974. Narrated `Abdullah: The Prophet (ﷺ) said, "Truthfulness leads to righteousness, and righteousness leads to Paradise. And a man keeps on telling the truth until he becomes a truthful person. Falsehood leads to Al-Fajur (i.e. wickedness, evil-doing), and Al-Fajur (wickedness) leads to the (Hell) Fire, and a man may keep on telling lies till he is written before Allah, a liar." (6094) ☐

1975. Narrated Abu Huraira: Allah's Messenger (ﷺ) said, "The strong is not the one who overcomes the people by his strength, but the strong is the one who controls himself while in anger." (6114) ☐

1976. Narrated Sulaiman bin Surd: While I was sitting in the company of the Prophet, two men abused each other and the face of one of them became red with anger, and his jugular veins swelled (i.e. he became furious). On that the Prophet said, "I know a word, the saying of which will cause him to relax, if he does say it. If he says: 'I seek Refuge with Allah from Satan.' then all is anger will go away." Some body said to him, "The Prophet has said, 'Seek refuge with Allah from Satan.'" The angry man said, "Am I mad?" (3282) □

1977. Narrated Abu Huraira: A man said to the Prophet (ﷺ), "Advise me!" The Prophet (ﷺ) said, "Do not become angry and furious." The man asked (the same) again and again, and the Prophet (ﷺ) said in each case, "Do not become angry and furious." (6116) □

1978. Narrated Abu As-Sawar Al-Adawi: `Imran bin Husain said: The Prophet (ﷺ) said, "Haya' (pious shyness from committing religeous indiscretions) does not bring anything except good." Thereupon Bashir bin Ka`b said, 'It is written in the wisdom paper: Haya' leads to solemnity; Haya' leads to tranquility (peace of mind)." `Imran said to him, "I am narrating to you the saying of Allah's Messenger (ﷺ) and you are speaking about your paper (wisdom book)?" (6117) □

1979. Narrated Abu Mas`ud: The Prophet (ﷺ) said, 'One of the sayings of the early Prophets which the people have got is: If you don't feel ashamed (from Haya': pious shyness from committing religeous indiscretions) do whatever you like." (6120) □

1980. Narrated Abu Musa: that when Allah's Messenger (ﷺ) sent him and Mu`adh bin Jabal to Yemen, he said to them, "Facilitate things for the people (treat the people in the most agreeable way), and do not make things difficult for them, and give them glad tidings, and let them not have aversion (i.e. to make the people hate good deeds) and you should both work in cooperation and mutual understanding, obey each other." Abu Musa said, "O Allah's Messenger (ﷺ)! We are in a land in which a drink named Al Bit' is prepared from honey, and another drink named Al-Mizr is prepared from barley." On that, Allah's Messenger (ﷺ) said, "All intoxicants (i.e. all alcoholic drinks) are prohibited." (6124) □

1981. Narrated `Aisha: I used to play with the dolls in the presence of the Prophet, and my girl friends also used to play with me. When Allah's Messenger (ﷺ) used to enter (my dwelling place) they used to hide themselves, but the Prophet would call them to join and play with me. (The playing with the dolls and similar images is forbidden, but it was allowed for `Aisha at that time, as she was a little girl, not yet reached the age of puberty.) (6130) □

1982. Narrated Abu Huraira: The Prophet (ﷺ) said, "A believer is not stung twice (by something) out of one and the same hole." (6133) □

1983. Narrated Abu Shuraih Al-Ka`bi: Allah's Messenger (ﷺ) said, whoever believes in Allah and the Last Day, should serve his guest generously. The guest's reward is: To provide him with a superior type of food for a night and a day and a guest is to be entertained with food for three days, and whatever is offered beyond that, is regarded as something given in charity. And it is not lawful for a guest to stay with his host for such a long period so as to put him in a critical position."

Narrated Malik: Similarly as above adding, "Who believes in Allah and the Last Day should talk what is good or keep quiet." (i.e. abstain from dirty and evil talk, and should think before uttering). (6135) □

1984. Narrated `Uqba bin 'Amir: We said, "O Allah's Messenger (ﷺ)! You send us out and it happens that we have to stay with such people as do not entertain us. What do you think about it?" Allah's Messenger (ﷺ) said to us, "If you stay with some people and they entertain you as they should for a guest, accept is; but if they do not do then you should take from them the right of the guest, which they ought to give." (6137) □

1985. Narrated Ubai bin Ka`b: Allah's Messenger (ﷺ) said, "Some poetry contains wisdom." (6145) □

1986. Narrated Al-Haitham bin Abu Sinan: that he heard Abu Huraira in his narration, mentioning that the Prophet (ﷺ) said, "A Muslim brother of yours who does not say dirty words." and by that he meant Ibn Rawaha, "said (in verse): 'We have Allah's Messenger (ﷺ) with us who recites the Holy Qur'an in the early morning time. He gave us guidance and light while we were blind and astray, so our hearts are sure that whatever he says, will certainly happen. He does not touch his bed at night, being busy in worshipping Allah while the pagans are sound asleep in their beds.'"

(6151) ☐

1987. Narrated Abu Huraira: Allah's Messenger (ﷺ); said, "It is better for anyone of you that the inside of his body be filled with pus which may consume his body, than it be filled with poetry." (6155) ☐

1988. Narrated Abu Bakra: A man praised another man in front of the Prophet. The Prophet (ﷺ) said thrice, "Wailaka (Woe on you)! You have cut the neck of your brother!" The Prophet (ﷺ) added, "If it is indispensable for anyone of you to praise a person, then he should say, "I think that such-and-such person (is so-and-so), and Allah is the one who will take his accounts (as he knows his reality) and none can sanctify anybody before Allah (and that only if he knows well about that person.)". (6162) ☐

1989. Narrated `Abdullah bin Mas`ud: A man came to Allah's Messenger (ﷺ) and said, "O Allah's Messenger (ﷺ)! What do you say about a man who loves some people but cannot catch up with their good deeds?" Allah's Messenger (ﷺ) said, "Everyone will be with those whom he loves." (6169) ☐

1990. Narrated `Aisha: The Prophet (ﷺ) said, "None of you should say Khabuthat Nafsi (My heart is heaving), but he is recommended to say 'Laqisat Nafsi (My heart is being annoyed)." (6179) ☐

1991. Narrated Abu Huraira: Allah's Messenger (ﷺ) said, "They say Al-Karm (the generous), and in fact Al-Karm is the heart of a believer." (6183) ☐

79. NAMING THE CHILD

1992. NARRATED JABIR (RA): A boy was born for a man among us, and the man named him Al-Qasim. We said to him, "We will not call you Abu-l-Qasim, nor will we respect you for that." The Prophet (ﷺ) was informed about that, and he said, "Name your son `Abdur-Rahman." (6186) ☐

1993. Narrated Al-Musaiyab: That his father (Hazn bin Wahb) went to the Prophet (ﷺ) and the Prophet (ﷺ) asked (him), "What is your name?" He replied, "My name is Hazn (rough, hard ground)." The Prophet (ﷺ) said, "You are Sahl (even, soft ground)." Hazn said, "I will not change the name with which my father has named me." Ibn Al-Musaiyab added: We have had roughness (in character) ever since. (6190) □

1994. Narrated Sahl: When Al-Mundhir bin Abu Usaid was born, he was brought to the Prophet (ﷺ) who placed him on his thigh. While Abu Usaid was sitting there, the Prophet (ﷺ) was busy with something in his hands so Abu Usaid told someone to take his son from the thigh of the Prophet (ﷺ). When the Prophet (ﷺ) finished his job, he said, "Where is the boy?" Abu Usaid replied, "We have sent him home." The Prophet (ﷺ) said, "What is his name?" Abu Usaid said, "(His name is) so-and-so." The Prophet (ﷺ) said, "No, his name is Al-Mundhir (the warner)." So he called him Al-Mundhir from that day. (6191) □

1995. Narrated Abu Huraira: Zainab's original name was Barrah (A kind and affectionate woman), but it was said' "By that she is giving herself the prestige of piety." So the Prophet (ﷺ) changed her name to Zainab (fragrant flower). (6192) □

1996. Narrated Jabir bin `Abdullah Al-Ansari: Allah's Messenger (ﷺ) said, "Name yourselves after me (by my name) but do not call (yourselves) by my Kuniya (nickname), for I am Al-Qasim (distributor), and I distribute among you Allah's blessings." This narration has also come on the authority of Anas that the! Prophet said so." (6196) □

1997. Narrated Abu Musa: I got a son and I took him to the Prophet (ﷺ) who named him Ibrahim, and put in his mouth the juice of a date fruit (which be himself had chewed?, and invoked for Allah's blessing upon him, and then gave him back to me. He was the eldest son of Abii Musa. (6198) □

1998. Narrated Anas: The Prophet (ﷺ) was the best of all the people in character. I had a brother called Abu `Umar, who, I think, had been newly weaned. Whenever he (that child) was brought to the Prophet (ﷺ) the Prophet (ﷺ) used to say, "O Abu `Umar! What did Al-Nughair (nightingale) (do)?" It was a nightingale with which he used to play. Sometimes the time of the Prayer became due while he (the Prophet) was in our house. He would order that the carpet underneath him be swept and sprayed with water, and then he would stand up (for the prayer) and we would line up behind him, and he would lead us in prayer. (6203) □

1999. Narrated Abu Huraira: The Prophet (ﷺ) said, "The most awful (meanest) name in Allah's sight." Sufyan said more than once, "The most awful (meanest) name in Allah's sight is (that of) a man calling himself king of kings." Sufyan said, "Somebody else (i.e. other than Abu Az-Zinad, a sub-narrator) says: What is meant by 'The king of kings' is 'Shahan Shah.," (6206) □

2000. Narrated Anas: The Prophet (ﷺ) was on a journey and a slave named Anjasha was chanting (singing) for the camels to let them go fast (while driving). The Prophet (ﷺ) said, "O Anjasha, drive slowly (the camels) with the glass vessels!" Abu Qilaba said, "By the glass vessels' he meant the women (riding the camels). (6210) □

2001. Narrated Anas bin Malik: Two men sneezed before the Prophet. The Prophet (ﷺ) said to one of them, "May Allah bestow His Mercy on you," but he did not say that to the other. On being asked (why), the Prophet (ﷺ) said, "That one praised Allah (at the time of sneezing), while the other did not praise Allah." (6221) □

2002. Narrated Abu Huraira: The Prophet (ﷺ) said, "Allah likes sneezing and dislikes yawning, so if someone sneezes and then praises Allah, then it is obligatory on every Muslim who heard him, to say: May Allah be merciful to you (Yar-hamuka-l-lah). But as regards yawning, it is from Satan, so one must try one's best to stop it, if one says 'Ha' when yawning, Satan will laugh at him." (6223) □

2003. Narrated Abu Huraira: The Prophet (ﷺ) said, " If anyone of you sneezes, he should say 'Al-Hamduli l-lah' (Praise be to Allah), and his (Muslim) brother or companion should say to him, 'Yar-hamuka-l-lah' (May Allah bestow his Mercy on you). When the latter says 'Yar-hamuka-llah", the former should say, 'Yahdikumullah wa Yuslih balakum' (May Allah give you guidance and improve your condition). (6224) □

80. Asking Permission

2004. Narrated Abu Sa`id Al-Khudri (ra): The Prophet (ﷺ) said, 'Beware! Avoid sitting on the roads." They (the people) said, "O Allah s Apostle! We can't help sitting (on the roads) as these are (our places) here we have talks." The Prophet (ﷺ) said, ' l f you refuse but to sit, then pay the road its right ' They said, "What is the right of the road, O Allah's Apostle?" He said, 'Lowering your gaze, refraining from harming others, returning greeting, and enjoining what is good, and forbidding what is evil." (6229) □

2005. Narrated Abu Huraira: The Prophet (ﷺ) said, "The young should greet the old, the passer by should greet the sitting one, and the small group of persons should greet the large group of persons." (6231) □

2006. Narrated Sahl bin Sa`d: A man peeped through a round hole into the dwelling place of the Prophet, while the Prophet (ﷺ) had a Midray (an iron comb) with which he was scratching his head. The Prophet (ﷺ) said, "Had known you were looking (through the hole), I would have pierced your eye with it (the comb)." Verily! The order of taking permission to enter has been enjoined because of that sight, (that one should not look unlawfully at the state of others). (6241) □

2007. Narrated Anas bin Malik: A man peeped into a room of the Prophet. The Prophet (ﷺ) stood up, holding an arrow head. It is as if I am just looking at him, trying to stab the man. (6242) □

2008. And added, "If someone is peeping (looking secretly) into your house without your permission, and you throw a stone at him and destroy his eyes, there will be no blame on you." (6888) □

2009. Narrated Abu Sa`id Al-Khudri: While I was present in one of the gatherings of the Ansar, Abu Musa came as if he was scared, and said, "I asked permission to enter upon Umar three times, but I was not given the permission, so I returned." (When Umar came to know about it) he said to Abu Musa, "Why did you not enter?'. Abu Musa replied, "I asked permission three times, and I was not given it, so I returned, for Allah's Messenger (ﷺ) said, "If anyone of you asks the permission to enter thrice, and the permission is not given, then he should return."' Umar said, "By Allah! We will ask Abu Musa to bring witnesses for it." (Abu Musa went to a gathering of the Ansar and said). "Did anyone of you hear this from the Prophet (ﷺ)?" Ubai bin Ka`b said, "By Allah, none will go with you but the youngest of the people (as a witness)." (Abu Sa`id) was the youngest of them, so I went with Abu Musa and informed Umar that the Prophet (ﷺ) had said so. (6245) ☐

2010. Narrated Abu Huraira: I entered (the house) along with Allah's Messenger (ﷺ). There he found milk in a basin. He said, "O Abu Hirr! Go and call the people of Suffa to me." I went to them and invited them. They came and asked permission to enter, and when it was given, they entered. (6246) ☐

2011. Narrated Anas bin Malik: that he passed by a group of boys and greeted them and said, "The Prophet (ﷺ) used to do so." (6247) ☐

2012. Narrated Jabir: I came to the Prophet (ﷺ) in order to consult him regarding my father's debt. When I knocked on the door, he asked, "Who is that?" I replied, "I" He said, "I, I?" He repeated it as if he disliked it. (6250) ☐

2013. Narrated Anas bin Malik: the Prophet (ﷺ) said, "If the people of the Scripture greet you, then you should say (in reply), 'Wa'alaikum (And on you).'" (6258) ☐

2014. Narrated Qatada: I asked Anas, "Was it a custom of the companions of the Prophet (ﷺ) to shake hands with one another?" He said, "Yes." (6263) ☐

2015. Narrated `Abdullah bin Hisham: We were in the company of the Prophet (ﷺ) and he was holding the hand of `Umar bin Al-Khattab. (6264) ☐

2016. Narrated Mu`adh: While I was a companion rider with the Prophet (ﷺ) he said, "O Muadh!" I replied, "Labbaik wa Sadaik." He repeated this call three times and then said, "Do you know what Allah's Right on His slaves is?" I replied, "No." He said, Allah's Right on His slaves is that they should worship Him (Alone) and should not join partners in worship with Him." He said, "O Muadh!" I replied, "Labbaik wa Sadaik." He said, "Do you know what the right of (Allah's) salves on Allah is, if they do that (worship Him Alone and join none in His worship)? It is that He will not punish them." (6267) ☐

2017. Narrated Ibn `Umar: The Prophet (ﷺ) forbade that a man should be made to get up from his seat so that another might sit on it, but one should make room and spread out. Ibn `Umar disliked that a man should get up from his seat and then somebody else sit at his place. (6270) ☐

2018. Narrated Ibn `Umar: I saw Allah's Messenger (ﷺ) in the courtyard of the Ka`ba in the Ihtiba.' posture putting his hand round his legs like this. (6272) ☐

2019. Narrated Thumama: Anas said, "Um Sulaim used to spread a leather sheet for the Prophet (ﷺ) and he used to take a midday nap on that leather sheet at her home." Anas added, "When the Prophet (ﷺ) had slept, she would take some of his sweat and hair and collect it (the sweat) in a bottle and then mix it with Suk (a kind of perfume) while he was still sleeping." When the death of Anas bin Malik approached, he advised that some of that Suk be mixed with his Hanut (perfume for embalming the dead body), and it was mixed with his Hanut. (6281) ☐

2020. Narrated Anas bin Malik: The Prophet (ﷺ) confided to me a secret which I did not disclose to anybody after him. And Um Sulaim asked me (about that secret) but I did not tell her. (6289) ☐

2021. Narrated `Abdullah: The Prophet (ﷺ) said, "When you are three persons sitting together, then no two of you should hold secret counsel excluding the third person until you are with some other people too, for that would grieve him." (6290) ☐

2022. Narrated Abu Musa: One night a house in Medina was burnt with its occupants. The Prophet (ﷺ) spoke about them, saying, "This fire is indeed your enemy, so whenever you go to bed, put it out to protect yourselves." (6294) □

81. Invocations (Dua)

2023. NARRATED ABU HURAIRA (RA): Allah's Messenger (ﷺ) said, "For every prophet there is one special invocation (that will not be rejected) with which he appeals (to Allah), and I want to keep such an invocation for interceding for my followers in the Hereafter." (6304) □

2024. Narrated Abu Huraira: I heard Allah's Messenger (ﷺ) saying." By Allah! I ask for forgiveness from Allah and turn to Him in repentance more than seventy times a day." (6307) □

2025. Narrated Al-Harith bin Suwaid: `Abdullah bin Mas`ud related to us two narrations: One from the Prophet (ﷺ) and the other from himself, saying: A believer sees his sins as if he were sitting under a mountain which, he is afraid, may fall on him; whereas the wicked person considers his sins as flies passing over his nose and he just drives them away like this." Abu Shihab (the sub-narrator) moved his hand over his nose in illustration. (Ibn Mas`ud added): Allah's Messenger (ﷺ) said, "Allah is more pleased with the repentance of His slave than a man who encamps at a place where his life is jeopardized, but he has his riding beast carrying his food and water. He then rests his head and sleeps for a short while and wakes to find his riding beast gone. (He starts looking for it) and suffers from severe heat and thirst or what Allah wished (him to suffer from). He then says, 'I will go back to my place.' He returns and sleeps again, and then (getting up), he raises his head to find his riding beast standing beside him." (6308) □

2026. Narrated Al-Bara bin `Azib: Allah's Messenger (s) said to me, "When you want to go to bed, perform ablution as you do for prayer, then lie down on your right side and say,

اللهُمَّ إِنِّي أَسْلَمتُ وَجهِي إِلَيكَ وفَوَّضتُ أمرِي إِلَيكَ وَألجَأتُ ظَهرِي إِلَيكَ رَغبَةً ورَهبَةً إِلَيكَ. لا مَلجَأَ ولامَنجا مِنكَ إلا إِلَيكَ. اللهُمَّ آمَنتُ بِكِتَابِكَ الَّذِي أنزَلتَ وبِنَبِيِّكَ الَّذِي أرسَلتَ۞

'Allahumma aslamtu wajhi ilaika, wa fawwadtu 'amri ilaika wa alja'tu dhahri ilaika, raghbatan wa rahbatan ilaika, la malja'a wa la manja minka illa ilaika. Amantu bikitabik al-ladhi anzalta wa binabiyyika al-ladhi arsalta'.

(O Allah! I surrender to You and entrust all my affairs to You and depend upon You for Your Blessings both with hope and fear of You. There is no fleeing from You, and there is no place of protection and safety except with You O Allah! I believe in Your Book (the Qur'an) which You have revealed and in Your Prophet (Muhammad) whom You have sent).

If you should die then (after reciting this) you will die on the religion of Islam (i.e., as a Muslim); so let these words be the last you say (before going to bed)" While I was memorizing it, I said, "Wa birasulika al-ladhi arsalta (in Your Apostle whom You have sent).' The Prophet (s) said, "No, but say Wa binabiyyika al-ladhi arsalta (in Your Prophet whom You have sent). (6311) □

2027. Narrated Hudhaifa: When the Prophet (s) went to bed at night, he would put his hand under his cheek and then say,

اللهم باسمك أموت وأحيا

"Allahumma bismika amutu wa ahya,"

"O Allah, with Your Name will I die and live (wake up)".

And when he got up, he would say,

الْحَمْدُ لِلَّهِ الَّذِي أَحْيَانَا بَعْدَ مَا أَمَاتَنَا وَإِلَيْهِ النُّشُورُ

"Al-Hamdu lil-lahi al-ladhi ahyana ba'da ma amatana, wa ilaihi an-nushur."

"All praise is to Allah Who gave us life after death (sleep) and unto Him is the return"

(6314) □

2028. Narrated Al-Bara' bin `Azib: When Allah's Messenger (s) went to bed, he used to sleep on his right side and then say,

اللَّهُمَّ أَسْلَمْتُ نَفْسِي إِلَيْكَ، وَوَجَّهْتُ وَجْهِي إِلَيْكَ، وَفَوَّضْتُ أَمْرِي إِلَيْكَ، وَأَلْجَأْتُ ظَهْرِي إِلَيْكَ، رَغْبَةً وَرَهْبَةً إِلَيْكَ، لاَ مَلْجَأَ وَلاَ مَنْجَا مِنْكَ إِلاَّ إِلَيْكَ، آمَنْتُ بِكِتَابِكَ الَّذِي أَنْزَلْتَ، وَنَبِيِّكَ الَّذِي أَرْسَلْتَ

"All-ahumma aslamtu nafsi ilaika, wa wajjahtu wajhi ilaika, wa fauwadtu `Amri ilaika, wa alja'tu zahri ilaika, raghbatan wa rahbatan ilaika. La Malja'a wa la manja minka illa ilaika. Amantu bikitabika al-ladhi anzalta wa nabiyyika al-ladhi arsalta"

"O Allah! I have submitted myself to You, I have turned myself to You, committed my affairs to You and sought Your refuge for protection out of desire for You and fear of You (expecting Your reward and fearing Your punishment). There is no refuge and no place of safety from You but with You. I believe in the Book You have revealed and in the Prophet (SAW) You have sent."

Allah's Messenger (s) said, "Whoever recites these words (before going to bed) and dies the same night, he will die on the Islamic religion (as a Muslim). (6315) □

2029. Narrated Ibn `Abbas: One night I slept at the house of Maimuna. The Prophet (s) woke up, answered the call of nature, washed his face and hands, and then slept. He got up (late at night), went to a water skin, opened the mouth thereof and performed ablution not using much water, yet he washed all the parts properly and then offered the prayer. I got up and straightened my back in order that the Prophet (s) might not feel that I was watching him, and then I performed the ablution, and when he got up to offer the prayer, I stood on his left. He caught hold of my ear and brought me over to his right side. He offered thirteen rak`at in all and then lay down and slept till he started blowing out his breath as he used to do when he slept. In the meantime Bilal informed the Prophet (s) of the approaching time for the (Fajr) prayer, and the Prophet offered the Fajr (Morning) prayer without performing new ablution. He used to say in his invocation,

اللَّهُمَّ اجْعَلْ فِي قَلْبِي نُورًا، وَفِي بَصَرِي نُورًا، وَفِي سَمْعِي نُورًا، وَعَنْ يَمِينِي نُورًا، وَعَنْ يَسَارِي نُورًا، وَفَوْقِي

نُورًا، وَتَحْتِي نُورًا، وَأَمَامِي نُورًا، وَخَلْفِي نُورًا، وَاجْعَلْ لِي نُورًا

"Allahumma ij`al fi qalbi nuran wa fi basari nuran, wa fi sam`i nuran, wa`an yamini nuran, wa`an yasari nuran, wa fawqi nuran, wa tahti nuran, wa amami nuran, wa khalfi nuran, waj`al li nuran." (Allah! Let my heart have light, and my sight have light, and my hearing (sense) have light; and let me have light on my right, and have light on my left, and have light above me, and have light under me, and have light in front of me, and have light behind me; and let me have light.)

Kuraib (a sub narrator) said, "I have forgotten seven other words, (which the Prophet (s) mentioned in this invocation). I met a man from the offspring of Al-`Abbas and he narrated those seven things to me, mentioning, '(Let there be light in) my nerves, my flesh, my blood, my hair and my body,' and he also mentioned two other things." (6316) □

2030. Narrated Ibn `Abbas: When the Prophet (ﷺ) got up at night to offer the night prayer, he used to say:

اللَّهُمَّ لَكَ الْحَمْدُ، أَنْتَ نُورُ السَّمَوَاتِ وَالْأَرْضِ وَمَنْ فِيهِنَّ وَلَكَ الْحَمْدُ، أَنْتَ قَيِّمُ السَّمَوَاتِ وَالْأَرْضِ وَمَنْ فِيهِنَّ وَلَكَ الْحَمْدُ، أَنْتَ الْحَقُّ، وَوَعْدُكَ حَقٌّ، وَقَوْلُكَ حَقٌّ، وَلِقَاؤُكَ حَقٌّ، وَالْجَنَّةُ حَقٌّ، وَالنَّارُ حَقٌّ، وَالسَّاعَةُ حَقٌّ، وَالنَّبِيُّونَ حَقٌّ، وَمُحَمَّدٌ حَقٌّ، اللَّهُمَّ لَكَ أَسْلَمْتُ، وَعَلَيْكَ تَوَكَّلْتُ، وَإِلَيْكَ أَنَبْتُ، وَبِكَ خَاصَمْتُ، وَإِلَيْكَ حَاكَمْتُ، فَاغْفِرْ لِي مَا قَدَّمْتُ وَمَا أَخَّرْتُ، وَمَا أَسْرَرْتُ وَمَا أَعْلَنْتُ، أَنْتَ الْمُقَدِّمُ، وَأَنْتَ الْمُؤَخِّرُ لَا إِلَهَ إِلَّا أَنْتَ أَوْ لَا إِلَهَ غَيْرُكَ

"Allahumma laka l-hamdu; Anta nuras-samawati wal ardi wa man fihinna. wa laka l-hamdu; Anta qaiyim as-samawati wal ardi wa man flhinna. Wa lakaI-hamdu; Anta-l-,haqqun, wa wa'daka haqqun, wa qauluka haqqun, wa liqauka haqqun, wal-jannatu haqqun, wannaru haqqun, was-sa atu haqqun, wan-nabiyyuna huqqun, Mahammadun haqqun, Allahumma laka aslamtu, wa Alaika tawakkaltu, wa bika amantu, wa ilaika anabtu, wa bika Khasamtu, wa ilaika hakamtu, faghfirli ma qaddamtu wa ma akh-khartu, wa ma asrartu, wa ma a'lantu. Anta al-muqaddimu, wa anta al-mu-'akhkhiru. La ilaha il-la anta (or La ilaha ghairuka)" (O Allah! All the praises are for you, You are the Light of the Heavens and the Earth, And whatever is in them. All the praises are for you, You are the Holder of the Heavens and the Earth, And whatever is in them. All the Praises are for You, You are the Lord of the Heavens and the Earth, And whatever is in them. All the praises are for You, You have the possession of the Heavens and the Earth, And whatever is in them. You are the Truth and Your Promise is the truth, Your Word is the Truth, and the Meeting with You is the Truth, and Paradise is the Truth, and the (Hell) Fire is the Truth, and the Day of Resurrection is true, And all the Prophets (Peace be upon them) are true; And Muhammad Sallallahu Alaihi Wasallam (Peace and Blessings of Allah be upon him) is true. O Allah! I surrender (my will) to You; I believe in You and depend on You. And repent to You, And with Your help I argue (with my opponents, the non-believers) And I take You as a judge (to judge between us). Allah! Forgive me my sins that I did in the past or will do in the future, and also the sins I did in secret or in public. You are my only God (Whom I worship) and there is no other God for me (I worship none but You). (6317) ☐

2030. Narrated `Ali: Fatima complained about the blisters on her hand because of using a mill-stone. She went to ask the Prophet for servant, but she did not find him (at home) and had to inform `Aisha of her need. When he came, `Aisha informed him about it. `Ali added: The Prophet (ﷺ) came to us when we had gone to our beds. When I was going to get up, he said, "'Stay in your places," and sat between us, till I felt the coolness of the feet on my chest. The Prophet (ﷺ) then said, "Shall I not tell you of a thing which is better for you than a servant? When you (both) go to your beds, say 'Allahu Akbar' thirty-four times, and 'Subhan Allah' thirty-three times, 'Al hamdu 'illah' thirty-three times, for that is better for you than a servant." Ibn Seereen said, "Subhan Allah' (is to be said for) thirty-four times." (6318) ☐

2031. Narrated Abu Huraira: The Prophet (s) said, "When anyone of you go to bed, he should shake out his bed with the inside of his waist sheet, for he does not know what has come on to it after him, and then he should say,

بِاسْمِكَ رَبِّي وَضَعْتُ جَنْبِي، وَبِكَ أَرْفَعُهُ، إِنْ أَمْسَكْتَ نَفْسِي
فَارْحَمْهَا، وَإِنْ أَرْسَلْتَهَا فَاحْفَظْهَا، بِمَا تَحْفَظُ بِهِ عِبَادَكَ الصَّالِحِينَ

"Bismika Rabbî wada'tu janbî, wa bika arfa'uhu, in amsakta nafî farhamha, wa in arsaltaha fahfazha bima tahfazu bihi 'ibâdakas-sâlihîn." (O my Lord! In Your Name I put my side over this bed and with Your Name I will lift it up therefrom. If You take my soul, bestow mercy on it, and if You release it, protect it as You protect Your righteous slaves.) (6320) □

2032. Narrated Abu Huraira: Allah's Messenger (ﷺ) said, "When it is the last third of the night, our Lord, the Blessed, the Superior, descends every night to the heaven of the world and says, 'Is there anyone who invokes Me (demand anything from Me), that I may respond to his invocation; Is there anyone who asks Me for something that I may give (it to) him; Is there anyone who asks My forgiveness that I may forgive him?'" (6321) □

2033. Narrated Shaddad bin 'Aus: The Prophet (s) said, "The most superior way of asking for forgiveness from Allah is,

" اللّهُمَّ أَنْتَ رَبِّي، لَا إِلٰهَ إِلَّا أَنْتَ، خَلَقْتَنِي وَأَنَا عَبْدُكَ، وَأَنَا عَلَى عَهْدِكَ وَوَعْدِكَ مَا اسْتَطَعْتُ، أَعُوذُ بِكَ مِنْ شَرِّ مَا صَنَعْتُ، أَبُوءُ لَكَ بِنِعْمَتِكَ عَلَيَّ وَأَبُوءُ لَكَ بِذَنْبِي، فَاغْفِرْ لِيْ، فَإِنَّهُ لَا يَغْفِرُ الذُّنُوْبَ إِلَّاأَنْتَ."

"Allahumma anta Rabbi la ilaha illa Anta Khalaqtani wa ana abduka, wa ana 'ala ahdika wa wa'dika mastata'tu, A'udhu bika min Sharri ma sana'tu, abu'u Laka bini'matika 'alaiya, wa Abu'u Laka bidhanbi faghfirli fainnahu la yaghfiru adhdhunuba illa anta" (O Allah! You are my Lord! None has the right to be worshipped but You. You created me and I am Your slave, and I am faithful to my covenant and my promise as much as I can. I seek refuge with You from all the evil I have done. I acknowledge before You all the blessings You have bestowed upon me, and I confess to You all my sins. So I entreat You to forgive my sins, for nobody can forgive sins except You.) If somebody recites this invocation during the night, and if he should die then, he will go to Paradise (or he will be from the people of Paradise). And if he recites it in the morning, and if he should die on the same day, he will have the same fate." (6323) □

2034. Narrated `Ikrima: Ibn `Abbas said, "Preach to the people once a week, and if you won't, then preach them twice, but if you want to preach more, then let it be three times (a week only), and do not make the people fed-up with this Qur'an. If you come to some people who are engaged in a talk, don't start interrupting their talk by preaching, lest you should cause them to be bored. You should rather keep quiet, and if they ask you, then preach to them at the time when they are eager to hear what you say. And avoid the use of rhymed prose in invocation for I noticed that Allah's Messenger (ﷺ) and his companions always avoided it." (6337) □

2035. Narrated Anas: Allah's Messenger (ﷺ) said, "When anyone of you appeal to Allah for something, he should ask with determination and should not say, 'O Allah, if You wish, give me.', for nobody can force Allah to do something against His Will. (6338) □

2036. Narrated Abu Huraira: Allah's Messenger (ﷺ) said, "The invocation of anyone of you is granted (by Allah) if he does not show impatience (by saying, "I invoked Allah but my request has not been granted.") (6340) □

2037. Narrated Ibn `Abbas: The Prophet (s) used to invoke Allah at the time of distress, saying,

" لاَ إِلَهَ إِلاَّ اللَّهُ الْعَظِيمُ الْحَلِيمُ، لاَ إِلَهَ إِلاَّ اللَّهُ رَبُّ السَّمَوَاتِ وَالأَرْضِ، رَبُّ الْعَرْشِ الْعَظِيمِ ".

"La ilaha illal-lahu Al-`Azim, al- Halim, La ilaha illal-lahu Rabbu-s-samawati wal-ard wa Rabbu-l-arsh il-azim." (There is no god except Allah, the All-Mighty, the Forbearing; there is no god except Allah, the Lord of the Mighty Throne; there is no god except Allah, Lord of the heavens, Lord of the earth and Lord of the noble Throne." (6345) □

2038. Narrated Abu Huraira: Allah's Messenger (ﷺ) used to seek refuge with Allah from the difficult moment of a calamity and from being overtaken by destruction and from being destined to an evil end, and from the malicious joy of enemies. Sufyan said, "This narration contained three items only, but I added one. I do not know which one that was." (6347) □

2039. Narrated Abu Huraira: that he heard the Prophet (ﷺ) saying, "O Allah! If I should ever abuse a believer, please let that be a means of bringing him near to You on the Day of Resurrection." (6361) □

2040. Narrated Mus`ab Sa`d used to recommend five (statements) and mentioned that the Prophet (s) I used to recommend it. (It was)

اللَّهُمَّ إِنِّي أَعُوذُ بِكَ مِنَ الْبُخْلِ، وَأَعُوذُ بِكَ مِنَ الْجُبْنِ، وَأَعُوذُ بِكَ أَنْ أُرَدَّ إِلَى أَرْذَلِ الْعُمُرِ، وَأَعُوذُ بِكَ مِنْ فِتْنَةِ "
الدُّنْيَا يَعْنِي فِتْنَةَ الدَّجَّالِ وَأَعُوذُ بِكَ مِنْ عَذَابِ الْقَبْرِ ".

"Allaahumma 'innee 'a'oothu bika minal-bukhli, wa 'a'oothu bika minal-jubni, wa 'a'oothu bika min 'an 'uradda 'ilaa 'arthalil-'umuri, wa 'a'oothu bika min fitnatid-dunyaa wa 'athaabil-qabri." (O Allah! I seek refuge with You from miserliness; and seek refuge with You from cowardice; and seek refuge with You from being sent back to geriatric old age; and I seek refuge with You from the affliction of this world (i.e., the affliction of Ad-Dajjal etc.); and seek refuge with You from the punishment of the grave.) (6365) □

2041. Narrated `Aisha: Two old ladies from among the Jewish ladies entered upon me and said' "The dead are punished in their graves," but I thought they were telling a lie and did not believe them in the beginning. When they went away and the Prophet (ﷺ) entered upon me, I said, "O Allah's Messenger (ﷺ)! Two old ladies.." and told him the whole story. He said, "They told the truth; the dead are really punished, to the extent that all the animals hear (the sound resulting from) their punishment." Since then I always saw him seeking refuge with Allah from the punishment of the grave in his prayers. (6366) □

2042. Narrated Anas bin Malik: Allah's Prophet used to say,

اللَّهُمَّ إِنِّي أَعُوذُ بِكَ مِنَ الْعَجْزِ وَالْكَسَلِ، وَالْجُبْنِ وَالْهَرَمِ، وَأَعُوذُ بِكَ مِنْ عَذَابِ الْقَبْرِ، وَأَعُوذُ بِكَ مِنْ فِتْنَةِ الْمَحْيَا "
وَالْمَمَاتِ ".

"O Allah! I seek refuge with You from incapacity and laziness, from cowardice and geriatric old age, and seek refuge with You from the punishment of the grave, and I seek refuge with You from the afflictions of life and death." (6367) □

2043. Narrated Anas bin Malik: The Prophet (s) used to say,

اللَّهُمَّ إِنِّي أَعُوذُ بِكَ مِنَ الْهَمِّ وَالْحَزَنِ، وَالْعَجْزِ وَالْكَسَلِ، وَالْبُخْلِ وَالْجُبْنِ، وَضَلَعِ الدَّيْنِ، وَغَلَبَةِ الرِّجَالِ

"Allaahumma 'innee 'a'oothu bika minal-hammi walhazani, wal'ajzi walkasali, walbukhli waljubni, wa dhala'id-dayni wa ghalabatir-rijaal" (O Allah, I seek refuge in You from grief and sadness, from weakness and from laziness, from miserliness and from cowardice, from being overcome by debt and overpowered by men (i.e. others)." (6369) □

2044. Narrated `Aisha: The Prophet (s) used to say,

اللَّهُمَّ إِنِّي أَعُوذُ بِكَ مِنْ فِتْنَةِ النَّارِ وَعَذَابِ النَّارِ وَمِنْ فِتْنَةِ الْقَبْرِ وَعَذَابِ الْقَبْرِ وَمِنْ شَرِّ فِتْنَةِ الْغِنَى وَشَرِّ فِتْنَةِ الْفَقْرِ وَمِنْ شَرِّ فِتْنَةِ الْمَسِيحِ الدَّجَّالِ اللَّهُمَّ اغْسِلْ خَطَايَاىَ بِمَاءِ الثَّلْجِ وَالْبَرَدِ وَنَقِّ قَلْبِي مِنَ الْخَطَايَا كَمَا نَقَّيْتَ الثَّوْبَ الأَبْيَضَ مِنَ الدَّنَسِ وَبَاعِدْ بَيْنِي وَبَيْنَ خَطَايَاىَ كَمَا بَاعَدْتَ بَيْنَ الْمَشْرِقِ وَالْمَغْرِبِ اللَّهُمَّ إِنِّي أَعُوذُ بِكَ مِنَ الْكَسَلِ وَالْهَرَمِ وَالْمَأْثَمِ وَالْمَغْرَمِ

"Allahum 'iiniy 'aeudh bik min alkisl walharam walmaghrim walmathima, llahuma 'iiniy 'aeudh bik min eadhab alnaar wafitnat alnaar waeadhab alqubri, washara fitnat alghunaa, washara fitnat alfuqr, wamin shari fitnat almasih aldijala, allahuma aghsil khitayaa bima' althalj walbarid, wanaq qalbi min alkhataya, kama yanqaa althawb al'abyad min aldanas , wabaeid bayni wabayn khatayaa kama baeadt bayn almashriq walmaghrib." (O Allah! I seek refuge with You from laziness from geriatric old age, from being in debt, and from committing sins. O Allah! I seek refuge with You from the punishment of the Fire, the afflictions of the grave, the punishment in the grave, and the evil of the affliction of poverty and from the evil of the affliction caused by Al-Masih Ad-Dajjal. O Allah! Wash away my sins with the water of snow and hail, and cleanse my heart from the sins as a white garment is cleansed of filth, and let there be a far away distance between me and my sins as You have set far away the East and the West from each other.) (6375) □

2045. Narrated Jabir: The Prophet (s) used to teach us the Istikhara for each and every matter as he used to teach us the Suras from the Holy Quran. (He used to say), "If anyone of you intends to do something, he should offer a two-rak`at prayer other than the obligatory prayer, and then say,

اللَّهُمَّ إِنِّي أَسْتَخِيرُكَ بِعِلْمِكَ وَأَسْتَقْدِرُكَ بِقُدْرَتِكَ وَأَسْأَلُكَ مِنْ فَضْلِكَ الْعَظِيمِ فَإِنَّكَ

تَقْدِرُ وَلَا أَقْدِرُ وَتَعْلَمُ وَلَا أَعْلَمُ وَأَنْتَ عَلَّامُ الْغُيُوبِ اللَّهُمَّ إِنْ كُنْتَ تَعْلَمُ أَنَّ هَذَا

الْأَمْرَ خَيْرٌ لِي فِي دِينِي وَمَعَاشِي وَعَاقِبَةِ أَمْرِي فَاقْدُرْهُ لِي وَيَسِّرْهُ لِي ثُمَّ بَارِكْ

لِي فِيهِ وَإِنْ كُنْتَ تَعْلَمُ أَنَّ هَذَا الْأَمْرَ شَرٌّ فِي دِينِي وَمَعَاشِي وَعَاقِبَةِ أَمْرِي

فَاصْرِفْهُ عَنِّي وَاصْرِفْنِي عَنْهُ وَاقْدُرْ لِيَ الْخَيْرَ حَيْثُ كَانَ ثُمَّ ارْضِنِي بِهِ

"Allahumma inni astakhiruka bi'ilmika, Wa astaqdiruka bi-qudratika, Wa as'alaka min fadlika al-'azlm Fa-innaka taqdiru Wala aqdiru, Wa ta'lamu Wala a'lamu, Wa anta 'allamu l-ghuyub. Allahumma, in kunta ta'lam anna hadha-l-amra Khairun li fi dini wa ma'ashi wa'aqibati amri (or 'ajili amri wa'ajilihi) Faqdirhu wa yas-sirhu li thumma barik li Fihi, Wa in kunta ta'lamu anna hadha-lamra shar-run li fi dini wa ma'ashi wa'aqibati amri (or fi'ajili amri wa ajilihi) Fasrifhu anni was-rifni anhu. Waqdir li al-khaira haithu kana Thumma ardini bihi." (O Allah! I ask guidance from Your knowledge, And Power from Your Might and I ask for Your great blessings. You are capable and I am not. You know and I do not and You know the unseen. O Allah! If You know that this job is good for my religion and my subsistence and in my Hereafter–(or said: If it is better for my present and later needs)–Then You ordain it for me and make it easy for me to get, And then bless me in it, and if You know that this job is harmful to me In my religion and subsistence and in the Hereafter–(or said: If it is worse for my present and later needs)–Then keep it away from me and let me be away from it. And ordain for me whatever is good for me, And make me satisfied with it.) Then he should mention his matter (need). (6382) □

2046. Narrated Abu Musa: We were in the company of the Prophet (s) on a journey, and whenever we ascended a high place, we used to say Takbir (in a loud voice).

الله أكبر "Allahu Akbar" (God is [the] greatest)

The Prophet (s) said, "O people! Be kind to yourselves, for you are not calling upon a deaf or an absent one, but You are calling an All-Hearer, and an All-Seer." Then he came to me as I was reciting silently, "La haul a wala quwwata illa bil-lah." He said, "O `Abdullah bin Qais! Say La haul a walaquwata illa bil-lah, for it is one of the treasures of Paradise." Or he said, "Shall I tell you a word which is one of the treasures of Paradise? It is,

لَا حَوْلَ وَلَا قُوَّةَ إِلَّا بِاللهِ "La haul a wala quwwata illa bil-lah." (There Is No Might Nor Power Except With Allah). (6384) □

2047. Narrated Ibn 'Abbas: The Prophet (s) said, "If anyone of you, when intending to have a sexual intercourse with his wife, says,

بِسْمِ اللهِ اللَّهُمَّ جَنِّبْنَا الشَّيْطَانَ وَجَنِّبِ الشَّيْطَانَ مَا رَزَقْتَنَا

'Bismillah, Allahumma jannibna-sh-shaitan, wa jannibi-sh-shaitan ma razaqtana,' "With the Name of Allah. O Allah, keep the I Devil away from us and keep the Devil away from that which You provide for us." And if the couple are destined to have a child (out of that very sexual relation), then Satan will never be able to harm that child." (6388) □

2048. Narrated Anas: The most frequent invocation of The Prophet (s) was,

رَبَّنَا آتِنَا فِي الدُّنْيَا حَسَنَةً وَفِي الْآخِرَةِ حَسَنَةً وَقِنَا عَذَابَ النَّارِ

"Rabbana Atina Fid-Dunya Hasanatan Wa Fil 'Akhirati Hasanatan Waqina 'Azaban-Nar" (O Allah! Give to us in the world that which is good and in the Hereafter that which is good, and save us from the torment of the Fire.) (2.201) (6389) □

2049. Narrated Abu Musa: The Prophet (s) used to invoke Allah with the following invocation:

رَبِّ اغْفِرْ لِي خَطِيئَتِي وَجَهْلِي وَإِسْرَافِي فِي أَمْرِي كُلِّهِ، وَمَا أَنْتَ أَعْلَمُ بِهِ مِنِّي، اللَّهُمَّ اغْفِرْ لِي خَطَايَاىَ وَعَمْدِي وَجَهْلِي وَهَزْلِي، وَكُلُّ ذَلِكَ عِنْدِي، اللَّهُمَّ اغْفِرْ لِي مَا قَدَّمْتُ وَمَا أَخَّرْتُ وَمَا أَسْرَرْتُ وَمَا أَعْلَنْتُ، أَنْتَ الْمُقَدِّمُ، وَأَنْتَ الْمُؤَخِّرُ، وَأَنْتَ عَلَى كُلِّ شَيْءٍ قَدِيرٌ ". وَقَالَ عُبَيْدُ اللهِ بْنُ مُعَاذٍ وَحَدَّثَنَا أَبِي، حَدَّثَنَا شُعْبَةُ، عَنْ أَبِي إِسْحَاقَ، عَنْ أَبِي بُرْدَةَ بْنِ أَبِي مُوسَى، عَنْ أَبِيهِ، عَنِ النَّبِيِّ صلى الله عليه وسلم بِنَحْوِهِ

'Rabbi-ghfir-li Khati 'ati wa jahli wa israfi fi `Amri kullihi, wa ma anta a'lamu bihi minni. Allahumma ighfirli khatayaya wa 'amdi, wa jahli wa jiddi, wa kullu dhalika'indi. Allahumma ighrifli ma qaddamtu wa ma akhartu wa ma asrartu wa ma a'lantu. Anta-l-muqaddimu wa anta-l-mu'akh-khiru, wa anta 'ala kulli shai'in qadir.' "O my Lord! Forgive my sins and my ignorance and my exceeding the limits (boundaries) of righteousness in all my deeds and what you know better than I. O Allah! Forgive my mistakes, those done intentionally or out of my ignorance or (without) or with seriousness, and I confess that all such mistakes are done by me. O Allah! Forgive my sins of the past and of the future which I did openly or secretly. You are the One Who makes things go before, and You are the One Who delays them, and You are the Omnipotent." (6398) □

2050. Narrated Abu Huraira: The Prophet (s) said, "When the Imam says 'Amin', then you should all say 'Amin' (آمين-so be it), for the angels say 'Amin' at that time, and he whose 'Amin' coincides with the 'Amin' of the angels, all his past sins will be forgiven." (6402) □

2051. Narrated Abu Huraira: Allah's Messenger (s) said," Whoever says:

لاَ إِلَهَ إِلاَّ اللَّهُ وَحْدَهُ لاَ شَرِيكَ لَهُ، لَهُ الْمُلْكُ، وَلَهُ الْحَمْدُ، وَهُوَ عَلَى كُلِّ شَىْءٍ قَدِيرٌ

"La ilaha illal-lah wahdahu la sharika lahu, lahu-l-mulk wa lahul- hamd wa huwa 'ala kulli shai'in qadir," (There is no true god except Allah. He is One and He has no partner with Him; His is the sovereignty and His is the praise, and He is powerful over everything). One hundred times (whoever recites) will get the same reward as given for manumitting ten slaves; and one hundred good deeds will be written in his accounts, and one hundred sins will be deducted from his accounts, and it (his saying) will be a shield for him from Satan on that day till night, and nobody will be able to do a better deed except the one who does more than he." (6403) □

2052. Narrated `Amr bin Maimun: Whoever recites,

لاَ إِلَهَ إِلاَّ اللَّهُ وَحْدَهُ لاَ شَرِيكَ لَهُ، لَهُ الْمُلْكُ، وَلَهُ الْحَمْدُ، وَهُوَ عَلَى كُلِّ شَىْءٍ قَدِيرٌ

"La ilaha illal-lah wahdahu la sharika lahu, lahu-l-mulk wa lahul- hamd wa huwa 'ala kulli shai'in qadir," Ten times (whoever recites) will be as if he manumitted one of Ishmael's descendants. Abu Aiyub narrated the same Hadith from the Prophet (s) saying, "(Whoever recites it ten times) will be as if he had manumitted one of Ishmael's descendants." (6404) □

2053. Narrated Abu Huraira: Allah's Messenger (s) said, "Whoever says,

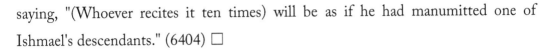

سُبْحَانَ اللَّهِ وَبِحَمْدِهِ

"Subhan Allah wa bihamdihi," (Glory and praise is to Allah). One hundred times a day, will be forgiven all his sins even if they were as much as the foam of the sea. (6405) □

2054. Narrated Abu Musa: The Prophet (ﷺ) said, "The example of the one who celebrates the Praises of his Lord (Allah) in comparison to the one who does not celebrate the Praises of his Lord, is that of a living creature compared to a dead one." (6407) □

2055. Narrated Abu Huraira: Allah 's Apostle said, "Allah has some angels who look for those who celebrate the Praises of Allah on the roads and paths. And when they find some people celebrating the Praises of Allah, they call each other, saying, "Come to the object of your pursuit.'" He added, "Then the angels encircle them with their wings up to the sky of the world." He added. "(after those people celebrated the Praises of Allah, and the angels go back), their Lord, asks them (those angels) ---- though He knows better than them----'What do My slaves say?' The angels reply, 'They say: Subhan Allah, Allahu Akbar, and Alham-du-li l-lah, Allah then says 'Did they see Me?' The angels reply, 'No! By Allah, they didn't see You.' Allah says, How it would have been if they saw Me?' The angels reply, 'If they saw You, they would worship You more devoutly and celebrate Your Glory more deeply, and declare Your freedom from any resemblance to anything more often.' Allah says (to the angels), 'What do they ask Me for?' The angels reply, 'They ask You for Paradise.' Allah says (to the angels), 'Did they see it?' The angels say, 'No! By Allah, O Lord! They did not see it.' Allah says, How it would have been if they saw it?' The angels say, 'If they saw it, they would have greater covetousness for it and would seek It with greater zeal and would have greater desire for it.' Allah says, 'From what do they seek refuge?' The angels reply, 'They seek refuge from the (Hell) Fire.' Allah says, 'Did they see it?' The angels say, 'No By Allah, O Lord! They did not see it.' Allah says, How it would have been if they saw it?' The angels say, 'If they saw it they would flee from it with the extreme fleeing and would have extreme fear from it.' Then Allah says, 'I make you witnesses that I have forgiven them.'" Allah's Messenger (ﷺ) added, "One of the angels would say, 'There was so-and-so amongst them, and he was not one of them, but he had just come for some need.' Allah would say, 'These are those people whose companions will not be reduced to misery.'" (6408) □

2056. Narrated Abu Huraira: Allah's Messenger (s) said,

اللَّهُمَّ ارْزُقْ آلَ مُحَمَّدٍ قُوتًا

"O Allah! Give food to the family of Muhammad." (6460) □

2057. Narrated Ibn `Abbas: The Prophet (ﷺ) used to seek Refuge with Allah for Al-Hasan and Al-Husain and say "Your forefather (i.e. Abraham) used to seek Refuge with Allah for Ishmael and Isaac by reciting the following:

أَعُوذُ بِكَلِمَاتِ اللَّهِ التَّامَّةِ مِنْ كُلِّ شَيْطَانٍ وَهَامَّةٍ، وَمِنْ كُلِّ عَيْنٍ لاَمَّةٍ

"A'uzu bi kalimatillah hit-taammati min kulli shaytaa new-wa hammah, wa min kulli ay nil-lammah"

'O Allah! I seek Refuge with Your Perfect Words from every devil and from poisonous pests and from every evil, harmful, envious eye.'" (3371) □

2058. Narrated Anas: The Prophet (s) used to say,

رَبَّنا ءاتِنا فِى الدُّنيا حَسَنَةً وَفِى الءاخِرَةِ حَسَنَةً وَقِنا عَذابَ النَّارِ

"Rabbanaa 'aatinaa fid-dunyaa hasanatan wa fil-'aakhirati hasanatan wa qinaa 'athaaban-naar." (2:201)

(Our Lord! Give us in this world that which is good and in the Hereafter that which is good, and save us from the torment of the Fire!") (4522) □

2059. Narrated Abu Huraira: Allah has ninety-nine Names, i.e., one hundred minus one, and whoever believes in their meanings and acts accordingly, will enter Paradise; and Allah is witr (one) and loves 'the witr' (i.e., odd numbers). (6410) □

82. HOPE AND DESIRE

2060. NARRATED IBN ʿABBAS: The Prophet (ﷺ) said, "There are two blessings which many people lose: (They are) Health and free time for doing good." (6412)

2061. Narrated Mujahid (ra): ʿAbdullah bin ʿUmar said, "Allah's Messenger (ﷺ) took hold of my shoulder and said, 'Be in this world as if you were a stranger or a traveler." The sub-narrator added: Ibn ʿUmar used to say, "If you survive till the evening, do not expect to be alive in the morning, and if you survive till the morning, do not expect to be alive in the evening, and take from your health for your sickness, and (take) from your life for your death." (6416) □

2062. Narrated ʿAbdullah: The Prophet (ﷺ) drew a square and then drew a line in the middle of it and let it extend outside the square and then drew several small lines attached to that central line, and said, "This is the human being, and this, (the square) in his lease of life, encircles him from all sides (or has encircled him), and this (line), which is outside (the square), is his hope, and these small lines are the calamities and troubles (which may befall him), and if one misses him, an-other will snap (i.e. overtake) him, and if the other misses him, a third will snap (i.e. overtake) him." (6417) □

2063. Narrated Anas bin Malik: The Prophet (ﷺ) drew a few lines and said, "This is (man's) hope, and this is the instant of his death, and while he is in this state (of hope), the nearer line (death) comes to Him." (6418) □

2064. Narrated Abu Huraira: The Prophet (ﷺ) said, "Allah will not accept the excuse of any person whose instant of death is delayed till he is sixty years of age." (6419) □

2065. Narrated Abu Huraira: I heard Allah's Messenger (ﷺ) saying, "The heart of an old man remains young in two respects, i.e., his love for the world (its wealth, amusements and luxuries) and his incessant hope." (6420) □

2066. Narrated Anas bin Malik: Allah's Messenger (ﷺ) said, "The son of Adam (i.e. man) grows old and so also two (desires) grow old with him, i.e., love for wealth and (a wish for) a long life." (6421) □

2067. Narrated `Utban bin Malik Al-Ansari: who was one of the men of the tribe of Bani Salim: Allah's Messenger (ﷺ) came to me and said, "If anybody comes on the Day of Resurrection who has said: La ilaha illal-lah, sincerely, with the intention to win Allah's Pleasure, Allah will make the Hell-Fire forbidden for him." (6423) □

2068. Narrated Abu Huraira: Allah's Messenger (ﷺ) said, "Allah says, 'I have nothing to give but Paradise as a reward to my believer slave, who, if I cause his dear friend (or relative) to die, remains patient (and hopes for Allah's Reward). (6424) □

2069. Narrated `Amr bin `Auf: (An ally of the tribe of Bani 'Amir bin Lu'ai and one of those who had witnessed the battle of Badr with Allah's Messenger (ﷺ)) Allah's Messenger (ﷺ) sent Abu 'Ubaida bin AlJarrah to Bahrain to collect the Jizya tax. Allah's Messenger (ﷺ) had concluded a peace treaty with the people of Bahrain and appointed Al 'Ala bin Al-Hadrami as their chief; Abu Ubaida arrived from Bahrain with the money. The Ansar heard of Abu 'Ubaida's arrival which coincided with the Fajr (morning) prayer led by Allah's Messenger (ﷺ). When the Prophet (ﷺ) finished the prayer, they came to him. Allah's Messenger (ﷺ) smiled when he saw them and said, "I think you have heard of the arrival of Abu 'Ubaida and that he has brought something." They replied, "Yes, O Allah's Messenger (ﷺ)!" He said, "Have the good news, and hope for what will please you. By Allah, I am not afraid that you will become poor, but I am afraid that worldly wealth will be given to you in abundance as it was given to those (nations) before you, and you will start competing each other for it as the previous nations competed for it, and then it will divert you (from good) as it diverted them."' (6425) □

2070. Narrated Abu Sa`id Al-Khudri: Allah's Messenger (ﷺ) said, "The thing I am afraid of most for your sake, is the worldly blessings which Allah will bring forth to you." It was said, "What are the blessings of this world?" The Prophet (ﷺ) said, "The pleasures of the world." A man said, "Can the good bring forth evil?" The Prophet (ﷺ) kept quiet for a while till we thought that he was being inspired divinely. Then he started removing the sweat from his forehead and said," Where is the questioner?" That man said, "I (am present)." Abu Sa`id added: We thanked the man when the result (of his question) was such. The Prophet (ﷺ) said, "Good never brings forth but good. This wealth (of the world) is (like) green and sweet (fruit), and all the vegetation which grows on the bank of a stream either kills or nearly kills the animal that eats too much of it, except the animal that eats the Khadira (a kind of vegetation). Such an animal eats till its stomach is full and then it faces the sun and starts ruminating and then it passes out dung and urine and goes to eat again. This worldly wealth is (like) sweet (fruit), and if a person earns it (the wealth) in a legal way and spends it properly, then it is an excellent helper, and whoever earns it in an illegal way, he will be like the one who eats but is never satisfied." (6427) □

2071. Narrated Mirdas Al-Aslami: The Prophet (ﷺ) said, "The righteous (pious people will depart (die) in succession one after the other, and there will remain (on the earth) useless people like the useless husk of barley seeds or bad dates. (6434)

2072. Narrated Ibn `Abbas: I heard the Prophet (ﷺ) saying, "If the son of Adam (the human being) had two valleys of money, he would wish for a third, for nothing can fill the belly of Adam's son except dust, and Allah forgives him who repents to Him." (6436) □

2073. Narrated `Abdullah: The Prophet (ﷺ) said, "Who among you considers the wealth of his heirs dearer to him than his own wealth?" They replied, "O Allah's Messenger (ﷺ)! There is none among us but loves his own wealth more." The Prophet (ﷺ) said, "So his wealth is whatever he spends (in Allah's Cause) during his life (on good deeds) while the wealth of his heirs is whatever he leaves after his death." (6442) □

2074. Narrated Abu Dhar: Once I went out at night and found Allah's Messenger (ﷺ) walking all alone accompanied by nobody, and I thought that perhaps he disliked that someone should accompany him. So I walked in the shade, away from the moonlight, but the Prophet (ﷺ) looked behind and saw me and said, "Who is that?" I replied, "Abu Dhar, let Allah get me sacrificed for you!" He said, "O Abu Dhar, come here!" So I accompanied him for a while and then he said, "The rich are in fact the poor (little rewarded) on the Day of Resurrection except him whom Allah gives wealth which he gives (in charity) to his right, left, front and back, and does good deeds with it. I walked with him a little longer. Then he said to me, "Sit down here." So he made me sit in an open space surrounded by rocks, and said to me, "Sit here till I come back to you." He went towards Al-Harra till I could not see him, and he stayed away for a long period, and then I heard him saying, while he was coming, "Even if he had committed theft, and even if he had committed illegal sexual intercourse?" When he came, I could not remain patient and asked him, "O Allah's Prophet! Let Allah get me sacrificed for you! Whom were you speaking to by the side of Al-Harra? I did not hear anybody responding to your talk." He said, "It was Gabriel who appeared to me beside Al-Harra and said, 'Give the good news to your followers that whoever dies without having worshipped anything besides Allah, will enter Paradise.' I said, 'O Gabriel! Even if he had committed theft or committed illegal sexual intercourse?' He said, 'Yes.' I said, 'Even if he has committed theft or committed illegal sexual intercourse?' He said, 'Yes.' I said, 'Even if he has committed theft or committed illegal sexual intercourse?' He said, 'Yes.'" (6443) □

2075. Narrated Abu Huraira: The Prophet (ﷺ) said, "Riches does not mean, having a great amount of property, but riches is selfcontentment." (6446) □

2076. Narrated Sahl bin Sa`d As-Sa`id: A man passed by Allah's Messenger (ﷺ) and the Prophet (ﷺ) asked a man sitting beside him, "What is your opinion about this (passer-by)?" He replied, "This (passer-by) is from the noble class of people. By Allah, if he should ask for a lady's hand in marriage, he ought to be given her in marriage, and if he intercedes for somebody, his intercession will be accepted. Allah's Messenger

(☪) kept quiet, and then another man passed by and Allah's Messenger (☪) asked the same man (his companion) again, "What is your opinion about this (second) one?" He said, "O Allah's Messenger (☪)! This person is one of the poor Muslims. If he should ask a lady's hand in marriage, no-one will accept him, and if he intercedes for somebody, no one will accept his intercession, and if he talks, no-one will listen to his talk." Then Allah's Messenger (☪) said, "This (poor man) is better than such a large number of the first type (i.e. rich men) as to fill the earth." (6447) □

2077. Narrated `Aisha: The Prophet (☪) was asked, "What deeds are loved most by Allah?" He said, "The most regular constant deeds even though they may be few." He added, 'Don't take upon yourselves, except the deeds which are within your ability." (6465) □

2078. Narrated Warrad: (the clerk of Al-Mughira bin Shu`ba) Muawiya wrote to Al-Mughira: "Write to me a narration you have heard from Allah's Messenger (☪)." So Al-Mughira wrote to him, "I heard him saying the following after each prayer: 'La ilaha illal-lahu wahdahu la sharika lahu, lahu-l-mulk wa lahuI-hamd, wa huwa 'ala kulli Shai-in qadir.' He also used to forbid idle (foolish and irrelevant) talk, asking too many questions (in religion), wasting money, preventing what should be given, and asking others for something (except in great need), being undutiful to mothers, and burying one's little daughters (alive) (6473) □

2079. Narrated Abu Huraira: That he heard Allah's Messenger (☪) saying, "A slave of Allah may utter a word without thinking whether it is right or wrong, he may slip down in the Fire as far away a distance equal to that between the east." (6477) □

2080. Narrated Abu Huraira: The Prophet; said, "A slave (of Allah) may utter a word which pleases Allah without giving it much importance, and because of that Allah will raise him to degrees (of reward): a slave (of Allah) may utter a word (carelessly) which displeases Allah without thinking of its gravity and because of that he will be thrown into the Hell-Fire." (6478) □

2081. Narrated Abu Huraira: I heard Allah's Messenger (☪) saying, "My example and the example of the people is that of a man who made a fire, and when it lighted what was around it, Moths and other insects started falling into the fire. The man tried (his best) to prevent them, (from falling in the fire) but they overpowered him and rushed into the fire. The Prophet (ﷺ) added: Now, similarly, I take hold of the knots at your waist (belts) to prevent you from falling into the Fire, but you insist on falling into it." (6483) □

2082. Narrated Abu Huraira: Allah's Messenger (ﷺ) said, "If anyone of you looked at a person who was made superior to him in property and (in good) appearance, then he should also look at the one who is inferior to him. (6490) □

2083. Narrated Ibn `Abbas: The Prophet (ﷺ) narrating about his Lord and said, "Allah ordered (the appointed angels over you) that the good and the bad deeds be written, and He then showed (the way) how (to write). If somebody intends to do a good deed and he does not do it, then Allah will write for him a full good deed (in his account with Him); and if he intends to do a good deed and actually did it, then Allah will write for him (in his account) with Him (its reward equal) from ten to seven hundred times to many more times: and if somebody intended to do a bad deed and he does not do it, then Allah will write a full good deed (in his account) with Him, and if he intended to do it (a bad deed) and actually did it, then Allah will write one bad deed (in his account) ." (6491) □

2084. Narrated Jundub: The Prophet (ﷺ) said, "He who lets the people hear of his good deeds intentionally, to win their praise, Allah will let the people know his real intention (on the Day of Resurrection), and he who does good things in public to show off and win the praise of the people, Allah will disclose his real intention (and humiliate him). (6499) □

2085. Narrated Abu Huraira: Allah's Messenger (ﷺ) said, "Allah said, 'I will declare war against him who shows hostility to a pious worshipper of Mine. And the most beloved things with which My slave comes nearer to Me, is what I have enjoined upon him; and My slave keeps on coming closer to Me through performing Nawafil (praying or doing extra deeds besides what is obligatory) till I love him, so I become his sense of hearing with which he hears, and his sense of sight with which he sees, and his hand with which he grips, and his leg with which he walks; and if he asks Me, I will give him, and if he asks My protection (Refuge), I will protect him; (i.e. give him My Refuge) and I do not hesitate to do anything as I hesitate to take the soul of the believer, for he hates death, and I hate to disappoint him." (6502) ☐

2086. Narrated 'Ubada bin As-Samit: The Prophet (ﷺ) said, "Who-ever loves to meet Allah, Allah (too) loves to meet him and who-ever hates to meet Allah, Allah (too) hates to meet him". `Aisha, or some of the wives of the Prophet (ﷺ) said, "But we dislike death." He said: It is not like this, but it is meant that when the time of the death of a believer approaches, he receives the good news of Allah's pleasure with him and His blessings upon him, and so at that time nothing is dearer to him than what is in front of him. He therefore loves the meeting with Allah, and Allah (too) loves the meeting with him. But when the time of the death of a disbeliever approaches, he receives the evil news of Allah's torment and His Requital (retaliation), whereupon nothing is more hateful to him than what is before him. Therefore, he hates the meeting with Allah, and Allah too, hates the meeting with him." (6507) ☐

2087. Narrated Abu Qatada bin Rib'i Al-Ansari: A funeral procession passed by Allah's Messenger (ﷺ) who said, "Relieved or relieving?" The people asked, "O Allah's Messenger (ﷺ)! What is relieved and relieving?" He said, "A believer is relieved (by death) from the troubles and hardships of the world and leaves for the Mercy of Allah, while (the death of) a wicked person relieves the people, the land, the trees, (and) the animals from him." (6512) ☐

2088. Narrated Anas bin Malik: Allah's Messenger (ﷺ) said, "When carried to his grave, a dead person is followed by three, two of which return (after his burial) and one remains with him: his relative, his property, and his deeds follow him; relatives and his property go back while his deeds remain with him." (6514) ☐

2089. Allah's Messenger (ﷺ) said: A time will come when any of you will love to see me rather than to have his family and property doubled." (3589) □

83. Qiyamah (Judgement Day)

2090. Narrated `Abdullah (ra): Allah's Messenger (ﷺ) said, "The key of the Unseen are five: Verily with Allah (Alone) is the knowledge of the Hour He sends down the rain and knows what is in the wombs. No soul knows what it will earn tomorrow, and no soul knows in what land it will die. Verily, Allah is All-Knower, All-Aware." (31.34) (4627) □

2091. Narrated Anas bin Malik: While the Prophet (ﷺ) and I were coming out of the mosque, a man met us outside the gate. The man said, "O Allah's Messenger (ﷺ)! When will be the Hour?" The Prophet (ﷺ) asked him, "What have you prepared for it?" The man became afraid and ashamed and then said, "O Allah's Messenger (ﷺ)! I haven't prepared for it much of fasts, prayers or charitable gifts but I love Allah and His Apostle." The Prophet (ﷺ) said, "You will be with the one whom you love." (7153). □

2092. Narrated Anas: I will narrate to you a Hadith and none other than I will tell you about after it. I heard Allah's Messenger (ﷺ) saying: From among the portents of the Hour are (the following): -1. Religious knowledge will decrease (by the death of religious learned men). -2. Religious ignorance will prevail. -3. There will be prevalence of open illegal sexual intercourse. -4. Women will increase in number and men will decrease in number so much so that fifty women will be looked after by one man. (81) □

2093. Narrated Abu Huraira: The Prophet (ﷺ) said, "The Hour (Last Day) will not be established until (religious) knowledge will be taken away (by the death of religious learned men), earthquakes will be very frequent, time will pass quickly, afflictions will appear, murders will increase and money will overflow amongst you. (1036) □

2094. Narrated `Aisha: Allah's Messenger (ﷺ) said, "An army will invade the Ka`ba and when the invaders reach Al-Baida', all the ground will sink and swallow the whole army." I said, "O Allah's Messenger (ﷺ)! How will they sink into the ground while amongst them will be their markets (the people who worked in business and not invaders) and the people not belonging to them?" The Prophet (ﷺ) replied, "all of those people will sink but they will be resurrected and judged according to their intentions." (2118) ☐

2095. Narrated Abu Huraira: The Prophet (ﷺ) said, "Dhus-Suwaiqa-tain (literally: One with two lean legs) from Ethiopia will demolish the Ka`ba." (1591) ☐

2096. Narrated Abu Sa`id Al-Khudri: The Prophet (ﷺ) said "The people will continue performing the Hajj and `Umra to the Ka`ba even after the appearance of Gog and Magog." Narrated Shu`ba extra: The Hour (Day of Judgment) will not be established till the Hajj (to the Ka`ba) is abandoned. (1593) ☐

2097. Narrated Ibn `Abbas: The Prophet (ﷺ) said, "As if I were looking at him, a black person with thin legs plucking the stones of the Ka`ba one after another." (1595) ☐

2098. Narrated Abu Huraira: Allah's Messenger (ﷺ) said, "The Hour will not be established until the son of Mary (i.e. Jesus) descends amongst you as a just ruler, he will break the cross, kill the pigs, and abolish the Jizya tax. Money will be in abundance so that nobody will accept it (as charitable gifts). (2476) ☐

2099. Narrated Abu Huraira: Allah's Messenger (ﷺ) said, "The Hour will not be established until you fight with the Turks; people with small eyes, red faces, and flat noses. Their faces will look like shields coated with leather. The Hour will not be established till you fight with people whose shoes are made of hair." (2928) ☐

2100. Narrated `Auf bin Mali: I went to the Prophet (ﷺ) during the Ghazwa of Tabuk while he was sitting in a leather tent. He said, "Count six signs that indicate the approach of the Hour: my death, the conquest of Jerusalem, a plague that will afflict you (and kill you in great numbers) as the plague that afflicts sheep, the increase of wealth to such an extent that even if one is given one hundred Dinars, he will not be satisfied; then an affliction which no Arab house will escape, and then a truce between you and Bani Al-Asfar (i.e. the Byzantines) who will betray you and attack you under eighty flags. Under each flag will be twelve thousand soldiers. (3176) ☐

2101. Narrated Abu Hurairah (ra): The Prophet (ﷺ) said, "The hour will not be established unless a man from the tribe of Qahtan appears, driving the people with his stick (ruling them with violence and oppression)." (3517) ☐

2102. Narrated Sahl bin Sa`d: I saw Allah's Messenger (ﷺ) pointing with his index and middle fingers, saying. "The time of my Advent and the Hour are like these two fingers." The Great Catastrophe will overwhelm everything. (4936) ☐

2103. Narrated Abu Huraira: Allah's Messenger (ﷺ) said, "The Day of (Judgment) will not be established till there is a war between two groups whose claims (or religion) will be the same. (Battle of Siffin)" (3608) ☐

2104. Ibn Mas`ud added: I heard Allah's Messenger (ﷺ) saying; (It will be) from among the most wicked people who will be living at the time when the Hour will be established." (7067) ☐

2105. Narrated Abu Huraira: Allah's Messenger (ﷺ) said, "The Hour will not be established till the buttocks of the women of the tribe of Daus move while going round Dhi-al-Khalasa." Dhi-al-Khalasa was the idol of the Daus tribe which they used to worship in the Pre-Islamic Period of ignorance. (7116) ☐

2106. Narrated Abu Huraira: Allah's Messenger (ﷺ) said, "The Hour will not be established till a fire will come out of the land of Hijaz, and it will throw light on the necks of the camels at Busra." (7118) ☐

2107. Narrated Abu Huraira: Allah's Messenger (ﷺ) said, "Soon the river "Euphrates" (Originating in the Turkey and travel southeast through northern Syria and Iraq to the head of the Persian Gulf) will disclose the treasure (the mountain) of gold, so whoever will be present at that time should not take anything of it." Al-A'raj narrated from Abii Huraira that the Prophet (ﷺ) said the same but he said, "It (Euphrates) will uncover a mountain of gold (under it). (7119) ☐

2108. Narrated Abu Huraira: Allah's Messenger (ﷺ) said, "The Hour will not be established (1) till two big groups fight each other whereupon there will be a great number of casualties on both sides and they will be following one and the same religious doctrine, (2) till about thirty Dajjals (liars) appear, and each one of them will claim that he is Allah's Messenger (ﷺ), (3) till the religious knowledge is taken away (by the death of Religious scholars) (4) earthquakes will increase in number (5) time will pass quickly, (6) afflictions will appear, (7) Al-Harj, (i.e., killing) will increase, (8) till wealth will be in abundance ---- so abundant that a wealthy person will worry lest nobody should accept his Zakat, and whenever he will present it to someone, that person (to whom it will be offered) will say, 'I am not in need of it, (9) till the people compete with one another in constructing high buildings, (10) till a man when passing by a grave of someone will say, 'Would that I were in his place (11) and till the sun rises from the West. So when the sun will rise and the people will see it (rising from the West) they will all believe (embrace Islam) but that will be the time when: (As Allah said,) 'No good will it do to a soul to believe then, if it believed not before, nor earned good (by deeds of righteousness) through its Faith.' (6.158) And the Hour will be established while two men spreading a garment in front of them but they will not be able to sell it, nor fold it up; and the Hour will be established when a man has milked his she-camel and has taken away the milk but he will not be able to drink it; and the Hour will be established before a man repairing a tank (for his livestock) is able to water (his animals) in it; and the Hour will be established when a person has raised a morsel (of food) to his mouth but will not be able to eat it." (7121) ☐

2109. Narrated Al--A`mash: Abu Huraira said, "Allah's Messenger (ﷺ) said, 'Between the two sounds of the trumpet, there will be forty." Somebody asked Abu Huraira, "Forty days?" But he refused to reply. Then he asked, "Forty months?" He refused to reply. Then he asked, "Forty years?" Again, he refused to reply. Abu

Huraira added. "Then (after this period) Allah will send water from the sky and then the dead bodies will grow like vegetation grows, There is nothing of the human body that does not decay except one bone; that is the little bone at the end of the coccyx of which the human body will be recreated on the Day of Resurrection." (4935) □

2110. Narrated Abu Huraira: The Prophet (ﷺ) said, "The sun and the moon will be folded up (deprived of their light) on the Day of Resurrection." (3200) □

2111. Narrated Sahl bin Sa`d: I heard the Prophet (ﷺ) saying, "The people will be gathered on the Day of Resurrection on reddish white land like a pure loaf of bread (made of pure fine flour)." Sahl added: That land will have no landmarks for anybody (to make use of). (6521) □

2112. Narrated Ibn `Abbas: Allah's Messenger (ﷺ) delivered a sermon and said, "O people! You will be gathered before Allah barefooted, naked and not circumcised." Then (quoting Qur'an) he said: -- "As We began the first creation, We shall repeat it. A promise We have undertaken: Truly we shall do it..." (21.104) The Prophet (ﷺ) then said, "The first of the human beings to be dressed on the Day of Resurrection, will be Abraham. Lo! Some men from my followers will be brought and then (the angels) will drive them to the left side (Hell-Fire). I will say. 'O my Lord! (They are) my companions!' Then a reply will come (from Almighty), 'You do not know what they did after you.' I will say as the pious slave (the Prophet (ﷺ) Jesus) said: And I was a witness over them while I dwelt amongst them. When You took me up. You were the Watcher over them and You are a Witness to all things.' (5.117) Then it will be said, "These people have continued to be apostates since you left them." (4625) □

2113. Narrated `Aisha: Allah's Messenger (ﷺ) said, "The people will be gathered barefooted, naked, and uncircumcised." I said, "O Allah's Messenger (ﷺ)! Will the men and the women look at each other?" He said, "The situation will be too hard for them to pay attention to that." (6527) □

2114. Narrated Abu Sa`id Al-Khudri: While Allah's Messenger (ﷺ) was sitting, a Jew came and said, "O Abul Qasim! One of your companions has slapped me on my face."

The Prophet (ﷺ) asked who that was. He replied that he was one of the Ansar. The Prophet (ﷺ) sent for him, and on his arrival, he asked him whether he had beaten the Jew. He (replied in the affirmative and) said, "I heard him taking an oath in the market saying, 'By Him Who gave Moses superiority over all the human beings.' I said, 'O wicked man! (Has Allah given Moses superiority) even over Muhammad I became furious and slapped him over his face." The Prophet (ﷺ) said, "Do not give a prophet superiority over another, for on the Day of Resurrection all the people will fall unconscious and I will be the first to emerge from the earth, and will see Moses standing and holding one of the legs of the Throne. I will not know whether Moses has fallen unconscious or the first unconsciousness was sufficient for him." (2412) □

2115. Narrated `Abdullah bin `Umar: The Prophet (ﷺ) said, "On the Day when all mankind will stand before the Lord of the Worlds, some of them will be enveloped in their sweat up to the middle of their ears." (4938) □

2116. Narrated Abu Huraira: Allah's Messenger (ﷺ) said, "The people will sweat so profusely on the Day of Resurrection that their sweat will sink seventy cubits deep into the earth, and it will rise up till it reaches the people's mouths and ears." (6532) □

2117. Narrated Abu Sa`id: Allah's Messenger (ﷺ) said, "Noah and his nation will come (on the Day of Resurrection and Allah will ask (Noah), "Did you convey (the Message)?' He will reply, 'Yes, O my Lord!' Then Allah will ask Noah's nation, 'Did Noah convey My Message to you?' They will reply, 'No, no prophet came to us.' Then Allah will ask Noah, 'Who will stand a witness for you?' He will reply, 'Muhammad and his followers (will stand witness for me).' So, I and my followers will stand as witnesses for him (that he conveyed Allah's Message)." That is, (the interpretation) of the Statement of Allah: "Thus we have made you a just and the best nation that you might be witnesses Over mankind..." (2.143) (3339) □

2118. Narrated Abu Huraira: Some (cooked) meat was brought to Allah Apostle and the meat of a forearm was presented to him as he used to like it. He ate a morsel of it and said, "I will be the chief of all the people on the Day of Resurrection. Do you know the reason for it? Allah will gather all the human being of early generations as well as late generation on one plain so that the announcer will be able to make them all-hear his voice and the watcher will be able to see all of them. The sun will come so close to the people that they will suffer such distress and trouble as they will not be able to bear or stand. Then the people will say, 'Don't you see to what state you have reached? Won't you look for someone who can intercede for you with your Lord' Some people will say to some others, 'Go to Adam.' So they will go to Adam and say to him. 'You are the father of mankind; Allah created you with His Own Hand, and breathed into you of His Spirit (meaning the spirit which he created for you); and ordered the angels to prostrate before you; so (please) intercede for us with your Lord. Don't you see in what state we are? Don't you see what condition we have reached?' Adam will say, 'Today my Lord has become angry as He has never become before, nor will ever become thereafter. He forbade me (to eat of the fruit of) the tree, but I disobeyed Him. Myself! Myself! Myself! (I am preoccuied with my own problems). Go to someone else; go to Noah.' So they will go to Noah and say (to him), 'O Noah! You are the first (of Allah's Messengers) to the people of the earth, and Allah has named you a thankful slave; please intercede for us with your Lord. Don't you see in what state we are?' He will say.' Today my Lord has become angry as He has never become nor will ever become thereafter. I had (in the world) the right to make one definitely accepted invocation, and I made it against my nation. Myself! Myself! Myself! Go to someone else; go to Abraham.' They will go to Abraham and say, 'O Abraham! You are Allah's Messenger (ﷺ) and His Khalil from among the people of the earth; so please intercede for us with your Lord. Don't you see in what state we are?' He will say to them, 'My Lord has today become angry as He has never become before, nor will ever become thereafter. I had told three lies (Abu Haiyan (the sub-narrator) mentioned them in the Hadith) Myself! Myself! Myself! Go to someone else; go to Moses.' The people will then go to Moses and say, 'O Moses! You art Allah's Messenger (ﷺ) and Allah gave you superiority above the others with this message and with His direct Talk to you; (please) intercede for us with your Lord

Don't you see in what state we are?' Moses will say, 'My Lord has today become angry as He has never become before, nor will become thereafter, I killed a person whom I had not been ordered to kill. Myself! Myself! Myself! Go to someone else; go to Jesus.' So they will go to Jesus and say, 'O Jesus! You are Allah's Messenger (﷽) and His Word which He sent to Mary, and a superior soul created by Him, and you talked to the people while still young in the cradle. Please intercede for us with your Lord. Don't you see in what state we are?' Jesus will say. 'My Lord has today become angry as He has never become before nor will ever become thereafter. Jesus will not mention any sin, but will say, 'Myself! Myself! Myself! Go to someone else; go to Muhammad.' So they will come to me and say, 'O Muhammad! You are Allah's Messenger (﷽) and the last of the prophets, and Allah forgave your early and late sins. (Please) intercede for us with your Lord. Don't you see in what state we are?" The Prophet (﷽) added, "Then I will go beneath Allah's Throne and fall in prostration before my Lord. And then Allah will guide me to such praises and glorification to Him as He has never guided anybody else before me. Then it will be said, 'O Muhammad Raise your head. Ask, and it will be granted. Intercede and It (your intercession) will be accepted.' So I will raise my head and Say, 'My followers, O my Lord! My followers, O my Lord'. It will be said, 'O Muhammad! Let those of your followers who have no accounts, enter through such a gate of the gates of Paradise as lies on the right; and they will share the other gates with the people." The Prophet (﷽) further said, "By Him in Whose Hand my soul is, the distance between every two gate-posts of Paradise is like the distance between Mecca and Busra (in Sham). (4712) □

2119. Narrated Abu Sa`id Al-Khudri: The Prophet (﷽) said, "Allah will say (on the Day of Resurrection), 'O Adam.' Adam will reply, 'Labbaik wa Sa`daik', and all the good is in Your Hand.' Allah will say: 'Bring out the people of the fire.' Adam will say: 'O Allah! How many are the people of the Fire?' Allah will reply: 'From every one thousand, take out nine-hundred-and ninety-nine.' At that time children will become hoary headed, every pregnant female will have a miscarriage, and one will see mankind as drunken, yet they will not be drunken, but dreadful will be the Wrath of Allah." The companions of the Prophet (﷽) asked, "O Allah's Apostle! Who is that (excepted) one?" He said, "Rejoice with glad tidings; one person will be from you and one-thousand will be from Gog and Magog." The Prophet (ﷺ) further said, "By Him in Whose Hands my life is, hope that you will be one-fourth of the people of Paradise." We shouted, "Allahu Akbar!" He added, "I hope that you will be one-third of the people of Paradise." We shouted, "Allahu Akbar!" He said, "I hope that you will be half of the people of Paradise." We shouted, "Allahu Akbar!" He further said, "You (Muslims) (compared with non Muslims) are like a black hair in the skin of a white ox or like a white hair in the skin of a black ox (your number is very small as compared with theirs). (3348) □

2120. Narrated Aisha: Allah's Messenger (ﷺ) said," (On the Day of Resurrection) any one whose account will be taken will be ruined (i.e. go to Hell)." I said, "O Allah's Messenger (ﷺ)! May Allah make me be sacrificed for you. Doesn't Allah say: "Then as for him who will be given his record in his right hand, he surely will receive an easy reckoning?" (84.7-8) He replied, "That is only the presentation of the accounts; but he whose record is questioned, will be ruined." (4939) □

2121. Narrated Abu Huraira: The Prophet (ﷺ) said, "The people will be gathered in three ways: (The first way will be of) those who will wish or have a hope (for Paradise) and will have a fear (of punishment), (The second batch will be those who will gather) riding two on a camel or three on a camel or ten on a camel. The rest of the people will be urged to gather by the Fire which will accompany them at the time of their afternoon nap and stay with them where they will spend the night, and will be with them in the morning wherever they may be then, and will be with them in the afternoon wherever they may be then." (6522) □

2122. Narrated `Abdullah: The Prophet (ﷺ) said, "The cases which will be decided first (on the Day of Resurrection) will be the cases of blood-shedding." (6533) □

2123. Narrated Ibn `Abbas: The Prophet (ﷺ) said, "The people were displayed in front of me and I saw one prophet passing by with a large group of his followers, and another prophet passing by with only a small group of people, and another prophet passing by with only ten (persons), and another prophet passing by with only five (persons), and another prophet passed by alone. And then I looked and saw a large multitude of people, so I asked Gabriel, "Are these people my followers?' He said, 'No, but look towards the horizon.' I looked and saw a very large multitude of people. Gabriel said. 'Those are your followers, and those are seventy thousand (persons) in front of them who will neither have any reckoning of their accounts nor will receive any punishment.' I asked, 'Why?' He said, 'For they used not to treat themselves with branding (cauterization) nor with Ruqya (get oneself treated by the recitation of some Verses of the Qur'an) and not to see evil omen in things, and they used to put their trust (only) in their Lord." On hearing that, 'Ukasha bin Mihsan got up and said (to the Prophet), "Invoke Allah to make me one of them." The Prophet (ﷺ) said, "O Allah, make him one of them." Then another man got up and said (to the Prophet), "Invoke Allah to make me one of them." The Prophet (ﷺ) said, 'Ukasha has preceded you." (6541) ☐

2124. Narrated Anas bin Malik: The Prophet (ﷺ) said, "Allah will say to the person who will have the minimum punishment in the Fire on the Day of Resurrection, 'If you had things equal to whatever is on the earth, would you ransom yourself (from the punishment) with it?' He will reply, Yes. Allah will say, 'I asked you a much easier thing than this while you were in the backbone of Adam, that is, not to worship others besides Me, but you refused and insisted to worship others besides Me.'" (6557) ☐

2125. Narrated Abu Sa`id Al-Khudri: During the lifetime of the Prophet (ﷺ) some people said: O Allah's Messenger (ﷺ)! Shall we see our Lord on the Day of Resurrection?" The Prophet (ﷺ) said, "Yes; do you have any difficulty in seeing the sun at midday when it is bright and there is no cloud in the sky?" They replied, "No." He said, "Do you have any difficulty in seeing the moon on a full moon night when it is bright and there is no cloud in the sky?" They replied, "No." The Prophet (ﷺ) said, "(Similarly) you will have no difficulty in seeing Allah on the Day of Resurrection as you have no difficulty in seeing either of them. On the Day of Resurrection, a call-maker will announce, "Let every nation follow that which they used to worship." Then none of those who used to worship anything other than Allah like idols and other deities but will fall in Hell (Fire), till there will remain none but those who used to worship Allah, both those who were obedient (i.e. good) and those who were disobedient (i.e. bad) and the remaining party of the people of the Scripture. Then the Jews will be called upon and it will be said to them, 'Who do you use to worship?' They will say, 'We used to worship Ezra, the son of Allah.' It will be said to them, 'You are liars, for Allah has never taken anyone as a wife or a son. What do you want now?' They will say, 'O our Lord! We are thirsty, so give us something to drink.' They will be directed and addressed thus, 'Will you drink,' whereupon they will be gathered unto Hell (Fire) which will look like a mirage whose different sides will be destroying each other. Then they will fall into the Fire. Afterwards the Christians will be called upon and it will be said to them, 'Who do you use to worship?' They will say, 'We used to worship Jesus, the son of Allah.' It will be said to them, 'You are liars, for Allah has never taken anyone as a wife or a son,' Then it will be said to them, 'What do you want?' They will say what the former people have said. Then, when there remain (in the gathering) none but those who used to worship Allah (Alone, the real Lord of the Worlds) whether they were obedient or disobedient. Then (Allah) the Lord of the worlds will come to them in a shape nearest to the picture they had in their minds about Him. It will be said, 'What are you waiting for?' Every nation have followed what they used to worship.' They will reply, 'We left the people in the world when we were in great need of them and we did not take them as friends. Now we are waiting for our Lord Whom we used to worship.' Allah will say, 'I am your Lord.' They will say twice or thrice, 'We do not worship any besides Allah.'" (4581) □

2126. Narrated `Abdullah bin `Amr: The Prophet (ﷺ) said, "My Lake-Fount is (so large that it takes) a month's journey to cross it. Its water is whiter than milk, and its smell is nicer than musk (a kind of Perfume), and its drinking cups are (as numerous) as the (number of) stars of the sky; and whoever drinks from it, will never be thirsty." (6579) □

2127. Narrated Anas bin Malik: The Prophet (ﷺ) said: "While I was walking in

Paradise (on the night of Mi'raj), I saw a river, on the two banks of which there were tents made of hollow pearls. I asked, "What is this, O Gabriel?' He said, 'That is the Kauthar which Your Lord has given to you.' Behold! Its scent or its mud was sharp smelling musk!" (The sub-narrator, Hudba is in doubt as to the correct expression.) (6581) ☐

2128. Narrated Abu Hazim from Sahl bin Sa`d: The Prophet (ﷺ) said, "I am your predecessor (forerunner) at the Lake-Fount, and whoever will pass by there, he will drink from it and whoever will drink from it, he will never be thirsty. There will come to me some people whom I will recognize, and they will recognize me, but a barrier will be placed between me and them." (6583) ☐

2129. Narrated Abu Huraira: The Prophet (ﷺ) said, "While I was sleeping, a group (of my followers were brought close to me), and when I recognized them, a man (an angel) came out from amongst (us) me and them, he said (to them), 'Come along.' I asked, 'Where?' He said, 'To the (Hell) Fire, by Allah' I asked, 'what is wrong with them' He said, 'They turned apostate as renegades after you left.' Then behold! (Another) group (of my followers) were brought close to me, and when I recognized them, a man (an angel) came out from (me and them) he said (to them); Come along.' I asked, "Where?' He said, 'To the (Hell) Fire, by Allah.' I asked, What is wrong with them?' He said, 'They turned apostate as renegades after you left. So I did not see anyone of them escaping except a few who were like camels without a shepherd." (6587) ☐

2130. Narrated Abu Huraira: I said, "O Allah's Messenger (ﷺ)! Who will be the luckiest person who will gain your intercession on the Day of Resurrection?" The Prophet (ﷺ) said, "O Abu Huraira! I have thought that none will ask me about this Hadith before you, as I know your longing for the (learning of) Hadiths. The luckiest person who will have my intercession on the Day of Resurrection will be the one who said, 'None has the right to be worshipped but Allah,' sincerely from the bottom of his heart." (6570) ☐

84. JANNAH AND JAHANNAM

2131. NARRATED SAHL BIN SA`D (RA): The Prophet (ﷺ) said, "Verily! 70,000 or 700,000 of my followers will enter Paradise altogether; so that the first and the last amongst them will enter at the same time, and their faces will be glittering like the bright full moon."(3247) □

2132. Narrated Anas bin Malik: A silken cloak was presented to the Prophet (ﷺ) and he used to forbid the usage of silk (by men). When the people were fascinated by the cloak. He said, "By Allah in Whose Hands the life of Muhammad is, the handkerchiefs of Sa`d bin Mu`adh in Paradise are better than this." (3248) □

2134. Narrated Abu Huraira: The Prophet (ﷺ) said "There is a tree in Paradise (which is so big and huge that) a rider could travel in its shade for a hundred years. And if you wish, you can recite: 'In shade long extended' (56. 30) (3252) □

2135. And a place in Paradise equal to an arrow bow of one of you, is better than (the whole earth) on which the sun rises and sets." (3253) □

2136. Narrated Abu Sa`id Al-Khudri: The Prophet (ﷺ) said, "The people of Paradise will look at the dwellers of the lofty mansions (i.e. a superior place in Paradise) in the same way as one looks at a brilliant star far away in the East or in the West on the horizon; all that is because of their superiority over one another (in rewards)." On that the people said, "O Allah's Messenger (ﷺ)! Are these lofty mansions for the prophets which nobody else can reach? The Prophet (ﷺ) replied," No! "By Allah in whose Hands my life is, these are for the men who believed in Allah and also believed in the Apostles." (3256) □

2137. Narrated Abu Huraira: Allah's Messenger (ﷺ) said, "Allah said, "I have prepared for My Pious slaves things which have never been seen by an eye, or heard by an ear, or imagined by a human being." If you wish, you can recite this Verse from the Holy Qur'an:--"No soul knows what is kept hidden for them, of joy as a reward for what they used to do." (32.17) (3244) □

2138. Narrated `Abdullah bin Qais Al-Ash`ari: The Prophet (ﷺ) said, "A tent (in Paradise) is like a hollow pearl which is thirty miles in height and on every corner of the tent the believer will have a family that cannot be seen by the others." (Narrated Abu `Imran in another narration, "The tent is sixty miles in height.") (3243) □

2139. Narrated Abu Huraira: Allah's Messenger (ﷺ) said, "The first batch (of people) who will enter Paradise will be (glittering) like a full moon; and those who will enter next will be (glittering) like the brightest star. Their hearts will be as if the heart of a single man, for they will have no enmity amongst themselves, and every one of them shall have two wives, each of whom will be so beautiful, pure and transparent that the marrow of the bones of their legs will be seen through the flesh. They will be glorifying Allah in the morning and evening, and will never fall ill, and they will neither blow their noses, nor spit. Their utensils will be of gold and silver, and their combs will be of gold, and the fuel used in their centers will be the aloeswood, and their sweat will smell like musk." (3246) □

2140. Narrated Abu Wail: Somebody said to Usama, "Will you go to so-and-so (i.e. `Uthman) and talk to him (i.e. advise him regarding ruling the country)?" He said, "You see that I don't talk to him. Really I talk to (advise) him secretly without opening a gate (of affliction), for neither do I want to be the first to open it (i.e. rebellion), nor will I say to a man who is my ruler that he is the best of all the people after I have heard something from Allah s Apostle ." They said, What have you heard him saying? He said, "I have heard him saying, "A man will be brought on the Day of Resurrection and thrown in the (Hell) Fire, so that his intestines will come out, and he will go around like a donkey goes around a millstone. The people of (Hell) Fire will gather around him and say: O so-and-so! What is wrong with you? Didn't you use to order us to do good deeds and forbid us to do bad deeds? He will reply: Yes, I used to order you to do good deeds, but I did not do them myself, and I used to forbid you to do bad deeds, yet I used to do them myself." (3267) □

2141. Narrated Abu Jamra Ad-Dabi: I used to sit with Ibn `Abbas in Mecca. Once I had a fever and he said (to me), "Cool your fever with Zamzam water, for Allah's Messenger (ﷺ) said: 'It, (the Fever) is from the heat of the (Hell) Fire; so, cool it with water (or Zamzam water). (3261) □

2142. Narrated Abu Huraira: Allah's Messenger (ﷺ) said, "Your (ordinary) fire is one of 70 parts of the (Hell) Fire." Someone asked, "O Allah's Messenger (ﷺ) This (ordinary) fire would have been sufficient (to torture the unbelievers)," Allah's Apostle said, "The (Hell) Fire has 69 parts more than the ordinary (worldly) fire, each part is as hot as this (worldly) fire." (3265) □

2143. Narrated Abu Huraira: The Prophet (ﷺ) said, "Paradise and the Fire (Hell) argued, and the Fire (Hell) said, "I have been given the privilege of receiving the arrogant and the tyrants.' Paradise said, 'What is the matter with me? Why do only the weak and the humble among the people enter me?' On that, Allah said to Paradise. 'You are My Mercy which I bestow on whoever I wish of my servants.' Then Allah said to the (Hell) Fire, 'You are my (means of) punishment by which I punish whoever I wish of my slaves. And each of you will have its fill.' As for the Fire (Hell), it will not be filled till Allah puts His Foot over it whereupon it will say, 'Qati! Qati!' At that time it will be filled, and its different parts will come closer to each other; and Allah will not wrong any of His created beings. As regards Paradise, Allah will create a new creation to fill it with." (4850) □

2144. Narrated `Abdullah bin Qais: Allah's Messenger (ﷺ) said, "Two gardens, the utensils and the contents of which are of silver, and two other gardens, the utensils and contents of which are of gold. And nothing will prevent the people who will be in the Garden of Eden from seeing their Lord except the curtain of Majesty over His Face." (4878) □

2145. Narrated `Abdullah bin Qais: Allah's Messenger (ﷺ) said, "In Paradise there is a pavilion made of a single hollow pearl sixty miles wide, in each corner of which there are wives who will not see those in the other corners; and the believers will visit and

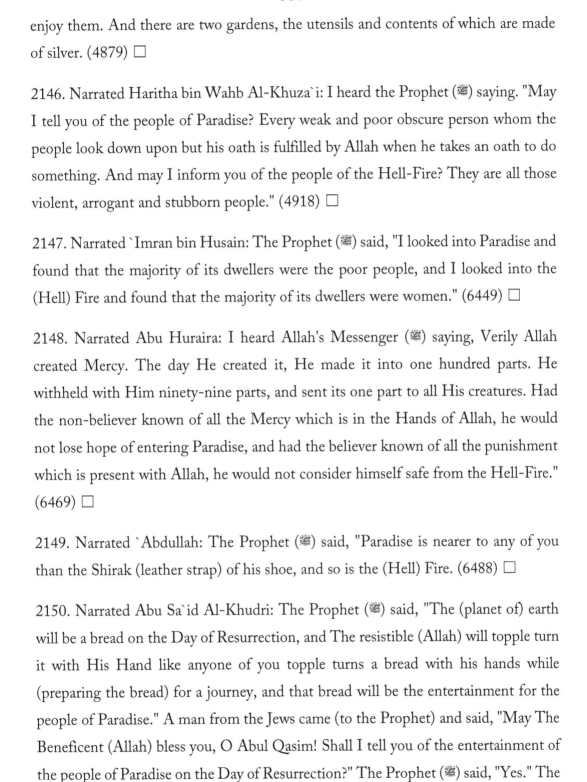

enjoy them. And there are two gardens, the utensils and contents of which are made of silver. (4879) ☐

2146. Narrated Haritha bin Wahb Al-Khuza`i: I heard the Prophet (ﷺ) saying. "May I tell you of the people of Paradise? Every weak and poor obscure person whom the people look down upon but his oath is fulfilled by Allah when he takes an oath to do something. And may I inform you of the people of the Hell-Fire? They are all those violent, arrogant and stubborn people." (4918) ☐

2147. Narrated `Imran bin Husain: The Prophet (ﷺ) said, "I looked into Paradise and found that the majority of its dwellers were the poor people, and I looked into the (Hell) Fire and found that the majority of its dwellers were women." (6449) ☐

2148. Narrated Abu Huraira: I heard Allah's Messenger (ﷺ) saying, Verily Allah created Mercy. The day He created it, He made it into one hundred parts. He withheld with Him ninety-nine parts, and sent its one part to all His creatures. Had the non-believer known of all the Mercy which is in the Hands of Allah, he would not lose hope of entering Paradise, and had the believer known of all the punishment which is present with Allah, he would not consider himself safe from the Hell-Fire." (6469) ☐

2149. Narrated `Abdullah: The Prophet (ﷺ) said, "Paradise is nearer to any of you than the Shirak (leather strap) of his shoe, and so is the (Hell) Fire. (6488) ☐

2150. Narrated Abu Sa`id Al-Khudri: The Prophet (ﷺ) said, "The (planet of) earth will be a bread on the Day of Resurrection, and The resistible (Allah) will topple turn it with His Hand like anyone of you topple turns a bread with his hands while (preparing the bread) for a journey, and that bread will be the entertainment for the people of Paradise." A man from the Jews came (to the Prophet) and said, "May The Beneficent (Allah) bless you, O Abul Qasim! Shall I tell you of the entertainment of the people of Paradise on the Day of Resurrection?" The Prophet (ﷺ) said, "Yes." The Jew said, "The earth will be a bread," as the Prophet (ﷺ) had said. Thereupon the Prophet (ﷺ) looked at us and smiled till his premolar tooth became visible. Then the

Jew further said, "Shall I tell you of the udm (additional food taken with bread) they will have with the bread?" He added, "That will be Balam and Nun." The people asked, "What is that?" He said, "It is an ox and a fish, and seventy thousand people will eat of the caudate lobe (i.e. extra lobe) of their livers." (6520) □

2151. Narrated Ibn `Umar: Allah's Messenger (ﷺ) said, "When the people of Paradise have entered Paradise and the people of the Fire have entered the Fire, death will be brought and will be placed between the Fire and Paradise, and then it will be slaughtered, and a call will be made (that), 'O people of Paradise, no more death ! O people of the Fire, no more death!' So the people of Paradise will have happiness added to their previous happiness, and the people of the Fire will have sorrow added to their previous sorrow." (6548) □

2152. Narrated Abu Sa`id Al-Khudri: Allah's Messenger (ﷺ) said, "Allah will say to the people of Paradise, 'O the people of Paradise!' They will say, 'Labbaik, O our Lord, and Sa`daik!' Allah will say, 'Are you pleased?" They will say, 'Why should we not be pleased since You have given us what You have not given to anyone of Your creation?' Allah will say, 'I will give you something better than that.' They will reply, 'O our Lord! And what is better than that?' Allah will say, 'I will bestow My pleasure and contentment upon you so that I will never be angry with you after for-ever.'" (6549) □

2153. Narrated Abu Sa'id: The Prophet (ﷺ) said: There is a tree in Paradise (so huge) that a fast (or a trained) rider may travel: for one hundred years without being able to cross it. (6553) □

2154. Narrated Sahl: The Prophet (ﷺ) said, "The people of Paradise will see the Ghuraf (special abodes) in Paradise as you see a star in the sky." (6555) □

2155. Narrated Hammad from `Amr from Jabir: The Prophet (ﷺ) said, "Some people will come out of the Fire through intercession looking like The Thaarir." I asked `Amr, "What is the Thaarir?" He said, Ad Dagh`Abis, and at that time he was toothless. Hammad added: I said to `Amr bin Dinar, "O Abu Muhammad! Did you hear Jabir bin `Abdullah saying, 'I heard the Prophet (ﷺ) saying: 'Some people will come out of the Fire through intercession?" He said, "Yes." (6558) ☐

2156. Narrated `Abdullah: The Prophet (ﷺ) said, "I know the person who will be the last to come out of the (Hell) Fire, and the last to enter Paradise. He will be a man who will come out of the (Hell) Fire crawling, and Allah will say to him, 'Go and enter Paradise.' He will go to it, but he will imagine that it had been filled, and then he will return and say, 'O Lord, I have found it full.' Allah will say, 'Go and enter Paradise, and you will have what equals the world and ten times as much (or, you will have as much as ten times the like of the world).' On that, the man will say, 'Do you mock at me (or laugh at me) though You are the King?" I saw Allah's Messenger (ﷺ) (while saying that) smiling that his premolar teeth became visible. It is said that will be the lowest in degree amongst the people of Paradise. (6571) ☐

2157. Narrated Anas bin Malik: The Prophet (ﷺ) said, "Some people will come out of the Fire after they have received a touch of the Fire, changing their color, and they will enter Paradise, and the people of Paradise will name them 'Al- Jahannamiyin' the (Hell) Fire people." (6559) ☐

2158. Narrated An-Nu`man: I heard the Prophet (ﷺ) saying, "The person who will have the least punishment from amongst the Hell Fire people on the Day of Resurrection, will be a man under whose arch of the feet a smoldering ember will be placed so that his brain will boil because of it." (6561) ☐

2159. Narrated `Adi bin Hatim: The Prophet (ﷺ) mentioned the Fire and turned his face aside and asked for Allah's protection from it, and then again he mentioned the Fire and turned his face aside and asked for Allah's protection from it and said, "Protect yourselves from the Hell-Fire, even if with one half of a date, and he who cannot afford that, then (let him do so) by (saying) a good, pleasant word." (6563) ☐

2160. Narrated Anas: Um (the mother of) Haritha came to Allah's Messenger (ﷺ) after Haritha had been martyred on the Day (of the battle) of Badr by an arrow thrown by an unknown person. She said, "O Allah's Messenger (ﷺ)! You know the position of Haritha in my heart (i.e. how dear to me he was), so if he is in Paradise, I will not weep for him, or otherwise, you will see what I will do." The Prophet (ﷺ) said, "Are you mad? Is there only one Paradise? There are many Paradises, and he is in the highest Paradise of Firdaus." The Prophet added, "A forenoon journey or an after noon journey in Allah's Cause is better than the whole world and whatever is in it; and a place equal to an arrow bow of anyone of you, or a place equal to a foot in Paradise is better than the whole world and whatever is in it; and if one of the women of Paradise looked at the earth, she would fill the whole space between them (the earth and the heaven) with light, and would fill whatever is in between them, with perfume, and the veil of her face is better than the whole world and whatever is in it." (6568) □

2161. Narrated Abu Huraira: The Prophet (ﷺ) said, "None will enter Paradise but will be shown the place he would have occupied in the (Hell) Fire if he had rejected faith, so that he may be more thankful; and none will enter the (Hell) Fire but will be shown the place he would have occupied in Paradise if he had faith, so that may be a cause of sorrow for him." (6569) □

2162. The Hell-fire of Hell complained to its Lord saying: O Lord! My parts are eating (destroying) one another. So Allah allowed it to take two breaths, one in the winter and the other in the summer. The breath in the summer is at the time when you feel the severest heat and the breath in the winter is at the time when you feel the severest cold." (537) □

2163. Narrated Anas: The Prophet (ﷺ) said, "A single endeavor (of fighting) in Allah's Cause in the afternoon or in the forenoon is better than all the world and whatever is in it. A place in Paradise as small as the bow or lash of one of you is better than all the world and whatever is in it. And if a houri from Paradise appeared to the people of the earth, she would fill the space between Heaven and the Earth with light and pleasant scent and her head cover is better than the world and whatever is in it." (2796) □

2164. Narrated `Abdullah bin `Umar: Allah's Messenger (ﷺ) said, "A lady was punished because of a cat which she had imprisoned till it died. She entered the (Hell) Fire because of it, for she neither gave it food nor water as she had imprisoned it, nor set it free to eat from the vermin of the earth." (3482) ☐

85. DIVINE WILL (DESTINY)

2165. NARRATED `ABDULLAH (RA): Allah's Messenger (ﷺ), the truthful and truly-inspired, said, "Each one of you collected in the womb of his mother for forty days, and then turns into a clot for an equal period (of forty days) and turns into a piece of flesh for a similar period (of forty days) and then Allah sends an angel and orders him to write four things, i.e., his provision, his age, and whether he will be of the wretched or the blessed (in the Hereafter). Then the soul is breathed into him. And by Allah, a person among you (or a man) may do deeds of the people of the Fire till there is only a cubit or an arm-breadth distance between him and the Fire, but then that writing (which Allah has ordered the angel to write) precedes, and he does the deeds of the people of Paradise and enters it; and a man may do the deeds of the people of Paradise till there is only a cubit or two between him and Paradise, and then that writing precedes and he does the deeds of the people of the Fire and enters it." (6594) ☐

2166. Narrated Anas bin Malik: The Prophet (ﷺ) said, "Allah puts an angel in charge of the uterus and the angel says, 'O Lord, (it is) semen! O Lord, (it is now) a clot! O Lord, (it is now) a piece of flesh.' And then, if Allah wishes to complete its creation, the angel asks, 'O Lord, (will it be) a male or a female? A wretched (an evil doer) or a blessed (doer of good)? How much will his provisions be? What will his age be?' So all that is written while the creature is still in the mother's womb." (6595) ☐

2167. Narrated `Imran bin Husain: A man said, "O Allah's Messenger (ﷺ)! Can the people of Paradise be known (differentiated) from the people of the Fire; The Prophet (ﷺ) replied, "Yes." The man said, "Why do people (try to) do (good) deeds?" The

Prophet said, "Everyone will do the deeds for which he has been created to do or he will do those deeds which will be made easy for him to do." (i.e. everybody will find easy to do such deeds as will lead him to his destined place for which he has been created). (6596) ☐

2168. Narrated Abu Huraira: Allah's Messenger (☺) said, "No child is born but has the Islamic Faith, but its parents turn it into a Jew or a Christian. It is as you help the animals give birth. Do you find among their offspring a mutilated one before you mutilate them yourself?" The people said, "O Allah's Messenger (☺)! What do you think about those (of them) who die young?" The Prophet (☺) said, "Allah knows what they would have done (were they to live)." (6599) ☐

2169. Narrated Abu Huraira: Allah's Messenger (☺) said, "No woman should ask for the divorce of her sister (Muslim) so as to take her place, but she should marry the man (without compelling him to divorce his other wife), for she will have nothing but what Allah has written for her." (6601) ☐

2170. Narrated Abu Sa`id Al-Khudri: That while he was sitting with the Prophet (☺) a man from the Ansar came and said, "O Allah's Messenger (☺)! We get slave girls from the war captives and we love property; what do you think about coitus interruptus?" Allah's Messenger (☺) said, "Do you do that? It is better for you not to do it, for there is no soul which Allah has ordained to come into existence but will be created." (6603) ☐

2171. Narrated `Ali: While we were sitting with the Prophet (☺) who had a stick with which he was scraping the earth, he lowered his head and said, "There is none of you but has his place assigned either in the Fire or in Paradise." Thereupon a man from the people said, "Shall we not depend upon this, O Allah's Apostle?" The Prophet (☺) said, "No, but carry on and do your deeds, for everybody finds it easy to do such deeds (as will lead him to his place)." The Prophet (☺) then recited the Verse: 'As for him who gives (in charity) and keeps his duty to Allah...' (92.5) (6605) ☐

2172. Narrated Aishah (ra): I heard the Prophet (☺), "Souls are like recruited troops:

Those who are like qualities are inclined to each other, but those who have dissimilar qualities, differ." (3336) □

86. OATHS AND VOWS

"Allah will not impose blame upon you for what is meaningless in your oaths, but He will impose blame upon you for [breaking] what you intended of oaths. So its expiation is the feeding of ten needy people from the average of that which you feed your [own] families or clothing them or the freeing of a slave. But whoever cannot find [or afford it] - then a fast of three days [is required]. That is the expiation for oaths when you have sworn. But guard your oaths. Thus does Allah make clear to you His verses that you may be grateful." (5:89) □

2173. NARRATED AISHA (RA): Once Allah's Messenger (ﷺ) heard the loud voices of some opponents quarreling at the door. One of them was appealing to the other to deduct his debt and asking him to be lenient but the other was saying, "By Allah I will not do so." Allah's Messenger (ﷺ) went out to them and said, "Who is the one who was swearing by Allah that he would not do a favor?" That man said, "I am that person, O Allah's Messenger (ﷺ)! I will give my opponent whatever he wishes." (2705) □

2174. Narrated `Abdur-Rahman bin Samura: The Prophet (ﷺ) said, "O `Abdur-Rahman bin Samura! Do not seek to be a ruler, because if you are given authority for it, then you will be held responsible for it, but if you are given it without asking for it, then you will be helped in it (by Allah): and whenever you take an oath to do something and later you find that something else is better than the first, then do the better one and make expiation for your oath." (6622) □

2175. Narrated Abu Musa: I went to the Prophet (ﷺ) along with a group of Al-Ash`ariyin in order to request him to provide us with mounts. He said, "By Allah, I will not provide you with mounts and I haven't got anything to mount you on." Then we stayed there as long as Allah wished us to stay, and then three very nice looking she-camels were brought to him and he made us ride them. When we left, we, or some of us, said, "By Allah, we will not be blessed, as we came to the Prophet (ﷺ) asking him for mounts, and he swore that he would not give us any mounts but then he did give us. So let us go back to the Prophet (ﷺ) and remind him (of his oath)." When we returned to him (and reminded him of the fact), he said, "I did not give you mounts, but it is Allah Who gave you. By Allah, Allah willing, if I ever take an oath to do something and then I find something else than the first, I will make expiation for my oath and do the thing which is better (or do something which is better and give the expiation for my oath). (6623) □

2176. Allah's Messenger (ﷺ) also said:"By Allah, if anyone of you insists on ful-filling an oath by which he may harm his family, he commits a greater sin in Allah's sight than that of dissolving his oath and making expiation for it." (6625) □

2177. Narrated Abu Huraira: Allah's Messenger (ﷺ) said, "Anyone who takes an oath through which his family may be harmed, and insists on keeping it, he surely commits a sin greater (than that of dissolving his oath). He should rather compensate for that oath by making expiation." (6626) □

2178. Narrated Ibn `Umar: The oath of the Prophet (ﷺ) used to be: "No, by Him who turns the hearts." (6628) □

2179. Narrated `Abdullah bin Hisham: We were with the Prophet (ﷺ) and he was holding the hand of `Umar bin Al-Khattab. `Umar said to Him, "O Allah's Messenger (ﷺ)! You are dearer to me than everything except my own self." The Prophet (ﷺ) said, "No, by Him in Whose Hand my soul is, (you will not have complete faith) till I am dearer to you than your own self." Then `Umar said to him, "However, now, by Allah, you are dearer to me than my own self." The Prophet (ﷺ) said, "Now, O `Umar, (now you are a believer). (6632) □

2180. Narrated Ibn Umar: Allah's Messenger (ﷺ) met Umar bin Al-Khattab while the latter was going with a group of camel-riders, and he was swearing by his father.

The Prophet (ﷺ) said, "Lo! Allah forbids you to swear by your fathers, so whoever has to take an oath, he should swear by Allah or keep quiet." (6646) □

2181. Narrated Abu Huraira: The Prophet (ﷺ) said, "Whoever swears saying in his oath, 'By Al-Lat and Al-`Uzza,' should say, 'None has the right to be worshipped but Allah; and whoever says to his friend, 'Come, let me gamble with you,' should give something in charity." (6650) □

2182. Narrated Thabit bin Ad-Dahhak: The Prophet (ﷺ) said, "Whoever swears by a religion other than Islam, is, as he says; and whoever commits suicide with something, will be punished with the same thing in the (Hell) Fire; and cursing a believer is like murdering him; and whoever accuses a believer of disbelief, then it is as if he had killed him." (6652) □

2183. Narrated Al-Bara: The Prophet (ﷺ) ordered us to help others to fulfill the oaths. (6654) □

2184. Narrated Abu Huraira: Allah's Messenger (ﷺ) said, "Any Muslim who has lost three of his children will not be touched by the Fire except that which will render Allah's oath fulfilled." (6656) □

2185. Narrated Haritha bin Wahb: I heard the Prophet (ﷺ) saying, "Shall I tell you of the people of Paradise? They comprise every poor humble person, and if he swears by Allah to do something, Allah will fulfill it; while the people of the fire comprise every violent, cruel arrogant person." (6657) □

2186. Narrated `Abdullah: The Prophet (ﷺ) said, "Whoever swears falsely in order to grab the property of a Muslim (or of his brother), Allah will be angry with him when he meets Him." Allah then revealed in confirmation of the above statement:-'Verily those who purchase a small gain at the cost of Allah's Covenant and their own oaths.' (3.77) Al-Ash'ath said, "This Verse was revealed regarding me and a companion of mine when we had a dispute about a well." (6659) □

2187. Narrated `Abdullah bin `Amr: The Prophet (ﷺ) said, "The biggest sins are: To join others in worship with Allah; to be undutiful to one's parents; to kill somebody unlawfully; and to take an oath Al-Ghamus. (6675) □

2188. Narrated `Abdullah: Allah's Messenger (ﷺ) said, "If somebody is ordered (by the ruler or the judge) to take an oath, and he takes a false oath in order to grab the property of a Muslim, then he will incur Allah's Wrath when he will meet Him." And Allah revealed in its confirmation: 'Verily! Those who purchase a small gain at the cost of Allah's covenants and their own oaths.' (3.77) (The sub-narrator added :) Al-Ash'ath bin Qais entered, saying, "What did Abu `Abdur-Rahman narrate to you?" They said, "So-and-so," Al-Ash'ath said, "This verse was revealed in my connection. I had a well on the land of my cousin (and we had a dispute about it). I reported him to Allah's Apostle who said (to me). "You should give evidence (i.e. witness) otherwise the oath of your opponent will render your claim invalid." I said, "Then he (my opponent) will take the oath, O Allah's Messenger (ﷺ)." Allah's Messenger (ﷺ) said, "Whoever is ordered (by the ruler or the judge) to give an oath, and he takes a false oath in order to grab the property of a Muslim, then he will incur Allah's Wrath when he meets Him on the Day of Resurrection." (6676) □

2189. Narrated Az-Zuhri: I heard `Urwa bin Az-Zubair, Sa`id bin Al-Musaiyab, 'Alqama bin Waqqas and 'Ubaidullah bin `Abdullah bin `Uqba relating from `Aisha, the wife of the Prophet (ﷺ) the narration of the people (i.e. the liars) who spread the slander against her and they said what they said, and how Allah revealed her innocence. Each of them related to me a portion of that narration. (They said that `Aisha said), "Then Allah revealed the ten Verses starting with: 'Verily! Those who spread the slander...' (24.11-21) All these verses were in proof of my innocence. Abu Bakr As-Siddiq who used to provide for Mistah some financial aid because of his relation to him, said, "By Allah, I will never give anything (in charity) to Mistah, after what he has said about `Aisha" Then Allah revealed: 'And let not those among you who are good and are wealthy swear not to give (any sort of help) to their kins men....' (24.22) On that, Abu Bakr said, "Yes, by Allah, I like that Allah should forgive me." and then resumed giving Mistah the aid he used to give him and said, "By Allah! I will never withhold it from him." (6679) ☐

2190. Narrated `Abdullah bin `Umar: The Prophet (ﷺ) forbade the making of vows and said, "It (a vow) does not prevent anything (that has to take place), but the property of a miser is spent (taken out) with it." (6693) ☐

2191. Narrated Zahdam bin Mudarrab: `Imran bin Hussain said, "The Prophet (ﷺ) said, 'The best of you (people) are my generation, and the second best will be those who will follow them, and then those who will follow the second generation." `Imran added, "I do not remember whether he mentioned two or three (generations) after his generation. He added, 'Then will come some people who will make vows but will not fulfill them; and they will be dishonest and will not be trustworthy, and they will give their witness without being asked to give their witness, and fatness will appear among them.'" (6695) ☐

2192. Narrated Ibn `Umar: `Umar said "O Allah's Messenger (ﷺ)! I vowed to perform I`tikaf for one night in Al-Masjid-al-Haram, during the Pre-Islamic Period of ignorance (before embracing Islam). "The Prophet (ﷺ) said, "Fulfill your vow." Ibn `Umar said to the lady, "Pray on her behalf." Ibn `Abbas said the same. (6697) ☐

2193. Narrated Sa`id bin 'Ubada Al-Ansari: that he consulted the Prophet (ﷺ) about a vow that had been made by his mother who died without fulfilling it. The Prophet (ﷺ) gave his verdict that he should fulfill it on her behalf. The verdict became Sunnah (i.e. the Prophet's tradition). (6698) ☐

2194. Narrated Ibn `Abbas: A man came to the Prophet (ﷺ) and said to him, "My sister vowed to perform the Hajj, but she died (before fulfilling it)." The Prophet (ﷺ) said, "Would you not have paid her debts if she had any?" The man said, "Yes." The Prophet (ﷺ) said, "So pay Allah's Rights, as He is more entitled to receive His rights." (6699) ☐

2195. Narrated `Aisha: The Prophet (ﷺ) said, "Whoever vowed to be obedient to Allah, must be obedient to Him; and whoever vowed to be disobedient to Allah, should not be disobedient to Him." (6700) ☐

2196. Narrated Ibn `Abbas: While the Prophet (ﷺ) was delivering a sermon, he saw a man standing, so he asked about that man. They (the people) said, "It is Abu Israil who has vowed that he will stand and never sit down, and he will never come in the shade, nor speak to anybody, and will fast." The Prophet (ﷺ) said, "Order him to speak and let him come in the shade, and make him sit down, but let him complete his fast." (6704) ☐

2319. Narrated Ibn Abu Mulaika: Two women were stitching shoes in a house or a room. Then one of them came out with an awl driven into her hand, and she sued the other for it. The case was brought before Ibn `Abbas, Ibn `Abbas said, "Allah's Messenger (ﷺ) said, 'If people were to be given what they claim (without proving their claim) the life and property of the nation would be lost.' Will you remind her of Allah and recite before her:--"Verily! Those who purchase a small gain at the cost of Allah's Covenant and their oaths..."(3.77) So they reminded her and she confessed. Ibn `Abbas then said, "The Prophet (ﷺ) said, 'The oath is to be taken by the defendant (in the absence of any proof against him). (4552) ☐

87. PUNISHMENTS

2197. NARRATED ABU SALAMA (RA): Abu Huraira said, "A man who drank wine was brought to the Prophet. The Prophet (ﷺ) said, 'Beat him!' Abu Huraira added, "So some of us beat him with our hands, and some with their shoes, and some with their garments (by twisting it) like a lash, and then when we finished, someone said to him, 'May Allah disgrace you!' On that the Prophet (ﷺ) said, 'Do not say so, for you are helping Satan to overpower him.'" (6777) ☐

2198. Narrated `Ali bin Abi Talib: I would not feel sorry for one who dies because of receiving a legal punishment, except the drunk, for if he should die (when being punished), I would give blood money to his family because no fixed punishment has been ordered by Allah's Messenger (ﷺ) for the drunk. (6778) ☐

2199. Narrated As-Sa'ib bin Yazid: We used to strike the drunks with our hands, shoes, clothes (by twisting it into the shape of lashes) during the lifetime of the Prophet, Abu Bakr and the early part of `Umar's caliphate. But during the last period of `Umar's caliphate, he used to give the drunk forty lashes; and when drunks became mischievous and disobedient, he used to scourge them eighty lashes. (6779) ☐

2200. Narrated Abu Huraira: The Prophet (ﷺ) said, "Allah curses a man who steals an egg and gets his hand cut off, or steals a rope and gets his hands cut off." Al-A`mash said, "People used to interpret the Baida as an iron helmet, and they used to think that the rope may cost a few dirhams." (6783) ☐

2201. Narrated `Aisha: The Quraish people became very worried about the Makhzumiya lady who had committed theft. They said, "Nobody can speak (in favor of the lady) to Allah's Messenger (ﷺ) and nobody dares do that except Usama who is the favorite of Allah's Messenger (ﷺ)." When Usama spoke to Allah's Messenger (ﷺ) about that matter, Allah's Messenger (ﷺ) said, "Do you intercede (with me) to violate one of the legal punishment of Allah?" Then he got up and addressed the people, saying, "O people! The nations before you went astray because if a noble person committed theft, they used to leave him, but if a weak person among them committed theft, they used to inflict the legal punishment on him. By Allah, if Fatima, the daughter of Muhammad committed theft, Muhammad will cut off her hand..!" (6788) ☐

2202. Narrated `Aisha: The Prophet (ﷺ) said, "The hand should be cut off for stealing something that is worth a quarter of a Dinar or more." (6789) ☐

2203. Narrated `Aisha: A thief's hand was not cut off for stealing something cheaper than a Hajafa or a Turs (two kinds of shields), each of which was worth a (respectable) price. (6793) ☐

2204. Narrated Ibn `Umar: Allah's Messenger (ﷺ) cut off the hand of a thief for stealing a shield that was worth three Dirhams. (6795) □

2205. Narrated `Aisha: The Prophet (ﷺ) cut off the hand of a lady, and that lady used to come to me, and I used to convey her message to the Prophet (ﷺ) and she repented, and her repentance was sincere. (6800) □

2206. Narrated 'Ikrima from Ibn 'Abbas: Allah's Messenger (ﷺ)s said, "When a slave (of Allah) commits illegal sexual intercourse, he is not a believer at the time of committing it; and if he steals, he is not a believer at the time of stealing; and if he drinks an alcoholic drink, when he is not a believer at the time of drinking it; and he is not a believer when he commits a murder," 'Ikrima said: I asked Ibn Abbas, "How is faith taken away from him?" He said, Like this," by clasping his hands and then separating them, and added, "But if he repents, faith returns to him like this, by clasping his hands again. (6809) □

2207. Narrated Ibn `Umar: A Jew and a Jewess were brought to Allah's Messenger (ﷺ) on a charge of committing an illegal sexual intercourse. The Prophet (ﷺ) asked them. "What is the legal punishment (for this sin) in your Book (Torah)?" They replied, "Our priests have innovated the punishment of blackening the faces with charcoal and Tajbiya." `Abdullah bin Salam said, "O Allah's Messenger (ﷺ), tell them to bring the Torah." The Torah was brought, and then one of the Jews put his hand over the Divine Verse of the Rajam (stoning to death) and started reading what preceded and what followed it. On that, Ibn Salam said to the Jew, "Lift up your hand." Behold! The Divine Verse of the Rajam was under his hand. So Allah's Apostle ordered that the two (sinners) be stoned to death, and so they were stoned. Ibn `Umar added: So both of them were stoned at the Balat and I saw the Jew sheltering the Jewess. (6819) □

2208. Narrated Anas bin Malik: While I was with the Prophet (ﷺ) a man came and said, "O Allah's Messenger (ﷺ)! I have committed a legally punishable sin; please inflict the legal punishment on me'.' The Prophet (ﷺ) did not ask him what he had done. Then the time for the prayer became due and the man offered prayer along with the Prophet (ﷺ), and when the Prophet (ﷺ) had finished his prayer, the man again got up and said, "O Allah's Messenger (ﷺ)! I have committed a legally punishable sin; please inflict the punishment on me according to Allah's Laws." The Prophet (ﷺ) said, "Haven't you prayed with us?' He said, "Yes." The Prophet (ﷺ) said, "Allah has forgiven your sin." or said, "your legally punishable sin." (6823) ☐

2209. Narrated Ibn `Abbas: When Ma'iz bin Malik came to the Prophet (in order to confess), the Prophet (ﷺ) said to him, "Probably you have only kissed (the lady), or winked, or looked at her?" He said, "No, O Allah's Messenger (ﷺ)!" The Prophet said, using no euphemism, "Did you have sexual intercourse with her?" The narrator added: At that, (i.e. after his confession) the Prophet (ﷺ) ordered that he be stoned (to death). (6824) ☐

2210. Narrated Abu Huraira: A man from among the people, came to Allah's Messenger (ﷺ) while Allah's Messenger (ﷺ) was sitting in the mosque, and addressed him, saying, "O Allah's Messenger (ﷺ)! I have committed an illegal sexual intercourse." The Prophet (ﷺ) turned his face away from him. The man came to that side to which the Prophet had turned his face, and said, "O Allah's Messenger (ﷺ)! I have committed an illegal intercourse." The Prophet (ﷺ) turned his face to the other side, and the man came to that side, and when he confessed four times, the Prophet (ﷺ) called him and said, "Are you mad?" He said, "No, O Allah's Messenger (ﷺ)!" The Prophet said, "Are you married?" He said, "Yes, O Allah's Messenger (ﷺ)." The Prophet (ﷺ) said, "Take him away and stone him to death." Ibn Shihab added, "I was told by one who heard Jabir, that Jabir said, 'I was among those who stoned the man, and we stoned him at the Musalla (Eid praying Place), and when the stones troubled him, he jumped quickly and ran away, but we overtook him at Al-Harra and stoned him to death (there).'" (6825) ☐

2211. Narrated Abu Huraira and Zaid bin Khalid: While we were with the Prophet (ﷺ), a man stood up and said (to the Prophet (ﷺ)), "I beseech you by Allah, that you should judge us according to Allah's Laws." Then the man's opponent who was wiser than him, got up saying (to Allah's Messenger (ﷺ)) "Judge us according to Allah's

Law and kindly allow me (to speak)." The Prophet (ﷺ) said, "'Speak." He said, "My son was a laborer working for this man and he committed an illegal sexual intercourse with his wife, and I gave one-hundred sheep and a slave as a ransom for my son's sin. Then I asked a learned man about this case and he informed me that my son should receive one hundred lashes and be exiled for one year, and the man's wife should be stoned to death." The Prophet (ﷺ) said, "By Him in Whose Hand my soul is, I will judge you according to the Laws of Allah. Your one-hundred sheep and the slave are to be returned to you, and your son has to receive one-hundred lashes and be exiled for one year. O Unais! Go to the wife of this man, and if she confesses, then stone her to death." Unais went to her and she confessed. He then stoned her to death. (6827) ☐

2212. Narrated Al-Mughira: Sa`d bin Ubada said, "If I found a man with my wife, I would kill him with the sharp side of my sword." When the Prophet (ﷺ) heard that he said, "Do you wonder at Sa`d's sense of ghira (self-respect)? Verily, I have more sense of ghira than Sa`d, and Allah has more sense of ghira than I." (6846) ☐

2213. Abu Huraira 'narrated from the Prophet who said Allah has written for Adam's son his share of adultery which he commits inevitably. The adultery of the eyes is the sight, the adultery of the tongue is the talk, and the inner self wishes and desires and the private parts testify all this or deny it. (6243) ☐

2214. Narrated Abu Burda: The Prophet (ﷺ) used to say, "Nobody should be flogged more than ten stripes except if he is guilty of a crime, the legal punishment of which is assigned by Allah." (6848) ☐

2215. Narrated `Abdullah bin `Umar: One of the evil deeds with bad consequence from which there is no escape for the one who is involved in it is to kill someone unlawfully. (6863) ☐

2216. Narrated `Abdullah: The Prophet (ﷺ) said, "The first cases to be decided among the people (on the Day of Resurrection) will be those of blood-shed." (6864) ☐

2217. Narrated Anas bin Malik: The Prophet (ﷺ) said, "The biggest of Al-Ka`ba'ir (the great sins) are (1) to join others as partners in worship with Allah, (2) to murder a human being, (3) to be undutiful to one's parents (4) and to make a false statement," or said, "to give a false witness." (6871) □

2218. Narrated Anas bin Malik: A girl wearing ornaments, went out at Medina. Somebody struck her with a stone. She was brought to the Prophet (ﷺ) while she was still alive. Allah's Messenger (ﷺ) asked her, "Did such-and-such a person strike you?" She raised her head, denying that. He asked her a second time, saying, "Did so-and-so strike you?" She raised her head, denying that. He said for the third time, "Did so-and-so strike you?" She lowered her head, agreeing. Allah's Messenger (ﷺ) then sent for the killer and killed him between two stones. (6877) □

2219. Narrated Anas: A Jew crushed the head of a girl between two stones. The girl was asked who had crushed her head, and some names were mentioned before her, and when the name of the Jew was mentioned, she nodded agreeing. The Jew was captured and when he confessed, the Prophet (ﷺ) ordered that his head be crushed between two stones. (2413) □

2220. Narrated `Abdullah: Allah's Messenger (ﷺ) said, "The blood of a Muslim who confesses that none has the right to be worshipped but Allah and that I am His Apostle, cannot be shed except in three cases: In Qisas for murder, a married person who commits illegal sexual intercourse and the one who reverts from Islam (apostate) and leaves the Muslims." (6878) □

2221. Narrated Abu Huraira: Allah's Messenger (ﷺ) said, if somebody is killed, his closest relative has the right to choose one of two things, i.e., either the Blood money or retaliation by having the killer killed." (6880) □

2222. Narrated Ibn `Abbas: For the children of Israel the punishment for crime was Al-Qisas only (i.e., the law of equality in punishment) and the payment of Blood money was not permitted as an alternate. But Allah said to this nation (Muslims): 'O you who believe! Qisas is prescribed for you in case of murder, ... (up to) ...end of the

Verse. (2.178) Ibn `Abbas added: Remission (forgiveness) in this Verse, means to accept the Blood-money in an intentional murder. Ibn `Abbas added: The Verse: 'Then the relatives should demand Blood-money in a reasonable manner.' (2.178) means that the demand should be reasonable and it is to be compensated with handsome gratitude. (6881) ☐

2223. Narrated Ibn `Abbas: The Prophet (ﷺ) said, "The most hated persons to Allah are three: (1) A person who deviates from the right conduct, i.e., an evil doer, in the Haram (sanctuaries of Mecca and Medina); (2) a person who seeks that the traditions of the Pre-lslamic Period of Ignorance, should remain in Islam (3) and a person who seeks to shed somebody's blood without any right." (6882) ☐

2224. Narrated Ya`la bin Umaiya: I fought in Jaish-al-Usra (Ghazwa of Tabuk) along with the Prophet (ﷺ) and in my opinion that was the best of my deeds. Then I had an employee, who quarrelled with someone and one of the them bit and cut the other's finger and caused his own tooth to fall out. He then went to the Prophet (ﷺ) (with a complaint) but the Prophet (ﷺ) canceled the suit and said to the complainant, "Did you expect him to let his finger in your mouth so that you might snap and cut it (as does a stallion camel)?" Narrated Ibn Juraij from `Abdullah bin Abu Mulaika from his grandfather a similar story: A man bit the hand of another man and caused his own tooth to fall out, but Abu Bakr judged that he had no right for compensation (for the broken tooth). (2265) ☐

2225. Narrated Anas: Ar-Rabi, the daughter of An-Nadr broke the tooth of a girl, and the relatives of Ar-Rabi` requested the girl's relatives to accept the Irsh (compensation for wounds etc.) and forgive (the offender), but they refused. So, they went to the Prophet (ﷺ) who ordered them to bring about retaliation. Anas bin An-Nadr asked, "O Allah"; Apostle! Will the tooth of Ar-Rabi` be broken? No, by Him Who has sent you with the Truth, her tooth will not be broken." The Prophet (ﷺ) said, "O Anas! Allah"; law ordains retaliation." Later the relatives of the girl agreed and forgave her. The Prophet (ﷺ) said, "There are some of Allah's slaves who, if they take an oath by Allah, are responded to by Allah i.e. their oath is fulfilled). Anas added, "The people agreed and accepted the Irsh." (2703) ☐

2226. Narrated Ibn `Abbas: The Prophet (ﷺ) said, "This and this are the same." He meant the little finger and the thumb [The diya (Blood Money) for fingers and thumb are the same)] (6895) ☐

2227. Ibn 'Umar said: A boy was assassinated. 'Umar said, "If all the people of San'a took part in the assassination I would kill them all." Al-Mughira bin Hakim said that his father said, "Four persons killed a boy, and 'Umar said (as above)." Abu Bakr, Ibn Az-Zubair, 'Ali and Suwaid bin Muqarrin gave the judgement of Al-Qisas (equality in punishment) in cases of slapping. And 'Umar carried out Al-Qisas for a strike with a stick. And 'Ali carried out Al-Qisas for three lashes with a whip. And Shuraih carried out for one last and for scratching. (6896) ☐

2228. Narrated Abu Raja: The freed slave of Abu Qilaba, who was with Abu Qilaba in Sham: `Umar bin `Abdul `Aziz consulted the people saying, What do you think of Qasama (Oath/Swear). They said, 'It is a right (judgment) which Allah's Apostle and the Caliphs before you acted on. (4193) ☐

2229. Narrated Abu Qilaba: Once `Umar bin `Abdul `Aziz sat on his throne in the courtyard of his house so that the people might gather before him. Then he admitted them and (when they came in), he said, "What do you think of Al-Qasama?" They said, "We say that it is lawful to depend on Al-Qasama in Qisas, as the previous Muslim Caliphs carried out Qisas depending on it." Then he said to me, "O Abu Qilaba! What do you say about it?" He let me appear before the people and I said, "O Chief of the Believers! You have the chiefs of the army staff and the nobles of the Arabs. If fifty of them testified that a married man had committed illegal sexual intercourse in Damascus but they had not seen him (doing so), would you stone him?" He said, "No." I said, "If fifty of them testified that a man had committed theft in Hums, would you cut off his hand though they did not see him?" He replied, "No." I said, "By Allah, Allah's Messenger (ﷺ) never killed anyone except in one of the following three situations: (1) A person who killed somebody unjustly, was killed (in

Qisas,) (2) a married person who committed illegal sexual intercourse and (3) a man who fought against Allah and His Apostle and deserted Islam and became an apostate." Then the people said, "Didn't Anas bin Malik narrate that Allah's Messenger (☻) cut off the hands of the thieves, branded their eyes and then, threw them in the sun?" I said, "I shall tell you the narration of Anas. Anas said: "Eight persons from the tribe of `Ukl came to Allah's Messenger (☻) and gave the Pledge of allegiance for Islam (became Muslim). The climate of the place (Medina) did not suit them, so they became sick and complained about that to Allah's Messenger (☻). He said (to them), "Won't you go out with the shepherd of our camels and drink of the camels' milk and urine (as medicine)?" They said, "Yes." So they went out and drank the camels' milk and urine, and after they became healthy, they killed the shepherd of Allah's Messenger (☻) and took away all the camels. This news reached Allah's Messenger (☻), so he sent (men) to follow their traces and they were captured and brought (to the Prophet). He then ordered to cut their hands and feet, and their eyes were branded with heated pieces of iron, and then he threw them in the sun till they died." I said, "What can be worse than what those people did? They deserted Islam, committed murder and theft." Then 'Anbasa bin Sa`id said, "By Allah, I never heard a narration like this of today." I said, "O 'Anbasa! You deny my narration?" 'Anbasa said, "No, but you have related the narration in the way it should be related. By Allah, these people are in welfare as long as this Sheikh (Abu Qilaba) is among them." I added, "Indeed in this event there has been a tradition set by Allah's Messenger (☻). The narrator added: Some Ansari people came to the Prophet (☻) and discussed some matters with him, a man from amongst them went out and was murdered. Those people went out after him, and behold, their companion was swimming in blood. They returned to Allah's Messenger (☻) and said to him, "O Allah's Apostle, we have found our companion who had talked with us and gone out before us, swimming in blood (killed)." Allah's Messenger (☻) went out and asked them, "Whom do you suspect or whom do you think has killed him?" They said, "We think that the Jews have killed him." The Prophet (☻) sent for the Jews and asked them, "Did you kill this (person)?" They replied, "No." He asked the Al-Ansars, "Do you agree that I let fifty Jews take an oath that they have not killed him?" They said, "It matters little for the Jews to kill us all and then take false oaths." He said, "Then would you like to receive the Diya after fifty of you have taken an oath (that the Jews have killed your man)?" They said, "We will not take the oath." Then the Prophet (ﷺ) himself paid them the Diya (Blood-money)." The narrator added, "The tribe of Hudhail repudiated one of their men (for his evil conduct) in the Pre-lslamic period of Ignorance. Then, at a place called Al-Batha' (near Mecca), the man attacked a Yemenite family at night to steal from them, but a. man from the family noticed him and struck him with his sword and killed him. The tribe of Hudhail came and captured the Yemenite and brought him to `Umar during the Hajj season and said, "He has killed our companion." The Yemenite said, "But these people had repudiated him (i.e., their companion)." `Umar said, "Let fifty persons of Hudhail swear that they had not repudiated him." So forty-nine of them took the oath and then a person belonging to them, came from Sham and they requested him to swear similarly, but he paid one-thousand Dirhams instead of taking the oath. They called another man instead of him and the new man shook hands with the brother of the deceased. Some people said, "We and those fifty men who had taken false oaths (Al-Qasama) set out, and when they reached a place called Nakhlah, it started raining so they entered a cave in the mountain, and the cave collapsed on those fifty men who took the false oath, and all of them died except the two persons who had shaken hands with each other. They escaped death but a stone fell on the leg of the brother of the deceased and broke it, whereupon he survived for one year and then died." I further said, "`Abdul Malik bin Marwan sentenced a man to death in Qisas (equality in punishment) for murder, basing his judgment on Al-Qasama, but later on he regretted that judgment and ordered that the names of the fifty persons who had taken the oath, be erased from the register, and he exiled them in Sham." (6899) □

2230. Narrated Ash-Shu`bi: I heard Abu Juhaifa saying, "I asked `Ali 'Have you got any Divine literature apart from the Qur'an?' (Once he said...apart from what the people have?) `Ali replied, 'By Him Who made the grain split (germinate) and created the soul, we have nothing except what is in the Qur'an and the ability (gift) of understanding Allah's Book which He may endow a man with and we have what is written in this paper.' I asked, 'What is written in this paper?' He replied, 'Al-`Aql (the regulation of Diya), about the ransom of captives, and the Judgment that a Muslim should not be killed in Qisas (equality in punishment) for killing a disbeliever." (6903) □

2231. Narrated Abu Huraira: Two women from the tribe of Hudhail (fought with each other) and one of them threw (a stone at) the other, causing her to have a miscarriage and Allah's Messenger (ﷺ) gave his verdict that the killer (of the fetus) should give a male or female slave (as a Diya). (6904) □

2232. Narrated Abu Huraira: Allah's Messenger (ﷺ) gave a verdict regarding an aborted fetus of a woman from Bani Lihyan that the killer (of the fetus) should give a male or female slave (as a Diya) but the woman who was required to give the slave, died, so Allah's Messenger (ﷺ) gave the verdict that her inheritance be given to her children and her husband and the Diya be paid by her 'Asaba. (6909) □

2233. Narrated Abu Huraira: Allah's Messenger (ﷺ) said, "There is no Diya for persons killed by animals or for the one who has been killed accidentally by falling into a well or for the one killed in a mine. And one-fifth of Rikaz (treasures buried before the Islamic era) is to be given to the state." (6912) □

2234. Narrated `Abdullah: When the Verse: 'It is those who believe and confuse not their belief with wrong (i.e., worshipping others besides Allah): (6.82) was revealed, it became very hard on the companions of the Prophet (ﷺ) and they said, "Who among us has not confused his belief with wrong (oppression)?" On that, Allah's Apostle said, "This is not meant (by the Verse). Don't you listen to Luqman's statement: 'Verily! Joining others in worship with Allah is a great wrong indeed.' (31.13) (6918) □

2235. Narrated Ibn Mas`ud: A man said, "O Allah's Messenger (ﷺ)! Shall we be punished for what we did in the Pr-elslamic Period of ignorance?" The Prophet (ﷺ) said, "Whoever does good in Islam will not be punished for what he did in the Pre-lslamic Period of ignorance and whoever does evil in Islam will be punished for his former and later (bad deeds). (6921) □

2236. Narrated `Ikrima: Some Zanadiqa (atheists) were brought to `Ali and he burnt them. The news of this event, reached Ibn `Abbas who said, "If I had been in his place, I would not have burnt them, as Allah's Messenger (ﷺ) forbade it, saying, 'Do not punish anybody with Allah's punishment (fire).' I would have killed them according to the statement of Allah's Messenger (ﷺ), 'Whoever changed his Islamic religion, then kill him.'" (6922) □

2237. Narrated Abu Burda: Abu Musa said, "I came to the Prophet (ﷺ) along with two men (from the tribe) of Ash`ariyin, one on my right and the other on my left, while Allah's Messenger (ﷺ) was brushing his teeth (with a Siwak), and both men asked him for some employment. The Prophet (ﷺ) said, 'O Abu Musa (O `Abdullah bin Qais!).' I said, 'By Him Who sent you with the Truth, these two men did not tell me what was in their hearts and I did not feel (realize) that they were seeking employment.' As if I were looking now at his Siwak being drawn to a corner under his lips, and he said, 'We never (or, we do not) appoint for our affairs anyone who seeks to be employed. But O Abu Musa! (or `Abdullah bin Qais!) Go to Yemen.'" The Prophet then sent Mu`adh bin Jabal after him and when Mu`adh reached him, he spread out a cushion for him and requested him to get down (and sit on the cushion). Behold: There was a fettered man beside Abu Muisa. Mu`adh asked, "Who is this (man)?" Abu Muisa said, "He was a Jew and became a Muslim and then reverted back to Judaism." Then Abu Muisa requested Mu`adh to sit down but Mu`adh said, "I will not sit down till he has been killed. This is the judgment of Allah and His Apostle (for such cases) and repeated it thrice. Then Abu Musa ordered that the man be killed, and he was killed. Abu Musa added, "Then we discussed the night prayers and one of us said, 'I pray and sleep, and I hope that Allah will reward me for my sleep as well as for my prayers.'" (6923) □

88. Coercion

2238. Narrated Abu Huraira (ra): While we were in the mosque, Allah's Messenger (ﷺ) came out to us and said, "Let us proceed to the Jews." So we went along with him till we reached Bait-al-Midras (a place where the Torah used to be recited and all the Jews of the town used to gather). The Prophet (ﷺ) stood up and addressed them, "O Assembly of Jews! Embrace Islam and you will be safe!" The Jews replied, "O Aba-l-Qasim! You have conveyed Allah's message to us." The Prophet (ﷺ) said, "That is what I want (from you)." He repeated his first statement for the second time, and they said, "You have conveyed Allah's message, O Aba-l- Qasim." Then he said it for the third time and added, "You should Know that the earth belongs to Allah and His Apostle, and I want to exile you from this land, so whoever among you owns some property, can sell it, otherwise you should know that the Earth belongs to Allah and His Apostle." (6944) □

2239. Narrated Khansa' bint Khidam Al-Ansariya: That her father gave her in marriage when she was a matron and she disliked that marriage. So she came and (complained) to the Prophets and he declared that marriage invalid. (6945) □

2240. Narrated Jabir: A man from the Ansar made his slave, a Mudabbar. And apart from that slave he did not have any other property. This news reached Allah's Messenger (ﷺ) and he said, "Who will buy that slave from me?" So Nu'aim bin An-Nahham bought him for 800 Dirham. Jabir added: It was a Coptic (Egyptian) slave who died that year. (6947) □

2241. Narrated Ibn `Abbas: Regarding the Qur'anic Verse: 'O you who believe! You are forbidden to inherit women against their will.' (4.19)

The custom (in the Pre-lslamic Period) was that if a man died, his relatives used to have the right to inherit his wife, and if one of them wished, he could marry her, or they could marry her to somebody else, or prevent her from marrying if they wished, for they had more right to dispose of her than her own relatives. Therefore this Verse was revealed concerning this matter. (6948) ☐

2242. And Safiyya bint 'Ubaid said:"A governmental male-slave tried to seduce a slave-girl from the Khumus of the war booty till he deflowered her by force against her will; therefore 'Umar flogged him according to the law, and exiled him, but he did not flog the female slave because the male-slave had committed illegal sexual intercourse by force, against her will." Az-Zuhri said regarding a virgin slave-girl raped by a free man: The judge has to fine the adulterer as much money as is equal to the price of the female slave and the adulterer has to be flogged (according to the Islamic Law); but if the slave woman is a matron, then, according to the verdict of the Imam, the adulterer is not fined but he has to receive the legal punishment (according to the Islamic Law). (6949) ☐

89. Interpretation of Dreams

2243. Narrated Anas bin Malik: Allah's Messenger (ﷺ) said, "A good dream (that comes true) of a righteous man is one of forty-six parts of prophetism." (6983) ☐

2244. Narrated Abu Sa`id Al-Khudri (ra): The Prophet (ﷺ) said, "If anyone of you sees a dream that he likes, then it is from Allah, and he should thank Allah for it and narrate it to others; but if he sees something else, i.e., a dream that he dislikes, then it is from Satan, and he should seek refuge with Allah from its evil, and he should not mention it to anybody, for it will not harm him." (6985) ☐

2245. Narrated Abu Huraira: Allah's Messenger (ﷺ) said, "Nothing is left of the prophetism except Al-Mubashshirat." They asked, "What are Al-Mubashshirat?" He replied, "The true good dreams (that conveys glad tidings). (6990) ☐

2246. Narrated Abu Huraira: I heard the Prophet (ﷺ) saying, "Whoever sees me in a dream will see me in his wakefulness, and Satan cannot imitate me in shape." Abu `Abdullah said, "Ibn Seereen said, 'Only if he sees the Prophet (ﷺ) in his (real) shape.'" (6993) □

2247. Narrated `Abdullah bin Salam: (In a dream) I saw myself in a garden, and there was a pillar in the middle of the garden, and there was a handhold at the top of the pillar. I was asked to climb it. I said, "I cannot." Then a servant came and lifted up my clothes and I climbed (the pillar), and then got hold of the handhold, and I woke up while still holding it. I narrated that to the Prophet (ﷺ) who said, "The garden symbolizes the garden of Islam, and the handhold is the firm Islamic handhold which indicates that you will be adhering firmly to Islam until you die." (7014) □

2248. Narrated Ibn `Umar: I saw in a dream a piece of silken cloth in my hand, and in whatever direction in Paradise I waved it, it flew, carrying me there. I narrated this (dream) to (my sister) Hafsa and she told it to the Prophet (ﷺ) who said, (to Hafsa), "Indeed, your brother is a righteous man," or, "Indeed, `Abdullah is a righteous man." (7015) □

2249. Narrated Abu Huraira: Allah's Messenger (ﷺ) said, "When the Day of Resurrection approaches, the dreams of a believer will hardly fail to come true, and a dream of a believer is one of forty-six parts of prophetism, and whatever belongs to propthetism can never be false." Muhammad bin Seereen said, "But I say this." He said, "It used to be said, 'There are three types of dreams: The reflection of one's thoughts and experiences one has during wakefulness, what is suggested by Satan to frighten the dreamer, or glad tidings from Allah. So, if someone has a dream which he dislikes, he should not tell it to others, but get up and offer a prayer." He added, "He (Abu Huraira) hated to see a Ghul (i.e., iron collar around his neck in a dream) and people liked to see fetters (on their feet in a dream). The fetters on the feet symbolizes one's constant and firm adherence to religion." And Abu `Abdullah said, "Ghuls (iron collars) are used only for necks." (7017) □

2250. Narrated Kharija bin Zaid bin Thabit: Um Al-`Ala an Ansari woman who had given the Pledge of allegiance to Allah's Messenger (ﷺ) said, "`Uthman bin Maz'un came in our share when the Ansars drew lots to distribute the emigrants (to dwell) among themselves, He became sick and we looked after (nursed) him till he died. Then we shrouded him in his clothes. Allah's Messenger (ﷺ) came to us, I (addressing the dead body) said, "May Allah's Mercy be on you, O Aba As-Sa'ib! I testify that Allah has honored you." The Prophet (ﷺ) said, 'How do you know that?' I replied, 'I do not know, by Allah.' He said, 'As for him, death has come to him and I wish him all good from Allah. By Allah, though I am Allah's Messenger (ﷺ), I neither know what will happen to me, nor to you.'" Um Al-`Ala said, "By Allah, I will never attest the righteousness of anybody after that." She added, "Later I saw in a dream, a flowing spring for `Uthman. So I went to Allah's Messenger (ﷺ) and mentioned that to him. He said, 'That is (the symbol of) his good deeds (the reward for) which is going on for him.'" (7018) □

2251. Narrated Ibn `Umar: Men from the companions of Allah's Messenger (ﷺ) used to see dreams during the lifetime of Allah's Messenger (ﷺ) and they used to narrate those dreams to Allah's Messenger (ﷺ). Allah's Messenger (ﷺ) would interpret them as Allah wished. I was a young man and used to stay in the mosque before my wedlock. I said to myself, "If there were any good in myself, I too would see what these people see." So when I went to bed one night, I said, "O Allah! If you see any good in me, show me a good dream." So while I was in that state, there came to me (in a dream) two angels. In the hand of each of them, there was a mace of iron, and both of them were taking me to Hell, and I was between them, invoking Allah, "O Allah! I seek refuge with You from Hell." Then I saw myself being confronted by another angel holding a mace of iron in his hand. He said to me, "Do not be afraid, you will be an excellent man if you only pray more often." So they took me till they stopped me at the edge of Hell, and behold, it was built inside like a well and it had side posts like those of a well, and beside each post there was an angel carrying an iron mace. I saw therein many people hanging upside down with iron chains, and I recognized therein some men from the Quraish. Then (the angels) took me to the right side. I narrated this dream to (my sister) Hafsa and she told it to Allah's Messenger (ﷺ). Allah's Messenger (ﷺ) said, "No doubt, `Abdullah is a good man." (Nafi` said, "Since then `Abdullah bin `Umar used to pray much.) (7028) □

2252. Narrated `Abdullah bin `Abbas: Allah's Messenger (ﷺ) said, "While I was sleeping, two golden bangles were put in my two hands, so I got scared (frightened) and disliked it, but I was given permission to blow them off, and they flew away. I interpret it as a symbol of two liars who will appear." 'Ubaidullah said, "One of them was Al-`Ansi who was killed by Fairuz at Yemen and the other was Musailama (at Najd). (7034) ☐

2253. Narrated Abu Musa: The Prophet (ﷺ) said, "I saw in a dream that I was migrating from Mecca to a land where there were date palm trees. I thought that it might be the land of Al-Yamama or Hajar, but behold, it turned out to be Yathrib (Medina). And I saw cows (being slaughtered) there, but the reward given by Allah is better (than worldly benefits). Behold, those cows proved to symbolize the believers (who were killed) on the Day of Uhud, and the good (which I saw in the dream) was the good and the reward and the truth which Allah bestowed upon us after the Badr battle (or the Battle of Uhud) and that was the victory bestowed by Allah in the Battle of Khaibar and the conquest of Mecca. (7035) ☐

2254. Narrated `Abdullah: The Prophet (ﷺ) said, "I saw a black woman with unkempt hair going out of Medina and settling at Mahai'a (Al-Juhfa). I interpreted that as a symbol of epidemic of Medina being transferred to that place. (7038) ☐

2255. Narrated Abu Musa: The Prophet (ﷺ) said, "I saw in a dream that I waved a sword and it broke in the middle, and behold, that symbolized the casualties the believers suffered on the Day (of the battle) of Uhud. Then I waved the sword again, and it became better than it had ever been before, and behold, that symbolized the Conquest (of Mecca) which Allah brought about and the gathering of the believers." (7041) ☐

2256. Narrated Ibn `Abbas: The Prophet (ﷺ) said, "Whoever claims to have seen a dream which he did not see, will be ordered to make a knot between two barley grains which he will not be able to do; and if somebody listens to the talk of some people who do not like him (to listen) or they run away from him, then molten lead will be poured into his ears on the Day of Resurrection; and whoever makes a picture, will be punished on the Day of Resurrection and will be ordered to put a soul in that picture, which he will not be able to do." Ibn `Abbas also narrated a similar hadith. (7042) ☐

2257. Narrated Ibn `Umar: Allah's Messenger (ﷺ) said, "The worst lie is that a person claims to have seen a dream which he has not seen." (7043) ☐

2258. Narrated Ibn `Abbas: A man came to Allah's Messenger (ﷺ) and said, "I saw in a dream, a cloud having shade. Butter and honey were dropping from it and I saw the people gathering it in their hands, some gathering much and some a little. And behold, there was a rope extending from the earth to the sky, and I saw that you (the Prophet) held it and went up, and then another man held it and went up and (after that) another (third) held it and went up, and then after another (fourth) man held it, but it broke and then got connected again." Abu Bakr said, "O Allah's Messenger (ﷺ)! Let my father be sacrificed for you! Allow me to interpret this dream." The Prophet (ﷺ) said to him, "Interpret it." Abu Bakr said, "The cloud with shade symbolizes Islam, and the butter and honey dropping from it, symbolizes the Qur'an, its sweetness dropping and some people learning much of the Qur'an and some a little. The rope which is extended from the sky to the earth is the Truth which you (the Prophet) are following. You follow it and Allah will raise you high with it, and then another man will follow it and will rise up with it and another person will follow it and then another man will follow it but it will break and then it will be connected for him and he will rise up with it. O Allah's Messenger (ﷺ)! Let my father be sacrificed for you! Am I right or wrong?" The Prophet replied, "You are right in some of it and wrong in some." Abu Bakr said, "O Allah's Prophet! By Allah, you must tell me in what I was wrong." The Prophet (ﷺ) said, "Do not swear." (7046) ☐

2259. Narrated Samura bin Jundub: Allah's Messenger (ﷺ) very often used to ask his companions, "Did anyone of you see a dream?" So dreams would be narrated to him by those whom Allah wished to tell. One morning the Prophet (ﷺ) said, "Last night two persons came to me (in a dream) and woke me up and said to me, 'Proceed!' I set out with them and we came across a man lying down, and behold, another man was standing over his head, holding a big rock. Behold, he was throwing the rock at the man's head, injuring it. The rock rolled away and the thrower followed it and took it back. By the time he reached the man, his head returned to the normal state. The thrower then did the same as he had done before. I said to my two companions, 'Subhan Allah! Who are these two persons?' They said, 'Proceed!' So we proceeded and came to a man lying flat on his back and another man standing over his head with an iron hook, and behold, he would put the hook in one side of the man's mouth and tear off that side of his face to the back (of the neck) and similarly tear his nose from front to back and his eye from front to back. Then he turned to the other side of the man's face and did just as he had done with the other side. He hardly completed this side when the other side returned to its normal state. Then he returned to it to repeat what he had done before. I said to my two companions, 'Subhan Allah! Who are these two persons?' They said to me, 'Proceed!' So we proceeded and came across something like a Tannur (a kind of baking oven, a pit usually clay-lined for baking bread)." I think the Prophet (ﷺ) said, "In that oven there was much noise and voices." The Prophet (ﷺ) added, "We looked into it and found naked men and women, and behold, a flame of fire was reaching to them from underneath, and when it reached them, they cried loudly. I asked them, 'Who are these?' They said to me, 'Proceed!' And so we proceeded and came across a river." I think he said, ".... red like blood." The Prophet (ﷺ) added, "And behold, in the river there was a man swimming, and on the bank there was a man who had collected many stones. Behold, while the other man was swimming, he went near him. The former opened his mouth and the latter (on the bank) threw a stone into his mouth whereupon he went swimming again. He returned and every time the performance was repeated. I asked my two companions, 'Who are these (two) persons?' They replied, 'Proceed! Proceed!' And we proceeded till we came to a man with a repulsive appearance, the most repulsive appearance, you ever saw a man having! Beside him there was a fire and he was kindling it and running around it. I asked my companions, 'Who is this (man)?' They said to me, 'Proceed! Proceed!' So we proceeded till we reached a garden of deep green dense vegetation, having all sorts of spring colors. In the midst of the garden there was a very tall man and I could hardly see his head because of his great height, and around him there were children in such a large number as I have never seen. I said to my companions, 'Who is this?' They replied, 'Proceed! Proceed!' So we proceeded till we came to a majestic huge garden, greater and better than I have ever seen! My two companions said to me, 'Go up' and I went up. The Prophet (ﷺ) added, "So we ascended till we reached a city built of gold and silver bricks and we went to its gate and asked (the gatekeeper) to open the gate, and it was opened and we entered the city and found in it, men with one side of their bodies as handsome as the handsomest person you have ever seen, and the other side as ugly as the ugliest person you have ever seen. My two companions ordered those men to throw themselves into the river. Behold, there was a river flowing across (the city), and its water was like milk in whiteness. Those men went and threw themselves in it and then returned to us after the ugliness (of their bodies) had disappeared and they became in the best shape." The Prophet (ﷺ) further added, "My two companions (angels) said to me, 'this place is the Eden Paradise, and that is your place.' I raised up my sight, and behold, there I saw a palace like a white cloud! My two companions said to me, 'That (palace) is your place.' I said to them, 'May Allah bless you both! Let me enter it.' They replied, 'As for now, you will not enter it, but you shall enter it (one day). I said to them, 'I have seen many wonders tonight. What does all that mean which I have seen?' They replied, 'We will inform you: As for the first man you came upon whose head was being injured with the rock, he is the symbol of the one who studies the Qur'an and then neither recites it nor acts on its orders, and sleeps, neglecting the enjoined prayers. As for the man you came upon whose sides of mouth, nostrils and eyes were torn off from front to back, he is the symbol of the man who goes out of his house in the morning and tells so many lies that it spreads all over the world. And those naked men and women whom you saw in a construction resembling an oven, they are the adulterers and the adulteresses. And the man whom you saw swimming in the river and given a stone to swallow, is the eater of usury (Riba). And the bad looking man whom you saw near the fire kindling it and going round it, is Malik, the gatekeeper of Hell. And the tall man whom you saw in the garden, is Abraham and the children around him are those children who die with Al-Fitra (the Islamic Faith). The narrator added: Some Muslims asked the Prophet, "O Allah's Messenger (ﷺ)! What about the children of pagans?" The Prophet (ﷺ) replied, "And also the children of pagans." The Prophet (ﷺ) added, "My two companions added, 'The men you saw half handsome and half ugly were those persons who had mixed an act that was good with another that was bad, but Allah forgave them.'" (7047) ☐

90. FITNA

2260. NARRATED USAMA BIN ZAID (RA): Once the Prophet (ﷺ) stood over one of the high buildings of Medina and then said (to the people), "Do you see what I see?" They said, "No." He said, "I see afflictions falling among your houses as rain drops fall." (7060) ☐

2261. Narrated Abu Sa`id Al-Khudri: Allah's Messenger (ﷺ) said, "There will come a time when the best property of a Muslim will be sheep which he will take to the tops of mountains and the places of rainfall so as to flee with his religion from the afflictions. (7088) ☐

2262. Narrated Abu Huraira: The Prophet (ﷺ) said, "The Hour will not be established till a man passes by a grave of somebody and says, 'Would that I were in his place.'" (7115) ☐

2263. Narrated Abu Huraira: The Prophet (ﷺ) said, "Time will pass rapidly, good deeds will decrease, miserliness will be thrown (in the hearts of the people) afflictions will appear and there will be much 'Al-Harj." They said, "O Allah's Apostle! What is "Al-Harj?" He said, "Killing! Killing!" (7061) ☐

2264. Narrated `Abdullah bin `Umar: Allah's Messenger (ﷺ) said, "Whoever takes up arms against us, is not from us." (7070) ☐

2265. Narrated Abu Huraira: The Prophet (ﷺ) said, "None of you should point out towards his Muslim brother with a weapon, for he does not know, Satan may tempt him to hit him and thus he would fall into a pit of fire (Hell)" (7072) ☐

2266. Narrated `Abdullah: The Prophet, said, "Abusing a Muslim is Fusuq (evil doing) and killing him is Kufr (disbelief). (7076) ☐

2267. Narrated Ibn `Umar: I heard the Prophet (صلى الله عليه وسلم) saying, "Do not revert to disbelief after me by striking (cutting) the necks of one another." (7077) ☐

2268. Narrated Hudhaifa bin Al-Yaman: The people used to ask Allah's Messenger (صلى الله عليه وسلم) about the good but I used to ask him about the evillest I should be overtaken by them. So I said, "O Allah's Messenger (صلى الله عليه وسلم)! We were living in ignorance and in an (extremely) worst atmosphere, then Allah brought to us this good (i.e., Islam); will there be any evil after this good?" He said, "Yes." I said, 'Will there be any good after that evil?" He replied, "Yes, but it will be tainted (not pure.)" I asked, "What will be its taint?" He replied, "(There will be) some people who will guide others not according to my tradition? You will approve of some of their deeds and disapprove of some others." I asked, "Will there be any evil after that good?" He replied, "Yes, (there will be) some people calling at the gates of the (Hell) Fire, and whoever will respond to their call, will be thrown by them into the (Hell) Fire." I said, "O Allah s Apostle! Will you describe them to us?" He said, "They will be from our own people and will speak our language." I said, "What do you order me to do if such a state should take place in my life?" He said, "Stick to the group of Muslims and their Imam (ruler)." I said, "If there is neither a group of Muslims nor an Imam (ruler)?" He said, "Then turn away from all those sects even if you were to bite (eat) the roots of a tree till death overtakes you while you are in that state." (7084) ☐

2269. Narrated Aisha: Allah's Messenger (صلى الله عليه وسلم) said, "If somebody innovates something which is not in harmony with the principles of our religion, that thing is rejected." (2697) ☐

2270. Narrated Hudhaifa: Allah's Messenger (صلى الله عليه وسلم) related to us, two prophetic narrations one of which I have seen fulfilled and I am waiting for the fulfillment of the other. The Prophet (ﷺ) told us that the virtue of honesty descended in the roots of men's hearts (from Allah) and then they learned it from the Qur'an and then they learned it from the Sunnah (the Prophet's traditions). The Prophet (ﷺ) further told us how that honesty will be taken away: He said: "Man will go to sleep during which honesty will be taken away from his heart and only its trace will remain in his heart like the trace of a dark spot; then man will go to sleep, during which honesty will decrease further still, so that its trace will resemble the trace of blister as when an ember is dropped on one's foot which would make it swell, and one would see it swollen but there would be nothing inside. People would be carrying out their trade but hardly will there be a trustworthy person. It will be said, 'in such-and-such tribe there is an honest man,' and later it will be said about some man, 'What a wise, polite and strong man he is!' Though he will not have faith equal even to a mustard seed in his heart." No doubt, there came upon me a time when I did not mind dealing (bargaining) with anyone of you, for if he was a Muslim his Islam would compel him to pay me what is due to me, and if he was a Christian, the Muslim official would compel him to pay me what is due to me, but today I do not deal except with such-and-such person. (7086) □

2271. Narrated Shaqiq: I heard Hudhaifa saying, "While we were sitting with `Umar, he said, 'Who among you remembers the statement of the Prophet (ﷺ) about the afflictions?' Hudhaifa said, "The affliction of a man in his family, his property, his children and his neighbors are expiated by his prayers, Zakat (and alms) and enjoining good and forbidding evil." `Umar said, "I do not ask you about these afflictions, but about those afflictions which will move like the waves of the sea." Hudhaifa said, "Don't worry about it, O chief of the believers, for there is a closed door between you and them." `Umar said, "Will that door be broken or opened?" I said, "No. it will be broken." `Umar said, "Then it will never be closed," I said, "Yes." We asked Hudhaifa, "Did `Umar know what that door meant?" He replied, "Yes, as I know that there will be night before tomorrow morning that is because I narrated to him a true narration free from errors." We dared not ask Hudhaifa as to whom the door represented so we ordered Masruq to ask him what does the door stand for? He replied, "`Umar." (7096)

☐

2272. Narrated Abu Maryam `Abdullah bin Ziyad Al-Aasadi: When Talha, Az-Zubair and `Aisha moved to Basra, `Ali sent `Ammar bin Yasir and Hasan bin `Ali who came to us at Kufa and ascended the pulpit. Al-Hasan bin `Ali was at the top of the pulpit and `Ammar was below Al-Hasan. We all gathered before him. I heard `Ammar saying, "`Aisha has moved to Al-Busra. By Allah! She is the wife of your Prophet in this world and in the Hereafter. But Allah has put you to test whether you obey Him (Allah) or her (`Aisha). (7100) ☐

2273. Narrated Abu Wail: Abu Musa and Abu Mas`ud went to `Ammar when `Ali had sent him to Kufa to exhort them to fight (on `Ali's side). They said to him, "Since you have become a Muslim, we have never seen you doing a deed more criticizable to us than your haste in this matter." `Ammar said, "Since you (both) became Muslims, I have never seen you doing a deed more criticizable to me than your keeping away from this matter." Then Abu Mas`ud provided `Ammar and Abu Musa with two-piece outfits to wear, and one of them went to the mosque (of Kufa). (7102) ☐

2274. Narrated Nafi`: When the people of Medina dethroned Yazid bin Muawiya, Ibn `Umar gathered his special friends and children and said, "I heard the Prophet (ﷺ) saying, 'A flag will be fixed for every betrayer on the Day of Resurrection,' and we have given the oath of allegiance to this person (Yazid) in accordance with the conditions enjoined by Allah and His Apostle and I do not know of anything more faithless than fighting a person who has been given the oath of allegiance in accordance with the conditions enjoined by Allah and His Apostle , and if ever I learn that any person among you has agreed to dethrone Yazid, by giving the oath of allegiance (to somebody else) then there will be separation between him and me." (7111) ☐

2275. Narrated Abu Al-Minhal: When Ibn Ziyad and Marwan were in Sham and Ibn Az-Zubair took over the authority in Mecca and Qurra' (the Kharijites) revolted in Basra, I went out with my father to Abu Barza Al-Aslami till we entered upon him in his house while he was sitting in the shade of a room built of cane. So we sat with him and my father started talking to him saying, "O Abu Barza! Don't you see in what dilemma the people has fallen?" The first thing heard him saying "I seek reward from Allah for myself because of being angry and scornful at the Quraish tribe. O you Arabs! You know very well that you were in misery and were few in number and misguided, and that Allah has brought you out of all that with Islam and with Muhammad till He brought you to this state (of prosperity and happiness) which you see now; and it is this worldly wealth and pleasures which has caused mischief to appear among you. The one who is in Sham (i.e., Marwan), by Allah, is not fighting except for the sake of worldly gain: and those who are among you, by Allah, are not fighting except for the sake of worldly gain; and that one who is in Mecca (i.e., Ibn Az-Zubair) by Allah, is not fighting except for the sake of worldly gain." (7112) □

2276. Narrated Abu Huraira: I heard the truthful and trusted by Allah (i.e., the Prophet (ﷺ)) saying, "The destruction of my followers will be through the hands of young men from Quraish." (7058) □

2277. Narrated `Ali: Whenever I tell you a narration from Allah's Apostle, by Allah, I would rather fall down from the sky than ascribe a false statement to him, but if I tell you something between me and you (not a Hadith) then it was indeed a trick (i.e., I may say things just to cheat my enemy). No doubt I heard Allah's Apostle saying, During the last days there will appear some young foolish people who will say the best words but their faith will not go beyond their throats (i.e. they will have no faith) and will go out from (leave) their religion as an arrow goes out of the game. So, where-ever you find them, kill them, for who-ever kills them shall have reward on the Day of Resurrection. (6930) □

2278. Narrated `Abdullah bin `Amr bin Yasar: That they visited Abu Sa`id Al-Khudri and asked him about Al-Harauriyya, a special unorthodox religious sect, Did you hear the Prophet saying anything about them? Abu Sa`id said, I do not know what Al-Harauriyya is, but I heard the Prophet saying, There will appear in this nation---- he did not say: From this nation ---- a group of people so pious apparently that you will consider your prayers inferior to their prayers, but they will recite the Qur'an, the teachings of which will not go beyond their throats and will go out of their religion as an arrow darts through the game, whereupon the archer may look at his arrow, its Nasl at its Risaf and its Fuqa to see whether it is blood-stained or not (i.e. they will have not even a trace of Islam in them). (6931) ☐

2279. Narrated Abu Sa`id: While the Prophet was distributing (something, `Abdullah bin Dhil Khawaisira at-Tamimi came and said, Be just, O Allah's Apostle! The Prophet said, Woe to you! Who would be just if I were not? `Umar bin Al-Khattab said, Allow me to cut off his neck! The Prophet said, Leave him, for he has companions, and if you compare your prayers with their prayers and your fasting with theirs, you will look down upon your prayers and fasting, in comparison to theirs. Yet they will go out of the religion as an arrow darts through the game's body in which case, if the Qudhadh of the arrow is examined, nothing will be found on it, and when its Nasl is examined, nothing will be found on it; and then its Nadiyi is examined, nothing will be found on it. The arrow has been too fast to be smeared by dung and blood. The sign by which these people will be recognized will be a man whose one hand (or breast) will be like the breast of a woman (or like a moving piece of flesh). These people will appear when there will be differences among the people (Muslims). Abu Sa`id added: I testify that I heard this from the Prophet and also testify that `Ali killed those people while I was with him. The man with the description given by the Prophet was brought to `Ali. The following Verses were revealed in connection with that very person (i.e., `Abdullah bin Dhil-Khawaisira at-Tarnimi): 'And among them are men who accuse you (O Muhammad) in the matter of (the distribution of) the alms.' (9.58). (6933) ☐

***Khawarij:** There are many Muslims who are troubled by ISIS and their vicious rhetoric and vicious actions. But this is not the first time that a rebel group of Muslims have emerged with extremist tendencies. And as the saying goes, those who do not heed history are doomed to repeat it.

Prophet Muhammad, peace be upon him, warned his followers of a group of people who would arise after his death. The Prophet mentioned their arrival and characteristics no less than 10 times. Among the characteristics he mentioned were:

- They would worship so much that "you shall consider your worship and your prayer and your recitation of the Qur'an to be nothing compared to theirs." Meaning, their outward actions, like praying and reciting the Qur'an, would be on overdrive. And yet...

- "They shall recite the Qur'an but it will not leave their throats." Meaning that their understanding of the Qur'an will not go any farther than their recitation, and they will not have religious knowledge or insight.

- "They are calling to the book of Allah, but they have nothing to do with the book of Allah." Meaning their call is great, but their actions are terrible.

- "They are speaking the best speech that you will ever hear of any man. But they will leave Islam like an arrow leaves its prey."

Surely enough, less than 20 years after the death of The Prophet, this group came into being.

The Beginning of the Khawarij: During the time of the fourth Caliph, Ali, (who ruled from 656 – 661 CE) there was a political war between him and another man named Mu'awiyah. Both were Companions (*sahaba*) of Prophet Muhammad, peace be upon him. Ali was also the Prophet's son-in-law and cousin.

At one point, Ali and Mu'awiyah had ceased fighting and began a process of arbitration to bring about peace. Arbitrators were selected from the two sides to bring an end to hostilities, based on the Qur'an and *sunnah* (traditions of The Prophet). However, among these people was a group who believed that arbitration was a sin, based on their own understanding of the verse of the Qur'an which states:

The judgement (hukm) is Allah's alone, He relates the truth and He is the Best of deciders. Qur'an, 6: 57

The group accused Ali of sin and disbelief and told him to repent. He defended himself, and said of them:

"The sentence is right but what *(they think)* it means is wrong. It is true that law-giving (*hukm*, judgement) is God's alone, but these people say that governance is God's alone…In short, the law does not get put into practice all by itself; there must be someone, or some group, who tries to put it into practice."

The group was adamant that Ali had sinned. In short, they believed that if Ali was following the truth, he had to kill Mu'awiyah and all his men for their insurrection. And if he was not following the truth, then Mu'awiyah and his men should have killed him.

6000 of them split away from Ali's rule and formed their own tribe. They became known as the Kharijites, or Khawarij. The title comes from the Arabic word "khuruj", meaning "revolt" or "insurrection". This group was the first group to exhibit extremist tendencies and the first sect to split away from mainstream Islamic thought—even before the Sunni-Shia split.

Features of the Khawarij: Initially, Ali left the group alone. In his wisdom, he did not want to force people to reform their beliefs or overpower them. He told them that they could practice however they wished, so long as they did not spread corruption in the land.

However, the extreme, overzealous practices of the Khawarij are what drove them into constant conflict and bloodshed. They would kill anyone who did not believe in their extremist ideology. Some of the many features of the Kharawij were among the following:

- They would pray so much that their foreheads would become calloused and their hands rough

- They would be malnourished from fasting so much

- They considered anyone who had committed a major sin (ie drinking alcohol, fornication, backbiting) to be a disbeliever, and that they should be killed

- They believed only they were on the correct path and everyone else was a disbeliever and had to be killed

- They questioned the religious scholarship of notables like Ibn Abbas, Ibn Masud, Aishah—and even The Prophet himself

- They were narrow-minded and short-sighted

- They lacked any sort of religious knowledge or scholarship

- They acted without knowledge or insight into the consequences of their actions

- They saw the need to openly fight whoever they considered to be an unjust ruler

In short, much of the Khawarij belief stemmed from an overzealous sense of righteousness. Their intention was noble: they were concerned for the purity of the religion. However, their extremist tendencies were incompatible with the realities of life, and showed a disregard for the maxim of Islam that calls for mercy and peace first and foremost.

Decline of the Khawarij: Caliph Ali sent the scholar and Companion Ibn Abbas to the Khawarij camp to debate with them. Ibn Abbas noted that they were ceaseless in their worship to the point where their camp was buzzing with Qur'an recitation in the afternoon heat, and their shirts were reduced to tatters. He debated with them and, using his knowledge and wisdom, won the debate.

One of the points he mentioned was related to what caused their split in the first place—the issue of arbitration between people. Ibn Abbas mentioned that arbitration between people is mentioned as something acceptable in the Qur'an, and quoted the verse that discusses appointing an arbiter from a husband and wife if the two fall into disagreement (4:35).

2000 of the Khawarij agreed with Ibn Abbas's arguments and returned with him, reforming their ways. However, the remaining 4000 refused to acknowledge his logic and remained stubbornly ingrate.

The turning point was when a man named Abdullah ibn-Khabbab, one of the children of the Companions, passed by the Khawarij with his pregnant wife. The Khawarij captured him and his wife and questioned him on his beliefs. When they asked what his opinion was on Ali—whom they regarded as a disbeliever—Abdullah told them Ali was more knowledgeable than either of them, and was the Caliph.

With that, the Khawarij killed his wife in front of him, cut her open and killed the baby, then tied him up and slaughtered him like an animal.

Upon hearing this, Caliph Ali went to war with them. He fought them for many years in many battles until they were practically eradicated in the Battle of Nahrawan in 659 CE. Though the bulk of them were killed, a few stragglers dispersed and fled.

They were Muslims—and yet Prophet Muhammad, peace be upon them, called them "the worst of creation" and said they were "the dogs of Hell". He said if they were to rise up in his midst, he would kill them.

The trials and troubles they caused Muslims were so great that after the Khawarij had been defeated, one of the men in Ali's army said: "Praise be to God who gave us rest with the death of these people."

But Ali said in response: "No. There will be amongst the loins of people this ideology until you will find them that they will fight with *Ad-Dajjal* (the Anti-Christ)."

Modern Times

The Prophet, peace be upon him, said that this group would continue to come and go until near the Day of Judgement. He described the Khawarij of our times like so:

"There will come towards the end of time a group of people, young men, they have the most grandiose visions, they are speaking the best speech that you will ever hear of any man. But they will leave Islam like an arrow leaves its prey." (Muslim)

There are a few noteworthy things to take from that hadith:

- They will be young men. Meaning they will be comprised mainly of overzealous young men. You won't see the old and wise among their ranks.

- They will have the most grandiose visions. They will, as young men do, dream of changing the world and will be able to inspire others with their dreams—though their dreams will be incompatible with reality.

- They will be speaking the best speech. Meaning, as the Prophet said before, they will call to Islam and to the Book of God, but their actions will be outwardly evil.

2280. Narrated Sa`id bin Jubair: `Abdullah bin `Umar came to us and we hoped that he would narrate to us a good Hadith. But before we asked him, a man got up and said to him, "O Abu `Abdur-Rahman! Narrate to us about the battles during the time of the afflictions, as Allah says: -- 'And fight them until there is no more afflictions (i.e. no more worshipping of others besides Allah).'" (2.193) Ibn `Umar said (to the man), "Do you know what is meant by afflictions? Let your mother bereave you! Muhammad used to fight against the pagans, for a Muslim was put to trial in his religion (The pagans will either kill him or chain him as a captive). His fighting was not like your fighting which is carried on for the sake of ruling." (7095) ☐

2281. Narrated Muawiya: I heard the Prophet (ﷺ) saying, "A group of my followers will keep on following Allah's Laws strictly and they will not be harmed by those who will disbelieve them or stand against them till Allah's Order (The Hour) will come while they will be in that state." (7460) ☐

2282. Narrated Abu Huraira: The Prophet (ﷺ) said, "The people of Yemen have come to you and they are more gentle and soft-hearted. Belief is Yemenite and Wisdom is Yemenite, while pride and haughtiness are the qualities of the owners of camels (i.e.bedouins). Calmness and solemnity are the characters of the owners of sheep." (4388) ☐

2283. Narrated `Abdullah bin `Umar: I saw Allah's Messenger (ﷺ) pointing towards the east saying, "Lo! Afflictions will verily emerge hence; afflictions will verily emerge hence where the (side of the head of) Satan appears." (3279) ☐

2284. Narrated `Uqba bin `Umar and Abu Mas`ud: Allah's Messenger (ﷺ) pointed with his hand towards Yemen and said, "True Belief is Yemenite yonder (i.e. the Yemenite, had True Belief and embraced Islam readily), but sternness and mercilessness are the qualities of those who are busy with their camels and pay no attention to the Religion where the two sides of the head of Satan will appear. Such qualities belong to the tribe of Rabi`a and Mudar." (3302) ☐

2285. Narrated Abu Huraira: I heard Allah's Messenger (ﷺ) saying, "Pride and arrogance are characteristics of the rural bedouins while calmness is found among the owners of sheep. Belief is Yemenite, and wisdom is also Yemenite i.e. the Yemenites are well-known for their true belief and wisdom)." Abu `Abdullah (Al-Bukhari) said, "Yemen was called so because it is situated to the right of the Ka`ba, and Sham was called so because it is situated to the left of the Ka`ba." (3499) ☐

2286. Narrated Abu Masud: The Prophet (ﷺ) beckoned with his hand towards Yemen and said, "Belief is there." The harshness and mercilessness are the qualities of those farmers etc, who are busy with their camels and pay no attention to the religion (is towards the east) from where the side of the head of Satan will appear; those are the tribes of Rabi`a and Mudar. (4387) □

2287. Narrated Ibn `Umar: The Prophet (ﷺ) said, "O Allah! Bestow Your blessings on our Sham! O Allah! Bestow Your blessings on our Yemen." The People said, "And also on our Najd." He said, "O Allah! Bestow Your blessings on our Sham (north)! O Allah! Bestow Your blessings on our Yemen." The people said, "O Allah's Apostle! And also on our Najd." I think the third time the Prophet (ﷺ) said, "There (in Najd) is the place of earthquakes and afflictions and from there comes out the side of the head of Satan." (7094) □

*The region of Syria (Arabic: ٱلشَّام, Ash-Shām), known in modern literature as "Greater Syria" (سُوْرِيَة ٱلْكُبْرَىٰ, Sūrīyah al-Kubrā), "Syria-Palestine", or the Levant, is an area located east of the Mediterranean Sea.

* Nejd is a geographical central region of Saudi Arabia. Najd consists of the modern administrative regions of Riyadh, Al-Qassim, and Ha'il.

The hadith of Najd is confusing in itself because there have been many opinions on the exact location of Najd today. We find a number of views of the scholars themselves who greatly differed with each other on the location of Najd.

Al-Nawawi said: "Najd is the area that lies between Jursh (in Yemen) all the way to the rural outskirts of Kufa (in Iraq), and its Western border is the hijaz. The author of al-Matali said: Najd is all a province of Al Yamama. Al-Fayruzabadi said: "Its geographical summit is Tihama and Yemen, its bottom is Iraq and Sham, and it begins at Dhat Irqin [= Kufa] from the side of the Hijaz. Al-Khattabi said: "Najd lies Eastward, and to those who are in Madina. Their Najd is the desert of Iraq and its vicinities, which all lie east of the people of Madina. The original meaning of Najd is 'elevated land' opposed to ghawr which means declivity. Thus, Tihama is all part of al-Ghawr, and Mecca is part of Tihama. This is confirmed by lbn al Athir's definition: "Najd is any elevated terrain and it is a specific name for what lies outside the Hijaz and adjacent to Iraq. Similarly lbn Hajar stated: "Al Dawudi said: 'Najd lies in the vicinity of lraq." Iraq itself lexically means river-shore or sea shore, in reference to the Euphrates and the Tigris.

All these explanations prove that those who say that Najd in the hadith denotes present-day Iraq exclusively of present-day Najd'" are mistaken, as Najd at that time included not only Iraq but also as in our present time everything East of Medina, especially the regions South of Iraq.

2288. Narrated `Abdullah bin `Umar: I heard Allah's Messenger (s) on the pulpit saying, "Verily, afflictions (will start) from here," pointing towards the east, "where the side of the head of Satan comes out." (3511) ☐

Najd" is in east direction from the Prophets pulpit.

2289. Narrated Abu Huraira: Allah's Messenger (صلى الله عليه وسلم) said, "The Hour will not be established until you fight with the Jews, and the stone behind which a Jew will be hiding will say, "O Muslim! There is a Jew hiding behind me, so kill him." (2926) ☐

2290. Narrated Abu Sa`id: The Prophet (صلى الله عليه وسلم) said, "You will follow the wrong ways, of your predecessors so completely and literally that if they should go into the hole of a mastigure, you too will go there." We said, "O Allah's Messenger (صلى الله عليه وسلم)! Do you mean the Jews and the Christians?" He replied, "Whom else?" (Meaning, of course, the Jews and the Christians.) (3456) ☐

2291. Narrated Abu Huraira: The Prophet (صلى الله عليه وسلم) said, "The Hour will not be established till there is a war between two groups among whom there will be a great number of casualties, though the claims (or religion) of both of them will be one and the same. And the Hour will not be established till there appear about thirty liars, all of whom will be claiming to be the messengers of Allah." (3609) □

2292. Narrated Ibn `Umar: `Umar set out along with the Prophet (ﷺ) with a group of people to Ibn Saiyad till they saw him playing with the boys near the hillocks of Bani Mughala. Ibn Saiyad at that time was nearing his puberty and did not notice (us) until the Prophet (ﷺ) stroked him with his hand and said to him, "Do you testify that I am Allah's Messenger (ﷺ)?" Ibn Saiyad looked at him and said, "I testify that you are the Messenger of illiterates." Then Ibn Saiyad asked the Prophet (ﷺ), "Do you testify that I am Allah's Messenger (ﷺ)?" The Prophet (ﷺ) refuted it and said, "I believe in Allah and His Apostles." Then he said (to Ibn Saiyad), "What do you think?" Ibn Saiyad answered, "True people and liars visit me." The Prophet (ﷺ) said, "You have been confused as to this matter." Then the Prophet (ﷺ) said to him, "I have kept something (in my mind) for you, (can you tell me that?)" Ibn Saiyad said, "It is Al-Dukh (the smoke)." The Prophet (ﷺ) said, "Let you be in ignominy. You cannot cross your limits." On that `Umar, said, "O Allah's Messenger (ﷺ)! Allow me to chop his head off." The Prophet (ﷺ) said, "If he is he (i.e. Dajjal), then you cannot overpower him, and if he is not, then there is no use of murdering him." (Ibn `Umar added): Later on Allah's Messenger (ﷺ) once again went along with Ubai bin Ka`b to the date-palm trees (garden) where Ibn Saiyad was staying. The Prophet (ﷺ) wanted to hear something from Ibn Saiyad before Ibn Saiyad could see him, and the Prophet (ﷺ) saw him lying covered with a sheet and from where his murmurs were heard. Ibn Saiyad's mother saw Allah's Apostle while he was hiding himself behind the trunks of the date-palm trees. She addressed Ibn Saiyad, "O Saf! (and this was the name of Ibn Saiyad) Here is Muhammad." And with that Ibn Saiyad got up. The Prophet (ﷺ) said, "Had this woman left him (Had she not disturbed him), then Ibn Saiyad would have revealed the reality of his case. (1354) □

2293. Narrated Ibn `Umar: We were talking about Hajjat-ul-Wada`, while the Prophet (ﷺ) was amongst us. We did not know what Hajjat-ul-Wada` signified. The Prophet (ﷺ) praised Allah and then mentioned Al-Masih Ad-Dajjal and described him extensively, saying, "Allah did not send any prophet but that prophet warned his nation of Al-Masih Ad-Dajjal. Noah and the prophets following him warned (their people) of him. He will appear amongst you (O Muhammad's followers), and if it happens that some of his qualities may be hidden from you, but your Lord's State is clear to you and not hidden from you. The Prophet (ﷺ) said it thrice. Verily, your Lord is not blind in one eye, while he (i.e. Ad-Dajjal) is blind in the right eye which looks like a grape bulging out (of its cluster). No doubt! Allah has made your blood and your properties sacred to one another like the sanctity of this day of yours, in this town of yours, in this month of yours." The Prophet (ﷺ) added: No doubt! Haven't I conveyed Allah's Message to you?" They replied, "Yes," The Prophet (ﷺ) said thrice, "O Allah! Be witness for it." The Prophet (ﷺ) added, "Woe to you!" (or said), "May Allah be merciful to you! Do not become infidels after me (i.e. my death) by cutting the necks (throats) of one another." (4402) □

2294. Narrated Zainab bint Jahsh: The Prophet (ﷺ) got up from his sleep with a flushed red face and said, "None has the right to be worshipped but Allah. Woe to the Arabs, from the Great evil that is nearly approaching them. Today a gap has been made in the wall of Gog and Magog like this." (Sufyan illustrated by this forming the number 90 or 100 with his fingers.) It was asked, "Shall we be destroyed though there are righteous people among us?" The Prophet (ﷺ) said, "Yes, if evil increased." (7059) □

2295. Narrated Ibn `Umar: Allah's Messenger (ﷺ) said, "If Allah sends punishment upon a nation then it befalls upon the whole population indiscriminately and then they will be resurrected (and judged) according to their deeds." (7108) □

2296. Narrated Abu Huraira: The Prophet (ﷺ) said, "A hole has been opened in the dam of Gog and Magog." Wuhaib (the sub-narrator) made the number 90 (with his index finger and thumb). (7136) □

2297. Narrated Ibn `Umar: Once Allah's Messenger (ﷺ) stood amongst the people, glorified and praised Allah as He deserved and then mentioned the Dajjal saying, "I warn you against him (i.e. the Dajjal) and there was no prophet but warned his nation against him. No doubt, Noah warned his nation against him but I tell you about him something of which no prophet told his nation before me. You should know that he is one-eyed, and Allah is not one-eyed." (3337) ☐

2298. Narrated Abu Huraira: Allah's Messenger (ﷺ) said, "Shall I not tell you about the Dajjal a story of which no prophet told his nation? The Dajjall is one-eyed and will bring with him what will resemble Hell and Paradise, and what he will call Paradise will be actually Hell; so I warn you (against him) as Noah warned his nation against him." (3338) ☐

2299. Narrated Anas: The Prophet (ﷺ) said, "No prophet was sent but that he warned his followers against the one-eyed liar (Ad-Dajjal). Beware! He is blind in one eye, and your Lord is not so, and there will be written between his (Ad-Dajjal's) eyes (the word) Kafir (i.e., disbeliever)." (7131) ☐

2300. Narrated `Abdullah bin `Umar: Allah's Messenger (ﷺ) said. "While I was sleeping, I saw myself (in a dream) performing Tawaf around the Ka`ba. Behold, I saw a reddish-white man with lank hair, and water was dropping from his head. I asked, "Who is this?' They replied, 'The son of Mary.' Then I turned my face to see another man with a huge body, red complexion and curly hair and blind in one eye. His eye looked like a protruding out grape. They said (to me), He is Ad-Dajjal." The Prophet (ﷺ) added, "The man he resembled most is Ibn Qatan, a man from the tribe of Khuza`a. " (7128) ☐

2301. Narrated Mujahid: I was in the company of Ibn `Abbas and the people talked about Ad-Dajjal and said, "Ad-Dajjal will come with the word Kafir (non-believer) written in between his eyes." On that Ibn `Abbas said, "I have not heard this from the Prophet (ﷺ) but I heard him saying, 'As if I saw Moses just now entering the valley reciting Talbyia.'" (1555) ☐

2302. Narrated Ibn 'Umar (ra): The Prophet (ﷺ) said (about Ad-Dajjal) that he is one eyed, his right eye is as if a protruding out grape." (7123) ☐

2303. Narrated Rabi bin Hirash: `Uqba bin `Amr said to Hudhaifa, "Won't you relate to us of what you have heard from Allah's Apostle?" He said, "I heard him saying, "When Al-Dajjal appears, he will have fire and water along with him. What the people will consider as cold water, will be fire that will burn (things). So, if anyone of you comes across this, he should fall in the thing which will appear to him as fire, for in reality, it will be fresh cold water." (3450) ☐

2304. Narrated Hudhaifa: The Prophet (ﷺ) said about Ad-Dajjal that he would have water and fire with him: (what would seem to be) fire, would be cold water and (what would seem to be) water, would be fire. (7130) ☐

2305. Narrated Al-Mughira bin Shu`ba: Nobody asked the Prophet (ﷺ) as many questions as I asked regarding Ad-Dajjal. The Prophet (ﷺ) said to me, "What worries you about him?" I said, "Because the people say that he will have a mountain of bread and a river of water with him (i.e. he will have abundance of food and water)" The Prophet (ﷺ) said, "Nay, he is too mean to be allowed such a thing by Allah"' (but it is only to test mankind whether they believe in Allah or in Ad-Dajjal.) (7122) ☐

2306. Narrated Anas bin Malik: The Prophet (ﷺ) said, "Ad-Dajjal will come to Medina and find the angels guarding it. So Allah willing, neither Ad-Dajjal, nor plague will be able to come near it." (7134) ☐

2307. Narrated Abu Bakra: The Prophet (ﷺ) said, "The terror caused by Al-Masih Ad-Dajjal will not enter Medina and at that time Medina will have seven gates and there will be two angels at each gate (guarding them). (7125) ☐

2308. Narrated Abu Sa`id: One day Allah's Messenger (ﷺ) narrated to us a long narration about Ad-Dajjal and among the things he narrated to us, was: "Ad-Dajjal will come, and he will be forbidden to enter the mountain passes of Medina. He will encamp in one of the salt areas neighboring Medina and there will appear to him a man who will be the best or one of the best of the people. He will say 'I testify that you are Ad-Dajjal whose story Allah's Messenger (ﷺ) has told us.' Ad-Dajjal will say (to his audience), 'Look, if I kill this man and then give him life, will you have any doubt about my claim?' They will reply, 'No,' Then Ad- Dajjal will kill that man and then will make him alive. The man will say, 'By Allah, now I recognize you more than ever!' Ad-Dajjal will then try to kill him (again) but he will not be given the power to do so." (7132) ☐

2309. Narrated Anas bin Malik: The Prophet (ﷺ) said, "Ad-Dajjal will come and encamp at a place close to Medina and then Medina will shake thrice whereupon every Kafir and hypocrite will go out (of Medina) towards him." (7124) ☐

2310. Narrated Salim from his father: No, By Allah, the Prophet (ﷺ) did not tell that Jesus was of red complexion but said, "While I was asleep circumambulating the Ka`ba (in my dream), suddenly I saw a man of brown complexion and lank hair walking between two men, and water was dropping from his head. I asked, 'Who is this?' The people said, 'He is the son of Mary.' Then I looked behind and I saw a red-complexioned, fat, curly-haired man, blind in the right eye which looked like a bulging out grape. I asked, 'Who is this?' They replied, 'He is Ad-Dajjal.' The one who resembled to him among the people, was Ibn Qatar." (Az-Zuhri said, "He (i.e. Ibn Qatan) was a man from the tribe Khuza`a who died in the pre-lslamic period.") (3441) ☐

2311. Narrated Abu Huraira: Allah's Messenger (ﷺ) said, "By Him in Whose Hands my soul is, surely (Jesus,) the son of Mary will soon descend amongst you and will judge mankind justly (as a Just Ruler); he will break the Cross and kill the pigs and there will be no Jizya (i.e. taxation taken from non Muslims). Money will be in abundance so that nobody will accept it, and a single prostration to Allah (in prayer) will be better than the whole world and whatever is in it." Abu Huraira added "If you wish, you can recite (this verse of the Holy Book): -- 'And there is none Of the people of the Scriptures (Jews and Christians) But must believe in him (i.e Jesus as an Apostle of Allah and a human being) Before his death. And on the Day of Judgment He will be a witness Against them." (4.159) (3448) ☐

2312. Narrated Khabbab bin Al-Arat: We complained to Allah's Messenger (ﷺ) (of the persecution inflicted on us by the infidels) while he was sitting in the shade of the Ka`ba, leaning over his Burd (i.e. covering sheet). We said to him, "Would you seek help for us? Would you pray to Allah for us?" He said, "Among the nations before you a (believing) man would be put in a ditch that was dug for him, and a saw would be put over his head and he would be cut into two pieces; yet that (torture) would not make him give up his religion. His body would be combed with iron combs that would remove his flesh from the bones and nerves, yet that would not make him abandon his religion. By Allah, this religion (i.e. Islam) will prevail till a traveler from Sana (in Yemen) to Hadrarmaut will fear none but Allah, or a wolf as regards his sheep, but you (people) are hasty. (3612) □

2313. Narrated Khalid bin Madan: That 'Umair bin Al-Aswad Al-Anasi told him that he went to 'Ubada bin As-Samit while he was staying in his house at the seashore of Hims with (his wife) Um Haram. 'Umair said. Um Haram informed us that she heard the Prophet (ﷺ) saying, "Paradise is granted to the first batch of my followers who will undertake a naval expedition." Um Haram added, I said, 'O Allah's Messenger (ﷺ)! Will I be amongst them?' He replied, 'You are amongst them.' The Prophet (ﷺ) then said, 'the first army amongst' my followers who will invade Caesar's City will be forgiven their sins.' I asked, 'Will I be one of them, O Allah's Messenger (ﷺ)?' He replied in the negative." (2924) □

2314. Narrated Abu Huraira: I enjoyed the company of Allah's Messenger (ﷺ) for three years, and during the other years of my life, never was I so anxious to understand the (Prophet's) traditions as I was during those three years. I heard him saying, beckoning with his hand in this way, "Before the Hour you will fight with people who will have hairy shoes and live in Al-Bazir." (Sufyan, the sub-narrator once said, "And they are the people of Al-Bazir.") (3591) □

2315. Narrated Abu Huraira: Allah's Messenger (ﷺ) said, "There will be afflictions (and at the time) the sitting person will be better than the standing one, and the standing one will be better than the walking, and the walking will be better than the running. And whoever will look towards those afflictions, they will overtake him, and whoever will find a refuge or a shelter, should take refuge in it." The same narration is reported by Abu Bakr, with the addition, "(The Prophet (ﷺ) said), 'among the prayers there is a prayer the missing of which will be to one like losing one's family and property." (3601) □

2316. Narrated Ibn Mas`ud: The Prophet (ﷺ) said, "Soon others will be preferred to you, and there will be things which you will not like." The companions of the Prophet (ﷺ) asked, "O Allah's Messenger (ﷺ)! What do you order us to do (in this case)?" He said, "(I order you) to give the rights that are on you and to ask your rights from Allah. (3603) □

2317. Narrated Abu Huraira: Allah's Messenger (ﷺ) said, "This branch from Quraish will ruin the people." The companions of the Prophet (ﷺ) asked, "What do you order us to do (then)?" He said, "I would suggest that the people keep away from them." (3604) □

2318. Narrated `Ikrima: that Ibn `Abbas told him and `Ali bin `Abdullah to go to Abu Sa`id and listen to some of his narrations; So they both went (and saw) Abu Sa`id and his brother irrigating a garden belonging to them. When he saw them, he came up to them and sat down with his legs drawn up and wrapped in his garment and said, "(During the construction of the mosque of the Prophet) we carried the adobe of the mosque, one brick at a time while `Ammar used to carry two at a time. The Prophet (ﷺ) passed by `Ammar and removed the dust off his head and said, "May Allah be merciful to `Ammar. He will be killed by a rebellious aggressive group. `Ammar will invite them to (obey) Allah and they will invite him to the (Hell) fire." (2812) □

***"Say, [O Muhammad], 'I do not tell you that I have the depositories [containing the provision] of Allah nor that I know the unseen, nor do I tell you that I am an angel. I only follow what is revealed to me.'" [al-An'ām 6: 50]

Only God has full access to the forgotten past and unseen future. As for predicting specifics about the future while never erring, that is only possible for the Knower of the Unseen, and whoever He may grant partial access to the unseen world. "[He is] Knower of the unseen, and He does not disclose His [knowledge of the] unseen to anyone—except whom He has approved of messengers..." [al-Jinn 72: 26-27]

1. The Globalization of Islam: Amidst the fiercest persecution and abuse that the Muslims faced in the earliest Meccan period, the Prophet Muhammad (s) would stand without wavering and convey to his followers God's promise of Islam spreading all over the world. Tamīm ad-Dāri (ra) reports that the Messenger of Allah (s) said, "This matter will certainly reach every place touched by the night and day. Allah will not leave a house of mud or [even] fur except that Allah will cause this religion to enter it, by which the honorable will be honored and the disgraceful will be disgraced. Allah will honor the honorable with Islam and he will disgrace the disgraceful with unbelief." In another narration, reported by Thawbān (ra), "Indeed, Allah gathered up the earth for me so that I saw its east and its west; and indeed the dominion of my nation will reach what was gathered up for me from it." The fact that these predictions were made at a time when Muslims were a powerless handful, and Islam was expected to be buried in its cradle, is nothing short of miraculous. At that point, presuming that the faith would even survive would be considered by most nothing short of a pipe-dream. But to predict that Islam would not just survive, but grow to thrive globally, was at that point inconceivable. For us nowadays, witnessing a quarter of this planet's population as subscribers to Islam makes it clear that this was no presumption, but instead another prophecy inspired by the Divine.

2. Six in Sequence: During the Battle of Tabūk, the Prophet (s) said to ʿAwf b. Mālik (ra), "Count six signs before the Hour; my death, the conquest of Jerusalem, two mortal plagues that will take you [in great numbers] as the plague of sheep [depletes them], then wealth will be in such surplus that a man will be given a hundred gold coins and still be unsatisfied, then there will be a tribulation that will not leave an Arab home without entering it, then there will be a truce between you [Muslims] and Banu al-Aṣfar (Byzantines) which they will betray, and march against you under eighty flags, and under each flag will be twelve thousand [soldiers]." Jerusalem was

conquered five years after his death (s), in the year 15H, followed by the plague of 'Amwās in 18H which took the lives of many Companions. An unprecedented surplus of wealth was then experienced during the caliphate of 'Uthmān (ra), 23H, as a result of conquests on every front. As for the tribulation that would spare no Arab home, this took place following the assassination of 'Uthmān, 37H, for it resulted in dissent and chaos everywhere. As for the truce and scourge of the Byzantines, traditional scholars seem to agree that this is a prophecy about the end-times.

3. Counting the Conquests: The Prophet Muhammad (s) foretold a multitude of Muslim conquests, including those of Rome, Persia, Egypt, Yemen, India, and Constantinople. None of these prophecies were described vaguely or with equivocation, but rather with an air of absolute certainty.

Jābir b. 'Abdillāh (ra) reports that while digging the trench outside Madinah to repel an approaching army, a massive boulder obstructed them that no ax would break. With time running out, and with people's fears and hunger eating away at them, the Prophet (s) walked over and picked up the ax. He said, "Bismillah (In God's name)," and hammered the boulder, reducing a chunk of it to rubble. He said, "Allāhu Akbar (God is Great)! I have been given the keys to Shām; I can see its red palaces at this very moment." Then he shattered another chunk and said, "Allāhu Akbar (God is Great)! I have been given the keys to Persia; I can see Madain's white palace." Then he shattered the last chunk and said, "Allāhu Akbar (God is Great)! I have been given the keys to Yemen. By Allah, I can see the Gates of Sana'a at this very moment from here."

Regarding Egypt, he (s) took its conquest for granted, knowing his Lord's promise was true. Abu Dharr (ra) narrated: The Prophet (s) said: "You will certainly conquer Egypt; a land in which [a currency] called al-qīrāṭ is customary. When you conquer it, be gracious to its people, for they are entitled to a covenant and [the right of] family bonds. And when you see two men disputing over the place of a brick, then leave [Egypt]." The Prophet (s) accurately spoke in the second person here, foretelling that none other than his personal Companions would conquer Egypt. Then he (s) instructed them to honor their peace treaty with the Egyptians and reminded them that their grandmother (Hājar; the mother of Ishmael) was from this land. In this same narration, Abu Dharr (ra) adds, "I witnessed 'Abdur-Raḥmān b. Shuraḥbīl b. Ḥasana and his brother, Rabī'a, disputing [in Egypt] over the place of a brick, so I left."

Regarding Constantinople, which is presently called Istanbul, the Prophet (s) determined that it would become a Muslim land nearly a millennium prior to that happening. 'Abdullāh b. 'Amr (ra) reports that they were once sitting with the Messenger of Allah (s) and writing, he (s) was asked, "Which city will be liberated first; Constantinople or Rome?" He said, "Indeed, the city of Heraclius will be liberated first," meaning Constantinople. An entire 800 years later, the Ottoman sultan, Muhammad al-Fātiḥ, accomplished this great feat. In another hadith, "Constantinople will certainly be liberated, and how excellent a leader will its leader be, and how excellent an army that army will be." Some scholars hold that this second hadith may refer to a second liberation of Constantinople which was also prophesied, but has not yet taken place.

4. Security will Prevail: 'Adi b. Ḥatim (ra) narrates: As I was with the Prophet (s) [prior to accepting Islam], a man came to him complaining of poverty, and then another came to him complaining of highway robbery. He (s) said, "O 'Adi, have you seen al-Ḥira (in Iraq)?" I said, "No, but I have been told about it." He said, "If you live long [enough], you will see a woman travel on camelback from al-Ḥira till she circles the Ka'ba while not fearing anyone but Allah." I said to myself, "Where then would the bandits of Tay' who have pillaged these lands be?" He (s) continued, "And if you live long [enough], the treasures of Chosroes, the son of Hurmuz, will be conquered." I said, "Chosroes, the son of Hurmuz?" He confirmed, "Chosroes, the son of Hurmuz. And if you live long [enough], you will see a man walking out, hand filled with gold or silver, seeking someone to accept it but he will not find anyone to accept it." Later in his life, 'Adi said, "I have [in fact] seen a woman travel on camelback from al-Ḥira till she circled the Ka'ba while not fearing anyone but Allah, and I was among those

who conquered the treasures of Chosroes, the son of Hurmuz. And if you live long [enough], you will see what the Prophet (s)—Abul Qāsim—said regarding a man walking out, hand filled…" Historians confirm that the inability to find someone eligible to accept charity took place during the reign of the Umayyad caliph, ʿUmar b. ʿAbdilʿAzīz (d. 91H).

5. The Last Emperors: When the Quraysh tribe embraced Islam, they feared being blocked from their trade routes to Greater Syria (Shām) and Iraq as a result, since these territories were under Byzantine and Sassanid rule and both had rejected the call to Islam. Jābir b. Samura (ra) reports the Prophet (s) addressing this concern by reassuring Quraysh that those empires would soon vanish from both regions. He said, "When Chosroes dies, there will be no Chosroes after him. And when Caesar dies, there will be no Caesar after him. And I swear by the One in whose hand is Muhammad's soul, their treasures will be spent in the path of God." Imam ash-Shāfiʿi (d. 820) and al-Khaṭṭābi (d. 988) explained that this meant there would never be another Caesar in Greater Syria, nor any other Chosroes in Iraq (Sassanid Persia). Indeed, the final Chosroes who rose to power during the Prophet's (s) life was Yazdegerd III (d. 651), and he, in fact, became the 38th and final king of the Sassanid Empire. The final Caesar during the Prophet's (s) life was Heraclius (d. 641), and Byzantium did in fact collapse and lose Christendom's holiest site of Jerusalem during his reign. After those individuals, neither empire maintained any presence in those two regions.

6. Inevitable Infighting: Saʿd b. Abi Waqqāṣ (ra) narrates that the Messenger of Allah (s) once visited the mosque of Banu Muʿâwiya. "He (s) entered, performed two units of prayer, which we prayed with him, and then he invoked his Lord for a long time. Then, he (s) turned to us and said, 'I asked my Lord for three things; He granted me two and withheld one. I asked my Lord not to destroy my nation with a widespread famine, and He granted me that, and I asked Him that He not exterminate my nation by drowning, and He granted me that. And I asked Him that He not let their aggression be against one another, but He withheld that from me.'" In another

narration, "Indeed, Allah has gathered the earth for me until I saw its east and its west, and the kingdom of my nation will reach whatever has been gathered for me of it. And I have been given the two treasures; the red and white (gold and silver). And I asked my Lord that He not destroy it with a widespread famine, and that He not empower against them an external enemy that will annihilate them. My Lord said, 'O Muhammad, when I decree a matter, it cannot be repelled. I have granted you, for your nation, that I not destroy them with a widespread famine, and that I not empower against them an external enemy that annihilates them—even if those from its (the earth's) every corner unite against them, but they will ultimately kill one another, and enslave one another. Once the sword is drawn within my nation, it will not be removed from them until the Day of Resurrection.'"

7. Tensions Among The Prophet's Household: Abu Rafiʿ (ra) reported that the Prophet (s) said to ʿAli, "There will be an issue between you and ʿAisha." He said, "Me, O Messenger of Allah?!" He said, "Yes." He said, "Me?!" He said, "Yes." He said, "Then [in that case] I would be the worst of them (all people)." He said, "No, but when this occurs, return her to her safe quarters." Just prior to her clash with ʿAli (ra), when ʿAisha (ra) heard dogs barking near Basra at a place called Haw'ab, she said, "Perhaps I must return home, for the Messenger of Allah (s) said to us (his wives), 'Which one of you will be barked at by the dogs of Haw'ab?'" Hopeful that her presence would effect a resolution, and that this was only a prophecy and not a prohibition, ʿAisha (ra) decided not to abort her journey.

8. The Fate of ʿAmmār: Abu Saʿīd al-Khudri (ra) narrated that, as the Muslims were building the mosque in Madinah, ʿAmmār b. Yāsir (ra) would carry two bricks at a time while others lifted one. When the Prophet (s) saw him, he began removing the dust [from ʿAmmār] with his hands and said, "Woe to ʿAmmār! He will be killed by the transgressing party; he will be inviting them to Paradise and they will be inviting him to the Fire." To that, ʿAmmār replied, "We seek refuge with Allah from the trials." When the Battle of Ṣiffīn took place, three decades after that prophecy, ʿAmmār was killed by the army of Shām who transgressed against the Muslim ruler

('Ali) while seeking to avenge the murdered caliph ('Uthmān). Interestingly, the army of Shām did not claim that this hadith had been fabricated (which proves that forging hadith was unfathomable by the Companions), but rather argued that those who called him to fight were the "transgressing party" ultimately responsible for his death. Thus, there was no question about the authenticity of the prophecy; they differed only in how to interpret it.

Finally, moments before the Battle of Ṣiffīn, as a glass of milk was passed to 'Ammār (ra), he smiled and said, "The Prophet (s) told me that the last thing I would drink before dying would be some milk." Then he rose to meet the promise of his Prophet (s) and fought until his death.

9. Repairing the Rift: Abu Bakra ath-Thaqafi (ra) narrated that the Prophet Muhammad (s) brought his grandson, al-Ḥasan (ra), out one day and ascended with him to the pulpit. Then, he (s) said, "This son of mine is a chief, and perhaps Allah will use him to reconcile between two [disputing] factions of Muslims." In truth, al-Ḥasan singlehandedly mended a long and tragic split between the Muslims of Kūfa and those of Shām upon becoming caliph, by abdicating his caliphate to Mu'āwiya b. Abi Sufyān (ra). By doing so, he unified two great factions of believers and allowed the progress of Islam to regain its momentum for decades. The Prophet (s) also foretold that at this precise point the Muslim nation would transition from a caliphate to a kingdom; "The caliphate will be for thirty years, then there will be a kingship after that." Abu Bakr ruled for approximately two years, then 'Umar for ten, then 'Uthmān for twelve, then 'Ali for five, before al-Ḥasan within months abdicated it to Mu'āwiya who founded the Omayyad dynasty. Ibn al-'Arabi (d. 1148) says, "And the promise of the Truthful (s) came to pass... [the period of the caliphate] neither exceeded nor fell short a day, so glory be to the All-Encompassing; there is no other Lord but He."

10. Cycling Back to Virtue is promised: In an explicit hadith about the forms of governance the Muslim nation would experience, Ḥudhayfa b. al-Yamān (ra) reported that the Prophet (s) said, "Prophethood will remain amongst you for as long as Allah

wishes. Then Allah will remove it whenever He wishes to remove it, and there will be a caliphate upon the prophetic methodology. It will last for as long as Allah wishes it to last, then Allah will remove it whenever He wishes to remove it. Then there will be an abiding dynasty, and it will remain for as long as Allah wishes it to remain. Then Allah will remove it whenever He wishes to remove it. Then there will be tyrannical (forceful) kingship, and it will remain for as long as Allah wishes it to remain. Then He will remove it whenever He wishes to remove it, and then there will be a caliphate upon the prophetic methodology."

11. Asmā' Sends a Tyrant Home: For confronting the tyranny of al-Ḥajjāj b. Yūsuf, 'Abdullāh b. az-Zubayr (ra) was crucified in front of the Sacred House in Mecca, and his body was thrown into the graveyard of the Jews. Then al-Ḥajjāj marched to his mother's house, 'Asmā' b. Abi Bakr (ra), the Prophet's (s) sister-in-law. He said to her, "What do you think of what I have just done to the enemy of Allah?" referring to her son, 'Abdullāh b. az-Zubayr. Though al-Ḥajjāj was trying to strike fear in her heart, lest a person of her position inspire more rebellion, this was a woman strengthened by a prophecy she had heard directly from the Prophet's (s) lips. Her response was, "I think you have destroyed his worldly life by destroying your own afterlife… The Messenger of Allah (s) has certainly told us that emerging from Thaqīf would be a liar and a murderer; the liar we have seen, and as far as the murderer is concerned, I have no doubt that you are him." Without saying a single word, al-Ḥajjāj rose and exited in disgrace. Hadith commentators agree that the liar from Thaqīf was al-Mukhtār b. Abi 'Ubayd, who claimed prophethood.

12. Um Ḥarām's Date with Destiny: Um Ḥarām b. Malḥān (ra) heard the Messenger of Allah (s) say, "The first army from my nation to ride the sea have guaranteed themselves [Paradise]." Um Ḥarām said, "O Messenger of Allah, will I be among them?" He said, "You will be among them." Later, he (s) said, "The first army from my nation to march in battle to the City of Caesar (Constantinople) will be forgiven." She said, "Will I be among them, O Messenger of Allah?" He said, "No." During the reign of Mu'āwiya (ra), Um Ḥarām b. Malḥān rode in the first Muslim naval fleet,

accompanying her husband, and died upon falling off her mount in enemy lands. Imam aṭ-Ṭabarāni and others report that the whereabouts of her gravesite on Cyprus Island were known. Ibn Ḥajar said, "This contains multiple prophecies by the Prophet (s) of what would take place, and it all occurred just as he said, and hence is considered among the signs of his prophethood. Of them is that his nation would remain after him, and that among them are those who would be strong, formidable, and a consequential force against the enemy, and that they would conquer territories until the army rides the sea, and that Um Ḥarām would live until that time, and that she would be with that army who rides the sea, and that she would not live to see the second military campaign [to Constantinople]."

13. An Unforgettable Sermon: Ḥudhayfa b. al-Yamān (ra) and ʿAmr b. Akhṭab (ra) report that the Prophet (s) once delivered a sermon, from dawn until sunset, in which he mentioned all the [major] things that would take place between then and the Day of Resurrection. Ḥudhayfa (ra) says that he sometimes forgot parts of it, until he saw those events unfold before his very eyes.

14. The Emergence of Selective Textualism: Miqdām b. Maʿd Karib (ra) reports that the Prophet (s) said, "Indeed, I have been given the Qurʾan and something similar to it along with it. But soon there will be a time when a man will be reclining on his couch with a full stomach, and he will say, 'You should adhere to this Qurʾan; what you find that it says is permissible, take it as permissible, and what you find it says is forbidden, take it as forbidden.' But indeed, whatever the Messenger of Allah forbids is like what Allah forbids." To this day, there continue to arise different groups of people who attempt to delegitimize the Sunnah (prophetic tradition) in order to escape the definitive interpretations it provides of the Qurʾan.

15. A Horrific Wildfire: Abu Hurayra (ra) narrates that the Prophet Muhammad (s) said, "The Hour will not take place until a fire emerges from the lands of Ḥijāz (central Arabia) that illuminates the necks of camels in Busra (Syria)." As numerous scholars—such as Ibn Ḥajar, Ibn Kathīr, and an-Nawawi—confirm, this enormous fire erupted in the city of Madinah on Friday, 5th of Jumāda Thāni, 654H, and lasted

for an entire month. The great historian, Abu Shāma, experienced it firsthand and documented much of its details, including its visibility from hundreds of miles away, and how the Madinans sought refuge in the Prophet's Mosque and collectively repented from the vices they had been engaging in. Historical records seem to indicate that this was a volcanic eruption, and the lava fields around Madinah remain observable until today.

16. Prosperity and Hedonism before the End-Times: Abu Hurayra (ra) reports that the Messenger of Allah (s) said, "The Hour will not commence before wealth becomes abundant and overflowing, to the point that a man brings out the Zakāt (charity due) on his wealth and cannot find anyone to accept it from him, and to the point that Arabia's lands become meadows and rivers." While acknowledging earlier manifestations of this prophecy about unprecedented affluence, current lifestyles in today's "first world" illustrate that they live in greater luxury than 99.9% of recorded human history. Even those financially struggling enjoy recliners at home that are cozier than any ancient king's royal throne, climate controls in every room, and access to modes of transport that have turned an excruciating month-long journey into a few entertaining hours. Perhaps even more intriguing is the Prophet (s) mentioning the agricultural transformation of Arabia in the same context as the surplus of wealth. Fourteen centuries ago, the extensive irrigation methods just invented through modern technology were downright inconceivable. In fact, we are the very first generations privileged to witness this geological phenomena (see: NASA Sees Fields of Green Spring up in Saudi Arabia).

Regarding how material prosperity will be a sign of the end-times, the Prophet Muhammad (s) said, "And if you see the barefoot, naked, shepherds of camels competing [for praise] in the construction of high-rise buildings, then this is from among the signs [of the Hour]." In a similar hadith about this egotism infesting the mosque atmosphere, he (s) said, "The Hour will not commence before people boast of their mosques." Ibn 'Abbās (ra), the narrator, added, "You will ornament your mosques just as the Jews and Christians did with their temples." This intense competition will involve exploitation of others, and thus we find parallel prophecies of hedonism and exploitation in the prophetic tradition as well. In the hadith of Miswar b. Makhrama (ra): "By Allah I do not fear poverty overtaking you, but I fear that you will have abundant wealth at your disposal as it became at the disposal of the nations before you, causing you to compete in it as they competed in it, and then it destroys you as it destroyed them."

17. The Unavoidability of Ribā (Interest): Prophet Muhammad (s) also foretold that ribā (interest/usury), which is one of the most unethical and exploitative transactions, would become inescapable. Abu Hurayra (ra) reports that the Messenger of Allah (s) said, "A time will come over the people when they will consume ribā." They asked him, "All of them?" He said, "Whoever does not consume it will [still] be reached by its dust." Whether for purchasing a property or vehicle, or simply for developing credit in today's world, interest-bearing clauses have permeated every dimension of contemporary financial dealings.

18. An Increase in Brutality and Killing: When people's greed causes them to see people's wealth as violable, seeing their lives that way is simply the next step on that continuum. Thus, the Prophet (s) said, "Beware of oppression, for oppression will result in darknesses on the Day of Judgment. And beware of greed, for greed is what destroyed those before you; it drove them to spill each other's blood, and violate each other's sanctities." The past century has seen atrocities in modern warfare, cycles of genocide, abusive policing, and senseless violence at large that are incomparable anywhere in human history and all traceable to selfish interests.

Abu Hurayra (ra) narrates that the Messenger of Allah (s) said, "By the One in whose hand is my soul, this world will not end until a day comes over the people where the killer has no idea why he killed, nor the killed why he was killed." It was said, "How will that be?" He said, "Chaos." In another hadith, "The Hour will not commence until knowledge is removed, earthquakes become frequent, time narrows, turmoil surfaces, and anarchy increases— namely killing, [lots of] killing." Again, the 21st century has been the bloodiest in human history. Even without the recent and ongoing nightmares of Bosnia, Iraq, Chechnya, Afghanistan, Kashmir, Palestine, Syria, and Burma; World War I alone claimed the lives of 65 million people, and World War II another 72 million. As for time passing rapidly, how often do people complain nowadays of time "flying" between gadgets and devices engineered to distract? As for knowledge becoming scarce, one can ask themselves what the average Muslim knows about their religion, and what kind of clarity the democratization of knowledge on the internet has offered.

19. The Plunge into Immorality: Abu Hurayra (ra) narrates that the Prophet (s) foretold that there will emerge in the future "women who are clothed yet naked, walking with an enticing gait, with something on their heads that looks like the humps of camels, leaning to one side. They will never enter Paradise or even smell its fragrance, although its fragrance can be detected from such and such a distance." Is it not remarkable how the Prophet did not only describe "provocative dress," but even predicted women's hairstyles?

The Prophet (s) also stated that even Muslim communities would participate in some of these trends; "There will be in the end of my nation men who ride chariots who are [in reality] pseudo-men; they will drop off their women, at the gates of the mosques, who are clothed [and yet] naked. Upon their heads will be the likes of a lean camel's hump."

'Abdullâh b. 'Umar (ra) narrated that the Messenger of Allah (s) also predicted the consequences of a hypersexualized popular culture; "And fornication never becomes prevalent among a people, to the degree that they practice it openly, except that epidemics become rampant among them which had never before existed in their ancestors." The link between sexual permissiveness and sexually transmitted diseases is not something any sensible person in our times can deny. Perhaps the unhinged pursuit of sexual gratification without liability is behind this next prophecy as well; "A woman will [one day] be taken and have her stomach cut open, then what is inside her womb will be taken and discarded, out of fear of having children." According to an extensive survey published in Guttmacher Institute Journal, the "fear of dramatic life changes" is by far the most common reason for abortions today, with more than half of those surveyed citing single motherhood as the reason for that fear.

Finally, 'Abdullah b. 'Amr (ra) narrates that the Prophet (s) said, "The Hour will not commence until people mate in the streets just as donkeys mate." I asked, "Will that really happen?" He said, "Yes, it most certainly will happen." Though this was stated as one of the last signs before the Day of Judgment, following major apocalyptic events, many of our modern cultures are clearly moving towards that degree of shamelessness, if not experiencing it already.

20. Muslims Becoming Easy Prey: The Prophet (s) also prophesied that carnal pursuits would not only infect his nation but would be the cause of their downfall and devastation. Thawbān (ra) reports that the Prophet (s) said, "The nations will soon invite one another to devour you, just as diners are invited to a dish." It was said, "Will it be because of our small number on that day?" He said, "No, rather you will be many on that day, but you will be [weightless] foam, like the foam on the river. And Allah will remove the fear of you from the hearts of your enemies, and will cast weakness into your hearts." Someone said, "O Messenger of Allah, what will this weakness be?" He said, "The love of this world, and the hatred of death."

Reinforcing this point, Anas (ra) narrates that the Prophet (s) said, "Once my nation considers five things permissible, then destruction will befall them: when cursing one another appears, wine is drunk, silk is worn [by men], musical instruments are played, and men suffice themselves with men and women suffice themselves with women." Certainly, Muslims today are not insulated from the ideologies demanding the acceptance of same-sex acts in the world around them. This is even imaginable for a practicing, mosque-goer Muslim, if they allow their religiosity to be reduced to a cultural identity, as the Prophet (s) said in a hadith narrated by 'Abdullah b. 'Amr (ra), "An age will surely come when people gather and pray in the mosques, while there is not a single believer amongst them."

21. The Immortality of This Ummah: In a multitude of reports, the Prophet (s)

declared, "There will never cease to be a group from my nation victorious upon the truth, unharmed by those who will oppose them, until Allah's decree comes to pass while they are like that." Despite the corruption and moral degradation, true believers will endure, even if their challenge is tantamount to holding onto a burning coal. They will be people who value their faith over their lives, and hence the Prophet (s) further described them by saying, "The Hour will not commence until a man passes by the grave of his brother and says, 'I wish I were in his place.'" Ibn Baṭṭāl (d. 1057) explains that this will not be due to any suicidal ideations, but rather an anxiety that the prevalent evils and the strength of their adversaries may cost them their religion.

22. Never Thought You Would Speak: Abu Sa'īd al-Khudri (ra) reports that the Prophet (s) said, "By the One in whose hand is my soul, the Hour will not commence until predators speak to people, and until the tip of a man's whip and the straps on his sandals speak to him, and his thigh informs him of what occurred with his family after he left." One can only assume how difficult these statements were for a seventh-century desert dweller to process, but the astronomical strides in electricity and electronics since then have now delivered us to these developments. In TIME's Best Inventions of 2002, a Japanese toy-maker is showcased for creating a dog translator; a device on its collar that interprets its yelps, growls, and whines into phrases such as "I can't stand it", "how boring", and "I am lonely." In November of 2006, the New York Times published an article entitled "These Shoes Are Made for Talking," hailing in a new age of futuristic sports training. In January of 2010, a security camera app was released which transformed the smart-phones on our hips and in our pockets into windows into our homes. Perhaps these are what the Prophet (s) intended, or perhaps other phenomena which we have yet to experience.

91. LEADERSHIP

2320. NARRATED `AISHA (RA): When Abu Bakr As-Siddiq was chosen Caliph, he said, "My people know that my profession was not incapable of providing substance to my family. And as I will be busy serving the Muslim nation, my family will eat from the National Treasury of Muslims, and I will practice the profession of serving the Muslims." (2070) ☐

2321. Narrated Ibn `Abbas: I used to teach (the Qur'an to) some people of the Muhajirln (emigrants), among whom there was `Abdur Rahman bin `Auf. While I was in his house at Mina, and he was with `Umar bin Al-Khattab during `Umar's last Hajj, `Abdur-Rahman came to me and said, "Would that you had seen the man who came today to the Chief of the Believers (`Umar), saying, 'O Chief of the Believers! What do you think about so-and-so who says, 'If `Umar should die, I will give the pledge of allegiance to such-andsuch person, as by Allah, the pledge of allegiance to Abu Bakr was nothing but a prompt sudden action which got established afterwards.' `Umar became angry and then said, 'Allah willing, I will stand before the people tonight and warn them against those people who want to deprive the others of their rights (the question of rulership). `Abdur-Rahman said, "I said, 'O Chief of the believers! Do not do that, for the season of Hajj gathers the riff-raff and the rubble, and it will be they who will gather around you when you stand to address the people. And I am afraid that you will get up and say something, and some people will spread your statement and may not say what you have actually said and may not understand its meaning, and may interpret it incorrectly, so you should wait till you reach Medina, as it is the place of emigration and the place of Prophet's Traditions, and there you can come in touch with the learned and noble people, and tell them your ideas with confidence; and the learned people will understand your statement and put it in its proper place.' On that, `Umar said, 'By Allah! Allah willing, I will do this in the first speech I will deliver before the people in Medina." Ibn `Abbas added: We reached Medina by the end of the month of Dhul-Hijja, and when it was Friday, we went quickly (to the mosque) as soon as the sun had declined, and I saw Sa`id bin Zaid bin `Amr bin Nufail sitting at the corner of the pulpit, and I too sat close to him so that my knee was touching his knee, and after a short while `Umar bin Al-Khattab came out, and when I saw him coming towards us, I said to Sa`id bin Zaid bin `Amr bin Nufail "Today `Umar will say such a thing as he has never said since he was chosen as Caliph." Sa`id denied my statement with astonishment and said, "What thing do you expect `Umar to say the like of which he has never said before?" In the meantime, `Umar sat on the pulpit and when the callmakers for the prayer had finished their call, `Umar stood up, and having glorified and praised Allah as He deserved, he said, "Now then, I am going to tell you something which (Allah) has written for me to say. I do not know; perhaps it portends my death, so whoever understands and remembers it, must narrate it to the others wherever his mount takes him, but if somebody is afraid that he does not understand it, then it is unlawful for him to tell lies about me. Allah sent Muhammad with the Truth and revealed the Holy Book to him, and among what Allah revealed, was the Verse of the Rajam (the stoning of married person (male & female) who commits illegal sexual intercourse, and we did recite this Verse and understood and memorized it. Allah's Messenger (ﷺ) did carry out the punishment of stoning and so did we after him. I am afraid that after a long time has passed, somebody will say, 'By Allah, we do not find the Verse of the Rajam in Allah's Book,' and thus they will go astray by leaving an obligation which Allah has revealed. And the punishment of the Rajam is to be inflicted to any married person (male & female), who commits illegal sexual intercourse, if the required evidence is available or there is conception or confession. And then we used to recite among the Verses in Allah's Book: 'O people! Do not claim to be the offspring of other than your fathers, as it is disbelief (unthankfulness) on your part that you claim to be the offspring of other than your real father.' Then Allah's Messenger (ﷺ) said, 'Do not praise me excessively as Jesus, son of Marry was praised, but call me Allah's Slave and His Apostles.' (O people!) I have been informed that a speaker amongst you says, 'By Allah, if `Umar should die, I will give the pledge of allegiance to such-and-such person.' One should not deceive oneself by saying that the pledge of allegiance given to Abu Bakr was given suddenly and it was successful. No doubt, it was like that, but Allah saved (the people) from its evil, and there is none among you who has the qualities of Abu Bakr. Remember that whoever gives the pledge of allegiance to anybody among you without consulting the other Muslims, neither that person, nor the person to whom the pledge of allegiance was given, are to be supported, lest they both should be killed. And no doubt after the death of the Prophet (ﷺ) we were informed that the Ansar disagreed with us and gathered in the shed of Bani Sa`da. `Ali and Zubair and whoever was with them, opposed us, while the emigrants gathered with Abu Bakr. I said to Abu Bakr, 'Let's go to these Ansari brothers of ours.' So we set out seeking them, and when we approached them, two pious men of theirs met us and informed us of the final decision of the Ansar, and said, 'O group of Muhajirin (emigrants)! Where are you going?' We replied, 'We are going to these Ansari brothers of ours.' They said to us, 'You shouldn't go near them. Carry out whatever we have already decided.' I said, 'By Allah, we will go to them.' And so we proceeded until we reached them at the shed of Bani Sa`da. Behold! There was a man sitting amongst them and wrapped in something. I asked, 'Who is that man?' They said, 'He is Sa`d bin 'Ubada.' I asked, 'What is wrong with him?' They said, 'He is sick.' After we sat for a while, the Ansar's speaker said, 'None has the right to be worshipped but Allah,' and praising Allah as He deserved, he added, 'To proceed, we are Allah's Ansar (helpers) and the majority of the Muslim army, while you, the emigrants, are a small group and some people among you came with the intention of preventing us from practicing this matter (of caliphate) and depriving us of it.' When the speaker had finished, I intended to speak as I had prepared a speech which I liked and which I wanted to deliver in the presence of Abu Bakr, and I used to avoid provoking him. So, when I wanted to speak, Abu Bakr said, 'Wait a while.' I disliked to make him angry. So Abu Bakr himself gave a speech, and he was wiser and more patient than I. By Allah, he never missed a sentence that I liked in my own prepared speech, but he said the like of it or better than it spontaneously. After a pause he said, 'O Ansar! You deserve all (the qualities that you have attributed to yourselves, but this question (of Caliphate) is only for the Quraish as they are the best of the Arabs as regards descent and home, and I am pleased to suggest that you choose either of these two men, so take the oath of allegiance to either of them as you wish. And then Abu Bakr held my hand and Abu Ubaida bin al-Jarrah's hand who was sitting amongst us. I hated nothing of what he had said except that proposal, for by Allah, I would rather have my neck chopped off as expiator for a sin than become the ruler of a nation, one of whose members is Abu

Bakr, unless at the time of my death my own-self suggests something I don't feel at present.' And then one of the Ansar said, 'I am the pillar on which the camel with a skin disease (eczema) rubs itself to satisfy the itching (i.e., I am a noble), and I am as a high class palm tree! O Quraish. There should be one ruler from us and one from you.' Then there was a hue and cry among the gathering and their voices rose so that I was afraid there might be great disagreement, so I said, 'O Abu Bakr! Hold your hand out.' He held his hand out and I pledged allegiance to him, and then all the emigrants gave the Pledge of allegiance and so did the Ansar afterwards. And so we became victorious over Sa`d bin Ubada (whom Al-Ansar wanted to make a ruler). One of the Ansar said, 'You have killed Sa`d bin Ubada.' I replied, 'Allah has killed Sa`d bin Ubada.' `Umar added, "By Allah, apart from the great tragedy that had happened to us (i.e. the death of the Prophet), there was no greater problem than the allegiance pledged to Abu Bakr because we were afraid that if we left the people, they might give the Pledge of allegiance after us to one of their men, in which case we would have given them our consent for something against our real wish, or would have opposed them and caused great trouble. So if any person gives the Pledge of allegiance to somebody without consulting the other Muslims, then the one he has selected should not be granted allegiance, lest both of them should be killed." (6830) □

2322. Narrated Abu Huraira: The Prophet (ﷺ) said, "The tribe of Quraish has precedence over the people in this connection (i.e the right of ruling). The Muslims follow the Muslims amongst them, and the infidels follow the infidels amongst them. People are of different natures: The best amongst them in the pre-lslamic period are the best in Islam provided they comprehend the religious knowledge. You will find that the best amongst the people in this respect (of ruling) is he who hates it (the idea of ruling) most, till he is given the pledge of allegiance."(3496)□

2323. Narrated Ibn `Umar: The 'Prophet said, "It is obligatory for one to listen to and obey (the ruler's orders) unless these orders involve one disobedience (to Allah); but if an act of disobedience (to Allah) is imposed, he should not listen to or obey it."

(2955) ☐

2324. Narrated Abu Huraira: That heard Allah's Messenger (ﷺ) saying, "We are the last but will be the foremost to enter Paradise." The Prophet added, "He who obeys me, obeys Allah, and he who disobeys me, disobeys Allah. He who obeys the chief, obeys me, and he who disobeys the chief, disobeys me. The Imam is like a shelter for whose safety the Muslims should fight and where they should seek protection. If the Imam orders people with righteousness and rules justly, then he will be rewarded for that, and if he does the opposite, he will be responsible for that." (2957) ☐

2325. Narrated Ibn `Abbas: The Prophet (ﷺ) said, "Whoever disapproves of something done by his ruler then he should be patient, for whoever disobeys the ruler even a little (little = a span) will die as those who died in the Pre-lslamic Period of Ignorance. (i.e. as rebellious Sinners). (7053) ☐

2326. Narrated Junada bin Abi Umaiya: We entered upon 'Ubada bin As-Samit while he was sick. We said, "May Allah make you healthy. Will you tell us a Hadith you heard from the Prophet (ﷺ) and by which Allah may make you benefit?" He said, "The Prophet (ﷺ) called us and we gave him the Pledge of allegiance for Islam, and among the conditions on which he took the Pledge from us, was that we were to listen and obey (the orders) both at the time when we were active and at the time when we were tired, and at our difficult time and at our ease and to be obedient to the ruler and give him his right even if he did not give us our right, and not to fight against him unless we noticed him having open Kufr (disbelief) for which we would have a proof with us from Allah." (7056) ☐

2327. Narrated Az-Zubair bin `Adi: We went to Anas bin Malik and complained about the wrong we were suffering at the hand of Al- Hajjaj. Anas bin Malik said, "Be patient till you meet your Lord, for no time will come upon you but the time following it will be worse than it. I heard that from the Prophet." (7068) ☐

2328. Narrated Abu Bakra: During the battle of Al-Jamal, Allah benefited me with a Word (I heard from the Prophet). When the Prophet heard the news that the people of the Persia had made the daughter of Khosrau their Queen (ruler), he said, "Never will succeed such a nation as makes a woman their ruler." (7099) ☐

2329. Narrated Anas bin Malik: Allah's Messenger (ﷺ) said, "You should listen to and obey, your ruler even if he was an Ethiopian (black) slave whose head looks like a raisin." (7142) ☐

2330. Narrated `Ali: The Prophet (ﷺ) sent an army unit and appointed a man from the Ansar as its commander and ordered them (the soldiers) to obey him. (During the campaign) he became angry with them and said, "Didn't the Prophet (ﷺ) order you to obey me?" They said, "Yes." He said, "I order you to collect wood and make a fire and then throw yourselves into it." So they collected wood and made a fire, but when they were about to throw themselves into it, they started looking at each other, and some of them said, "We followed the Prophet (ﷺ) to escape from the fire. How should we enter it now?" So while they were in that state, the fire extinguished and their commander's anger abated. The event was mentioned to the Prophet (ﷺ) and he said, "If they had entered it (the fire) they would never have come out of it, for obedience is required only in what is good." (7145) ☐

2331. Narrated `Abdur-Rahman bin Samura: The Prophet (ﷺ) said, "O `Abdur-Rahman! Do not seek to be a ruler, for if you are given authority on your demand then you will be held responsible for it, but if you are given it without asking (for it), then you will be helped (by Allah) in it. If you ever take an oath to do something and later on you find that something else is better, then you should expiate your oath and do what is better." (7146) ☐

2332. Narrated Abu Huraira: The Prophet (ﷺ) said, "You people will be keen to have the authority of ruling which will be a thing of regret for you on the Day of Resurrection. What an excellent wet nurse it is, yet what a bad weaning one it is!" (7148) ☐

2333. Narrated Abu Musa: Two men from my tribe and I entered upon the Prophet. One of the two men said to the Prophet, "O Allah's Messenger (ﷺ)! Appoint me as a governor," and so did the second. The Prophet (ﷺ) said, "We do not assign the authority of ruling to those who ask for it, nor to those who are keen to have it." (7149) ☐

2334. Narrated Ma'qil: I heard the Prophet (ﷺ) saying, "Any man whom Allah has given the authority of ruling some people and he does not look after them in an honest manner, will never feel even the smell of Paradise." (7150) ☐

2335. Narrated Ma'qil: Allah's Messenger (ﷺ) said, "If any ruler having the authority to rule Muslim subjects dies while he is deceiving them, Allah will forbid Paradise for him." (7151) ☐

2336. Narrated Tarif Abi Tamima: I saw Safwan and Jundab and Safwan's companions when Jundab was advising. They said, "Did you hear something from Allah's Messenger (ﷺ)?" Jundab said, "I heard him saying, 'Whoever does a good deed in order to show off, Allah will expose his intentions on the Day of Resurrection (before the people), and whoever puts the people into difficulties, Allah will put him into difficulties on the Day of Resurrection.'" The people said (to Jundab), "Advise us." He said, "The first thing of the human body to purify is the `Abdomen, so he who can eat nothing but good food (Halal and earned lawfully) should do so, and he who does as much as he can that nothing intervene between him and Paradise by not shedding even a handful of blood, (i.e. murdering) should do so." (7152) ☐

2337. Narrated 'Abdullah bin As-Sa'di: That when he went to 'Umar during his Caliphate. 'Umar said to him, "Haven't I been told that you do certain jobs for the people but when you are given payment you refuse to take it?" 'Abdullah added: I said, "Yes." 'Umar said, "Why do you do so?" I said, "I have horses and slaves and I am living in prosperity and I wish that my payment should be kept as a charitable gift for the Muslims." 'Umar said, "Do not do so, for I intended to do the same as you do. Allah's Messenger (ﷺ)'s used to give me gifts and I used to say to him, 'Give it to a needier one than me.' Once he gave me some money and I said, 'Give it to a needier person than me,' whereupon the Prophet (ﷺ) said, 'Take it and keep it in your possession and then give it in charity. Take what ever comes to you of this money if you are not keen to have it and not asking for it; otherwise (i.e., if it does not come to you) do not seek to have it yourself.'" (7163) ☐

2338. Narrated Muhammad bin Zaid bin `Abdullah bin `Umar: Some people said to Ibn `Umar, "When we enter upon our ruler we say in their praise what is contrary to what we say when we leave them." Ibn `Umar said, "We used to consider this as hypocrisy." (7178) ☐

2339. Narrated Abu Huraira: Allah's Messenger (ﷺ)'s said, "The worst of all mankind is the double-faced one, who comes to some people with one face and to others, with another face." (7179) ☐

2340. Narrated `Abdullah: The Prophet (ﷺ) said, "If somebody on the demand of a judge takes an oath to grab (a Muslim's) property and he is liar in it, he will meet Allah Who will be angry with him". So Allah revealed: -- 'Verily! those who purchase a small gain at the cost of Allah's Covenant and their oaths..' (3.77) 'Al- Ashath came while `Abdullah was narrating (this) to the people. Al-Ashath said, "This verse was revealed regarding me and another man with whom I had a quarrel about a well. The Prophet (ﷺ) said (to me), "Do you have any evidence?' I replied, 'No.' He said, 'Let your opponent take an oath.' I said: I am sure he would take a (false) oath." Thereupon it was revealed: 'Verily! those who purchase a small gain at the cost of Allah's Covenant....' (7183) ☐

2341. Narrated Bishr: The Prophet (ﷺ) was reclining (leaning) and then he sat up saying, "And I warn you against giving a false statement." And he kept on saying that warning so much so that we said, "Would that he had stopped." (6274) ☐

2342. Narrated Abu Huraira: The Prophet (ﷺ) said, "Allah said, 'I will be an opponer to three types of people on the Day of Resurrection: -1. One who makes a covenant in My Name, but proves treacherous; -2. One who sells a free person and eats his price; and -3. One who employs a laborer and takes full work from him but does not pay him for his labour.'" (2270) ☐

2343. Kharija bin Zaid bin Thabit said that Zaid bin Thabit said, "The Prophet (ﷺ) ordered me to learn the writing of the Jews. I even wrote letters for the Prophet (ﷺ) (to the Jews) and also read their letters when they wrote to him."

And 'Umar said in the presence of 'Ali, 'Abdur-Rahman, and 'Uthman, "What is this woman saying?" (The woman was non-Arab) 'Abdur-Rahman bin Hatib said:"She is informing you about her companion who has committed illegal sexual intercourse with her."

Abu Jamra said, "I was an interpreter between Ibn 'Abbas and the people." Some people said, "A ruler should have two interpreters." (7195) □

2344. Narrated Abu Sa`id Al-Khudri: The Prophet (ﷺ) said, "Allah never sends a prophet or gives the Caliphate to a Caliph but that he has two groups of advisors: A group advising him to do good and exhorts him to do it, and the other group advising him to do evil and exhorts him to do it. But the protected person (against such evil advisors) is the one protected by Allah.'" (7198) □

2345. Narrated 'Ubada bin As-Samit: We gave the oath of allegiance to Allah's Messenger (ﷺ) that we would listen to and obey him both at the time when we were active and at the time when we were tired and that we would not fight against the ruler or disobey him, and would stand firm for the truth or say the truth wherever we might be, and in the Way of Allah we would not be afraid of the blame of the blamers. (7199) □

2346. Narrated Jabir bin `Abdullah: I gave the Pledge of allegiance to the Prophet (ﷺ) that I would listen and obey, and he told me to add: 'As much as I can, and will give good advice to every Muslim.' (7204) □

2347. Narrated Al-Miswar bin Makhrama: The group of people whom `Umar had selected as candidates for the Caliphate gathered and consulted each other. `Abdur-Rahman said to them, "I am not going to compete with you in this matter, but if you wish, I would select for you a caliph from among you." So all of them agreed to let

`Abdur-Rahman decide the case. So when the candidates placed the case in the hands of `Abdur-Rahman, the people went towards him and nobody followed the rest of the group nor obeyed any after him. So the people followed `Abdur-Rahman and consulted him all those nights till there came the night we gave the oath of allegiance to `Uthman. Al-Miswar (bin Makhrama) added: `Abdur-Rahman called on me after a portion of the night had passed and knocked on my door till I got up, and he said to me, "I see you have been sleeping! By Allah, during the last three nights I have not slept enough. Go and call Az-Zubair and Sa`d.' So I called them for him and he consulted them and then called me saying, 'Call `Ali for me." I called `Ali and he held a private talk with him till very late at night, and then 'Ali, got up to leave having had much hope (to be chosen as a Caliph) but `Abdur-Rahman was afraid of something concerning `Ali. `Abdur-Rahman then said to me, "Call `Uthman for me." I called him and he kept on speaking to him privately till the Mu'adh-dhin put an end to their talk by announcing the Adhan for the Fajr prayer. When the people finished their morning prayer and that (six men) group gathered near the pulpit, `Abdur-Rahman sent for all the Muhajirin (emigrants) and the Ansar present there and sent for the army chief who had performed the Hajj with `Umar that year. When all of them had gathered, `Abdur- Rahman said, "None has the right to be worshipped but Allah," and added, "Now then, O `Ali, I have looked at the people's tendencies and noticed that they do not consider anybody equal to `Uthman, so you should not incur blame (by disagreeing)." Then `Abdur-Rahman said (to `Uthman), "I gave the oath of allegiance to you on condition that you will follow Allah's Laws and the traditions of Allah's Apostle and the traditions of the two Caliphs after him." So `Abdur-Rahman gave the oath of allegiance to him, and so did the people including the Muhajirin (emigrants) and the Ansar and the chiefs of the army staff and all the Muslims. (7207) □

2348. Narrated `Abdullah bin `Umar: It was said to `Umar, "Will you appoint your successor?" `Umar said, "If I appoint a Caliph (as my successor) it is true that somebody who was better than I (i.e., Abu Bakr) did so, and if I leave the matter undecided, it is true that somebody who was better than I (i.e., Allah's Messenger

(🕊)) did so." On this, the people praised him. `Umar said, "People are of two kinds: Either one who is keen to take over the Caliphate or one who is afraid of assuming such a responsibility. I wish I could be free from its responsibility in that I would receive neither reward nor retribution I won't bear the burden of the caliphate in my death as I do in my life." (7218) □

2349. Narrated Anas bin Malik: That he heard `Umar's second speech he delivered when he sat on the pulpit on the day following the death of the Prophet (🕊) `Umar recited the Tashahhud while Abu Bakr was silent. `Umar said, "I wish that Allah's Messenger (🕊) had outlived all of us, i.e., had been the last (to die). But if Muhammad is dead, Allah nevertheless has kept the light amongst you from which you can receive the same guidance as Allah guided Muhammad with that. And Abu Bakr is the companion of Allah's Messenger (🕊) He is the second of the two in the cave. He is the most entitled person among the Muslims to manage your affairs. Therefore get up and swear allegiance to him." Some people had already taken the oath of allegiance to him in the shed of Bani Sa`ida but the oath of allegiance taken by the public was taken at the pulpit. I heard `Umar saying to Abu Bakr on that day. "Please ascend the pulpit," and kept on urging him till he ascended the pulpit whereupon, all the people swore allegiance to him. (7219) □

2350. Narrated Jabir bin Samura: I heard the Prophet (🕊) saying, "There will be twelve Muslim rulers." He then said a sentence which I did not hear. My father said, "All of them (those rulers) will be from Quraish." (7222) □

2351. Narrated Abu Huraira: The Prophet (🕊) said, "The Israelis used to be ruled and guided by prophets: Whenever a prophet died, another would take over his place. There will be no prophet after me, but there will be Caliphs who will increase in number." The people asked, "O Allah's Messenger (🕊)! What do you order us (to do)?" He said, "Obey the one who will be given the pledge of allegiance first. Fulfil their (i.e. the Caliphs) rights, for Allah will ask them about (any shortcoming) in ruling those Allah has put under their guardianship." (3455) □

92. WISHES

2352. NARRATED ABU HURAIRA (RA): The Prophet (ﷺ) said, "If I had gold equal to the mountain of Uhud, I would love that, before three days had passed, not a single Dinar thereof remained with me if I found somebody to accept it excluding some amount that I would keep for the payment of my debts." (7228) □

2353. Narrated Abu Huraira: Allah's Messenger (ﷺ) said, "Not to wish to be the like except of two men. A man whom Allah has given the (knowledge of the) Qur'an and he recites it during the hours of night and day and the one who wishes says: If I were given the same as this (man) has been given, I would do what he does, and a man whom Allah has given wealth and he spends it in the just and right way, in which case the one who wishes says, 'If I were given the same as he has been given, I would do what he does.'" (7232) □

2354. Narrated `Abdullah bin Abi `Aufa: Allah's Messenger (ﷺ) said, "Do not long for meeting your enemy, and ask Allah for safety (from all evil)." (7237) □

2355. Narrated `Abdullah: Today a man came to me and asked me a question which I did not know how to answer. He said, "Tell me, if a wealthy active man, well-equipped with arms, goes out on military expeditions with our chiefs, and orders us to do such things as we cannot do (should we obey him?)" I replied, "By Allah, I do not know what to reply you, except that we, were in the company of the Prophet (ﷺ) and he used to order us to do a thing once only till we finished it. And no doubt, everyone among you will remain in a good state as long as he obeys Allah. If one is in doubt as to the legality of something, he should ask somebody who would satisfy him, but soon will come a time when you will not find such a man. By Him, except Whom none has the right to be worshipped. I see that the example of what has passed of this life (to what remains thereof) is like a pond whose fresh water has been used up and nothing remains but muddy water." (2964)

93. ACCEPTING INFORMATION GIVEN BY A TRUTHFUL PERSON

2356. NARRATED `ABDULLAH (RA): The Prophet (ﷺ) led us in Zuhr prayer and prayer five rak`at. Somebody asked him whether the prayer had been increased." He (the Prophet (ﷺ)) said, "And what is that?" They (the people) replied, "You have prayed five rak`at." Then the Prophet (ﷺ) offered two prostrations (of Sahu) after he had finished his prayer with the Taslim. (7249) □

2357. Narrated `Abdullah bin `Umar: While the people were at Quba offering the morning prayer, suddenly a person came to them saying, "Tonight Divine Inspiration has been revealed to Allah's Messenger (ﷺ) and he has been ordered to face the Ka`ba (in prayers): therefore you people should face it." There faces were towards Sham, so they turned their faces towards the Ka`ba (at Mecca). (7251) □

2358. Narrated Hudhaifa: The Prophet (ﷺ) said to the people of Najran, "I will send to you an honest person who is really trustworthy." The Companion, of the Prophet (ﷺ) each desired to be that person, but the Prophet (ﷺ) sent Abu 'Ubaida. (7254) □

94. HOLDING FAST TO THE QUR'AN AND SUNNAH

2359. NARRATED ANAS BIN MALIK (RA): That he heard `Umar speaking while standing on the pulpit of the Prophet (ﷺ) in the morning (following the death of the Prophet), when the people had sworn allegiance to Abu Bakr. He said the Tashah-hud before Abu Bakr, and said, "Amma Ba'du (then after) Allah has chosen for his Apostle what is with Him (Paradise) rather than what is with you (the world). This is that Book (Qur'an) with which Allah guided your Apostle, so stick to it, for then you will be guided on the right path as Allah guided His Apostle with it." (7269) ☐

2360. Narrated Abal Minhal: Abu Barza said, "(O people!) Allah makes you self-sufficient or has raised you high with Islam and with Muhammad."). (7271) ☐

2361. Narrated `Abdullah: The best talk (speech) is Allah's Book 'Qur'an), and the best way is the way of Muhammad, and the worst matters are the heresies (those new things which are introduced into the religion); and whatever you have been promised will surely come to pass, and you cannot escape (it). (7277) ☐

2362. Narrated Abu Huraira and Zaid bin Khalid: We were with the Prophet (ﷺ) when he said (to two men), "I shall judge between you according to Allah's Book (Laws)." (7278) ☐

2363. Narrated Abu Huraira: Allah's Messenger (ﷺ) said, "All my followers will enter Paradise except those who refuse." They said, "O Allah's Messenger (ﷺ)! Who will refuse?" He said, "Whoever obeys me will enter Paradise, and whoever disobeys me is the one who refuses (to enter it)." (7280) ☐

2364. Narrated Jabir bin `Abdullah: Some angels came to the Prophet (ﷺ) while he was sleeping. Some of them said, "He is sleeping." Others said, "His eyes are sleeping but his heart is awake." Then they said, "There is an example for this companion of yours." One of them said, "Then set forth an example for him." Some of them said, "He is sleeping." The others said, "His eyes are sleeping but his heart is awake." Then they said, "His example is that of a man who has built a house and then offered therein a banquet and sent an inviter (messenger) to invite the people. So whoever accepted the invitation of the inviter, entered the house and ate of the banquet, and whoever did not accept the invitation of the inviter, did not enter the house, nor did he eat of the banquet." Then the angels said, "Interpret this example to him so that he may understand it." Some of them said, "He is sleeping." The others said, "His eyes are sleeping but his heart is awake." And then they said, "The houses stands for Paradise and the call maker is Muhammad; and whoever obeys Muhammad, obeys Allah; and whoever disobeys Muhammad, disobeys Allah. Muhammad separated the people (i.e., through his message, the good is distinguished from the bad, and the believers from the disbelievers). (7281) □

2365. Narrated Hammam: Hudhaifa said, "O the Group of Al-Qurra! Follow the straight path, for then you have taken a great lead (and will be the leaders), but if you divert right or left, then you will go astray far away." (7282) □

2366. Narrated Abu Musa: The Prophet (ﷺ) said, "My example and the example of what I have been sent with is that of a man who came to some people and said, 'O people! I have seen the enemy's army with my own eyes, and I am the naked warner; so protect yourselves!' Then a group of his people obeyed him and fled at night proceeding stealthily till they were safe, while another group of them disbelieved him and stayed at their places till morning when the army came upon them, and killed and ruined them completely So this is the example of that person who obeys me and follows what I have brought (the Qur'an and the Sunna), and the example of the one who disobeys me and disbelieves the truth I have brought." (7283) □

2367. Narrated Abu Huraira: The Prophet (ﷺ) said, "Leave me as I leave you, for the people who were before you were ruined because of their questions and their differences over their prophets. So, if I forbid you to do something, then keep away from it. And if I order you to do something, then do of it as much as you can." (7288) □

2368. Narrated Sa`d bin Abi Waqqas: The Prophet (ﷺ) said, "The most sinful person among the Muslims is the one who asked about something which had not been prohibited, but was prohibited because of his asking." (7289) □

2369. Narrated Anas: We were with `Umar and he said, "We have been forbidden to undertake a difficult task beyond our capability (i.e. to exceed the religious limits e.g., to clean the inside of the eyes while doing ablution). (7293) □

2370. Narrated Ibn `Umar: The Prophet (ﷺ) wore a gold ring and then the people followed him and wore gold rings too. Then the Prophet said, "I had this golden ring made for myself. He then threw it away and said, "I shall never put it on." Thereupon the people also threw their rings away. (7298) □

2371. Narrated Abu Huraira: The Prophet (ﷺ) said (to his companions), "Do not fast Al-Wisal (continuous fasting for two days)." They said, "But you fast Al-Wisail." He said, "I am not like you, for at night my Lord feeds me and makes me drink." But the people did not give up Al-Wisal, so the Prophet (ﷺ) fasted Al-Wisal with them for two days or two nights, and then they saw the crescent whereupon the Prophet (ﷺ) said, "If the crescent had delayed, I would have continued fasting (because of you)," as if he wanted to vanquish them completely (because they had refused to give up Al Wisal). (7299) □

2372. Narrated `Aisha: The Prophet (ﷺ) did something as it was allowed from the religious point of view but some people refrained from it. When the Prophet (ﷺ) heard of that, he, after glorifying and praising Allah, said, "Why do some people refrain from doing something which I do? By Allah, I know Allah more than they." (7301) □

2373. Narrated Al-A`mash: I asked Abu Wail, "Did you witness the battle of Siffin between `Ali and Muawiya?" He said, "Yes," and added, "Then I heard Sahl bin Hunaif saying, 'O people! Blame your personal opinions in your religion. No doubt, I remember myself on the day of Abi Jandal; if I had the power to refuse the order of Allah's Messenger (ﷺ), I would have refused it. We have never put our swords on our shoulders to get involved in a situation that might have been horrible for us, but those swords brought us to victory and peace, except this present situation.'" Abu Wail said, "I witnessed the battle of Siffin, and how nasty Siffin was!" (7308) □

2374. Narrated Jabir bin `Abdullah: When the (following) Verse was revealed to Allah's Messenger (ﷺ): 'Say: He has power to send torment on you from above,'... (6.65) he said, "O Allah! I seek refuge with Your Face (from that punishment)." And when this was revealed: '...or from beneath your feet.' (6.65) he said, "O Allah! I seek refuge with Your Face (from that)." And when this Verse was revealed: '...or to cover you with confusion in partystrife, and make you to taste the violence of one another,'... (6.65) he said: "These two warnings are easier (than the previous ones). (7313) ☐

2375. Narrated Abu Sa`id Al-Khudri: The Prophet (ﷺ) said, "You will follow the ways of those nations who were before you, span by span and cubit by cubit (i.e., inch by inch) so much so that even if they entered a hole of a mastigure (a lizard), you would follow them." We said, "O Allah's Messenger (ﷺ)! (Do you mean) the Jews and the Christians?" He said, "Whom else?" (7320) ☐

2376. Narrated `Ali bin Abi Talib: That Allah's Messenger (ﷺ) came to him and Fatima the daughter of Allah's Messenger (ﷺ) at their house at night and said, "Won't you pray?" `Ali replied, "O Allah's Messenger (ﷺ)! Our souls are in the Hands of Allah and when he wants us to get up, He makes us get up." When `Ali said that to him, Allah's Messenger (ﷺ) left without saying anything to him. While the Prophet (ﷺ) was leaving, `Ali heard him striking his thigh (with his hand) and saying, "But man is quarrelsome more than anything else." (18.54) (7347) ☐

2377. Narrated `Amr bin Al-`As: That he heard Allah's Messenger (ﷺ) saying, "If a judge gives a verdict according to the best of his knowledge and his verdict is correct (i.e. agrees with Allah and His Apostle's verdict) he will receive a double reward, and if he gives a verdict according to the best of his knowledge and his verdict is wrong, (i.e. against that of Allah and His Apostle) even then he will get a reward." (7352) ☐

2378. Narrated Jundab bin `Abdullah: Allah's Messenger (ﷺ) said, "Recite (and study) the Qur'an as long as you are in agreement as to its interpretation and meanings, but when you have differences regarding its interpretation and meanings, then you should stop reciting it (for the time being.) (7364) ☐

95. Oneness, Uniqueness of Allah

2379. NARRATED MU`ADH BIN JABAL (RA): The Prophet (ﷺ) said, "O Mu`adh! Do you know what Allah's Right upon His slaves is?" I said, "Allah and His Apostle know best." The Prophet (ﷺ) said, "To worship Him (Allah) Alone and to join none in worship with Him (Allah). Do you know what their right upon Him is?" I replied, "Allah and His Apostle know best." The Prophet (ﷺ) said, "Not to punish them (if they do so). (7373) ☐

2380. Narrated `Aisha: The Prophet (ﷺ) sent (an army unit) under the command of a man who used to lead his companions in the prayers and would finish his recitation with (the Sura 112): 'Say (O Muhammad): "He is Allah, the One."' (112.1) When they returned (from the battle), they mentioned that to the Prophet. He said (to them), "Ask him why he does so." They asked him and he said, "I do so because it mentions the qualities of the Beneficent and I love to recite it (in my prayer)." The Prophet; said (to them), "Tell him that Allah loves him." (7375) ☐

2381. Narrated Abu Musa Al-Ash`ari: The Prophet (ﷺ) said, "None is more patient than Allah against the harmful and annoying words He hears (from the people): They ascribe children to Him, yet He bestows upon them health and provision. (7378) ☐

2382. Narrated Masruq: `Aisha said, "If anyone tells you that Muhammad has seen his Lord, he is a liar, for Allah says: 'No vision can grasp Him.' (6.103) And if anyone tells you that Muhammad has seen the Unseen, he is a liar, for Allah says: "None has the knowledge of the Unseen but Allah." (7380) ☐

2383. Narrated Abu Huraira: The Prophet (ﷺ) said, "On the Day of Resurrection Allah will hold the whole earth and fold the heaven with His right hand and say, 'I am the King: where are the kings of the earth?'" (7382) ☐

2384. Narrated Ibn `Abbas: The Prophet (ﷺ) used to say, "I seek refuge (with YOU) by Your 'Izzat, None has the right to be worshipped but You Who does not die while the Jinns and the human beings die." (7383) □

2385. Narrated Abu Huraira: The Prophet (ﷺ) said, "Allah says: 'I am just as My slave thinks I am, (i.e. I am able to do for him what he thinks I can do for him) and I am with him if He remembers Me. If he remembers Me in himself, I too, remember him in Myself; and if he remembers Me in a group of people, I remember him in a group that is better than they; and if he comes one span nearer to Me, I go one cubit nearer to him; and if he comes one cubit nearer to Me, I go a distance of two outstretched arms nearer to him; and if he comes to Me walking, I go to him running.'" (7405) □

2386. Narrated Abu Huraira: Allah's Messenger (ﷺ) said, "Allah's Hand is full, and (its fullness) is not affected by the continuous spending, day and night." He also said, "Do you see what He has spent since He created the Heavens and the Earth? Yet all that has not decreased what is in His Hand." He also said, "His Throne is over the water and in His other Hand is the balance (of Justice) and He raises and lowers (whomever He will)." (7411) □

2387. Narrated `Abdullah: A Jew came to the Prophet (ﷺ) and said, "O Muhammad! Allah will hold the heavens on a Finger, and the mountains on a Finger, and the trees on a Finger, and all the creation on a Finger, and then He will say, 'I am the King.'" On that Allah's Messenger (ﷺ) smiled till his premolar teeth became visible, and then recited: "They have not appraised Allah with true appraisal, while the earth entirely will be [within] His grip on the Day of Resurrection, and the heavens will be folded in His right hand. Exalted is He and high above what they associate with Him." (39.67) `Abdullah added: Allah's Apostle smiled (at the Jew's statement) expressing his wonder and belief in what was said. (7414) □

2388. Narrated Al-Mughira: Sa`d bin 'Ubada said, "If I saw a man with my wife, I would strike him (behead him) with the blade of my sword." This news reached Allah's Messenger (ﷺ) who then said, "You people are astonished at Sa`d's Ghira. By Allah, I have more Ghira than he, and Allah has more Ghira than I, and because of

Allah's Ghira, He has made unlawful Shameful deeds and sins (illegal sexual intercourse etc.) done in open and in secret. And there is none who likes that the people should repent to Him and beg His pardon than Allah, and for this reason He sent the warners and the givers of good news. And there is none who likes to be praised more than Allah does, and for this reason, Allah promised to grant Paradise (to the doers of good)." `Abdul Malik said, "No person has more Ghira than Allah." (7416) □

2389. Narrated Abu Huraira: The Prophet (ﷺ) said, "When Allah had finished His creation, He wrote over his Throne: 'My Mercy preceded My Anger.' (7422) □

2390. Narrated Ibn `Abbas: The Prophet (ﷺ) used to say at the time of difficulty,

لَا إِلَهَ إِلَّا اللَّهُ الْعَظِيمُ الْحَلِيمُ، لَا إِلَهَ إِلَّا اللَّهُ رَبُّ الْعَرْشِ الْعَظِيمِ، لَا إِلَهَ إِلَّا اللَّهُ رَبُّ السَّمَوَاتِ وَرَبُّ الْأَرْضِ رَبُّ الْعَرْشِ الْكَرِيمِ".

'La ilaha il-lallah Al-`Alimul-Halim. La-ilaha illallah Rabul- Arsh-al-Azim, La ilaha-il-lallah Rabus-Samawati Rab-ul-Ard; wa Rab-ul-Arsh Al- Karim.' (None has the right to be worshipped but Allah, the Majestic, the Most Forbearing. None has the right to be worshipped but Allah, the Lord of the Tremendous Throne. None has the right to be worshipped but Allah, the Lord of the Heavens and the Lord of the Honourable Throne.) (7426) □

2391. Narrated 'Ata' bin Yazid Al-Laithi: On the authority of Abu Huraira: The people said, "O Allah's Messenger (ﷺ)! Shall we see our Lord on the Day of Resurrection?" The Prophet (ﷺ) said, "Do you have any difficulty in seeing the moon on a full moon night?" They said, "No, O Allah's Messenger (ﷺ)." He said, "Do you have any difficulty in seeing the sun when there are no clouds?" They said, "No, O Allah's Messenger (ﷺ)." He said, "So you will see Him, like that. Allah will gather all the people on the Day of Resurrection, and say, 'whoever worshipped something (in the world) should follow (that thing),' so, whoever worshipped the sun will follow the sun, and whoever worshiped the moon will follow the moon, and whoever used to worship certain (other false) deities, he will follow those deities. And there will remain only this nation with its good people (or its hypocrites). (The sub-narrator, Ibrahim is in doubt.) Allah will come to them and say, 'I am your Lord.' They will (deny Him and) say, 'We will stay here till our Lord comes, for when our Lord comes, we will recognize Him.' So Allah will come to them in His appearance which they know, and will say, 'I am your Lord.' They will say, 'You are our Lord,' so they will follow Him.

Then a bridge will be laid across Hell (Fire)' I and my followers will be the first ones to go across it and none will speak on that Day except the Apostles. And the invocation of the Apostles on that Day will be, 'O Allah, save! Save!' In Hell (or over The Bridge) there will be hooks like the thorns of As-Sa'dan (thorny plant). Have you seen As-Sa'dan?" They replied, "Yes, O Allah's Messenger (ﷺ)!" He said, "So those hooks look like the thorns of As-Sa'dan, but none knows how big they are except Allah. Those hooks will snap the people away according to their deeds. Some of the people will stay in Hell (be destroyed) because of their (evil) deeds, and some will be cut or torn by the hooks (and fall into Hell) and some will be punished and then relieved. When Allah has finished His Judgments among the people, He will take whomever He will out of Hell through His Mercy. He will then order the angels to take out of the Fire all those who used to worship none but Allah from among those whom Allah wanted to be merciful to and those who testified (in the world) that none has the right to be worshipped but Allah. The angels will recognize them in the Fire by the marks of prostration (on their foreheads), for the Fire will eat up all the human body except the mark caused by prostration as Allah has forbidden the Fire to eat the mark of prostration. They will come out of the (Hell) Fire, completely burnt and then the water of life will be poured over them and they will grow under it as does a seed that comes in the mud of the torrent.

Then Allah will finish the judgments among the people, and there will remain one man facing the (Hell) Fire and he will be the last person among the people of Hell to enter Paradise. He will say, 'O my Lord! Please turn my face away from the fire because its air has hurt me and its severe heat has burnt me.' So he will invoke Allah in the way Allah will wish him to invoke, and then Allah will say to him, 'If I grant you that, will you then ask for anything else?' He will reply, 'No, by Your Power, (Honor) I will not ask You for anything else.' He will give his Lord whatever promises and covenants Allah will demand.

So Allah will turn his face away from Hell (Fire). When he will face Paradise and will see it, he will remain quiet for as long as Allah will wish him to remain quiet, then he will say, 'O my Lord! Bring me near to the gate of Paradise.' Allah will say to him, 'Didn't you give your promises and covenants that you would never ask for anything more than what you had been given? Woe on you, O Adam's son! How treacherous you are!' He will say, 'O my lord,' and will keep on invoking Allah till He says to him, 'If I give what you are asking, will you then ask for anything else?' He will reply, 'No, by Your (Honor) Power, I will not ask for anything else.'

Then he will give covenants and promises to Allah and then Allah will bring him near to the gate of Paradise. When he stands at the gate of Paradise, Paradise will be opened and spread before him, and he will see its splendor and pleasures whereupon he will remain quiet as long as Allah will wish him to remain quiet, and then he will say, O my Lord! Admit me into Paradise.' Allah will say, 'Didn't you give your covenants and promises that you would not ask for anything more than what you had been given?' Allah will say, 'Woe on you, O Adam's son! How treacherous you are! '

The man will say, 'O my Lord! Do not make me the most miserable of Your creation,' and he will keep on invoking Allah till Allah will laugh because of his sayings, and when Allah will laugh because of him, He will say to him, 'Enter Paradise,' and when he will enter it, Allah will say to him, 'Wish for anything.' So he will ask his Lord, and he will wish for a great number of things, for Allah Himself will remind him to wish for certain things by saying, '(Wish for) so-and-so.' When there is nothing more to wish for, Allah will say, 'This is for you, and its equal (is for you) as well."

'Ata' bin Yazid added: Abu Sa'id Al-Khudri who was present with Abu Huraira, did not deny whatever the latter said, but when Abu Huraira said that Allah had said, "That is for you and its equal as well," Abu Sa'id Al-Khudri said, "And ten times as much, O Abu Huraira!" Abu Huraira said, "I do not remember, except his saying, 'That is for you and its equal as well.'" Abu Sa'id Al-Khudri then said, "I testify that I remember the Prophet (ﷺ) saying, 'that is for you, and ten times as much.'" Abu Huraira then added, "That man will be the last person of the people of Paradise to enter Paradise." (7437) ☐

2392. Narrated Abu Huraira: The Prophet (ﷺ) said, "Allah said: "The son of Adam hurts Me by abusing Time, for I am Time; in My Hands are all things and I cause the revolution of night and day.'" (7491) ☐

2393. Narrated Abu Huraira: Allah's Messenger (ﷺ) said, "Every night when it is the last third of the night, our Lord, the Superior, the Blessed, descends to the nearest heaven and says: Is there anyone to invoke Me that I may respond to his invocation? Is there anyone to ask Me so that I may grant him his request? Is there anyone asking My forgiveness so that I may forgive him?" (7494) ☐

2394. Narrated Abu Huraira: I heard the Prophet (ﷺ) saying, "If somebody commits a sin and then says, 'O my Lord! I have sinned, please forgive me!' and his Lord says, 'My slave has known that he has a Lord who forgives sins and punishes for it, I therefore have forgiven my slave (his sins).' Then he remains without committing any sin for a while and then again commits another sin and says, 'O my Lord, I have committed another sin, please forgive me,' and Allah says, 'My slave has known that he has a Lord who forgives sins and punishes for it, I therefore have forgiven my slave (his sin). Then he remains without Committing any another sin for a while and then commits another sin (for the third time) and says, 'O my Lord, I have committed another sin, please forgive me,' and Allah says, 'My slave has known that he has a Lord Who forgives sins and punishes for it I therefore have forgiven My slave (his sin), he can do whatever he likes." (7507) ☐

2395. Narrated Safwan bin Muhriz: A man asked Ibn `Umar, "What have you heard from Allah's Messenger (ﷺ) regarding An-Najwa?" He said, "Every one of you will come close to His Lord Who will screen him from the people and say to him, 'Did you do so-and-so?' He will reply, 'Yes.' Then Allah will say, 'Did you do so-and-so?' He will reply, 'Yes.' So Allah will question him and make him confess, and then Allah will say, 'I screened your sins in the world and forgive them for you today.'" (7514) □

2396. Narrated `Abdullah: I asked Allah's Messenger (ﷺ) "What is the biggest sin in the sight of Allah?" He said, "To set up rivals unto Allah though He alone created you." I said, "In fact, that is a tremendous sin," and added, "What next?" He said, "To kill your son being afraid that he may share your food with you." I further asked, "What next?" He said, "To commit illegal sexual intercourse with the wife of your neighbor." (7520) □

2397. Narrated `Abdullah: Two person of Bani Thaqif and one from Quarish (or two persons from Quraish and one from Bani Thaqif) who had fat bellies but little wisdom, met near the Ka`ba. One of them said, "Did you see that Allah hears what we say?" The other said, "He hears us if we speak aloud, but He does not hear if we speak in stealthy quietness (softly)." The third fellow said, "If He hears when we speak aloud, then He surely hears us if we speak in stealthy quietness (softly)." So Allah revealed the Verse: -- 'And you have not been screening against yourselves, lest your ears, and your eyes and your skins should testify against you...' (41.22) (7521) □

2398. Narrated Abu Huraira: Allah's Messenger (ﷺ) said, "When Allah completed the creation, He wrote in His Book which is with Him on His Throne, "My Mercy overpowers My Anger." (3194) □

9 798640 953879